Politics in Dark Times
Encounters with Hannah Arendt

This outstanding collection of essays explores Hannah Arendt's thought against the background of world-political events unfolding since September 11, 2001. It engages in a contentious dialogue with one of the greatest political thinkers of the past century, with the conviction that she remains contemporary. Themes such as moral and political equality, action, natality, judgment, and freedom are reevaluated with fresh insight by a group of thinkers who are themselves well known for their original contributions to political thought. Other essays focus on novel and little-discussed themes in the literature by highlighting Arendt's views on sovereignty, international law and genocide, nuclear weapons and revolutions, imperialism and Eurocentrism, as well as her contrasting images of Europe and America. Each essay displays not only superb Arendt scholarship but also stylistic flair and analytical tenacity.

Seyla Benhabib is the Eugene Meyer Professor of Political Science and Philosophy at Yale University. She is the author of *Critique, Norm and Utopia: A Study of the Normative Foundations of Critical Theory* (1986); *Situating the Self: Gender, Community and Postmodernism in Contemporary Ethics* (2002); *Feminist Contentions: A Philosophical Exchange* (coauthored with Judith Butler, Drucilla Cornell, and Nancy Fraser, 1996); *The Reluctant Modernism of Hannah Arendt* (1996); *The Claims of Culture: Equality and Diversity in the Global Era* (2002); *The Rights of Others: Aliens, Citizens and Residents* (2004); and *Another Cosmopolitanism: Hospitality, Sovereignty and Democratic Iterations* (2006). She has edited and coedited seven volumes, most recently with Judith Resnik, *Mobility and Immobility: Gender, Borders and Citizenship* (2009). Her work has been translated into fourteen languages, and she was the recipient of the 2009 Ernst Bloch Prize for her contributions to cultural dialogues in a global civilization.

Politics in Dark Times

Encounters with Hannah Arendt

Edited by

SEYLA BENHABIB
Yale University

With the assistance of
ROY T. TSAO

PETER J. VEROVŠEK
Yale University

CAMBRIDGE
UNIVERSITY PRESS

CAMBRIDGE UNIVERSITY PRESS
Cambridge, New York, Melbourne, Madrid, Cape Town, Singapore,
São Paulo, Delhi, Dubai, Tokyo, Mexico City

Cambridge University Press
32 Avenue of the Americas, New York, NY 10013-2473, USA

www.cambridge.org
Information on this title: www.cambridge.org/9780521127226

First published 2010

Printed in the United States of America

A catalog record for this publication is available from the British Library.

Library of Congress Cataloging in Publication data

Politics in dark times : encounters with Hannah Arendt / edited by Seyla Benhabib.
  p. cm.
Includes bibliographical references and index.
ISBN 978-0-521-76370-7 (hardback) – ISBN 978-0-521-12722-6 (paperback)
1. Arendt, Hannah, 1906–1975. 2. Political science – Philosophy.
I. Benhabib, Seyla. II. Title.
JC251.A74P66 2010
320.5092–dc22   2010024375

ISBN 978-0-521-76370-7 Hardback
ISBN 978-0-521-12722-6 Paperback

This publication has been supported by a generous grant from the John K. Castle Fund housed in
Yale's Program on Ethics, Politics and Economics. The Castle Fund was established in honor of
Reverend James Pierpont, one of Yale's original founders.

Contents

Notes on Contributors

Andrew Arato is Dorothy H. Hirshon Professor in Political and Social Theory at the New School for Social Research. He is the author of *Constitution Making under Occupation: The Politics of Imposed Revolution in Iraq* (2009); *Civil Society, Constitution and Legitimacy* (2000); and *From Neo-Marxism to Democratic Theory* (1993) and coauthor of *Civil Society and Political Theory* (1992). He is currently working on a book on constituent authority and an essay volume on dictatorship and modern politics.

Benjamin R. Barber is a Distinguished Senior Fellow at Demos in New York and Walt Whitman Professor Emeritus at Rutgers University. His seventeen books include the classic *Strong Democracy* (1984), issued in a new twentieth-anniversary edition in 2004; the international best-seller *Jihad vs. McWorld*, now in thirty languages (1995); and, most recently, *Consumed: How Markets Corrupt Children, Infantilize Adults and Swallow Citizens Whole* (2008). He is president and founder of CivWorld, the nongovernmental organization (NGO) that since 2003 has convened the annual Interdependence Day Forum and Celebration in a global city on September 12.

Seyla Benhabib is Eugene Meyer Professor of Political Science and Philosophy at Yale University. Some of her books include *The Reluctant Modernism of Hannah Arendt* (1996; reissued in 2003); *The Rights of Others: Aliens, Citizens and Residents* (2004; winner of the Ralph Bunche Award of the American Political Science Association); *Another Cosmopolitanism*, with responses by Jeremy Waldron, Bonnie Honig, and Will Kymlicka, based on her Berkeley Tanner Lectures and edited by Robert Post (2006); and most recently *Mobility and Immobility: Gender, Borders and Citizenship* (2009), edited with Judith Resnik.

Richard J. Bernstein is Vera List Professor of Philosophy at the New School for Social Research. His books include *Hannah Arendt and the Jewish Question*

(1996); *Freud and the Legacy of Moses* (1998); *Radical Evil: A Philosophical Interrogation* (2002); and *The Abuse of Evil: The Corruption of Politics and Religion since 9/11* (2005). His most recent book is *The Pragmatic Turn* (2010).

Leora Bilsky is Professor of Law at Tel-Aviv University and the author of *Transformative Justice: Israeli Identity on Trial* (2004).

Jean L. Cohen is Professor of Political Theory at Columbia University. She is the author of *Class and Civil Society: The Limits of Marxian Critical Theory* (1982); *Civil Society and Political Theory* (1992) with Andrew Arato; and *Rethinking Intimacy: A New Legal Paradigm* (2002). She is completing a book for Cambridge University Press on legality and legitimacy in the epoch of globalization.

Bryan Garsten is Professor of Political Science at Yale University and author of *Saving Persuasion: A Defense of Rhetoric and Judgment* (2006). He has also written articles on themes related to representative government in the thought of Hobbes, Rousseau, Tocqueville, and Benjamin Constant.

Dick Howard is Distinguished Professor of Philosophy at the State University of New York at Stony Brook. He is the author of fourteen books, most recently *The Specter of Democracy* (2002); *La naissance de la pensée politique américaine* (2005); and *La démocratie à l'épreuve: Chroniques américaines* (2006). *The Primacy of the Political: A History of Political Thought from the Greeks to the American and French Revolutions* was published in 2010.

George Kateb is William Nelson Cromwell Professor of Politics Emeritus at Princeton University. His books include *Hannah Arendt: Politics, Conscience, Evil* (1984); *The Inner Ocean: Individualism and Democratic Culture* (1992); *Emerson and Self-Reliance* (1994, 2002); *John Stuart Mill, On Liberty*, coedited with David Bromwich (2003); and *Patriotism and Other Mistakes* (2006).

Richard H. King is Professor Emeritus of American Intellectual History at the University of Nottingham, UK. He is the author of *Race, Culture and the Intellectuals, 1940–1970* (2004), and coeditor of *Hannah Arendt and the Uses of History: Imperialism, Nation, Race and Genocide* (2007). He is currently at work on *The American Arendt*, which will focus on Arendt's impact on American thought and the impact of her experience in America on her own thought.

Karuna Mantena is Assistant Professor of Political Science at Yale University. She has researched and written on empire and imperialism in modern political thought and, especially, on nineteenth-century British imperial ideology. She is the author of *Alibis of Empire: Henry Maine and the Ends of Liberal Imperialism* (2010).

Patchen Markell is Associate Professor of Political Science at the University of Chicago and the author of *Bound by Recognition* (2003). He is currently writing a book-length study of Hannah Arendt's *The Human Condition* and is pursuing a longer-term project on conceptions of power, agency, and rule in democratic theory.

Susan Neiman is Director of the Einstein Forum in Berlin, Germany. Her most recent books are *Evil in Modern Thought* (2004), which has been translated into nine languages, and *Moral Clarity: A Guide to Grown-Up Idealists* (2008), a *New York Times* Notable Book.

Jonathan Schell is the author of *The Fate of the Earth* (1982) and *The Unconquerable World: Power, Nonviolence, and the Will of the People* (2004), among other books. His most recent book is *The Seventh Decade: The New Shape of Nuclear Danger* (2008). He is a Peace Fellow at the Nation Institute and a lecturer in international studies and ethics, politics, and economics at Yale University.

Roy T. Tsao has taught political theory at Yale, Georgetown, and Brown universities. He has published numerous articles on aspects of Arendt's thought.

Peter J. Verovšek is a Ph.D. candidate in political science at Yale University. Before coming to Yale, he spent a year on a Fulbright Grant researching how memories of World War II continue to affect politics within the former Yugoslavia and in the relations of its successor states with Italy. His dissertation examines the connection between memory and political community through the development of the European Union.

Christian Volk received his doctoral degree from Aachen University (Germany) in 2009. He is the author of *Die Ordnung der Freiheit. Recht und Politik im Denken Hannah Arendts* (2010). He currently holds a postdoctoral position at the Humboldt-University in Berlin and is working on his *Habilitationsprojekt* "The Paradigm of Post-Sovereignty: Law and Democracy in a Global Order."

Jeremy Waldron is University Professor at New York University School of Law. He is the author of *Law and Disagreement* (1999) and *God, Locke and Equality* (2002) among other books. He is the author of "Arendt's Constitutional Politics" in Dana Villa (ed.), *The Cambridge Companion to Hannah Arendt* (2001) and "What Would Hannah Say?" in *The New York Review of Books*, March 15, 2007.

Introduction

Seyla Benhabib

Few if any political thinkers of the twentieth century have attracted public attention and scholarly discussion as wide-ranging as has Hannah Arendt. Her theoretical reflections on the human condition have attained classic status in political philosophy, while her writings on the political crises of her time are a continuing source of intellectual inspiration and provocation.

A former student of Martin Heidegger and Karl Jaspers and a comrade in exile from Nazi Germany with Walter Benjamin, Arendt first came to public prominence ten years after her emigration to the United States, with the publication of *The Origins of Totalitarianism* (1951). That celebrated work's highly original analyses of antisemitism, imperialism, and totalitarianism immediately established her as a leading commentator on the political upheavals and catastrophes of the era. With that book, she not only offered a uniquely clear-sighted, broad account of twentieth-century totalitarian politics and their antecedents; she also provided an exceptionally subtle and penetrating analysis of the modern mentalities that gave succor to those politics. Within those same pages, she also made a landmark contribution to the discourse of international human rights, with a strong critique of the misuse of the institution of citizenship in the modern nation-state. She followed that achievement with even more far-reaching analyses of the exhausted traditions and neglected resources of Western political thought, culminating in her books *The Human Condition* (1958) and *On Revolution* (1963). Her fearlessness in exploring the nature of political evil and personal responsibility found further expression in *Eichmann in Jerusalem* (1963), the source of her famous, much-misunderstood phrase, "the banality of evil." All of these books – along with the numerous other volumes, essays, and lectures that constitute the corpus of Arendt's work – were the focus of extensive critical notice and often controversy in her lifetime, and in more recent years they have gained an ever-widening circle of attentive readers, both within and outside the academy.[1] With the passage of time, her stature as a major thinker of the twentieth century has received ample confirmation.

In the fall of 2006, the centenary of Hannah Arendt's birth was celebrated with conferences from New York to Istanbul, from Paris to Lima, from Berlin to Sofia and beyond. These not only marked her worldwide recognition and reputation,[2] they also revealed an urgent need, an intellectual hunger, "to think with Arendt, against Arendt."[3] This need was increased by the global struggles that ensued after the September 11, 2001, attacks on the World Trade Center and the Pentagon, and the subsequent American-led wars in Afghanistan and Iraq. Many have presented the conflict between the resurgent forces of an Islamist Jihadi movement, spearheaded by al-Qaeda, against the 'West,' as a confrontation between liberal democracies and the new face of totalitarianism in the twenty-first century. In this context, Arendt's epochal analysis of Nazi and Stalinist totalitarianism has often been invoked as a source of analytical insight about current problems and also to support entrenched ideological positions, with which Arendt most likely would not have agreed.[4]

The month of October 2006 was a particularly dark one for the American republic in Arendtian terms: With congressional midterm elections only a month away, it appeared to many that nothing less than the future of constitutional government in the United States was at stake. Guantanamo and Abu Ghraib were only the most infamous of the sites of illegality where the U.S. Constitution was hemorrhaging in the hands of those who claimed that executive power, beyond the rule of domestic and international law, would determine the status of enemy combatants. Evidence was mounting daily that

---

[1] See Samantha Power, "Introduction," *The Origins of Totalitarianism* (New York: Schocken, 2004), pp. ix–xxiv.

[2] See the two volumes published by *Social Research* documenting these conferences: *Hannah Arendt's Centenary: Political and Philosophical Perspectives*, Part I, edited by Arienne Mack and Jerome Kohn, 74, 3 (Fall 2007); *Hannah Arendt's Centenary: Political and Philosophical Perspectives*, Part II, edited by Arienne Mack and Jerome Kohn, 74, 4 (Winter 2007).

[3] I introduced this phrase in Seyla Benhabib, "Preface to the New Edition," *The Reluctant Modernism of Hannah Arendt* (new edition, New York: Rowman and Littlefield, 2003; first published by Thousand Oaks, CA: Sage, 1996), pp. xix–xx.

[4] In the fall of 2001, shortly after the September 11 attacks on the World Trade Center, a conference was held at the New School for Social Research that had been originally planned to mark the fiftieth anniversary of the publication of *The Origins of Totalitarianism*. Impassioned participants debated whether the al-Qaeda movement and Islamic Jihadism could be considered "totalitarian" in the way spelled out by Hannah Arendt. Cf. *The Origins of Totalitarianism. Fifty Years Later*, *Social Research*, edited by Arienne Mack and Jerome Kohn, 69, 2 (Summer 2002).

The thesis of "Islamo-fascism" has been put forward by Paul Berman, who has called for an "anti-totalitarian war." Paul Berman, *Terror and Liberalism* (New York: W.W. Norton, 2003); Cf. also Christopher Hitchens, *A Long-Short War: The Postponed Liberation of Iraq* (London: Penguin, 2003); and Thomas Cushman, Simon Cottee, and Christopher Hitchens, *Christopher Hitchens and His Critics: Terror, Iraq and the Left* (New York and London: New York University Press, 2008).

Cf. Chapter 11 in this book, by Benjamin Barber, who radically disagrees with these views of Islam.

torture, including waterboarding, was used by the American military as well as paramilitary contractors working for Blackwater Security in Iraq. U.S. Attorney General Alberto Gonzales issued a memo that declared that all acts besides those leading to severe organ failure and malfunctioning did *not* constitute torture – again, in violation of international covenants.[5] The "Global War on Terror," which had murky legal and even strategic justifications at best, was under way. Jonathan Schell observes that " . . . the President's bid to achieve global military dominance by the United States [was] presented to the public as a kind of colossal footnote to the war on terror. The interplay, enacted on the electoral stage, between the attempt at dominance abroad and one-party rule at home,"[6] was probably the most important generator of this constitutional crisis.

Although the chapters in this book were composed with the vivid memory of these political crises in the background, their engagement with Arendt's work

---

[5] Cf. the article, Scott Shane, David Johnston, and James Riesen, "Secret U.S. Endorsement of Severe Interrogations," *New York Times* (October 4, 2007): "From the secret sites in Afghanistan, Thailand and Eastern Europe where C.I.A. teams held al-Qaeda terrorists, questions for the lawyers at C.I.A. headquarters arrived daily. Nervous interrogators wanted to know: Are we breaking the law against torture?"

Several controversial memos and briefs of the G. W. Bush Administration sought to establish that neither Article III of the Geneva Convention (1949), to which the United States was a High Contracting Party, nor the War Crimes Act (1996) applied to a non-state actor such as the al-Qaeda organization. See "Memorandum for Alberto Gonzales, Counsel to the President and William J. Haynes, II, General Counsel of the Department of Defense," prepared by the Office of the Assistant Attorney General, Bybee, on January 22, 2002 and the Alberto R. Gonzales Memos of January 25, 2002 and August 1, 2002. Once the protection of al-Qaeda and of captured Taliban prisoners under the Geneva Conventions and the War Crimes Act was lifted, they became fair game to be tortured and the U.S. government avoided the onus of violating international obligations and customary international law. The August 1 memo states with respect to "Standards of Conduct for Interrogation under 18 U.S.C. #2340–2340 A that . . . certain acts may be cruel, inhuman or degrading, but still not produce pain and suffering of the requisite intensity to fall within section 2340A's proscription against torture. . . . Physical pain amounting to torture must be equivalent in intensity to the pain accompanying serious physical injury, such as organ failure, impairment of bodily function or even death. For purely mental pain or suffering to amount to torture under Section 2340, it must result in significant physical harm of significant duration, e.g. lasting for months or even years."

Gonzales' memo in effect sanctioned the use of torture by the United States. That the reasoning of the Office of the U.S. Attorney General was faulty is widely accepted in the legal community and has been proven by subsequent U.S. Supreme Court decisions to close down the Guantanamo Bay Prison. In a series of related decisions over a number of years, the U.S. Supreme Court has concluded that "United States courts have jurisdiction to consider challenges to the legality of the detention of foreign nationals captured abroad in connection with hostilities and incarcerated at Guantanamo Bay. (July 2004). See http://news.bbc.co.uk/2/hi/americas/3867067.stm. And on December 15, 2008, the justices ordered a Washington appeals court to review its January 2008 ruling quashing the lawsuit against former defense secretary Donald Rumsfeld and ten senior U.S. military officers. This decision was the latest in a string of legal rebukes to the military justice system set up by the administration of President George W. Bush to try "enemy combatants" seized as part of the government's "war on terrorism."

[6] Jonathan Schell, "The Torture Election," *The Nation,* October 30, 2006. Accessible online at http://www.thenation.com/doc/20061113/schell.

goes far beyond them.[7] Many of the contributors to this book have written on Hannah Arendt before; others have not. In some cases, these chapters revisit with fresh eyes themes such as evil, equality, action, judgment, freedom, morality, and natality, which are crucial to any account of Arendtian politics. In other cases, they address themes such as sovereignty, jurisdiction, international law, genocide, nuclear holocaust, and Arendt's contrasting views on Europe and America that have not been much discussed in the literature. They explore and evaluate critically Arendt's multifaceted achievements as a theorist of political principles and institutions; as a philosopher of political judgment and a witness to political evil; and, throughout, as a thinker who alerts us to the simultaneous claims of these manifold public roles.

Freedom, Equality, and Responsibility

Hannah Arendt is indebted to the republican tradition of political thought insofar as for her the republic is the "res publica," the public thing – or more appropriately, the edifice – in which freedom is housed.[8] Like Cicero, Rousseau, Montesquieu, and Jefferson, she believes in government in which laws and not men rule; in which the balance of powers among different branches is constitutionally secured. Above all, she is convinced that a republic cannot be maintained unless its citizens display and exercise certain capacities of character and intellect that privilege the concern for the common good in their hearts and minds over narrowly understood self-interest.

As Jeremy Waldron notes in Chapter 1, "Arendt on the Foundations of Equality," the republican ideal of civic participation is often thought to privilege an elite and is not easily reconcilable with the idea of democratic participation based on universal suffrage. But Waldron undertakes to clarify the philosophical bases of Arendt's concept of human equality to show that while Arendt denied that egalitarian principles in politics have an imperative force apart from our own decision to recognize them, this does not mean that those principles are purely arbitrary. Rather, she insisted, human equality *supervenes* upon a basic fact of the human condition, namely, the ever-present capacity to initiate the new and the unprecedented. By showing how this relation of supervenience informs her insistence on establishing republican politics on an inclusive, egalitarian basis, Waldron defends the theoretical coherence of

---

7 On September 29–30, 2006, Yale University's Program in Ethics, Politic and Economics and the Whitney Humanities Center convened a conference under the title "Crises of Our Republics: Hannah Arendt at One Hundred." Some of the essays collected in this book were originally delivered during that conference. All have been revised for inclusion in this book.

8 For further discussions see Margaret Canovan, *Hannah Arendt: A Reinterpretation of her Political Thought* (Cambridge: Cambridge University Press, 1992), and for a comprehensive overview of some of the debates surrounding various aspects of Arendt's political philosophy, cf. *The Cambridge Companion to Hannah Arendt*, edited by Dana Villa (Cambridge: Cambridge University Press, 2000).

Arendt's egalitarian principles and attempts to reconcile her republican elitism with her democratic egalitarianism.

Arendt often reiterates that every human being who comes upon this earth has the capacity to initiate a new set of words and actions that are uniquely hers and that no human life can ever be the replica of any other. This principle, which is at the source of all that is new and unprecedented in politics, prompts both hope and dread; yet it can also harbor the hubris that modern men can tolerate only what they have made or can consider themselves to have created. The modern belief in autonomy, that humans are worthy of respect insofar as they can fashion and create the conditions of their lives, also breeds a dangerous impatience with whatever men have not produced and cannot change. In a subtle analysis of the paradoxes of autonomy and acceptance, freedom and reconciliation with the given, Roy Tsao returns to Arendt's dissertation of 1929 on *Der Liebesbegriff bei Augustin* and her subsequent rewritings and musings of Augustinian themes.

Arendt often quotes Augustine, "that there be a beginning, man was created before whom there was nobody" (*HC*, 177).[9] Augustine was referring specifically to the creation story in Genesis; Arendt nonetheless takes his dictum as a touchstone for her concept of natality, the universal human capacity for fresh initiative. In Chapter 2, "Arendt's Augustine," Roy Tsao suggests that Arendt's penchant for quoting Augustine in this connection is a sign that even when celebrating human initiative, her thoughts were never far from recognizing the limitations upon human action, and the perils in failure to recognize and accept those limitations. In her dissertation, Arendt had examined Augustine's sense that an adequate human self-understanding depends crucially on the recognition that all human beings share a common historical situation: All inherit the same dead weight of the past; none are denied the chance to be redeemed from that burden; each must continually seize on that chance for himself or herself, while also benefiting from others' example and encouragement. Tsao underscores the importance of this same pattern of argument – transposed to a secular context – to Arendt's later thinking about the human predicament. In Tsao's view, this pattern can be seen most clearly in *The Origins of Totalitarianism*, where Arendt warns darkly of the "perversions of human self-consciousness" that arise when men refuse to acknowledge their common humanity with all others, whatever their failings or limitations.

If *The Origins Of Totalitarianism* can be considered the crowning achievement of Arendt as a political and historical analyst, *The Human Condition* – which she titled *Vita Activa* (life of action or active life) in its German edition, in contradistinction to *vita contemplativa* (the contemplative life or the life of the mind) – is clearly her most philosophically challenging work. In Chapter 3, "The Rule of the People: Arendt, *Arché*, and Democracy," Patchen Markell examines how Arendt's understanding of human action informs her account

---

[9] Hannah Arendt, *The Human Condition* (University of Chicago Press: Chicago, 1958), p. 177. The quotation is from St. Augustine, *De Civitate Dei*, Book XII, 21.

of democratic politics. Arendt's signature notion of action as a "beginning" figures in her recurrent polemic against the particular conception of "rule," which she deems pervasive in Western political thought. Politics has often been thought to be about ruling and being ruled, but through a careful analysis of Arendt's discussion of action in *The Human Condition* and related texts, Markell shows how this critique of the concept of "rule" poses a challenge to the standard dichotomies of order versus anarchy in contemporary theories of democratic politics.

Markell, like Tsao, returns to the Augustinian motto, "that there be a beginning, man was created before whom there was nobody," and asks what such a beginning can possibly mean. Noting that most commentators understand "beginning" as the interruption of some sequence or some series, he suggests instead a novel reading: " ... when an event passes from possibility to actuality ... something changes in a different register; namely, the register in which happenings are not only caused states of affairs but also meaningful events, features of a world, and, in particular, occasions for a response." For Markell, as for Tsao, beginning does not mean a defiant act of autonomous assertion, but rather, "a state of practical engagement with events." The principle of natality, then, on which Waldron wants to rest supervenience, is open to many readings, but in each case there is a new modality of practical engagement with the world, beyond banal understandings of autonomy as self-mastery.

Hannah Arendt's *The Origins of Totalitarianism* has a structure that has long puzzled commentators: Part One is called "Anti-Semitism," Part Two is named "Imperialism," and it is only in Part Three, "Totalitarianism," that the origin and structure of totalitarian movements are addressed. How is one to interpret this structure? Did Arendt see antisemitism and imperialism as causally linked to European totalitarianism? If so, how can one explain the fact that French antisemitism in the Dreyfus Affair did not culminate in French totalitarianism, despite Vichy France's capitulation to the Germans? Likewise, the British experience of imperialism in India, which is given such a prominent place in Arendt's account, does not lead to the rise of totalitarian movements in the United Kingdom. It is not countries which engaged in "overseas imperialism," but rather those that ventured into "continental imperialism," such as Germany and Russia, that became the homes of Nazism and Stalinism respectively. What does Arendt mean by her insight that the experience of the "heart of darkness" in the white imperialist encounter with Africa, in which all European nations more or less participated, culminated in the "heart of darkness" in Europe itself?

The relationship between imperialism and totalitarianism is at the center of Chapter 4, "Genealogies of Catastrophe: Arendt on the Logic and Legacy of Imperialism," by Karuna Mantena. Noting that Arendt sharply distinguished imperialism from totalitarianism, as if consigning the former to a subordinate place in her survey of the catastrophes of her time, Mantena nonetheless sees in Arendt's analysis of imperialism a considerable achievement in its own right. Mantena undertakes to delineate both the insights and the limitations of that analysis, comparing it to the near-contemporary treatment of the same phenomenon in the *Discourse on Colonialism* of Aimé Césaire.[10] While Césaire charged that the European experience of living with the gap between the theory of universalism and the practice of imperial domination led to the moral corruption that made fascism possible, Arendt refused to posit either imperialism or fascism as *inevitable* developments of European history. Instead, she focused on the contingent and inadvertent play of political forces that led the European colonizers to adopt "race" and bureaucracy as political devices to control and justify the violent hypocrisy of their imperialist forays. It was this union of bureaucratic rule with the ranking of peoples into "higher" and "lower" races that transformed the imperialist experience eventually into the attempted extermination of a people. Mantena concludes, "If the new imperialism inaugurated a distinct era of global politics and global rivalry, when every nation saw its economic livelihood intimately connected to the expansion of political power and race and economics drew every nation into world politics, it is an era to which our politics are still held captive, with all its calamitous consequences."

Retrieving themes from Waldron's chapter on Arendt's concept of equality, Richard H. King subjects Arendt's egalitarianism to a different order of critical scrutiny in Chapter 5, "On Race and Culture: Hannah Arendt and Her Contemporaries." King's particular concern is with Arendt's representation of non-Western peoples in *The Origins of Totalitarianism*, which has often been criticized for expressing the cultural biases that were prevalent among European intellectuals of her generation. Without denying the substance of that criticism, King insists on distinguishing Arendt's position from that of her contemporaries in Germany, such as Theodor Adorno, Leo Strauss, Eric Voegelin, and Karl Löwith. By reconstructing the cultural terms in which "the crises of the West" were articulated, King argues that Western thinkers of the time attempted to reimagine European humanism often at the cost of positing European cultural superiority over Asia and Africa. Arendt, however, had no interest in revitalizing the Western cultural tradition per se. Part of her critique of colonialism was a rejection of the philosophy of history that grounded the narrative of Western superiority. King counters that charge of ethnocentric discourse in her writings by arguing that Arendt was committed to equality as a *political* concept, not as a factual statement about human capabilities. Both Waldron and King disclose for us the originality of Arendt's concept of equality, which is poised to steer clear of naturalism and pure normativism. Instead, equality is an ethico-political practice of human relations, actualized through the building of republican institutions.

Sovereignty, the Nation-State, and International Law

Arendt celebrated the American Revolution and the decolonization movements in Asia and Africa because of the opportunities they allowed for national

---

[10] Aimé Césaire, *Discourse on Colonialism*, translated by Joan Pinkham (New York: Monthly Review Press, 1972).

sovereignty. But can the division of power *within* a country actually benefit from greater constraints on sovereignty imposed by the international system? This is Andrew Arato and Jean Cohen's question in Chapter 6, as they explore the relationship between external sovereignty – freedom from international domination and constraints – and internal sovereignty – the finality of decision making within a republic. Arendt saw the dangers of allowing one institution or person to have complete sovereignty and thus praised the American republic for "banishing the sovereign." However, Arato and Cohen find that Arendt's characterization of the American case as a paradigm of divided sovereignty does not take into account the long history of belief in American exceptionalism and executive privilege that have marked U.S. foreign policy. "Sovereign immunity" and "sovereign privilege" were never absent from American state and legal doctrine. If anything, in the wake of September 11, 2001, the idea of a "unified sovereign" gained ground in the United States with assertions of "unitary executive" authority by President George W. Bush.

Arato and Cohen claim that Arendt's position on the concept of external sovereignty, as opposed to internal sovereignty, is ambiguous. She understands external sovereignty to be necessary to create the type of republic she cherishes, but the protection of this kind of republic may require that both internal and external sovereignty be limited by a regime built on international law – about which she remains ambivalent.

The tensions between international law and republican politics recurs frequently in Hannah Arendt's writings: In her discussion of the "right to have rights" in *The Origins of Totalitarianism*, with the question of territorial versus universal jurisdiction in the trial of Nazi official Adolf Eichmann and the status of genocide, we uncover a theme that has been little explored in the literature.

In her chapter on "The Decline of the Nation-State and the End of the Rights of Man" in *The Origins of Totalitarianism,* Arendt showed why European nation-states had tendencies to forsake their republican traditions in the service of nationalist aspirations. No longer guaranteeing equality to all their citizens, particularly in the interwar period, the European nation-states instead created millions of stateless peoples, refugees, and political minorities. In Chapter 7, "The Decline of Order: Hannah Arendt and the Paradoxes of the Nation-State," Christian Volk claims that for Arendt, the notion of political order represented by the nation-state system was inappropriate to deal with problems of an interdependent Europe.

By linking the concept of the rule of law with that of the nation-state, Arendt followed in the footsteps of German state-theorists and their critique of the "System of Weimar." This group includes Max Weber, Hans Kelsen, Hermann Heller, and also Carl Schmitt. Volk argues that despite topical similarities among their works, Arendt distanced herself from German state-theorists' traditional solutions to the problem of order. Unlike her, they insisted that a "homogeneous" society was a precondition for a well-ordered political community. For Arendt, the search for such homogeneity would prove politically disastrous and morally abhorrent.

In Chapter 8, "The Eichmann Trial and the Legacy of Jurisdiction," Leora Bilsky turns to Arendt's writings on the 1961 trial of Eichmann in order to stimulate fresh thinking on the abiding problem of jurisdiction in international political trials. In defending its jurisdiction over Eichmann, the Jerusalem Court put forth a theory of "universal jurisdiction," according to which every national court had the power to try crimes against humanity as a delegate of the international community. Arendt, by contrast, thought that the legitimacy of the Jerusalem Court rested not on "universal" but on "territorial" jurisdiction. The concept of territory over which a court has jurisdiction should be interpreted politically and culturally, and not purely geographically, she argued. The state of Israel was the legitimate representative of the Jewish people, even though the crimes of the Holocaust were not committed on its territory, because it could be said to "represent" the Jewish people. Through close attention to Arendt's unusual justification for the legitimacy of the Jerusalem Court, Bilsky identifies Arendt's key insight as the need for criminal law to acknowledge that it is embedded simultaneously in two orders of moral community: that of a political state and that of humanity. On the basis of this insight, Bilsky proposes a framework for resolving the seemingly intractable dilemmas associated with the prosecution of heads of state and their agents for genocide and other crimes against humanity.

What is the foundation of the concept of genocide? Why is it considered the principal crime against humanity? In Chapter 9, "International Law and Human Plurality in the Shadow of Totalitarianism: Hannah Arendt and Raphael Lemkin," I engage in a comparative analysis of the thought of Arendt and Raphael Lemkin, the "father" of the Genocide Convention. Both arrived in New York in 1941, albeit from different directions: Arendt and her husband Heinrich Bluecher came from Portugal and Lemkin from Japan, via Sweden; they both sought to understand the European catastrophe as it befell them personally, she as a German Jewish refugee and he as a Polish Jewish refugee. They lived in New York City and developed their analyses of the European catastrophe through the categories of totalitarianism and genocide. No evidence exists that they were aware of each other's work. In fact, many of Arendt's references to the futility of declarations of human rights – and in particular her statement that " . . . all attempts to arrive at a new bill of human rights were sponsored by marginal figures – by a few international jurists without political experience or professional philanthropists supported by the uncertain sentiments of professional idealists"[11] – lead one to believe that she had no particular use at that point for the Convention on the Recognition of Genocide, which was passed only three years earlier in 1948 through Lemkin's great efforts.

I argue that between 1951, when *The Origins of Totalitarianism* was composed, and 1963, when *Eichmann in Jerusalem* was published, a reorientation took place in Arendt's thought. This is most manifest in her condemnation

---

[11] Hannah Arendt, *The Origins of Totalitarianism* (1951) (New York: Harcourt, Brace, Jovanovich, 1979), p. 292; in the new Schocken Books edition (New York: 2004), p. 371.

of Eichmann, who in the dramatic epilogue of the book she finds guilty of destroying human plurality in wanting to exterminate the Jews. Genocide violates a fundamental human condition, namely, that of plurality. I then examine the ontological foundation of the concept of the group for Arendt and Lemkin. I trace Lemkin's concept to a Herderian notion of groups as creators and carriers of human culture. Arendt's principle of plurality, by contrast, is not centered on the creation and preservation of any one culture per se but on the importance of protecting the varied perspectivality and manifoldness of the world as it appears to human beings. Genocide, in wanting to destroy this, is an attempt by humans to play God. It is the ultimate hubris of modern man, as Roy Tsao has also emphasized, to want to revolt against human difference and to wish to manipulate it at will.

Politics in Dark Times

One global issue about which Arendt herself did not say much was the question of nuclear weapons and nuclear proliferation. Although genocide and totalitarianism were at the center of her thought, she did not address the possibility of a nuclear holocaust, the genocide of all life on earth. Jonathan Schell calls his moving reflections on this matter, "In Search of a Miracle: Hannah Arendt and the Atomic Bomb," beginning with his personal encounter with Hannah Arendt. The phrase "in search of a miracle" is Arendt's own. In her only recently published fragment, called "Introduction into Politics," she writes:

No matter how hard we try to understand the situation or take into account the individual factors that this twofold threat of totalitarian states and atomic weapons represents – a threat only made worse by their conjunction – we cannot so much as conceive of a satisfactory solution, not even with the best will on all sides. Only some sort of miracle might break the impasse.[12]

Instead of thus bringing matters to a dreary conclusion, Schell notes in Chapter 10 that Arendt makes a startling "U-turn" and acknowledges that miracles are indeed possible in the political realm, just as life on earth itself emerged out of an infinite improbability. Schell reprieves the central themes of Arendtian politics that run through so many of the chapters in this book – natality, plurality, and the meaning of freedom – so that one can "understand the new stakes that have been put on the historical table." Totalitarianism destroys "the political," in the Arendtian sense, as the space in which, through action and discussion, individuals find the meaning of freedom in and through their "action in concert." "The atomic bomb," observes Schell, "of course threatens the common world from another angle – not by destroying all freedom but simply by destroying all life." Central to both traditional conceptions of politics as rule and domination (already analyzed by Markell in Chapter 3) and

---

[12] Hannah Arendt, "Introduction into Politics," in *The Promise of Politics*, edited and with an Introduction by Jerome Kohn (New York: Schocken, 2005), p. 111.

the technical invention that paved the way for the bomb is the view that "the political, public space had itself become an arena of force both in the modern world's theoretical self-perception and its brutal reality."[13]

Is there any reason, then, to hope for a miracle, a new beginning? The Hungarian Revolution of 1956 suggested to Arendt (who died in 1976, before she could witness the crumbling of the Soviet system in Russia and in Eastern and Central Europe after 1989) that totalitarianism could indeed find an end. She also did witness the emergence of a stable liberal democracy in post–World War II Germany. Could an end likewise to the threat of nuclear annihilation be envisaged? "Neither Arendt nor history has written that story," concludes Schell.

The poles of hope and despair – faith in the capacity of ordinary human agents to initiate the new and the unprecedented, and despair in the face of so much that goes so wrong most of the time – are a motif in Chapter 11, "Hannah Arendt between Europe and America: Optimism in Dark Times," Benjamin Barber's exploration of Arendt's love/hate relationship with the American republic. Very early on, Arendt expressed this ambivalence with a pithy phrase about the United States: "politische Freiheit und soziale Knechtschaft," that is, "political freedom and social servitude." Despite the fact that she appreciated and praised American republican political traditions, Arendt was also deeply skeptical about America's cheerful optimism, which, paradoxically much like European totalitarianism, exuded the belief that "everything is possible." Distancing herself from American social science and scientifically enlightened public policy, which was at the foundation of this optimistic belief, Arendt harbored a profound pessimism about modernity's belief in mutability without forsaking faith in American political institutions.

Barber points out that in the new post-9/11 skepticism, Americans have caught up to Hannah Arendt, ready finally by opening themselves to a confrontation with radical evil. But does this reality warrant the inflationary application of the term "totalitarian" to the new Islamic fundamentalist movements? Barber argues that it does not, and concludes provocatively: "The real lesson of *Origins* for our time is not that our enemies represent the new totalitarianism, but that we ourselves are no longer wholly immune from the dreadful seductions that pave the way to its Hellishness."

Arendt's engagement with the American political legacy is also at the center of Chapter 12, "Keeping the Republic: Reading Arendt's *On Revolution* after the Fall of the Berlin Wall." Dick Howard asks, what questions led her to write *On Revolution*? And what questions would make us receptive to her thought today? In trying to understand post-totalitarian politics after the fall of the Berlin Wall and the emergence of what seemed like "Arendtian revolutions" (Jonathan Schell) throughout the world in the late-1990s, Howard advises that Arendt's essay on "Civil Disobedience" may provide a better lens than *On Revolution* through which to assess these transformations. Furthermore, although

---

[13] Ibid., p. 147.

On Revolution is a prime example of Arendt's ability to "think the political," Arendt misses the uniqueness of the American Revolution. Arendt intuited but did not fully articulate a broader view of the dynamics of democratic politics, in which politics and antipolitics constantly have to compete. With this argument, Howard rejoins the problem with which Markell opens Chapter 3, namely, the vacillation among theorists of modern democracy between privileging order as opposed to insurrection; the rule of law as opposed to the outburst of the constitutive power of the people.

Judging Evil

What about Arendt's thesis of the "banality of evil"? How illuminating is this category for our times? In Chapter 13, "Are Arendt's Reflections on Evil Still Relevant?," Richard J. Bernstein faces this question directly. Considering that her reflections on evil arose in conjunction with her analysis of totalitarian regimes, Bernstein asks what pertinence those reflections can have for us today, in a world no longer so plainly menaced by the global power of the sort of regime she classified as totalitarian. Whereas Benjamin Barber is skeptical that Arendt's reflections on evil are relevant for politics in our world, Bernstein identifies three insights of enduring political significance. The first is the corruption of political discourse occasioned by the rhetoric of *absolute good and evil*. The second insight concerns the *radical dehumanization* that is suffered whenever people are deprived of juridical status in a political community that denies their "right to have rights." Thirdly, the notion of the much maligned "banality of evil" itself contains the insight that the most devastating evil in politics may be carried out by perpetrators whose psychology is perfectly ordinary, even nondescript. And this, alas, is not a truth that our world has faced up to or transcended. That evil can be perpetrated by the most banal among us, especially in the world of bureaucratically and technologically interconnected modernity, calls for continuous vigilance. Treating each of these insights in turn, Bernstein concludes that Arendt's writings on evil offer as much of a stimulus to reflection for our time as they did for hers.

In Chapter 14, "Banality Reconsidered," Susan Neiman hails Arendt's *Eichmann in Jerusalem* as the most significant and successful attempt to revive theodicy for the modern age. Neiman undertakes to show how Arendt sought to make the most horrifying instances of modern evil humanly explicable. Arendt reveals her love of the world, what she called "*amor mundi*," by arguing that evil is neither an inherent part of the world nor of human nature. Evil is not inexplicable, argues Arendt.

In this chapter, Neiman also undertakes to explicate and extend the theory of strict moral responsibility that underlies Arendt's damning portrayal of Eichmann, a theory in which the agent's private intentions are vastly subordinate to the meaning of his or her acts. Arendt dispels the myth that evil must be intentional; whether we *will* good or evil may have little impact on how we actually affect the world; rather than our intentions, actions are what matter most. Eichmann's guilt, Arendt argued, was not a question of his subjective state of mind but of objective fact. Even though Eichmann often claimed that he was not an antisemite, by participating in the attempted extermination of the Jewish race, he committed crimes against humanity. In this context, it is fascinating to compare the significant divergences in Arendt's and Lemkin's understanding of the significance of intentionality in the perpetration of evil. For Lemkin, establishing genocidal intent is crucial, while it is not so for Arendt.

Another perspective on Arendt's response to the Eichmann trial is provided by Bryan Garsten in Chapter 15, "The Elusiveness of Arendtian Judgment." Here Garsten examines the conception of judgment that Arendt adumbrated in her writings after the Eichmann trial. In particular, he focuses on Arendt's consideration of Eichmann's invocation of ostensibly Kantian formulae to relieve himself of the burden of personal judgment. Garsten shows how Eichmann's disturbing use of such Kantian language prompted Arendt to turn to Kant's conception of representative thinking – found in his analysis of aesthetic judgment – to serve as the template for an alternative account of the activity of judging in politics. Arendt's moral theory seeks to make the individual beholden to no one or thing beside herself, while at the same time rejecting Nietzsche's invitation to move beyond good and evil. Arendt's conception of judgment remains *moral* in that it allows for right and wrong answers, but it is faced with finding a ground for its moral validity. Therefore, the judging individual remains a solitary one. Moral judgment, claims Garsten, lies in the ability to look at oneself from a distance, to imagine oneself as one voice among others. Moral failure occurs when, as with Eichmann, our identities are fixed by bureaucratic, nationalist or other contexts and our imaginations become too inert.

Arendt was not a moral philosopher in the ordinary sense. She was neither concerned with meta-ethics nor the foundations of ethics, nor was she interested in writing a book about virtues and principles. Yet moral preoccupations, and above all moral judgments about the right thing to do and the appropriate attitude and comportment to show, range from her reflections on antisemites to the story of Billy Budd (the paragon of blind innocence) and to Socrates as well as Heidegger, whom she called "the fox."[14] In Chapter 16, "Existential Values in Arendt's Treatment of Evil and Morality," George Kateb contends that the values that dominate Arendt's understanding of politics – and even her reflections on evil – are fundamentally existential in character. By "existential," Kateb means those characteristics that contribute to *human status*, that is, to one's survival as part of the species, and to *human stature*, such as the qualities of courage, selflessness, love, and friendship, among others. Kateb argues that Arendt had a great distaste for distinctions between morality and immorality, while at the same time a fascination with questions of evil and responsibility. Morality still takes various forms in Arendt's work, including social convention, Socratic morality, God's commandments, the teaching of Jesus, and the

---

[14] See Hannah Arendt, "Heidegger the Fox," in *Essays in Understanding. 1930–1954*, edited by Jerome Kohn (New York and London: Harcourt, Brace, 1994), pp. 361–3.

morality of authentic politics. Agreeing with Bernstein and Neiman, Kateb also holds that evil cannot be reduced to immorality and that Arendt was most concerned with the processes of dehumanization set into motion by evils that aimed at eradicating the existential principles of human status and human stature.

The highest type of morality for Arendt is Socratic morality. It is a morality that refuses to do harm even when one cannot expect recognition or reciprocation. Kateb asks whether Arendt is indeed calling for such a high model of self-sacrifice; he concludes instead that her model is the person who judiciously confronts evil rather than suffers it. It is courage above all that is the highest existential value. Courage is the virtue that comes to the fore in all genuinely political moments of resistance and in the emergence of the new in politics. In dark times, we search for courage.

PART I

FREEDOM, EQUALITY, AND RESPONSIBILITY

I

Arendt on the Foundations of Equality

Jeremy Waldron

1.1 Artificial Equality

Treating people as equals: Is this something that a political community can just decide to do regardless of what people are like, regardless of their similarities and differences? Is it something we can do even when we are not compelled to do it by what we know of human nature?

Hannah Arendt's affirmative answers to these questions are among the best-known features of her political philosophy. Arendt suggested that we might adopt a principle of treating one another as equals, not because of any similarities among us, but because such a principle makes possible a form of political community that we could not otherwise have. This is something the ancient Athenians did, she says; they identified a class of persons to treat as equal citizens even though others physically indistinguishable from them were subordinated as slaves (OR, 30–1).[1] And this is something she says we can do too. By nature, we may be quite different from one another. But by convention, we *hold* ourselves to be one another's equals.[2] We promised in the Declaration of Independence (and moved toward fulfillment of that promise in the Thirteenth Amendment and the Civil Rights Act) that, unlike the Athenians, we would not consign a race of people to permanently inferior status as slaves and non-citizens. But nothing, she says – neither God nor nature – compelled us to take that position. "We are not born equal; we become equal as members of a group on the strength of our decision to guarantee ourselves mutually equal rights"

[1] Hannah Arendt, *On Revolution* (Harmondsworth: Penguin, 1973), pp. 30–1. (Hereafter abbreviated OR.)

[2] See the reflections on the wording of the Declaration of Independence, in OR, pp. 192–3, and in Hannah Arendt, "Truth and Politics," in *Between Past and Future: Eight Exercises in Political Thought* (Harmondsworth: Penguin, 1977), pp. 246–7. See also, on this point, Philip Selznick, *The Moral Commonwealth: Social Theory and the Promise of Community* (Berkeley: University of California Press, 1992), pp. 482–3, and the discussion in Pauline Maier, *American Scripture: Making the Declaration of Independence* (New York: Vintage, 1997), pp. 123 ff.

(*OT,* 301).[3] Arendt understood political equality not as something inherent in human nature, but as something conventional and artificial, the product of human effort, an artifact of social and political institutions in a man-made world.[4] "Our political life," she said, "rests on the assumption that we can produce equality through organization," even when nature has not produced it for us (*OT,* 301). For our engagement in the joint enterprise of politics, the law can create for each of us an artificial *persona* – the citizen – that takes its place on the public stage, presenting us not exactly as the beings we naturally are, but as equals for political purposes.

As Seyla Benhabib has noticed, these and similar remarks (pervasive in Arendt's work) have generated a great deal of excitement among those of Arendt's commentators who want to claim her for the antifoundationalist party in modern political theory.[5] Like Benhabib, I am skeptical that Arendt's view of equality is best understood as an antifoundationalist claim.[6] Arendt sometimes finds it convenient, for rhetorical purposes, to *pretend* that she thinks that we could just hold a group of entities to be one another's political equals, irrespective of what the entities are like. But that proposition – which in itself is slightly mad (as though we could just decide to treat trees, tigers, teapots, and teenagers as one another's equals for political purposes) – is not what Arendt thinks. Her work makes it clear that we can be held to be one another's equals because of certain facts about ourselves (our nature and our condition). I suspect that those who recoil from this position, those who cling to the antifoundationalist interpretation, do so because they have not really thought through what it is to articulate a view about equality in political theory.

In this chapter, I shall set out what I think is involved in the articulation of a view – any view – about basic equality, and I shall relate that view step by step to what we know of Arendt's account. A lot of what follows involves an exploration of certain ideas and concepts from analytic moral and political philosophy.[7] In section 8, I shall try to delineate the exact shape of Arendt's equality commitment and the facts on which it is grounded. I shall argue that Arendt believed not only that a happy few can construct equality among themselves for political purposes, but that humans in general have the potential to be among those who can be treated as equals in politics, so that in this very indirect and background way, it makes sense to hold that all humans are born or created equal.

[3] Hannah Arendt, *The Origins of Totalitarianism,* new edition (New York: Harcourt, Brace, Jovanovich, 1973), p. 301. (Hereafter abbreviated *OT.*)

[4] This is a close paraphrase of *OR,* pp. 30–1.

[5] Seyla Benhabib, *The Reluctant Modernism of Hannah Arendt* (Thousand Oaks, CA: Sage, 1996), p. 197.

[6] Ibid., pp. 196–7.

[7] It draws on an unpublished manuscript of mine entitled "Basic Equality," which can be accessed at http://ssrn.com/abstract=1311816.

1.2 A Normative Theory?

For Hannah Arendt, equality is a principle or a commitment, something that operates in the practical political realm.[8] We do not do a study and discover that people are equal; we *hold* that they are equal. Equality is not an idle description of anything (though whether it is based on anything descriptive is something that will occupy us for much of this chapter). It is an "ought," not an "is." It is normative, not descriptive.

On the other hand, it is not easy to regard any of Arendt's work as straight-forwardly and cheerfully normative, like an article on global justice in *Philosophy and Public Affairs*. Arendt is not urging us to do anything or telling us what she would do if she ruled the world.[9] She once said that it was presumptuous for a theorist to issue instructions concerning political action: "[M]y God! These are adults! We are not in the nursery!"[10] And in any case, there is no clear sense in her work that what she values or the principles she embraces have any real chance now of being implemented in the world. Often her tone is one of lamentation, close to despair, that certain things that might have been done are now impossible, that we have closed off certain practical possibilities in the way we have nurtured our political heritage.[11] It is not quite despairing; there is always a muted, "And yet . . . ," in her writing. But mostly it is autumnal and elegiac in the spirit of the sentence that opens section 4 of the final chapter of *On Revolution*: "It is a strange and sad story that remains to be told and remembered . . . " (*OR*, 255).

So if anyone asks, "What does Arendt recommend we do about equality now, in 2010, in the United States?" the answer may well be a sad and stoic, "Nothing. It's too late." But still, she had a position on equality and it was a practical political position, not just an idle contemplative one. The bitterness of defeat that characterizes much of her writing does not transform the logical character of her position (from practical to merely contemplative), though it certainly alters the prospect of its "implementation." We should bear all this in mind in everything that follows.

---

[8] This has two meanings. Almost any principle of equality will operate in the political realm inasmuch as it goes to the issue of what we are to do together (about our political system, our economy, our family structures, or whatever). Arendt's principle is also political in a second sense: She is interested (politically) in political equality – the equality of participants in a political process. She was much less interested in – and rather feared the application of – principles of social and economic equality.

[9] See also Jeremy Waldron, "What Plato Would Allow," in Ian Shapiro and Judith Wagner DeCew, eds., *Nomos XXXVII: Theory and Practice* (New York University Press, 1995), 138, at pp. 167–70.

[10] Hannah Arendt, "On Hannah Arendt," in Melvyn Hill, ed., *Hannah Arendt: The Recovery of the Public World* (New York: St. Martin's Press, 1979), 301, at p. 310.

[11] See Margaret Canovan, "The Contradictions of Hannah Arendt's Political Thought," *Political Theory*, 6 (1978), 5, for discussion of the trajectory of Arendt's thought in this regard.

1.3 Equality and Supervenience

Arendt's position on equality is (in this ambivalent sense) practical and political. However, despite what she sometimes says, I do not believe that that her position is unrelated to a view about what human beings are factually like. We need to proceed carefully, to consider what that factual view might be and what its relation might be to Arendt's practical position.

One thing that Arendt insists on is that we are not driven or compelled to any particular position on equality by facts about ourselves (our nature and our condition).[12] Equality is a matter of value, decision, and attitude; it is not itself a fact. And the value, decision, or attitude that it embodies is not something we are compelled to adopt by the way the world is.

But the proposition that we are not compelled by the facts to take any particular position on human equality does not mean that the position we do decide to take has no relation to facts about ourselves (our nature and our condition). To use the technical language of analytic philosophy, our value position on equality can *supervene* upon certain factual propositions even though it is not entailed by those propositions.

Everything in this last paragraph needs amplification. Let us begin with Arendt's view about what we are compelled to think or do in relation to equality. Like everyone else in the world, Arendt believes there are differences and similarities among human beings. A common type of egalitarian view holds that the differences among humans are not so great or important while at least some of the similarities among humans are very considerable and important. So important are the similarities, according to this view, that all people of good faith will just see that humans ought to be regarded as equal; and – the view continues – the differences among humans are not so great as to drive us away from the recognition of equality. Arendt is convinced that this view is wrong, at least in its psychological predictions about how most people respond to the differences and similarities. Some of the differences among humans arouse "dumb hatred, mistrust, and discrimination," while some of the more striking similarities lead us to recoil from our common biological humanity (*OT,* 190, 301). Certainly there does not seem to be anything in our common humanity that compels any sort of moral or practical response: "The world found nothing sacred in the abstract nakedness of being human" (*OT,* 297).

Of course, the psychological fact that people do not move from proposition P to proposition Q does not show that Q is not a logical entailment of proposition P. People may be bad reasoners. But I think Arendt at this stage is associating herself with a perfectly intelligible philosophical position – namely, that facts themselves do not dictate values or principles. The fact that people often do not adopt an egalitarian principle when confronted with the commonalities of

---

[12] Cf. Margaret Canovan, *Hannah Arendt: A Reinterpretation of Her Political Thought* (Cambridge: Cambridge University Press, 1992), p. 242: "Arendt did not believe that 'nature' prescribed criteria to human beings."

human nature pays tribute to the point that you cannot *derive* an "ought" from an "is."

Now, some people *do* say that humans are one another's equals. And they say that when they are confronted with exactly the same evidence that drives others to inequality or racism. So what does this show? It shows, presumably, that the egalitarian position is possible, though not necessary, in the face of this evidence. Some people hold it, and others do not. It is, as Arendt puts it, a matter of opinion, not truth.[13] But what it does not show is that those who hold the equality position take no notice of the facts from which their inegalitarian opponents recoil. They do take notice of those facts; they just respond in a different way. And it misrepresents their position to omit the point that it is a response to these facts; it would certainly misrepresent their position to say that they just decided to treat people as equals irrespective of the facts.

Philosophers use the term "supervenience" to refer to the relation between moral qualities and the descriptive characteristics in virtue of which the moral qualities hold or apply. As Simon Blackburn puts it:

Properties of one kind, F, supervene upon those of another kind, G, when things are F in virtue of being G. Thus a person cannot just be good, but must be good in virtue of possessing other properties, such as courage or kindness. The supervening property relates to the underlying qualities in at least this way: if one thing possesses the underlying properties and is F, then any other thing with the same underlying properties must share the resultant property F.[14]

If I say that one particular piece of pottery is good and another is not, it must be by virtue of some difference between them, and then the distinction of value is supervenient upon that difference. It doesn't matter what sort of difference it is – a difference in their physical properties or appearance, a difference in the order in which I viewed them, a difference in their history or their manufacture. The important point is that it is part of the logic of value predicates that evaluations do not float free of other characteristics as though two objects could differ only in their value without any other basis for discrimination between them.

Also, the supervenience thesis is perfectly compatible with the view that each person or community decides for itself how to organize and structure its

[13] Arendt, "Truth and Politics," p. 246.

[14] Simon Blackburn, *The Oxford Dictionary of Philosophy* (Oxford: Oxford University Press, 1996), p. 368. See also R. M. Hare, "Supervenience," *Proceedings of the Aristotlean Society*, 58 (1984); Simon Blackburn, *Essays in Quasi-Realism* (New York: Oxford University Press, 1983), pp. 114 ff.; and Robert Stalnaker, "Varieties of Supervenience," *Noûs*, 30 (1996), Supplement: 221. For some discussions of why supervenience is true of moral properties, see Jonathan Dancy, "On Moral Properties," *Mind*, 90 (1981): 367; and James Klagge, "An Alleged Difficulty Concerning Moral Properties," *Mind*, 93 (1984): 370. Note that supervenience is not just about value properties. It is also true of the relation between mental and physical properties: If at one moment I am in mental state M_1 and a moment later in a different mental state M_2, that must be in virtue of the fact that the physical state of my body or central nervous system has changed. This is not reductionism: It does not reduce mental states to physical states, but it insists that the former supervene upon the latter.

values. One person's (or one culture's) evaluative distinction between x and y may rest on fact F_1, another person (or culture) may refuse to make such a discrimination, or if they do, they may base it on a different fact F_2. So supervenience is not about moral objectivity, moral truth, or moral universals or being forced by the way things are to adopt one value position or another. It simply indicates that if one does make an evaluative discrimination, one must have in mind some underlying reference to other differences on which one's evaluative discrimination is based.

My point then is that Arendt need not be read as denying that equality supervenes upon certain facts simply because she denies that any facts about our nature compel us to adopt the principle. Or to put it the other way around, there is no reason to be scared off by her remarks about what nature does or does not compel us to think, from exploring the facts that she thinks are important to the position she holds and recommends concerning human equality.

I suppose it is possible that Arendt could (in effect) be denying the supervenience thesis. Some political philosophers have sometimes talked about equality in tones that indicate they do not accept supervenience. An example is Margaret Macdonald, a follower of Ludwig Wittgenstein, writing in the late 1940s. Beginning from a noncognitivist perspective, Macdonald wrote:

... value-utterances are more like records of *decisions* than propositions. To assert that "Freedom is better than slavery" or "All men are of equal worth" is not to state a fact but to *choose* a side. It announces *This is where I stand*.[15]

Macdonald acknowledged that this invited the following question:

Upon what grounds or for what reasons are decisions reached? Consider the expression of the doctrine of equality; that all human beings are of equal worth, intrinsic value, or are ends in themselves. Is there an answer to the question, Why?[16]

But she responded defiantly:

I affirm that no natural characteristic constitutes a reason for the assertion that all human beings are of equal worth. Or, alternatively, that all the characteristics of any human being are equally reasons for this assertion.... Do we, then, decide without reason? Are decisions determined by chance or whim?[17]

No, she says, but the problem is a little bit like asking someone why he or she loves his or her friends or children. They just do.[18]

---

[15] Margaret Macdonald, "Natural Rights" (1947), reprinted in Jeremy Waldron, ed., *Theories of Rights*, (Oxford: Oxford University Press, 1984), 21, at p. 35.

[16] Ibid., p. 36.

[17] Ibid., pp. 36–7.

[18] At ibid., p. 37, Macdonald quoted this from Montaigne's essay "On Friendship": "If a man urge me to tell him wherefore I loved him, I feel it cannot be expressed but by answering, because it was he, because it was myself.... It is not one especial consideration, nor two, nor three, nor four, nor a thousand. It is I know not what kind of quintessence of all this commixture which seized my will" (idem.).

It is not clear whether Macdonald is really saying in this passage that equality is based on nothing or whether she is saying – something that is perfectly compatible with the supervenience principle – that it is hard to pin down *anything in particular* that it is based on, though it is certainly based on something. What I want to emphasize, however, is that it would be a mistake to associate the rejection of supervenience with Macdonald's noncognitivism – her view that value judgments express decisions rather than report facts. Maybe some noncognitivists do reject supervenience. But most do not – Simon Blackburn and R. M. Hare being two very prominent examples of people who believe, on the one hand, that it is the function of value judgments to express attitudes, and, on the other hand, that the expression of an attitude in a value judgment is always supervenient on some range of facts.

1.4 A Shallow Grounding?

Another possibility is that Arendt might accept supervenience but give equality a fairly shallow grounding. I think this is not the case, but it is worth exploring the possibility anyway. I will begin with an analogy between shallow versions of equality and shallow versions of racism.

Some versions of racism are shallow. The racist makes a discrimination of value as between *x* and *y*, and when asked what the discrimination is based on, he or she cites a difference in skin color or physiognomic characteristics: The racist says *x* is white and *y* is black. When asked why that matters, he or she may or may not have anything interesting to say: The racist may come up with some theory about the infrastructure of racial difference, or may simply retreat to the position that "color matters." That position is compatible with the supervenience thesis; the supervenience simply reveals how shallow the racist's position is. (The racist is, in R. M. Hare's terms, a color fanatic.)[19]

A view about equality might be shallow in a similar way. A person who treats *x* and *y* as equals but not *z* might, when challenged for an explanation, simply respond that *x* and *y* belong to the human species, whereas *z* is a dolphin. If we ask what is it about that species that makes this great difference, he or she might say: "It's just the species itself. Everyone's moral positions start from somewhere (Bentham starts from the pleasure principle, Kant from the categorical imperative, etc.). This is the starting point of my position. I just happen to place a fundamental nonderivative value on being human." (This kind of superficiality tends to enrage animal-rights defenders.)

Now one has to get at least that far – at least as far as this very superficial supervenience – just to have one's egalitarianism identified as a principle of *human* equality (as opposed to a principle of the equality of all things – trees, teapots, tigers, teenagers, etc.). But most theories of human equality go much further than this. Their supervenience is deeper. They offer an explanation of *why* humanness makes a difference. They do that in terms of certain capacities

[19] R. M. Hare, *Freedom and Reason* (Oxford: Clarendon Press, 1963), p. 161.

and vulnerabilities that all humans have or that come as standard equipment with being human – and they might explain, too, why having those capacities is more important than having them to any particular degree. (They identify them as range properties, in John Rawls's phrase.[20])

If it is political equality that such theories are talking about, they may go further and also identify features of individuals in response to which we accord them equal standing. For example, the fact that x has a life to lead in this land just as y does was as important to Colonel Rainsborough's political egalitarianism in the 1647 Putney Debates as any commonality of capacity as between x and y.[21] And they will relate these facts about capacity and standing to the rights that equality is supposed to confer. When an account of equality is articulated in this way – in terms of principles about standing as well as capacity – then it begins to become not just a position supervening on certain facts, but a full-blooded theory.

Is there any reason to suppose that Hannah Arendt's view of equality is not a theory in this sense? Is there any reason to consign her to the ranks of those superficial egalitarians who say, "I just hold humans to be one another's equal because they are humans. I just do." I think not. Occasionally she is reputed to have announced an aversion from "theory." But on other occasions, Arendt indicated she thought conceptual structure and articulation were essential and that Americans were the worse for their lack of it (*OR*, 220). Whether we call it a theory or not, we shall see shortly that her position on equality is complex and articulate. But first let me develop two or three further philosophical points about supervenience.

---

[20] John Rawls, *A Theory of Justice* (Cambridge: Harvard University Press, 1971), p. 508, proposes the notion of *a range property* as a way of capturing the fact that basic equality responds to the mere presence of a capacity as opposed to the degree to which people possess it:

> [I]t is not the case that founding equality on natural capacities is incompatible with an egalitarian view. All we have to do is to select a range property (as I shall say) and to give equal justice to those meeting its conditions.

For an example of a range property, consider the characteristic which a municipality might have of *being in New Jersey* (e.g., as opposed to *being in New York*). Though Princeton is in central New Jersey, well away from the state line, and Hoboken just over the river from New York, they are both *in* New Jersey to the same extent, so far as the law is concerned. One could point to a scalar geographical difference between them; but jurisdictionally, it is irrelevant. *Being in New Jersey*, then, is a range property, ranging over all the points within the boundaries of the state. On Rawls's view, the relevant range property for equality to supervene upon is "the capacity for moral personality":

> [W]hile individuals... have varying capacities for a sense of justice, this fact is not a reason for depriving those with a lesser capacity of the full protection of justice. Once a certain minimum is met, a person is entitled to equal liberty on a par with everyone else. (ibid., pp. 505–6)

[21] I am thinking of Colonel Rainsborough's great exclamation at Putney: "[T]ruly I think that the poorest he that is in England has a life to lead as the greatest he." Extract from "The Debates at the General Council of the Army, Putney, 29 October 1647," in Andrew Sharp, ed., *The English Levellers* (Cambridge: Cambridge University Press, 1998), p. 103.

1.5 Shapelessness

We have already seen that it is no part of the supervenience position that moral judgments supervene on very simple or easily identifiable factual properties. As George Fletcher argues, even if humans are equal in virtue of something, there is no reason to suppose that that something is a single property of human nature.[22] Fletcher points out that when Shakespeare's Shylock attempted to persuade Venetian gentiles that he was their equal, he cited not one characteristic but a whole array of features, as though to get his audience to see things in terms of a *Gestalt*:

Hath not a Jew eyes? [H]ath not a Jew hands, organs, dimensions, senses, affections, passions? [F]ed with the same food, hurt with the same weapons, subject to the same diseases, healed by the same means, warmed and cooled by the same winter and summer as a Christian is? If you prick us, do we not bleed? If you tickle us, do we not laugh? [I]f you poison us, do we not die? – And if you wrong us, shall we not revenge?[23]

There is a further point that follows from this. We may associate equality with certain characteristics and capabilities. But there is no reason to suppose that a commitment to equality must supervene upon a set of properties that is intelligible, or makes sense as a package, apart from the commitment. When we say that a moral commitment is a subjective response to a factual feature or a set of factual features of the world, we do not necessarily mean that it is a composite of two independently intelligible judgments – one of fact, one of value – that can be understood quite separately from one another. Consider an analogy. It is tempting to say that the term "courage" refers descriptively to a certain steadfastness in the face of danger and (as a separate matter) that it connotes an evaluative attitude of approval to that character trait. But singling out *this* character trait may make no sense apart from our interest in judging people courageous. And the same may be true of other "thick" moral predicates, particularly virtue words such as "temperance," "honesty," "fidelity," and so forth. It is not the case that for these words, we already understand a certain character trait and *then* decide to adopt and express an evaluative attitude toward it. Instead, the attitude itself shapes the trait we are interested in, and the trait may seem odd or shapeless apart from the interest that the attitude defines.[24]

---

[22] George P. Fletcher, "In God's Image: The Religious Imperative of Equality under Law," 99 *Columbia Law Review* 1608 (1999).

[23] Ibid., pp. 1619–20, citing William Shakespeare, *The Merchant of Venice*, Act 3, scene 1.

[24] This position is set out for value language generally by John McDowell, "Non-Cognitivism and Rule-Following," in Steven Holtzman and Christopher Leich, eds., *Wittgenstein: To Follow a Rule* (London: Routledge, 1981), p. 144. Reacting against the view that we can always separate a factual and evaluative component of our value judgements, McDowell says we should

be skeptical about whether the disentangling manouevre . . . can always be effected: specifically, about whether, corresponding to any value concept, one can always isolate a genuine feature

Applying this to equality, it is possible that the descriptive features underlying equality are weird or "shapeless" – who would be interested in *them*, under exactly *this* description? – apart from the attitude (commitment to equality) that is supposedly a response to them. Seeing people in a certain way may be inseparable from resolving to treat them as one's equals, and someone who has not resolved to treat them as his equals may complain that he does not really "get" the description to which his adversaries say they are responding. All this is perfectly plausible for equality, particularly because egalitarians often base their commitment to equality on range properties (such as the property of operating cognitively above a certain threshold) or having a certain capacity (irrespective of the degree to which one has it). Seeing people under the description of a certain range property – focusing on kinds of capacity, rather than degrees of capacity[25] – may be something that egalitarians do and inegalitarians refuse to do. But this is all quite consistent with supervenience.

I believe that Arendt's position is of this kind. She does not believe that we first have a theory of human nature and once we are convinced of that, then we arrive at a commitment to equality on the basis of it. Instead, the things we notice about human nature and the human condition are themselves part and parcel of our willingness to adopt an egalitarian perspective. We buy into a theory (of the sort mentioned at the end of section 4) as a whole, as a package, and that is one of the reasons she resists any claim that we have been driven to this theory by preexisting independent observations of human nature. But, again, the fact that we buy into it as a whole does not mean that it is necessarily inarticulate or that there is nothing that can be said to explain, ground, or characterize our commitment to equality.

1.6 Natural and Non-Natural Accounts

Readers may worry that I am trying, one way or another, to saddle Hannah Arendt with some sort of naturalism about equality. I am not. The position I am attributing to her does not require that an equality commitment be based on natural or biological features. Our animality, the shape of our bodies, our natural givenness – she had no interest in resting equality on any of this and

---

of the world –...that is, a feature that is there anyway, independently of anyone's value-experience being as it is – to be that to which competent users of the concept are to be regarded as responding when they use it; that which is left in the world when one peels off the reflection of the appropriate attitude.... If the disentangling manouevre is always possible, that implies that the extension of the associated term...could be mastered independently of the special concerns which...show themselves in admiration or emulation of actions seen as falling under the concept.... But is it at all plausible that this singling out can always be brought off?

McDowell insists that the "shapelessness" thesis need not involve a denial of "supervenience": "Supervenience requires only that one be able to find differences expressible in terms of the level supervened upon whenever one wants to make different judgements in terms of the supervening level. It does not follow...that the set of items to which a supervening term is correctly applied need constitute a kind recognizable as such at the level supervened upon" (ibid., pp. 144–5).

[25] Rawls, *Theory of Justice*, pp. 504–12. See note 22.

she regarded all efforts to do so as dangerous (*OT,* 300–2). She did not deny that one *could* found a principle of equality on this basis, but it would be an equality of animal need – "Insofar as we all need bread, we are indeed all the same" (*OR,* 94) – and as a social ideal it would be liable to flatten and destroy the more active political equality she was interested in (*OT,* 54).[26]

Fortunately, the supervenience I have been talking about does not imply anything about the *character* of the properties supervened upon. It does not require that they be biological, natural, or even social properties. They may be non-natural or metaphysical properties. It does not even require that they be non-value properties, so long as two conditions are satisfied: first, the supervened-upon property must be distinct from the supervening property; and secondly, if the supervened-upon property is evaluative, then there is also some further property upon which it in turn supervenes.

There is, for example, no affront to supervenience in suggesting that humans' equal worth is based on their all having a soul, their being all children of God, or their having some noumenal capacity for moral will of the sort that Immanuel Kant wrote about. When Justice McLean, dissenting in *Dred Scott,* protested that the plaintiff was entitled to justice because "[h]e bears the impress of his Maker, . . . and he is destined to an endless existence,"[27] he was not just repeating himself. He was pointing to facts, albeit non-natural facts, in virtue of which it was hideously wrong to treat Dred Scott as a "mere chattel." George Fletcher associates the holism for which (as we saw in section 5) he argues in his recent article on equality with the idea that humans are one another's equals because they are created in the image of God.[28] This bases equality on a complex relational property with serious theological and non-natural components. Of course, all such claims require explication and they may be problematic for those who are convinced that basic equality has to be characterized and defended on secular grounds.[29] But they should not be ruled out a priori.

I am not saying that Arendt held a view of this kind. She distinguished her view from any sort of equality before God, equality as sinners, or equality in the face of death (*HC,* 215).[30] But there are other non-natural elements that might be important.

Think, for example, of the way Kant articulated the moral equality basic to his system of thought. In his account of why humans were to be respected as ends in themselves,[31] Kant emphasized the common human capacity to grasp and respond to the moral law: "To satisfy the categorical command of morality

---

[26] See also Benhabib, *Reluctant Modernism,* p. 27.

[27] *Dred Scott v. Sandford* 60 U.S. 393, 550 (1856), McLean J. dissenting.

[28] Fletcher, "In God's Image."

[29] See the account of "public reason" in John Rawls, *Political Liberalism,* New Edition (New York: Columbia University Press, 1996).

[30] Hannah Arendt, *The Human Condition* (Chicago: University of Chicago Press, 1958), p. 215. (Hereafter abbreviated *HC.*)

[31] I introduce Kant at this stage as an analogy, to help us focus on different ways of grounding human equality. But I do not forget the rather severe things that Arendt had to say about Kant's

is within everyone's power at all times."[32] Now, from one point of view, such a capacity is the most mundane thing imaginable. It is a range property that covers a whole variety of ordinary human abilities. It covers not just the effete sensibility of the moral specialist, but also the unsophisticated scruples of the ordinary man,[33] the uneasy conscience of "the boldest evildoer,"[34] even the "child of around eight or nine years old," who will undoubtedly answer in the negative if asked whether it is all right to appropriate to one's own use money with which one has been entrusted.[35] It ranges over the good and the bad, the self-aware and the self-deluded, the scrupulous and the unscrupulous, the morally learned and the morally illiterate.[36] From another point of view, however, Kantian moral capacity is momentously otherworldly. He sees it as a feature of the noumenal rather than the phenomenal aspect of our being.[37] It is an awe-inspiring form of metaphysical freedom, it distinguishes us as creatures who can rise above our given natural heritage, and it reveals for us "a life independent of animality and even of the whole sensible world."[38] So much is this so that some modern philosophers regard Kant's theory of basic equality as hopelessly inappropriate for the modern world.[39]

formula of "ends-in-themselves" in *HC*, pp. 155–6, and her qualified enthusiasm for his account of freedom in Hannah Arendt, "What Is Freedom?" in *Between Past and Future*, pp. 144–5.

[32] Kant, The *Critique of Practical Reason*, in Immanuel Kant, *Practical Philosophy*, edited by Mary Gregor (Cambridge: Cambridge University Press, 1996), 137, at p. 169 (V: 36 in the Prussian Academy edition of Kant's *Werke*).

[33] Ibid., p. 210 (V: 88).

[34] Ibid., p. 204 (V: 80).

[35] Immanuel Kant, "On the Common Saying: "This May be True in Theory, but it does not Apply in Practice," in *Kant: Political Writings*, edited by Hans Reiss (Cambridge: Cambridge University Press, 1991), p. 70.

[36] Kant does not mean by this to suggest that people's unequal moral achievements are unimportant. On the contrary: "Before a humble common man, in whom I perceive uprightness of character in a higher degree than I am aware of in myself my spirit bows, whether I want it or whether I do not." (Kant, *Critique of Practical Reason*, p. 202 (V: 77)) But far from being incompatible with our fundamental equality, the importance of our awareness of this inequality is precisely that it confirms that the righteous man and I are basically one another's equals. For as Kant goes on immediately to say: "His example holds before me a law that strikes down my self-conceit when I compare it with my conduct, and I see observance of that law and hence its practicability proved before me in fact" (idem).

[37] See Immanuel Kant, *Groundwork of the Metaphysics of Morals*, in Kant, *Practical Philosophy*, p. 103 (4: 457).

[38] Kant, *Critique of Practical Reason*, pp. 269–70 (5: 161–2).

[39] See Bernard Williams, "The Idea of Equality" (originally 1962), in his collection *Problems of the Self* (Cambridge: Cambridge University Press, 1973) 230, at p. 235: "The very considerable consistency of Kant's view is bought at what would generally be agreed to be a very high price. The detachment of moral worth from all contingencies is achieved only by making man's characteristic as a moral or rational agent a transcendental characteristic; man's capacity to will freely as a rational agent is not dependent on any empirical capacities he may have – and, in particular, is not dependent on empirical capacities which men may possess unequally – because in the Kantian view, the capacity to be a rational agent is not itself an empirical capacity at all.... The ground of the respect owed to each man thus emerges in the Kantian theory as a kind of secular analogue of the Christian conception of the respect owed to all men as equally

Arendt is not Kant, but I believe her commitment to equality is like his in many ways. It is not grounded in any natural characteristic if by that is meant biological, animal, or even social-psychological nature. But it is grounded in our nature in another sense: in the sense in which "human nature" means *what we are like*.[40] (Analogously, Kant's account of our noumenal capacity to will morally even in the face of contrary inclination is an account of our nature, of what we are like, even though it is not an account of any natural or empirical characteristic.) And for Arendt, too, the key element is a form of non-natural or even antinatural freedom: the remarkable ability of human individuals to embark on new beginnings. I will say more about this – which is the key to Arendt's theory of equality – in section 8.

1.7 Human Nature and the Human Condition

One other point about equality and supervenience is worth mentioning. It is often thought that the facts on which egalitarian commitments supervene must be properties of isolated individuals: Each human has certain needs or each human has a certain capability, and this is something about each individual that can be understood quite apart from his or her relation to others. There is no reason why an articulate egalitarianism has to have this shape. Equality might be based on relational facts about humans – that each human may be capable of entering into certain relations with others.

Some Christian thinkers have pursued a theory of this kind, suggesting that humans are equals because they equally have the capacity to love one another.[41] If God is (in a sense) love, then our loving might be our bearing the image of God. There is nothing individually about us that makes us worth loving, but that we *can* love one another – that is the key to our equality. I do not want to pursue these theological matters any further. For us, the point is this: There is no particular reason why we should start with an account of human characteristics rather than human relations in our quest for an understanding of to what (if anything) basic equality is a response.

Again, Arendt's account is not theological, but I think it is of this shape. Unlike Kant, who spoke of the moral will as a distinct capability of each

---

children of God. Though secular, it is equally metaphysical.... This transcendental Kantian conception cannot provide any solid foundation for the notions of equality among men, or of equality of respect owed to them. Apart from the general difficulties of such transcendental conceptions, there is the obstinate fact that the concept of 'moral agent,' and the concepts allied to it such as that of responsibility, do and must have an empirical base."

[40] For Arendt's allergy to talk of "human nature" and her preference for talk of "the human condition," see *HC*, p. 10. For the idea that Arendt nevertheless developed a "universal anthropology" of the human species, see Benhabib, *Reluctant Modernism*, pp. 195–6.

[41] Karl Barth has suggested that we should emphasize the plurals in Genesis 1:26: "Then God said: 'Let *us* make human beings in *our* image, after *our* likeness...'" See the discussion of Barth's *Dogmatik* in David Cairns, *The Image of God in Man* (London: SCM Press, 1953), pp. 24 and 167 ff. Barth emphasizes particularly the relation between male and female. God created "man-and-woman" in his image: "... male and female created he them."

person considered in isolation from others (a capability that might be directed as much to self-regarding moral choices as to other-regarding moral choices), the freedom that in my view lies at the base of Arendt's theory of equality is definitively other-related.[42] It is like Aristotle's view that man is a political animal and that our capacity to speak to one another is the leading mark of this (*HC*, 25–8).[43]

This may be one way of explaining Arendt's extreme allergy to all talk of human nature, even though (as we said at the end of section 6) "human nature" need not be understood naturalistically. She preferred to speak of "the human condition," which seemed to leave open the possibility that it is something about the way in which we live or can live with others (our being with others), not taxonomic facts about ourselves, that is key to any claim about our equality. Plurality, for Arendt, was key to the human condition – "not one man, but men, inhabit the earth" (*HC*, 234) – and "specifically *the* condition – not only the *conditio sine qua non*, but the *conditio per quam* – of all political life" (*HC*, 7–8).

1.8 Equality, Participation, and Self-selecting Elites

It is time to stop saying what Arendt's conception of equality is not and state clearly what I think it is. My exposition will be brief. It is not the aim of this short chapter to give a comprehensive view of this aspect of Arendt's political thought. I have mostly wanted to understand its structure and to relate it – I hope fruitfully – to discussions in political philosophy, a discipline from which consideration of her ideas has been isolated too long.

In acknowledgment of her position that one is not driven to any view about equality by noticing certain facts about ourselves, I begin my affirmative account of Arendt on equality not with her view of human nature or the human condition but with her account of the normative work that a principle of political equality has to do. Equality operates in Arendt's thought as a principle about political participation. It embodies two positions:

1. The position that anyone might participate in the actions and discussions of a free republic
2. The position that the actions and discussions of a free republic are possible only among equals

These positions work together in Arendt's thinking and they need to be understood in light of each other.

---

[42] I would say "social" except that that has a particular meaning in Arendt's vocabulary (*HC*, 38 ff.). See Hanna Pitkin, *The Attack of the Blob: Hannah Arendt's Concept of the Social* (Chicago: University of Chicago Press, 1998).

[43] See Aristotle, *The Politics*, edited by Stephen Everson (Cambridge: Cambridge University Press, 1988), p. 3 (Book I, chapter 2, 1253a).

Of the two positions I have mentioned, position (1) is roughly democratic in character: It argues against any sort of a priori exclusion of persons of any category from the political life of a republic (e.g., on the grounds that people of that sort are unworthy or do not have what it takes). Position (2) is more republican than democratic in spirit. It emphasizes that if there is to be action and discussion in politics, those who participate must hold themselves to be equals, because only among equals can the relevant kinds of interaction take place.

Too often, Arendt's position is understood in the light of (2) only. But position (2) by itself is egalitarian only in the sense that apartheid South Africa was democratic: apartheid South Africa empowered a demos of white citizens to interact as equals (as voters, as potential legislators, etc.) in the governance of the republic; but it did that while excluding millions of South Africans from the franchise and from political life generally. There was no equivalent in apartheid South Africa of a commitment to (1); indeed, position (1) was explicitly denied. Those who think of Arendt as an elitist often come close to saying that she denied (1). But she did not: (1) was an integral part of her view about equality.

How do the two positions work together? Position (2) puts a lot of strain on (1), because it requires that those for whom position (1) secures entry to politics must be capable of being equals in the sense that position (2) requires. Put the other way around, position (1) not only demands that people not be excluded from politics, but promises that the basis of that demand is consistent with the requirement that position (2) imposes. Both positions have to make claims about those to whom they apply. Position (2) is predicated on certain assumptions about those who are likely to engage in political life: It assumes that they can submit to the discipline of (artificial) equality. (I shall say more about this in a moment.) And position (1) assumes that the promise I mentioned can be fulfilled: that humans in general are such that in principle no exclusion from political participation of any class of them is necessary to ensure that republican politics is possible. Working together in this way, the two principles add up to an egalitarian commitment, which as we will see is both rooted in Arendt's account of what humans (but not trees, teapots, and tigers) are like, and credible in the light of that account.

As we detail these principles, it is necessary – more than ever – to bear in mind what was said in section 2 of this chapter. Arendt was not offering cheerful normative recommendations about what should be done in public life; but she was articulating (sadly, sometimes with precious little hope) a political position of a certain kind, and it went something like this.

A form of action and enterprise together can be imagined (and has shown itself from time to time to be possible) that involves speech, debate, and res-olution on action among people interacting as equals on matters of common concern. This is the gist of position (2) that I have mentioned. We imagine large groups of people participating in the public realm addressing matters that concern them all. The primary mode of this participation is speech, though of course when speech issues an action, there is also the cooperative undertaking of the enterprise itself and the keeping of faith with whatever was resolved or instituted (*OR*, 174). In this business, people will speak freely; they will make speeches with proposals, cautions, criticisms, and modifications of each other's proposals; they will distinguish themselves in these affairs, pay attention to each other, and hold themselves ready to modify their own positions in the light of others' distinctive contributions. If resolution and action subsequent to debate are necessary, then there will also need to be some means such as voting and majority decision (*OR*, 164) for settling on action in the face of any remaining disagreement, and people will participate in this too and act together in and on the basis of it.

This realm of action is undeniably political, but among the participants it is not a system of rule (*OR*, 30, and *HC*, 32). It is a system of determination and action in common. Arendt calls it "freedom in a positive sense" (*OR*, 275), because participants experience it as a mode of action, attentive and responsive to others but unconstrained by them. No one's opinion is entitled to dominate the others. Instead, opinion is filtered through the process of debate – "formed and tested in a process of exchange of opinion against opinion" (*OR*, 227). And no one's practical conclusion dominates others: This is not like a king listening to his counselors. The decision procedure, like the debate, is something in which all are involved.

Arendt adopts the position that none of this can take place without each participant regarding every other participant as his peer and recognizing and treating each of his peers as his equals. "Freedom in a positive sense is possible only among equals" (*OR*, 275). As George Kateb puts it, "[i]f political actors were not equal, they could not understand each other and work together."[44] Though politics may be (in some agonistic way) a striving for distinction, it is not oblivious display. Each seeks to be seen and heard, and participants in the processes that Arendt describes must pay attention to each other. They do so not just as an admiring audience but because each recognizes the possibility of learning from others (and contributing to others) as he might learn from (and contribute to) dialogic consideration with himself. So openness is required, as are toleration, patience, and the ability to reflect and reconsider. No one is above the debate and no one's contributions are beneath the attention of others.

Arendt emphasizes the artificiality of all this. Of course, there are important senses in which likely participants in public life differ radically from one another, not just in being diverse – which is affirmatively important in this conception – but in being worthy or unworthy of each other's respect and consideration. But to make possible a public realm of action in common, we construct a persona for each that occludes such differences of worth, and we

---

[44] George Kateb, *Hannah Arendt: Politics, Conscience, Evil* (Totowa: Rowman & Allenheld, 1984), p. 14.

establish (by our determination to fall in and persist with this form of life) equal standing for each (*OR,* 106–7).

Creating these personae, this equality, is not easy.[45] It has certain structural requirements – a public space and a constitution (*OR,* 124–5, 157).[46] And it makes exacting demands on its human participants. To understand these demands is to understand something of the theory of human nature or the human condition that underlies this part of Arendt's conception of equality. For all sorts of things might be true of human beings that would make this project impossible. There might be no one who had a taste for these proceedings and for the artifice it required. There might be many who had a taste for public affairs but were incapable of submitting to the discipline of equality – men like the "Jason" whom Aristotle mentioned, who "felt hungry when he was not a tyrant."[47] Or, to stick with Aristotle for a moment, there might be

some one person, or more than one... whose excellence is so pre-eminent that the excellence or the political capacity of all the rest admit of no comparison with his or theirs.... Such a man may truly be deemed a God among men.[48]

Aristotle said this was the reason democratic states instituted ostracism.[49] Be that as it may, such beings intermingled among humanity would pose serious difficulties for an Arendtian egalitarianism. Further, it would be impossible to sustain an Arendtian political process if humans were not capable of diversity. If whenever they came together they fell into unanimity and spoke with one voice – if that was what humans were like and there were no possibility to the contrary – then the artificial construction of this political equality among participants to hear and be heard would make no sense.

To understand the grounding of this part of Arendt's egalitarianism, then, we just turn each of these troubling hypotheses around. Though political equality is an artificial construct, it presupposes that some humans *will* have the impulse to participate, that they *do* have what it takes to submit to the discipline of equality, and that neither the superiority of the few nor the inevitable unanimity of the many makes the project of equality irrational. We assume that when men exert their reason coolly and freely on public questions, "they inevitably fall into different opinions on some of them,"[50] and that they are the kinds of beings who associate their interest in the subject of these opinions with a willingness to hear and entertain what others have to say on these matters. We assume that we are alike in these regards, but not so alike as to make positive, active equality redundant. As Arendt puts it at the beginning of *The Human*

[45] See *HC,* p. 215: "[T]he equality attending the public realm is necessarily an equality of unequals who stand in need of being equalized in certain respects and for specific purposes."

[46] See also Jeremy Waldron, "Arendt's Constitutional Politics," in Dana Villa, ed., *The Cambridge Companion to Hannah Arendt* (Cambridge, New York: Cambridge University Press, 2001).

[47] Aristotle, *Politics,* p. 56 (Book III, chapter 4, 1277a).

[48] Ibid., p. 71 (Book III, chapter 13, 1284a).

[49] Ibid., p. 72 (Book III, chapter 13, 1284a).

[50] *The Federalist Papers,* number 50, quoted in *OR,* p. 225.

Condition, "[p]lurality is the condition of human action because we are all the same, that is, human, in such a way that nobody is ever the same as anyone else who ever lived, lives, or will live" (*HC*, 8).

These relational attributes of human beings are probably of interest only to those who care to set up a political system of this kind.[51] As I said in my discussion of supervenience, at the end of section 5, we do not first note something about what humans are like and then decide what political system to set up on the basis of it; we are certainly not *driven* to institute a republic of equals once we have noted these characteristics. A supporter of monarchy may be uninterested in these facts or regard them as curiosities or nuisances. The things we notice about human nature and the human condition are themselves part and parcel of our willingness to adopt an egalitarian perspective. We buy into a whole package.

So far, we have concentrated on position (2). But position (1) gives Arendt's egalitarianism its real bite. It indicates that anyone – any human – might choose to engage in political participation and that that engagement must be respected. Position (2) supervened upon the characteristics of those actually involved in politics. But position (1) must supervene on something about all humans. What could that be?

Before we answer this question, we have to consider a challenge. Did Arendt really hold position (1)? Did she really believe that all humans were in principle capable of participating in a politics governed by position (2), even if most of them lacked the inclination? Margaret Canovan has noted one or two things that Arendt wrote that suggested that political participation among equals "is possible only among an aristocratic leisured class undisturbed by compassion for their serfs."[52] That accusation of elitism and aristocracy is quite common and there is some warrant for it. Certainly Arendt believed that the concerns and the mentality of mass society, the preoccupations of a demos obsessed with the conditions of life and labor, would make republican politics impossible.[53] And she believed it was much more difficult for a person mired in poverty to come forward and act in politics than for a person with wealth and leisure. But that is not the same as saying that there is a category of humans unfit for republican politics.[54]

Or consider this. In *On Revolution,* Arendt wrote that the equality associated with political freedom is "by no means a universally valid principle

---

[51] Cf. Hannah Arendt, "Truth and Politics," in *Between Past and Future,* 227, at p. 247: "That all men are created equal is not self-evident nor can it be proved. We hold this opinion because freedom is possible only among equals, and we believe that the joys and gratifications of free company are to be preferred to the doubtful pleasures of holding dominion."

[52] Canovan, "Contradictions," p. 15.

[53] See *OR,* 59–114, and *HC,* pp. 58, 126–35, 214–6.

[54] Besides Canovan, "Contradictions," the best piece on this problem is Jeffrey Isaacs, "Oases in the Desert: Hannah Arendt on Democratic Politics," *American Political Science Review,* 88 (1994): 156.

but . . . applicable only within limitations and even within spatial limits" (*OR*, 275). The limitations she speaks of may be understood in a number of ways:

(a) The claim could mean that political equality is associated with the conduct of the affairs of a particular community, and only the members of that community are eligible for participation in its public business: New Zealanders do not get to participate in Australia and vice versa. That's a familiar limitation, and quite compatible with ordinary notions of political equality (assuming that there is universal suffrage in both countries and that the same general principles of republican organization might apply to each).

(b) It could also mean that political equality needs to be structured in certain institutional settings, that these settings will have to restrict behavior in certain ways (and draw lines in that sense), and that each such institution would probably have to limit the number of participants.[55] That certainly seems to be the context of the "limitations" remark in *On Revolution*.

(c) One might try to associate Arendt's comment about limitations to some sort of Schmittian friend/enemy principle. But this would be irresponsible, just as it would be wrong to infer anything normative for modern politics from Arendt's observation that, among the ancient Greeks, "equality of the political realm . . . presupposed the existence of 'unequals' who, as a matter of fact, were always the majority of the population in a city-state" (*HC*, 32).[56] Her comment about limitations is best understood along the lines of (a) and (b).

The key to what we called position (1) in Arendt's political equality is the notion of self-selection. She certainly envisages that a relatively small proportion of the population will choose to participate in politics (and take on the mask of equality that such participation requires). And it may be natural to describe those who do this – "those few from all walks of life who have a taste for public freedom and cannot be happy without it" (*OR*, 279) – as an elite. They take responsibility for the fate of the others and they need to protect this choice against its being overwhelmed by the cares of the life process (*OR*, 276). Arendt calls these few "the best" and says it is "the sign of a well-ordered republic to assure them of their rightful place in the public realm" (*OR*, 279). Yet she insists that they are not an independently identifiable aristocracy. They are identifiable only by virtue of their own political initiative: They selected themselves to participate (*OR*, 277–8). And those who show no interest in the matter are not exactly disqualified from politics; they are "self-excluded" (*OR*, 280). There is no principle excluding them. They emancipate themselves from politics, as they go about other aspects of their business. This negative political

---

[55] See *OR*, 236: "[T]he room will not hold all." But there might be a great many such settings, related to one another through federal structure: see ibid., pp. 249, 267.

[56] See also Waldron, "Arendt's Constitutional Politics," pp. 205–6.

freedom – freedom from politics – is important for all people some of the time, and for most people most or all of the time (*HC*, 199).

Still there is no telling who might emerge from the darkness of nonpolitical life into the light of action among equals in the political realm. It might be gentlemen or it might be workers. It might be any human. And this "might be" is not just an artifact of our not knowing what people are like. It is grounded on something about each of us, even those who never participate.

In Arendt's thought, the view that *anyone might participate* in free republican politics is predicated in the final analysis on something distinctive about humanity – what she calls in the essay "What Is Freedom?" the faculty of freedom itself, "the sheer capacity to begin, which animates and inspires all human activities and is the hidden source of the production of all great and beautiful things."[57] She says that the birth of every human being represents the possibility of a new beginning, an occurrence in the world *once again* (for the sixth billionth time) of the faculty of interrupting the life process with something new (*HC*, 246–7). She says that something of this capacity for new beginning, this *natality*, is present in all that humans do, political and nonpolitical (*HC*, 9). It is "a supreme gift which only man, of all earthly creatures, seems to have received, of which we can find traces and signs in almost all his activities."[58]

We might be tempted to play down this universality, to regard these traces and this potential as purely notional and inconsiderable except as manifested in those few who put it publicly on display. There is something of this in Arendt's writing, when she says that this "supreme gift... develops fully only when action has created its own worldly space where it can come out of hiding, as it were, and make its appearance."[59] In adverse circumstances, where political life has become stultified or overwhelmed by mass society, this potential for freedom lies dormant. Or in most people's lives, even under propitious circumstances, there is no inclination to awaken it. It is just an occluded potential. Until it comes out of hiding, it may "dwell in men's hearts as desire or will or hope or yearning; but the human heart, as we all known, is a very dark place, and whatever goes on in its obscurity can hardly be called a demonstrable fact."[60]

Still, Arendt's ontology of the human has this capacity there in each of us as a permanent possibility. We cannot read her remarks on natality any other way. When she writes in "What Is Freedom?" that "[m]an does not possess freedom so much as he, or better his coming into the world, is equated with the appearance of freedom in the universe,"[61] we need to associate that concretely

---

57 Hannah Arendt, "What Is Freedom?" p. 169.
58 Ibid.
59 Ibid.
60 Ibid., p. 149.
61 Ibid., p. 167.

with *each* man or woman coming into the world not just with some sort of lofty Hegelian emergence of the idea of freedom as such.

[M]en are equipped for the...task of making a new beginning because they themselves are new beginnings and hence beginners, [and] the very capacity for beginning is rooted in natality, in the fact that human beings appear in the world by virtue of birth. (*OR*, 211)

There are pages in *The Origins of Totalitarianism* where Arendt indicates that this natality is disturbing – that there can be "a deep resentment against the disturbing miracle contained in the fact that each of us is made as he is – single, unique, unchangeable" (*OT*, 301). It is certainly not a fact about us that compels anyone to treat each and every human as an equal or a potential equal. But for those who are disposed to establish a politics among equals, this is the basis of the assurance that humans are capable of bearing the weight of equality and that politics among equals can be open to anyone. It is our assurance that, however rare the inclination to politics is, the most basic attribute for it, the basic thing that it requires, is something given to us all.[62] In this sense, Arendtian natality, this permanent possibility of freedom and initiative in the nature and condition of men, is the fact about us on which her commitment to equality supervenes.[63] It is a relational fact, because it concerns what we can do with others. It is a non-natural fact, at least in the sense that our freedom and our natality transcend our biological animality. It is a complicated fact, in the sense that this is the foundation for a complex array of important political skills. And it is a fact that is unlikely to be of any interest to anyone who does not have a taste for this enterprise of the institution of politics. It is a fact of exactly the sort that supervenience calls for in the case of equality.

1.9 Reclaiming Arendt for Equality

There is not much that is new in this chapter. I have not tried to bring out any startling nuance in Arendt's lesser-known writings or to make her thinking any more delicate or extraordinary than it is already known to be. If anything

---

[62] As George Kateb states this part of Arendt's position in his book *Hannah Arendt*, p. 15: "Only in political life are the talents that are needed potentially in all men."

[63] In Benhabib, *Reluctant Modernism*, p. 195, Seyla Benhabib speaks of Arendt's "anthropological universalism." She treats human beings, says Benhabib,

as members of the same species, to whom life on earth is given under certain conditions, namely those of natality, plurality, labor, work, and action. This philosophical anthropology proceeds from a level of abstraction that treats all forms of cultural, social, and historical differentiation among humans as irrelevant when measured up against the fundamentals of their condition. There is an implicit ethical gesture in approaching the human condition from this level of abstraction, one that proceeds from our fundamental equality and commonality as members of the same species.

I think this is right and important and that Benhabib is right, too, in saying (ibid., p. 196) that something of this is presupposed, if not argued for, in Arendt's account of political equality.

I have tried to do the opposite – I have tried to reclaim Arendt for a familiar tradition of thinking about equality. Though she writes in ways that seem to set some distance between her own position and the usual way of approaching these matters – that is, defending an equality commitment on the basis of some commonality in human nature – her position turns out not to be the existentialist leap in the dark without foundations that some commentators think it is. She has a view about what humans are like and though, as she says, that view does not drive her or anyone to adopt a principle of equality, it is nevertheless what her principle of equality responds to and is grounded on. I have found it helpful to use the philosophical concept of supervenience to elucidate what such grounding may or may not involve. Others may understand the relation less analytically. That does not matter. What matters is that the depth and complexity of her position on equality should not be trivialized or discredited by associating it with a sort of ungrounded decisionism that represents the principle of basic equality as arbitrary and the practice of treating one another as equals as just something we happen to do around here.

2

Arendt's Augustine

Roy T. Tsao

"Initium ergo ut esset, creatus est homo" – "that there be a beginning, man was created" (*HC*, 177).[1] These words of Augustine's, from *The City of God*, recur as a *leitmotiv* in the writings of Hannah Arendt, where they invariably are associated with a concept of great importance to her: natality, the condition of having come into the world through birth. Augustine's dictum appears in this way in numerous essays and books of hers over a two-decade span, from the mid-1950s to the end of her life – from the time of *The Human Condition* (1958), where the idea receives its most elaborate exposition, to that of *The Life of the Mind*, left incomplete at her death in 1975.[2] On each of these occasions, Arendt tends to make it sound as if Augustine's point in this statement were closely connected with her own idea that our having been born into the world is a condition for the human capacity for action, "whereby we confirm and take upon ourselves the naked fact of our original physical appearance" (*HC*, 176). Augustine's actual point is about something different: He is referring specifically, and solely, to God's creation of the first man, from whom all humankind was descended. Arendt cannot have been unaware of this, but it did not keep her from quoting the line in this context. Apparently she found it congenial with her more general point that "men, though they must die, are

[1] Hannah Arendt, *The Human Condition* (Chicago: 1958), p. 177, quoting Augustine, *De civitate Dei* XII.21. Compare Augustine, *The City of God against the Pagans*, edited and translated by R. W. Dyson (New York: Cambridge University Press, 1998), p. 532. Subsequent references to *The Human Condition* are abbreviated as *HC*.

[2] *On Revolution* (New York: Penguin, 1965), p. 211; *Between Past and Future* (New York: Penguin, 1968), 167; *The Life of the Mind: Willing* (New York: Harcourt, 1978), pp. 109–10, 216–7. In each of these passages, excepting the first of the two from *The Life of the Mind*, the citation is slightly inaccurate, given as XII.20.

The author would like to thank David Bromwich, David Cobb, Stephan Jaklitsch, George Kateb, Mark Larrimore, Adam Trettel, and especially Spencer Salovaara for their encouragement and reproaches.

not born in order to die, but to begin" (*HC*, 246). It is an interesting question why she did.

Arendt's involvement with Augustine's thought goes back decades before she picked up the habit of quoting him in this connection. Augustine had been the subject of her first book, *Der Liebesbegriff bei Augustin* (Augustine's Concept of Love, 1929).[3] Based on her doctoral dissertation, it is a slender volume, dense with Latin quotations and recondite philosophical categories. Arendt was only twenty-three when it was published, and it would be many years before Augustine's name would appear in her writings with any frequency. Even so, her reading of Augustine from that time had a profound and lasting impact on her. It was still reverberating in her mind twenty years later, when she wrote *The Origins of Totalitarianism* (published in 1951, but completed in 1949). In *The Human Condition*, too, there are traces of *Liebesbegriff* – but their pattern is very different from that in *The Origins of Totalitarianism*. The differences between *The Origins of Totalitarianism* and *The Human Condition* in this regard are significant and instructive, in that they betoken a basic reorientation in Arendt's thinking between the writing of those two works. The concept of natality belongs to the later period only.

This is difficult to perceive from Arendt's books in the form they are commonly read today, however. Every edition of *The Origins of Totalitarianism*, except for the first, contains that very statement of Augustine's about the creation of man, quoted by Arendt in just the same way that she does in *The Human Condition* and subsequent works. It comes in a chapter that Arendt added for the expanded German edition of 1955, and which was based on an essay first published in 1953. In other ways, too, the added material reflects Arendt's thinking in the period of *The Human Condition*, so the reader encountering this statement may come away with the impression of an unbroken consistency in Arendt's thought in all of the works of her maturity. Going back to the text of the first edition reveals a significant turnabout on Arendt's part in the space of just a few years. This can be seen very clearly when the added material – and specifically, the passage referring to Arendt's idea of natality – is compared with certain statements from the first edition's "Concluding Remarks," which were dropped from the text at the time the new chapter was added. Even in its revised editions, *The Origins of Totalitarianism* contains a number of formulations, scattered throughout the text, that are flatly inconsistent with her treatment of similar matters in *The Human Condition* and thereafter.

The text of Arendt's early Augustine book presents much the same difficulty – at least for readers of the only available English-language edition, published in 1995 as *Love and Saint Augustine*.[4] Readers of *Love and Saint*

---

[3] Hannah Arendt, *Der Liebesbegriff bei Augustin: Versuch einer philosophischen Interpretation* (1929), edited by Ludger Lütkehaus (Berlin: Philo, 2003). (Subsequent references are to this edition, hereafter abbreviated *LA*.)

[4] Hannah Arendt, *Love and Saint Augustine*, edited by Joanna Vecchiarelli Scott and Judith Chelius Stark (Chicago: University of Chicago Press, 1996).

Augustine find Arendt quoting Augustine's statement about the creation of man with reference to her idea of natality. And yet, *Love and Saint Augustine* is not in fact a strict translation of *Der Liebesbegriff bei Augustin* as published in 1929. It is based on the text of a translation that was made, but never published, in the early 1960s – and which Arendt herself had a hand in revising, making substantial cuts and additions.[5] Only then, thirty years after writing the book, did she add the passages about natality. The original German text of *Liebesbegriff* contains nothing of this, nor any reference to the statement from *The City of God* she would later associate with the idea. It is not even clear whether Arendt's later use of that statement is compatible with her original reading of Augustine; the added passages sit awkwardly in the text, incongruous with her original argument.

The truth is that the concept of natality first emerges in Arendt's work only in the 1950s. It belongs to an understanding of human freedom that she first arrived at only after she had written *The Origins of Totalitarianism*. To the extent that this concept is associated in her mind with Augustine, it expresses a different response to his example than what is seen in her earlier work. Considering those responses in sequence, and locating each in relation to Arendt's earlier reading of Augustine in *Liebesbegriff*, is one way to tell the story of her maturation and development as a thinker.

This is not the only way for that story to be told. *Liebesbegriff* is not only the register of Arendt's early encounter with Augustine; it is also a record of what she had learned in her studies with Martin Heidegger. Arendt wrote her dissertation under not Heidegger's supervision, but that of Karl Jaspers; yet it attests to Heidegger's influence on every page. Her studies with him, just a few years before, had been during the very period in which Heidegger was refining his project of fundamental ontology, with its analysis of the conditions for meaning in human existence. She had already left to study with Jaspers in Heidelberg by the time Heidegger was ready to publish *Being and Time*, in 1927, but she was well-enough schooled in its presuppositions and procedures to be able to put them to elegant use in her dissertation. The questions posed, the inferences drawn, and the distinctions insisted upon all lie within the ambit of Heidegger's fundamental ontology, and conform with exactitude to its protocols. Her passage from *Liebesbegriff* to the works of her maturity

---

[5] On the serious difficulties with taking the text published as *Love and Saint Augustine* as a reliable proxy for Arendt's views at the time she wrote her dissertation thirty years previously, see Stephan Kampowski, *Arendt, Augustine, and the New Beginning: The Action Theory and Moral Thought of Hannah Arendt in Light of Her Dissertation on St. Augustine* (Grand Rapids, MI: Eerdmans, 2008), 13–24. Kampowski also rightly observes there is reason to wonder whether Arendt's later reworking of the text for the English translation may be taken as a fair indication of her considered positions, even for the period when the revisions were made. Only about half of the text was revised before Arendt laid the project aside – defaulting on her contractual obligations with the publisher and forfeiting a payment she had already received for the anticipated edition. It is perhaps worth noting, too, that the revised portion of the text breaks off abruptly just a few pages after those with the added references to natality.

can be told not only as one of successive responses to Augustine's example, but also as one of the vicissitudes in her attitude toward Heidegger's formal ontology. Viewed from that angle, the swerve in her thinking between *The Origins of Totalitarianism* and *The Human Condition* is the manifestation of her renewed appreciation for those aspects of Heidegger's work that had been most important for *Liebesbegriff* – after a period of many years during which that side of her education had been effectively disowned.

These two stories are complementary; they deserve to be fitted together. That might be more than is wise to attempt in a single essay, however. Of the two, the one about Arendt's responses to Augustine is by far the less familiar to students of her work; it holds more than enough interest in itself to be told on its own, leaving Heidegger out of the picture.

2.1 *Der Liebesbegriff bei Augustin*

Der Liebesbegriff bei Augustin – Augustine's concept of love. A theme is announced in the title; a question is posed on its opening page: "the relevance of the neighbor" in Augustine's understanding of love (*LA*, 23). Yet the study provides no detailed exposition of Augustine's ethical teachings. Instead, it offers a complex analysis of the conceptual basis of Augustine's understanding of human existence. Arendt's focus on Augustine's concept of love reflects Augustine's own oft-stated belief that it is only through loving properly that we gain access to truth. Her question concerning the neighbor's relevance is really a question about the bearing of social relations on human self-understanding.

Whether the neighbor has any relevance in Augustine's understanding of love, or *why* – those matters stand in no need of philosophical clarification, as Arendt sees it. Augustine is a Christian; he is enjoined to love God with all his heart, mind, and soul, and also to love his neighbor as himself. The interesting question, for Arendt, concerns how he understood the last phrase in the latter commandment: to love the neighbor "as oneself" (*LA*, 107). Arendt supposes, with some support from Augustine's writings, that he took this phrase to imply something more than an equivalence in the degree or the magnitude of the love to be given to neighbor and self. The neighbor is to be loved *as* the self: A *manner* of love is prescribed, as would be consistent with recognizing some ontological commonality between self and neighbor. What manner of love might this be, whereby neighbor and self are thus understood? In what sense am I to understand the concerns or the interests of other people as proximate to my own? In what sense is the neighbor's existence to be seen as relevant to my own, or mine to his? Strange questions, perhaps – but interesting ones, when brought to bear on Augustine's thinking more generally. For if Augustine had the means to make intelligent sense of all this – and Arendt assumes that he did – then how might this complicate his oft-expressed sense that the Christian must sever himself from the cares of this world and seek the meaning of his existence nowhere but in God? What might this say of his understanding of self and world?

Augustine's sense of the neighbor's relevance thus offers a *point d'appui* for examining Augustine's thinking on human existence more generally. What allows her to frame this investigation in relation to Augustine's understanding of love is his own emphasis on the correspondence between our capacity to love properly, and our grasp of the truth. As any reader of Augustine knows, this emphasis is inseparable. If love opens the way to the truth, in Augustine's eyes, it must be love as informed by Christian belief. Arendt correctly recognizes this as the central axis to his thinking on all things human; she keeps this in view throughout her investigation. From the outset, she disclaims any intention to deal with the dogmatic basis of Augustine's Christian beliefs (*LA*, 25). But by this all she means is that she sets aside such questions as how his thinking was influenced or constrained by his acceptance of the Christian Scriptures or by his deference to the Nicene Creed and other doctrinal formulations. Instead, she limits herself to considering how Augustine took Christian beliefs to make better sense of what otherwise is seen only confusedly or incompletely. And in this her interest is not to evaluate the cogency of Augustine's Christian apologetics, but to analyze the concepts at work in his sense of what there is that stands in need of clarification through Christian beliefs, and of what manner of greater lucidity is the result. Her basic thesis is that those concepts are heterogeneous, belonging to three distinct "conceptual contexts" – corresponding to three different ways of conceiving the self and the world, and both in relation to God. Two of these three conceptual contexts tend to be dominant, at least when it comes to Augustine's own propensities when expressing himself in formal conceptual language. It is neither of these, however, that Arendt will deem the operative one for his making sense of the neighbor's relevance.

According to the first conceptual context, the world is made up of material things, possessing a greater or lesser degree of fixity and subsistence. Within this conceptual context, to love is to want; love is felt as desire to have and to hold – and is limned with a constant fear of loss (*LA*, 30). Seen in the light of desire such as this, the world appears as a scene of mutability and transience, of perishing and evanescence; love as desire chases at wisps, knowing nothing of true enjoyment – except for those who seek their enjoyment in God. To love God in this sense is to cleave to that which alone is eternal and incorruptible. By aligning oneself with a cosmic order transcending all temporal flux, those who order their loves properly may then also appreciate merely transient things, insofar as these too point toward that cosmic order, and thereby participate in it. Except – what then can be said of the relevance of the neighbor – or even the self? Neighbor and self alike are disowned and forgotten, reduced to bit parts in the great scheme of things (*LA*, 53).

As Arendt is hardly the first to observe, this side of Augustine's thought owes more to his schooling in Stoic and Neoplatonic philosophy than to his Christian beliefs (*LA*, 44). The next conceptual context is more closely tied to Christianity. Within this second conceptual context, the things of the world are known not in light of their sufficiency in themselves, but with regard to their serviceability. The world so construed is a site of human activity, available for human use, hospitable to human purposes. Or so it would seem – so long as its denizens stay absorbed in their business and pleasures, avoiding the fact that this seemingly well-stocked world fails to supply the one item they need to keep carrying on like this indefinitely: security against death. As with the first conceptual context, true enjoyment is spoiled – this time not merely by fear of loss, but by anxious foreboding in the face of death, and consequent sense of estrangement from the world (*LA*, 77).

As with the prior conceptual context, Augustine holds that the situation can be properly illuminated only by turning to God. This time, however, God is understood in a sense that is proper to Christianity: God as Creator (*LA*, 92). The insight granted the Christian is understood, this time around, not as a glimpse of a rational order beyond all transience and perishing, but instead as a view to the goodness of Creation – a view that is lost to all those who, in their prideful esteem for things human, have forgotten their Creator. With the recovery of this perception comes a revaluation of self and world – all within the same conceptual context. The world is not seen as something made to order for men, but as Creation, the work of God's hand, made for God's purposes; instead of panicking when things fall apart, the Christian confesses a brokenness all his own, in his incapacity to serve God adequately (*LA*, 98).

This second conceptual context, then, is the one that informs Augustine's thinking when he famously speaks, in his *Confessions*, of having become a problem to himself, a riddle he lacked the means to solve. Out of his own most painstaking efforts at self-recollection came only an inchoate sense of himself as a creature of God, a longing to be restored to the presence of his Creator. And with this, Arendt's question about the neighbor's relevance asserts itself again: If this were how Augustine had to understand his existence vis-à-vis God, what place could there be for a neighbor? How can the neighbor be seen as someone close to oneself, if even the self is grasped only by God (*LA*, 101).

Having found each of the two dominant conceptual contexts unsuited for making sense of the neighbor's relevance, Arendt proceeds at last to discuss Augustine's actual understanding of that relevance, with the aim of supplying that answer with a degree of conceptual articulacy that she supposes it lacks. To pinpoint what Augustine takes the neighbor's relevance to be, she looks to his conception of the Christian community – that is, the True Church, the company of the faithful (*LA*, 108). She does not delve into Augustine's ecclesiology per se, but limits herself to the implicit criteria in his understanding of fellowship among Christians – in particular, those which the prior conceptual contexts fail to illuminate. The Church has to be a community that lays claim to its members' truest sense of themselves, while being based on a faith that is common to all. Moreover, it must be a community into which any human being anywhere might be included; its members must be able to recognize every last human being on earth as potentially one of their number, whether presently so or not. How is this to be conceived?

The crux of the answer, as Arendt sees it, lies in the specific historical content of Augustine's Christian faith – a matter left to the side of Arendt's interpretation up to this point. The God in whom Augustine places his faith is not merely the Neoplatonic Highest Good, nor is He understood only as Maker of heaven and earth. For the Christian, the order of Creation is restored through the action of redemption – and fulfilled through the life-giving history of salvation. If the Christian has hope for redemption, it is because he finds himself part of that history – and this means to understand his own situation as one that is common to all human beings (*LA*, 110). All are descended alike from a common progenitor; none are exempt from the doom of the Fall. Yet all are potentially to be counted among the elect who are freed from that doom, through Christ's cancellation of Adam's sin; there is none who might not be destined for citizenship in the Heavenly City (*LA*, 112). But only potentially: Redemption is already won, but salvation is not yet accomplished. It is thus that Augustine understands the situation of humankind: to inherit the past as a doom, to be granted the hope for a future unmarred by that burden – but a hope to be realized only through constant striving (*LA*, 110).

This then is where Arendt locates Augustine's sense of the neighbor's relevance. The individual Christian's existence is poised between the inherited curse and the hoped-for regeneration; his passage on earth takes the form of continuous struggle against the dead weight of the past, a striving for newness of life. And he sees all human beings in just the same situation. To fail to recognize this is to misunderstand one's own situation – for it would be to forget one's own helplessness in securing one's own salvation. In the conduct of others, the Christian is to find constant inducements to greater effort, and greater humility. In the conduct of some, he is to find models to emulate in his striving; from others, a humbling reminder of his own former condition (*LA*, 117). In his own conduct, he is to take thought to the example he sets for his fellows – whether by way of encouragement or rebuke.

2.2 The Origins of Totalitarianism

Twenty years separate *Der Liebesbegriff bei Augustin* from *The Origins of Totalitarianism*. The latter book seems to come from a different world than that of her doctoral dissertation – and not simply because of the difference in topic and scope. In *Liebesbegriff*, Arendt kept her own beliefs in the background; the reader is met with an account of Augustine's understanding of human existence – with the final accent on Augustine's irreducibly Christian sense of the meaning of history. Speaking in her own voice these two decades later, Arendt maintains an emphatically secular – that is to say, agnostic – perspective from the start, and by the book's end has cast her lot with the Enlightenment project of "modern man's coming of age." In an era in which mass deportations, police terror, and concentration camps had darkened the fate of humanity, she calls upon her contemporaries to establish "a new law on earth," to affirm and uphold human dignity – in none but humanity's name. "If there is any sense in the eighteenth-century formula that man has come of age," she writes (in the "Concluding Remarks" to the book's first edition), "it is that from now on man is the only possible creator of his own laws and the only possible maker of his own history" (*OT*, 437).[6]

Yet there is also another, less commonly noticed, side to Arendt's thinking in this book. She may speak in Promethean tones when she calls for the completion of modern man's "coming of age," yet she also shows herself – in the very same passages – to be haunted by a quite different sense of the human condition. "The first disastrous result of man's coming of age," she says at the end of the book, "is that modern man has come to resent everything given, even his own existence – to resent the very fact that he is not the creator of the universe and himself" (*OT¹*, 438). What is this but that most characteristically Augustinian theme: man's attempt to usurp the position of God, and coming to grief when he finds he cannot? The only difference is that Arendt avoids making any positive reference to God; she seems determined to describe the same syndrome without making any claims one way or another about God's existence. Statements with this same pattern can be found throughout *The Origins of Totalitarianism*.

"The more highly developed a civilization," Arendt observes, "the more accomplished the world it has produced, the more at home men feel within the human artifice – the more they will resent everything they have not produced, everything that is merely and mysteriously given to them" (*OT*, 301). This remark introduces a passage of great concentrated density, at the close of the chapter titled "The Decline of the Nation-State and the End of the Rights of Man." Her immediate concern in this passage is a pressing political problem, modern nation-states' resistance to assimilating aliens through naturalization. Why is it, she asks, that even liberal polities are averse to admitting persons of foreign birth to full citizenship? Why is it that political communities so often are loath to welcome persons of differing ethnic origins into their midst, even where it is understood that political life is "based the assumption that we can produce equality through organization" – that is, through equal treatment under law?

Arendt's answer is unexpected. She claims that it is *because* civilized peoples base their political life upon that assumption, and stake their pride on this fact, that they incline to xenophobia. The more they identify with the norms of civilized life, the more they take pride in human achievements, and the less they are able to cope with conspicuous ethnic differences, the manifestation of traits that neither are chosen nor alterable at will. The antipathies that are aroused in this situation are ultimately much the same, she suggests, whether those differences are of appearance or manner, whether due to descent or to upbringing. Either way, they bespeak the inescapable limits to human freedom, and therefore present a standing rebuke to civilization's engrained self-conceit.

---

[6] Arendt, *The Origins of Totalitarianism* (New York: Harcourt, 1951), 437. The statement quoted is from the "Concluding Remarks," dropped from every edition of the book after the first. References to passages found only in this first edition are cited as *OT¹*; references to material added to subsequent editions (those of 1958 and after) as *OT²*. References to material contained in all editions are cited simply as *OT*.

The émigré's accented speech, his awkward retention of manners anomalous in his present milieu, his imperfect mastery of the local customs and usages – all of this constitutes an unwelcome reminder that no man is truly self-made. As Arendt puts it,

The reason why highly developed political communities...so often insist on ethnic homogeneity is that they hope to eliminate as far as possible those natural and always present differences and discriminations which by themselves arouse dumb hatred, mistrust and discrimination because they indicate all too clearly those spheres where men cannot act at and change at will, i.e., the limitations of the human artifice. The "alien" is a frightening reminder of difference as such, of individuality as such, and indicates those realms in which man cannot change and cannot act, and therefore has a distinct tendency to destroy. (*OT*, 301)

Why should men who feel themselves at home in the human artifice be so loath to accept strangers into their midst? Because it arouses their own "deep resentment against the disturbing miracle contained in the fact that each of us is made as he is – single, unique, unchangeable." Why should that resentment be provoked simply by the sight of those strangers' inability to make themselves fit in? Because it reminds them of a truth about themselves that they would sooner evade: that they too are strangers in this world, unable to choose or control the conditions of their existence. Why should they find this reminder so unnerving? Because, Arendt goes on to suggest, they stake their pride on the human artifice, "having forgotten that man is only the master, not the creator of the world" (*OT*, 302).

Arendt's reasoning here is peculiarly reminiscent of the Augustinian pattern of thought that she had examined, twenty years previously, in *Der Liebesbegriff bei Augustin*. She even mentions Augustine by name – and with reference to his notion of love. When speaking about those aspects of who we are that we are unable to change, she says,

This mere existence, that is, all that which is mysteriously given by birth and which includes the shape of our bodies and the talents of our minds, can be adequately dealt with only by the unpredictable hazards of friendship and sympathy, or by the great and incalculable grace of love, which says with Augustine, "*Volo ut sis* (I want you to be)," without being able to give any particular reason for such supreme and unsurpassable affirmation. (*OT*, 301)

Volo ut sis: This very phrase had been used by Arendt in her dissertation, when paraphrasing a longer statement from Augustine's *Tractates* on the First Epistle of John (*LA*, 102). In *Liebesbegriff*, the Latin phrase is used to stand for Augustine's conceptualization of the love he believes must be shown to all human beings because they are fellow creatures of God. Perhaps that original context is still somehow in Arendt's mind when she now adds, rather too cryptically, that this love "is unable to give any particular reason for such supreme and surpassable affirmation."

Why she might want to mention that here is not easy to say, and it is probably best not to make too much of the allusion. Even without it, the passage gives ample reason to suppose that Arendt was thinking of Augustine in pursuing this unsettling line of thought. And this is just one of several key passages in *The Origins of Totalitarianism* where continuing reverberations of *Liebesbegriff* can be felt. Consider this statement from the "Concluding Remarks," where Arendt broaches the question of what might be needed to give human community a more adequate basis:

No divine command, derived from man's having been created in the image of God, and no natural law, derived from man's "nature," are sufficient for the establishment of a new law on earth, for rights spring from human plurality, and divine command or natural law would be true even if there existed only a single human being. (*OT¹*, 437)

Read apart from *Liebesbegriff*, the statement is deeply obscure. It may not be surprising to find Arendt doubting the usefulness of appeals to divine command or natural law in the circumstances, given her secular outlook, but why offer *this* as the grounds for rejecting them – the fact they "would be true even if there existed only a single human being"? When the statement is read in light of *Liebesbegriff*, the point comes into focus. A natural law might direct our aspirations; the command of our Maker might chasten our pride. But neither can tell us the relevance of our neighbor, in the sense that this had been understood by Augustine. Neither suffices for making sense of a basis of solidarity with other people; neither can show us our own situation reflected in theirs.

What we most sorely lack, as Arendt sees it, is not some more authoritative moral standard – she is satisfied that we know well enough how to tell apart right and wrong. What we lack is a way to make sense of the fact that human beings fall short, so often fail to conduct themselves responsibly. "The more peoples know about one another," Arendt says, "the less they want to recognize other peoples as their equals, the more they recoil from the ideal of humanity" (*OT*, 235). The *more* peoples know about one another – such knowledge may be founded on actual experience, so far as that goes. She insists that racist thinking is not to be understood merely as an expression of self-serving bias or ignorant prejudice – for to see it that way is to miss what makes it so insidious. She latches instead on to an aspect of racist thought that is not easily grasped by the liberal imagination: its connection with moral indignation. If there is hope for us to hold on to a sense of our common humanity, it must be an idea of humanity that extends not just to the decent and the innocent, the admirable and the diligent, but also to the backward and the compromised, the brutal and the misguided.

The problem comes most clearly into focus in the chapters devoted to the subject of racism. When discussing the rise and proliferation of overtly racist political doctrines and ideologies in the nineteenth century, she lays particular stress on such doctrines' denial of a common *origin* of all peoples – thus repudiating the traditional Judeo-Christian belief in a common progenitor for all humankind. She sees this not only in formal doctrines of polygenism, but equally in the claims that Russians, say, or Germans, were set off from all other peoples on account of some special, divinely infused quality of their souls. Her remarks about this are worth quoting at length:

The untruth of this theory is as conspicuous as its political usefulness. God created neither men – whose origin clearly is procreation – nor peoples, who come into being as the result of human organization. Men are unequal according to their natural origin, their different organization, and fate in history. Their equality is an equality of rights only, that is, an equality of human purpose; yet behind this equality of human purpose lies, according to Jewish-Christian tradition, another equality, expressed in the concept of one common origin beyond human history, human nature, and human purpose – the common origin in the mythical, unidentifiable Man who alone is God's creation. This divine origin is the metaphysical concept on which the political equality of purpose may be based, the purpose of establishing mankind on earth. (*OT*, 234)

She goes to some trouble here to specify that it is *only* the first progenitor of the human race who is to be seen as God's creation, all others having originated in procreation. It is revealing that Arendt would lay such emphasis on this particular tenet of Western religious traditions – even when she herself is so quick to call it no more than a myth. Here again, Augustine figures in the background of her thinking.

"God chose to create one individual for the propagation of many," Augustine writes in *City of God*, "so that men should thus be admonished to preserve unity among their whole multitude."[7] The statement was noted by Arendt in *Liebesbegriff*; the idea it expresses was pivotal to her account of how Augustine understood the neighbor's relevance (*LA*, 114). As she had then explained Augustine's view, it is the descent of the whole human race from Adam – together with Christ's undoing of Adam's sin – that define the historical situation in which the Christian discovers the relevance of all human beings to himself. All stand under the same dispensation of judgment and mercy; none has a special access to grace. To refuse to acknowledge this common origin (in the context of Christian belief) means something far worse than to refuse ties of natural kinship; it amounts to claiming to merit salvation on the strength of one's own achievements. To deny any basis of commonality with all human beings – the standing temptation of those who would make themselves judges of righteousness when confronted with human wickedness – can be done, but at the cost of losing one's sense of one's humanity.

All of this resonates in Arendt's account of the consequences of racist and tribalist thinking – minus the content of Augustine's Christian beliefs. It is no wonder, then, that she might be disposed to echo Augustine's emphasis on the singular origin of the human race, even if without ever asserting the truth of that proposition. She invokes this very same Biblical teaching in the book's

---

[7] Augustine, *De civitate Dei* XII.28, quoted (in part) in *LA* at 114. The English version given here is from Augustine, *The City of God*, 539.

final pages, suggesting that it holds the "insight" needed if we are to come to terms with human diversity:

We can reconcile ourselves to the variety of mankind, to the differences between human beings – which are frightening precisely because of the essential equality of rights of men and our consequent responsibility for all deeds and misdeeds committed by people different from ourselves – only through insight into the tremendous bliss that man was created with the power of procreation, that not a single man but Men inhabit the earth. (*OT¹*, 438–9)

Man was created with the power of procreation – "man" in the singular, "created" in the past tense. There is something peculiarly cagey in this, the way Arendt alludes to the "insight" – even the "bliss" – connected somehow to a religious belief, the truth of which she does not assert. And there is something revealing, too, in that caginess. The pattern of her thinking here consists in transposing the Augustinian pattern into a strictly secular register – and therefore, inevitably, compressing its range, reassigning its parts.

Paradoxically, this very pattern seems also to be the impetus for Arendt's most Promethean-sounding assertions, those calling on man to become "creator of his own laws" and "maker of his own history." For when she speaks of the need for "a new law on earth," she means something larger, more awesome and elusive, than the practical business of treaties and federations. It is to be nothing less than "a consciously-planned beginning of history" (*OT¹*, 439). In the absence of eschatological hope, how else are we to meet all human beings on earth as part of the same perilous striving? We are left alone with our day, and the time is short, and

The Rights of Man can be implemented only if they become ... the, so to speak, prehistorical fundament from which the history of mankind will derive its essential meaning, in much the same way Western civilization did from its own fundamental origin myths. (*OT¹*, 439)

2.3 The Human Condition

It was in the years immediately after she completed *Origins of Totalitarianism* that Arendt first arrived at her notion of natality. The notion (but not the term itself) first enters Arendt's published writings in 1953, in the closing lines of "Ideology and Terror," an essay that would later be appended to *Origins of Totalitarianism* in its revised editions. As its title indicates, that chapter consists primarily of a further discussion of aspects of totalitarianism, but it closes with a more general reflection on human history and hope. There she makes her first use of Augustine's statement from *The City of God* about how a beginning came into being with the creation of man:

But there remains also the truth that every end in history necessarily contains a new beginning; this beginning is the promise, the only "message" which the end can ever produce. Beginning, before it becomes a historical event is the supreme capacity of man;

politically, it is identical with man's freedom. *Initium ut esset homo creatus est* – "that a beginning be made man was created," said Augustine. This beginning is guaranteed by every new birth. It is indeed every man. (*OT²*, 478–9)

As on later occasions, Arendt identifies the notion of "beginning" thus evoked with the human capacity of freedom, associating both with the phenomenon of human birth. The gloss she provides in *The Human Condition* is characteristic: "This beginning is not the same as the beginning of the world; it is not the beginning of something but of somebody, who is a beginner himself" (*HC*, 177).

This marks a departure from her thinking from the time she wrote *The Origins of Totalitarianism*. Before she had spoken of the need for a "self-consciously planned beginning of history"; she now speaks instead of beginnings *in* history, and suggests they take care of themselves. Before she had referred to "the disturbing miracle" of human birth as a reminder of the *limits* of human freedom, the emblem for all those natural qualities and inherited circumstances that we are helpless to alter (*OT*, 301). Now human birth is offered instead as an emblem for the fact that human beings are capable of acting on their own initiative. As if to reinforce this latter difference, moreover, she now suggests that this very capacity is to be seen as nothing short of miraculous. "The fact that man is capable of action means that the unexpected can be expected from him, that he is able to perform what is infinitely improbable" (*OT*, 178). She goes so far as to call this capacity for human initiative as "the one miracle-working faculty in man" (*OT*, 246).

These changes correspond to one that is still more fundamental, in Arendt's conception of human agency. The 1953 text that was pressed into service as the new last chapter of *The Origins of Totalitarianism* is also the first in which this is adumbrated (*OT²*, 475); it would come to the fore in Arendt's next book, *The Human Condition*. The hallmark of Arendt's new way of thinking is her emphatic insistence on strictly distinguishing among different modes of human activity, each with a basis for intelligibility of its own. In this way, she conceives "action" in contradistinction to "fabrication" (and both in contradistinction to a third, "labor").

That this constitutes a break with her own former practice, from just a few years before, can be seen from a glance at any of the various passages in *The Origins of Totalitarianism* in which comparable themes are addressed. There, she had consistently identified human action with the fulfillment of chosen purposes, the achievement of self-given ends. Its limiting condition was said to be nature's resistance to human purposes; its enabling one, participation in a "human artifice" in which human purposes are recognized and respected. Thus, for instance, when discussing the plight of stateless refugees, deprived "the right to action" by being denied recognition in any state's legal system, she had seen fit to compare their condition to that of people who "inhabit an unchanged nature which they cannot master, yet upon whose abundance or frugality they depend for their livelihood, [and who] live and die without leaving any trace, without having contributed anything to a common world" (*OT*, 296, 300). Mastery over "nature," contributions to a common world, and participation in a juridical order – all of these had been treated by Arendt then as expressions of the same human capacity.

All this would change in *The Human Condition*. Whereas before she had employed such concepts as purposiveness and instrumentality when speaking of human agency generally, she now deems this appropriate only with reference to that mode of activity whereby we produce and use the nonhuman things that compose our human world – not so with reference to action, defined as that "activity that goes on directly between men without the intermediary of things or matter" (*HC*, 7). Action, so defined, is to be understood as a response to the acts and words of others, so as to elicit some further response in return. For this reason alone, the meaning of action cannot be reckoned in terms of successful achievement of purposes, of employing suitable means to determinate ends. For this reason, she argues, any idea of autonomous self-determination is not only unattainable, but illusory and chimerical. "If it were true that sovereignty and freedom are the same, then indeed no man could be free, because sovereignty, the ideal of uncompromising self-sufficiency and mastership, is contradictory to the very condition of plurality" (*HC*, 234).

This new understanding of human agency is the impetus for Arendt's concept of natality. "With word and deed we insert ourselves into the human world," she says, "and this insertion is like a second birth, in which we confirm and take upon ourselves the fact of our original physical appearance" (*HC*, 176–7). A *second* birth. It is not within normal human capacities to be born at one's own free initiative; none of us chooses the time or the circumstances of our actual birth. No mere human being has ever been born at his own initiative; none of us chose the circumstances into which we were born. The initiative of which we are capable consists in our owning up to those circumstances, speaking up for ourselves. It is a matter of responding to that situation in which we find ourselves, so as to engage and sustain the attention of others – so that they might take interest in our situation, see it as part of their own (*HC*, 178–9). It is *because* human beings are capable of such initiative – or more to the point, it is because this is how we understand human beings – that our original, physical birth, too, carries the sense of a beginning (*HC*, 9). The actual event of our birth in the world is meaningful as a beginning only in retrospect – or in others' anticipation.

So much for the theoretical basis for Arendt's idea of natality. Now to the puzzle: What could this possibly have to do with that statement of Augustine's, from *The City of God*, that she habitually quotes when broaching this theme – not just once, but in book after book, over a two-decade span? "*That a beginning be made, man was created*": The statement refers to a singular act, God's creation of Adam. The statement comes from the very same part of *The City of God* in which Augustine makes so much of the difference between this singular act of creation and the subsequent generation of the human race through procreation. And it is hard to believe that Arendt would not have been mindful of this, for not only had she written of that in *Liebesbegriff*, but it had made enough of an impression on her to reverberate in her mind when she wrote *The Origins of Totalitarianism*. There is even a reference to it in *The Human Condition* itself, tucked away at the end of a footnote (*HC*, 8n.1). Augustine does also speak, elsewhere, of each human being as owing his existence directly to God. But that way of speaking – as Arendt had emphasized, properly, in *Liebesbegriff* – belongs to a different *conceptual* context entirely. How can she have found this quotation even remotely appropriate to her purposes? Why should she be quoting from Augustine at all?

A clue can be found in the fact that natality is closely connected in Arendt's mind with the practice of forgiveness. This connection goes unmentioned on many occasions when Arendt discusses natality, including the sections of *The Human Condition* in which that concept is first introduced and explained. It comes to the fore only when Arendt takes up the topic of forgiveness itself, late in the book. There it emerges that natality and forgiveness are opposite sides of the same coin: Only because we are able to seek and offer forgiveness is natality of any significance, because it is only thus that we are capable of making *new* beginnings at all. "Without being forgiven, released from the consequences of what we have done, our capacity to act would, as it were, be confined to one single deed from which we could never recover; we would remain the victims of its consequences forever" (*HC*, 237). Arendt emphasizes that the disburdening is mutual: If the party receiving forgiveness is spared any blot on his name, the party forgiving, too, is freed from the past, obtaining what Arendt calls "freedom from vengeance" (*HC*, 241). Through seeking and offering forgiveness, we are spared the otherwise irrevocable doom of mischance and resentment, opprobrium and indignation.

It might sound like an exaggeration to say that new beginnings are possible only because of forgiveness – or, if not an exaggeration, a truth that is applicable only within a narrow range of situations, where some palpable wrong stands in need of rectification. This is not how Arendt would have us see it, however. Her point can be seen in its proper proportions when put together with her conception of human action generally. If the initiative taken in action consists in newly inserting oneself in a realm of human affairs, in response to what others have done and are doing; if it is in asserting a claim on others' attention that this is meaningful, and in eliciting some further response from them that it becomes significant – if all that is so, then action *consists in* a taking of liberties, a trespass on others' time and attention. Our every venture is in principle an impertinence – not unwelcome, we hope, but that is not for us to determine. The most we can do, if our impertinence is ill received, is to ask that it be forgiven – and that is to say, to ask to be given another chance.

In pursuing this theme, Arendt is clearly revisiting the concerns that had haunted her when writing *The Origins of Totalitarianism*. The telltale sign of this is her emphasis on the "freedom from vengeance" to be had through the willingness to forgive others the burden of their past mischances and misdoings. As before, she seeks an insight into the human predicament that might counter men's tendency toward self-righteous resentment and sterile indignation in the face of the limits of human freedom. The difference in her approach is as much as anything due to her understanding of human freedom. Whereas before, she had conceived those limitations in terms of the recalcitrance of "nature" – which had been obscurely linked in her mind with a tendency toward evil – she now focuses instead on limitations that are simply the obverse of the conditions for action as such. That difference is of great enough moment to prompt quite a different sense of the requisite insight. But despite that difference, the motivating concern is still much the same. So it should come as no surprise that Arendt's thoughts would have turned once again to Augustine, just as they had in that earlier period. She has come back once again to the question posed in her dissertation: the relevance of the neighbor.

Forgiveness had not been addressed explicitly in *Liebesbegriff*. Even so, Arendt's treatment of this subject in *The Human Condition* recalls the themes of her early study of Augustine. "The discoverer of the role of forgiveness in the realm of human affairs," Arendt now writes, "was Jesus of Nazareth" (*HC*, 238). Now, Arendt makes it plain that she is speaking of Jesus solely in human terms: "The fact that he made this discovery in a religious context and articulated it in religious language is no reason to take it any less seriously in a strictly secular sense." The Jesus of Christian faith – Jesus as Christ, Redeemer, and Judge – lies outside the scope of her discussion, and properly so. And yet she is more closely attuned to the specific Christian context of Jesus' teachings than the phrase "strictly secular sense" might seem to imply. All that she really means is that she believes she can set aside the theme of God's forgiveness of sins, so as to focus on Jesus' insights regarding the role of forgiveness in men's dealings with one another. She does not mean to say that Jesus' precepts can be extracted straightforwardly from their setting in the Gospel, as if to yield moral rules of general applicability. On the contrary, what interests her most about Jesus' precepts is that they were framed specifically for "the closely-knit community of his followers." What manner of fellowship is this, if its members must seek and grant forgiveness of one another?

In naming Jesus as "the discoverer of the role of forgiveness in human affairs," Arendt does not mean to suggest that he was the first to recognize or to teach the importance of forgiveness generally. What she considers decisive is simply his having recognized that forgiveness is needed not just where there has been animosity or conflict, but even among those who see themselves as brethren, the company of his disciples. Justice would be rendered by God at the Last Day; even so, he commanded his followers to be unstinting in forgiving one another their trespasses (*HC*, 240). In this she sees a crucial insight regarding the conditions for human action generally. "Trespassing," she observes, "is an everyday occurrence which is in the very nature of action's constant establishment of new relationships within the web of relations, and it needs forgiving, dismissing, in order to make it possible for life to go on by constantly releasing men from what they have done unknowingly" (*HC*, 240).

There is a further, more specific sense in which Arendt's discussion of this is reminiscent of her reading of Augustine's sense of the neighbor's relevance. In a typically Augustinian vein, she stresses that the readiness to forgive, as commanded by Jesus, is not to be confused with complaisance or tolerance. (In this she might well be taking a page out of Augustine's homilies.) The proper response to a brother's trespass may well be reproach and rebuke; forgiveness comes next, but only upon the offender's repentance. What makes Jesus' mandate a difficult one is that forgiveness is *always* to follow upon repentance, no matter how often the situation repeats itself.[8] Our fellows are not to be written off, no matter how many times they have failed in the past; the prodigal is always to be welcomed back. There is no question here of recommending Jesus' teaching as a general ethical rule; it is no part of her business to offer what Jesus did not, a secular reason for granting unlimited second chances to those who repent. So far as she is concerned, the lesson is not that we *must* grant forgiveness when it is asked, but simply that we *might*. Not the command to forgive, but the capacity, is her theme; it is there that she locates the basis for human natality.

Why then her habitual use of that statement from *The City of God*, about the beginning arising with man's creation? The tie between natality and forgiving may suffice to account for her having had Augustine somehow in mind when her thoughts turned to this topic, yet it sheds little light on her penchant for quoting that particular statement. That may be a puzzle without a real answer, but there is one further clue to consider. It involves one further, allusive reference to another statement of Augustine's, which is found in *The Human Condition* just after the section on forgiveness. The allusion comes in a passage addressing the relation between natality and mortality – considered in relation to the meaningfulness of human affairs. "If left to themselves," she says, "human affairs can only follow the law of mortality, which is the most certain and the only reliable law of a life spent between birth and death." It is only because of natality, she continues, that the realm of human affairs yields more than a chronicle of ruin and futility:

The life-span of man running toward death would inevitably carry everything human to ruin and destruction, if it were not for the faculty of interrupting it and beginning something new, a faculty which is inherent in action like an ever-present reminder that men, though they must die, are not born in order to die, but in order to begin. (*HC*, 246)

The life span of man running toward death: From the very beginning of our existence in this body, "there is not a moment when death is not at work in us" – so Augustine wrote in *The City of God*, in a well-known passage noted in

---

[8] Arendt cites Luke 17:3–4, quoting from the King James Version. "If thy brother trespass against thee, rebuke him; and if he repent, forgive him. And if he trespass against thee seven times in a day, and seven times in a day turn to thee, saying, I repent; thou shalt forgive him."

Arendt's dissertation.[9] We are all hurtling forward toward death all the time, every hour of our lives, with never a respite or slackening in our pace – for those who live longest have simply been given a greater distance to run. Arendt does not contest that description – if anything, she takes it for granted. She simply insists that this need not be the last word on human affairs – that awareness of this need not drain human action of meaning or significance. In this much at least, she is in perfect accord with Augustine's sentiment in the statement she echoes.

The clue lies in how she proceeds to develop this thought, a few sentences on: "The miracle that saves the world, the realm of human affairs, from its normal, 'natural' ruin is ultimately the fact of natality, in which the faculty of action is ontologically rooted" (HC, 247). *The miracle that saves the world.* Arendt cannot mean to claim that natality, as a general human capacity, does the work of that world-saving miracle in which Augustine, or any Christian, places his hope. What is "saved" in this manner is simply "the realm of human affairs," and the only sense in which it is saved is that it is able to exist for us *as* such a realm. All that Arendt actually means with the phrase, strictly speaking, is that natality may be counted among the (existential) conditions for the possibility of meaning in human affairs. In calling the condition of natality "the miracle that saves the world," Arendt is speaking figuratively, making self-conscious use of the religious overtones of the phrase, but only as a kind of allegory, to describe an aspect of the human condition. It is just the same with her penchant for quoting Augustine's words about the beginning made with man's creation – which for her is but the opposite pole of the same allegory. Whereas Augustine speaks of actual events – corresponding to divine actualities, from both of which together proceeds all meaning in human history – Arendt intends no more than to clarify the corresponding conceptual context, so far as this might be intelligible from a secular standpoint alone. In drawing on Augustine's language for this, she is ultimately doing no more than recording her debts to the pattern of thought in which she had found that conceptual context to be most vividly illuminated.

The Human Condition contains one further reference to Augustine that deserves to be noticed in connection with this, if only to indicate something of the care Arendt takes, at least in this period, not to stray beyond the bounds of her secular standpoint. It comes near the beginning of the book, where Arendt is explaining why her inquiry takes as its theme the human condition rather than human nature. "The problem of human nature," she remarks, "the Augustinian *quaestio mihi factus sum* ('I have become a question for myself') seems unanswerable in both its individual psychological sense and its general philosophical sense" (HC, 10). We can no more answer that question than jump over our shadows; those who make the attempt "almost invariably end with some construction of a deity, that is, with the god of the philosophers"

---

[9] Augustine, *De civitate Dei*, XIII.10; compare *City of God*, pp. 550–1.

(*HC*, 11). But then again, she observes, this is something that Augustine knew very well. Rounding out that thought, in a footnote, she adds: "The question of the nature of man is no less of a theological question than the question about the nature of God; both can be settled only within the framework of a divinely revealed answer" (*HC*, 11n.2).

3

The Rule of the People

Arendt, Archê, *and Democracy*

Patchen Markell

Perhaps the very fact that these two elements, the concern with stability and the spirit of the new, have become opposites in political thought and terminology... must be recognized to be among the symptoms of our loss.

Hannah Arendt[1]

3.1 Arendt and the Paradox of Rule

"Democracy," writes David Held, "means a form of government in which, in contradistinction to monarchies and aristocracies, the people rule."[2] One important kind of democratic theory is devoted to filling in the details of this basic formula and to debating the merits of the resulting array of models of democracy: classical, modern, direct, representative, participatory, minimalist, deliberative, aggregative, and so on. Another important kind of democratic theory, however, lingers over the "elementary idea" of democracy itself, exploring problems that lurk in and behind its basic terms.[3] Lately, for instance, many democratic theorists have been preoccupied with the fraught idea of "the people," asking what sorts of things peoples are and how their boundaries are to be settled. This is a question about identity; about who the people are. There is, however, an equally vital but relatively neglected question to be asked

---

[1] Hannah Arendt, *On Revolution,* revised edition (New York: Viking Compass, 1965), p. 223.

[2] David Held, *Models of Democracy.* 2nd ed. (Stanford: Stanford University Press, 1996), p. 1.

[3] Robert A. Dahl, *Democracy and Its Critics* (New Haven: Yale University Press, 1989), p. 3.

This is a condensed and amended version of an essay that first appeared in the *American Political Science Review* 100, 1 (February 2006), pp. 1–14; in addition to the people and institutions thanked there, I am grateful to Seyla Benhabib for her suggestions for further revision.

about activity – about what the people do.[4] What does it mean to say that in democracy the people *rule*?

In mainstream democratic theory, the term *rule* has received relatively little attention, not because it has been thought to be unimportant, but because its meaning has seemed comparatively straightforward. To "rule," Webster's tells us, means "to have power or command," to "exercise supreme authority," and "to exercise control."[5] To say that democracy is a form of rule, then, is just to say that it is one distinctive way of arranging the institutions and practices through which authoritative decisions are made and executed in a polity.[6] One important strand of democratic theory, however, throws the idea of rule as such into relief, and it does so by drawing in an unexpected way on a species of antidemocratic polemic. From classical Athens onward, critics of democracy have argued that because the people are nothing but a formless multitude, incapable of government, their rule would in effect be no rule at all, but monstrous disorder. Many democratic theorists respond to this charge by straightforwardly defending the people's qualifications for rule, but some refuse to accommodate themselves to the terms of this critique. Sheldon Wolin, for example, has famously proposed "accepting the familiar charges that democracy is inherently unstable, inclined toward anarchy, and identified with revolution, and using these traits as the basis for a different, *a*constitutional conception of democracy."[7] Skeptical of the very idea of democracy as a regime, Wolin reminds us that subjection inhabits every form of rule, even those in which we exercise considerable control over our rulers, or rule ourselves; and he warns that, in conceiving of democracy as a system of command and obedience, we risk sacrificing the spirit of insubordination that animates it.[8]

---

[4] For similar efforts to shift attention from identity to agency see Michaele Ferguson, *Sharing and Sharing Alike: Political Unity in Diverse Democracies* (Ph.D. diss., Harvard University, 2003); Jill Frank, *A Democracy of Distinction: Aristotle and the Work of Politics* (Chicago: University of Chicago Press, 2004); James Tully, "The Agonic Freedom of Citizens." *Economy and Society* 28 (May 1999): 161–82; and Linda M. G. Zerilli, *Feminism and the Abyss of Freedom* (Chicago: University of Chicago Press, 2005).

[5] *Webster's Third New International Dictionary of the English Language Unabridged*, s.v. "Rule."

[6] The disagreements that have dominated mainstream democratic theory – Does democratic rule require the existence of a sovereign people with a common will, or merely the balancing of the competing interests of a multiplicity of groups? Does it require the choice of rulers in competitive elections, or more intensive and direct forms of popular participation? – are ultimately about the question of identity; that is, about whether it's really *the people* who are ruling under this or that institutional arrangement. The thought that politics is at bottom a matter of ruling, and that ruling consists in the exercise of authoritative control, remains part of the taken-for-granted background against which these debates take place.

[7] Sheldon S. Wolin, "Norm and Form: The Constitutionalizing of Democracy," in J. Peter Euben, Josiah Ober, and John R. Wallach, eds., *Athenian Political Thought and the Reconstruction of American Democracy* (Ithaca: Cornell University Press, 1994), p. 37.

[8] For similar argument made in terms of liberalism, see Richard E. Flathman, "Ruling, Rules, and Rule Following: Mainstay or Mirage, Miracle or Misfortune?," in *Reflections of a Would-Be Anarchist: Ideals and Institutions of Liberalism* (Minneapolis: University of Minnesota Press, 1998).

Wolin's appreciation of the uncomfortable fit between democracy and rule resonates with the ideas of a wide range of democratic theorists working in otherwise disparate traditions. Michael Hardt and Antonio Negri, drawing on Spinoza, embrace what they call the "maddeningly elusive" and nonsovereign power of the "multitude." Jacques Rancière identifies democracy with a "rupture in the logic of *archê*," or rule, that takes place when those who have no recognized part within a regime suddenly appear and speak in public without authorization. Ernesto Laclau, inspired by Claude Lefort, characterizes democracy as constitutively torn between rule and the suspension of rule – or, in his terms, between the "occupation" of the "place of power" by particular groups who claim to represent universal values, and the equally ongoing exposure of the ideological character of every such claim, which keeps the place of power open or "empty."[9] Although some of these authors flirt with a simple rejection of rule, all ultimately acknowledge that rule is unavoidable, perhaps even (partly) beneficial; and the resulting tension between the rejection and acceptance of rule troubles their work in various ways, leading them to characterize democracy in terms that can sometimes seem self-contradictory.[10] Still,

---

[9] Michael Hardt and Antonio Negri, *Multitude: War and Democracy in the Age of Empire* (New York: Penguin Press, 2004), pp. 192, 340; Ernesto Laclau, "Democracy and the Question of Power." *Constellations* 8 (March 2001), p. 7; Ernesto Laclau and Chantal Mouffe, *Hegemony and Socialist Strategy* (London: Verso, 1985); Claude Lefort, *Democracy and Political Theory*, translated by David Macey (Minneapolis: University of Minnesota Press, 1988), p.17; Jacques Rancière, *Disagreement: Politics and Philosophy*, translated by Julie Rose (Minneapolis: University of Minnesota Press, 1999), 20–30; idem, "Ten Theses on Politics." *Theory & Event* 5, 3 (2001), available online at http://muse.jhu.edu/journals/theory_and_event/v005/5 .3ranciere.html, accessed July 15, 2005, par. 14.

[10] Wolin, for example, is left caught between two pictures of democracy – as an episodic, "fugitive" rebelliousness and as a continuous practice of cooperative decision making – that he cannot quite reconcile. Sheldon S. Wolin, "Fugitive Democracy," in Seyla Benhabib, ed., *Democracy and Difference: Contesting the Boundaries of the Political* (Princeton: Princeton University Press, 1996); idem, *Politics and Vision: Continuity and Innovation in Western Political Thought,* expanded ed. (Princeton: Princeton University Press, 2004), pp. 601–6; and see Nicholas Xenos, "Momentary Democracy," in Aryeh Botwinick and William E. Connolly, eds., *Democracy and Vision: Sheldon Wolin and the Vicissitudes of the Political* (Princeton: Princeton University Press, 2001). Hardt and Negri alternate between invocations of the unlimited potential of the multitude to exceed every form or order, and characterizations of the activity of the multitude in terms of "decision-making" and "the rule of everyone by everyone." Hardt and Negri, *Multitude,* pp. 237, 339; see also Paul A. Passavant, "From Empire's Law to the Multitude's Rights: Law, Representation, and Revolution," and Kam Shapiro, "The Myth of the Multitude," in Paul A. Passavant and Jodi Dean, eds., *Empire's New Clothes: Reading Hardt and Negri* (New York: Routledge, 2004). For Rancière, the tension gives rise to an account of democracy as an ephemeral practice, "always on the shore of its own disappearance," as the unauthorized voices that interrupt rule find themselves incorporated into a new regime. Rancière, "Ten Theses on Politics," par. 25; Jean-Philippe Deranty, "Jacques Rancière's Contribution to the Ethics of Recognition." *Political Theory* 31 (February 2003): 136–56, at 152–3. And Laclau is drawn toward what sometimes sound like self-contradictory descriptions of democratic political action as "the ambiguous practice of trying to fill [a] gap" – the empty space signified by universal terms like "the people" – "while keeping it permanently open." Ernesto Laclau, "Deconstruction,

as Alan Keenan has suggested, these tensions may also be signs of responsiveness to a paradox intrinsic to the very notion of democracy: On the one
hand, democracy's radical inclusiveness and self-grounding character mean that
"democratic politics renders everything provisional and open to question"; on
the other hand, if "the people" is to "regulate its own collective life," democracy must embrace some degree of closure, stability, and institutional form.
From this perspective, democracy is an ideal "at odds with itself, torn between
the closure necessary for the people's identity and rule, and the openness of
contestation and revisability."[11]

The contours of this conversation about democracy and rule are echoed in
contemporary treatments of the political thought of Hannah Arendt. For some
readers, Arendt's most obvious contribution to our thinking about rule lies in
her forceful denial that "ruling" has any proper place in politics at all, notwithstanding its central position in the tradition of Western political thought. In
The Human Condition, for instance, Arendt argues that "the concept of rule"
is at the center of the philosophical tradition's long-standing effort to escape
from the uncertain world of politics, typically by substituting the logic of "making," or *poiêsis,* in which a craftsman applies an already-given set of "rules and
standards" to his material, for the unruliness of genuine action.[12] Likewise,
in *On Revolution,* Arendt seems to embrace an idea of freedom as what she
calls "no-rule," a kind of political life "without a division between rulers
and ruled," and from which "the notion of rule" is "entirely absent" (*OR,*
30). This rejection of "rule" has led some readers to identify Arendt, whether
approvingly or disapprovingly, with an anarchic tradition of political thought
that sees freedom as intrinsically opposed to form and associated instead with
revolutionary events, or with perpetual movement and the transgression of
borders.[13] Other readers of Arendt take her to be more ambivalent toward the
phenomenon of rule, but their readings remain structured by the presuppo-
sition of an opposition between rule and freedom, closure and openness. On
Keenan's interpretation, for example, Arendt's conception of political freedom
in terms of novelty "illuminate[s] in profound ways the constitutive openness of
democratic politics," which, properly understood, is never a closed system but

---

Pragmatism, Hegemony," in Chantal Mouffe, ed., *Deconstruction and Pragmatism* (New York:
   Routledge, 1996), p. 59.

[11] Alan Keenan, *Democracy in Question: Democratic Openness in a Time of Political Closure*
   (Stanford: Stanford University Press, 2003), pp. 10, 13.

[12] Hannah Arendt, *The Human Condition* (Chicago: University of Chicago Press, 1958), pp. 222,
   227 (hereafter *HC*); see also Dana R. Villa, *Arendt and Heidegger: The Fate of the Political*
   (Princeton: Princeton University Press, 1996), p. 51.

[13] See, for instance, Annabelle Herzog, "Political Itineraries and Anarchic Cosmopolitanism in
   the Thought of Hannah Arendt." *Inquiry* 47 (February 2004): 20–41; Miguel Vatter, *Between
   Form and Event: Machiavelli's Theory of Political Freedom* (Dordrecht: Kluwer Academic,
   2000), p. 14. For a more disapproving stance toward Arendt's account of action as "eruptive,"
   revolutionary creativity, see George Kateb, "Political Action: Its Nature and Advantages,"
   in Dana Villa, ed., *The Cambridge Companion to Hannah Arendt* (Cambridge: Cambridge
   University Press, 2000).

is permanently exposed to the possibilities of critique, contestation, expansion, transformation, and reinvention. At the same time, Arendt also sees that freedom understood as beginning is, on its own, an evanescent phenomenon: As Keenan says, it "needs the support of political foundations in order to be more than an occasional or marginal occurrence." As she tries (and fails) to identify a kind of foundation that could be made perfectly consistent with freedom – looking first, in *The Human Condition*, to the phenomenon of promising, and then, in *On Revolution*, to the American Constitution – Arendt, on this reading, expresses both poles of the fundamental tension between democracy's unruliness and its need for rule.[14]

Both of these ways of interpreting Arendt's critique of rule fit well with, and are sustained by, a common way of understanding her larger theoretical project, one that sees her as attempting to purify politics of a whole host of supposedly nonpolitical phenomena, such as rule, violence, sovereignty, embodiment, sentiment, and many others. There is good reason to read Arendt this way: She often presents herself precisely as a policer of boundaries, reminding us of the differences among the various components of the vita activa so that we can keep each one in its "proper location in the world" (*HC*, 73). In particular, because it is *action* that seems to be most in danger of being smothered by these other phenomena, keeping these components in their proper locations seems to require that she "discover a set of criteria that will isolate genuinely political action from its various simulacra." It is at this point, however, that the substantive problem of the relationship between democracy and rule joins up with a long-standing interpretive problem about the meaning of Arendt's concept of action, for it has proved maddeningly difficult for her readers to flesh out these criteria and so to determine "what specific activities *count*" for her as instances of action.[15] The trouble is that, strictly understood, genuine action can seem vanishingly rare (and rarefied), hemmed in by irresistible social forces as well as by Arendt's own puritanical insistence that action be undertaken for the sake of nothing but itself; while, capaciously understood, action can lose its specificity, as though anything could be action if it were regarded in the right way or done in the right spirit.[16] Just as democracy has come to seem torn between rule and novelty, order and change, Arendt's idiosyncratic conception of action has also come to seem torn between the extremes of narrowness and ubiquity.

---

[14] Keenan, *Democracy in Question*, pp. 17, 80. For a more recent reading of Arendt on human rights structured around a similar paradox, see Étienne Balibar, "(De)constructing the Human as Human Institution: A Reflection on the Coherence of Hannah Arendt's Practical Philosophy," *Social Research* 74, 3 (Fall 2007): 727–38.

[15] Villa, *Arendt and Heidegger*, pp. 20, 28.

[16] For an especially vivid account of this problem see Hanna Fenichel Pitkin, *The Attack of the Blob: Hannah Arendt's Concept of the Social* (Chicago: University of Chicago Press, 1998), pp. 177–83; see also Mary Dietz, *Turning Operations: Feminism, Arendt, and Politics* (New York: Routledge), 2002, chs. 5–6; Bonnie Honig, *Political Theory and the Displacement of Politics* (Ithaca: Cornell University Press, 1993), chapter 4.

Nevertheless, there is reason to suspect that Arendt does more than simply reproduce the paradox of democracy and rule, and, relatedly, that the function of her conception of action is different than we have supposed. Consider her comments about rule more closely. In *The Human Condition* and elsewhere, Arendt argues that "rule" in its ordinary sense of a power of command over others is a deeply antipolitical concept, the "hallmark" of various efforts by political actors and philosophers, starting with Plato, to "escape from politics altogether" (*HC*, 222). Yet the dominance of "rule" in this sense, Arendt claims, actually represents the loss of a vital ambiguity in the Greek words *archê* and *archein*, the terms that are now conventionally translated into English as the noun *rule* and the verb *to rule*, and which are often rendered *Herrschaft* and *herrschen* in German.[17] These Greek words, Arendt observes, originally had to do with "beginning," with setting something into motion, as well as with leading; while the complementary verb *prattein* (whence *praxis*) originally referred to the achievement or completion of a course of action (*HC*, 189, 222–5).[18] The interrelatedness of these two action terms, *archein* and *prattein*, captured something of the mutual vulnerability that Arendt says characterizes action: "the dependence of the beginner and leader upon others for help and the dependence of his followers upon him for an occasion to act themselves" (*HC*, 189).

Actors and theorists alike, however, experienced this vulnerability as a limitation, and their efforts to insulate themselves from the uncertainties of action – to "make sure that the beginner would remain the complete master of what he had begun" – are reflected in the subsequent transformations in the meaning of these terms. "In the realm of action," their thinking went, "this isolated mastership can be achieved only if the others are no longer needed to join the enterprise of their own accord, with their own motives and aims, but are

---

[17] Arendt's own translation of *The Human Condition* into German (under the title *Vita Activa*) consistently uses *herrschen, Herrschaft*, and so on, where the English edition has "rule," and her comments about the Greek *archê* and *archein* in her German-language notebooks focus on the interpretation of *archê* as *Herrschaft*. Hannah Arendt, *Denktagebuch, 1950–1973*, edited by Ursula Ludz and Ingeborg Nordmann (Munich: Piper, 2002), e.g., p. 161. Her close association of "rule" with *Herrschaft* may explain why Arendt does not try to reclaim the English term: *Herrschaft*, which can be traced back to medieval German words designating superior rank as well as seniority, does not bear the same productive ambiguity that she finds in *archê* and *archein*. Peter Moraw, "Herrschaft. II. Herrschaft im Mittelalter," in Otto Brunner, Werner Conze, and Reinhart Koselleck, eds., *Geschichtliche Grundbegriffe*, vol. 3 (Stuttgart: Klett-Cotta, 1982), pp. 5–6. Indeed, when Arendt translates the phrase "new form of government" into German twice in the space of one paragraph in *The Human Condition*, initially to refer to totalitarianism and then to refer to the "people's councils" to which she was famously sympathetic – she renders it "*neu[e] Staats- und Herrschaftsform*" in the first instance and "*neue Staats- und Regierungsform*" in the second (*HC*, 216; *Vita Activa*, p. 211), which suggests that she is willing to use derivatives of the Latin *rego* (to which both *regieren* and "rule" are related) when she could contrast them with *herrschen* and *Herrschaft*. (This does not mean that *rego*-derivatives are, for her, unambiguously positive; for a contrasting case, see her discussion of "rules" [*Regeln*] in *HC*, 225–7; thanks to Roy Tsao on this point.)

[18] See also "What Is Freedom," pp. 165–6; *OR*, 213; *Denktagebuch*, pp. 161, 327.

used to execute orders, and if, on the other hand, the beginner who took the initiative does not permit himself to get involved in the action itself" (*HC*, 222). As a consequence, *archein* and *prattein* "split into two altogether differ- ent functions: the function of giving commands, which became the prerogative of the ruler, and the function of executing them, which became the duty of his subjects" (*HC*, 189).[19] Once *archein* and *prattein* were separated in this way, *archein* itself – now recognizable as what we conventionally call "rul- ing" – began to lose its ambiguity, and the idea of "beginning" came to play an increasingly insignificant role in the conceptualization of action and politics. Plato himself did still exploit the "equivocal significance of the word *archein*" by appealing to the soul's status as the beginning (*archê*) of all motion in order to explain why the soul ought to rule (*archein*) the body.[20] Yet to think about beginning in this way, which reduced it to a kind of "legitimation" of rule, actually prepared the ground for the ultimate disappearance of "the element of beginning," in the sense of the initiation of an undertaking, "from the concept of rulership." "With it," Arendt concludes, "the most elementary and authen- tic understanding of human freedom disappeared from political philosophy" (*HC*, 224–5).

Two features of this critique of rule deserve special attention. First and most fundamental is its attention to language. For Arendt, the elements of our political vocabulary are not just ways of pointing to given things in the world: the capacity of a word like *rule* to refer to something always also involves an interpretation of the world, an explicit or tacit sense of why some phenomena belong together, what they are like, and why they are significant. By focusing specifically on the language of rule – that is, on the gaps between the meanings of terms that are often thought to be equivalent, such as *archê* and *rule*, or on differences in the use of *archê* and *archein* themselves across time or from one author to another – Arendt signals that her concerns about rule lie at *this* level: Instead of reversing the positive valence traditionally assigned to the phenomenon called "rule," she aims her critique at the interpretation of the world that the word *rule* carries with it (and which underlies both positive and negative assessments of rule's place in politics). Second, among the particular features of this interpretation that draw Arendt's critical attention, one of the most important is the close association it posits between relationships of subordination on the one hand, and such phenomena as stability, regularity, and continuity on the other. The conceit of the idea of rule, Arendt tells us, is "the notion that men can lawfully and politically live together only when some are entitled to command and the others forced to obey" (*HC*, 222). Yet the fact that structures of subordination often *do* produce more or less stable orders

---

[19] See also *HC*, 222–3.

[20] Arendt says that "it is decisive for Plato, as he says expressly at the end of the *Laws*, that only the beginning (*archê*) is entitled to rule (*archein*)" (*HC*, 224); as her notebooks indicate, this is a gloss on *Laws* 895b and 967d. Plato, *Laws, Books VII–XII*, translated by R. G. Bury (Cambridge, MA: Harvard University Press, 2004). See Arendt, *Denktagebuch*, pp. 323–4.

does not mean that they are the only forms of human relationship that can do so, nor does it mean that their strategies for ensuring stability are sustainable: The ideal of isolated mastership, as Arendt repeatedly reminds us, misleads rulers about the sources of their own power and so exposes them to failure and reversal (*HC*, 189).[21] This, too, indicates that the point of her critique of rule and her recovery of beginning is not to celebrate those phenomena that are conventionally taken to be rule's opposites, such as disorder, instability, interruptions of regularity, or radical breaks in continuity, but to prise apart phenomena that the idea of rule has taught us to see as inseparably connected.

Understood in these terms, Arendt's work intersects with debates in contemporary democratic theory in an unexpected way. It suggests that the whole matrix of oppositions that structures democratic theory (between rule, stability, continuity, and order on the one hand, and freedom, change, novelty, and openness on the other) is itself an artifact of the ongoing dominance of political theory and practice by a set of background assumptions about what ruling is and how it works, including especially the assumption that stability, continuity, order, and related phenomena are to be understood as the products of the exercise of supreme authoritative control. These assumptions were originally employed to rationalize hierarchical social and political forms, but they are now held in common by those who see democracy as a structure of authoritative control, *and* by those who reject such regime-oriented views of democracy in the name of revolutionary insubordination, *and* by those whose work is structured by their acknowledgment of the simultaneous appeal of both positions.[22] Correspondingly, Arendt's aim is not simply to rehabilitate those phenomena that, within that matrix, are positioned as rule's opposites; instead, she works to accustom us to unfamiliar ways of using and relating some of these familiar terms – ways that cannot be captured within this matrix of oppositions, because they express an alternative interpretation of the political world. In what follows, I shall develop this interpretation of Arendt through a consideration of her idiosyncratic use of the idea of "beginning," which I shall suggest is meant to pick out not the spontaneous disruption of existing patterns, but the sense in which action, whether disruptive or not, involves attention and responsiveness to worldly events. This reworking of the idea of beginning will shed light on

---

[21] See also *HC*, 222, 227.

[22] Arendt's critique of conventional views of ruling thus fits well with Wittgenstein's critique in the *Philosophical Investigations* of conventional views of rules and rule following – at least as long as Wittgenstein is not understood as saying merely that rules, as instruments for the production of control, leave more room than we sometimes believe for non–rule-bound freedom. What is radical about both Arendt and Wittgenstein is that they refuse the opposition between rules as sources of determination and freedom as the power to exceed or transform rule, thereby letting us see the fundamental *similarity* (though not identity) of breaking or subverting a rule; modifying a rule; *and* going on as before. See, e.g., Hanna Fenichel Pitkin, *Wittgenstein and Justice: With a New Preface* (Berkeley: University of California Press, 1993); Tully, "The Agonic Freedom of Citizens"; Linda M. G. Zerilli, "Doing without Knowing: Feminism's Politics of the Ordinary," in Cressida J. Heyes, ed., *The Grammar of Politics: Wittgenstein and Political Philosophy* (Ithaca: Cornell University Press, 2003).

the nature of Arendt's critique of rule; it will illuminate the broader problem I have described in her account of action; and, ultimately, it will open a new way of thinking about the nature of the impediments faced by democratic politics in the modern world – for what threatens "beginning" as Arendt understands it is not the enforcement of regularity, but the erosion of the contexts in which events call for responses and, thus, in which it makes sense to act at all.

3.2 What Is Beginning?

Given the unusual nature of Arendt's critique of rule – and given, in particular, her insistence on linking "beginning" back to words such as *archê* and *archein* that have come to suggest the stifling of novelty – we should expect that her appeals to the phenomenon of beginning will turn out to be more than just an effort to rehabilitate unruliness. However, it is not obvious what else "beginning" could mean. Arendt's readers typically suppose that the paradigmatic instance of beginning is an act that *interrupts* an existing series or a given order,[23] and thus that beginning is, precisely, that which is closed down by rule – by the making of decisions, the application of principles, the consolidation of identities, the issuing of commands. Arendt's work sometimes seems to support this understanding of beginning. In "What Is Freedom," for instance, she seems to contrast action, in the sense of beginning, with the operation of "automatic processes," which generate only "stagnation" and "petrifaction." Against this background, she says, a new beginning "breaks into the world"; it is experienced as an "infinite improbability."[24] Such characterizations echo Arendt's phenomenology of "natality," which is her name for that aspect of the human condition in virtue of which we possess "the capacity of beginning something anew, that is, of acting" (*HC*, 9). This condition is manifest in those acts in which "something new is started which cannot be expected from whatever may have happened before," which take place "against the overwhelming odds of statistical laws and their probability" (*HC*, 178). "Beginning," thus understood, refers to a human possibility that is the very opposite of regularity: It means, as James Tully puts it, "the freedom of speaking and acting *differently* in the course of the game."[25]

One problem with this reading, however, is that it treats Arendt's concepts of beginning and natality as something akin to restrictive clauses in grammar – that is, as qualifications that pick out the particular subset of human acts that actualize the power to break with an existing series or pattern. The trouble with that approach is twofold. The first issue has to do with the formal function

---

[23] See, e.g., Ronald Beiner, "Action, Natality, and Citizenship: Hannah Arendt's Concept of Freedom," in Zbigniew Pelczynski and John Gray, eds., *Conceptions of Liberty in Political Philosophy* (New York: St. Martin's Press, 1984), p. 355; Maurizio Passerin d'Entrèves, *The Political Philosophy of Hannah Arendt* (London: Routledge, 1994), p. 68.

[24] Arendt, "What Is Freedom," 168–9.

[25] Tully, "The Agonic Freedom of Citizens," p. 164, emphasis added.

of the concept of action (with which beginning and natality are associated) in Arendt's text: Arendt's famous triad of "labor," "work," and "action" does not operate straightforwardly as a set of categories into which different instances of human activity are to be sorted; indeed, she herself suggests that activities may belong to more than one of these at once.[26] (As I have suggested, however, it seems equally problematic to think of these categories as something like a set of dimensions that inhere in *every* instance of human activity, because part of the point of the book seems to be to warn against the loss of certain capacities or possibilities; if that is right, then there must be *something* restrictive about these concepts. I shall return to this problem.) The second issue is substantive: At crucial points, Arendt says things that seem inconsistent with the conventional reading of beginning or natality as the power to break with a series, change direction, or act differently. Consider a passage from "Understanding and Politics," one of the most important transitional essays Arendt wrote after the publication of *Origins of Totalitarianism*, as she was undertaking the work on the tradition of political philosophy that would eventually find expression in *The Human Condition*. After criticizing appeals to laws of cause and effect in historical writing, Arendt offers a different characterization of the task of the historian:

Just as in our personal lives our worst fears and best hopes will never adequately prepare us for what actually happens – because the moment even a foreseen event takes place, everything changes, and we can never be prepared for the inexhaustible literalness of this "everything" – so each event in human history reveals an unexpected landscape of human deeds, sufferings, and new possibilities which together transcend the sum total of all willed intentions and the significance of all origins. It is the task of the historian to detect this unexpected *new* with all its implications in any given period and to bring out the full power of its significance.[27]

What is crucial about this passage is the puzzling claim that a kind of unexpectedness and novelty – which Arendt immediately equates with *arché* and "beginning," and ties not just to the activity of the historian but also to political science and political action – is a feature of *all* events, including those that are hoped for, feared, or foreseen. Several years later, Arendt amplifies the same thought in "What Is Freedom," where she writes that "every act" is, from a certain perspective, a "miracle," and that "it is because of this element of the 'miraculous' present in all reality that events, no matter how well anticipated in fear or hope, strike us with a shock of surprise once they have come to pass."[28]

---

[26] For instance, she says that action is typically "about some worldly objective reality" in addition to being "a disclosure of the acting and speaking agent," which suggests a kind of "over-grow[th]" of the work world with the action world, rather than a sharp separation between them (*HC*, 182–3; see Roy T. Tsao, "Arendt against Athens," *Political Theory* 30 (February 2002): 97–123, at 101.

[27] Arendt, "Understanding and Politics," p. 320.

[28] Arendt, "What Is Freedom," pp. 169–70.

In what sense could something "foreseen" or "anticipated" nevertheless also be "unexpected"? Arendt's point cannot be to claim that even those things of which we count ourselves certain are, as matters of scientific fact, uncertain, or that even those acts that conform to our expectations count as beginnings if the agent could have chosen to act differently: Even to dwell on the margins of error in our expectations, or on the space of underdetermination, is still to remain in the register of cause and effect, and that, she insists, is never enough to account for the phenomenon of beginning.[29] Instead, her point is that when an event passes from possibility to actuality – regardless of how probable or improbable we may have taken it to be while it was still only a possibility – *something* changes in a different register; namely, the register in which happenings are not only caused states of affairs but also meaningful events, features of a world, and, in particular, occasions for response.[30] Even the most purely strategic kinds of response are crucially affected by the passage between the possible and the actual: What might have invited preemption or prevention now invites retaliation or compensation, for instance, and the significance of this difference is no less when it comes to other modes of response, from holding liable, to forgiving, to narrating, to thanking, to following, and so on. To say that *all* events exhibit unexpectedness in this sense, then, is to say that no degree of certainty about whether something will or will not happen, and what it will turn out to be, can smooth over the difference between "not yet" and "already." Beginning is tied to the perspective or stance in which *that* difference matters: The novelty of a new beginning, its eruptiveness, arises not out of the degree of qualitative difference it manifests with respect to what has come before, as though the features of this act were being compared with the features of its predecessors by a neutral observer of history, standing outside of time, but precisely out of an agent's attunement to its character as an irrevocable event, and therefore also as a new point of departure.[31]

Some further evidence for this way of understanding beginning comes from the fact that it helps make sense of Arendt's characterization of natality as a *condition* of human life rather than a feature of human nature or a property of the will. Although Arendt's capsule account of natality is well known, it is also deceptively simple. The word "natality" refers to the fact that human beings are born; at the same time, it refers to the capacity of human beings to engage in action – to give birth, as it were, to new beginnings (HC, 8–9). These two senses of natality are, somehow, connected: We are "newcomers and beginners *by virtue of* birth"; our words and deeds are "like a second birth" (HC, 176–7,

---

[29] Arendt, "Understanding and Politics," pp. 319–20.

[30] On the terms "occasion" and "response" in Arendt, see Kimberly Curtis, *Our Sense of the Real: Aesthetic Experience and Arendtian Politics* (Ithaca: Cornell University Press, 1999), chapter 5.

[31] This seems close to what Stanley Cavell means by "presentness." Stanley Cavell, "The Avoidance of Love: A Reading of King Lear," in *Disowning Knowledge in Six Plays of Shakespeare* (Cambridge: Cambridge University Press, 1987), pp. 118–19. On the "event" as involving a "strange coincidence" of expectation and surprise, see Françoise Dastur, "Phenomenology of the Event: Waiting and Surprise," *Hypatia* 15 (Fall 2000): 178–89.

emphasis added). That connection is captured in Arendt's beloved passage from Augustine – "that there be a beginning, man was created before whom there was nobody" – which means, on her gloss, that "with the creation of man, the principle of beginning came into the world" (*HC*, 177).[32] Yet the precise nature of this connection is uncertain. If we lean toward a literal reading of Arendt's deployment of Augustine, we might take her to mean that the power of beginning is a faculty that each human being possesses, implanted in us with the creation of the species and passed on from generation to generation; but that would seem to be a claim about human *nature* – that is, about the essential properties that mark us off as beings of a certain kind, rather than the basic structures of our existence, which are not *in* us. Conversely, if we incline toward a less literal reading of the passage from Augustine, matters are not much better. If Arendt simply means that the Biblical account of Creation is a vivid metaphor that figures the subsequent birth of each individual human being, and if she means, in turn, that the phenomenon of beginning as manifest in action is *like* both of these sorts of "birth," then "natality" would seem to be little more than an analogy: useful, perhaps, for drawing attention to a certain human capacity, but not a *condition* of anything.

There is another possibility, however. If, as I have suggested, the phenomenon of action as beginning turns not on the degree of qualitative difference between one state of affairs and its predecessor, but rather on the irreducible further difference introduced by the happening, the actuality of every event, then to call natality in the sense of birth a "condition" of beginning would be to say that birth is the fundamental phenomenon on the basis of which *this* difference becomes meaningful: It is that in virtue of which the actuality of events acquires its weight. This reading seems to be confirmed by Arendt's account of the phenomenon of time. The individual life story, she says, which has a beginning and an end, is "distinguished from all other things by the rectilinear course of its movement, which, so to speak, cuts through the circular movement of biological life" (*HC*, 19). Birth and death, in other words, are the conditions of the experience of linear time.[33] This is why she calls the appearance and disappearance of individual human beings the "*supreme* events" (*HC*, 97, emphasis added). It is also why she ties action, in the sense of a new beginning, so closely to what she calls the "disclosure" of the uniqueness of the individual agent: not, as is sometimes supposed, because action necessarily expresses an individualistic or self-centered attitude on the part of the actor, but simply because she thinks that the lives of distinct persons, whose beginnings and ends are the markers that lend our experience of time its linear character, are for

---

[32] See also "Understanding and Politics," p. 321; "What Is Freedom," p. 167.

[33] This point is suggested by Patricia Bowen-Moore, who says that "man and temporality are affirmed by the miracle of birth"; but she more often stresses the opposite thought, that beginning involves the insertion of a human being into an already-existing "time continuum." Patricia Bowen-Moore, *Hannah Arendt's Philosophy of Natality* (New York: St. Martin's Press, 1989), pp. 22–3.

this reason the medium of action: the points into which meaning gathers and from which it disperses, dependent upon but never determined by the initiative of individuals (*HC*, 175ff).[34]

On Arendt's understanding, then, beginning is by no means only manifest in acts that depart from an existing series or constitute a "radical break with our ordinary expectations."[35] Instead, the term "beginning" points to a kind of novelty that can also be present in moments that satisfy our expectations, follow existing patterns, or continue observable regularities, but which comes into view only from a stance of practical engagement with events. Correspondingly, the reason the dominance of the concept of rule tends to obscure beginning is not that beginning is diametrically opposed to the phenomena conventionally associated with rule, since nothing about beginning requires a break with the terms of an existing order, or resistance to regularity as such. Rather, the concept of rule obscures beginning by blocking this posture of practical attunement; and it can do so in more than one way. By teaching us to associate phenomena such as regularity and continuity with hierarchical relations of command and obedience, the idea of rule can encourage the sort of withdrawal from practical engagement that is required to maintain the illusion of mastery (*HC*, 222–3). However, the same background assumption of a close connection between subordination and regularity can equally well inform democratic *critiques* of rule, leading us to embrace a countervailing commitment to openness and interruption – which, however, we seem to be tragically bound to violate every time we make a decision, indeed, every time we move in one direction rather than another, and which can therefore produce paralysis.[36]

Still, all this leaves us with some unanswered questions about Arendt's conception of beginning. The source of the eruptiveness of beginning in Arendt's sense lies in what I called "our attunement" to events – but this phrase glosses over some difficulties too quickly. Whose "attunement"? What is attunement,

---

[34] Arendt's notes from a lecture she gave at Brandeis University in 1960, called "The Productivity of Life and Work," offer some confirmation of this interpretation. There, under the heading "Newness," she writes: "Nature is forever, no beginning and no end. Men comes [sic] into nature, hence beginning and end. By acting, he begins a STORY." As others have shown, we can also understand the relationship of beginning to birth in Arendt by seeing "birth" as the paradigmatic case of an "event" to which the actor responds: As Arendt says, in action we "confirm and take upon ourselves the naked fact of our original physical appearance" (*HC*, 176). On this view, as Françoise Collin emphasizes, the importance of the moment of birth lies not in its association with a spontaneous "creation" but in its exemplification of the givenness to which action is always a response. François Collin, "Birth as Praxis," in Joke J. Hermsen and Dana R. Villa, eds., *The Judge and the Spectator: Hannah Arendt's Political Philosophy* (Leuven, Belgium: Peeters, 1999), p. 106; see also Marguerite Durst, "Birth and Natality in Hannah Arendt," *Analecta Husserliana* 79 (2004): 777–97. On the relationship between the physical and intersubjective dimensions of natality, see Peg Birmingham, *Hannah Arendt and Human Rights: The Predicament of Common Responsibility* (Bloomington: Indiana University Press, 2006), chap. 1.

[35] Beiner, "Action, Natality, and Citizenship," p. 84.

[36] See Keenan, *Democracy in Question*, pp. 20–2.

anyway? Does this just mean that something is a beginning if the person who undertakes it thinks it is? Or if he or she has some other kind of mental state in relation to other events in the world? These answers might seem to constitute a way to deal with the formal problem about the nature of the category of "action" that I bracketed earlier: Perhaps Arendt's apparent hesitation between an inclusive use of that category, in which every instance of activity can be seen from the perspective of action, and a restrictive use of that category, in which action names something we are in danger of losing, can be resolved by thinking of action as an attitude or stance that is available to be taken toward any activity, but which we do not necessarily always take up. The turn to the difference between possibility and actuality in this idea is right, but the implicit intellectualism is misleading, to the extent that it suggests either that it is an actor's mental states that determine whether his or her activity counts as action, or that the recovery of action might simply be a matter of theoretical reflection, of seeing what we are always already doing *as* action in a way that leaves the shape of our activity untouched. To see why, to develop a fuller account of what it is that makes a beginning a beginning, and to prepare the way for a return to democratic theory, we need to go back to Arendt's text, approaching the problem this time via the intersection between the ideas of action and rule.

3.3 Action and Rule: Arendt's Dante

The chapter on action in *The Human Condition* begins with two epigraphs. The first, from Isak Dinesen, reads: "All sorrows can be borne if you put them into a story or tell a story about them." The second, from the first book of Dante's *De Monarchia*, is printed first in Latin and then in Arendt's own English translation:

Nam in omni actione principaliter intenditur ab agente, sive necessitate naturae sive voluntarie agat, propriam similitudinem explicare; unde fit quod omne agens, in quantum huiusmodi, delectatur, quia, cum omne quod est appetat suum esse, ac in agendo agentis esse modammodo amplietur, sequitur de necessitate delectatio.... Nihil igitur agit nisi tale existens quale patiens fieri debet.

For in every action what is primarily intended by the doer, whether he acts from natural necessity or out of free will, is the disclosure of his own image. Hence it comes about that every doer, in so far as he does, takes delight in doing; since everything that is desires its own being, and since in action the being of the doer is somehow intensified, delight necessarily follows.... Thus, nothing acts unless [by acting] it makes patent its latent self. (*HC*, 145)

In a recent study of Arendt, Susannah Gottlieb explores the meaning of these epigraphs, and of the passage from Dante in particular. Noting the irony involved in Arendt's use of a passage drawn from a philosophical defense of universal monarchy, Gottlieb brilliantly tracks the ways in which Arendt turns Dante's passage into "a plea for a nonmonarchial politics," a transformation that, she observes, turns on a distinctive translation of Dante's "*explicare*" as well as a mistranslation of the crucial last sentence.[37] Yet there are further layers of significance in this epigraph. One of these comes into view when we notice the importance of the concept of rule in Dante's work. Although he uses a variety of other terms to refer to political authority, including *monarchia*, *imperium*, *regnum*, and related words, he also frequently calls the monarch *princeps* and his rule *principatus*, which suggests a connection between monarchy and the "principle," *principium*, of humanity.[38] Indeed, Dante's defense of monarchy rests on his claim that a single, universal *princeps* is uniquely able to produce peace, which is the prerequisite of the fulfillment of the *principium* of humankind. Moreover, unlike many other terms for political authority, *princip*-words (which were used to render *archê* and related terms in medieval Latin translations of Greek texts) also bear some of the same semantic complexity that Arendt finds in *archê* and *archein*: *Princeps* can also mean first in time; and both *principatus* and, more commonly, *principium* can refer to a beginning or origin.[39] Against this background, it seems plausible to treat Arendt's brief but rich engagement with Dante as an extension of her critical engagement with the ideas of rule and beginning.

Another layer of significance in the epigraph becomes visible when we attend to the role of Aristotle in the first book of *De Monarchia*, and in particular to Dante's use of categories drawn from Aristotle's philosophy. Dante's inquiry into the principle of humankind takes the form of an investigation of humankind's highest power (*potentia*); the principle – that is, for Dante, the goal or end – of humanity is to actualize this potential (*actuare*, also *reducere de potentia in actum*, "reduce" from potential to act).[40] Among the functions of the monarch is to "dispose" (*disponere*) humankind rightly for this task, which involves a kind of arrangement and ordering of humanity that strengthens certain human potentials (and weakens others) – for instance, by intensifying the power of justice and minimizing the power of greed.[41] And the passage that Arendt uses as her epigraph is drawn from that section of the *Monarchia* in which Dante argues that the monarch is best able to dispose others well in this way – an argument that turns explicitly on a citation of Aristotle's account of potentiality and actuality (*dunamis* and *energeia*) in the *Metaphysics*.[42] Perhaps, then, Arendt's use of Dante is also tied to her own,

---

37 Susannah Young-Ah Gottlieb, *Regions of Sorrow: Anxiety and Messianism in Hannah Arendt and W.H. Auden* (Stanford: Stanford University Press, 2003), p. 163.

38 Dante, *Dante's Monarchia,* edited and translated by Richard Kay (Toronto: Pontifical Institute of Mediaeval Studies, 1998), 1.2. Unless otherwise indicated, all quotations from Dante's *De Monarchia* are from Kay's edition of *Monarchia*.

39 Charlton T. Lewis and Charles Short, *A Latin Dictionary* (Oxford: Clarendon Press, 1879). Available online at http://www.perseus.tufts.edu/cgi-bin/ptext?doc=Perseus%3Atext% 3A1999.04.0059. Accessed July 15, 2005. For Arendt's recovery of the language of "principle," see, e.g., "What Is Freedom," p. 152.

40 Dante, *De Monarchia* 1.4.1, 1.3.8.

41 Ibid., 1.11, 1.13.

42 Ibid., 1.13.1–3.

distinctive use of Aristotle's metaphysical vocabulary in the chapter on action –
for instance, in her account of the relationship between power (*dunamis*) and
activity (*energeia*) (*HC*, 100–206, passim).

Gottlieb's reading of Arendt's epigraph begins with an observation about
her translation of Dante's "*explicare*" in the phrase "*propriam similitudinem
explicare,*" which Arendt renders as "the disclosure of his own image."
Gottlieb notes that "*explicare* ('uncoiling' or 'unfolding') can characterize a
purely internal occurrence – and this is indeed the direction of Dante's thought
as he seeks to justify the institution of monarchy"; for this reason, she argues,
Arendt's translation of *explicare* as "disclosure" shatters Dante's solipsism,
highlighting the fact of plurality, the existence of others to whom the agent's
disclosure is directed.[43] (Though it may seem implausible to say that Dante's
analysis is "entirely absorbed with the relation of the agent to itself," given
that he is concerned precisely with the power of the monarch to shape and
dispose *others*, Gottlieb's point is, presumably, that the monarch's effort at
self-propagation does not really count as a relation to *others*: There is no
acknowledgment of separateness here, no plurality except as a function of
divine self-division and self-unfolding.) Gottlieb then goes on to discuss the
rendering of the last sentence of the epigraph, "*nihil igitur agit nisi tale existens quale patiens fieri debet,*" which Arendt translates as "thus, nothing acts
unless [by acting] it makes patent its latent self." As Gottlieb notes, and as
the context indicates, this is evidently a mistranslation;[44] Prue Shaw's edition
has "nothing acts unless it has the qualities which are to be communicated
to the thing acted upon"; and Richard Kay's translation reads "nothing acts
unless it is already what the patient ought to become."[45] What, exactly, has
Arendt done? Since the "patient" or the "thing acted upon" is the *patiens*,
Gottlieb concludes that Arendt has transformed "*patiens*" into "patent" by
"subtracting an *i.*"[46] This cannot be right, however, for it leaves us with no
plausible account of where Arendt finds "latent" in this sentence, or of what
she would mean by that word. It seems more likely that Arendt has read "*exis-
tere*" as "to make patent," and "*patiens*" as "the latent self," in which case
her crucial departure from Dante would lie not in dropping an *i* but in tying
existens and *patiens* to the same subject, rather than treating *patiens* as the
separate recipient of the actor's action. (From two subjects to one: It is Arendt,
notice, who is letting herself be absorbed into the question of the agent's
self-relation – but sometimes it may be more effective to approach plurality
indirectly.)

The first part of this hypothesis is plausible enough, for *exsistere* can mean
to be, but also to emerge, appear, or be made manifest; and it would be no

---

[43] Gottlieb, *Regions of Sorrow,* p. 162.
[44] Ibid., p. 162.
[45] Dante, *Monarchy, Monarchy,* edited and translated by Prue Shaw (Cambridge: Cambridge
University Press, 1996), 1.13.3; Dante, *Dante's Monarchia,* 1.13.3.
[46] Gottlieb, *Regions of Sorrow,* p. 162.

surprise for Arendt, the student of Heidegger, to stress these latter senses.[47] Moreover, both parts of the hypothesis receive some support and elaboration later in Arendt's discussion of action, when she says that "the meaning of the last sentence of the Dante quotation at the head of this chapter," which "defies translation," is as follows: "The human sense of reality demands that men actualize the sheer passive givenness of their being, not in order to change it but in order to make articulate and call into full existence what otherwise they would have to suffer passively anyhow" (HC, 208). Here, Arendt unpacks "the latent self" into an even richer notion, "what one has to suffer passively anyhow"; and *that* phrase is identifiably a rendering – albeit a misrendering, ungrammatical and unmoored from the context of Dante's words – of "*tale . . . quale patiens fieri debere.*"

Reading Arendt's mistranslation this way has a chain of important consequences. The first is that it clarifies what Arendt means here by "the latent self." When Arendt's Dante says that "nothing acts unless [by acting] it makes patent its latent self," it is tempting to think of this as a kind of unveiling: the identity of the self rests, fully formed but unseen, under the cover of darkness, until the actor steps into the light of the public, putting his persona – carefully crafted back in the private workshop – on public display. Yet Arendt's own comments about the "nonsovereign" character of action belie this reading. "Nobody knows whom he reveals when he discloses himself in deed and word," she says (HC, 180), and this is because this "who" is formed in the crucible of disclosure itself, where it is shaped by the unpredictable reactions it provokes; the "unchangeable identity of the person" only comes into being as such in retrospect, once an actor's life "has come to its end" (HC, 193).[48] Does this mean, then, that the "latent self" in this epigraph is merely the symptom of a kind of ideological misrecognition, the falsely naturalized sediment of a series of performatives, which good Arendtian political actors should attempt to expose as such and to resist?[49] Yes and no: *Sometimes* the rhythm of Arendtian beginning may involve making spaces for subversion of existing norms, or for the creation of something that looks substantially different from what has preceded it, but, as we have seen, such unruliness is not constitutive of what it means to be engaged in action on Arendt's account; and anyway, Arendt's talk of "making patent," "making articulate," and "calling into full existence" does not fit well with the thought that "the latent self" is a misrecognition to be unmasked.

The phrase "what otherwise they would have to suffer passively anyhow," however, suggests another possibility, one that lies outside this all-too-familiar

---

[47] As Shadi Bartsch has pointed out to me, on this reading Arendt is also mistranslating *exsistere* by treating it as a transitive verb; but this, too, seems like a plausible mistranslation to ascribe to her, since one way to read her larger philosophical point is that the kind of "existence" involved in acting is not self-contained but involves a practical relation to circumstances and events.

[48] Ibid., 193; see also 233–4.

[49] See, e.g., Honig, *Political Theory and the Displacement of Politics*; Honig, "Toward an Agonistic Feminism."

dichotomy between the self as settled in advance and the self, if it can still be called that, as in perpetual flux. It suggests that what Arendt calls the latent self is not an *identity*, real *or* illusory; instead, it is action's point of departure, the constellation of circumstances, events, and forces to which each new act is a response. To say that this is not a *real* identity is to say that action, in responding to such a point of departure, always does more than merely reveal an always already established character; to say that it is not an *illusory* identity is to say that this point of departure cannot be unmasked – to do that would be like pulling oneself out of that matrix in which there are occasions to do things, in which acting makes sense at all. Of course, because circumstances, events, and forces are usually things that we regard as external to the self, it may seem problematic to say that they are among the self's constituents; doing so may still seem to dissolve the self into its surroundings. Yet it is important to notice that Arendt's account of the latent self is not reductive in this way. For her, we might say, the latent self exists at – indeed, it *is* – the intersection between these worldly happenings and circumstances, on the one hand, and the biologically individuated human beings for whom they are meaningful, whose bodily trajectories from birth to death serve as the threads that organize this latent stuff into *selves* and make it possible to speak intelligibly of an individual actor's initiatory response to the circumstances and events with which he or she is confronted (and which will turn out to have made up part of the story of who he or she is).

All of this suggests that there is a close connection between Arendt's account of the "latent" self, that in relation to which one is *patiens*, on the one hand, and the idea of the event that I spelled out earlier, on the other. Yet there is also a subtle temporal twist here. Recall that what makes a beginning a beginning for Arendt, what lends it its eruptiveness, is not its degree of departure from what preceded it, but rather our attunement to its character as an irrevocable event, which also means as an occasion for response. This suggests that the status of being a beginning is not acontextual: Beginnings are always beginnings *for* some agent or agents – specifically, for those from whom the beginning calls for a response. Now, however, Arendt has also told us that what it means to act is to "call into full existence" something that one would otherwise merely suffer passively. To do that, it would seem, is precisely to be attuned to the character of this latent stuff as a set of irrevocable events and an occasion for action. There is no way to undo what has been done, no way *not* to suffer it – but you can do more than *merely* suffer it: You can take it as your point of departure. You can, in short, begin. Taking these two points together: what makes an act an instance of beginning? That, against its background, someone begins. What makes *that* a beginning? That it becomes an occasion to begin – and so on.[50]

---

[50] In "Understanding and Politics," Arendt characterizes the complementary relationship between understanding and action in these terms: "we can *understand* an event only as the end and the culmination of everything that happened before, as 'fulfillment of the times'; only in action will

This temporal structure has several crucial implications. Notice, first, that it immediately does away with the notion that the question of whether an instance of activity is a beginning might be decided by the attitude or mental state of its agent. To the contrary, whether your activity is a beginning is not wholly under your control: It is, instead, a matter of the character of the responses and reactions it provokes (or fails to provoke) in you and others. In this sense, the structure of intersubjective vulnerability that Arendt discusses in *The Human Condition* under such rubrics as the "boundlessness" and "unpredictability" of action applies to more than just individual instances of action: *It also applies to the very status of action as action.* Second, this also suggests that the being of beginnings is a *public* matter – not in the sense that it is to be decided by rational-critical discourse, nor in the sense that it is a question of the common good rather than the private interest, nor in the sense that it involves the exposure of a hidden truth – but simply in the sense that it is a worldly phenomenon, which exists only in the sometimes face-to-face, sometimes impersonal, but always uncertain circulation of address and response.[51] Third, it also indicates that the being of a beginning is actually *not* best conceived as a state. Action, understood as beginning, is an ongoing activity whose future is uncertain – and indeed whose past is in a certain sense uncertain as well, insofar as the character of one act as a beginning hangs on its future reception. For this reason, it might be better to speak of action as something that is, at various times and places, coming into being or passing away, as the intensity of responsiveness in a space of potential circulation waxes and wanes, but which never simply or definitively *is*.

We are now in a position to return to the interpretive problem deferred earlier, about the curious difficulty in knowing whether Arendt means concepts such as action and beginning to pick out a specific subset of human activity or to point to a dimension of significance that might be found in *any* instance of human activity. This difficulty, recall, is closely related to the trouble that readers of Arendt often have in finding a suitable criterion in her work by which to decide whether an example of human activity *counts* as action. We should now be able to identify some of the sources of this trouble. First, it may sometimes be the result of a focus on relatively individualized examples of activity, abstracted from the sequences of occasion and response in which they are embedded. Such abstraction makes the examples more manageable, but it also extracts them from the contexts in relation to which Arendt's account of action as beginning makes sense: Trying to decide whether *this* instance of activity, on its own, is a beginning is like trying to decide whether *this* instance of me flexing my knee, on its own, is running. Second, this difficulty is also the result of trying to *decide* whether an instance of activity is or is not a beginning,

we proceed, as a matter of course, from the changed set of circumstances that the event has created, that is, treat it as a beginning" (p. 319).

[51] For this conception of publicity, see Michael Warner, *Publics and Counterpublics* (New York: Verso, 2002).

for beginning, as we have seen, is not a finally settled property, but a possibility we actualize – though never completely – by responding to it. From the stance of the classifier, who sorts specimens of activity into categories, action and beginning are bound to seem paradoxical.

Together, these features of Arendt's account of beginning shed light on her transformative appropriation of Dante. As I indicated earlier, rule, on Dante's account, is a matter of the realization of the highest possibility of human beings through their "disposition" by a sovereign, who is himself already a maximal embodiment of the virtuous dispositions that remain merely possible – latent – in his subjects, and whose activity of disposition is a kind of reproduction of his own likeness in those he governs. This is why the passage that Arendt mistranslates is so crucial to Dante's argument: "nothing acts unless it is already what the patient ought to become." Indeed, in the sentence immediately following this – which Arendt does not quote – Dante adds the authority of Aristotle to his conclusion: "This is why the Philosopher says in the *Metaphysics* that everything that is brought from potentiality into actuality is produced by something similar to itself that already exists in actuality; for if anything tried to act otherwise, it would try in vain."[52] The passage to which Dante seems to be referring is part of Aristotle's account of the various ways in which actuality, *energeia,* is prior to potentiality, *dunamis.* For example, "the actual member of the species is prior to the potential member of the same species," and helps to produce it: "man [is produced] by man, musician by musician."[53] Or again, in a slightly different sense, actuality is prior to potentiality in the sense that the actuality of a thing is its end, and the end, as that for the sake of which the thing is, is prior to the thing qua potentiality; hence "animals do not see in order that they may have sight, but have sight that they may see."[54] Dante here translates such ideas about the priority of actuality into a doctrine of hierarchical rule, treating the monarch as, at once, the one who activates the potentiality of the multitude (as the one who disposes) and the one who *defines* its potentiality (as the embodiment of the *telos* of human beings).

By contrast, Arendt's mistranslation of Dante is a perfect miniature of her critique of the concept of rule in the philosophical tradition. Dante's separation of the monarch from the multitude – expressed in the conventional translation of the crucial sentence, in which *existens* and *patiens* relate to two separate subjects – is an example of the breakdown of the original interdependence between beginner and responder, and of the transformation of that relationship into the *Herrschaft* exercised by one who already knows what is to be done

---

[52] Dante, *De Monarchia* 1.13.3. Some editions have Dante quoting Aristotle's *Metaphysics* 1049b24–2 (e.g., Dante, *Monarchy*); Kay's edition (*Dante's Monarchia*) suggests that Dante was merely paraphrasing Aristotle.

[53] Aristotle, *Metaphysics,* translated by W. D. Ross, in *The Complete Works of Aristotle, The Revised Oxford Translation,* edited by Jonathan Barnes (Princeton: Princeton University Press, 1984) 1049b19–20, 25. The following discussion is especially indebted to conversations with Jill Frank and to Frank, *A Democracy of Distinction.*

[54] Aristotle, *Metaphysics* 1050a7–11.

(who is always already actual) over one who obeys (who has to be brought from potentiality to actuality). In collapsing *existens* and *patiens* back into the "patent" and "latent" selves of a single agent – the action one undertakes, and the constellation of irrevocable events within which, and in response to which, one takes it – Arendt peremptorily denies the claim of *any* agent to be a full embodiment, always already actualized, of human potentiality. In so doing, she also tacitly rejects the reading of Aristotle on which Dante relies. Whereas Dante tends to understand *energeia* as *actuality* in the sense of a state of complete development or perfection, Arendt restores to that concept its association with *activity*: As Aristotle also states, it is because of the priority of *energeia* to *dunamis* that we say that "it is thought impossible to be a builder if one has built nothing or a harpist if one has never played the harp; for he who learns to play the harp learns to play by playing it, and all other learners do similarly."[55] Here, as in the case of beginning, to be "actual" is not to have a certain set of qualities at a particular time, nor is it to realize a possibility always already implanted in you. It is, instead, to be engaged in an activity, making and remaking (in ways at once orderly *and* unruly) that activity and its possibilities as you proceed, and sustaining your attunement to the events that call for your response.

3.4 Conclusion: Democracy's Beginning

Although Hannah Arendt was not a democratic theorist in the usual sense of the term – indeed, her occasional remarks about the reality of democratic politics in the twentieth century were often unflattering – her critique of rule and her unorthodox interpretation of beginning have much to offer democratic theory, because they invite us to think differently about the nature of the political activity we ascribe to "the people." Different characterizations of this activity, as we have seen, produce starkly different versions of the democratic ideal: Sometimes we imagine the people jointly ruling themselves, in control of their own destinies, free from subjection to alien forces or sinister interests; at other times we imagine the people insurgent, rising up in opposition to a regime or order, and so displaying the irreducibility of popular power to a fixed form. Arendt herself has been enlisted in support of both sorts of democratic vision; yet from her perspective, I have suggested, these positions are equally problematic – and not because of the distance between them, but because of what they share. To conceive of democratic politics as the rule of the people over itself is, she claims, to reduce it to a variation on monarchy, in which the "collective body" of the people takes the place of the king (*HC*, 221); to conceive of it as the perpetual interruption or destabilization of order is merely to invert this picture of politics as rule, reducing freedom to a matter of "liberation" (*OR*, 142) – in many circumstances a worthwhile aim, but one that, when generalized into the defining feature of political action as such,

---

[55] Ibid. 1049b30–32.

seems to demand an impossible escape from the contexts in which action is situated and which give it sense. Neither seeking a middle ground between these positions nor affirming them as the poles of a constitutive paradox, Arendt instead and more radically draws our attention to a dimension of activity that they jointly obscure, one defined not by the opposition between determination and undertermined spontaneity, but by the complementarity between events and the responses they occasion, provoke, or summon.[56]

What does this view of political activity mean for our understanding of democratic politics? To begin with, it highlights a distinctive way in which democratic political activity can be obstructed or impeded, thereby providing political theorists and actors with a new target for, and language of, democratic critique. We are used to thinking of the impediments to democracy as, on the one hand, forces that interfere with the autonomous self-determination of the people or, on the other hand, forces that constrict the space of underdetermination in which popular action can operate – for instance, by channeling it into a constitutional form. From an Arendtian perspective, however, the most fundamental threat to democratic political activity lies in the loss of responsiveness to events: the erosion of the contexts in which action makes sense. To experience an event – if "experience" is the right word – as irrelevant; to have it be imperceptibly distant (whether at a distance of one mile or a thousand); for it to signify *only* as an observation or datum, made from a posture of scientific disengagement; for it to be imperceptibly close, so much the medium of your being that it never occurs to you that it might be something to which you *could* respond; to feel it as a force that rips up, or rips you out of, the contexts in which you might be able to imagine *how* to respond; to experience an event generically, as something significant for you only insofar as you belong to a category or type, which does not engage you as the locus of a separate, as-yet-unfinished life: these are signs of the contraction of the dimension of activity that concerns Arendt, and they become particularly significant for democracy when they systematically characterize the experience either of citizens generally or of a subset of citizens disproportionately.

To conceive of the impediments to democracy in these terms is, crucially, to locate them in the mode of presence or appearance of events, and not merely in the states or capacities of persons. In mainstream, regime-oriented democratic theory, the failure of democratic rule is often cast as a failure in or of the citizens who exercise democratic rule: For democratic government to be genuinely autonomous *self*-government, the citizen body must form a "people" that possesses and displays a general will, without lapsing into irrationality or

---

[56] Insofar as our neglect of this dimension of activity is itself part of the legacy of the concept of rule and of the relationships of subordination that it has been employed to rationalize, Arendt's effort to recover this distinctive perspective on activity is already antihierarchical and egalitarian in spirit; hence her insistence that the "attempt to replace acting with making is manifest in the whole body of arguments against 'democracy,' which, the more consistently and better reasoned it is, will turn into an argument against the essentials of politics" (*HC*, 220).

partiality – but the prior work of molding and forming that this requires may belie the autonomy it is supposed to produce.[57] Likewise, for democratic critics of rule, genuinely democratic agency lies in a power of spontaneous interruption that needs somehow to be awakened or instilled in those who are subject to the controlling force of regimes – but the very nature of spontaneity so conceived makes it difficult in principle to locate or produce. Both of these approaches, however, render it difficult to understand how democratic activity might be generated when or where it is weak or absent, for they imagine that what makes action democratic is one or another kind of purity at its origin. Arendt's account of beginning, by contrast, shows us that action, as a response to events, is, you might say, always a *second* step rather than a first: If we can never quite lose our capacity to act altogether, this is because there never ceases to be a fund of doings and happenings – beginnings – in the world to which we might respond (*HC*, 323).[58] Arendt thus replaces the unanswerable question of how to generate something (autonomy, spontaneity) from nothing (heteronomy, determination) with the more tractable question of how to sustain, intensify, and democratize the beginnings with which we are already confronted; and that is less a question about the qualities or virtues of persons than about the worldly intersections *among* persons, or between persons and the happenings they encounter, or fail to.

Importantly, identifying breakdowns of the nexus of event and response is not a matter of the top-down application of an authoritative philosophical criterion: Just as, for Arendt, the status of human activity as "action" cannot be apprehended from the disengaged stance of the classifier, the significance of events is also a matter of judgment and, often enough, a matter for dispute, undertaken within the horizons of practical engagement. Some of the most important work of democratic politics thus consists in the interpretation of particular events – that is, in the re-presentation of happenings that, although they may or may not be widely known as matters of fact, are not (as) widely experienced as practically significant. This does not mean, however, that theoretical reflection has no role to play here. The patterns of engagement and responsiveness we confront are not merely accidental: They are, in part, the effects of social and political practices and institutions, which structure and mediate people's experiences of the world. In addition to (and often in conjunction with) the public interpretation of particular events, then, the problem of democratic political activity can be engaged at a higher level of generality, by asking how these practices and institutions expose us to the imperatives of

---

[57] See, e.g., Honig, *Democracy and the Foreigner*; Keenan, *Democracy in Question*.

[58] Pitkin, *The Attack of the Blob*, 282; as Pitkin puts it, "the only place to begin is where we are, and there are a hundred ways of beginning" (p. 283). Perhaps because Pitkin casts beginning as what I have called a "first" step rather than as a "response," however, her account of Arendtian action sometimes sounds like an invocation of spontaneity: "if you wait for your own action to befall you, it will not; you have to just do it" (p. 284), and "once we do begin... we may find others already under way" (p. 283). Yet it is also because things – events – befall us, and because we encounter others already under way, that we have occasions and ways to begin.

events or render them practically inert. This is in part a question of the responsiveness that institutions foster or suppress toward the work they themselves perform: Institutions may be more or less peremptory, more or less dependent for their successful operation upon their insulation from the engagement, whether cooperative or critical, of those whom they affect.[59] Yet practices and institutions – and not just institutions with formalized decision-making powers – also have much wider consequences for the shape of political activity. The contours of the built environment; the aesthetics of print, televisual, and electronic media; the discursive forms through which events are distinguished, measured, scaled, organized, and presented; the practices of representation and patterns of identification that make some events but not others "our" business: These are among the mechanisms of what Susan Bickford calls "attention orientation," which may heighten or diminish responsiveness to events as Arendt understands it.[60] They are properly objects of democratic criticism not because they produce order and stability, but – in keeping with Arendt's distinctive critique of rule – just insofar as they predicate the order and stability they produce on the narrowing of some or all of citizens' practical horizons.

We can see an example of this way of thinking about institutions in Arendt's own writing, when, near the end of *On Revolution* and after an extensive discussion of the failure of the American founders and their successors to preserve the "revolutionary spirit," she waxes enthusiastic about Jefferson's unrealized "ward system" – a division of the nation into local "elementary republics" – and, relatedly, about the council movements of the nineteenth and twentieth centuries (*OR*, 248ff). From the point of view of mainstream accounts of democracy as a form of rule, Arendt's invocation of the ward system and council movement would look like a call – perhaps nostalgiac and unrealistic – for a return to direct popular decision making. For much radical democatic theory, the wards would seem instead to be mechanisms of popular unruliness: Arendt herself notes that Jefferson saw wards as a "non-violent alternative" to revolution (*OR*, 250). Recall, however, that in *On Revolution*, Arendt claims that the American revolutionaries failed to comprehend the nature of their own experiences, in part because they "channelled" those experiences "into concepts that had just been vacated" (*OR*, 155) – a phrase that should remind us of Lefort's story of democratic revolution as an evacuation of the place

---

[59] It is at this point that Arendt's concerns would intersect fruitfully with the tradition of participatory democratic theory. However (as Archon Fung has recently noted) much of that tradition focuses on citizens' participation in "moments of initial decision" rather than on their responses to those decisions and their ongoing involvement in the "postdecision" phases of the operation of institutions. Archon Fung, *Empowered Participation: Reinventing Urban Democracy* (Princeton: Princeton University Press, 2004), p. 232. Arendt might suggest that such a focus is an artifact of our continuing tendency to see political institutions primarily as sites of rule.

[60] Susan Bickford, "Constructing Inequality: City Spaces and the Architecture of Citizenship." *Political Theory* 28 (June 2000): 307–36, at 356. (Bickford's focus here is the democratic significance of city spaces.)

of power.[61] For Arendt, the paradoxes in which the revolutionaries came to feel themselves caught – including especially the apparently intractable conflict between permanence and novelty, exemplified by Jefferson's own oscillation from an "identification of action with rebellion" to an "identification with founding anew and building up" – are the symptoms of a "fallacy" in their thought that "becloud[ed]" their understanding of action (*OR* 234, 133). They failed to take measure of the fact that their own revolutionary activity, although not determined in advance, had not appeared out of nowhere: Sensitized to the abuses of Crown and Parliament, they had set out to restore their traditional liberties, but found themselves, in response both to events and to the "charms" they discovered in action itself, doing far more than they had intended (*OR*, 33, 28–9, 37). If, as Arendt suggests, the ward system represents an unfollowed route that might have helped to preserve political freedom, this is neither because the wards would have institutionalized popular sovereignty nor because they would have generated rebelliousness, but because they would have organized political experience so as to sustain the same kind of attunement to events that had drawn the revolutionaries into action, and along its path.[62]

[61] Lefort, *Democracy and Political Theory*, p. 17.
[62] For a more extended discussion of this aspect of *On Revolution*, see Patchen Markell, "The Experience of Action," in Roger Berkowitz, Jeff Katz, and Thomas Keenan, eds., *Thinking in Dark Times: The Legacy of Hannah Arendt* (New York: Fordham University Press, 2010).

4

Genealogies of Catastrophe

Arendt on the Logic and Legacy of Imperialism

Karuna Mantena

> ... colonization ... dehumanizes even the most civilized man; that colonial activity, colonial enterprise, colonial conquest, which is based on contempt for the native and justified by that contempt, inevitably tends to change him who undertakes it; that the colonizer, who in order to ease his conscience gets in the habit of seeing the other man as *an animal*, accustoms himself to treating him like an animal, and tends objectively to transform *himself* into an animal. It is this result, this boomerang effect of colonization that I wanted to point out.
>
> Aimé Césaire[1]

> The much-feared boomerang effect of the "government of the subject races" (Lord Cromer) on the home government during the imperialist era meant that rule by violence in faraway lands would end by affecting the government of England, that the last "subject race" would be the English themselves.
>
> Hannah Arendt[2]

Hannah Arendt's work has had an extraordinarily wide and deep impact on contemporary political theory. From debates on democratic theory and pluralism, theories of political action and judgment, to constitutionalism and human rights, the ubiquity and intensity of recourse to Arendt's work has cemented her status as one of the twentieth century's preeminent political philosophers. At the same time, in this canonization, her most overtly political works, critical essays, and public interventions have curiously played a less decisive role.[3] This is arguably the case even with respect to Arendt's acknowledged masterwork, *The Origins of Totalitarianism*, which in her own lifetime defined her public

---

[1] Aimé Césaire, *Discourse on Colonialism* (New York: Monthly Review Press, 2001), p. 41.

[2] Hannah Arendt, "On Violence," in *Crises of the Republic* (New York: Harcourt Brace, 1972), p. 153.

[3] For a critical view of some of the tendencies of current Arendt scholarship, see Corey Robin's review essay, "Dragon-Slayers," *London Review of Books* 29, 2 (January 4, 2007): 18–20.

For their perceptive comments and obliging discussion of the arguments presented here, I am grateful to Kathleen Arnold, Noah Dauber, Sam Moyn, and David Scott.

reception and reputation and now occupies a more ambiguous place in current scholarship. Though commentators still consider *Origins* to be fundamental for framing Arendt's political horizon – and even setting the agenda of her future work[4] – the *theoretical* contributions of the work are often construed in more limited terms, principally confined to the conceptualization of totalitarianism as a novel form of government. Tellingly, recent analyses of *Origins* tend to focus upon and emphasize the elements of that work that prefigure aspects of her more accomplished political philosophy.[5] In this sense, the importance of *Origins* has been overshadowed by Arendt's later works, especially *The Human Condition*, but also *Between Past and Future* and *On Revolution*, which together are taken to "constitute her most enduring legacy in political theory."[6]

If *Origins* has come to hold a relatively subordinate place in the context of analyses and assessments of Arendt's political philosophy as a whole, then her account of imperialism – which occupies the large middle section of *Origins* – has left little or no imprint on the mainstream of Arendt scholarship.[7] This neglect is all the more perplexing as Arendt's analysis of imperialism, especially her suggestive hypothesis linking imperialism to totalitarianism, has

[4] Commentators such as Richard Bernstein and Bernard Crick have emphasized the importance of *Origins*. Indeed, Crick often remarked that Arendt's later work was like "a giant footnote" to *Origins*. See Richard Bernstein, *Hannah Arendt and the Jewish Question* (Cambridge, MA: MIT Press, 1996); Bernard Crick, "Arendt and *The Origins of Totalitarianism*: An Anglocentric View," in Steven E. Aschheim, ed., *Hannah Arendt in Jerusalem* (Berkeley: University of California Press, 2001). But it is Margaret Canovan's *Hannah Arendt: A Reinterpretation of Her Political Thought* (Cambridge: Cambridge University Press, 1992), which has offered the most compelling and extensive interpretation of Arendt's work in which *Origins* and the political problem of totalitarianism play a defining role.

[5] See Mary Dietz, "Arendt and the Holocaust," in Dana Villa, ed., *The Cambridge Companion to Hannah Arendt* (Cambridge: Cambridge University Press, 2000), and Jacques Taminiaux, "The Philosophical Stakes in Arendt's Genealogy of Totalitarianism," *Social Research* 69, 2 (Summer 2002): 23–46, who both analyze in different ways how the central themes of *The Human Condition* are shaped by and prefigured by *Origins*.

[6] Dana Villa, "Introduction: The Development of Arendt's Political Thought," in *The Cambridge Companion to Hannah Arendt*, p. 9.

[7] Even the major interpretative work on *Origins* has little to say directly about her analysis of imperialism. The essays in *Social Research* (Summer 2002), the special issue dedicated to revisiting *Origins* fifty years later, make only passing reference to the Imperialism section. Stephen Whitfield's *Into the Dark: Hannah Arendt and Totalitarianism* (Philadelphia: Temple University Press, 1981), one of the first full-length historical treatments of Arendt's theory of totalitarianism, focuses entirely on the last part of *Origins*. Important exceptions to this trend in Arendt scholarship include Kateb's brief but penetrating analysis in his *Hannah Arendt: Politics, Conscience, Evil* (Totowa: Rowman, 1983); Shiraz Dossa, "Human Status and Politics: Hannah Arendt on the Holocaust," *Canadian Journal of Political Science* 13, 2 (June 1980): 308–23; more recently, Norma Moruzzi, *Speaking through the Mask: Hannah Arendt and the Politics of Social Identity* (Ithaca: Cornell University Press, 2000); and Patricia Owens, *Between War and Politics: International Relations and the Thought of Hannah Arendt* (Oxford: Oxford University Press, 2009). The recent edited volume by Richard King and Dan Stone, *Hannah Arendt and the Uses of History: Imperialism, Nation, Race, and Genocide* (New York: Berghahn, 2007), was animated by a need to overcome this neglect in Arendt studies.

undergone a remarkable resurgence in recent years.[8] The new interest in and engagement with Arendt's analysis, however, has been driven largely by work in imperial and German history, genocide and Holocaust studies, and postcolonial theory and criticism, that is, from outside the core of Arendt scholarship in political theory and philosophy. Substantively, the theoretical (and political) framework of this revival is marked by a deep investment in understanding European empire as a central – indeed, constitutive – historical process in the making of modernity. The central aim of this chapter will be to revisit the main lines of Arendt's analysis of imperialism in light of these new turns in critical interpretation, with a view toward assessing its internal coherence, theoretical significance, and political implications. The focus on the question of imperialism enables a different angle for exploring the relationship among history, politics, and philosophy in Arendt's work, as well as a reconsideration of *Origins* and its legacies for our new political moment.

The initial Cold War reception of *Origins* was marked by a singular focus on Arendt's concept of totalitarianism – especially its equation of Nazism and Stalinism as exemplary cases, and its emphasis on the role of ideology and terror in the workings of totalitarian government. In a postwar context also shaped by the struggles over decolonization, excavating the connection between imperialism and fascism was a theme pursued mainly by anticolonial critics and European radicals.[9] In general, the liberal-right appropriation of Arendt's account of totalitarianism as ammunition in ideological debates on communism, terrorism, and, more recently, "Islamo-Fascism" has been quick to ignore her concerns about imperialism, to the point of actively disavowing any linking of historical and contemporary practices of imperialism to the instabilities of the global order. Likewise, liberal-left interpreters of Arendt who draw upon her now prescient concerns about the problem of statelessness and the limits of the nation-state as a guarantor of human rights also take little notice of the ways in which, for Arendt, the very crisis of the nation-state was intimately bound up with its imperial career.[10]

Arendt herself, in her 1967 preface, noted how the political preoccupation with totalitarianism had blinded observers from more apt comparisons between postwar global politics and the period of imperialism. From proxy

---

[8] For an indication of the breadth of this revived interest see King and Stone, eds., *Hannah Arendt and the Uses of History*.

[9] The link between imperialism and fascism was noted by many prominent anticolonial and radical black intellectuals from Ralph Bunch (as early as 1936), W. E. B. DuBois, George Padmore, C. L. R. James, to Aimé Césaire and Frantz Fanon. See also Michael Rothberg, *Multidirectional Memory: Remembering the Holocaust in the Age of Decolonization* (Stanford: Stanford University Press, 2009).

[10] See Robin's criticism of recent attempts, notably by Elisabeth Young-Bruehl and Samantha Power, to make Arendt relevant by loosely and speciously extending her theory of totalitarianism to the analysis of radical Islamist political movements. Young-Bruehl also identifies some features of totalitarianism in the Bush presidency. See Robin, "Dragon-Slayers"; Young-Bruehl, "On the Origins of a New Totalitarianism," *Social Research* 69, 2 (Summer 2002): 567–78.

wars orchestrated by great powers to fabricating pretexts for intervention, what appeared as a stalemate was, for Arendt, nothing other than "a competitive struggle for predominance in more or less the same regions in which European nations had ruled before," and thus she warned, "we are back, on an enormously enlarged scale, where we started from, that is, in the imperialist era and on the collision course that led to World War I" (*OT*, xvii–xviii).[11] While Cold War ideologues (and, we may add, their contemporary counterparts) sought to justify the aggressive use of force "in terms of analogies with Munich" and the crisis of the interwar years, for Arendt, "the threats of today's policies in deeds and words bear a much more portentous resemblance to the deeds and verbal justifications that preceded the outbreak of World War I" (*OT*, xxi) and thus are resolutely tied to the dynamics of imperialist politics.

These suggestive comments, though never elaborated in Arendt's later work, invite a more serious engagement with and reconsideration of Arendt's early attempt in *Origins* to locate in European imperialism nascent ideological and political formations that can be genealogically linked to the catastrophes of the Second World War. Indeed, these comments imply that political processes unleashed in the era of imperialism may not only culminate in, but also endure beyond, twentieth-century totalitarianism. But what Arendt understood to be the exact nature of imperialism – its dynamics, novelty, and content – as well as its precise connection to totalitarianism, however, are neither straightforward nor free from contention. *Origins* as a whole has often been charged with lacking unity, and, in method and choice of subject matter, the imperialism section is perhaps even more unwieldy, controversial, and at times decidedly obscure. The analysis moves at breakneck speed from the European bourgeoisie's rise to political power, the origins of race-thinking and racism, the Boers in South Africa, British imperialism in India and Egypt, to continental nationalism (i.e., the pan-German movement), with all of these disparate streams cascading toward the institutional and ideological decay of the nation-state.

Admirers of Arendt tend to declare (rather than demonstrate) the exceptional novelty of this analysis and uncritically rehearse and endorse its main contours. By contrast, critics often hone in on Arendt's more controversial statements and extravagant claims to contest their historical accuracy and political undertones. Neither view, however, attends very closely to the overall analytical coherence of Arendt's arguments and often mistakenly attributes views to her that she does not in fact hold. In this chapter, therefore, I want to reconstruct and critically analyze Arendt's understanding of the logic and legacy of imperialism, with a view toward elucidating its theoretical implications. I take Arendt's central contention to be that imperialist expansion necessitated the invention of race and bureaucracy as instrumentalities of rule, which served both to exacerbate the inner contradictions of the nation-state and to degrade Western moral principles and political institutions so as to make the extermination of peoples

---

[11] Hannah Arendt, *The Origins of Totalitarianism* (New York: Harcourt Brace, 1973), pp. xvii–xviii. Hereafter cited as *OT*.

appear to be acceptable state policy. In this respect, I argue that the strength of Arendt's hypothesis about the structural dynamic between late-nineteenth-century imperialism and totalitarianism, evocatively figured as the boomerang effect of imperialism, lies in its attention to the ways in which the *experience* of overseas empire instigated and intensified the moral vacuum that made Nazi genocide possible.[12] Viewed in this way, Arendt's understanding of imperialism contains her strongest statement about the fragility of moral and political universals in the face of practices of domination. And, as a warning about the limits of moral principles to restrain politics and of political institutions to respond to power, the significance of Arendt's understanding comes to bear not just on her theorization of totalitarianism but on her political thought more generally.

4.1 The Boomerang Effect

According to Arendt, the thirty-year period (1884–1914) from the Berlin Conference that formalized the so-called scramble for Africa to the outbreak of the First World War witnessed fundamental ideological and institutional innovations that "appear so close to totalitarian phenomena of the twentieth century that it may be justifiable to consider the whole period a preparatory stage for coming catastrophes" (*OT*, 123). This is the period of *imperialism,* spun into motion by the capture of state power by the bourgeoisie – what Arendt termed "the political emancipation of the bourgeoisie" – and culminating in the eruption of global war and the destabilization of the nation-state system. Its central political idea was competitive *expansion* as the "permanent and supreme aim of politics" (*OT*, 125), with the European bourgeoisie seeking to radically extend its newly acquired political power overseas without the accompanying extension of its body politic. This meant that, in the colonial theater, the official instruments of conquest (i.e., the army and the police) reigned supreme without political and legal institutions to constrain the accumulation of power and the escalation of violence. The explosive impact of these "breathtaking developments in Asia and Africa" (*OT*, 123) – the intensifying rivalry between projects of limitless expansion and the growth of (unrestrained) technologies of violence – first came to be felt in Europe itself in the devastations of the First World War, its undoing of the foundations of the nation-state, and, thus, experientially and institutionally, setting the stage for the calamities to come.

   Less than advancing a new theory of imperialism, Arendt offered a historical-theoretical account of the nature and consequences of imperialism framed by

---

[12] In this chapter, the term *totalitarianism* will be used with primary reference to Nazism (and thus with little or no mention of Stalinism). This is partially in keeping with Arendt's original outline of *Origins* as a study of Nazi "race-imperialism," since the historical analysis contained in the imperialism section is still largely framed by that outline. Also, the recent literature on Arendt's account of analysis of imperialism focuses almost exclusively on the historical relationship between imperialism and Nazi genocide.

two overarching conceptual claims. Firstly, Arendt insisted on the *novelty* of imperialism, that the practices it generated and gave it sustenance introduced wholly new principles for the ordering of politics. The two most important innovations were the elevation of *expansion* to a legitimate political principle and the very idea of *world politics*, in which politics could no longer be contained within national boundaries and no state could remain indifferent to global political and economic imperatives. Arendt took the principle of "expansion for expansion's sake" to be "an entirely new concept in the long history of political thought and action" (*OT*, 125). But there were also less visible but no less momentous inventions in forms of government – the organization of polities on the principle of race and bureaucratic domination as a replacement for government – that enabled the conscious use of violence as an instrument for the management of subject peoples and its accretion into normal state policy.

For Arendt, imperialism's ideas and practices, from global conquest and racial domination to administrative massacres and extermination campaigns, established a repertoire of legitimating ideologies and practical precedents for Nazism and its genocidal program. The novelty of imperialism thus stands with a second claim about a consequential or causal relationship between imperialism and totalitarianism. Arendt famously characterized this as imperialism's *boomerang effect*, whereby dehumanizing and destabilizing practices in the periphery eventually return to infiltrate European politics. Indeed, it is Arendt's proposed boomerang effect that has been especially singled out as a seminal thesis to be celebrated and elaborated.[13]

Arendt evoked imperialism's boomerang effect in a variety of ways: from the return of colonial violence and racism, the quickened alliance of mob and capital, to the infiltration of bourgeois privacy into norms of public policy. But whether it is was in reference to colonial atrocities, or new sociological and political formations that were solidified overseas, the metaphor marked the extra-European world – especially Africa – as a space of political exception, of practical experiments in lawlessness and violence that eventually return to deform domestic politics. For Arendt, up to the period of the new imperialism, the notion that empire and conquest posed a danger to domestic democratic institutions was a well-established political maxim, exemplified in the classic republican thesis on the fall of the Roman republic. Yet, even statesmen such as Gladstone and Clemenceau, who "knew by instinct rather than insight" that overseas adventures had this potential for devastation, could not themselves fully comprehend or resist the new tide of competitive expansion (*OT*, 125).

As a starting point, then, Arendt's boomerang effect may be usefully described as an attempt to revise and update the republican critique of empire in which imperial despotism is seen to threaten and undo liberty at home. Yet,

---

[13] The introduction by King and Stone to their edited volume *Hannah Arendt and the Uses of History* provides an excellent overview and analysis of recent scholarly engagements with Arendt's boomerang thesis.

as a revival of the classic thesis, Arendt's account appears underspecified and even misplaced. What has puzzled many readers is Arendt's relative lack of attention to the specific case of Germany, to the ways in which its political culture and Nazism in particular – its personnel, ideologies, and institutions – were shaped by German colonial experience.[14] This is especially curious as Arendt does make repeated and striking reference to the notorious figure of Carl Peters, the colonial commissioner much admired by Hitler, who was convicted of atrocities against native subjects in German East Africa. For Arendt, Peters was the model for Mr. Kurtz of Joseph Conrad's *Heart of Darkness*, the true precursor of the Nazi personality. Peters arose from the mob and found that in Africa, through sheer force, he could make himself part of the "master race" (*OT*, 189–90, 206). Thus, Peters embodies most straightforwardly the boomerang effect in which "African colonial possessions became the most fertile soil of the flowering of what later was to become the Nazi elite" (*OT*, 206). This observation of Arendt's, however, is neither elaborated in great detail nor returned to in the final sections on totalitarianism. Not Peters, but Cecil Rhodes, Lord Cromer, and T. E. Lawrence were the imperial personalities whom Arendt took great care to depict, making the British experience in Africa (alongside the Boers in South Africa) the core of Arendt's substantive analysis of imperialism. But this focus on Britain only heightens our original paradox, for Arendt claims that Britain, the most expansive and successful imperial nation of the nineteenth century, was also, counterintuitively, the most effective at protecting its domestic institutions from the perversions of empire.[15]

That Arendt left unfulfilled the claims about the German colonial origins of Nazism can be partially accounted for by her late decision to incorporate Stalinism/Bolshevism to what was initially a study of the elements of Nazi

---

[14] A prominent stream in the recent revival of Arendt's thesis has precisely sought to fill in this gap. See Pascal Grosse, "From Colonialism to National Socialism to Postcolonialism: Hannah Arendt's *The Origins of Totalitarianism*," *Postcolonial Studies* 9, 1:35–52; Isabel V. Hull, "Military Culture and the Production of 'Final Solutions' in the Colonies: The Example of Wilhelminian Germany," in *The Spectre of Genocide: Mass Murder in Historical Perspective*, eds. Robert Gellately and Ben Kiernan (New York: Cambridge University Press, 2003); Benjamin Madley, "From Africa to Auschwitz: How German South West Africa Incubated and Ideas and Methods Adopted and Developed by the Nazis in Eastern Europe," *European History Quarterly* 35, 3 (2005): 429–64; and especially, Jürgen Zimmerer, "The Birth of the *Ostland* out of the Spirit of Colonialism: A Postcolonial Perspective on the Nazi Policy of Conquest and Extermination," *Patterns of Prejudice*, 39, 2 (2005): 197–219.

[15] That Britain neither became a totalitarian state nor were its political institutions undermined by imperialism is often taken, even in the sympathetic and sophisticated readings by Benhabib and Canovan, to be the strongest rebuttal of the causal claims of Arendt's analysis of imperialism. See Seyla Benhabib, *The Reluctant Modernism of Hannah Arendt* (Lanham: Rowman & Littlefield, 2003), p. 76; Canovan, *The Political Thought of Hannah Arendt*, p. 38; I want to show, however, that this is an overly strict interpretation of the role of overseas imperialism in Arendt's understanding of the boomerang effect and one upon which the logic of her analysis does not in the end rest.

"race-imperialism."[16] This decision radically reshaped the very nature of the project and introduced two important disjunctures into the narrative arc of the text of *Origins* as a whole: firstly, a thematic imbalance between the historical treatment of Nazism and Bolshevism[17] and, secondly, a formal disjuncture between a primarily *historical* analysis of antisemitism and imperialism and a more *conceptual* account of totalitarianism.[18] One can speculate that if Arendt had followed her original plan, she might have specified with greater precision the carrier links between imperialism and Nazism. But the shift in emphasis towards the theorization of totalitarianism, and especially the insistence on its "horrible originality,"[19] seemingly rendered the question of historical antecedents – and thus the question of imperialism's relationship to totalitarianism – conceptually less coherent and less compelling.

Arendt maintained that she had not sought to write a conventional history of totalitarianism (or of antisemitism or imperialism), "but an analysis in terms of history." It was to be a historical analysis, a tracing back into history of the chief elements "which eventually crystallized into totalitarianism." In this sense, despite its title, the study was never meant to pinpoint the definite or absolute *origins* of totalitarianism, but only aspects of those historical elements – such as antisemitism and imperialism – that "were still clearly visible and played a decisive role in the totalitarian phenomenon itself."[20] For Arendt, the term *origins* hinted too strongly of a deterministic sense of historical causality – of sequences of ideas and events that having once emerged are seen to culminate necessarily in full-blown totalitarianism.[21] By contrast, for Arendt, a proper understanding of totalitarianism had to avoid the temptations of a teleological account of its origins or a philosophy of history that would emplot imperialism and fascism as so many moments in the inevitable degeneration

---

[16] Indeed, one of the working titles for *Origins* had been *The Elements of Shame: Antisemitism-Imperialism-Racism*. On Arendt's early conceptualization of *Origins* as a study of racial imperialism, see especially Roy Tsao's excellent analysis in "The Three Phases of Arendt's Theory of Totalitarianism," *Social Research* 69 (Summer 2002): 579–619; and also Elisabeth Young-Bruehl, *Hannah Arendt: For Love of the World* (New Haven: Yale University Press, 2004), pp. 58, 200–8.

[17] Arendt considered redressing this neglect of a proper historical analysis of Stalinism/Bolshevism in a never-completed follow-up work on the "The Marxist Elements of Totalitarianism." See Canovan, *Hannah Arendt*, pp. 63–99; Young-Bruehl, *Hannah Arendt*, p. 211.

[18] By this contrast, I do not mean to imply that the earlier parts were more empirical or less theoretical. Rather, I want to draw attention to the difference between the diachronic frame of the first two sections of *Origin* and the more synchronic account of the structural dynamics of totalitarianism.

[19] Hannah Arendt, "Understanding and Politics (The Difficulties of Understanding)," in *Essays in Understanding, 1930–1945*, edited by Jerome Kohn (New York: Harcourt Brace, 1994), p. 309.

[20] Hannah Arendt, "A Reply," *Review of Politics* 15, 1 (January 1953): 78. Also reprinted in *Essays in Understanding*.

[21] Arendt was always unsatisfied with the final title of *Origins* and struggled to find one that more appropriately captured its tone and purpose. In fact, the first British edition was published as *The Burden of Our Time*. See Young-Bruehl, *Hannah Arendt*, p. 200.

of Western civilization. One way of countering this tendency would be to seek out and emphasize the historical specificity and distinctiveness of the phenomena considered. The hallmark of Arendt's historical analysis would thus be an emphasis on the contingent, conjunctural, and unintended crystallization of political forces and events that, only in retrospect, could be seen to have contained the kernels of the catastrophes to come.

Arendt's concerns about how to write a history of totalitarianism, and indeed her strong rejection of causal determinism, however, should not lead us to disavow or undervalue the nature of the connections she does in fact draw between imperialism and totalitarianism. Richard King in a seminal essay suggests that given both her underdevelopment of the direct links between imperialism and Nazism and her sharp criticism of causality, Arendt's thesis should be understood as one that identifies imperialism less as strictly a causal force than the "historical prefiguration or foreshadowing" of totalitarian phenomena.[22] While I agree with King that Arendt underspecified, and may indeed have underestimated, these genetic connections, I think Arendt nevertheless intended a more potent link, one that is framed less by the logic of analogy (implied in the idea of foreshadowing) than a question of cumulative precedents, of historical conditions of possibility.[23] Here George Kateb's arresting formulation is especially useful:

[T]otalitarianism is not conceivable, not conceptually possible, not superficially recognizable, not experientially familiar, not able to receive welcome and adherence and cooperation, without several generations of anti-Semitism, other kinds of racism, and imperialism (not only in Africa). At the same time, totalitarianism is not their causal derivative or logical outcome.[24]

The aftereffects of imperialism would not therefore be strictly causal in the sense of historically determinate, for example, that imperialist racism once invented necessarily had to lead to genocide. Nevertheless, the experience of racist ideology and racial atrocity can be understood to be precedent setting, making genocide experientially and conceptually possible if not inevitable. In this sense, a notion of historical conditions of possibility indicates a historical "causality" that is neither determinative nor logically entailed, but is still framed by a distinct temporal trajectory. It is a trajectory premised on the accumulation of experience, but because it eschews causal determination, it can only fully come to light as such in retrospect; only after the emergence of the phenomena of totalitarianism can its constitutive elements be pieced apart and genealogically reconstructed.

---

[22] Richard H. King, *Race, Culture, and the Intellectuals, 1940–1970* (Baltimore: Johns Hopkins Press, 2004), p. 107.

[23] Along these lines, King also concludes that Arendt seemed to say that imperialism "created an ethos in which total domination and mass extermination might more easily take hold in Europe." Ibid.

[24] Kateb, *Hannah Arendt*, p. 57.

Foregrounding the precedent-setting nature of imperialism also allows us to see how Arendt reformulates the republican anxiety about empire as the harbinger of despotism on a purposefully *enlarged* and *escalating* scale.[25] In schematic terms, the series of cumulative effects begins with the moral hazards created and legitimated in overseas empire and its emulation in the expansionist programs of continental nationalism and totalitarian movements, which together culminate in the institutional breakdown of the nation-state and a crisis of Western civilization. The historically consequential boomerang effects, then, have less to do with the undoing of a specific mother country's liberal institutions than the step-by-step degeneration and disruption of the underlying principles of Western politics tout court. This fundamental difference from the traditional republican critique of empire is most apparent when Arendt's thesis is set against J. A. Hobson's seminal work, *Imperialism: A Study*, the key text that defined the critical debate on the new imperialism and one whose influence on *Origins* was pronounced. Though better known for his influential economic theory of imperialism, Hobson, like Arendt, also investigated "the theory and practice of Imperialism" with a view toward outlining "its political and moral reactions upon the conduct and character of the Western nations engaging in it."[26] The political significance of imperialism, for Hobson, was defined by the myriad threats that the spectacular expansion of despotism abroad posed to home politics, that, is, how "the arts and crafts of tyranny, acquired and exercised in our unfree Empire, should be turned against our liberties at home."[27] The threats Hobson warned against thus replay classic republican tropes concerning the ill effects of empire: the centralization of power and the growth of militarism that produce imperialist classes that "usurp the authority and voice of the people," are "hostile to the institutions of popular self-government," lead to the "diminution of the power of representative institutions," "poison the springs of democracy," and "strike at the very root of popular liberty."[28]

Yet, for Arendt, these dire warnings, while well founded, did not in the end correctly predict the sequence of events that led to institutional collapse. Neither in Britain nor in France – that is, in the leading imperial nations – were overtly imperialist parties and movements able to fully undermine the home country's basic political structure. This recognition, however, was not meant to lessen the significance of overseas of imperialism. The specific reverberations of

---

[25] If critics read the boomerang thesis too narrowly in order to condemn it, many admirers often read it too broadly, with the effect that Arendt's argument loses both its specificity and analytical coherence. That modern European thought and culture were implicated in and shaped by the imperial encounter is certainly a claim that Arendt's thesis would support and one with which I sympathize. But my contention that Arendt's boomerang effect works on an enlarged scale is not a claim of this sort but rather tries to capture the distinct causal sequences outlined by Arendt.

[26] J. A. Hobson, *Imperialism: A Study* (Ann Arbor: University of Michigan Press, 1965), p. xvii. First published in 1905.

[27] Ibid., pp. 151–2.

[28] Ibid., pp. 113–52; especially 127, 133, 147, 150.

overseas imperialism that interested Arendt, I want to emphasize, were more ideological than institutional, or more precisely, they were transformations in habits of mind that led to the loss of respect for the institutional foundations of the nation-state. Arendt sought to demonstrate how the *experience* of imperial rule worked to undermine the universal validity of law and the aspirational universality of the rights of man – how it laid the grounds, morally and psychologically, for a new ideological landscape in which violent exclusion, degradation, and extermination enter the language of everyday politics.

4.2 Imperialism versus Empire-Building

The key to Arendt's understanding of overseas imperialism and its corrosive moral and political effects lies in her insistence on its fundamental novelty. As noted earlier, Arendt cites the principle of expansion and the invention of global politics as the overarching political innovations of the imperialist period. More importantly, these principles underscored, in Arendt's view, radically new and aberrant forms of imperial practice. The newness of the new imperialism, in Arendt's analysis, was grounded in a sharp conceptual distinction between the *political* forms of imperialism and those of classical empire-building. And it was the disjuncture between the two that engendered the explosive mix of racist ideology and bureaucratic governance and the systematized, escalating violence in the conquest and management of subject peoples, making way for the eventual acceptance of these strategies of domination as legitimate instruments of state policy.

Some critics have been quick to question this characterization of late-nineteenth-century imperialism as a distinct and necessarily more destructive phase of Western imperial history, and further object to an implied normativity in distinguishing imperialism from allegedly more moderate, respectable forms of colonialism and empire-building. They charge that such an opposition overlooks the brutality of centuries of settlement, genocide, and slavery coincident with European empire and functions to shield the Western tradition from a deep complicity with this history.[29] These criticisms register legitimate anxieties about the accuracy of Arendt's highly stylized account of the historical formation of overseas empires (and will be taken up later in this chapter). At the same time, critics are mistaken to assume that Arendt's conceptual distinction between earlier and later forms of imperial expansion necessarily betrays a deep normative investment in colonialism and classical empire-building as idealized models of political life. In *Origins*, Arendt employs a number of similar

---

[29] See especially Kathryn Gines, "Race Thinking and Racism in Hannah Arendt's *The Origins of Totalitarianism*," in King and Stone, eds., *Hannah Arendt and the Uses of History*; A. Dirk Moses, "Hannah Arendt, Imperialism, and the Holocaust," in Volker Langbehn and Mohammed Salma, eds., *Colonial (Dis)-Continuities: Race, Holocaust, and Postwar Germany* (New York: Columbia University Press, 2010); Gail Presbey, "Critique of Boers or Africans? Arendt's Treatment of South Africa in *The Origins of Totalitarianism*," in Emmanuel Chukwudi Eze, ed., *Postcolonial African Philosophy: A Critical Reader* (Oxford: Blackwell, 1997).

historical contrasts – that is, Jew-hatred versus antisemitism, and race-thinking versus racism – that function to highlight a historical discontinuity and ideological escalation. In so doing, Arendt neither absolves the prior forms of prejudice and political practice of their unsavory associations and consequences nor seeks their nostalgic redemption.

More often, the importance of Arendt's claim about the political novelty of imperialism, and the substantive distinction it is premised upon, is overlooked or mischaracterized, especially when the Marxist undertones of her account of imperialism are overemphasized. Of course, Arendt herself located the "originality" of the principle of expansion as stemming in part from it being an economic doctrine uncannily transferred to the political realm (*OT*, 125). This understanding of the interruption of the logic of capitalist accumulation into the sphere of politics was built upon the previous generation's (primarily Marxist) debate on the new imperialism and origins of the First World War. Indeed, Arendt's very marking of the period of 1884 to 1914 as the period of imperialism is indebted to the debates initiated by Hobson at the turn of the century and subsequently elaborated in the Marxist tradition by V. I. Lenin, Karl Kautsky, Rudolf Hilferding, and Rosa Luxembourg. Despite Arendt's adherence to the basic tenets concerning the economic roots of imperialism, her analysis does not in fact examine in any great detail the actual process by which the nation-state was captured by economic actors (whether they be financiers, bankers, or industrial cartels), nor indeed does she spend much time on the precise dynamics of inter-state rivalry and competition, two themes that dominated the earlier literature on the new imperialism. Her primary interest was in understanding the political consequence of imperialism, that is, how the capture of the military and political machinery of the nation-state for securing economic adventures abroad enabled the subsequent liquidation of both the nation-state and the capacity of the bourgeoisie to control the forces it had helped to unleash.

Though Arendt was a great admirer of Luxembourg, in this respect, her analysis was much closer to the political aspects of Hobson's seminal work.[30] What Hobson noted, and Arendt developed, as the underlying novelty of imperialism was its profound difference from both the classical idea of *imperium* and the liberal model of colonialism. Whereas older notions of *imperium* signified universal dominion, a single (cosmopolitan) political unit encompassing the known world, modern imperialism was structured by the dynamic of multiple and competing empires. For Hobson, while the former could be idealized as a kind of normative internationalism and a potential model for a pacific federation, imperialism was spurred by and engendered forms of militarism, protectionism, and jingoistic nationalism that corrupted classical empire's cosmopolitan universalism into a competitive struggle for global

---

[30] Hobson's book is divided in two parts: the much more well-known Part One on "The Economics of Imperialism" and Part Two on "The Politics of Imperialism."

domination.[31] In Arendt, this contrast was starkly articulated as: "Imperialism is not empire building and expansion is not conquest" (*OT*, 130). For Arendt, "true empire building Roman-style" was premised on the eventual creation of an integrated legal unit; classical empires as a political form were aggregative or incorporative structures, whose legitimacy was framed by a necessary fusion of the domain of *ius* (law/justice) and *imperium* (rule/sovereignty). Unlike imperialism, which was governed by infinite expansion as its political goal, traditional empire-building was defined by this built-in limit. Either through assimilation or absorption in a federal arrangement, conquest would terminate in the foundation of a new body politic (*OT*, 125, 127–9). For Arendt, modern imperialism and its policy of expansion consciously refused any path of incorporation or assimilation for its non-European subject populations. On the one hand, a permanent refusal to incorporate subject peoples into a single political and legal entity implied the permanent suspension of the universality of law. On the other, it severed any grounds for political and moral connections between rulers and ruled, the imbrication of interests that function, even in despotic governments, as immanent limits to the violence of domination.

In this respect, Arendt's distinction between expansion and conquest developed a very Burkean point. Given Arendt's recurrent use of Burke's epitaph, the "breakers of law in India," as a general designation for British imperial rulers, it is not implausible to consider Arendt as extending Burke's prescient analysis of the unprecedented character of modern empire. For Burke, previous conquerors of India had settled among their subject populations, producing a natural link between the interests of the rulers and the ruled in the welfare of the country. Conquest by the East India Company, however, entailed a turbulent government by an ever-changing supply of "boys" who never developed a common bond with the people over whom they were given the grave responsibility to rule.[32] While past conquerors may have been more "ferocious, bloody, and wasteful" than the Company's initial acquisition of territories in India, Burke contended that "the Asiatic conquerors very soon abated of their ferocity, because they made the conquered country their own."[33] In permanently settling among the conquered people, the ruling power would feel the adverse consequences of "acts of rapacity or tyranny" equally, and thus conquerors themselves had an incentive to mitigate and temper them with the

---

[31] Hobson, *Imperialism*, pp. 8–11. He also emphasized how imperialism self-consciously distinguished itself from liberal empire, that is, it discredited the older liberal language of educating natives for industry and self-government.

[32] Edmund Burke, "Speech on Opening of Impeachment," February 15, 1788, *Writings and Speeches of Edmund Burke*, Volume VI, *India: The Launching of the Hastings Impeachment*, edited by P. J. Marshall (Oxford: Clarendon Press, 1991), pp. 285–6. See also Edmund Burke, "Speech on Fox's India Bill," December 1, 1873, *Writings and Speeches of Edmund Burke*, Volume V, *India: Madras and Bengal, 1774–1785*, edited by P. J. Marshall (Oxford: Clarendon Press, 1981), p. 402.

[33] Burke, "Speech on Fox's India Bill," *Writings and Speeches of Edmund Burke*, Volume V, p. 401.

establishment of regular government. The conquerors in settling had tied their prosperity and prestige (and that of future generations) with "the rise and fall of the territory they lived in," thus producing over time a sustained interest in the general well-being, safety, and happiness of the subject people.[34]

Company rule in Bengal, however, had thoroughly distorted this natural trajectory of a conquest that ends in assimilation, one that may begin in violence but ought to resolve into the constitution of a new polity. The Company was always a peculiarly hybrid entity, "a State in disguise of a Merchant," whose revolving personnel attempted to give institutional form only to acts of temporary looting. Burke likened these new conquerors to migrating "birds of prey," who in their transience and avarice necessarily failed to build lasting political institutions and social networks, leaving "no monument, either of state or beneficence, behind."[35] Having no common interest with the people over whom they rule, and loosed from the legal constraints of their home country, Company rule heralded an unprecedented and dangerous new imperial form, a power lacking all counterbalancing checks from above or below.[36]

For Arendt, the refusal to truly integrate imperial and national institutions into a new imperial polity was exacerbated in the age of imperialism by the historical triumph of the nation-state, for the ideological underpinnings of the nation constantly came into conflict with the imperative of expansion. Imperialism and nationalism could often embolden the other; overseas adventures served as a rallying cry for national unity, an interest "above party" that could also function as a safety valve for domestic class conflict. For Arendt, however, this was only a temporary and transitory alliance, to be undone by the "inner contradiction between the nation's body politic and conquest as a political device" (*OT*, 128). The nation-state was especially unsuccessful at imitating classical empire-building, which in its successful Roman form integrated "the most heterogeneous peoples by imposing upon them a common law" (*OT*, 125). The unity of the modern nation-state was premised not upon law but homogeneity and active consent; such integration demanded strict forms of assimilation, an enforced consent rather than justice, and thus degenerated into tyranny (*OT*, 125). Moreover, when the nation appeared as a conqueror, and conquest was used as a vehicle for assimilation, it encountered engendered nationalist resistance and rebellion. Thus, the British, as Arendt observed, were

---

[34] For it was in the conquered lands that "their lot was finally cast; and it is the natural wish of all, that their lot should not be cast in a bad land." Ibid., p. 401.

[35] "Young men (boys almost) govern there, without society, and without sympathy with the natives. They have no more social habits with the people, than if they still resided in England; nor indeed any species of intercourse but that which is necessary to making a sudden fortune, with a view to a remote settlement. Animated with all the avarice of age, and all the impetuosity of youth, they roll in one after another; wave after wave; and there is nothing before the eyes of the natives but an endless, hopeless prospect of new flights of birds of prey and passage, with appetites continually renewing for a food that is continually wasting." Ibid., p. 402.

[36] Burke, "Speech on Opening of Impeachment," *Writings and Speeches of Edmund Burke*, Volume VI, p. 286.

most adept in pursuing "the Greek model of colonization" rather than "the Roman art of empire building." From Ireland to India, the most successful modern empire had utterly failed to integrate or assimilate its longest-held dependencies (*OT*, 127). For Arendt, the French were the only modern imperial nation that tried to combine *ius* and *imperium* in the Roman style, resulting only in more brutal forms of exploitation (*OT*, 128–9). The eventual British solution actively demurred from this model, and instead proffered indirect rule as allegedly a more humane and cultural sensitive alternative to the imposition of British law and culture.

Modern imperialism, by resisting empire's telos of political incorporation, had entailed a form of government "without name or precedent" (*OT*, 213). The "philosophy of the bureaucrat," exemplified for Arendt in the figure of Lord Cromer, sought to fill the political and moral vacuum entailed by this precarious and unprecedented form of rule. Cromer, former finance minister in the government of India and eventual proconsul of Egypt, was considered to be a leading imperial administrator of his generation, and for Arendt represented the culmination of the British imperial experience. It was an experience which had convinced Cromer that "free institutions in the full sense of the term . . . [were] wholly unsuitable to countries such as India and Egypt.[37] Unlike their ancient counterparts, modern empires had resolutely failed at any "effective fusion of the Western and Eastern races."[38] The striking inability of liberal models of empire to secure political allegiance and consent from subject races underpinned Cromer's vehement critique of "the reckless adaptation of Western ideas to Eastern requirements,"[39] especially the liberal call to propagate principles of representative government abroad. The best imperial rule could hope for was to "foster some sort of respect always according superior talents and unselfish conduct."[40] In lieu of building lasting political ties through assimilation or education toward self-government, for Cromer, the basis of imperial rule would be founded upon the moral character of the imperial bureaucrat. In other words, rule over subject peoples was best maintained through a strict demarcation between ruler and ruled, a domination that would be moderated

---

[37] Evelyn Baring, Earl of Cromer, "The Government of the Subject Races," in *Political and Literary Essays, 1908–1913* (London: Macmillan, 1913), p. 26.

[38] Evelyn Baring, Earl of Cromer, *Ancient and Modern Imperialism* (New York: Longmans, Green, 1910), p. 82. Cromer argued that this failure at "effective fusion" was due in part to modern race consciousness and differences in religion, which worked as "powerful dissolvent forces . . . which act in favor of disunion" (p. 82). Even when modern empires – the French more aggressively, but also British liberal imperialists – actively encouraged the dissemination of Western civilization to dependencies, this policy failed to inculcate political loyalty to the empire, despite, for example, the successful spread of the English language and English education. Whereas, in Rome, knowledge of Latin had served to "knit the subject race to its conquerors" (p. 104), in India, Egypt, and Ireland, common language served instead to disrupt unification, as it furnished colonized peoples "with a very powerful arm against their alien rulers" (p. 107).

[39] Ibid., p. 70.

[40] Ibid., p. 13.

not by balancing institutions but by the imperial officer's sense of duty (itself cemented by consciousness of belonging to a superior civilization).

For Arendt, the refusal to extend British laws and institutions to Asia and Africa, in effect, declared a permanent severance between the interests of rulers from the ruled to which the only solution would be the development and defense of a "permanent government by administrative measures" (*OT*, 183). Bureaucratic elites whose only function was rule, and neither settlement nor any sort of political identification with subject peoples, emboldened a distinct form of race consciousness. What was particularly perverse about the justification of bureaucracy was how it so easily wrapped itself around an exaggerated language of moral duty, deeming aloofness a virtue and equating political responsibility with a (boyish) ethic of fairness. It was the British who had veiled the contempt for those over whom they ruled with the paternalistic language of protecting the "lesser" races. For Arendt, this philosophy of rule saw its culmination in indirect rule in Africa, a device of rule that was wholly negative in character and never producing "a new way for peoples to live together" (*OT*, 131). The justification of indirect rule, such as Rudyard Kipling's notion of the "white man's burden," exemplified the ability of British imperialism to make a policy essentially premised on a dangerous aloofness – and, indeed, absolute division between ruler and ruled – appear to be a gesture of cultural compromise and a mark of British integrity and tolerance.

The force of Arendt's analysis of the imperialist character in the portrayal of Cromer was to demonstrate how the imperial experience had functioned to caricature, degrade, and infantilize Western moral standards. Premised upon a radical and immutable separation between rulers and ruled, imperial bureaucratic domination produced and legitimated "a more dangerous form of governing than despotism and arbitrariness" (*OT*, 212). The posture of aloofness eliminated any social, political, or moral connection between rulers and subjects, and government was made "more inhuman and more inaccessible to its subjects than Asiatic rulers or reckless conquerors had ever been" (*OT*, 212).[41] Constrained neither by domestic political institutions nor human ties over whom they ruled, rulers themselves came to assume "a responsibility that no man can bear for his fellowman and no people for another people" (*OT*, 207). Thus, British rule in Africa, in glorifying the imperial bureaucrat's innate capacity to dominate, abandoned any commitment to the universal validity of law and set the stage for the general acceptance of illegality and racial exceptionalism as valid principles for organizing political orders.

What enabled the British imperial experience to become precedent-setting in a more overarching sense, for Arendt, was closely tied to the second novel aspect underlying the expansionist dynamics of the new imperialism. Arendt's

---

[41] Ibid. "In comparison, exploitation, oppression, or corruption look like safeguards of human dignity, because exploiter and exploited, oppressor and oppressed, corruptor and corrupted live in the same world, still share the same goals, fight each other for possession of the same things; and it is this *tertium comparationis* which aloofness destroyed."

account of an enlarged and escalating boomerang thesis was sustained, and I would argue made more persuasive, by her insistence that political develop-ments in the era of imperialism, whether within or beyond Europe, could no longer be contained within national or local boundaries. For it was the impe-rialist era that had invented *world politics*, that is, a global structure of com-petition and emulation that not only threatened to enfold local conflicts within great power politics but also, more tellingly, forced imperial rivals to imitate and learn from their competitors' successes in the struggle for survival and/or dominance. The most straightforward example of this kind of explicit emula-tion of imperialist aims and patterns of rule can be found in the pan-German program for continental expansion, which itself served as the outline for Nazi programs of continental conquest. The unprecedented territorial expansion that defined the period of the new imperialism opened the door for radical claims for territorial enlargement within Europe in those countries left out of the competition for land and resources overseas. It was the success of overseas imperialism that "captured the imagination of broader strata" (*OT*, 222) and enabled the crystallization of mass movements for continental imperialism. As more recent scholarship has argued, the debt Hitler owed to overseas imperi-alism not only lay in the ideological underpinning of claims for *Lebensraum*, but also shaped the settlement policies and organizational structure of Hitler's eastern empire. The admiration Hitler and other leaders of the Third Reich held for the British empire (especially its rule over India) led to the drafting of colonial experts to oversee the project of eastward expansion, the setting up of eastern protectorates on the model of the colonial mandate system, and, more broadly, the adoption of well-worn colonial legal instruments from systems of extraterritorial jurisdiction to race-based legal pluralism.[42]

The irony, for Arendt, was that the continental imperialisms that first applied colonial techniques of conquest and subjugation in Europe themselves lacked overseas colonies and did not directly emerge from contradictions of empire – that is, from their own imperial experience of the institutional disjuncture between nation and colony. Yet, they were more brutal and successful in attempts to "imperialize the whole nation ... to combine domestic and for-eign policy in such a way as to organize the nation for the looting of foreign territories and the permanent degradation of alien peoples" (*OT*, 155). Thus, continental imperialism proved to be much more efficacious than overseas

---

[42] On the specific influence of British empire on Nazi ideology, practices, and aspirations, see Dan Stone, "Britannia Waves the Rules: British Imperialism and Holocaust Memory," in *His-tory, Memory and Mass Atrocity: Essays on the Holocaust and Genocide* (London: Vallentine Mitchell, 2006); Zimmerer, "The Birth of the *Ostland* out of the Spirit of Colonialism"; and especially Mark Mazower, *Hitler's Empire: How the Nazi's Ruled Europe* (New York: Penguin Press, 2008). On the more general question of colonial precedents to Nazi policies of depopu-lation, forced transfers, and genocide, see Sven Lindqvist, *"Exterminate All the Brutes": One Man's Odyssey Into the Heart of Darkness and the Origins of European Genocide* (New York: New Press, 1996); Enzo Traverso, *The Origins of Nazi Violence* (New York: New Press, 2003); Zimmerer, "The Birth of the *Ostland* out of the Spirit of Colonialism."

imperialism in directly rejecting, attacking, and undermining domestic political institutions and safeguards: "The nation-state system's ruin, having been
prepared by its own overseas imperialism, was eventually carried out by those
movements which had originated outside its realm" (*OT*, 250). The final disintegration of the nation-state as the protective shield and guarantor of the rights
of man was thus effected by a *double* detour, through the experience of overseas
imperialism and its emulation and adoption by continental imperialism. In this
sense, the structural dynamics of the new imperialism themselves necessitated
a revised understanding of empire's boomerang effect as an expanded causal
nexus in which imperial violence and illegality harbor wider repercussions and,
indeed, global reverberations.

4.3 The Crisis of the West

This brings us to the most expansive and most elusive register of the boomerang
effect of imperialism, in which the policies and practices it instigated and intensified, according to Arendt, are seen to have "led to an almost complete break
in the continuous flow of Western history as we had known it for more than
two thousand years" (*OT*, 123). For Arendt, the imperialist elements of totalitarianism did not originate, and could not be contained, in purely German or
British history, and ultimately came to constitute a usurpation and breakdown
of "the Western tradition" itself. This adds a special inflection to Arendt's
repetition of Conrad's famous line: "All Europe contributed to the making of
Kurtz" (*OT*, 191). Figuring the imperialist Kurtz as the forerunner of Nazi
personality, in Arendt's analysis, not only designates a genealogy of Nazi race-
imperialism, it also exemplifies the ways in which Western political thinking
dangerously habituated itself to racism's suspension of the idea of a single
humanity. It was in this sense that, for Arendt, the ubiquitous appearance of
racial consciousness – from tribal nationalism to the "white man's burden" –
could be seen as carrying

the doom of the Western world and, for that matter, of the whole of human civilization.
When Russians have become Slavs, when Frenchmen have assumed the role of commanders of a *force noire*, when Englishmen have turned into "white men," as already
for a disastrous spell all Germans became Aryans, then this change will itself signify the
end of Western man. For no matter what learned scientists may say, race is, politically
speaking, not the beginning of humanity but its end, not the origins of peoples but their
decay, not the natural birth of man but his unnatural death. (*OT*, 157)

That totalitarianism can be see as coincident with and as an exemplification of
an overarching crisis of Western man brings Arendt's analysis into a complex
dialogue with another major postwar intervention in the debate concerning the
relationship between imperialism and fascism, namely Aimé Césaire's near-
contemporary polemic, *Discourse on Colonialism* (1950/1955).[43] Césaire's

---

[43] Césaire, *Discourse on Colonialism*.

searing indictment of the complicity of European humanism with the rise of "Hitlerism" was likewise marked by a deep sense that the atrocities of the Second World War had been set in motion by Europe's imperial experience.

Origins appeared just as the great wave of postwar anticolonialism was gaining momentum, and between the two existed fundamental differences in political agendas and preoccupations. Arendt's interest in the legacies of late-nineteenth-century imperialism was subsumed by her attempted deconstruction of the elements of totalitarianism, never extending to any sustained engagement with the crisis of decolonization or the global political shifts entailed by the collapse of European empires. In this sense, the political stakes of *Origins* were pointedly framed and contained by the need to understand the unprecedented dangers that totalitarianism posed. By contrast, Césaire mobilized the connection between imperialism and fascism to articulate a critical stance vis-à-vis the increasingly violent struggles over decolonization, namely, to expose claims of Western civilizational superiority and to catalyze indignation against continued colonial violence. In his view, the fascist practices so recently denounced in Europe seemed unabated, even emboldened, in the colonies.[44]

Situating Arendt's work in relation to Césaire's, I think, usefully clarifies both the differences in their conceptualization of relationship between empire and Western civilization as well as the resonances in their phenomenological account of the moral erosion effected by the imperial experience. Writing from the vantage point of a Martinique recovering from Vichy rule, Césaire unveiled what he took to be the historical entailments of modern empire in a language strikingly parallel to Arendt's. He wrote, "colonial enterprise is to the modern world what Roman imperialism was to the ancient world: the prelude to Disaster and the forerunner of Catastrophe."[45] In a remarkable overlap, Césaire likewise conceives of the emergence of fascism in Europe as "un choc en retour" of colonial violence, a reverse shock that in English translations of the *Discourse* is often rendered as "boomerang effect." While Césaire's view of Nazi genocide as the culmination of European colonialism was meant most pointedly to direct attention to colonial injustices and incite moral condemnation in relation to ongoing enactments of this brutal history, something more was at stake. For Césaire, the concentration camps signaled nothing less than the end of the *idea* of Europe, of Europe as the apotheosis of civilization, of Europe as the beacon of humanism.

Hitlerism, and the European bourgeoisie's inadequate moral response to it, was thus conceived as a symptom of a simmering crisis in Europe's articulation of the rights of man and the supposed universality that undergirded them. Césaire contended that

what he [the bourgeois humanist] cannot forgive Hitler for is not *the crime* in itself, *the crime against man*, it is not *the humiliation of man as such*, it is the crime against the

---

[44] On this point, see Rothberg, *Multidirectional Memory*, chapter 2.

[45] Césaire, *Discourse on Colonialism*, p. 74.

white man, the humiliation of the white man, and the fact that he applied to Europe colonialist procedures which until then had been reserved exclusively for the Arabs of Algeria, the "coolies" of India, and the "niggers" of Africa.[46]

Moreover, even as European elites slowly realized that Nazism was indeed "the supreme barbarism, the crowning barbarism that sums up all barbarism," they continued to blind themselves from the fact "that before they were its victims, they were its accomplices; that they tolerated Nazism before it was inflicted on them, that they absolved it, shut their eyes to it, legitimated it, because, until then, it had been applied only to non-European peoples."[47] Césaire here puts forward what one might call two classic arguments of anticolonial critique: the charges of hypocrisy and complicity, which together proved, for Césaire, irrefutably and nakedly, that Europe's humanism was only ever a "pseudo-humanism... that its concept of rights has been... narrow and fragmentary, incomplete and biased, and, all things considered, sordidly racist."[48]

Alongside the rhetoric of indignation also lies a forceful proposition about the corrupting effects of experiencing and living with the moral contradictions of colonialism. I would argue that the important contention at the heart of Césaire's claim is less that European colonial history exposes a dissoluble logical gap between the theory and practice of universalism, but rather that the long-term habituation to that gap is what led to the moral corruption that made fascism possible and thus to the final – in the sense of irredeemable – degradation of Europe itself:

[C]olonization works to *decivilize* the colonizer, to *brutalize* him in the true sense of the word, to degrade him, to awaken him to buried instincts, to covetousness, violence, race hatred, and moral relativism;... each time a head is cut off or an eye put out in Vietnam and in France they accept the fact, each time a little girl is raped and in France they accept the fact, each time a Madagascan is tortured and in France they accept the fact, civilization acquires another dead weight, a universal regression takes place, a gangrene sets in, a center of infection begins to spread; and that at the end of all these treaties that have been violated, all these lies that have been propagated, all these punitive expeditions that have been tolerated, all these prisoners who have been tied up and "interrogated," all these patriots who have been tortured, at the end of all the racial pride that has been encouraged, all the boastfulness that has been displayed, a poison has been distilled into the veins of Europe and, slowly but surely, the continent proceeds toward *savagery*.[49]

In the path from imperialism to fascism, Europe had been led down "a blind alley"; Césaire's boomerang effect of violence in the periphery is not an example of blowback but rather a slow dehumanization where the most civilized man "transforms *himself* into an animal."[50]

[46] Ibid., p. 36. Emphasis in the original text.
[47] Ibid., p. 36.
[48] Ibid., p. 37.
[49] Ibid., pp. 35–6. Emphasis in the original text.
[50] Ibid., p. 41. Emphasis in the original text. The full quote is given as an epigraph to the essay.

As I had emphasized in the previous section, Arendt saw imperialism as necessitating the invention of race and bureaucracy as instrumentalities of rule that function to veil, reconcile, and dangerously habituate European consciousness to precisely the same forms of moral corruption and complicity that Césaire so eloquently denounced. Yet, for Césaire, the moral and spiritual degradation of the West set in as soon as conquest and plunder were justified as "harbinger[s] of a superior order," and thus were coeval with the centuries-long history of modern European expansion.[51] By contrast, one of the most distinctive features of Arendt's analysis is how it was strictly delimited – spatially to Africa and temporally to the relatively short period of the new imperialism. While Arendt rightly insisted on the specificity of late-nineteenth-century imperialism,[52] especially in its implication of a world of competitive and coexisting empires, critics are not wrong to suggest that this strict temporal delimitation between earlier and later moments in the history of European empire is not entirely persuasive. Indeed, Arendt's acknowledgment of the violence that accompanied earlier regimes of colonial conquest, settlement, and slavery betrays the artificiality of her strict demarcation and implies that the longer history of modern European expansion prefigured the calamities that so marked the heyday of imperialism. But what seems to have most piqued critics is how in the attempt to define the *qualitative* difference of totalitarian genocide from its colonial precursors, Arendt seems cavalier or even callous in her seeming lack of moral outrage at the scale of colonial violence.[53] However, it is a stretch to conclude from this that Arendt's portrait of British imperialism was intended as either an apologia or redemption of the British Empire.[54] Arendt can be legitimately charged with Eurocentrism, but this has less to do with any purported idealization of European imperialism than the underlying fact that, for all her critical attention to it, imperialism appears only as an episode of and for European history. That is, Arendt's interest in imperialism is limited to

---

[51] Ibid., p. 33.

[52] Indeed, the very term *imperialism* was a relatively late linguistic phenomenon in the history of empire and specific to the late nineteenth century. See Richard Koebner and Helmut Dan Schmidt, *Imperialism: The Story and Significance of a Political Word, 1840–1960* (London: Cambridge University Press, 1964).

[53] See Robert Bernasconi, "When the Real Crime Began: Hannah Arendt's *The Origins of Totalitarianism* Dignity of the Western Philosophical Tradition," in King and Stone, eds., *Hannah Arendt and the Uses of History*, p. 62; Kateb, *Hannah Arendt*, p. 61; Presbey, "Critique of Boers or Africans?" p. 167; Moruzzi, *Speaking through the Mask*, p. 88.

[54] Arendt's scathing portrait of indirect rule in Africa and the pretensions supplied to justify it should counter this surprising criticism of Arendt's treatment of British imperialism. She is often taken to task for being "soft" on British imperialism and even producing an apologia for it. While Arendt did see British imperialism as comparatively less violent and genocidal, this does not mean that she glorified it as a model for empire building. Though Arendt praised Britain's parliamentary system for being able to resist the formation of extreme imperialist parties, she still insisted on the corrosive moral effects of the experience of imperial rule. For criticism of Arendt's portrait of British imperialism, see Moses, "Hannah Arendt, Imperialism, and the Holocaust"; Presbey, "Critque of Boers or Africans?"

how imperialism impinges upon, and indeed radically disrupts, the moral and political coordinates of Europe, and has very little to say in terms of its specific and catastrophic legacy for the ex-colonial world.

This points to a fundamental divergence in the political horizons that animated Arendt's and Césaire's concern to link imperialism to Nazi totalitarianism, a divergence that helps makes sense of their respective understanding of, and proposed response to, the crisis of Western civilization. For Césaire, this crisis is defined in terms of the crisis of European humanism. Césaire charged European humanism with a deep complicity in the crimes of colonialism, which, in turn, enabled the brutal return of this barbarism in the form of fascism and Hitlerism. In fascism, the inner contradictions of humanism came fully to light, and thus it could no longer serve as a model to be admired nor blindly emulated in the age of decolonization. Thus, for anticolonial criticism, the evocation of Europe's degradation into fascism not only serves to puncture its claims to moral superiority, but to urge newly independent countries to supersede Europe's compromised humanism in the name of a new postcolonial political order.[55]

Arendt, in resisting a conceptual narrative in which imperialism and totalitarianism appear as immanent to the logic of Western civilization, more often figured their emergence as constituting a break with, and collapse of, the Western tradition. As she remarked, totalitarianism's originality was "horrible, not because some new 'idea' came into the world, but because its very actions constitute a break with all our traditions; they have clearly exploded our categories of political thought and our standards of moral judgement" (*OT*, 310). To figure the crisis as a disruption or usurpation of the Western tradition by subterranean or liminal elements, and thus not an irredeemable or constitutive corruption at its core, Arendt could hope for its future reconstitution.[56] Thus, the task of political theory in the aftermath of totalitarianism required both a serious reckoning with the profound moral and political collapse that it signified as a well as a bold attempt to rethink political concepts anew – in other words, not its supersession but rather a fundamental interrogation *and* reconstruction of the Western tradition itself.

Arendt's proposed diagnoses of (and response to) the crisis of Western civilization were thus dependent upon a unified and exalted sense of *the* Western tradition with which it was identified, so much so that the demise of one was

---

[55] Recall Fanon's famous exhortation to the Third World: "Leave this Europe that never stops talking of man but massacres him at every one of its street corners, at every corner of the world," and begin again "a new history of man." Frantz Fanon, *The Wretched of the Earth* (New York: Grove Press, 2005), pp. 235, 238.

[56] Critics see this as Arendt's attempt to shield the West from true complicity with either imperialism or totalitarianism. See especially Bernasconi, "When the Real Crime Began"; Moses, "Hannah Arendt, Imperialism, and the Holocaust." Arendt's later work seemed to move away from the image of totalitarianism as something radically liminal to the mainstream of Western political philosophy, especially in her long engagement with Marx. See Dana Villa, "Totalitarianism, Modernity, and the Tradition," in Aschheim, ed., *Hannah Arendt in Jerusalem*.

necessarily linked to disintegration of the other. One can rightly question the Eurocentrism of this construction of a historically continuous, two-thousand–year-old Western tradition and the reverence it is meant to evoke. But we should also be attentive to the rhetorical effects of this evocation. On the one hand, the assertion of a (European) unity works against attempts to construe totalitarianism as peculiar to a specific national history or national character, that is, to render it a purely German question. Though conditions in Germany after the defeat in the First World War made it especially fruitful for the growth of totalitarian movements, for Arendt, the *crisis* "from which Nazism sprang" was a *European-wide* affair, namely "the vacuum resulting from an almost simultaneous breakdown of Europe's social and political structures."[57] It is a striking feature of *Origins* that its most resonant descriptions of historical antecedents to totalitarianism are French and British; this is the case not only in terms of the analysis of imperialism, but also the chapters on antisemitism and race-thinking, where French examples are particularly central.[58] On the other hand, the invocation of reverence for the achievements of Western civilization – and Western political philosophy – works to direct our attention continually to perhaps the central paradox running throughout *Origins*: How did a tradition of thinking that seemed to reach a grand achievement in the eighteenth-century declaration of human rights collapse so spectacularly? Evoking such heights of achievement dramatizes the catastrophic fall.

4.4 Race and Imperial Violence

Nowhere is this fall or seeming collapse of eighteenth-century universalism more acute than in Arendt's account of the rise of racism as an all-encompassing ideology. The disastrous implications of imperialist racism were everywhere apparent in the unprecedented scale, speed, and rapacity of genocidal killing that accompanied European expansion in Africa. Arendt herself had in mind the Boers' destruction of the Khoikhoi (Hottentot), the German extermination of the Herero, and the genocide in Leopold's Congo, which in her own speculative estimate amounted to the deaths of over 20 million people (*OT*, 185). For Arendt, what made the bureaucratic principle of rule uniquely dangerous in Africa was that it had cemented "the new imperialist consciousness of a fundamental, and not just temporary superiority of man over man, of the 'higher' over the 'lower breeds'" (*OT*, 130). In Africa, the older language of

---

[57] Hannah Arendt, "Approaches to the 'German Problem,'" in *Essays in Understanding*, p. 111. Moreover, Arendt argued that to insist that it was a peculiarly German problem was to delude people "into believing that the crushing of Germany is synonymous with the eradication of fascism" and "to close one's eyes to the European crisis which has by no means been overcome and which made possible the German conquest of the continent" (pp. 107–8).

[58] The only sustained examination of a direct German precursor to Nazism was chapter 8 on "Continental Imperialism," on the pan-German movement and the decline of continental party systems.

gradation of races would be transformed into a full-blown racism that expelled the so-called lower races from the category of the human altogether.

Though extreme race consciousness was a byproduct of imperialism, for Arendt, racism as ruling device also had a distinct and separate genealogy from that of bureaucratic domination. For Arendt, it had originated in southern Africa, specifically rooted in the history of the Boers and their elevation of race as the supreme ordering principle of society. With the gold rush of 1880s and 1890s, South Africa attracted a new breed of imperialist adventurers, who adopted and exacerbated the existing coordinates of race society. For Arendt these new adventurers were the "refuse" of Europe, those who had been rendered "superfluous" by industrial capitalism and cast aside by bourgeois society (*OT*, 189). In South African race society, these men could effortlessly find not only social status but an elevated one as a member of the master race. This experience proved to the mob and its leaders, the future personnel of totalitarian movements, how "peoples could be converted into races" and how, through sheer violence, "one might push one's own people into the position of the master race" (*OT*, 206). In Africa itself, "outside of all social restraint and hypocrisy . . . the gentlemen and the criminal felt not only a closeness of men who share the same color of skin, but the impact of a world of infinite possibilities for crimes committed in the spirit of play" (*OT*, 190).

Yet, as many critics have pointed out, there is something troubling in Arendt's insistence that it was in Africa that all these various imperial elements crystallized into unprecedented forms of violence. For, in this insistence, lay a deeper claim about an element of *experiential* truth at the heart of imperialist racism. For Arendt, "before imperialism had exploited it as a major political idea," racism as a ruling device had emerged out of the dynamics of race society in Africa. That is, "its basis, and its excuse, were still experience itself, a horrifying experience of something alien beyond imagination or comprehension" (*OT*, 195). For Arendt, the European encounter with Africa was indeed a radically dissonant experience, understandably registered as "shocking" and "frightful." In the African, European settlers and adventurers had encountered a species of man so different to what they had known that it necessitated a reopening of the question of the unity of man. In her words, "what made them different from other human beings was not at all the color of their skin but the fact that they behaved like a part of nature. . . . They were as it were, 'natural' human beings who lacked the specifically human character, the specifically human reality, so that when European men massacred them they somehow were not aware that they had committed murder" (*OT*, 193). As critics have rightly noted, this description of the European encounter with Africa, and in particular Arendt's contradictory and controversial characterization of Africans, relied on Eurocentric and racist stereotypes that, though mobilized to explain rapacious violence against natives, instead seemingly excused it.[59]

---

[59] There has been extensive criticism of the Eurocentrism and/or racism of Arendt's depictions of Africans in *Origins*. See Richard H. King's chapter 5 in this book, "On Race and Culture:

In rejecting the racism of Arendt's portrait of Africa, however, I also want to attend to Arendt's strong investment in this portrait and consider its theoretical function in her larger argument.[60]

The supposedly novel and frightful experiences that accompanied European expansion into Africa unleashed a brutality and rapaciousness that necessitated the invention of racism into a full-blown ideology precisely to legitimate, explain, and excuse its "senseless slaughter" and "wild murdering." Arendt would go so far as to suggest that "if the 'scramble for Africa' and the new era of imperialism had not exposed Western humanity to new and shocking experiences," race-thinking "would have disappeared in due time with other irresponsible opinions of the nineteenth century" (*OT*, 183). This controversial claim is linked to two underlying theoretical contentions that run throughout the entire text of *Origins*. Arendt's distinction between race-thinking and racism underscores her emphasis on the historical specificity of imperialist and totalitarian ideological/political formations. Secondly, the question of historical specificity itself is understood through Arendt's complication of the relationship between ideas and practices. As was noted before, the argument of *Origins* is punctuated by a number of key historical contrasts, especially between Jew-hatred and antisemitism and between race-thinking and racism, that are specifically intended to point to a historical rupture and escalation that the latter ideologies represented. Indeed, for Arendt, the assumption of continuity worked, in the case of antisemitism and racism, to insulate observers from recognizing the unprecedented nature of the dangers they came to pose. Arendt is often criticized for not acknowledging earlier forms of racism and race consciousness, especially those forms that underpinned modern slave regimes and prior programs of colonial conquest, and for not attending to how these also laid the groundwork for later, more virulent, racial formations. At the same time, though Arendt may not have given a full account of the genealogy of modern racism, there was some basis for her marking the late nineteenth century as the high point of racial theory and racial ideology. That is, whether one associates this development with the rise of scientific racism, the fallout from the politics of emancipation, or the birth of extreme, messianic nationalism in the era of imperialist competition (as Arendt emphasized), few historians or critics of the race concept would doubt the unparalleled ubiquity and popular legitimation

Hannah Arendt and Her Contemporaries," and his earlier treatment in *Race, Culture, and the Intellectuals*, chapter 5. See also the seminal essays by Dossa, "Human Status and Politics: Hannah Arendt on the Holocaust," and, more recently, Anne Norton, "Heart of Darkness: Africa and African Americans in the Writings of Hannah Arendt," in Bonnie Honig, ed., *Feminist Interpretations of Hannah Arendt* (University Park: Penn State University Press, 1995).

[60] Though many commentators have tried to locate the source of Arendt's racial prejudices – for example, in her reliance on Conrad or simply as representative of German or European culture at the time – the more important and interesting question seems to be what the theoretical stakes are in her depictions. However misguided or empirically baseless, Arendt's reference to Africans in *Origins* are not casual but highly stylized and meant to carry a philosophical weight that we ought to try to account for.

that it enjoyed at the dawn of the twentieth century.[61] Moreover, in viewing them as "reaction formations to the ideals of universal equality, human rights, and the brotherhood of men propagated by the French Revolution,"[62] Arendt was alluding to something important in the very nature of nineteenth-century discourses of race. This reconstitution of racial ideology *after* the age of emancipation and equality could only be accounted for by attending to historical discontinuities and distinctions.

Arendt contended that the "incapacity for making distinctions" was the unfortunate and growing tendency of modern historical and political sciences, "where everything distinct disappears and everything that is new and shocking is (not explained but) explained away either through drawing some analogies or reducing it to a previously known chain of causes and influences."[63] Moreover, the challenge of historical specificity – of recognizing and trying to account for what might be new and unprecedented in politics – was not only a problem of or for positivist social science, but also, and perhaps even more acutely, for intellectual histories of political concepts and ideologies. Arendt was particularly wary of a philosophical "histories of ideas" approach for understanding the historical novelty of political phenomena. In the central case of totalitarianism, Arendt objected to the mode of reconstructing chains of "intellectual influences and affinities" as distinguished from proceeding "from facts and events," a method of analysis that she viewed as spuriously casting the search for origins too widely and too deeply. As she caustically remarked, "from Plato to Nietzsche there is hardly a philosopher left who has not been either praised by Nazi intellectuals – or accused by their foes – of having been a forerunner of their monstrosities."[64] Though this kind of criticism was directed most pointedly at Eric Voegelin's contention that the roots of totalitarianism lay in the late Middle Ages (in the "rise of immanentist sectarianism" and the concomitant history of secularization), for Arendt, a tracing of protototalitarian elements in the history of philosophy tended to function like a loose historical determinism. When totalitarianism is figured as the historical fruition of a certain set of ideas and concepts, the historical and political conditions of its emergence cannot be adequately accounted for. Indeed, for Arendt, totalitarianism's originality was "not primarily its ideological content, but the *event* of totalitarian domination itself."[65]

For Arendt, intellectual or philosophic histories that served as *explanations* for historical processes or events also suffered from a second kind of theoretical

---

[61] Arendt was particularly interested in understanding how racial ideology served to mobilize mass movements. This was closely tied to ways in which the race concept was remade and radicalized in the era of imperialist competition, where the existence of one's race was seen to be secured only by annihilating or dominating all others.

[62] Benhabib, *The Reluctant Modernism of Hannah Arendt*, p. 83.

[63] Arendt, "A Reply," pp. 82–3.

[64] Hannah Aendt, "Race-Thinking before Racism," *Review of Politics* 46, 1 (January 1944), p. 40. This line does not appear in the reprinted version of the essay in *Origins*.

[65] Arendt, "A Reply," p. 80.

confusion. They assumed or posited an immediate relationship between ideas and reality, or ideas and practices, such that the very emergence of an idea or concept implied specific effects. For Arendt, there was an irreducible gulf between ideas/opinions and reality. In *Origins*, the clearest discussion of this comes with respect to the history of racism. The emergence of racism and racist ideology, for Arendt, was not the "history of an idea endowed by some 'immanent logic.'"[66] Indeed, in this context, she contended there was "an abyss between men of brilliant and facile conceptions and the men of brutal deeds and active bestiality which no intellectual explanation is able to bridge" (*OT*, 183). That is, the relationship between race-thinking and racism is also mediated and traversed by ideology, by the transformation of ideas into political practices and programs. The appeal of racist ideology is a political phenomenon and cannot be understood or explained purely in terms of its intellectual genealogy (or its purported scientific validity). Moreover, the reverse is equally true. Even the most admired ideas, concepts, and principles – such as the eighteenth-century discovery of the rights of man – prove susceptible to perversion, corruption, or irrelevance in political practice, a transformation that traditional forms of intellectual history can perhaps track but never fully explain.

Moreover, Arendt's understanding of the gulf between ideas and practices was linked to her attempt to make sense of the moral psychology that made possible the transformation of ideas and opinions into fully fledged political ideologies. Here, the category of experience played an especially crucial role. Successful ideologies must "attract and persuade a majority of people," and this persuasion itself "is not possible without an appeal to either experience or desires, in other words to immediate political needs" (*OT*, 159). Thus, in relation to both antisemitism and racism, Arendt attempted to discern the underlying perceptual and experiential rationale for their appeal and acceptance. Perhaps most disconcertingly, Arendt contended that "an ideology which has to persuade and mobilize people cannot choose its victims arbitrarily" (*OT*, 7). In the case of antisemitism, Arendt formulated a complex history of Jewish privilege and status as being closely imbricated with first the absolutist and then the national state in such a way that growing hostility to the state brought the Jews to the center of any conflict between state and society. Moreover, the height of antisemitism coincided with the loss of real power – their public function and influence – of formerly advantaged Jewish groups, making them and their wealth appear parasitic. In this sense, antisemitism primarily originated in varied forms of *misrecognition* of the Jews' assumed dominance in the backrooms of state power (*OT*, 4, 11–42).

By contrast, in Arendt's account of racism in Africa, there is no similar acknowledgment of processes of misidentification in the targeted dehumanization

---

[66] This is most likely a reference to Voegelin's *Rasse und Staat* (1933), which Arendt took to be the best example of a "history of ideas" analysis of race-thinking (*OT*, 158). See *The Collected Works of Eric Voegelin*, Volume 2, *Race and State*, and Volume 3, *The History of the Race Idea: From Ray to Carus* (Baton Rouge: Louisiana State University Press, 1998).

of Africans. Nor is there in Arendt's account, as Kateb subtlely noted, an interval of time between the allegedly original "experience" of race and the atrocities that are legitimated in its name.[67] Without such mediations, Arendt, when articulating the psychological rationale for imperialist racism rather than offering a critical explanation, can only restate it in its already ideologized terms. In this respect, a basic paradox emerges in Arendt's attempt to unearth the relationship between race experience and racial ideology, for one can never be certain that the original experience or perception is not itself already ideologically constituted. However, Arendt's own conceptualization of the emergence of racism as *ideology* in point of fact can turn the analysis more fruitfully in the opposite direction. If imperialism "invented" racism as "the only possible 'explanation' and excuse for its deed," then racism may also be conceived as a purely ideological consequence, and not the cause, of imperial politics (*OT*, 183–4).[68] As the product of practices of domination, rather than their originating source, imperialist racism highlights the process by which ideological possibilities can be radically redrawn by political processes.

Arendt insisted that the "task of the historian" interested in a critical understanding of ideology cannot simply rest in unveiling its key tenets as falsehoods, for example, in exposing the "Protocols of the Elders of Zion" to be a forgery or (in our case) proving that Africans were not purely "natural" beings incapable of creating a truly human reality. Rather, what needs to be confronted is "the chief political and historical fact of the matter," that is, why such falsehoods are "being believed" (*OT*, 7). In this respect, Arendt (in my view) correctly perceived that there was something unprecedented about both the scale and rapacity of racial violence in colonial Africa, even if she was wrong to locate the source of that distinctness in the "overwhelming monstrosity of Africa" (*OT*, 185) – in the hostility of the African climate and the otherness of the Africans. Arendt was perfectly aware that this was not Europe's first encounter with societies considered to be "savage" or "pre-historic"; in fact, she puzzles as to why these earlier encounters had not elicited similarly radical reactions and consequences. Arendt herself has no real answer to the crucial question she posed, without which one cannot fully comprehend the conundrum that initiates and frames Arendt's own analysis, namely why the colonization of Africa was accompanied by such "wild murdering" and "senseless slaughter."

Rather than seeking to answer this question as Arendt did, in terms of how African "savages" differ from other primitive peoples, a more effective critical account would perhaps consider the larger circumstances that shaped the subjective experience of race in colonial Africa. The European adventurer and settler of the late nineteenth century was formed by not only a different set

---

[67] Kateb, *Hannah Arendt*, pp. 61–3.

[68] A similar kind of reversal is put forward in Arendt's claim that scientific racism was a consequence, and not the cause, of race-thinking (*OT*, 160).

of racial assumptions about the relationship among peoples, but he was also armed with unprecedented instruments of violence. The colonization of Africa was embarked upon at the height of Europe's military and technological superiority relative to the non-European world, and this discrepancy had devastating consequences during the scramble for Africa. When Winston Churchill wrote of the battle of Omdurman as "the most signal triumph ever gained by the arms of science over barbarians,"[69] he was attesting to the shocking ease in which the British could within a few short hours decimate eleven thousand native troops while losing only forty-eight of their own men (of a contingent of twenty-five thousand). This radical asymmetry itself contributed to the simultaneous dehumanization of victims and the sense of omnipotence of victors as colonial war seemed less like war and more like "a sporting element in a splendid game."[70] Rather than a new experience of radical otherness, the catastrophic alliance among novel technologies of violence, racist ideology, and bureaucratic amorality "resulted in the most terrible massacres in recent history . . . and perhaps worst of all, it resulted in the triumphant introduction of such means of pacification into ordinary, respectable foreign policies" (*OT*, 185). And with this, the conscious extermination of peoples had been proven to be technologically, and thus experientially, possible.

4.5 Conclusion

If the new imperialism inaugurated a distinct era of global politics and global rivalry, when every nation saw its economic livelihood intimately connected to the expansion of political power, it is an era to which our politics are still held captive, with all its calamitous consequences. In our own times, when asymmetrical war has reemerged as the norm in global conflict, and military observers recognize that the technological gap has widened to levels not seen since the late nineteenth century, Arendt's cautionary tale about the moral and political hazards of imperialist politics attains a new urgency and significance. Arendt's analysis of imperialism's role in setting the stage for totalitarianism attests not to the inevitability of imperialism leading to genocide but the ways in which the habituation to domination presents a recurring threat to principles of moral universalism and equality. That is, despite the recognition and sanctification of universal norms of human equality and dignity, these principles can all too easily be corrupted and degenerate when tied to and subsumed by the dynamics of nation-state rivalry, war and occupation, and the quest for global dominance. Though Arendt thought the search for new political concepts was an urgent moral and political task, she was anxious that politics could not be given anything like permanent or impenetrable foundations. In this particular

---

[69] Winston Churchill, *The River War: An Historical Account of the Reconquest of the Soudan* (London: Longmans, 1898). Quoted in Lindqvist, *"Exterminate All the Brutes,"* p. 67.
[70] Churchill, *The River War*. Quoted in Lindqvist, *"Exterminate All the Brutes,"* p. 54.

sense, Arendt's antifoundationalism is more melancholic than celebratory, for it underscored her sense that even though imperialism and totalitarianism were not the logical fulfillment of the Western tradition and European humanism, the latter were still culpable for proving to be dangerously vulnerable, and even irrelevant, when confronted with violence and domination.

5

On Race and Culture

Hannah Arendt and Her Contemporaries

Richard H. King

In recent years, Hannah Arendt has been criticized for the way she characterized the people of sub-Saharan Africa as they faced invasion and occupation by
European imperial powers. Such criticism has become more frequent, even as
her "boomerang" thesis in *The Origins of Totalitarianism* (1951) – the idea that
the European imperial experience in Africa was among the main factors contributing to the emergence of totalitarianism in Europe – has received renewed
attention, even from academic historians. Thus her critique of imperialism
places her among the forerunners of anticolonial thought and of postcolonial studies, while her attitude toward sub-Saharan African cultures makes her
sound eerily like the very European settler population she was condemning.[1]

Some defend Arendt by suggesting that what she did was to capture the
racist mentality of the white settlers in southern Africa through an act of
narrative ventriloquism. By entering into the consciousness of the early Boer
settlers and Europeans generally, she revealed, according to Seyla Benhabib,
the "temptation of regression to a condition in which everything is possible."
Yet even before Chapter 7 ("Race and Bureaucracy") in *Origins*, where Arendt
took up this topic directly, she wrote that the eighteenth-century European
"enthusiasm for the diversity in which the all-present identical nature of man
and reason could find expression" met a stern test when it was "faced with
tribes which, as far as we know, never had found by themselves any adequate
expression of human reason or human passion in either cultural deeds or popular customs, and which had developed human institutions only to a very low

---

[1] The first person explicitly to raise this issue was Shiraz Dossa in his "Human Status and Politics:
Hannah Arendt on the Holocaust," *Canadian Journal of Political Science* 13, 2 (June 1980):
309–23. Later, Anne Norton widened the discussion in "Heart of Darkness: Africa and African
Americans in the Writings of Hannah Arendt," in Bonnie Honig, ed., *Feminist Interpretations
of Hannah Arendt* (University Park: Pennsylvania State University Press, 1995), pp. 247–62. See
also several of the essays in Richard H. King and Dan Stone, eds., *Hannah Arendt and the Uses
of History: Imperialism and Nation, Race and Genocide* (New York and Oxford: Berghahn,
2007).

level."[2] Her view here clearly characterized sub-Saharan Africans not as in- or subhuman but as culturally underdeveloped.[3] In the words Sankar Muthu has used to describe the capacity that anti-imperialist European thinkers variously attributed to non-European peoples, Arendt denied much, if any, "cultural agency" to black Africans.[4]

But how, it might be asked, does her stance on racial and cultural difference compare with the way her German contemporaries expressed themselves on such matters? Without trying to make excuses for Arendt, a look at the work of such figures as Theodor Adorno, Leo Strauss, Karl Löwith, Eric Voegelin, and their mentors, including Edmund Husserl and of course Martin Heidegger, reveals that they spoke of racial and crosscultural matters in ways remarkably similar to, or even more ethnocentric than, Arendt. Thus this controversy has to do not only with views of a particular individual, Hannah Arendt, but also with a specific *discourse* about racial and cultural difference that was not only "German" but also lasted well beyond World War II in the West generally.[5] This is not to say that the dominant discourse on race and culture was inescapable, since one of Arendt's mentors, Karl Jaspers, as well as Arendt herself, broke with some of its central tenets. But, it was very powerful.

Moreover, although the 1940s saw the emergence of powerful intellectual and moral critiques of racism in the West, not every thinker who challenged the theoretical or scientific basis of white supremacy or of antisemitism had fully developed views on the new egalitarianism as it related to Western colonialism and imperialism.[6] Except for certain French intellectuals and Francophone intellectuals of the black diaspora, post–World War II anticolonialism failed to attract much active support from (white) Western intellectuals. This reluctance

---

[2] See Seyla Benhabib, *The Reluctant Modernism of Hannah Arendt* (Thousand Oaks, CA.: Sage, 1996), p. 84, as well as Hannah Arendt, *The Origins of Totalitarianism*, 2nd ed. (Cleveland: Meridian, 1958), pp. 176–7; hereafter abbreviated *OT*. The problem with the phrase "temptation of regression" is that it can (too easily) be read as a way of blaming sub-Saharan culture for undermining a supposedly superior European culture. Moreover, Arendt's claim that "slave-holding peoples" were not "race-conscious before the nineteenth century" (p. 177) is highly questionable, to say the least.

[3] T. Carlos Jacques, "From Savages and Barbarians to Primitives: Africa, Social Typologies, and History in Eighteenth-Century French Philosophy," *History and Theory*, 36, 2 (May 1997): 190–215.

[4] Sankar Muthu, *Enlightenment against Empire* (Princeton: Princeton University Press, 2003).

[5] See James Clifford, "On *Orientalism*," in *The Predicament of Culture: Twentieth Century Ethnography, Literature and Art* (Cambridge, MA: Harvard University Press), pp. 266–9, for his use of "discourse," a term clearly related to "paradigm" (Kuhn) and "episteme" (Foucault). See Michael Foucault, *The Order of Things: An Archaeology of the Human Sciences* (New York: Pantheon, 1970); Thomas S. Kuhn, *The Structure of Scientific Revolution*, 2nd ed., enlarged (Chicago: University of Chicago Press, 1970). The use of such synchronic concepts raises in particularly clear fashion the persisting tension between structure versus agency in the social sciences and historical studies.

[6] In Richard H. King, *Race, Culture and the Intellectuals, 1940–1970* (Washington and Baltimore: Woodrow Wilson/Johns Hopkins Presses, 2004), I did not emphasize enough the uneven absorption of cultural and racial egalitarianism among Western intellectual elites, though I did analyze the rhetoric Arendt used to describe African cultures (pp. 115–9).

to take a strong stand on this issue continued a post-Enlightenment reluctance by white intellectuals to attack European imperialism or colonialism. A list of imperialism's defenders would include classic nineteenth-century liberals such as Alexis de Tocqueville and John Stuart Mill, as well as Karl Marx and G. W. F. Hegel.[7] Clearly, a commitment to the Enlightenment culture of progress through reason led all too easily – though not inevitably– to the assumption of Western cultural superiority, including the West's right, even duty, to "instruct" traditional – that is, non-Western – cultures in the ways of modernity.

On nearly all counts, Arendt was more aware of the pressing need to come to terms with the European sense of racial and cultural superiority than most other intellectuals of her time. She concluded "Organized Guilt and Universal Responsibility" (1945) with a set of sobering observations. The awareness of "the idea of humanity and of the Judeo-Christian faith in the unitary origin of the human race," she noted, had created a moral burden that many simply did not care to shoulder. Indeed, some have rejected these ideas and "become more susceptible to the doctrine of race, which denies the very possibility of common humanity." In a time of global expansion and awareness: "To follow a non-imperialistic policy and to maintain a non-racist faith becomes daily more difficult because it becomes daily clearer how great a burden mankind is for man."[8]

Nor had her deep opposition to race as a way of defining humanity, organizing politics, or understanding history diminished by 1951 when *Origins* appeared. For instance, just before the beginning of the imperialism section, she contended that:

When Russians have become Slavs, when Frenchmen have assumed the role of commanders of a *force noire*, when Englishmen have turned into "white men," as already for a disastrous spell all Germans became Aryans, then this change will itself signify the end of Western man. For no matter what learned scientists may say, race is, politically speaking, not the beginning of humanity but its end, not the origin of peoples but their decay, not the natural birth of man but his unnatural death. (*OT*, 157)

It is hard to imagine a stronger statement *against* the politicization of race and the racialization of politics and *for* the idea of common humanity. All of this underlines the centrality of "racial imperialism" to her conception of what *Origins* was "about." Finally, in her 1957 essay "Karl Jaspers: Citizen of the World?," Arendt returned to the idea that "mankind" was a normative concept, almost a utopian ideal, as it were. But she went on to note that the moral "fact" of mankind is one that has become possible because of the "technical development of the Western world" rather than because of the ideas of "the humanists" or "reasoning of philosophers."[9] That is, faced by

---

[7] See Muthu, *Enlightenment against Empire*, p. 259, for this point.

[8] Arendt, "Organized Guilt and Universal Responsibility," in *Essays in Understanding, 1930–1954*, edited by Jerome Kohn (New York: Harcourt, Brace, 1994), p. 131.

[9] Arendt, "Karl Jaspers: Citizen of the World?" (1957), in *Men in Dark Times* (New York: Harvester, 1968), p. 82.

the undeniable evidence of human interconnectedness through technology, the unity of mankind must be accepted and nurtured.

However, the great majority of those who thought about cultural difference, especially vis-a-vis Africa and Asia, assumed that the West was not only different from, but superior to, those cultures. The considerable irony (not to mention hypocrisy) here is that in response to the crisis of the West in the interwar years, several of Arendt's contemporaries were moved to emphasize precisely that superiority, even as European culture was abandoning rather than strengthening its own best ideals. In what follows, I want to establish the historical and intellectual context within which we might better understand *both* Arendt's forthright and often courageous attacks on modern racism and her problematic characterization of certain African cultures. It is not correct to see Arendt's views as just like those of her contemporaries, but it is also a mistake to think that she totally escaped the pervasive hold that the discourse of European superiority had over them.

5.1 Spiritual Renewal and Greek Reason

Though the groundwork had been well prepared philosophically for the death of God and the collapse of the dream of (Enlightenment) reason, it was the experience of World War I that triggered the deep cultural crisis in Europe. References to "the crisis of historicism" (Ernst Troeltsch), "European nihilism" (Karl Löwith), "the revolution of nihilism" (Hermann Rauschning), "German nihilism" (Leo Strauss), and cultural "catastrophe" (Martin Heidegger) indicate the dominant mood of post-1918 European, especially German, thought. If much of this was to become philosophical and spiritual cliché, the crisis of both faith and reason was still a very real and very pressing one.

Specifically, there was a crisis of reason *within* modern secular culture. As illustrated in the trajectory of Max Weber's thought, reason was no longer the spiritual-intellectual power that transformed historical events into a coherent whole and made individual life an exercise of autonomy rather than blind obedience to the irrational or social compulsion. Rather, it was the more limited capacity to control and direct natural and human processes but at the cost of the spiritual and emotional impoverishment of the culture. Broadly speaking, it was Weber's distinction between substantive and instrumental reason that many young Marxists, including Georg Lukacs and members of the Frankfurt School, incorporated into their thought.[10] But even this neo-Marxist critique of reason needs to be seen in the context of a more general crisis among "bourgeois" thinkers, as I have already indicated. For instance, Edmund Husserl's "Philosophy and the Crisis of European Man" (1935) contrasted modern science's "objectivism" and "naturalism" with "rationality in that noble and genuine sense, the original Greek sense." In a move that was familiar in German intellectual history, he identified the "spiritual birthplace" of the West

---

[10] Though the story of the crisis in Western reason was central to the Frankfurt School "project," I will not take it up here.

as "the ancient Greek nation." Greek reason aimed to achieve "infinity" and entailed a spiritual complexity beyond its function as an instrument for practical results.[11] For Husserl, "Nature belongs to the sphere of the spirit," and it was "the West's mission to humanity"[12] to emphasize this claim. Though his essay began by positing a deep spiritual/philosophical crisis in the West, it ended by looking to the saving power of Greek reason as the basis for the West's superiority.

Meanwhile, Leo Strauss had sketched in the broad outlines of his mature position by around 1940. In "The Living Issues of German Postwar Philosophy" (1940), Strauss, by then living in America, rejected the culture of modernity, including Enlightenment rationality, by claiming that the answer to the modern crisis lay in the origins of the Western philosophical tradition: "It is after all possible that the truth, or the right approach to the truth, has been found in a remote past and forgotten for centuries." Not only focusing on epistemology but also political ethics, he wrote of the "inability of modern science or philosophy to give man an evident teaching as regards the fundamental question, the question of the right life."[13] In his magnum opus, *Natural Right and History* (1953), Strauss, also powerfully influenced by Weber but in a negative way, rejected the latter's fact-value distinction as one of the disastrous developments in modern thought.

Like Husserl, Strauss looked back to the Greeks for spiritual replenishment. He came to the conclusion that "classical natural right thinking" was the original source of Western values and traditions. Only with such a foundation in mind could the characteristics of modern rationality – positivism, relativism, and ultimately nihilism – be combated. Finally, though Strauss was to respect both civilizational underpinnings of the Western tradition, his own commitment was to "Athens" over "Jerusalem," to a life of (classical) reason over a life guided by biblical revelation.[14] Almost anticlimactically, Strauss sought to repair the break in the tradition by, as Alfons Soellner has put it:

pursuing intellectual history as reestablishment of tradition.... it was not the absolute *Zivilisationsbruch* (breakdown of civilization), symbolized by Auschwitz, which came

---

[11] Edmund Husserl, "Philosophy and the Crisis of European Man," in *Phenomenology and the Crisis of Philosophy* (New York: Harper Torchbooks, 1965), pp. 179, 158, 181. A much more recent essay in the Husserlian spirit is Klaus Held, "The Origin of Europe with the Greek Discovery of the World," *Epoche* 7, 1 (Fall 2002): 81–105.

[12] Husserl, "Philosophy and the Crisis of European Man," pp. 190, 192.

[13] Leo Strauss, "Living Issues of Postwar German Philosophy," in Heinrich Meier, ed., *Leo Strauss and the Theological-Political Problem* (Cambridge: Cambridge University Press, 2006), pp. 125, 129. See also "German Nihilism" (1941), *Interpretation* 26, 3 (Spring 1999): 353–78, which is the companion essay to "Living Issues."

[14] See Leo Strauss, *Natural Right and History* (Chicago: University of Chicago Press, 1953), chapters 1 and 2; Leo Strauss, "Jerusalem and Athens: Some Introductory Reflections," *Commentary* (June 1967): 45–57; along with David N. Myers, *Resisting History: Historicism and Its Discontents in German Jewish Thought* (Princeton: Princeton University Press, 2003), pp. 106–29.

to the fore in his [Strauss's] American phase, but rather the study of the Greek classics, which evaded (and leveled?) this break through abstraction.[15]

Thus, for Strauss, Athens stood at the opposite moral and spiritual pole to Auschwitz rather than having a subterranean connection to it.

It is significant that later in *The Human Condition* (1958), when Arendt located the origins of Western politics in the Greek experience, it was not some grand concept of substantive reason, as with Husserl, or anything like Strauss's classical natural right thinking that she resurrected. It was rather a worldly concept of public speech and action that she placed at the center of the normative experience of politics. It was not *logos* as an authoritative word but as spoken *dialogue* or interchange, not the Truth but the exchange of opinions, not contemplation but action that she identified as the great Greek contribution.[16]

5.2 The Mission of the West

How can we understand the appeal of Greek thought as an antidote to Western modernity? Grounded in the centrality of classical languages, literature and thought, the focus on Greece in the *Bildung* of German thinkers avoided any sort of renewed *religious* commitment to Christianity or to Judaism. Thus, what Elizabeth Butler famously called "the tyranny of Greece over Germany" was central to modern, nonreligious critiques of modernity in the German tradition.

The most influential figure in this post-Enlightenment tradition was of course Friedrich Nietzsche, who looked to a pre-Socratic or Dionysian Greece to revitalize the modern, history-ridden West.[17] His commitment to a vision of a pre-Socratic Greek sensibility anticipated Heidegger's embrace of Greek primordiality/autochtonicity (*Bodenständigkeit*) as uniquely resonant with the German language and *Geist*. Heidegger assumed that German language and culture possessed greater philosophical depths than other languages and thus was uniquely attuned to the pre-Socratic understanding of Being. But Heidegger characterized Greek reason much as Husserl and Strauss characterized modern scientific reason as "the triumph of ratiocinative-technological *logos* over the Heraclitean-Sophoclean logos of oracular speech and poetic thought." Thus, Heidegger located the fall of the West's *logos* in ancient Greece rather than

---

[15] Alfons Soellner, "Leo Strauss: German Origins and American Impact," in Peter Graf Kielmansegg et al., eds., *Hannah Arendt and Leo Strauss: German Emigres and American Political Thought after World War II* (Cambridge and Washington: Cambridge University Press, 1995), p. 125.

[16] Roy T. Tsao, "Arendt against Athens: Rereading *The Human Condition*," *Political Theory*, 30, 1 (February 2002): 97–123, has recently questioned the extent to which Arendt was an uncritical admirer of the Greek polis.

[17] Karl Löwith, *My Life in Germany before and after 1933* (Urbana and Chicago: University of Illinois Press, 1994/1940), p. 20.

early-modern Europe or the eighteenth-century Enlightenment.[18] By returning to the pre-Socratic Greeks, Heidegger placed his faith in the capacity of German thought to recapture the essence of the West's grasp of Being before its "fall" into the opposition between temporal and eternal and the emergence of the (*other*) tradition of humanism associated with Roman thought and culture. It was in response to this Heideggerian "turn" against classical Greek thought that Husserl, Strauss, and later Arendt reacted.

In retrospect, there was an obvious danger in the German embrace of Greece as a saving "other" that turned out to be the "same." As Karl Löwith noted, this return to pre-Socratic Greece was part of German thought's "distancing itself from the Old Europe" and "our Roman-Christian heritage" and the embrace of a "'nordically' interpreted Hellenism directed against Rome and Christendom."[19] Many Jewish thinkers would have found it particularly difficult to commit themselves to the West defined in terms of the "Roman-Christian heritage," since few Jewish thinkers would find a compelling spiritual home in the Middle Ages, the Roman Christian culture par excellence.[20] To return to classical Greek thought was paradoxically a way of remaining modern – that is, secular – without being committed to the modern Cartesian-Enlightenment idea of reason.

Furthermore, an "orientalist" motif was central to the whole idea of modern humanism as developed in Germany. As Löwith began his powerful essay "European Nihilism: Reflections on the European War" (1940):

Europe is a concept that develops not out of itself but rather from out of its essential contrast with Asia.... Europe is primordially and, as long as it remains true to itself, politically and spiritually a power that is opposed to the Asiatic.[21]

---

[18] See Martin Heidegger, "The Self-Assertion of the German University," in Richard Wolin, ed., *The Heidegger Controversy* (Cambridge, MA: MIT Press, 1993), pp. 29–39; also Hans Sluga, *Heidegger's Crisis: Philosophy and Politics in Nazi Germany* (Cambridge, MA: Harvard University Press, 1993), p. 120. On Heidegger's notion of rootedness, see Charles Bambach, *Heidegger's Roots: Nietzsche, National Socialism, and the Greeks* (Ithaca and London: Cornell University Press, 2003), p. xxi.

[19] Karl Löwith, "European Nihilism: Reflections on the Spiritual and Historical Background of the European War," in Richard Wolin, ed., *Martin Heidegger and European Nihilism* (New York: Columbia University Press, 1995), p. 179. This long essay sums up Löwith's 1941 classic *From Hegel to Nietzsche* (Garden City, NY: Anchor, 1967). For more on Löwith, see Jurgen Habermas, "Karl Löwith: Stoic Retreat from Historical Consciousness (1963)," in *Philosophical-Political Profiles* (London: Heinemann, 1983); Richard Wolin, "Karl Löwith: The Storic Response to Modern Nihilism," in *Heidegger's Children: Hannah Arendt, Karl Löwith, Hans Jonas and Herbert Marcuse* (Princeton: Princeton University Press, 2001), pp. 70–100 Löwith.

[20] Philip Rieff once made this point polemically in *Fellow Teachers* (New York: Harper and Row, 1973).

[21] Löwith, "European Nihilism," p. 173. Incidentally, Thomas Mann's *The Magic Mountain* also reflects (on) the German obsession with the lure of the East, though it is figured more in the appeal of the Russian soul than anything further east or south. Thomas Mann, *The Magic Mountain*. trans by John E. Woods (New York and London: Alfred A. Knopf, 2005).

Though Edward Said was wrong to imply that Max Weber all but agreed "that there was a sort of ontological difference between Eastern and Western economic (as well as religious) 'mentalities,'"[22] the driving force behind much of Weber's work was the question as to why the West had become so different than the rest of the world – specifically, why and how it had developed "rational" forms of culture, law, thought, and economics. Indeed, Weber's work perfectly illustrated the ambivalence about the modern West among German thinkers. On the one hand, it had far outstripped the rest of the globe in economic and political power, as witnessed by European domination of much of Asia and Africa. Yet, the West seemed to have lost its way and succumbed to a spiritual crisis of major proportions.

Not surprisingly, this Weberian sense of Western cultural superiority – and even mission – constantly recurs in the thought of Arendt's contemporaries. This was not a major issue but more of a tacit assumption in *Natural Right and History*, wherein Strauss drew a clear distinction between the classical Greeks and people of "lesser" cultures when he observed that "one ought not to expect any real knowledge of natural right among savages." Although the difference between those who are "civilized" and those who are "savages" is, he assumed, clear, he was pessimistic about the culture of "savages": "One ought not even to expect any real knowledge of natural right among savages." Yet later in the book he writes:

As long as man has not cultivated his reason properly, he will have all sorts of fantastic notions . . . he will elaborate absurd taboos. But what prompts the savages in their savage doings is not savagery but the divination of right.[23]

Though not denying human status to the "savage," Strauss clearly drew a strong line between civilized peoples and savages. (Strauss cited no modern anthropologist to back such claims, but only the usual ancient and early-modern sources to which he habitually repaired.) A few fugitive comments throughout his work suggested that Strauss differentiated between the advanced cultures of the Far East (and medieval Islam) and so-called primitive cultures of Asia, Africa, and the Americas. But cultural relativism for Strauss and his followers was one of the cardinal sins of modernity.[24] The assumption of Western superiority was not a careless or unconsidered judgment in Strauss's thought, but basic to it.

Husserl was much more explicit about the cultural superiority of the West. In the 1935 essay "Philosophy and the Crisis of European Man," he defined Europe as a "unity of one spiritual image." Still, he was anxious to differentiate this claim to spiritual unity from the idea that culture and geography coincide;

---

[22] Edward W. Said, *Orientalism* (New York: Vintage, 1979), p. 259.

[23] Strauss, *Natural Right and History*, pp. 9, 130.

[24] Leo Strauss, "What Is Liberal Education," in *Liberalism: Ancient and Modern* (Chicago: University of Chicago Press, 1995), pp. 3–9.

nor was he making a racial claim: "there is essentially no zoology of peoples."[25] And yet, Husserl excluded certain peoples living in Europe from that spiritual unity: "the Eskimos and Indians of the county fairs, or the Gypsies who are constantly wandering about Europe."[26] By contrast: "No matter how inimical the European nations may be toward each other, still they have a special inner affinity of spirit."[27] Europe possessed an "innate entelechy" not toward a predetermined destination but toward an infinite spirit of reflection upon itself and the human condition. This was what made Europe's culture special and what other cultures tried to imitate and even join.

However, this will to imitation was not reciprocated by Europe. Other cultures, he noted, have a "motivation . . . – despite their determination to retain their spiritual autonomy – constantly to Europeanize themselves, whereas we, if we understand ourselves properly, will never, for example, Indianize ourselves."[28] Though the philosophical-cultural ideal that Husserl championed was far from Heidegger's German primordiality, it unquestioningly assumed the West's superiority to other cultures. Overall, the Greek-derived notion of spiritualized reason was clearly a trans-European ideal to be counterposed to the cultural particularism of fascism and Nazism. Yet insofar as it entailed the West's mission to the world, it suggested not just difference from, but superiority to, non-Western cultures. It was far from the kind of cosmopolitanism proposed by thinkers such as Karl Jaspers after the war.[29]

Significantly, Karl Löwith's exploration of the crisis of European nihilism was developed in Japan, where he taught (from 1936 to 1941) after having fled Germany and Italy. Along with Strauss and Eric Voegelin, Löwith was a practitioner of "the history of ideas";[30] that is, he attributed a primacy, or at least great causal importance, to ideas in the development of the modern West. Like Strauss and Voegelin, his work was organized around the central question of modernity: Was "the essence and meaning of history determined absolutely within history itself; and, if not, then how?"[31] According to Löwith, Europe's problem was one of no longer having "faith in a genuine mission." But, his remarks implied that economic and political imperialism were symptoms of, rather than answers to, Europe's spiritual crisis.[32] More explicitly cosmopolitan than Husserl, Löwith also insisted that the "unity of Europe" was "neither

---

[25] Husserl, "Philosophy and the Crisis of European Man," pp. 156, 158.

[26] Ibid., p. 155.

[27] Ibid., p. 157.

[28] Ibid., p. 157.

[29] See, for examples, Joanne Myang Cho, "The German Debate over Civilization: Troeltsch's Europeanism and Jaspers's Cosmopolitanism," *History of European Ideas*, 25, 6 (November 1999): 305–19; Ned Curthoys, "The Émigré Sensibility 'World-Literature': Historicizing Hannah Arendt and Karl Jaspers' Cosmopolitan Intent," *Theory and Event*, 8, 3 (2005).

[30] See *OT*, 158 note 3; Arendt, "A Reply to Eric Voegelin" (1953), in *Essays in Understanding*, pp. 401–8, where she identified Voegelin as someone who practices the history of ideas. Strauss too, I think, belongs in this category, though she does not mention him.

[31] Löwith, *From Hegel to Nietzsche*, p. vi.

[32] Löwith, "European Nihilism," p. 175.

geographic nor racial and is defined neither by 'blood' nor 'soil.'" Rather it was a historically based "kind of shared feeling, willing and thinking that has developed in the course of Europe's history.... "[33] He blamed the loss of European unity and mission in part on the German Reformation, which had initiated "the destruction of the religious and moral unity of the Christian West," while the French Revolution betokened the "destruction of its political tradition."[34]

Yet in tracing "the history of decline" from Hegel to Nietzsche, Löwith hardly mentioned antisemitism or racism, specifically "blood," as one of the substitutes for reason or *Geist* in the German/European tradition. He did note Nietzsche's attack on antisemitism and cited approvingly his attribution of a large part of German creativity to its Jewish thinkers and artists, while also referring to Paul Lagarde's "essentially anti-Jewish" line of thought. Beyond that, Löwith was largely silent.[35] He concluded that Nietzsche "spiritually opened up the path for the Third Reich," though it was not a path that he himself "traverse[d]," and also observed that Nietzsche had drawn the historical link between democratization and the appeal of "dictatorial leadership."[36]

Löwith's "Afterword to the Japanese Reader," which he appended to the long essay "European Nihilism," revealed his particular perspective on the Western cultural-spiritual mission in the world. In light of the growing links between Japan and Germany as war broke out in Europe, his short piece attacked the German (and European) embrace of dictatorship as well as the Japanese failure to absorb the "authentic" or "true" meaning of the West. If this had been merely an example of "spiritual condescension" on Löwith's part, it would hardly have been worth attending to.[37] But Löwith's short essay also attempted to explain what prevented the Japanese from grasping the inner spiritual essence of the West, while clearly and successfully adopting its "material civilization." In a general way, he was aware that no culture really understood and appropriated another culture's "spirit" and "history."[38] He also implied what became a cliché about the Japanese – that they were good imitators, but lacked a creative spirit. All that said, Löwith did not assume that the Japanese were inherently incapable of changing their ways, either.

Löwith's real indictment was couched in broader terms. Like the "high cultures of the ancient Orient," the Japanese lacked the "kind of free emergence out of oneself and the consequent power of appropriation." In that respect, they were not good enough imitators, since they only appropriated the most external aspects of the West. The Japanese lacked the will to see other cultures not only for what they were but for what can be learned from them about one's

---

[33] Ibid., p. 174.
[34] Ibid., p. 181.
[35] See Habermas, "Karl Löwith: Stoic Retreat from Historical Consciousness," p. 82; Löwith, *From Hegel to Nietzsche*, pp. 191 note 59, 425, 372.
[36] Löwith, "European Nihilism," p. 208.
[37] Ibid., p. 228.
[38] Ibid., p. 230.

own culture, that is, "for themselves." "They," writes Löwith, "are not with themselves in Being-other."[39] Lacking the cultural habit of deep self-scrutiny, the Japanese also failed to understand the dynamic inherent in the self-critical spirit of the West, which nevertheless transcended mere negativism. Though he identified a number of Western characteristics, he emphasized "individuality," that is, the capacity of the self to gain perspective on itself, and also to distinguish one's own self from others and from existing values and traditions.

According to Löwith, this Japanese failure derived ultimately from the Asian spirit that valued "life in an attunement that blurs boundaries; a unity between human beings and the natural world that lacks an opposite because it is grounded in mere feeling...." He cited Hegel on the "Greek spirit" as antithetical to this: "It does not know uniformity; it lives in a dispersion and multiplicity, which correspond to the variety of Greek peoples...."[40] The Greeks had possessed the spirit and curiosity to imagine themselves as "other" before taking that otherness into themselves and making it their own. In *My Life in Germany*, Löwith also identified in the Jews a capacity for "self-criticism" and the capacity to "do justice to something really different."[41] Indeed, the political implications of this deep individuality and diversity – which Löwith undoubtedly intended to apply to contemporary Europe and not just to ancient Greece – were "that we should not yield silently to world monarchies and theocracies like the *Orient*," and should resist "oppressive power which makes everything uniform, be it in the service of *one* state or *one* leveling intention...."[42]

Of course, Löwith's scarcely concealed reference here was to the contemporary world situation in which Nazi Germany and the Soviet Union vied for supremacy. (Such a passage indicates that Löwith saw the essence of National Socialism to lie in its desire to augment state power, not in its racial ideology.) His message also anticipated Arendt's later celebration of human plurality as an ontological condition. At the same time, however, Löwith's message *was* an example of "spiritual," that is, cultural, condescension. Even in its self-betrayal, the West was superior to Japan and the Orient, since it was aware of its own failure and demanded more of itself than it did of others. Finally, even one of the most perceptive among the German Jewish émigré thinkers remained wedded to the sense that the West in its darkest hour was, and should be, the object of emulation by other cultures.

5.3 From Asia to Africa, Orientalism to Africanism

Over the last three decades, thinking about the West's relationship to the Middle East and Asia has been dominated by Edward Said's *Orientalism* (1978). But Europe has created itself by creating its own Africa as well, an imaginary

---

[39] Löwith, *My Life in Germany*, p. 103; "European Nihilism," pp. 231–2.
[40] Löwith, "European Nihilism," p. 233.
[41] Löwith, *My Life in Germany*, p. 103.
[42] Ibid., p. 234.

entity quite differently imagined than the East.[43] In Hegel's *Philosophy of History*, one of the canonical sources of European cultural superiority, Asia was seen as the birthplace of civilization, even though its historical-cultural dominance was a thing of the past and its political legacy consisted of what would later be called "Oriental despotism." Hegel compared world-historical development down to and including the modern world to the course of individual development: Greece is the "adolescence" of the World Spirit, while the modern age represents its "Old Age" but also "its perfect maturity and strength."[44] Thus a paradox characterizes the Hegelian history of the Spirit. As the site of the "birth" of civilization, the Orient is prior to and older than the West, while the modern West is older insofar as it inherits and carries forward human self-consciousness that originated and developed elsewhere.

For Hegel, however, Africa had yet to attain historical or cultural status of any significance: "It is no historical part of the World" and is the "Unhistorical, Undeveloped Spirit." Reflecting the (modern) belief that Egypt lacked any essential tie with the rest of Africa, Hegel identified it as the site of the "passage of the human mind from its Eastern to its Western phase, but it does not belong to the African Spirit."[45] Sub-Saharan Africa had yet to enter history properly so-called, since it lacked the political entity called the state and thus could not be rightly named a "people" or set of "peoples." Africa thus stood *outside* the basic Greek-Aristotelian paradigm, according to which full humanity is defined by life in a law-governed polis or political unit.[46] Being historical and having a state were also linked with the relative closeness to/distance from nature and the relationship to sensory/sensual existence. This position did not deny human status to Africans nor claim that they were incapable, in principle, of attaining the levels of achieved by Europe. But it did suggest a strong distinction between the fundamental moral equality of all human beings and the hierarchy of "spiritual" (cultural) attainment with Europe at the pinnacle.[47] Indeed, this is an area where Arendt's evaluation of African culture echoed not only Hegel but

43 Though there is no comparable book that has defined the West's historical orientation toward Africa or Africa's response to Western intellectual and cultural penetration in the same way as Said's *Orientalism*; V. Y. Mudimbe's *The Invention of Africa: Gnosis, Philosophy, and the Order of Knowledge* (Bloomington and Indianapolis: Indiana University Press, 1988); and Kwame Anthony Appiah's *In My Father's House: Africa in the Philosophy of Culture* (New York: Oxford University Press, 1992), deserve much more attention than they have received.

44 G. W. F. Hegel, *The Philosophy of History* (London and New York: Colonial Press, 1900), pp. 106, 108–9.

45 Ibid., p. 99. See also Martin Bernal, *Black Athena: The Afroasiatic Roots of Classical Civilization* (London: Free Association, 1987).

46 See Ivan Hannaford, *Race: The History of an Idea in the West* (Washington and Baltimore: Wilson Press/Johns Hopkins University Press, 1996), p. 167, for the Greek origins of this essentially political understanding of what it means to be human, which is replaced by the "race" idea in the modern world.

47 To show the pervasiveness of this view of Africa(ns) in German thought, we need only to refer to Martin Heidegger. According to Robert Bernasconi, he shared "the longstanding idea that the Negro has no history," even though he did not, according to Sonia Sikka, entirely foreclose the possibility of blacks acquiring one. See Bernasconi, "Heidegger's Alleged Challenge to the Nazi

also Heidegger, though in *Origins*, she emphasized the absence both of lasting cultural achievement and of political existence under law in sub-Saharan Africa (*OT*, 177).

There were other, nonhistorical ways of conceptualizing the differences between Africans and Europeans in the German tradition. Kant traced racial differences back to climatic and geographical factors while objecting strongly to European imperial domination of other races. According to Kant, Africans and Americans (that is, Native Americans) were located at the bottom of the racial hierarchy.[48] In addition, a common distinction in German anthropology between *Kultur*- and *Naturvölker* emerged in the late nineteenth century. Such a typological distinction was combined with an evolutionary framework according to which "primitive" peoples could become "civilized" at some point in the future. In *Origins*, for instance, Arendt suggested that as Africans came into contact with European civilization through urban life and labor, they became more aware of their specifically human powers.[49]

Yet, there was also a tradition in German thought that took into account the specifically historical nature of African cultures rather than treating Africa as an undifferentiated mass of primitive beings whose life was enmeshed in sensory immediacy and lacked a sense of historical differentiation. The main source of this tradition was Johann Gottfried von Herder.[50] Herder's philosophy of culture was based on the idea that the essence of every culture develops in its own terms rather than in reference to a universal goal or essence, though there was also something like "humanity" shared by all people. As Isaiah Berlin has explained, *Fortgang* refers to "internal development of a culture in its own habitat, toward its own goals."[51] From this, it followed that each culture, equipped with reason and language, should be respected by other cultures. If there were such things as races, and Herder was reluctant to use the term, there were more than four or five. Besides, it was "language" that was the source of

Concept of Race," in T. Faulconer and M. Wrathall, eds., *Approaching Heidegger* (Cambridge: Cambridge University Press, 2000), p. 51; Sonia Sikka, "Heidegger and Race," in Robert Bernasconi with Sybol Cook, eds., *Race and Racism in Continental Philosophy* (Bloomington and Indianapolis: Indiana University Press, 2003), pp. 76–7. For Sikka, Heidegger's judgment is a "not yet" rather than a "never."

[48] Emmanuel Chukwudi Eze, ed., *Race and the Enlightenment* (Oxford: Blackwell, 1979), pp. 42–8, 58–64. For Kant's anti-imperialist views, see Muthu, *Enlightenment against Empire*, pp. 120–209. As David Krell has observed, we want Kant to be "transcendentally enlightened," even if "empirically benighted." See Krell, "The Bodies of Black Folk: From Kant and Hegel to Du Bois and Baldwin," *boundary* 2 ("Sociology Hesitant: Thinking with W. E. B. DuBois"), 27, 3 (Fall 2000): 109.

[49] For a wider discussion of this issue, see King, *Race, Culture and the Intellectuals*, pp. 115–19.

[50] Isaiah Berlin, "Herder and the Enlightenment," in *Vico and Herder: Two Studies in the History of Ideas* (New York: Vintage, 1977), pp. 143–216; Eze, *Race and the Enlightenment*, pp. 70–8; Muthu, "Pluralism, Humanity and Empire in Herder's Political Thought," in *Enlightenment against Empire*, pp. 210–58. Interestingly, Eze and Muthu consider Herder an Enlightenment thinker, while Berlin makes Herder's objection to abstract universalism central to his thought and thus one of the sources of Romanticism.

[51] Berlin, "Herder and the Enlightenment," p. 192.

differences among peoples.[52] In rejecting the "myth of the Dominant Model" – that is, the idea of one single trajectory of human development – Herder laid the groundwork for cultural relativism.[53] Put another way, Herder's legacy was to reject the idea that cultural differences also entailed cultural or racial hierarchy.

Like many Jews, Arendt was drawn to Herder's thought early in her career, since Herder was "fascinated by the survival of the Jews"[54] (Isaiah Berlin) and urged them to retain a link with their own history rather than jettisoning it for assimilation. Herder also emphasized the political nature of the "Jewish question," which appealed to Arendt, as did his general emphasis upon (cultural) diversity. One can easily see in Herder one of the sources of Arendt's lifelong commitment to plurality[55] and her resistance to identifying the state with any one race, religion, or ethnic group. According to Herder, concluded Berlin, "Nature creates nations not states."[56] Still, there remains a profound tension – and thus an ambiguity – in Herder's thought between "global diversity among nations" and "diversity within nations."[57] When a minority culture draws on Herder to justify its cultural rights within a polity, it is one thing. But when a majority culture uses Herder to assert its dominance within a state structure over various minority cultures, it is quite another. The latter implies that ethnic and racial diversity *within* a state – as opposed to *among* states – is not a desirable thing and that minorities have no cultural rights that the majority is bound to observe. Thus the notion of separate but equal cultures can be used to justify the "mono-ethnic state."[58] Indeed, by (illicitly) joining Herder and Hegel, the idea emerged that only in and through the state can a people enjoy full cultural development, a view that seemed to preoccupy German thought in particular.

Overall, what was most striking about the European/German view of Africa was the profound ignorance that informed it. Africa's alleged lack of a history and of its absence from the history of the Spirit were more plausibly traced back to European ignorance of African history than to anything inherent in the history of Africa itself. As already emphasized, Arendt very much shared the idea that the cultures of sub-Saharan Africa were culturally underdeveloped. But she did break decisively with the idea that the state should be linked to

---

[52] Muthu, "Pluralism, Humanity and Empire in Herder's Political Thought," pp. 245–6, 249.

[53] Berlin, "Herder and the Enlightenment," p. 189.

[54] Ibid.

[55] Ibid., p. 159. For Arendt on Herder, see Elizabeth Young-Bruehl, *For Love of the World* (New Haven: Yale University Press, 1982), pp. 93–4, 304. There are several references to Herder in *Origins* and even more in her *Rahel Varnhagen: The Life of a Jewess*, edited by Liliane Weissberg (Baltimore: Johns Hopkins University Press, 1997). See also, Arendt, "The Enlightenment and the Jewish Question," in Jerome Kohn and Ron H. Feldman, eds., *The Jewish Writings* (New York: Schocken, 2007), pp. 11–16.

[56] Berlin, "Herder and the Enlightenment," p. 158.

[57] Muthu, *Enlightenment against Empire*, p. 224.

[58] See Sikka, "Heidegger and Race," for a discussion of this in relationship to nonracial interpretations of Heidegger's thought.

cultural, ethnic, and religious homogeneity or that it had any sort of cultural mission.

5.4 Race, Theory, and History: Arendt and Voegelin

In focusing on Arendt's relationship with Eric Voegelin, we move from drawing parallels between Arendt and her contemporaries to considering a direct influence on her thinking about race, though how much is difficult to determine with any precision. For instance, Arendt's essay "Race-Thinking before Racism" (1944), which appeared in *Review of Politics*, cited Voegelin's *Race and State* (1933) in a footnote that appeared in the chapter of the same name in *Origins*: "The best historical account of race-thinking in the pattern of a 'history of ideas' is Erich Voegelin, *Rasse und Staat*, Tuebingen, 1933."[59] After the publication of *Origins*, she wrote to Karl Jaspers that Voegelin's *New Science of Politics* (1952) was "important," though it had taken "a wrong turn." Then, two notes in her essay "Religion and Politics" (1953) referred to the importance of Voegelin's *The Political Religions* (1938) and again to *The New Science of Politics*. Although Voegelin's review of *Origins* claimed that it was infected with the same gnosticism that he saw as the downfall of modern Europe and Arendt responded with considerable force to this critique, the two thinkers apparently became good friends, to the degree that Arendt was one of the editors of a 1962 *Festschrift* for Voegelin.[60] Overall, aside from this one mention of Voegelin's book on race, Arendt's explicit references to Voegelin's work concerned the relationship of politics and religion and his theory of modernity, matters only tangentially related to the issue of race. Neither thinker even mentioned the topic of race in their exchange on *Origins*, aside from Arendt's explanation of why she had avoided a conventional treatment of antisemitism. Most interesting in Arendt's response to Voegelin was her rejection of what might be called his "essentializing" of modernity as uniformly a product of gnosticism as opposed to her emphasis upon the history of modernity as shaped by "facts" and "events."

Voegelin's works on race written while he still lived in Austria have been both controversial and seriously neglected. According to David Levy, Voegelin offered what was perhaps the only intellectually respectable attempt in German-speaking Europe to analyze what he called the "race concept" and the "race

---

[59] See *OT*, 158, note 3, and Hannah Arendt, "Race-Thinking before Racism," *Review of Politics*, 6, 1 (January 1944): 37, note 2.

[60] Actually, Arendt's letter was directed to Gertrud Jaspers, whom she asked to inquire whether her husband had read Voegelin's *The New Science of Politics*. See *Hannah Arendt–Karl Jaspers Briefwechsel, 1926–1969*, edited by Lotte Koehler and Hans Saner (Munchen: Piper Verlag, 1985), p. 240; Arendt, "Religion and Politics, and "A Reply to Eric Voegelin," in *Essays in Understanding*, notes 10 and 11, and pp. 401–8; Eric Voegelin, "The Origins of Totalitarianism (1953)," in *The Collected Works of Eric Voegelin (Published Essays 1953–1965*, Vol. 11, edited and introduced by Ellis Sandoz (Columbia and London: University of Missouri Press, 2000), pp. 15–23.

idea."[61] A political philosopher influenced by Max Weber and especially Max Scheler's philosophical anthropology, Voegelin wrote at the beginning of "The Growth of the Race Idea":

And finally we do not intend to deal with the problem of political and social relationships between the white and colored races. . . . we have in mind chiefly the idea as it is used by modern creeds of the type of National Socialism, in order to integrate the community spiritually and politically.[62]

Once in the United States, Voegelin never actually dealt with the race issue in print, something that may be linked to the fact that he taught at Louisiana State University, a Deep South university, until his return to Germany in the late 1950s. In America, he was considered one of the philosophical mentors of post-1945 conservative intellectuals and exerted particular influence over southern conservatives such as Cleanth Brooks and Richard Weaver and helped shape the thinking of Catholic writers such as Walker Percy and Flannery O'Connor. Even his engagement with the issue of antisemitism over the rest of his career was, in fact, pretty minimal.

Both *Race and State* and *History of the Race Idea* appeared in 1933 while Voegelin was teaching in Vienna, and they were eventually withdrawn since they were at odds with Nazi racial orthodoxy and thus too controversial. Still, it is difficult to explain the serious neglect of his work on race since then.[63] Levy has recently suggested several reasons for this, one of them being the fact that Voegelin's work is difficult and confusingly organized. It is also difficult for many scholars in the post-Holocaust world to take an intellectually rigorous analysis of racial theory seriously.[64] But Levy suggests that Voegelin's work reminds us of the degree to which race was once a respectable topic in Western thought. Overall, "race studies" in Anglophone countries was handled in sociology and anthropology (not to mention psychology and biology) departments, while in Germany, the West's most philosophically advanced nation, race was also dealt with by philosophers, theorists of the human sciences, and philosophically inclined historians.

Though I want to explore Voegelin's influence on Arendt primarily, the overall shape of Voegelin's work on race needs clarification. Levy has suggested that

[61] Eric Voegelin, "The Growth of the Race Idea," *Review of Politics* (July 1940): 283.

[62] Ibid., p. 283.

[63] This is true even of Voegelin specialists and of historians of racial thought, at least until Ivan Hannaford's *Race: The History of the Idea in the West* (1996), in which Voegelin and Arendt were central to the author's conceptual framework. See also Thomas Heilke, *Voegelin on the Idea of Race: An Analysis of Modern European Racism* (Baton Rouge: Louisiana State University Press, 1990); and "Science, Philosophy, and Resistance: On Eric Voegelin's Practice of Opposition," *Review of Politics*, 56, 4 (Autumn 1994): 727–52; David J. Levy, "Ethos and Ethnos: An Introduction to Eric Voegelin's Critique of European Racism," Bernasconi with Cook, eds., *Race and Racism in European Philosophy*, pp. 98–114. A recent intellectual biography of Voegelin follows suit in avoiding the race issue. See Michael P. Federici, *Eric Voegelin: The Restoration of Order* (Wilmington, DL: ISI, 2002).

[64] Levy, "Ethos and Ethnos," pp. 98–101.

there are at least four analytical levels to Voegelin's analysis. First there is "the empirical fact of race or ethnic differences," that is, the sociology of race. Second is "the political idea of race as a mobilizing principle," which belongs to political science (what Voegelin called "the race idea"). Third, Voegelin was concerned with the possibility of an "explanatory science of race," or the "race concept." And, fourth, he wanted to develop a "philosophically adequate theory of race," something he felt would only emerge from an adequate philosophical anthropology.[65]

But while Voegelin believed a philosophically adequate notion of race might be achievable, it had been hindered by a mid-nineteenth century shift from considering race in terms of a complex interaction among body, mind, and spirit to considering it in purely biological and materialistic terms. Indeed, Voegelin was much opposed to the idea that race was a purely biological entity. As he wrote in *Race and State*:

> ...we have not the least doubt that there are connections between body, soul, and mind; we are fully convinced that blood inheritance is of paramount importance to man's total spiritual nature; but we are equally convinced that this significance can only be discovered by the most thorough inquiry into the mental structure itself.[66]

It is worth noting Voegelin's ambivalence in this passage. On the one hand, all three dimensions – body, mind, and spirit – are crucial to the formation of a race, yet he stresses the particular importance of "blood inheritance."[67] In addition, he rejected the vast majority of National Socialist theorizing about race, insofar as it was crudely materialistic, that is, based purely on biology. However, not all National Socialists believed in a purely biological theory of race, and some, such as Heidegger, explicitly rejected such a position. Voegelin himself acknowledged this, at least as regards antisemitism.[68]

Specifically, theories of race that *sounded* biological sometimes referred to what Alan Steinweis refers to as "race of the second order,"[69] that is, a people of mixed race that over time had became a *Volk*. In fact, the difference between *Rasse* and *Volk* was never very clear in Nazi ideology, which tended to make heavier use of the latter than the former term. However, there was an ominous aspect to the idea that race was a composite rather than purely biological entity, since it made it easier to think of a race as something to be constructed rather than already fixed by descent from common ancestors. Sophisticated National

---

[65] Ibid., p. 110.

[66] *The Collected Works of Eric Voegelin* [*Race and State*], Vol. 2, edited and introduced by Klaus Vondung (Baton Rouge and London: Louisiana State University Press, 1997), p. 86.

[67] Levy downplays Voegelin's clear emphasis on the biological in passages such as this. Of course, the idea that race was in part but not entirely a biological entity was still common in the rest of Europe and the United States. For instance, W. E. B. DuBois held such a view, as did many a good number of Jews.

[68] See Voegelin, "The Growth of the Race Idea," p. 309, where he notes the noncoincidence in Nazi ideology of racial spirit and biology. See also Alan E. Steinweis, *Studying the Jew: Scholarly Antisemitism in Nazi Germany* (Cambridge, MA.: Harvard University Press, 2006).

[69] Steinweis, *Studying the Jew*, p. 41.

Socialist racial ideology tended to be future- rather than past-oriented. Thus it was a radical, not a conservative, ideology to the extent that it proposed policies for "constructing" Aryans, as it were. Thus, Voegelin's work, itself contemp-tuous of the crudity of most Nazi racial ideologists, was hardly unambiguously harmless in its implications for the Nazi idea of race in Nazi Germany.[70]

Still, Voegelin's work shaped the way Arendt treated race in *Origins*. For instance, there she focused on what Voegelin referred to as race as an "idea," that is, as a "symbol" to mobilize and consolidate political opinion. She was not at all concerned with its "scientific" status or whether it was "empirically verifiable," since it was, asserted Voegelin, "not the function of an idea to describe social reality, but to assist in its constitution."[71] On the other hand, at the end of the "Race-Thinking before Racism" chapter in *Origins*, Arendt got in a dig at Voegelin when she insisted that "it is not the history of an idea endowed by some 'immanent logic' with which we are concerned" (*OT*, 185).[72] The term "immanent logic" alludes to Voegelin's focus on the purely secular-historical nature of modernity. Moreover, Arendt firmly objected to the notion that racial totalitarianism was an ersatz religion and thus a replacement for Christianity, while Voegelin made such a notion central to his understand-ing of political religion. For him, race as an idea – that is, race as a way of organizing and manipulating political identity – was a distinctively modern response to the decline of Christianity.[73] That said, Arendt *did* correlate the emergence of biological racism in the late nineteenth century with the decline of religious antisemitism. Moreover, in Chapter 9 of *Origins,* she also suggested in several cryptic formulations that race was the last in a series of attempts to provide a foundation for human nature and a lasting political and social order. But Arendt's analysis hinged much more directly upon historical events (for example, the *fact* of the camps) rather than whether modern ideas of race emerged inexorably from the "immanent logic" of modernity.

Even though Arendt was correct that Voegelin's emphasis fell upon the logic of ideas in history, his work did sometimes allude to historical forces and trends. His explanation of the strength of racial politics in Germany in comparison with Britain and France was that German unification emerged in the latter part of the century when Darwinism and biological science in general enjoyed tremendous prestige. This contrasted with the emergence of liberal democracies

---

[70] This future orientation of a constructivist theory of race is suggested by Helmut Walser Smith, "The Talk of Genocide, the Rhetoric of Miscegenation: Notes on Debates in the German Reichstag Concerning Southwest Africa, 1904–1914," in Sara Friedrichsmeyer et al., eds., *The Imperialist Imagination: German Colonialism and Its Legacy* (Ann Arbor: University of Michigan Press, 1998), 107–23.

[71] Voegelin, "The Growth of the Race Idea," p. 284.

[72] Arendt does not footnote the allusion and added the closing paragraph to the original article when it became part of *Origins*.

[73] For Arendt's rejection of this functionalist view of totalitarianism as an ersatz religion, see her "Reply to Eric Voegelin," pp. 406–7. Voegelin makes clear the post-Christian importance of race in "The Growth of the Race Idea," pp. 302–4.

in the late eighteenth century, when the dominant political language had to do with natural rights and other liberal-republican notions. Nor did Voegelin see anything inevitable in a metahistorical or spiritual sense about the prominent role that race thinking and racism played in German political thought. Indeed, in most European fascist movements, including Mussolini's fascism, race had not been the central focus or motivating force. Overall, then, he suggested that the eighteenth-century nation-states made "personal freedom" central and presupposed a "spiritual and corporeal unity," while those he designated as "imperial peoples," such as Germany and Italy, believed that the essence of a particular group preexisted and overrode rights or other aspects of liberal institutions. Thus French and American polities did not depend exclusively on a racial or ethnic understanding of the idea of "the people" to give them coherence, while the idea of Germany rested on a racial-ethnic notion of *das Volk*.[74]

In general, Voegelin placed almost no emphasis upon the causal importance of imperialism and colonialism in the development of European and German racial thought. Yet, he did anticipate, and perhaps helped shape, Arendt's general contention that the geographical-historical expansion of Europe had increased racial consciousness in the modern world. He noted that in the eighteenth century, "the white race [was] the normal type" and the rest were "exotic variations." The eighteenth and early nineteenth century, noted Voegelin, still applied the notion of race "with significant hesitations."[75] This is all very reminiscent of Arendt's distinction between "race-thinking," which she contended preserved a common humanity in spite of racial differences, and "racism," which posited a fundamental inequality among races. The binary opposition Voegelin proposed to capture this difference referred to "open" versus "closed" historical settings. Racism, he contended, flourished when openness to the "transcendental point of union" was undermined by the process of secularization and the purely "mundane" or "immanent" connections among individuals might express themselves in exclusivist forms of union such as race.[76] He also observed that Arthur de Gobineau's thought arose in the vacuum left by the extermination of the French aristocracy, an idea that Arendt developed in *Origins*. But most interestingly, he suggested that racism and nationalism were potentially inimical to one another: "a consistent racial policy would destroy the national unit from within."[77] With this, Voegelin anticipated one

---

[74] Voegelin, "The Growth of the Race Idea," pp. 286–90; 310–12. His emphasis upon the importance of the "bodily" in formulating ideas of the political – for example, the "mystic body" of Christ or the "body politic" – reminds us that an emphasis on the body in politics is no guarantee of a progressive or egalitarian politics.

[75] Ibid., p. 296. We might think here of Jefferson's hesitancy in *Notes on Virginia* to assign clear inferiority to people with black skin, however subjectively certain he may have been of that inferiority.

[76] Voegelin, "The Growth of the Race Idea," p. 303.

[77] Ibid., p. 300. Arendt initially emphasized this point in her discussion of racism and nationalism in the ideology of Pan-Slavism and related movements. See *OT*, 223.

of Arendt's most radical, and still least understood, points about the relationship between Nazi racial ideology and "normal" state-based nationalism – that after a point they undermined rather than reenforced one another.

Voegelin's work was provocative in other areas. All but abandoning his general agnosticism on the topic, he expressed doubt that the Jews "are a race at all in any reasonable meaning of the word." Yet he also suggested that "the idea that men are different, and that their differences may be due to differences in their biological structure, is not more unrealistic than the idea that all men are equal." Overall, then, Voegelin contended that both belief in the causal efficacy of race *and* the dismissal of this belief tended to be presuppositions brought to, rather then conclusions to be drawn from, "sense data and quantitative analysis."[78]

None of this is to say that Arendt's conceptions of race thinking and racism were derived mechanically from Voegelin's work. If nothing else, her discussion of antisemitism was much more morally charged and sociologically and historically nuanced than his. Her interest lay in understanding the social-historical psychology of Jewish assimilation and their reception by Gentile society rather than tracing the intellectual history of race as it reflected the loss of the spiritual dimension to modern life. Overall, what she most clearly took from Voegelin's thought was a heightened understanding of the powerful social and political function that the "race idea" had in European modernity.

5.5 Arendt and Her Contemporaries

Though Arendt came to intellectual and spiritual maturity in the midst of the crisis of religious faith and of secular reason, she seems to have been immune to the alternatives – whether race or Greek reason, the proletariat or *Volk*, God or History, Jerusalem or Athens – over which her contemporaries often agonized. What Max Weber once said of himself – that he was religiously "tone-deaf" – may also, I think, be applied to Arendt. Indeed, it was not so much the spiritual dimension of the crisis of modernity, but the *instantiation* of nihilism in the camps that most haunted her.

As we have seen, Arendt also rejected any conception of history as the working out of the logic of an idea or ideas. Arendt's rejection of the philosophy of history or a theory of progress in particular made it *more* difficult for her to speak in terms of a master narrative of Western superiority. Though at times her analysis of modernity sounded like it derived from a typical conservative "decline" narrative, her *On Revolution* (1963) was devoted to an account of the modern emergence of a "different" (and preferable) tradition of revolution from the Jacobin-Leninist one, though her neglect of the Haitian Revolution has been noted.[79]

---

[78] Ibid., pp. 309, 312, 313.

[79] In his *Conscripts of Modernity: The Tragedy of Colonial Enlightenment* (Durham and London: Duke University Press, 2004), David Scott wonders about Arendt's "curious 'silencing'... of

To be specific about the theme at issue here, Arendt certainly never championed Western imperialism or colonialism; nor did she elevate Western thought and culture above the other great world cultures. Even before the Holocaust, the German mission to revitalize the Western tradition failed to impress her or win her assent. In a 1933 letter to Karl Jaspers, she rejected Max Weber's (and Jasper's) exceptionalist view of the German commitment to "reason" and "humanity" while still identifying herself with the German "mother tongue, philosophy and poetry."[80] Three decades later, she answered her own question of "what remains?" with "the language remains. . . . It wasn't the German language that went crazy. . . ."[81] She was strongly opposed to organizing political and legal institutions, much less understanding the history of her time, in terms of race, ethnicity, religion, or ideology. Equality was for her a crucial *political* concept, whatever else might be said about equality among human beings and human cultures as such. For Arendt, it was disastrous to have a polity in which some citizens had more rights, more privileges and immunities, than others did, whatever their race or ethnicity.

Finally, as we have seen, it was the historical threat that sheer racial and cultural variety posed to belief in the unity of humanity that concerned Arendt. Unlike Leo Strauss and most of the other German Jewish émigré intellectuals of whatever political ideology, she was deeply worried by the state of race relations in the United States and in Africa. A partial explanation for her mistaken analysis of the Little Rock School Crisis of 1957 was the desire to protect social and cultural diversity against state power by defending the right of white parents to send their children to the school of their choice – but at the expense, of course, of the right of black parents to send their children to integrated schools. In the early 1960s, she corresponded with Jaspers about the importance of publicly recognizing those who worked for better race relations in South Africa and the United States. Then, later on in the 1960s, she was scathing about what she felt were racist political, educational, and cultural demands of Black Power advocates. It is a long way from the late-nineteenth-century "heart of darkness" of Europeans in Africa to Little Rock, Arkansas, and to the racially explosive American cities of the late 1960s. We will probably never know whether and how Arendt linked them together, whether her responses were determined by the specifics of the historical situation or whether she had some sort of blind spot concerning people of African descent.

---

the Haitian Revolution, her complete elision of it and its place in the story of the revolutionary tradition and its legacy" (p. 217).

[80] The terms she used were *Vernunftigkeit* and *Menschlichkeit*. See Arendt's letter of January 1, 1933, to Jaspers in *Hannah Arendt—Karl Jaspers: Briefwechsel 1926–1969*, p. 52.

[81] Arendt, "'What Remains? The Language Remains': A Conversation with Gunter Gaus," in *Essays in Understanding*, pp. 12–13. One of the missing concepts in Arendt's thought – and perhaps in modern Western thought – is some cultural equivalent of political citizenship. One's political and cultural homes are a mixture of contingent circumstances and explicit choices. The modern appeal of race and ethnicity has been in part an attempt to give people a sense of cultural belonging.

Finally, it is also important that we become more complex and careful in our understanding of these matters of racial and cultural difference. It is disappointing that contemporary intellectuals and academics fail to explore with greater complexity the persisting claims about the cultural superiority of the West *and* the automatic preference for cultural relativism. In neither case do the positions seem to be particularly well thought through. One of the points I have wanted to make here is that claims about the superiority of the West have historically hardly been intellectual "slips of the tongue" or mere afterthoughts. The assumption of its superiority has been – and remains – central to the very idea of the West. That it is so rarely challenged on whatever grounds testifies to the fear many have of being called "cultural relativists."

On the other hand, it is also important to recognize that belief in Western cultural superiority does not necessarily entail support for Western imperialism and the right to dominate other cultures that are "weaker" or allegedly less "developed." Nor, for that matter, were or are all opponents of imperialism firm advocates of cultural or racial equality. Just as most abolitionists, not to mention Abraham Lincoln, did not believe in black equality in the modern sense, but still worked to destroy slavery, so Arendt and (some of) her contemporaries could indict imperialism and colonialism, yet speak of African people and culture in what seem to be stereotypical ways. Finally, the question to ask is whether and to what extent such judgments invalidate the rest of her thought on racial and cultural concerns. Interestingly, many African studies specialists both acknowledge the problematic nature of Arendt's views and recognize the importance of her early effort to link European imperialism with totalitarianism in Europe and racist colonial societies in Africa, not to mention the importance of her thought for analyzing the historical and political importance of truth, reconciliation, and forgiveness in the recent history of Africa.[82] Perhaps the answer is to learn to distinguish Arendt's own particular positions (and biases) from what might be called an Arendtian position on these matters.

[82] See King and Stone, eds., *Hannah Arendt and the Uses of History*, particularly the chapters by Elisa von Joeden-Forgey and Christopher Lee and the Conclusion by Richard H. King.

PART II

SOVEREIGNTY, THE NATION-STATE, AND THE RULE OF LAW

6

Banishing the Sovereign?

Internal and External Sovereignty in Arendt

Andrew Arato and Jean L. Cohen

According to Hannah Arendt, "the great and, in the *long run*, perhaps the greatest American innovation in politics as such was the consistent abolition of sovereignty within the body politic of the republic, the insight that in the realm of human affairs sovereignty and tyranny are the same."[1] This statement can profitably be put together with Hans Kelsen's 1920 "Die Souveränitätsvorstellung freilich muss radikal verdrängt werden."[2] He best explained this idea twenty-five years later, when he defined (as before) sovereignty as the nonderivability of the domestic legal order from, and its supremacy over, all other sources of law, including and even in particular international law. Under a sovereignty regime, international law gains its validity only because it is so recognized by a domestic system, and the laws of *other* domestic systems, even more indirectly, are seen as valid only because of the requirements of international law. Sovereignty regimes are thus epistemologically solipsistic, and politically even worse, potentially. "A person whose political attitude is nationalism and imperialism will naturally be inclined to accept the hypothesis of the primacy of national law. A person whose sympathies are for internationalism and pacifism will be inclined to accept the hypothesis of the primacy of international law."[3] The latter will therefore seek (politically, or morally at least) to suppress sovereignty regimes.

---

[1] Hannah Arendt, *On Revolution* (1963) (London: Penguin, 1990), p. 153. (Hereafter abbreviated *OR*.)

[2] Hans Kelsen, *Das Problem der Souveränität* (1920) (2nd unchanged ed. Tübingen: J.C. B. Mohr, 1928), p. 320. Chapter 2 defines *sovereignty*; see especially pp. 97–8. See P. Caldwell, *Popular Sovereignty and the Crisis of German Constitutional Law* (Durham: Duke University Press, 1997), pp. 90–1. The essential point regarding the absence of sovereignty if there is a primacy of international law is already made in *Das Problem der Souveränität* on p. 40, and in detail in the second part.

[3] Hans Kelsen, *General Theory of State and Law* (Cambridge: Harvard University Press, 1945), pp. 383–8. As he often explained, he interpreted such statements as political rather than

An earlier version of this piece has appeared in *Constellations. A Journal of Critical and Democratic Theory*, 16, 2 (June 2009): 307–31.

Leaving for another occasion consideration of Kelsen's remarkable though not wholly convincing argumentation for this position, we note that the two perspectives, his and Arendt's, could be seen as entirely incompatible or as complementary. Arendt's statement is about supposed historical fact, whereas Kelsen's is about a moral-political norm rather than a legal norm. An unconvincing way of reconciling them would be to say that what is both *fact* and a *norm* in America is mere *norm* elsewhere, and Arendt's appeal to "the long run" seems to suggest such a relationship between a model and its desired normative influence. But it is doubtful that Kelsen would have thought that in the period of the rejection of the League of Nations or at the time of the founding of the United Nations Americans were not confronted with the same fateful choice as other states. More relevant here is that it is very clear that Arendt considers the American abolition of sovereignty to pertain to *internal* affairs only, first, because she explicitly says "within the body politic," and second because she even implies (very rightly) that the point or one of the points of forming a more perfect union was to enhance *external* sovereignty. The task was to "reconcile the advantages of monarchy in foreign affairs with those of republicanism in domestic policy" (*OR*, 152). It would be absurd to call this a chance or careless remark, given that the correspondence of its thrust with the intentions of the authors of *The Federalist* had to be entirely clear to Arendt.[4]

To Kelsen, however, the suppression of sovereignty would mean that the supremacy of international law would be established vis-à-vis both the internal and external legal orders of states. More classically, then, he considered the external and internal dimensions of sovereignty to be inseparable.[5] On the

---

"scientific." The pure theory of law is equally compatible with nationalism and internationalism, imperialism, and pacifism. We do not agree, nor would have Hannah Arendt, with such a sharp distinction between the two cognitive attitudes, ideology and knowledge. See, e.g., Hans Kelsen, "Legal Formalism and the Pure Theory of Law" (1929), in B. Schlink and A. Jacobson, eds., *Weimar: A Jurisprudence of Crisis* (Berkeley: University of California Press, 2000).

[4] To state the obvious, that is what the first nine papers written by Jay and Hamilton were all about: the meaning of and reasons for constructing a sufficiently large, united, organized federal state or a union that would be able compete with all other states on an equal basis if that was required. In general, the *Federalist Papers* handles the question of sovereignty from this point of view, and to the extent that previously independent sovereignties had to be surrendered and pooled in a new sovereignty to achieve it. Even Madison's (#39) famous discussion of the mixing of national and federal elements in the Union belongs in this context, and so does the idea of what came to be called "direct effect" (#s15,16, as we can see in #39) of the federal government acting on individuals rather than the states. Admittedly, it is difficult to portray the latter as not being sovereignty in internal affairs, but as we will see, Arendt's critique is directed at an entirely different level of sovereignty. Even direct effect could be understood as part of the state sovereignty that is at the same time external and internal, and Hamilton's argument against a federation that does not have direct effect is that its members then remain in an international law relation, where only warlike coercion can enforce compliance. Direct effect then creates a domestic space from a previous international space. There is thus a good case to be made for sovereignty being in general an international law category in the *Federalist Papers*.

[5] Kelsen, *Das Problem der Souveränität*, p. 38.

other hand, in his two cited works, assuming sovereignty, its suppression in the internal life of the state would be without meaning. There is no way, by definition, that he can thus explore the internal constitutional conditions required for the abolition of "sovereignty." And that is just the strength of Arendt's reconstruction of American history, or at least of the path that her reconstruction commences though hardly completes. If she does not explore what in the internal constitutional design's link to sovereignty promotes imperialism, Kelsen could not in principle do so.[6]

6.1 The Abolition of Sovereignty?

What did Arendt's famous statement really mean? It is certainly not difficult to discover why she thought sovereignty and tyranny were the same in human affairs.

Arendt saw the discourse of sovereignty (including popular sovereignty) as the claim to control, rule, and assert jurisdictional supremacy by an undivided, single political instance within a territorial body politic. Sovereignty, in short, is construed as a matter of the assertion of the will, as the command and ultimate discretion of an uncommanded commander who is *legibus solutus* – the source of law and so unbound by law – thus arbitrary, hierarchical, leveling, homogenizing, and solipsistic by definition (*OR*, 30–1). To her, the discourse of sovereignty is deeply antipolitical. It is the discourse of rule and domination (a projection from the sort of *dominium* characteristic of paternalistic rule over a household). Its unifying logic involves the attempt to conjure away the ineluctable contingency and plurality of political action and the public sphere. The concept of freedom associated with the ideal of sovereignty is freedom of the unimpeded will, an uncompromising self-sufficiency and mastership divorced from action in concert.[7] It is liberty, "freedom of choice," ultimately

---

[6] Entirely independent of his views of sovereignty, Kelsen was hostile to the presidential government that will play a key role in this chapter, a form that he considered between democracy and autocracy and close to a monarchical form. Kelsen, *General Theory of State and Law*, p. 301. The only place where his political fears were clearly articulated on this score was in the 1931 debate with Schmitt concerning constitutional guardianship: "Wer soll der Hüter der Verfassung sein?" *Die Justiz* 6(1930–1): 576–628. Kelsen's quest to suppress sovereignty has recently been interpreted as bringing the state entirely under the heading of legal order. M. Loughlin, "Ten Tenets of Sovereignty," in N. Walker, ed., *Sovereignty in Transition* (Oxford: Hart, 2003), pp. 76–7. But (aside from the fact that Kelsen did not interpret his idea this way) in itself this move could, in his system given its permissive definition of the "rule of law," mean the opposite, depending on a particular *Grundnorm* (e.g., act so as the father of the Constitution, the absolute monarch, has willed), namely bringing law entirely under the rule of a will. Even H. L. A. Hart's critique of sovereignty (*Concept of Law* [Oxford: Oxford University Press, 1961], chapter IV) does not eliminate the possibility of "organ" or "ruler" sovereignty; it only makes it unnecessary from the point of view of the existence of a legal order. At least he thematizes what would be the meaning of the elimination of internal sovereignty in Arendt's sense.

[7] Hannah Arendt, *The Human Condition*, (New York: University of Chicago Press, 1958) p. 234. (Hereafter abbreviated *HC*.)

in a monological sense, as opposed to political freedom in a republic, a concept that is inseparable from acting and speaking in the public sphere.[8]

Thus sovereignty (rule) and politics (no rule) are antithetical; the former is monological, the latter communicative or at least interactive. The former involves the solipsistic freedom and assertion of the will, and as such is antithetical to freedom, plurality, and the exercise of political judgment by a multiplicity of actors communicating, deliberating, and acting together in concert. Sovereignty involves command and obedience; it is an institution of rulership and political hierarchy, not equality (*OR*, 30–1).

Sovereignty is thus antithetical to the rule of law, *political* plurality, and the existence of counterpowers, equal citizenship, and ultimately constitutionalism itself. Accordingly, sovereignty, at least in internal matters, is unbridled discretion – that is, tyranny (today we would say dictatorship).

Arendt in addition understood sovereignty as by definition absolute and linked irrevocably to an embodiment model of representation and thus locatable in one single political instance. It makes no difference whether sovereignty is asserted by the king, by a parliament, or in the name of the people. In every case, this discourse unleashes the attempt to appropriate it by a single "representative" instance and thus leads to tyranny and the abolition of politics and the rule of law. For her, the discourse of popular or national sovereignty does not avoid this dynamic, as evidenced by the case of the French Revolution, for it too is perforce a discourse of the will – in this case, the indivisible general will, which must be unitary and homogeneous (*OR*, 156).[9] Will and power set above the law as the source of law can refer to "the people" as well as to "the king." The attempt of continental democratic theory and practice, from Rousseau to Sieyès and Carl Schmitt, to put the sovereignty of people in the place of the king involved the correlate that as the constituent power, the people are prior to and unbound by law, hence able to change the constitution through revolution when they so will.

In Arendt's view too, popular sovereignty as the revolutionaries understood it led inexorably to what Claude Lefort has called the embodiment model of representation first articulated by Sieyès.[10] Since the people cannot rule directly in modern society, their sovereignty must be represented, that is, embodied by a single political instance, be it an assembly, a committee, or a president, who, as sovereign representative, tends to appropriate the political for itself or himself, to the exclusion of all other actors. The outcome is equally disastrous for political plurality and freedom as it would be under an absolute monarchical

---

[8] Hannah Arendt, "What Is Freedom," in *Between Past and Future* (New York: Penguin, 1968), pp. 143–71.

[9] Ibid., p. 156. "What else did Sieyès do but simply put the sovereignty of the nation into the place which had been vacated by a sovereign king?"

[10] Claude Lefort, "Permanence du theologico-politique," *Essais sur le politique* (Paris: du Seuill, 1986). We will develop this view in relation to the concept of organ sovereignty in Raymond Carré de Malberg, *Contribution à la Théorie générale de l'état* (Paris: Editions Dalloz, 2004), pp. 199–410.

sovereignty. Thus the continental theory of popular sovereignty, and especially the concept of constituent power, is a receipt for arbitrariness, populist distortion of republican principles and an invitation to an institutional organ, be it the legislative assembly or the executive, to claim to embody the will and unity of the people, ultimately undermining both the rule of law and political freedom. The discourse of popular sovereignty is, like monarchical sovereignty, associated with the absolute and with unity and hence ultimately incompatible with constitutionalism. Accordingly, Arendt wanted to be done with the discourse of sovereignty altogether. She wanted to keep the place of sovereign power empty.[11]

It is quite significant to affirm that, given her own normative theory, this train of thought does not tautologically put Arendt in opposition to "external sovereignty." This is so, first, because presenting a united front ("the advantages of monarchy") toward the outside does not, in spite of the contrary logic of Carl Schmitt's argument (in *Concept of the Political*[12]), exclude the public, deliberative interaction domestically of equal citizens who initially disagree as long as there are mechanisms allowing the generation and enforcement of collective decisions. And it is also the case, second, because Arendt never described or imagined external "politics" as *political* in her demanding sense of the term. That may leave her and us with the lamentable conclusion that, in external affairs too (where states are often seen as kinds of super-individuals or supermen – see also H. L. A. Hart's *Concept of Law*[13]), sovereignty is tyranny at least with respect to states incapable of full sovereignty, a conclusion Arendt seemed to draw in the context of late-nineteenth-century imperialism[14] without insisting or at least settling on either of the two obvious remedies implied by Kelsen's quest to abolish sovereignty, both of which will be discussed in the conclusion: world government and sovereign equality.

The conceptual link between external and internal sovereignty is nevertheless strong, in spite of Arendt's concept of the political that seems to sever it. There is much to recommend the historically dominant view in legal theory, articulated by Carré de Malberg, for example, that internal and external sovereignty must be treated as inseparable and even identical.[15] According to this view, a state indeed could not be supreme at home if it had a state that was its external superior, whose legislators or decision makers could then use whatever advantages they had to dictate the foreign policy of the dependent state to dictate

---

[11] Lefort, "Permanence du theologico-politique."

[12] Carl Schmitt, *Concept of the Political* (New Jersey: Rutgers, 1976).

[13] Hart, *Concept of Law*, pp. 215–21.

[14] Hannah Arendt, *The Origins of Totalitarianism* (1951, 1968) (New York: Harcourt, 1994), pp. 269–70 (hereafter abbreviated *OT*): "Modern power conditions . . . make national sovereignty a mockery except for giant states, the rise of imperialism and the pan-movements undermined the stability of Europe's nation state system from the outside."

[15] Carré de Malberg, *Contribution à la théorie générale de l'état*, I, pp. 70–2. It is easy to retranslate this point to a conception of sovereignty like Kelsen's, where sovereignty has to do only with the question of which legal order is supreme. See footnote 3.

its internal policies as well. The means of violence used to enforce each are the same, even if, for pragmatic reasons, they are used in one case and not the other. Leaving aside when the break really occurred, the Canadian federation, for example, was not sovereign as long as Canada was under a colonial status. The East and Central European satellites of the Soviet Union were also not sovereign at home. A sovereign state is a supreme political organization that has not only inferiors internally (supremacy) but also at most equals externally (independence). Inequality externally vitiates the supremacy internally. Conversely, however, can a state be at least equal to all others abroad if it is not supreme at home? The classical theory would have denied this also, and this is another reason for the inseparability of external and internal sovereignty. But how could then Arendt imagine that external sovereignty could be erected and maintained in America without internal sovereignty?

In her spirit, Arendt's efforts can be saved from a serious contradiction only by using the distinction insisted on by Carré de Malberg, that between "state" and "organ" sovereignty.[16] Such a distinction was fudged by the theorists of absolutism or monarchical sovereignty, but became crucially important to make, according to Carré de Malberg, in the epoch of "national" or "popular" sovereignty, when the body of the whole could not rule directly, and claims that it could do so would inevitably lead to usurpation. An "organ" (a person, an assembly, an institution) may exercise all the powers of sovereignty that Jean Bodin assigned alternately to the state and its organ, the monarch, but there may be (and ought to be, according to Carré de Malberg, under "national sovereignty," if not Bodin, Thomas Hobbes, and John Austin!) state sovereignty without such an organ. It is more or less the latter that was the basis of Kelsen's understanding of sovereignty, and even of the sovereign state, as the supremacy of the domestic legal order, though he wrongly neglected the problem of organ sovereignty altogether.

Arendt did not differentiate between state and organ sovereignty,[17] but with respect to internal affairs, her fire is directed almost exclusively against

---

[16] Ibid. The distinction comes from the German *Staatslehre* of the imperial period (Gerber, Laband, Jellinek), and referred back to the battle over the budget between the king and the Landtag under the 1850 Constitution of Prussia. See Caldwell, *Popular Sovereignty and the Crisis of German Constitutional Law*, pp. 18–22. Carré de Malberg, influenced by German theory, developed his whole jurisprudence and critique of revolutionary public law around the distinction that led to his unique concept of national sovereignty. Recently, the distinction between organ and state sovereignty has been often restated as "ruler" and "rule" sovereignty, not quite accurately in our view, because "rule" sovereignty implies something like the constitution or the laws are sovereign, and that to us is not necessarily the meaning of state sovereignty even when it is not exercised or usurped by an organ.

We are inclined to think that the attempt to constitutionalize stateness has nowhere fully succeeded; and if it did, perhaps all sovereignty regimes would indeed have been suppressed, as Kelsen thought still in 1945.

[17] This may be because she seemed to regard Bodin's treatise the last serious word on the subject, and did not seem to be aware of its critiques in German *Staatslehre* and French public law. See, e.g., *OT*. The implicit role of Schmitt in her argument, however, makes up for some of the difficulty, because of course *Political Theology* (*Politische Theologie. Vier Kapitel zur Lehre*

the latter. And it is only organ sovereignty that the Americans banished in her reconstruction. Accordingly, the American state is sovereign with respect to the outside, but with respect to the internal life of the republic, at least no organ, institution, person, or power holder ever has undivided supremacy, complete legal independence. Each is under law and checked by other powers. If it were otherwise, as Carré de Malberg argued, "national" (or to the Americans, popular) sovereignty would be confiscated in an act of usurpation by a mere branch or organ of power. Organ sovereignty is modern dictatorship or, as Arendt anachronistically says, tyranny.

Note that *state* sovereignty is compatible with Arendt's communicative conception of the political (and is implicitly treated as such in *Origins of Totalitarianism*). This is so because the idea of the state's law being supreme no more excludes the public, deliberative interaction of equal citizens than does external sovereignty. The reasons are partly the same as in the case of external sovereignty, because in state sovereignty the external and internal are closely linked, as we have said, and according to some are even identical. It is of course otherwise with the concept of organ sovereignty. To understand how Arendt came to concentrate on that issue without using the actual concept and locate the domains from which she thought it must be banished, it is important to uncover Carl Schmitt's direct or (since she has not left us with the needed references) indirect role in her train of thought. Smarting from attacks on sovereignty by positivists such as Carré de Malberg and Kelsen, Schmitt admitted that the traditional concept based on the omnipotence of the hidden God was political theology – the wrong political theology. Sovereignty, which always presupposes representation by and personalization in an actor or *an organ* capable of decision, requires a different political theology with the miracle or the extraordinary as its central concept.[18] Thus Schmitt came to concentrate on two extraordinary contexts in which sovereignty – *organ* sovereignty *capable of decision* – reappears in the modern world: revolutionary constitution making and states of constitutional exception.[19] He had no problems with affirming both as dictatorships: the sovereign and the commissarial, both of which overcome all divisions and separations in the structure of power, and temporarily all limitation by law. To Arendt, this way of thinking (which she had to know well from the 1920s when it was advanced both in the form of pamphlets and more serious studies) became of course unacceptable and even reprehensible given her political conception to which we have already alluded. Evidently, her conception of the political in *Human Condition* already stood the Schmitt of *The Crisis of Parliamentary Democracy* on his head by adopting the deliberative model derided by the latter as the normatively preferred one.

---

von der Souveränität [Berlin: Duncker & Humblot, 1922]) contained a critique of Bodin even as it tried to link him, implausibly, to the decisionist position.

[18] Schmitt, *Political Theology.*

[19] In reverse order in Carl Schmitt, *Die Diktatur* (Berlin: Duncker & Humblot, 1922), and in Carl Schmitt, *Verfassungslehre* (Berlin: Duncker & Humblot, 1928). (The subtitle of Schmitt's 1922 work was, in English, "From the Origins of the Modern Theory of Sovereignty to the Proletarian Class Struggle.")

Now, in *On Revolution*, her strategy was to use the Americans against Schmitt (whose stand-in textually is Sieyès interpreted in the same one-sided manner of Schmitt himself!).[20]

Accordingly, on every possible level of internal politics, the American Framers differentiated rather than unified power. First and foremost, they truly differentiated, legalized, and tamed the constituent power itself. Instead of conceiving that revolutionary power in the state of nature, they located it in organized bodies. Instead of making the organized bodies of the people the source of both power and law, they separated the two dimensions and conceived themselves to be always under law. And, Arendt could have added, instead of fashioning a constituent assembly with the plenitude of powers, unchecked or checked only by a plebiscite, they constructed a many-stage, dualistic constitution-making effort where the drafting assembly was supposed to recommend only. (We are not now concerned with the small errors and omissions she made in this context.)

When it came to the constituted powers, the division of powers involved their segmental differentiation while the separation of powers entails their functional differentiation. According to the Madisonian formula of blending sovereignty between the states and the federal union, sovereign *powers* monopolized by absolute monarchies (and some American state legislatures) were shared among these instances. Arendt is a staunch advocate of "federalism" and even states rights, and remained so in spite of the fact that she clearly saw the misuse of the principle both in the period before the Civil War and in the period of the civil rights movement.[21] In fact, as far as we can tell, the idea that the Americans dispensed with sovereignty appeared first in the famous (we think misguided) essay on Little Rock (1959), where she identified (and defended) the states' rights principle "as that of the division of power and ... the conviction that the body politic is strengthened by the division of power." That was not the American experience with the doctrine, and states' rights were of course only one version of the idea of division of power and of federalism. In American history, states' rights have indeed been a challenge to national sovereignty if not to the sovereignty principle as such, but it has also been, repeatedly, a source of disunity and deep conflict. Arendt nevertheless called the doctrine one of

---

[20] It is demonstrable that Sieyès had strong American influences on him; that he accepted the idea of a sovereign constituent assembly with the plenitude of powers reluctantly; that he had two concepts of the nation, one under law and one in the state of nature, and so on; and that he was always seeking some model for constitutional guardianship and was uncomfortable with applying the doctrine of sovereignty to the constituent power as well. For a different Sieyès, see P. Pasquino, *Sieyes et l'invention de la constitution en France* (Paris: Editions Odile Jacob, 1998). In our view, both sides are present in Sieyès, the Rousseauian side dominating from 1788 to 1791 and the Montesquieuian side after 1794. Characteristically, Arendt, like Schmitt, sees only the former. Her citations are almost identical to those of Schmitt.

[21] Hannah Arendt, "Civil Disobedience" (1970 or 1971), in *Crises of the Republic* (New York: Mariner, 1972), pp. 75–7; Hannah Arendt, "Reflections on Little Rock" (1959), in *Responsibility and Judgement* (New York: Schocken, 2003), pp. 209–11.

the most authentic sources of power for the republic as a whole.[22] How that worked she never tried to demonstrate beyond entirely abstract considerations about the supposed nature of power, which unlike "strength" increases when it is divided. As late as the epoch of Watergate, Arendt defended the principle and, quite implausibly, saw the "enormous growth of federal power at the expense of states' rights" as an issue to which movements of civil disobedience should respond.[23]

While less is said about the separation of powers, the Montesquieuian scheme, reinterpreted in terms of checks and balances, is also consistently presented as actually a framework for the enhancement and increase of power. This may be a stretch, but in effect this argument, partially right and partially wrong, served among other things as the answer to Schmitt's presidentialism, and within that his second extraordinary context in which organ sovereignty inevitably reappears as the state of exception: war and internal emergency. Historically, as Arendt well knew, from the Romans to the present, "dictatorship" is commonly justified as the need to overcome temporarily the weakness of dualistic or mixed or functionally separated forms of government. The Americans accordingly would have banished sovereignty from internal affairs and answered Schmitt by designing a form of division and separation of powers that generates rather than diminishes power and eliminated the need for exceptional or emergency breakthroughs or suspensions of the Constitution even in grave crises of the republic.[24]

Of course, she may not have had the problem of emergency and exceptional powers in mind in *On Revolution,* a text written before the Vietnam crisis and Watergate. But the train of argument allows her to maintain a consistent and very curious disinterest in the institution of presidency in American affairs and almost miss the tendency of the immense secular strengthening of the institution in the *material* constitution of the country, in spite of using many texts that do not make the same obvious mistake.[25] Admittedly, in "Civil Disobedience," focusing on unconstitutional undeclared wars in Vietnam and

---

[22] Arendt, "Reflections on Little Rock," p. 210.

[23] Arendt, "Civil Disobedience," p. 75.

[24] Arendt recognizes the persistence of the Roman idea of dictatorship in today's states of emergency and martial law administrations, but never makes a reference of the relevance of these forms also in America. Hannah Arendt, "Personal Responsibility under Dictatorships," in *Responsibility and Judgement,* p. 32.

[25] In particular, James Bryce, *The American Commonwealth* (London: Macmillan, 1906), chapter 6; W. Wilson, *Congressional Government* (Cleveland: Meridian, 1956), with its Preface to the 15th ed. on presidential power and foreign affairs, and relevant introduction by W. Lippman (Arendt did not use *Constitutional Government* [New York: Columbia University Press, 1908], with its synthesis of the plebiscitary conception and the absolutist one for foreign affairs); H. S. Commager, "Can We Limit Presidential Power?" cited in "On Violence," *Crises of the Republic,* p. 153. Perhaps she was convinced by the cyclical view in Bryce and Lippman, which seems to indicate the growth of presidential power to be a temporary matter of emergencies. Wilson on his part realized that crises can be produced and that there could be attempts to break the cycle.

Cambodia, she speaks of attempts to deprive the Senate of its constitutional powers, of the proper balance of government threatened by the executive branch, and even of "the increasingly impatient claim to power of the executive branch of government."[26] But again in "Lying in Politics" (written in 1971 or 1972),[27] she describes the president only as "allegedly the most powerful man of the most powerful country ... [who] may be the only person likely to be an ideal victim of complete manipulation ... the only person in this country whose range of choices can be predetermined." The fault may of course lie with the particular executive for cutting himself off from the deliberative body of the Senate, which could have been his only shield from "the antics of the consumer society and the public relations managers that cater to it." But the source of the pathology cited in both essays lies certainly not in the constitutional office of the executive. When a president such as Eisenhower "is old-fashioned enough to believe in the Constitution," we get consultation with Congress and no undeclared presidential wars or "open" interventions or "acts of war."[28] Arendt does not seem to realize that in the same passage she attests to the same Eisenhower ordering a covert war instead, which testifies both to the immense powers of his office and his ability, apparently legal even to her, to escape the strictures of the written constitution.[29]

When it finally came to Nixon in one of her last lectures ("Home to Roost," 1975), she still had a chance to see matters more clearly. She did not, not really, in spite of the eloquence of her condemnation of the phenomenon. The ultimate culprit (unconvincingly) is still consumer society, with its agent, public relations, that has infected American foreign policy and has turned it into (more convincingly) an imperialism seeking the permanent goal of the image of the greatest power on earth. When this image had to be sustained by a campaign of lies incompatible with the free press and the constitutional system, there was a recourse to criminality. Nixon and Watergate represented a criminal conspiracy *against* the Constitution, or at least some of its laws, even if it was not as serious as some might have thought, and certainly not a potential *of* this constitutional regime itself. More deeply and plausibly, the Nixon presidency was seen as certainly a dangerous boomerang effect of a special type of imperialism dedicated not to expansion and annexation but to image creation, where this imperialism itself, much less convincingly, had nothing whatever to do with the American system of government.[30]

---

[26] Arendt, "Civil Disobedience," pp. 74–5, 93.

[27] Arendt, "Lying in Politics," *Crises of the Republic*, p. 9.

[28] Ibid., p. 21.

[29] It takes little imagination and a knowledge of only a little American history to see how even a small covert war, in itself possibly barely (but only barely) legal under the commander-in-chief clause, produces and has produced situations where American troops are "attacked" and a president claims to use his (again) barely legal authority to repel attack, this time openly, with (as in the Mexican War) or without a congressional declaration of war (as in Vietnam and Cambodia).

[30] Arendt, *Responsibility and Judgement*, pp. 263–6, 271.

In the end, she winds up in the circle of theorists who seem to maintain that all that is wrong with American politics is usurpation, and things would be right if we stayed with the original Constitution. Implausibly, given what she has said about declarations of war, for example, the Nixon conspiracy and its failure are used as proof that *only* in the United States does the (written) Constitution still function as a genuine basic law of the land.

6.2 The American Revival of Organ Sovereignty

We may wish that it were so. On balance, Arendt's reading of the *main* trend of the intentions of the framing as well as the persistence of constitutionalism still has merit, even if her notion of the "long run" can only be read today with irony. But there are deep flaws and lacunae in her reconstruction of the tradition. In particular, she has simply misread two fundamental issues in relation to the problem of *internal* sovereignty. The first had to do with popular sovereignty, the second with governmental sovereignty, and our contention is that in the United States both of these issues tended to come together in the office and the personality of the plebescitary presidency.

To begin with, something was clearly wrong with her treatment of popular sovereignty, wrong on the face of it in light of the ubiquitous use of the idea if not always the words themselves in the period of the founding and memorialized by the Preamble. Arendt's argument again is directed against the famous set of substitutions first suggested by none other than Sieyès himself.[31] The monarch is put in the place of the omnipotent God, then the people in the place of the king – and one could continue and go on to nation, class, party, and so on. She is right that the Americans were not on the whole guilty of such a substitution of one "absolute" for another, but the claim that they did without the concept of popular sovereignty is simply too sweeping. A glance at not only the Preamble, but more importantly Hamilton's argument for judicial review in Federalist 78,[32] followed by Marshall in *Marbury*, should have convinced her of this. What is possible to argue, however, is that here too there were two traditions, one compatible with Arendt's argument against organ sovereignty and another potentially undermining it. It is possible to claim (and so interpret Federalist 78!) that the role of popular sovereignty, all the way down to the process of the founding itself, was to point to the impossibility and illegitimacy of any single democratic organ to speak for the people as a totality. A single (in extremis, usurping) organ trying to do so should be stopped by the devices of the Constitution, including judicial review (in the case of Congress), impeachment (in the case of the president), and the use of the amendment rule (in the

---

[31] Sieyès, "Opinion de Sieyès, Sur plusieurs articles de titres IV et V du projet de constitution" 2 Thermidor Year III (1795), in *Oeuvres III*, p. 7.

[32] "Nor does this conclusion by any means suppose a superiority of the judicial to the legislative power. It only supposes that the power of the people is superior to both...." No. 78 *The Federalist Papers* (New York: Signet Classics, 2003), p. 466.

case of the Supreme Court). This was more or less the meaning that Carré de Malberg gave to "national sovereignty," and there are both American as well as French revolutionary texts to support the notion. The popular sovereign here would not be embodied within the Constitution, within the body politic, but stand outside it as an ultimate limiting concept. But what happens when the negative source of all authority, A.V. Dicey's slumbering sovereignty, actually awakes?[33]

It was inevitable that popular sovereignty also in America would come to mean the will of the majority, expressed in elections, incorporated in assemblies, and, after 1800, periodically mobilized by plebiscitary leaders. If this be called a usurpation in light of the written Constitution, and the explicit warning of Federalist 78, it could not be so in cases of the "solemn and authoritative act" by the people Hamilton is forced to admit into the system.[34] Though a minor tendency among the makers of the Constitution at least, the early Jeffersonian appearance of the plebescitary presidency, of the president as the unique leader of the people as whole, reconstructed by Bruce Ackerman in his recent *Failure of the Founding Fathers*,[35] indicates that this view was becoming if not the hegemonic one, then at least one permanently available one for cyclical "reconstructions."[36] And it was the bringing together of the plebescitary presidency with another doctrine – of inherent, unenumerated powers of the executive in foreign affairs first proposed by Hamilton, at that time in the face of Jefferson's (and Madison's) strong opposition – that represented the most dangerous possibility for the republic. It was these two doctrines in particular, of the two antagonists, that when mixed together provided the most explosive fuel propelling the dramatic reentry of sovereignty on the scene. Even if Jefferson did not have in mind inherent, constitutional, or extraconstitutional powers, when pioneering a particular emergency regime based on Locke's prerogative, he certainly benefited from his plebescitary democratic legitimacy.[37]

---

[33] Albert Venn Dicey, *Introduction to the Study of the Law of the Constitution*, 8th ed. (Indianapolis: Liberty, 1982), p. 81.

[34] Federalist 78, p. 468. A close reader of just these texts, Ackerman combines both meanings of popular sovereignty, negative and positive, in the early version of his dualistic theory. In normal politics, popular sovereignty is negative, in constitutional politics it turns positive, plebiscitary, and embodied. See Bruce Ackerman, *We the People I: Foundations* (Cambridge: Harvard University Press, 1991), pp. 181–6, 217–18.

[35] Bruce Ackerman, *The Failure of the Founding Fathers* (Cambridge, MA: Harvard University Press, 2006).

[36] S. Skowronek, *The Politics Presidents Make: Leadership from John Adams to Bill Clinton* (Cambridge: Harvard University Press).

[37] The dominant view is that Jefferson, in founding the Locke-Jefferson-Lincoln model, did not claim inherent powers, accepted the illegality of his actions, and appealed to the future judgment of other branches of power. He is thus seen as the founder of a liberal model. See L. Fisher, *Presidential War Power* (Lawrence: University of Kansas Press, 1995), pp. 25–7; A. Schlesinger, *Imperial Presidency* (Boston: Houghton Mifflin, 1973), pp. 23–5; J. Lobel, "Emergency Power and the Decline of Liberalism," *Yale Law Journal* 98, 7 (May 1989): 1392ff. There is a case to be made, however, for a republican Jefferson, who despite this earlier opposition to the Roman

And conversely, the later importance of the plebescitary presidency was reinforced precisely by the ability of executives in periods of war and crisis to appeal to their allegedly superior popular mandate (noted by Marx, Tocqueville, and Schmitt) as a source of legitimacy in the face of stalemates and immobility produced by the legal-constitutional system.

Today, the existence of an American emergency regime with presidential powers in its center (as Clinton Rossiter has already conclusively demonstrated) and linked to sovereignty claims is hardly deniable.[38] This was the second dimension of sovereignty missed by Arendt, having to do with extraordinary state or governmental powers outside the law and the Constitution. Admittedly it was easy to miss, focusing on a Constitution that allowed only a single congressional suspension of one of its fundamental safeguards, habeas corpus, and on commentaries such as *The Federalist* that seemed to guarantee that the federal Constitution would build an unusually strong political union that would not be exposed to the hazards of the then-distant European state system.[39] Thus, the best-known texts of Jefferson on the subject, especially the *Notes on Virginia* that Arendt well knew, could adopt an "absolutist" attitude excluding any suspensions of the Constitution and especially classical dictatorships. What she could have noticed admittedly on the other side were in bits and pieces in the founding period on which she concentrated. There were first the same Jefferson's early warnings, based on the Constitution, about the future threat of a president capable of reelection (in effect the plebescitary or Caesarist danger).[40] Second, if the *Federalist* accepted (like the early Jefferson)

---

idea of dictatorship revived it here, as evident in his letter to Brown ("To Dr. James Brown," October 27, 1808, cited by A. M. Schlesinger, *The Imperial Presidency* [New York: Houghton Miflin, 1973 [2004], p.24]). The highest duty of saving the country in the face of ultimate danger, appealed to in another letter (J. B. Colvin, September 20, 1810), higher than to law itself, is the Roman "salus publica suprema lex" or "salus rei publicae suprema lex esto." The fact that this is combined with traditional British safeguards (the possibility of impeachment and legal action) can be said to be a function of a common law context where otherwise the Roman insitution would be entirely unchecked. But it is probably wrong to say that Jefferson thought that his actions were not legitimate, even if they were not legal. That comes close to an inherent power, even if not an unlimited one.

[38] Clinton Rossiter, *Constitutional Dictatorship* (Princeton: Princeton University Press, 1948), pp. 210–11, 217–21.

[39] If Arendt had read Rossiter's *Constitutional Dictatorship*, she would have found confirmation for the view that the traditional theory of the Constitution, including the debates at the Convention, and the *Federalist Papers* were "clearly hostile to the establishment of any crisis institutions and procedures" and believed "that the Constitution will be equal to any emergency" (p. 212). Federalist 23, which Rossiter cites, referring to an unlimited power without "constitutional shackles," does not sustain this position. Moreover, the whole thrust of his book indicates that America's material Constitution is different than the formal one.

[40] Most famously, "Notes on Virginia" attacks the legislature's plans to set up a temporary dictatorship and defines republican organization as one that "proscribes under the name of *prerogative* the exercise of all powers undefined by the laws." Thomas Jefferson, *The Life and Selected Writings of Thomas Jefferson* (1821), edited by Adrienne Koch and William Piden (New York: Random House, 1944), pp. 244–5. In a sense going even further, he was dissatisfied

that there was no need for emergency powers, there were two points on which Hamilton at least went beyond the rest of the text. First, in the case of national exigencies in Federalist 23, he sought unlimited powers without "constitutional shackles" for the federal state.[41] Second, he considered the one-person presidency (Federalist 70) a functional substitute for the Roman dictatorship, needed because in Rome the executive power was divided.[42] This point could be read as consistent with the refusal of drawing a distinction between normal and emergency constitutions. Accordingly, the ordinary functionary can carry out the functions under normal safeguards that in Rome an extraordinary magistrate had to assume, suspending many of the laws. But it could be read as constitutionalizing dictatorship, with the president being available to assume the unlimited powers of Federalist 23 when the need for dictatorship arose. At worst, and least plausibly, it could be read even as the desire for the normalization of a dictator-like presidency.[43] The same Hamilton (as Pacificus) a few years later went on to argue for the doctrine of inherent powers of the chief executive in war and foreign affairs, a doctrine that in the correct reading of Madison (as Helvidius) took what was "inherent" from the British prerogative and insisted that the only (congressional) limits on such powers had to be explicitly enumerated.[44]

Finally, Jefferson as president came to be the spokesman for the doctrine of the Lockean prerogative, according to which violations of the law and the Constitution by the president and his executive agents, though based on no inherent powers, were justified as long as "necessity" required them and the actor exposed himself to subsequent condemnation or indemnification by the

---

with the right of Congress under the 1787 Constitution to suspend habeas corpus and sought, unsuccessfully, a bill of rights that would anchor habeas more firmly. All this was initially also coupled with a fear of the presidency created by the Federal Convention. See Letters to Madison December 20, 1787; July 31, 1788; March 15, 1789, the last with the famous prediction: "[The tyranny] of the executive will come in its turn, but it will be at a later period" (pp. 438, 451, 464). Jefferson's autobiography, in *The Life and Selected Writings of Thomas Jefferson*, still reflects an earlier position on pp. 81–2 (habeas and the presidency in the same sentence). It is weird that the editors studiously included these texts, but excluded the important letters after Jefferson's switch to the prerogative. The situation is better with the more recent Thomas Jefferson, *Writings* (New York: Viking, 1984), which has two of the relevant letters, to Gov. C. C. Claiborne (1807) and to John B. Colvin (1810).

[41] Federalist 23, p. 149. The phrase "same councils which are appointed to preside over common defense" in the *Federalist Papers* must have meant the president and Congress together. But speaking of the powers dealing with "national exigencies," No. 23 goes on to say: "these powers ought to exist without limitation . . . no constitutional shackles can be wisely imposed on the power to which the care of it is committed."

[42] Federalist 70, pp. 421–2.

[43] That was sometimes Jefferson's inclination: He depicts Hamilton (perhaps not entirely reliably) as calling Julius Caesar the greatest man in history. Thomas Jefferson, "To Benjamin Rush," January 16, 1811, in *The Life and Selected Writings of Thomas Jefferson*, p. 609.

[44] Hamilton, Madison, "Helvidius" No. 1, *Writings* (New York: Library Classics, 1999), pp. 538ff; 545 ff.

other branches of government.[45] Where the author of the *Notes on Virginia* sought to banish all traces of the prerogative, of the state not under the Constitution, Jefferson as president appealed to just such a prerogative, an obvious "sovereignty remnant" even in its Lockean version, exercised (at least in the moment of the emergency) by himself when he saw, for example, the integrity of the state threatened in a crisis of potential secession.[46] Arendt, had she read the relevant passage, knowing Schmitt's famous theses from *Political Theology* or Dicey's treatment of the prerogative as a sovereignty remnant, should have had no difficulty in deciphering a sovereignty claim behind Jefferson's insistence that the Constitution should be transgressed or bypassed when the state (the laws as a whole or "the union" or "the country") were in danger.

Admittedly, only in retrospect (from the point of view of Woodrow Wilson[47] and especially the era of Franklin Roosevelt and thereafter) do these fragments of sovereignty doctrine add up to a perspective of a plebescitary presidency, with inherent powers, justified to take extraconstitutional actions in grave emergencies with very limited control on the president's actions by the other

---

[45] "To Dr. James Brown," October 27, 1808: "under the maxim of the law itself, that *inter arma silent leges,* that in an encampment expecting daily attack from a powerful enemy, self-preservation is paramount to all law, I expected that instead of invoking the forms of the law to cover traitors, all good citizens would have concurred in securing them. Should we have ever gained our Revolution, if we had bound our hands by manacles of the law, not only in the beginning, but in any part of the revolutionary conflict? There are extreme cases where the laws become inadequate even to their own preservation, and where, the universal resource is a dictator, or martial law. Was N(ew) O(orleans) in that situation?" And "To John B. Colvin," September 20, 1810: "an hourly expectation of the enemy, salvation of the city, and of the Union itself, which would have been convulsed to its center . . . all these constituted a law of necessity and self-preservation, and rendered the *salus populi* supreme over written law." Jefferson, *Writings*, p. 1233.

[46] Fisher, *Presidential War Power*, pp. 25–7, and Schlesinger, *Imperial Presidency*, pp. 23–5, make convincing cases that for Jefferson, there was no question of using *inherent* powers of the presidency, thus a Blackstonian *royal* prerogative. The powers were of the American government as a whole, and their abuse could be subsequently punished by the other branches of government. Arguably, their use too had to be subsequently upheld by the legislature and the actor indemnified. Jefferson indeed writes: "The officer who is called upon to act on this superior ground, does indeed risk himself on the justice of the controlling powers of the constitution, and his station makes it his duty to incur this risk." "Letter to Colvin," Jefferson, *Writings*, p. 1235. Nevertheless, the appeal to *salus populi* as higher than written law indicates several things. First, Jefferson is adopting a republican, and not merely a liberal, model of emergency, as Lobel argues. Second, he is close to considering "state" or "respublica" different and more than the constitutional order. Third, he considers executive action on behalf of the Union or republic legitimate even when extralegal. All this makes his use of the prerogative a sovereignty remnant even if he is occupying the place of a minister, strictly speaking, and not that of the king (who is beyond legal responsibility). The sovereignty in this model, as Gouverneur Morris said at the Convention, is the following: The people are the King, and the magistrate the prime minister with legal responsibility. See footnote 71.

[47] We get the first real synthesis of inherent, nearly absolute powers in foreign affairs and plebescitary ideas of legitimation for the presidency in Woodrow Wilson, *Constitutional Government in the United States* (New York: Columbia University Press, 1909), pp. 58–60, 66–70, 77, 80.

branches. Historically, it is right to see three originally competing interpretive perspectives here, as does J. Lobel, and, following him, to trace the relative victory of the relativist-statist one (against the absolutist one assumed by Arendt, and even the Locke-Jefferson-Lincoln one stylized by Arthur Schlesinger and still attributed to FDR[48]) as related to America's turn to the world and to imperialism. There are indeed important changes in how this emergency regime is conceived from the founding to Jefferson and Lincoln, and from them to Theodore Roosevelt, Wilson, FDR, the judges who decided *Quirin and Korematsu*, and finally to our time: in general, from temporal-spatial-legal limitations toward their removal, and from the idea of shared sovereign powers, to the inherent powers of the presidency alone. What becomes clear, however, is that the absolutist position that made a stance around the written Constitution and their enforcement by the courts in war as well as peace, the position that Arendt's banishment of the sovereign presupposes was never the only one and it suffered defeat very early.[49] And we need not suspect any unconstitutional usurpation behind this outcome. Whatever can be said about the theoretical possibility of the American brand of the separation and division of powers enhancing power, an equal case could be made for their limiting and even stalemating power. Clearly, in some historical junctures, it was this second dimension that came to the fore, producing crises that could not be resolved within the same separation and division. At such moments, the banished sovereign tended to reemerge, and its preferred vehicle was the presidency. As we can see in retrospect, this was so because of the executive powers lodged in the president for reasons of maintaining the external sovereignty of the federal state.

6.3 External Sovereignty and the Boomerang Effect

Here are the issues that are opened up by Arendt's own concession of external sovereignty and denial of internal sovereignty. What should be the powers of external sovereignty? How can the line between external and internal be maintained? Who should exercise these formidable powers and how?

According to a dictum, both highly influential and much derided,[50] of Justice Sutherland in the famous case *U.S. v. Curtiss Wright*, the American Union

---

[48] Schlesinger, *Imperial Presidency*, p. 109; Lobel, otherwise close, does not follow Schlesinger here.

[49] Justice Davis's dictum in ex parte *Milligan* was the last authentic hurrah of this position, and was followed by more or less sincere accomodationist uses. The opinion of Davis too was legally vulnerable, because the minority of four would have decided the case on more flexible, narrower grounds that anticipated Justice Jackson's three zone theory. At the time, it was also interpreted as an attack on the Reconstruction. On all this, see I. Zuckerman "One Law for Peace and War?" *Constellations* (December 2006).

[50] We do not think that the terms "badly reasoned" and "badly grounded" apply to all aspects of the decision or even to all of Sutherland's dictum. Fisher, *Presidential War Power*, pp. 57 ff. Fisher himself admits that it may be reasonable to delegate more broadly in foreign than in domestic affairs, though his case elsewhere against congressional blank checks to go to war

(or federal state) as a whole inherits its sovereign powers not from the Constitution but, at the moment of the Declaration of Independence, from the British Crown (meaning the king's prerogative power or the "king in parliament" he is not initially clear!), and these are all the powers of which a state in a Westphalian order is capable. This was in fact consistent with Lincoln's view that "The Union is much older than the Constitution. It was formed in fact by the Articles of Association in 1774. It was matured and continued by the Declaration of Independence in 1776."[51] The aim of the Constitution was accordingly only "to form a more perfect union." Evidently, the position could not become a politically dominant one until after the Civil War, during which it was only the perspective of one of the warring sides, notably Lincoln's views on state sovereignty. But after the Civil War, down to our time, there is remarkable vitality to this particular conception in American theory.

Of course, this idea is not exclusive to American theory. Its most important intellectual roots and development are indeed elsewhere. Reflecting the reality of Imperial Germany and its states, in the classical state theory (*Staatslehre*) developed by German theorists of the late nineteenth century, such as Georg Jellinek, and continued in this respect by Schmitt, the state is prior to the constitution, and the constitution can at best only partially constitutionalize the state (in Schmitt, variously, sovereignty and the constituent power).[52] When Dicey described the French *droit administratif*, in an analysis relied upon by Hannah Arendt, it was still a relatively large domain where state power, state action, and the servants of the state have not been brought under the rule of the constitution, in spite of evolutionary trends in that direction.[53] Finally, the English prerogative, partially tamed by the conventions of the constitutions, has been well represented by the same Dicey "as the residue of discretionary or arbitrary authority, which at any time is legally left in the hands of the Crown. . . . whether such a power is exercised by the King or by his Ministers."[54] Dicey calls this power a residue of the time when the king was in fact sovereign, or "by far the most powerful part of sovereign power," of a time indeed when England could have but did not develop its own *droit administratif*.[55]

---

is well taken. Admittedly, the dictum was legally unnecessary, and the step to presidential power (the "sole organ" theory) was logically and constitutionally fallacious. Even the British Crown did not have the type of prerogative Sutherland imagined. But the idea that there was a state, or stateness, before the Constitution was reasonable, however it is dated, and that of its nonsubsumption under the Constitution is at least arguable.

[51] Abraham Lincoln, "First Inaugural Address," March 4, 1861, in *Selected Speeches and Writings* (New York: Vintage, 1992).

[52] See Jacobson and Schlink, "Introduction," in *Weimar. A Jurisprudence of Crisis.*

[53] Arendt, "Personal Responsibility under Dictatorships," pp. 37–8; Dicey, *The Law of the Constitution*, chapter XII.

[54] Dicey, *The Law of the Constitution*, chapter XIV, p. 282.

[55] Ibid., pp. 242–4. However, Dicey makes clear that the prerogative is not beyond the reach of parliamentary sovereignty that could abolish it (pp. 20–1). Given a veto by one of the components of that sovereignty, this step in constitutionalization was illusory, but with the conventional

In America, an argument can be and has often been made for the (federal) state being entirely a product of the Constitution as well as being completely subsumed by it,[56] and that here the royal prerogative that was supposedly tamed only by relatively weak conventions in Britain was securely constitutionalized.[57] It is this doctrine that (in our view) at least Jefferson as president but certainly Lincoln[58] as well as Justice Sutherland disputed, the latter two affirming the non-identity of state and Constitution. The theoretical arguments are relatively strong on both sides, but the historical development of the material Constitution has favored the Lincoln-Sutherland side.

When Arendt first alluded to this problem, in the form of the acts of state or reason of state doctrine[59] concerning the ability of sovereign states and their servants to act beyond all legal and moral limitations when political existence is at stake, there was no mention of America.[60] But, as we have seen, banishing the sovereign from the internal life of the body politic would have meant that powers rooted in the state (including emergency and war powers) would have been fully constitutionalized. This has been the view of Jefferson in *Notes on Virginia* and of Justice Davis in, for example, *ex parte Milligan* (1865); however, the view has been rejected by Justice Sutherland in *Curtiss Wright* precisely to the extent that the matter in question was of foreign (or inherently executive) affairs. Note, however, that Davis too dealt with a time (if not space) of war, and his dictum allowed for no exceptions. Normatively, and in terms of the historical analysis of *On Revolution*, Arendt is on Davis's side of this debate, whether or not she was aware of it. But in the end, she was

rule that has eliminated the veto, it is now shakily established. That would still mean that there is an element of nonconstitutionalized statehood left in parliamentary sovereignty itself.

[56] See Jacobson and Schlink, "Introduction."

[57] As Dicey reports, while it is the prerogative of the Crown to declare war and to make treaties, it was a convention of the British constitution that the Crown or its ministers go to war or make treaties only when they have the Commons behind them. Dicey, *The Law of the Constitution*, chapter XIV. All conventions can be broken, and when they are, there is no legal recourse against the ministers responsible. Ibid., chapter XV. The U.S. Constitution has constitutionalized these conventions. It is another matter that today the clause on the declaration of war is indeed treated as a convention in the United States that can be broken with impunity. Tony Blair, however, followed the British convention in the recent Iraq War, all the while making clear that it was only a convention, thereby degrading its constitutional significance.

[58] As to Lincoln contesting the subsumption of the Union under the Constitution, we would refer to the equally famous all-laws-but-one argument ("Message to Congress," July 4, 1861), which could admittedly be interpreted as defending the spirit of the Constitution, when following the letter would lead to its destruction. We think it would be hard to deny that the Union, and saving the Union, represented an independent principle of legitimation in Lincoln's whole argumentation, and all his constitutional illegalities, the Lincoln dictatorship so well described by Rossiter (*Constitutional Dictatorship*, chapter xv) were justified by this principle, for which, in the manner of the users of the English prerogative, he even asked for and received congressional acts of indemnity that were not called that.

[59] Using Dicey's analysis of the French *droit administratif*, not fully cited, the important text is *The Law of the Constitution*, chapter XII, especially p. 226ff on "acts of state."

[60] Arendt, "Personal Responsibility under Dictatorship," in *Responsibility and Judgement*, pp. 37–8.

forced to admit that for her own time at least, those who claimed that the state was not entirely subsumed by the American Constitution were right, at least on the level of the facts. This meant that the banished sovereign could return after all.

The argument was presented in the 1971 essay "Civil Disobedience"[61] and it is interesting for several reasons, not least because Arendt provides us with one important additional argument of how she thought of the expulsion of sovereignty from the internal body of the American republic. She quotes James Wilson, then (1793) Supreme Court Justice of the United States, who supposedly said or wrote (we get no source) the following: "to the Constitution of the United States the term sovereignty is totally unknown." This could have meant literally only that the term "sovereignty" was unmentioned in the federal Constitution. Clearly and rightly, Arendt meant to make the more serious point that according to Wilson (who was earlier in fact a staunch advocate of popular sovereignty as the source of and authority behind the Constitution[62]), all dimensions of the state were constitutionalized, leaving nothing over to a pre or extraconstitutional raison d'état (as in French and German theories of raison d'état and *Staatsräson*, as well as of the French *droit administratif* and the continental traditions influenced by it) that could act outside of the Constitution in war or emergencies when the laws must be silent. No organ can act outside the law, and the state itself is identified with a fully constitutionalized legal order, a point that Kelsen would have agreed with, except that his idea of a constitution was not a very demanding one and he would have called this order sovereign unless subordinated to international and not only constitutional law. Arendt insisted on – and, according to her, the Americans tried to achieve (and in the 1963 version, did achieve) "only" – the constitutionalization of the entire state. This constitutionalization was meant to be enforced by the Supreme Court, according to her. Yet, revealingly, the same passage of 1971 goes on to say that neither that Court nor especially any international tribunal would be able to enforce decisions that would (or were deemed to) hurt the interests of sovereign states, the United States being the one explicitly under discussion.[63] The question only is whether unsubsumed sovereignty with respect to the outside remains sovereignty internally, and if so, even more importantly, what kind of sovereignty would it then be?

At issue was the "political question doctrine" in "Civil Disobedience" and the refusal of the U.S. Supreme Court to consider the constitutionality of the war in Vietnam.[64] Following well-known legal analysts of the issue, Arendt was led to the conclusion that the political question doctrine is "that loophole

---

[61] Arendt, "Civil Disobedience," p.100 ff.
[62] For example, he supported direct popular election of both chambers as well as of the president. See James Madison, *Notes of Debates of the Federal Convention of 1787* (New York: Norton, 1987), pp. 48–9.
[63] Arendt, "Civil Disobedience," p. 101.
[64] Ibid., pp. 100–1.

through which the sovereignty principle and the reason of state doctrine are permitted to filter back into a system of government which in principle denies them."[65] The formulation is apt, though the doctrine was by no means the only such loophole. Arendt's source, Graham Hughes, referring to *inter arma silent leges*, went on to deny that when the political question doctrine is appealed to, it is a Constitution that is being expounded. To Justice Sutherland, however, the decision would have meant only that in foreign affairs, the Constitution does not, ought not, and indeed cannot subsume the state and its sovereignty. To Arendt's way of thinking, this admission (of the "does not," if not of the "cannot" and "ought not") was doubly disastrous, because of its possible foreign policy outcomes and because of their possible consequences eventually on the internal institutions of the republic.

And this brings us to the second issue, whether the boundary between the external and the internal can be maintained, an issue that Arendt liked to treat under the heading of "the boomerang effect." The line could not be kept in the Civil War for obvious reasons, because the war was internal, and it is without doubt that in that great struggle, the president's prerogative – armed with an initially illegal suspension of habeas corpus, an after-the-fact illegal (or partially illegal, that is, in states where the regular courts were open) use of military commissions, massive detentions in the face of court opposition, and so on – became a fundamental tool for internal repression. In Rossiter's terms, the United States was indeed a constitutional dictatorship[66] and sovereignty was not absent from the internal life of the republic. The president managed to conquer even a portion of the constituent power when the Emancipation Proclamation did what, according to Lincoln, only a constitutional amendment but no act of Congress could do. But so did Congress, during the Reconstruction, in the period of its own "constitutional dictatorship" when the Fourteenth and Fifteenth Amendments to the Constitution were rammed through in an extra-constitutional manner.[67] This was all to great and good purpose, we might of course say. At least as far as the president's actions go, the structures and the precedents have been established for whatever purpose.

While the line between external and internal was also threatened subsequently, nothing in this respect could resemble the Civil War. Note that even Justice Sutherland's dictum applies only to foreign affairs, and if some critics doubted that inherent powers could be so confined, the depth of the problem did not become clear until World War II and after, when the U.S mainland was never threatened, yet the internal security measures undertaken became very drastic. Thus during Korea, Justice Jackson's polemic was especially harsh against a president who can now start wars on his own, and by that fact would make himself commander-of-chief of the country. Even the "d" word appears

[65] Ibid., p. 100.

[66] Dicey, *The Law of the Constitution*, chapter XV.

[67] Ackerman's treatment in *We the People II Transformations* is comprehensive and convincing on this score.

in this famous warning. Less than a generation later, however, the country confronted Watergate; and now, in another generation, without a new criminal conspiracy, a series of presidential initiatives, starting with the November 2001 Military Order, threatened to abolish fully the outside-inside distinction and to deform completely the constitutional order that Arendt revered.

Arendt did not think the system was already gravely deformed, but she feared the boomerang effect of imperialist policy. She imagined a battle between domestic republican institutions and imperial external policy and its agents, and at least in America, where the domestic institutions were not based on the brittle structure of the nation-state nor linked to an imaginary national homogeneity. She thought the advantage lay with the domestic institutions *unless* internal political processes were successfully invaded, with the help of invisible government, by "sheer criminality." It is this judgment that was tied to the epoch of Watergate and has become obsolete today. As it turned out, we were far better protected against political criminality than the internal possibilities of the Constitution itself.

6.4 Analytical Flaws and the Flawed American Constitution

What really went wrong with Arendt's analysis? Of course, history entered, and the United States has entered the world as a major (and, there is little question, imperial) power. Arendt at least had no questions regarding this state of affairs, and she understood the consequences for internal politics well enough. Incredibly powerful, the United States was also incredibly exposed. "It was this world power, rather than national existence, that was challenged by the revolutionary power of Moscow directed communism" (*OT*, xx), she wrote in 1967, and, slightly altered, the sentence could be repeated forty years later. The first time tragedy, the philosopher had written, the second time, farce. All this was something that was unimaginable at the time of the framing.[68] But the presidency and its dangers were imagined at that time,[69] and it is the interaction

---

[68] We do not buy the thesis of the imperial constitution of Michael Hardt and Antonio Negri, *Empire* (Cambridge, MA: Harvard University Press, 2000). Even the project of a *small* empire *isolated* from the world system was restricted to some of the founders, and it is not an important feature of the text of the federal Constitution. A large republic is not the same as an empire, in spite of the Roman language of American republicanism. The decentralized American relation to military force and militarism was completely non-Roman in the founding period. The destruction of an aboriginal population, horrible as it is, leads to no imperialism in itself. Australia is not an empire and is only a minor subimperialist state. Whether the Louisiana Purchase or the Monroe Doctrine brought the really decisive change is an academic matter; for us the key if not first precedent from a constitutional point of view remains the annexation of Texas and the Mexican War.

[69] Madison-Pacificus speaking, while the revered and pacific Washington is president: "War is in fact the true source of executive aggrandizement.... the executive is the department of power most distinguished by its propensity to war: hence it is a propensity of all states, in proportion that they are free, to disarm this propensity of its influence." Cited by Fisher, *Presidential War Power*, p. 21.

of that institution with imperial expansion that made a still episodic presence of sovereign power in American life at the time of the Civil War a much more regular challenge in the next century as well as ours.[70] The issue has to do with our third question, namely, the agent that was to exercise the powers of sovereignty external in the American regime, and the meaning of this for the problem of the return of internal sovereignty.

The most spectacular answer focusing on the presidency was provided by Justice Sutherland in *Curtiss Wright*. Sutherland, starting with state sovereignty prior to the Constitution, proceeds further with an astonishing logical leap: According to him, it is the president, our chief executive ("sole organ" of executive power), who inherits all the powers (the royal prerogative) of the British Crown, their chief executive. This view could be attributed to the spirit of an imperialist epoch, that Sutherland enthusiastically and "belligerently" shared[71] and the needs of a minor (it seems exceptionally pacific) intervention in Latin America in 1930s, except for one fact: It was anticipated by the Hamilton of the "Pacificus-Letters" arguing for peace, neutrality, and nonintervention.

In the history of presidential powers, this view triumphed against Madison's alternative, Lincoln's protest against Polk's presidential war, and even Jackson's opinion in *Youngstown Steel* that is the jurisprudential foundation for *Hamdan*. Indeed, there was secular development on both sides of the argument, with each great step in building an emergency regime using precedents of previous ones, and with each step in opposition hoping to save and extend preceding forms of limitation. What is important here is that with respect to presidential powers, there was thus a developmental line (in spite of paradigmatic shifts) from Hamilton-Pacificus to the Jefferson of the prerogative, the later Lincoln's war power, to Theodore Roosevelt's inherent powers and then to Justice Sutherland of the *Curtiss Wright* dictum of 1936 and even to John Yoo, just as there is a line from Madison's Helvidius papers to the early Lincoln, to the Milligan majority, to Justice Jackson's opinion in *Youngstown Steel*, to *Hamdan,* and now to those opposed to the Bush emergency regime.[72] Yet, however weak its foundations in formal constitutional history may be, and however much opposition and occasional reversals it encountered, the presidentialist or "relativist" (Lobel) position was thus well grounded in the history of the material or real Constitution or constitutional regime. To be sure, the view triumphed at first only in regard to the so-called war power, and it is to this that Jackson tried to limit it.[73] But he already understood (after having

[70] Lobel is highly persuasive on this point, and so was Schlesinger, even if he was insensitive to the institutional roots of the problem and the needs of institutional reform. Both are right, of course, on the need to end the imperial role in the world if we want to see the return of liberalism or something better.

[71] Fisher, *Presidential War Power*, p. 58.

[72] A. Arato, "Their Creative Thinking and Ours: Ackerman's *Emergency Constitution* after Hamdan," *Constellations*, pp. 13, 14.

[73] According to Lobel, the doctrine of inherent powers asserted by Theodore Roosevelt (anticipating Truman, Nixon, and now George W. Bush) already did not contain this limitation. Lobel, "Emergency Power and the Decline of Liberalism," p. 1404.

served as attorney general for FDR, whose views he was forced to later repudiate in *Youngstown*) that giving the president the whole nation's elect awesome powers in external affairs and then trying to limit them internally would be a very difficult task.[74]

Justice Jackson, in other words, ran into the frightening combination of the plebescitary presidency and the (claim of) *inherent* war powers of the "sole organ of the executive" interpreted as emergency powers, transgressing the line between the external and the internal. One might think that both doctrines and their mix violated the original Constitution, its text and structure as well as intent, and on balance, such a view would be correct. Yet we think the roots of the difficulty can still lie in that original Constitution and its illusory solution to the problem of sovereignty. Proceeding in the reverse order than before, it is clear that the separation of powers structure by which the framers hoped to contain legislature and executive both was a poor model. We know this now from a long line of analysis from Marx and Tocqueville to Linz and Sartori, but admittedly the framers had no way of knowing it and had no convincing alternative model available for the republican executive. In any case, they restructured a not yet fully constitutional version of monarchy (because of the existence of the royal prerogative) by giving it an elective and term-bound form and tried to deal with all the potentially pernicious implications by cutting away or rather sharing out (pace Yoo) the elements of the royal prerogative and by creating the antiplebiscitary electoral college. Only Gouverneur Morris, as far as we can tell, had a sense that they were creating a system of dual democratic legitimacy where the president, as the elect of the whole people, would be able to appear in the name of the popular sovereign as "the guardian of the people.... the protector of the whole mass of the people," in a system where the president is "not the King, but the prime minister. The people are the King."[75] Here the famous substitution was operative anticipating Jefferson's reduction of the royal prerogative to a ministerial one, on behalf of the people. While at the Convention direct election was rejected in part to counter just such claims, and in part to shore up the Southern role otherwise diminished by slaves being unable to vote,[76] the plebescitary model nevertheless came into its own with the formation of parties, at the latest though not yet definitively, by 1800. What was in effect created, as only Gouverneur Morris clearly saw when facing the

---

[74] "Executive power has the advantage of concentration in a single head in whose choice the whole Nation has a part, making him the focus of public hopes and expectations. In drama, magnitude and finality his decisions so far overshadow any others that almost alone he fills the public eye and ear. No other personality in public life can begin to compete with him in access to the public mind through modern methods of communications. By his prestige as head of state and his influence upon public opinion he exerts leverage upon those who are supposed... to check and balance his power which often cancels their effectiveness...." *Youngstown Co. v. Sawyer*, concurrence 653–4.

[75] Madison, *Notes*, pp. 322–3, 335.

[76] See ibid., p. 327, for Madison's relevant remarks. This calculation worked out, because in the election of 1800, John Adams lost because of how the three-fifths compromise affected the electoral college. That did not deprive the winner of his plebescitary legitimacy.

intractable issue of presidential reelection, was a weak structural position with a superior legitimacy; a potential leader who has the incentive to increase his power through the accumulation of precedents and practices in the material Constitution that are initially of questionable legality.[77]

No one saw this more clearly or earlier than John C. Calhoun[78] in the service of material interests. Even Jefferson's and Andrew Jackson's states' rights perspectives did not mollify him: He saw the presidency as an organ of both federal sovereignty and future authoritarianism.[79] In fact, the Madisonian mélange of national and segmental sovereignty never fully worked; it was continually challenged by both nationalists on behalf of the whole and states' rightists on behalf of the units. Between them, in the end only force could decide. The Civil War decided this issue once and for all. It was also the first time when the tremendous powers of (federal) state sovereignty and first presidential and then congressional organ sovereignty (ex parte *McCardle* being a case in point for the latter[80]) were united. What the country did not get, pace Ackerman's constitutional revolution, was a new constitution capable of dealing with this new reality.

Moving on to the division of powers and the constituent power together, as they met in Article V of the Constitution, on this one point, the banishing of sovereignty from the internal life of the republic was perhaps too successful, much more successful than Ackerman's brilliant model of informal amendments would have us believe. The very much states' rightist Article V indeed follows the Arendtian recipe of locating the (amending or derived) constituent power in organized bodies, in so many of them, in fact, and with such consensus requirements that it is almost impossible to change the American Constitution legally. It is for this reason that an interpreter such as Dicey referred to the American sovereign as "slumbering" except for the Civil War. And yet after the Civil War, after having seen terrible emergency powers in operation for four years – indeed, many more if we count the Reconstruction – Americans had no constitutional reconstruction except as pertaining to the problem they could not avoid after the Emancipation Proclamation: the problem of slavery and its heritage, a problem that on balance they solved remarkably badly as far as the material or real regime was concerned. All the rest was entrusted to the judges, who remarkably could argue (as did Justice Davis in *Milligan*) that the U.S. Constitution was (or should be) exactly the same in peace and war,

---

[77] See Madison, *Notes*, pp. 322–5, for Morris's very admirable, even self-critical, speech on the dangers of both reeligibility and its exclusion; the speech anticipated Tocqueville's and Marx's critiques of the plebescitary presidency he promoted.

[78] John C. Calhoun, "A Discourse on the Constitution and the Government of the United States," in *Union and Liberty* (Indianapolis: Liberty Fund, 1992).

[79] Interestingly, Arendt's one reference to Calhoun is positive, but she does not pick up at all on his antipresidential and anti–Supreme Court views. Instead, she refers positively to the doctrine of concurrent majorities in distinction to majority rule. She recognizes, of course, the cause on behalf of which the intellectual effort was generated. See Arendt, "Civil Disobedience," p. 76.

[80] On this, see Ackerman, *We the People* II, pp. 223–7.

in normal and exceptional times. Surprisingly, given her republican argument (and inconsistently given her partiality for several famous Jeffersonian formulas!), Arendt bought into this conception of a constitution of judges, putting a glowing senatorial aura on Woodrow Wilson's rather negative depiction of the Court as "a kind of constitutional assembly in permanent session" (*OR*, 192).

That was still in the era of "congressional government." America was soon to enter the world, using, as Wilson was to soon realize (in *Constitutional Government*), the preferred vehicle of the presidency. The causal arrow seems to suggest imperialism led to strengthening of presidency that in turn led to more imperialism, if for no other reason than Grover Cleveland's rejection of imperialism and even McKinley's initial reluctance to engage in overseas ventures. But the weakness of the constitutional structure of the executive implied that in the future (as well as the past, if we think of the Mexican War), the causal relationship could also work in the other direction, because as Wilson realized and then came to promote, presidents could come to understand that strengthening their institutional and personal powers was possible mainly through the domains of war and foreign involvements.[81] "Emergency powers would tend to kindle emergencies," wrote Justice Jackson in the *Youngstown* decision, and the point applies apparently just as much to executive war powers, as Madison knew. And now we also know that it applies to implied, inherent, and unenumerated powers as well as to the formal ones that Madison did not give, and Jackson still feared, at least under given world-political conditions.

Arendt's silence about American imperialism in the great essay of the main body of *Origins* is rather deafening. But in the new (1967) preface to this part, she comes to remedy the fault partially though without however adequate historical and especially constitutional analysis. "The initiative for overseas expansion has shifted westward from England and Western Europe to America, and the initiative for continental expansion . . . is exclusively located in Russia" (*OT*, xix). This was the Cold War, and it was according to her at least half true that American imperialism, like British imperialism, supposedly begins in a "fit of absent mindedness" rather than being the result of deliberate policy. "Whatever the causes for American ascendancy to world power, the deliberate pursuit of foreign policy leading to it or any claim of global rule are not among them" (*OT*, xx). But the result is all the same "limitless pursuit of power that could roam and lay waste the whole globe with no certain nationally or

---

[81] "The President," Wilson wrote, "is at liberty, both in law and conscience, to be as big a man as he can." "Our President must always, henceforth be one of the great powers of the world. . . . The President can never again be a mere domestic officer. . . . He must stand always in the front of our affairs, and the office will be as big and influential as the man who occupies it." Wilson, *Congressional Government in the United States*, pp. 70, 78–9. These lines (as well as the rest of the argument) make clear that it is only by holding on to the new external policy emphasis that the president can escape the mechanical constraints of the formal Constitution. Wilson did not advocate illegality in internal affairs for the same purpose, but believed that in foreign policy there was no need for illegality because of the nearly absolute powers he attributed to the chief executive. Ibid., pp. 71ff v. pp. 77–8.

territorially prescribed purpose." And once again the internal institutions of the old republics are under threat, by the rise of "invisible government." Yet nothing in these institutions themselves that constitute the American form of government represents such a predisposition or even potential. On the contrary, this "form of government is less fitted [for imperialist power politics] than that of any other country" (*OT*, xix–xx).

It is hard to believe that she did not know something about the facts of the Mexican or Spanish–American wars, the history of U.S. policy in Latin America, the colonization of the Philippines and Cuba, the U.S. rivalry with Japan in the Pacific, and the role of the presidency in each of these conflicts, which are theoretically explained as well as justified by Woodrow Wilson, whose writings she knew. Astonishingly enough, in one place she speaks of "the colonialism and imperialism of the European nations . . . [as] the one great crime in which America was never involved."[82] What puzzles us equally on a theoretical level is why she thought that the external sovereignty sought and created by the American framers, untouched in her analysis, would work differently (less tyrannically!) toward weaker states in the case of the United States than in the case of the other great powers that reduced, according to her, the sovereignty of smaller and weaker nation states to illusions.

In other words, the link between Westphalian sovereignty and imperialism, that for Kelsen was a logical relationship, was recognized by Arendt in the case of the traditional European great powers, but not the United States. That would have been perhaps a small problem had she been able to come up with a convincing solution concerning the direction of change needed to "domesticate" external sovereignty in general, but unfortunately she could not.

6.5 Federation and Sovereignty

It is odd that Arendt never dedicated an essay to the problem of external sovereignty, for she broached the issue at several points in her career. For example, she made it quite clear in *Origins* that the international system of states' attribution of absolute sovereignty to the nation-state over internal matters contributed to the willingness and ability to deprive both citizens and noncitizens of basic rights (*OT*, 278–80). But the reverse is also true, as she understood theoretically though routinely neglected, in the American case. If nothing tempers its sovereignty in the international arena, the internal limits to (organ) sovereignty so carefully erected by constitutional republics and so closely analyzed are also at risk at the first moment of crisis.[83] Moreover, from the external standpoint there is not the difference that she sometimes imagined between federal republics and nation-states – both are territorial states equally sovereign regarding matters of emigration, naturalization, nationality, expulsion, and foreign policy generally. Arendt did provide a systematic analysis of

---

[82] Arendt, "Reflection on Little Rock," p. 198.
[83] As she herself stated. See ibid., p. 176.

this issue in one respect. Her analysis of nineteenth-century imperialism and the threat that the lawless exercise of external sovereign power in the peripheries poses to republican institutions in the mother country revealed that she grasped the connection between the external and the internal. She called this the "boomerang effect." But isn't the connection even closer, because "monarchical sovereignty" in foreign affairs seems to be the same absolute, unlimited, solipsistic imperial sovereignty usually claimed and exercised by the executive power posing such threats to domestic republican institutions and to civil rights? For either reason, shouldn't external sovereignty also be limited?

Arendt had some of the conceptual tools for approaching the issue of legally limiting sovereignty in the international arena, such as the idea that the authority of political institutions derives from acts and agreements of political actors; her "Roman" understanding of law as establishing connections and relationships through alliances and treaties (instead of the Austinian concept of law as the will and command of the sovereign); and the principle of federalism (and confederation), which could be applied in new ways in the supranational domain. With these concepts, Arendt could have seen international law and supranational institutions, produced by the consent of states but as creating binding law (rather than simply positive morality in the Austinian sense), able to limit and transform (without abolishing) state sovereignty through a process that embeds states in larger frameworks that nonetheless preserves the identity and equality of each polity while augmenting their power.[84]

Yet Arendt never used her concepts to develop these ideas *systematically* despite the fact that in her lifetime, developments – starting with the UN Charter itself, and including a wide range of treaties, covenants and conventions, such as the genocide convention and the human rights covenants – signaled the transformation of the old "Westphalian" state system that ascribed *absolute sovereign power*, including the right to go to war, to member states. These developments installed a new sovereignty regime based on the legal principle of sovereign equality (and human rights), the banning of aggression, the loss of the right to go to war apart from self-defense, the illegitimacy of forceful annexation, and the emergence of an effective principle of self-determination, applied during the epoch of decolonization to imperial powers. Overseas imperialism was in effect rendered illegal, while the principles of nonintervention and domestic jurisdiction were strongly affirmed. All of this – together with the idea of collective security and the new status and trajectory for international law and multilateral institutions on the one hand and the institutionalization of human rights in a global legal regime on the other – called for (and still does) a rethinking of the concept of sovereignty itself and of the nature of the

---

[84] For example, the European Union is a new form of supranational polity that ascribes sovereign equality to member states while embedding them in a larger political and legal framework that enhances their combined and individual power. The UN does this but in an entirely different way.

international system.[85] The starting point should be reflection on the new legal principle of sovereign equality articulated in the UN Charter and its relation to the shifting interpretation and institutionalization of a particular set of human rights. At the very least, the new sovereignty regime installed in the UN Charter system carries the implication that grave violation of certain rights (such as genocide or mass enslavement) is no longer deemed to be within the domestic jurisdiction of sovereign states.

So why did Arendt not take this route? Evidently, the Cold War and the violations of international law by both superpowers made that law and the UN Charter system seem as weak and irrelevant in the third quarter of the twentieth century as the League of Nations seemed in the second. But there may also have been a theoretical reason that she could not pursue a systematic analysis of the new sovereignty regime. As already indicated, Arendt was unable to get beyond the absolutist conception of sovereignty and the embodiment model of representation that seemed to go with it. What she imagined could be done about it was ultimately the same internally and externally, namely, to abolish it in favor of a constitutional order based on the division and separation of powers, including a constituent power always under the law. She clearly favored such an abolition internally, and believed moreover (this is her greatest mistake as we see it) that it could be done, and the Americans have done it by entirely separating the internal and the external. Was the mistake also a function of her skepticism concerning the application of the one formula she knew for taming the sovereign or the sovereigns to the international realm?

A 1970 interview, "Thoughts on Politics and Revolution," is the one place where she explicitly takes up the question of what to do with external sovereignty, but very inconclusively. The (external) sovereignty of the state, identified with the Westphalian model, means that "conflicts of an international character can ultimately be settled only by war. . . . there is no other last resort."[86] Today (not in 1787!), war can no longer serve as a last resort and therefore "we must have a new concept of the state." Interestingly but cryptically, she says that this new concept would be a *transformation* of the old one, not a *different* one, involving the preservation of the notion of "national independence, namely freedom from foreign rule," but not its identification with the "sovereignty of the state."[87] Consistently with *On Revolution,* to which she refers, Arendt hesitantly first advances "federalism" and then the "councils"

---

[85] Hans Kelsen was the first to attempt to do this. See Hans Kelsen, "The Principle of Sovereign Equality or States as a Basis for International Organization," *Yale Law Journal,* 53, 2 (March 1944), pp. 207–20. See also Bardo Fassbinder, "Sovereignty and Constitutionalism in International Law," in Neil Walker, ed., *Sovereignty in Transition* (Oxford: Hart, 2003), pp. 115–44; Jean L. Cohen, "Whose Sovereignty: Empire versus International Law," *Ethics and International Affairs* 18, 3 (Winter 2008): 1–24.

[86] Arendt, "Thoughts on Politics and Revolution," in *Crises of the Republic,* p. 229.

[87] Ibid., p. 229. Here we are cobbling two texts together, the interviewer having quoted a passage from the German version of "On Violence" that is not in the English versions.

as elements or models of such a new concept of the state, but it is unclear how exactly they are supposed to help now that we are in the international rather than domestic terrain. The federal state is a sovereign state, a world federation would be either a world state or a supra (or, as she says, supernational) entity. The new order according to her, however, must be international rather than *super*national, the latter being identified with world government or the slippery slope to it. But international then again cannot mean the then-current system of international law, or even a new international court or a new league of nations, all of which are interpreted as merely different forms of the same system of sovereign or "ostensibly sovereign" states. The cryptic statement that in the last version, the conflicts of sovereign states would be "played out there all over again...on the level of discourse...which is more important than usually thought," is left hanging without elaboration or demonstration of how discourse and war as a last resort would be still the "same."[88]

Arendt was deeply skeptical of cosmopolitan discourses on human or minority rights – reasoning from the failures of the League of Nations. She deemed these to be ineffectual within a system of international law that in her view was still one of absolutely sovereign states (*OT*, 298). She maintained that in spite of that experience, it now made sense to speak of "human" rights that somehow ought to be guaranteed by "humanity" itself. But she did not know whether this was possible because she was deeply suspicious of the only historically plausible method of realization she entertained, the idea of a world government with direct effect on individuals. To her, as to Kant before her, such a supernational project would most likely mean world despotism and heteronomy because such an enormous state responsible for the welfare of an enormous number of people would be most likely guided by a utilitarian ethics to which rights and freedom will be easily sacrificed (*OT*, 298–9). "The bigger the country becomes in terms of population, of objects, and of possessions, the greater will be the need for administration and with it the anonymous power of administrators."[89] But this issue she confronted in *On Revolution*, with federalism and the federal state being the American answers to the dilemma. In another context she argued, more powerfully, that a world state would be predicated on the end of true political plurality. She insists that

No matter what form a world government with centralized power over the whole globe might assume, the very notion of one sovereign force ruling the whole earth, holding the monopoly of all means of violence, *unchecked and uncontrolled by other sovereign powers* is not only a forbidding nightmare of tyranny, it would be the end of all political life as we know it.... The establishment of one sovereign world state, far from the prerequisite for world citizenship, would be the end of all citizenship.[90]

---

[88] Ibid., pp. 230–1.
[89] Arendt, "On Violence," p. 180.
[90] Hannah Arendt, "Karl Jaspers: Citizen of the World?" in *OR*, 81–2. Emphasis added.

Finally, she argued that a supernational entity, if not yet a world state, would most likely be captured by the most powerful nation and then transformed into a world government as possibly the most frightful tyranny, because of its necessarily all-powerful "police" forces.[91]

The matter cannot be decided on an abstract level comparing schemes for the cosmopolitan organization of the world; designs for a decentralized world state institutionalizing fundamental rights could be imagined that are compatible with internal political plurality as well as constitutional government. Arendt's third argument, focusing on the transformation of a cosmopolitan scheme into an imperial one given existing power relations, is the one that should be worthy of the most serious attention, and the problem is even graver than she briefly outlined because it is not connected only to the possible designs of the strongest. As Kant (who experienced the wars of the French Revolution) certainly realized, in the existing condition of world-political plurality, strong (and even weak) states would violently resist the abolition of their sovereignty, and only an imperial strategy could force them to submit to worldwide integration no matter how beautifully designed. The historical examples of federation are no argument against this, because whether they are Swiss cantons, American states, or members of the European Union, states have decided to "pool" their sovereignty, among other things, in the face of external challenges that smaller units could not meet on their own. To federate in a pluralistic world could thus be voluntary in order to enhance and defend the goods that smaller-scale sovereignty was meant to protect. To federate to abolish plurality is, however, a very different matter. Here the units are meant only to surrender powers without gaining any new ones through the collective. And this they would, rightly or wrongly (we think rightly), resist, turning cosmopolitanism, no matter how well intentioned, into an imperial project of conquest.

Thus we believe Arendt was right, even if for not the best, clearest, or most consistent reasons, against strong, centered versions of political and legal cosmopolitanism: Political plurality and the rule of law are crucial domestically and internationally to establishing and protecting freedom. She was also right that the domestic and autonomous legal system of a polity, backed up by sanctions, with direct effect on individuals who also have full legal standing (legal personhood), is indispensable for instituting and protecting the rights asserted by a citizenry. Political concepts are indeed based on plurality, diversity, and mutual limitations. An autonomous polity provides the space wherein political freedom becomes possible: It is the primary context of politics. What she did not understand was that it is ultimately the internal sovereignty of the territorial state that institutes the autonomy of the polity and enables the project of self-government under law – the political (as distinct from the ethical) meaning of self-determination. To be sure, that sovereign power also can violate rights and undermine political freedom. That is why she and we construe civil and

---

[91] Hannah Arendt, "Thoughts on Politics and Revolution," p. 230.

political rights as legal mechanisms that help ensure that state power is exercised within the limits of law and the rule of law, alongside institutionalized counterpowers and an active citizenry. Yet this insight apparently puts Arendt in the "statist" camp against cosmopolitan visions of a world order without autonomous polities.

On the other hand, she knew perfectly well, as already indicated, that unlimited external state sovereignty also puts rights and political freedom at risk and her concept of the right to have rights must be understood accordingly. It is, after all, a cosmopolitan idea, since the addressee of such a right is every person qua person. This concept thus pushes in the direction of global international institutions and laws capable of enunciating and backing up such a right. The circle could be squared only through a rethinking of the concepts and relations between sovereignty and rights.

Arendt's reflections on "world citizenship" in her Karl Jaspers essay and on the meaning of a crime against humanity in the Adolf Eichmann book take a few steps in this direction.[92] In the former, she reflected on the historical emergence of what she calls a "factual unity of mankind," based on technology and the global system of communication that now covers the surface of the Earth.[93] Today we call this globalization. According to Jaspers and to Arendt, all peoples on Earth now have a common present and every man feels the shock of events that take place on the other side of the globe. "But this common factual present is not based on a common past and does not in the least guarantee a common future. Technology, having provided the unity of the world, can just as easily destroy it and the means of global communication were designed side by side with the means of possible global destruction."[94] Indeed, the most potent symbol of this factual, technologically produced unity is atomic weaponry, which thus far has yielded a merely negative solidarity based on fear of global destruction.

Arendt argues that the step toward a positive solidarity of mankind would require the assumption of political responsibility by citizens for what their governments do, but that this could emerge within two rather different forms of "cosmopolitanism." The first version, which she rejects, would be based on a dogmatic conception of truth and entail a conception of world citizenship that sees historical, cultural, and political diversity as obstacles on the road to a horridly "shallow unity of mankind."[95] The "real abstraction" required to produce "mankind" would involve a leveling down and bland homogenization, most probably through the "universalization" of one cultural or civilizational set of understandings, institutions, and "truths." Let us call this imperial

---

[92] Ibid.; Hannah Arendt, *Eichmann in Jerusalem* (New York: Penguin), 1963; Arendt, "Karl Jaspers: Citizen of the World?"

[93] Ibid., pp. 83, 88.

[94] Ibid., p. 83.

[95] Ibid., p. 87.

universalism.[96] The other route would proceed through horizontal communication and entail faith in the communicability of all truths and the good will to reveal and listen. It would enable the creation of solidarity and the discovery of commonalities about our shared human condition while preserving the key features of that condition: plurality, diversity, and difference. This could yield a unity of mankind that would be political, embedded, and guaranteed in a framework of universal mutual agreements that would lead eventually to a worldwide federated structure. According to Arendt, this was Jaspers' vision: His conception of world citizenship would require a world federation involving a cosmopolitanism of nations such that "the national of every country can enter this world history of humanity only by remaining and clinging stubbornly to what he is."[97] The principle to follow in order to get there would be that nothing should happen in politics today that would be contrary to the actually existing solidarity of mankind. This is presented as a variant on Kant's dictum that nothing should happen in war that would make peace impossible.[98]

However, even in this essay Arendt seems to think, along with Jaspers, that the prerequisite of world federation would be the abolition of sovereignty, in part because it would have to rule out war as a political means since any war would affect immediately and directly all mankind in the current context.[99] This makes her nervous, and rightfully so, in my view. She states that

The abolition of war, like the abolishment of a plurality of sovereign states, would harbor its own peculiar dangers; the various armies would be replaced by federated police forces, and our experiences with modern police states and totalitarian governments where the old power of the army is eclipsed by the rising omnipotence of the police, are not apt to make us overoptimistic about this prospect.[100]

Indeed. The preceding ambivalence toward either meaning of a cosmopolitan order or of a world federation notwithstanding, Arendt did come to see that international law would have an important new role to play in the future when she had to confront the issue of the Eichmann trial: the meaning of a "crime against humanity" and the significance of the 1948 Genocide Convention. On her famous interpretation, the concept of the crime against humanity was based not on the abstract idea of human rights and their grave violation, but on her particular conception of the human condition as one of diversity and plurality and the attempt to alter this. Accordingly, the project of annihilating the Jews was viewed in terms of the later concept of genocide, that is, as a crime against humanity perpetrated upon the Jewish people, insofar as the perpetrators were unwilling to share the earth with a particular group and thus sought to destroy that entire group. Unlike the crime of murder, which violates the order of a

[96] Arendt states that, "A world citizen, living under the tyranny of a world empire, and speaking and thinking in a kind of glorified Esperanto, would be . . . a monster. . . ." Ibid., p. 89.
[97] Ibid.
[98] Ibid., p. 93.
[99] Ibid., pp. 84, 93.
[100] Ibid., pp. 93–4.

particular state, the crime against humanity and genocide violate an altogether different order and different community: the human condition.[101] Expulsion of nationals violates an offense against humanity understood as the comity of nations (because the expelled appear at one's borders) and thus does concern the international community, but genocide is an attack upon human diversity, a characteristic of the "human status" as such without which "mankind" would be devoid of meaning.[102] This reveals another dimension, then, of the "right to have rights."

With great prescience, Arendt insisted on looking at genocide as an actual possibility of the future, and given that possibility, she insisted that without the help and protection of international law, no people on Earth could be sure of its continued existence.[103] Accordingly, she argued for the creation of an international penal code and for a permanent international criminal court.[104]

How can these various positions on international law be reconciled? Thinking with and beyond Arendt, we argue that her own best impulses point toward the need to rethink rather than abandon the concept of state sovereignty, to rethink the discourse of human rights and their role within the context of a new sovereignty regime, and finally to rethink the relation among sovereignty, international law, and international justice.

6.6 Conclusion

In the spirit of the Arendtian theory, we come to the following conclusion: We must *transform* rather than abolish both internal and external sovereignty. Abolition of sovereignty, on the contrary, is impossible in the modern world; projects that aim at this end are counterproductive and strengthen the wrong sovereignty regimes. First, the American attempt to abolish internal sovereignty, if it was a project at all, failed. Arendt's analysis contains the seeds of failure: namely, her mistake about the supposed abandonment of the idea of popular sovereignty; her idea that in America, unlike anywhere else, the state was entirely constitutionalized; and the eventually revisited but, for America, never revised separation of the problem of internal sovereignty from that of the transformation of the external world of states. Historically, at the crossroads of the legitimation resources of popular sovereignty, and the functional requirements as well as the imperial temptation of external sovereignty, the American presidency periodically managed to renew the organ sovereignty that Arendt sought to banish. It is better to see this phenomenon that often appears in the form of "constitutional dictatorship" as inherent in our sovereignty regime, rather than crime or usurpation, the effect of popular or consumer culture as mediated by public relations, or the pernicious effect of bureaucracy. This sovereignty

---

[101] Arendt, *Eichmann in Jerusalem*, p. 272.
[102] Ibid., pp. 268–9.
[103] Ibid., p. 273.
[104] Ibid., p. 270.

regime, and indeed the U.S. constitutional system, should be redesigned, but there is little chance of that. Though we suffer from its consequences year after year, we tend to, like Arendt, pronounce it the most if not only healthy component of the American body politic. Even if it were redesigned, a new project of banishing internal sovereignty and eliminating the possibility of organ sovereignty would predictably not succeed entirely, because the motor for its reappearance is on the level of the state, or the material rather than the formal Constitution, and that state will continue to respond to challenges and opportunities in an unstable international world in a more or less traditional way if that world itself is not reorganized. And this is especially so if that state does not divest itself of its imperial role.

With respect to the world of states, Arendt was right: We do indeed need to abandon once and for all two dangerous myths: the myth of a homogeneous nation-state and the myth of absolute, legally unlimited sovereignty as prerogative, discretion, and unbridled will. But we also should resist, as she rightly argued, the cosmopolitan utopia of a unitary global legal and political order, centralized or federal, that replaces the principle of the sovereign equality of a plurality of autonomous polities with justice to persons and human rights.

Her critique of the absolute conception of sovereignty is of course right on the mark. But the concept of sovereignty need not be absolute or interpreted in the one-sided way we find in her work. Arendt's dichotomous conception of sovereignty and politics and of sovereignty and law, her identification of sovereignty with the will, rule, unity, homogeneity, arbitrariness, and ultimately lawlessness, prevented her from seeing the complexity of the concept. Sovereignty as a concept, as a discourse, and as an institution always was and is irrevocably dual: It always involves a *relation* of law and power, politics and rule, voluntas and ratio, fact and norm, legitimacy and legality, unity and plurality – a relation that can be contested and be reconfigured. It is always also symbolic (of the political autonomy of a polity and as popular sovereignty, of self-government under law) and never simply factual (control, effective rule). Indeed, the external sovereignty of a state requires recognition and today it is also the UN and not only individual states that afford such recognition and the legal status and prerogatives that go with it. Sovereignty involves legal and political relationships, and indeed without the unity provided by the sovereign state, and the legal equality among them, the diversity, the plurality, the rule of law, political freedom, and the contestation that is politics would have no framework within which to exist and no common ground to contest. It is thus mistaken to assume that sovereignty is the opposite of law or political freedom or that sovereignty inexorably entails homogenization, embodiment, tyranny, or dictatorship. Had Arendt reflected adequately on this, she would have been able to see that there could be *different sovereignty regimes* and that effective international institutions and law, including global human rights law, need not spell the end of the sovereign state any more than constitutionalism requires the abandonment of the discourse of (popular or state) sovereignty internally. But neither must it entail a wholesale shift to an abstract and overly utopian cosmopolitanism.

If we try to reconceive sovereignty in its deep dualities, we can come to the real task before us: how to rethink the institutionalization of sovereign equality and human rights, of genuine political plurality and global justice that has been on the agenda since 1945 in a way that protects the autonomy and self-determination and thus political freedom of and within each polity while simultaneously ensuring that everyone's right to have rights (and thus to the protection of the law and the rule of law) is accepted as a principle and ensured by all members of the international community.

In short, international law can bind sovereignty without abolishing it; just as constitutional law can do domestically. But to see this, one would have to theorize the dualistic character of the international/global regime as a dualistic international society based on sovereign equality with important cosmopolitan legal elements – human rights – that enunciate shifts in the prerogatives ascribed to sovereign states based on changing conceptions of the principles and mechanisms of global justice. Through the legal principle of sovereign equality and the rules for recognizing states, internal law authorizes states to exercise sovereign power, with certain provisos. Sovereign equality is and remains the organizing legal principle of international law and politics. Yet it is indicative of an important shift in the understanding of sovereignty and certainly is not "Westphalilan" or absolutist. The "cosmopolitan" dimension of what we call our dualistic international order, however, has a global dimension, meaning, at the very least, that there can be no "lawless" zones, implying that the project of recreating absolute imperial sovereignty and zones of pure discretion symbolized by the Guantanamo detention center is illegal and can be challenged legally. In this sense, it meets Arendt's concern regarding the right to have rights, namely, that all individuals should be covered by a legal persona. This must operate on national and global levels, as she came to see. Of course, the human rights of those detained are at issue. But the way to understand legal human rights, including those at stake in grave violations of international law such as genocide, ethnic cleansing, or mass enslavement, is to see them as mechanisms aimed at regulating the effects of the ascription of legal sovereignty and its exercise, not as indications of its abolition.[105] We believe that this project of rethinking sovereignty and rights is true to the spirit if not in the letter of Arendt's work.

---

[105] See the interesting paper by Patrick Macklem, "What Is International Human Rights Law?" on file with the author.

7

The Decline of Order

Hannah Arendt and the Paradoxes of the Nation-State

Christian Volk

Even beyond political theory, Hannah Arendt's analysis of the minority and refugee problem in the European interwar period has found broad appeal.[1] Authors such as Michael Marrus, Claudena Skran, Gérard Noiriel, and Aristide Zolberg all refer to Arendt's work in their studies on minorities and refugees. Zolberg, for instance, states that Arendt's analysis of the interwar period "provides the principal key for understanding how refugees come about."[2] He concludes that in her work Arendt links the refugee and minority problems directly to the spread of the idea of the nation-state to eastern and southeastern states. In agreement with Arendt, Claudena Skran maintains that from the perspective of the new national governments, the minorities posed a problem "because

---

[1] Within political theory, Arendt's considerations on statelessness are mainly discussed under the scope of human rights. Cf. Seyla Benhabib, *The Rights of Others* (Cambridge: Cambridge University Press, 2004); Peg Birmingham, *Hannah Arendt and Human Rights: The Predicament of Common Responsibility* (Bloomington: Indiana University Press, 2006); Hauke Brunkhorst, "Sind Menschenrechte Aporien? Kritische Bemerkungen zu einer These Hannah Arendts," *Kritische Justiz* 29, 3 (1996): 335–42; Frank I. Michelman, "Parsing a Right to Have Rights," *Constellations* 3, 2 (1996): 200–8; Serena Parekh, "A Meaningful Place in the World: Hannah Arendt on the Nature of Human Rights," *Journal of Human Rights* 3, 1 (2004): 41–53. In their recent works, Wolfgang Heuer and Waltraud Meints-Stender address the same issue from the perspective of the political problem of exclusion. Cf. Wolfgang Heuer, "Europa und seine Flüchtlinge. Hannah Arendt über die notwendige Politisierung von Minderheiten," in Heinrich-Böll-Stiftung, ed., *Hannah Arendt: Verborgene Tradition – Unzeitgemäße Aktualität?* (Berlin: Akamdemie-Verlag, 2007), pp. 331–41; Waltraud Meints-Stender, "Hannah Arendt und das Problem der Exklusion – eine Aktualisierung," in Heinrich-Böll-Stiftung, ed., *Hannah Arendt: Verborgene Tradition – Unzeitgemäße Aktualität?* (Berlin: Akamdemie-Verlag, 2007), pp. 251–8.
[2] Aristide Zolberg, "The Formation of New States as a Refugee-Generating Process," *Annals of the American Academy of Political and Social Science*, 467, 24 (1983): 24–38, at 30.

This article is a translated, revised, and altered version of the first chapter, "Die Paradoxien des Nationalstaats," of my book *Die Ordnung der Freiheit. Recht und Politik im Denken Hannah Arendts* (Baden-Baden: Nomos, 2010). I would like to thank Claudia Mason for her great help with the English language.

they do not fit within the normal parameters of a world of nation-states." The massive streams of refugees, Skran continues, were "by-products of efforts to achieve ethnically pure nation-states and ideologically homogeneous political systems."[3] As Michael Marrus points out, for authors dealing with refugee and minority issues, the main reason for referring to Arendt's studies is that Arendt was one of the first to highlight "the singular predicament of refugees" and to describe "how they were reduced to a lonely, savage existence, hounded from place to place by national governments that alone accorded to people elementary rights."[4]

Although Zolberg, Skran, and Marrus emphasize an important argument within Arendt's considerations, I argue that the narrative they base their arguments upon is problematic. With respect to their object of inquiry, all three speak of the nation-state as a sovereign actor that pursues its interests independently and that thus bears responsibility for the precarious humanitarian situation of the refugees. Yet, if one considers Arendt's analysis from the perspective of political theory, that narrative of the nation-state as a sovereign actor is misleading. The refugee and minority problem, I argue, discloses the "internal disintegration"[5] of an order of nation-states and the impracticality of its concepts in a globalized world. For Arendt, the minority problem does not show the sovereignty of the nation-state but its inappropriateness as a form of government and the concurrent fall of a Europe composed of nation-states. Against the background of the interwar period, the question of the reliability, stability, and durability of a political order represented by the nation-state becomes the linchpin of her analysis.

To argue that Arendt is concerned with the problem of political order stands out for two reasons. Generally, Arendt is not considered as a thinker of order but as a thinker of contingency, of revolutionary beginning. Accordingly, Albrecht Wellmer stresses Arendt's "revolutionary universalism,"[6] which "no extra-political normative foundation secures or justifies."[7] If one examines her work purely from the perspective of contingency and revolutionary beginnings, it might not be apparent how one can associate her thinking with the questions on political order.[8] Irrespective of questions about order and

---

[3] Claudena Skran, *Refugees in Inter-War Europe: The Emergence of a Regime* (Oxford: Oxford University Press, 1995), p. 29.

[4] Michael Marrus, *The Unwanted: European Refugees in the Twentieth Century* (Oxford and New York: Oxford University Press, 1985), p. 4.

[5] Hannah Arendt, *The Origins of Totalitarianism* (New York: Harcourt, 1994), p. 270. (Hereafter abbreviated *OT*.)

[6] Albrecht Wellmer, "Arendt on Revolution," in R. Dana Villa, ed., *The Cambridge Companion to Hannah Arendt* (Cambridge: Cambridge University Press, 2005), pp. 220–41, at 224.

[7] Ibid., p. 229.

[8] The fact that order and new beginning are directly connected with each other results from the loss of power and authority of an old order that precedes a new political beginning, such as a revolution. In *On Revolution*, Arendt, therefore, writes that "a revolution did not end with the abolition of state and government but, on the contrary, aimed at the foundation of a new state

revolution, about contingency and new beginnings, my evaluation might irritate for a second reason: Discussing the interwar period under the perspective of the decline of order directly concurs with the tenor of the debates within state theory of that time. Since Bodin, the question of political order has been the central question of state theory; in the interwar period, German political thinkers in particular centered their critique of the "Weimar System" on the question of order – regardless of their political and ideological positions. Max Weber, for instance, states that the main purpose of the state was "to enforce its system of order."[9] Hans Kelsen asserts "the modern state is essentially a coercive order – a centralized coercive order."[10] For Carl Schmitt, Kelsen's strongest critic, "public safety and order" represent not only the highest "state interest,"[11] but also the basis for his theory of sovereignty. Additionally, later he describes his own state theory as "concrete order thinking."[12] Rudolf Smend, a further opponent of Kelsen, defines the state as a rule that exists "by virtue of an order."[13] For Hermann Heller, the "question of the relation between rule and order" is the "basic problem of all state-theories."[14] Because none of Arendt's books *seem* to deal with the triad of state, law, and order explicitly, it is deemed a remote notion to link Arendt to these discussions on state theory.

In what follows, I will fill this void and show how far Arendt's thinking is indeed occupied with the relation among the state, law, and order. However, Arendt does not reflect on political order on the basis of anthropological, moral, or ethical assumptions. Rather, her criticism is *immanent* and starts with the self-perception and self-description of nation-states. What does this mean? Seen from a system-analytical perspective, the nation-state is a form of government that, according to Arendt, is based on specific principles, which interact and then result in a certain form of order – the national government. Without claiming comprehensiveness, Arendt lists, for example, peoples' right to self-determination, the identity of state and nation, the idea of democratic sovereignty of the people, state sovereignty, *Rechtstaatlichkeit* (rule of law), and

and the establishment of a new form of government." Hannah Arendt, *On Revolution* (New York: Penguin, 1963), p. 265.

9 Max Weber, *Economy and Society: An Outline of Interpretive Sociology* (2 vols) (Berkeley: University of California Press, 1978), p. 55.

10 Hans Kelsen, *Pure Theory of Law,* translation from the second German edition by Max Knight (Berkeley: University of California Press, 2002), p. 54.

11 Carl Schmitt, *Politische Theologie. Vier Kapitel zur Lehre von der Souveränität* (Berlin: Duncker & Humblot, 2004), p. 13.

12 Carl Schmitt, *Über die drei Arten des rechtswissenschaftlichen Denkens* (Berlin: Duncker & Humblot, 1993), p. 10.

13 Rudolf Smend, "Staat und Politik," in *Staatsrechtliche Abhandlungen und andere Aufsätze* (Berlin:,1994), pp. 363–79, at 368.

14 Hermann Heller, "Die Souveränität. Ein Beitrag zur Theorie des Staats- und Völkerrechts," in *derselbe: Gesammelte Schriften. Zweiter Band* (Recht, Staat, Macht, Leiden: Sijthoff, 1971), pp. 31–202, at 57.

so on.[15] Constitutionality and rule of law are especially pivotal for the stability, security, and reliability of a nation-state order. The nation-state, Arendt writes, is "characteristically a constitutional state."[16] In her analysis of the interwar period, she compares the actual behavior of the European states with their self-perception and attempts to secure peace after the disastrous experiences of World War I. Arendt comes to the conclusion that a Europe of nation-states, due to the principles of order to which it was committed and with which it attempted to grasp reality, at no time was in a position to solve or to defuse the problems posed by refugees and minorities. Because of this, the legal and political foundation of the nation-states started dissolving and – both facts are directly linked – the relationship between the different states got poisoned. This points to Arendt's assumption that within a Europe based on the principles of a nation-state order, "a guaranteed peace on Earth is as utopian as the squaring of the circle."[17]

I demonstrate that Arendt's assertion of the decline of a constitutional order can be determined mainly by four paradoxes of the nation-state. I present her argument of the "collapse of the system of nation-state" (*OT*, 22) and provide tangible and concrete characteristics for the understanding of the paradoxes of the system of the nation-state. These inner contradictions – the *paradox of the right to self-determination*, the *paradox of deassimilation and denaturalization*, the *paradox of lawlessness*, the *paradox of human rights* – which are a direct result of the principles of the nation-state, developed their subversive potential in the interwar period. There is not one single paradox that justifies the claim of a Europe-wide breakdown of the national-state order by itself. It also does not coincide with Arendt's idea of "fragmentary historiography"[18] to try and find a closed theory or a historic chronology behind her discussion of the disintegration of order. The aim, rather, must be to span a kind of net in which

---

[15] For Arendt, the United States is a republic, not a nation-state, just like Great Britain. Moreover, she does not consider National Socialist Germany, fascist Italy, authoritarian Poland, or Hungary under the regent of Horthy as nation-states. Fundamental characteristics of a nation-state form of government had been dissolved. In all mentioned cases, the principle of legal government and the idea of the peoples' sovereignty had been perverted. Above all, the Nazis' racism and ideology – with regard to territory and to the term people – abolished the idea of nation-states. In addition, the National Socialist ideas based on party and movement destroyed the institutional structure of the state.

[16] Hannah Arendt, "Nationalstaat und Demokratie," 2006, available online at HannahArendt.net, Documents 2/06. Here I quote from "Nationalstaat und Demokratie." The German text says: "*Denn dass der Nationalstaat in seinem Wesen ein Rechts- und Verfassungsstaat und nur als solcher lebensfähig war, hatte sich bereits in Anfängen vorher erwiesen und sollte vor allem nach dem zweiten Weltkrieg ganz offenbar werden.*" Arendt delivered this paper on a German broadcast Westdeutscher Rundfunk (West German Broadcasting) in 1963 during a discussion with Eugen Kogon. Whenever it is appropriate, I will also mention the German text on which I base my own translation.

[17] Hannah Arendt, "Thoughts on Politics and Revolution: A Commentary," in Hannah Arendt, *Crisis of the Republic* (New York: Mariner, 1972), pp. 199–233, at 229.

[18] Seyla Benhabib, *The Reluctant Modernism of Hannah Arendt* (Lanham: Rowman & Littlefield, 2003), p. 94.

the relation between the order-endangering potential of the paradoxes becomes apparent and thus provides an impression of the *Totalgeschehen*.[19]

However, the "decline of the nation-state" (*OT*, 267) is more than just the end of a form of government. Along with the nation-state "*a whole way of life*"[20] perished and its moral standards and values vanished from public life. At least this was one precondition for what Arendt later had described as the "totality of the moral collapse"[21] in Europe.

7.1 The Paradox of the Right to Self-Determination

The first paradox that endangers the order of the nation-state can be identified as the right to national self-determination, one of the fundamental principles of the European nation-state model. Sieyès was one of the first who stipulated, "[E]very nation ought to be . . . free."[22] Ernest Renan sees in "the wish of the nation . . . the sole legitimate criterion, the one to which one must always return,"[23] and thus further develops the liberating and emancipating idea of self-determination, more than one hundred years after the French Revolution. Since only a few nations could be accorded "national self-determination and sovereignty," Arendt elucidates how this liberating idea of self-determination became an instrument of repression. She argues that against this background, the newly established states quickly found themselves in the role of the oppressor. The "nationally frustrated peoples" (*OT*, 271), on the other hand, became aware "that true freedom, true emancipation, and true popular sovereignty could be attained only with full national emancipation, that people without their own national government were deprived of human rights" (*OT*, 272). Understood as a sign of national emancipation, the right to self-determination was considered a universal justification according to international law for oppressive political actions by the new nation-states as well as for independence movements of minority groups. This dialectic of repression and autonomy coexisted with ethnic hatred that "began to play a central role in public affairs everywhere" (*OT*, 268) in the interwar period, and which reflected

---

[19] Walter Benjamin, "Das Passagen-Werk. Aufzeichnungen und Materialen," in *Gesammelte Schriften*, Volume 1, edited by Rolf Tiedemann (Frankfurt a. M.: Suhrkamp 1991), pp. 79–654, at 575.

[20] Hannah Arendt, *Was ist Politik. Fragmente aus dem Nachlaß*, edited by Ursula Ludz (Munich: Piper, 2003), p. 226. (Hereafter abbreviated *WiP*.) Italics in the original text. Ursula Ludz alludes that Arendt points out in a lectures given in 1963 in Chicago that the term "forms of government" is misleading. Arendt argues, as does Ludz, that much more is at stake when we speak of forms of governments, namely a "*whole way of life*" (cf. *WiP*: 226).

[21] Hannah Arendt, *Eichmann in Jerusalem: A Report on the Banality of Evil* (New York: Penguin, 2006), p. 125.

[22] Emmanuel Joseph Sieyès. "What Is the Third Estate?" in *Political Writings: Including the Debate between Sieyes and Tom Paine in 1791*, edited by Michael Sonenscher (Indianapolis: Hackett Publishing Company, 2003), pp. 92–162, at 77.

[23] Ernest Renan, *Was ist eine Nation? Rede am 11. März 1882 an der Sorbonne, Mit einem Essay von Walter Euchner* (Hamburg: Europäische Verlagsanstalt, 1996), p. 36.

Arendt's assumption of the "internal disintegration" of Europe's nation-state system.

Despite peace agreements, minority contracts, and other political treaties, the European nation-states were not "capable of bringing order to this chaos of reciprocal hate."[24] Arendt notes that in such an atmosphere of ethnic hatred, "practical consideration and the silent acknowledgment of common interests" (OT, 278) as the idea of nation-states once envisaged, became impossible. Instantly it became apparent *"that full national sovereignty was possible only as long as the comity of European nations existed."* Only as long as the *"spirit of unorganized solidarity and agreement"* (OT, 278) existed among the sovereign states was it possible that a balance of the different interests on the one hand and respect for the sovereignty of the other nation-states on the other could lead to a functioning political order. Without that spirit, the situation very quickly resulted in those *"deadly conflicts"* (OT, 278; emphasis in the original text) that should have been prevented from the perspective of the established nation-states and against the backdrop of the experiences of the disaster of World War I. Kelsen's assertion of "national legal order as state subjectivism"[25] and his theory that any idea of national sovereignty can function only if it is based on reciprocal recognition coincides with Arendt's skepticism on such things as absolute sovereignty. Nevertheless, if one perceives self-determination against the background of ethnic hatred, the first question is how, according to Arendt, the principle of national self-determination could gain such a determining influence on European politics.

Even before 1914, approximately one hundred million people in Europe were denied the right to self-determination.[26] After World War I, this situation was no longer tenable. For one, political constraints forced the established nation-states to fill the power void that ensued after the collapse of the Austro-Hungarian monarchy, the rule of the Russian czar, and the Ottoman Empire. As the old European nation-states were being confronted with independence movements in their colonies, it would only have been possible to deny the ethnic groups in eastern and southeastern Europe national self-determination with military violence – an option that was deemed unimaginable after the shocking experiences of modern war. Arendt argues that in view of this historic-political

---

[24] Hannah Arendt, *Elemente und Ursprünge totaler Herrschaft Antisemitismus, Imperialismus, totale Herrschaft* (Munich: Piper, 2003), p. 561. (Hereafter abbreviated *ETH*.) This is my own translation from the German version *Elemente und Ursprünge totaler Herrschaft*. Arendt writes: "Selbst die Friedensverträge, welche die Nationalitäten in 'Staatsvölker' und Minderheiten aufteilten, haben in dieses Chaos gegenseitigen Hasses keine Ordnung bringen können" (*ETH*: 561). Since some passages or phrases were added to the German version of Arendt's book on totalitarianism, sometimes I will refer to *Elemente und Ursprünge totaler Herrschaft*. In that case, whenever it is appropriate, I will give the German version on which I base my translation; if not, I will just cite the quotation.

[25] Kelsen, "Pure Theory of Law," p. 345.

[26] Arendt takes these numbers from the studies of English historian and diplomat Sir Charles Kingsley Webster. (Cf. *OT*, 272.)

background, the peace agreements of 1919 through 1920 were to pave the way for national emancipation of all ethnic groups and all European countries. In addition, for Arendt, the peace agreements represented the attempt to preserve a Europe organized in nation-states, to defend the idea of nation-states as the basis of a new peace order of the twentieth century and "to conserve the European status quo" (*OT*, 271). Since a different federal-supranational solution was not feasible, the idea of national self-determination was extended to the whole of Europe.

However, it was not possible simply to apply the nation-state theme to eastern and southeastern Europe. None of the newly structured regions could fulfill the requirements on which traditional nation-states such as France rested; none of these territories was uni-national. On the contrary, Arendt stresses that these regions all comprised a colorful mix of ethnic groups that defined themselves as political groups. She agrees with Mussolini, who maintained that the fundamental problem of Czechoslovakia was that it was not Czecho-Slovakia only, but rather "Czech-Germano-Polono-Magyaro-Rutheno-Rumano-Slovakia" (*OT*, 270). The aim was to create nation-states on the grounds of the right to self-determination, yet the result was "nationalities-states" (*ETH*, 567).[27] Moreover – and this is a decisive point in Arendt's considerations – the ethnic groups involved were people whose national consciousness had only recently been awakened following the example of the Western nations. Instead of looking back to a history of stateness and linking nationality with the legal institutions of the state, Arendt argues in the tradition of Meinecke, distinguishing between the concept of state-nation and cultural nation, that in these ethnic groups, the concept of nationality "had not yet developed beyond the inarticulateness of ethnic consciousness." In contrast to the Western understanding of nationality, "their national quality appeared to be much more a portable private matter, inherent in their very personality, than a matter of public concern and civilization" (*OT*, 231). In short, in eastern and southeastern Europe, the concept of a nation-state had an ethnic connotation from the beginning.

Arendt assumed that the leading politicians of old nation-states thought or hoped that the nationality problems in eastern and southeastern Europe could be channeled with the help of minority treaties. The minority system that they had designed warranted that the important ethnic groups could participate in administration and government, according to their proportion in the population. The other smaller ethnic splinter groups were to surrender their political rights, especially the right to national emancipation, in favor of the right to use their own language, to run their own schools, to practice their own religion, and so on. Arendt stresses that the adjective "national" was avoided at all accounts when determining these minorities. Thus a "Czech-Germano-Polono-Magyaro-Rutheno-Rumano-Slovakia" became a Czechoslovakia in which 7 million Czechs were under the auspices of the minority group of Slovaks

---

[27] The German version says "Nationalitätenstaaten" (*ETH*, 567).

with 2 million people. Describing the actual intention of the minority treaties, Arendt refers to former British foreign minister Sir Austen Chamberlain:

[T]he object of the Minority Treaties (is)... to secure... that measure of protection and justice which would gradually prepare them to be merged in the national community to which they belonged. (*OT*, 273)

While identifying one nation – as in Poland, Romania, and Lithuania – or two nations – such as in Czechoslovakia or Yugoslavia – as the state's nation in order to guarantee the constitutional requirements for a national identity, European statesmen believed that the decisive steps had been undertaken to secure a robust statutory future in those parts of Europe. The reality that was emerging in Europe refuted the vision that Chamberlain had described. *Firstly*, the minority treaties that had been designed as exceptions became the rule. There was no one region in eastern and southeastern Europe that was not coveted by several nationalities simultaneously. Moreover, when the idea was conceived, many ethnic groups had simply not been identified. Therefore, the territorial divisions, no matter which kind, seemed arbitrary from the start. *Secondly*, the classifications into nations based on these divisions seemed equally artificial. One ethnic group was elevated to the status of a state's nation, whose political will was declared "the sole legitimate criterion" and was internationally recognized with reference to self-determination, whereas the other group only managed to achieve an ethnic, religious, or language group status.[28] This situation, which was deemed unacceptable by the minorities and led to separatist attempts everywhere, was accompanied by a policy of "systematic obstruction" (*ETH*, 576). Looking at their own minorities across the border, many newly created states considered the drawing of the borders unsatisfactory as well, which led to numerous border conflicts that partially escalated into border wars. The border conflicts on the other hand spurred inner-state conflicts among different ethnic groups and revealed, in Pearson's words, "*hybrid nature of the new states.*"[29] Early on it became apparent that, if the constellations were "unsuited," *intra*state conflicts between population and minorities or even between minorities themselves could very quickly lead to *inter*state conflicts.

Arendt describes how the leading European politicians, who were worried by the increasingly conflict-ridden situation, clearly and expressly "pointed out the 'duties' the minorities owed to the new states" (*OT*, 272). Here it became obvious what the minority term actually entailed. Arendt quotes French politician Aristide Briand, who noted, "The process... at which we should aim is not the disappearance of the minorities, but a kind of assimilation" (*OT*, 272). For Arendt, from the beginning on, the nation-state aimed at the assimilation of minorities. On this basis, Arendt detects two different versions

[28] Cf. *OT*, 270.
[29] Raymond Pearson, *National Minorities in Eastern Europe, 1848–1945* (London: Palgrave Macmillan, 1983), p. 184. Emphasis added.

of the concept of minority. On the one hand, we see the understanding of a minority as a splinter group separated from the majority but which is protected by the neighbor state where the minority is not the minority but the majority of the population. On the other hand, the idea of a nation-state minority according to Arendt was modeled on the situation of the Jews. Because Jews lived in all countries and were content with the status of a minority, they exemplify the "minorité par excellence" (*OT*, 289).

What is significant about this equation is that a specific inherent focus ensued from the "minority term," which coincided with the expectations of the old nation-states and also the demands for absolute sovereignty of the newly created states. Since the Jews did not have their own state but advanced to the model of a new concept of minority, the political notion of minority changed; the "minority" term was deprived of its power. A powerless "minority" term was in the interest of the fundamental idea of a nation-state, as it could change a section of the population into a silent minority that had to behave accordingly toward the majority. Arendt maintains that this silent wish, which shortly afterward was asserted in Briand's political claim for assimilation, was not fulfilled. On the one hand, a "powerless" understanding of minorities did not reflect the actual situation. It depended strongly on the minority involved how "powerless" or "powerful" a minority actually was. What de facto applied to the unprotected Jewish minorities or the Sinti and Roma in all European states did not necessarily apply to the German minority in Czechoslovakia as the crisis in the Sudetenland showed. On the other hand, many ethnic groups were not happy with the situation. Most minorities defined themselves as political groups and therefore considered themselves the "unlucky remaining rest" (*ETH*, 565), who due to power political concerns or sinister interests were prevented from being united with their country of origin. The call for assimilation was, therefore, *thirdly*, absolutely unacceptable to them.

At the same time, the tradition of the nation-state thinking that had been generally accepted since the French Revolution assumed that the people and the nation had to be the same and that minorities were, if anything, temporary anomalies. This in turn spurred the nationalization of minorities because only sustained political and permanent emphasis of their national identity could prevent the threatening absorption by the majority people in the long term. In this fashion, as Zolberg maintains, the minorities changed into "*political misfits*."[30] It is undisputed that this process of nationalization fell on the fertile ground of an ethnic notion of nationality that comprised additional conflict potential. Arendt stresses in her reflections that the minority system intensified the political escalation of the nationality question. In other words, the "means" with which the established nation-states tried to solve the nationality issue and to secure a European peace only incited further conflict. The nation-state demand for assimilation turned into the protest of the minorities and highlighted

---

[30] Zolberg, "The Formation of New States as a Refugee-Generating Process," p. 28. Emphasis added.

[T]hat the European status quo could not be preserved and that it became clear only after the downfall of the last remnants of European autocracy that Europe had been ruled by a system which had never taken into account or responded to the needs of at least 25 percent of her population. (*OT*, 271)

Moreover, very early on it became clear that the older powers were not willing to consider the minorities or the minority system. From the start, the new states complained of "an open breach of promise and discrimination" (*OT*, 270) between the newly created and the established states, such as France, that excluded themselves without compromise from the minority system. Arendt emphasizes that this stance on the part of the older states was understandable when viewed from a national perspective, because the minority treaties "implied restriction on national sovereignty [that] would have affected the national sovereignty of the older European powers" (*OT*, 273). Arendt points out that not one of the older powers was prepared to do this. Thus, the potential for conflict that the minority system carried was not only evident in eastern and southeastern Europe, but gradually affected the relationships between the new and the older powers. In this spirit, Pearson underlines how the new states were inspired "to discriminate against minorities as a matter of national bravado, a continuous declaration of independence."[31] The one-sided implementation of the minority system led the new states to believe that the "spirit of solidarity" was not adopted by the older powers and they felt forced to manifest their national sovereignty in other ways. Arendt comes to the conclusion that the "atmosphere of disintegration" (*OT*, 268) created by an intentionless and aimless hate was the direct consequence of the fact that no party could really be helped with the available political instruments that a nation-state order could provide. Every new nation-state that attempted to gain political freedom on the grounds of international principles and sought membership in the community of nations found itself in the role of the oppressor. On the other hand, the national minorities that pursued their right to their own nation-state or sought the affiliation with their country of origin were declared criminals and enemies of the state. In a situation in which every party implored the "dogma of state sovereignty,"[32] communication and exchange became impossible. The ethnic hatred in the "chronically insecure, over-ambitious and unconscionably competitive"[33] states escalated in such a way that the minorities saw themselves confronted with the alternative "*fight or flight*,"[34] as Pearson concludes in his study. However, the end result of both alternatives was that many were driven away from their home countries or that they fled, creating masses of people seeking protection in West Europe. The political and historic context in which this migration took place created a new political category that until then had not been known – namely, the "stateless persons." Now the new phenomenon

---

[31] Pearson, *National Minorities in Eastern Europe*, p. 142.
[32] Kelsen, *Pure Theory of Law*, p. 346.
[33] Pearson, *National Minorities in Eastern Europe,* p. 185. Emphasis added.
[34] Ibid., p. 84. Emphasis added.

of statelessness was to confront the older nation-states with massive problems
as well.

7.2 The Paradox of Deassimilation and Denaturalization

The second paradox of the nation-state, the *paradox of deassimilation and
denaturalization*, contained in Arendt's discourse on the collapse of a Europe
of nation-states, begins with the phenomenon of statelessness. Arendt attempts
to prove that within the framework of the nation-state, no means existed with
which to restore the "right to act" that the phenomenon of massive statelessness had brought about. The core of Arendt's critique is that the path to an
agreement on international asylum and refugee regulations was obstructed by
the general atmosphere of chauvinistic ethnic hatred and the fear of the loss
of sovereignty. Therefore, the European countries, paradoxically, lost those
sovereignty rights that, apart from *ius ad bellum*, had been the domain of
national sovereignty, namely "sovereignty . . . in matters of 'emigration, naturalization, nationality, and expulsion'" (*OT*, 278).

In order to unpack the paradox of deassimilation and denaturalization,
the political and legal implications of statelessness need to be explicated. For
Arendt, statelessness is not only "the newest mass phenomenon in contemporary history" (*OT*, 277), but also the clearest expression of "the first great
damage [of] the nation-states" (*OT*, 280). Before World War I, statelessness
had just been an oddity where countries had renounced the citizenship of a
person because he or she had moved to another country. During World War
I, "de-naturalization through decree"[35] had become more common in Europe.
However, this was "only" effected on naturalized citizens who had their roots
in countries that had become enemy states in the course of hostilities. Even so,
the political impact of statelessness was insignificant until the October revolution; after the revolution, the millions of Russians who fled the country in the
face of the revolutionary events were deprived of their citizenship by the new
government. In chronological order and in a short period of time, the Russians
were followed by hundreds of thousand of Armenians, Hungarians, Germans,
Slovaks, and Jews, who were all fleeing systematic persecution, genocide, border conflicts, civil wars, riots, or pogroms and were forced to leave their home
countries.[36] But what was the exact problem of statelessness and how far did
the "destruction of nation-states" become apparent through it?

Although refugees are anything but unknown in history, in Arendt's eyes
the refugees of the interwar period were fundamentally different from those
of previous ages. At no other point in time had there been such masses of
people who were in a "fundamental situation of rightlessness" (*OT*, 296). The
fact that rightlessness followed statelessness occurred only due to the formation of nation-states. Arendt elucidates that as long as the medieval principle
quidquid est in territorio est de territorio was valid, all persons present in the

[35] Cf. *OT*, 277.
[36] Cf. ibid., 278.

state territory were subject to jurisdiction of the sovereign.[37] However, since with the establishment of the nation-state as the main paradigm of a political order, the will of the people became the only source of law; the identity and the cohesion of a people had to be determined by the principle of exclusion and inclusion. The consequence was that a state granted legal protection only to those who belonged among the "included," the ones who possessed citizenship on the grounds of their nationality or whose country had signed certain treaties that ensured that the foreign citizenship was recognized in the respective countries.

The older states, just like the new ones, tried to deal with the refugee problem by "making the problem disappear from the world through juridical interpretations" (*ETH*, 582).[38] One of these, for Arendt, was the untenable distinction between refugees and stateless people. This was nothing but the "non-recognition of statelessness" (*ETH*, 579) as a mass phenomenon and the attempt to declare the refugee problem a "passing anomaly" (*ETH*, 582). According to Arendt, all these judiciary aspirations failed due to the fact that "all refugees in effect were stateless and nearly all stateless people were virtually refugees" (*OT*, 276).[39] These attempts to veil the actual situation with the help of legal tricks, for Arendt, were more than simple ignorance: Hitherto people who had lost all legal rights due to statelessness had been unknown. In this new identification of statelessness and rightlessness lay the silent acceptance of the collapse of one of the oldest and nearly sacred laws of political communities: the right to asylum. The state's capacity to allow persons to stay on its territory is based on the option to expel them to neighboring countries or to the persons' home countries. Only where the state is legally as well as factually in the position to refuse residency is the state in the position to grant the right to residency. With the de facto stateless refugees of the interwar period, this possibility was abolished. The state was not to expel them because no country would take them. Since they do not belong to a state, they were "undeportable" (*OT*, 276). This "undeportability" of the refugees and the ensuing collapse of the asylum system had consequences for the sovereignty of the nation-state when determining those who were granted permission to stay and those who had to leave the country. Arendt writes,

The whole naturalization system of European countries fell apart when it was confronted with stateless people, and this for the same reason that the rights of asylum had been set aside. Essentially naturalization was an appendage to the nation-state's legislation that reckoned only with "nationals," people born in its territory and citizens by birth. Naturalization was needed in exceptional cases, for single individuals whom

---

[37] Cf. ibid., 280.

[38] The German version says: "Sobald sich die ungeheuren Proportionen des Problems herausstellten, begannen die nicht enden wollenden Versuche, durch juristische Interpretationen das Phänomen aus der Welt zu deuten" (*ETH*, 582).

[39] Apart from the stateless Russian and Armenian refugees who were officially recognized as stateless persons and "protected" by the Nansen-Office and, therefore, count as a kind of "aristocracy" within the millions of stateless refugees, most of the other refugees were de facto stateless. Cf. *OT*, 271.

circumstances might have driven into a foreign territory. The whole process broke down when it became a question of handling mass applications for naturalization. (*OT*, 284)

Although the solution to defusing this increasingly volatile refugee problem would have been, at least theoretically, to guarantee fundamental rights and naturalization, Arendt points out that this possibility was blocked in numerous ways. *Firstly*, it is obvious that such a naturalization process could only be carried out on the basis of international agreements to which all nation-states would have to adhere. A single state would never have been in the position to implement such a policy on its own. But every country as a prisoner of a nation-state order insisted on its sovereignty, and this, complemented by the poisonous atmosphere of ethnic hatred, made an international solution to the refugee and statelessness problem unthinkable. To underline Arendt's arguments, we can refer to Gérard Noiriel, who illustrated how in this time "the asylum issue became a real problem for international law, because now norms had to be defined that could be recognized by most states."[40] As Noiriel highlights by referring to the French Home Secretary's views of a refugee and minority agreement that was drawn up in 1928, the general opinion was that "social order and French security"[41] could be realized only unilaterally and that any binding refugee agreement would mean a loss of sovereignty regarding security questions. Obviously, this restricted any effective political action on an international level.

Setting Arendt's rather speculative argument aside, no bureaucracy would ever have been able to manage and organize the naturalization of millions of refugees. *Secondly*, the refugees' acceptance to assimilate as a prerequisite for naturalization was not to be assumed. Aside from sparking the wish for national self-determination, the renaissance of nationalism also changed the refugee profile. Before this, refugees had been single, persecuted individuals who fled over the frontier. Now entire ethnic groups were on the move who, due to group dynamics, were unable to assimilate. Instead, they actually triggered a process of "deassimilation" in the already naturalized citizens who had the same ethnic roots in the host countries. Arendt writes,

Where a wave of refugees found members of their own nationality already settled in the country to which they immigrated – as was the case with Armenians and Italians in France, for example, and with Jews everywhere – a certain retrogression set in in the assimilation of those who had been there longer. For their help and solidarity could be mobilized only by appealing to the original nationality they had in common with the newcomers. (*OT*: 285)

What she outlines here is the transformation of an ethnic notion of nationality to a decisive political factor. This does not mean though that the minorities in eastern and southeastern Europe did not have an ethnonationalistic feeling of belonging together before. Now, however, under the situation of

[40] Gérard Noiriel, *Die Tyrannei des Nationalen* (Lüneburg: zu Klampen, 1994), p. 86.
[41] Ibid., p. 97.

exile and deportation, the affiliation with an ethnic group attained new decisive importance in the old nation-states as well. When people lose all their
external worldly securities such as their rights and even their home countries,
their origin becomes the central reference point and a crucial source of solidarity. The "humanitarianism of brotherhood" – which means nothing else than
"that the element common to all men is not the world, but human nature"[42] –
for Arendt has always compensated, by its warmth, the light of a mutual world
all humiliated people lost in dark times. Although nationality had no political
significance for the now naturalized and assimilated members of the same ethnic
group and was only a question of cultural background, these people now felt
attracted by this new notion of nationality. The negative effects that the waves
of refugees spawned in the already settled people and their feelings of belonging
increased the fear in the old nation-states that an influx of refugees would lead
to a "dangerous" multinational state. This fear was not without reason and
originated in the difficulties of the nation-states in dealing with other national
groups and prevented, *thirdly*, any considerations of a naturalization policy.

Nevertheless, the nation-state governments had to react to the increasing
number of refugees and the accompanying process of deassimilation. Arendt
argues that when it became clear that frontiers could not completely be sealed
by any means, and that ever more refugees were streaming into the countries,
the governments started to revoke already granted naturalizations. The problem was that denaturalization was just as ineffectual as naturalization and did
not really offer a solution – neither in nation-states nor Europe-wide. On the
contrary, the tragedy of "the legislation of denationalization" (*ETH*, 585)[43] in
the 1920s was that once a state started nullifying the once-granted citizenships
as a reaction to the influx of refugees, the bordering states felt forced to follow suit. The result was that the denaturalization laws were passed across all
of Europe and led to a "wave of mass-denationalization" (*ETH*, 585).[44] In a
long footnote, Arendt depicts how in 1922 the denaturalization laws started in
Belgium and how states such as Turkey, Austria, France, and so on followed
suit.[45] The legal foundations for these denaturalization laws were so vaguely
formulated that they did not express more than the police guidelines for the
treatment of "undesirable aliens" (*OT*, 283). Far beyond referring to any actual
offense, the laws were dressed in hardly tangible formulations and spoke of
"*manquant gravement à leurs devoirs de citoyen belge*," or of a "not 'worthy of Italian citizenship,'" or denationalized those of its new citizens "who
committed acts contrary to the interests of France."[46]

As the denationalization laws spread from country to country, statelessness increased, which in turn started a process of deassimilation, to which

---

[42] Hannah Arendt, "On Humanity in Dark Times: Thoughts about Lessing," in *Men in Dark Times* (New York: Mariner, 1995), pp. 3–31, at 16.
[43] The German version speaks of "Denaturalisierungsgesetzgebung" (*ETH*, 585).
[44] The German versions speaks of "einer Welle von Massendenaturalisationen" (*ETH*, 585).
[45] Cf. *OT*, 279.
[46] Cf. ibid., 279.

states reacted with the further withdrawal of citizenship. This only set off the whole process again in an escalated form. Not only the living conditions of the refugees were affected by this escalation, but also the situation of the nation-states, whose scope for action declined from "denationalization round" to "denationalization round." As more and more states followed denationalization laws and produced ever more stateless people, the number of countries that could expel their stateless persons legally decreased. Arendt describes a spiral of denationalization and deassimilation or deassimilation and denationalization that made the legal tools of the nation-state of naturalization and deportation ineffectual. This clearly highlighted how far and under what conditions national jurisdiction could affect international response and how little national sovereignty was prepared and capable of reacting to. The importance and effect of the legal decisions of neighboring countries on the legal and political scope of the other nation-states became clear. The inability to find a legal and political regulation for the treatment of stateless refugees impacted all those "foreigners" who had a foreign citizenship and whose residency was legalized in some form, usually with a work permit. The deciding difference between stateless people and the people Arendt called "foreigners" (*OT*, 227) was deportability. Consequently, state sovereignty could manifest itself in questions of residency and nonresidency for "foreigners." Arendt points out that the presumable advantages of statelessness were not lost on the "foreigners," who then tried everything to obtain this status. For governments to manage questions of residency or deportation legally, it is essential to determine or to recognize the legal status of a person. However, the "inextricable chaos" (*ETH*, 588) escalated so that it became increasingly more difficult to distinguish who was refugee, who was stateless, and who was a "foreigner," and more and more people became "legally undeterminable" (*ETH*, 581).[47] As the governments' fear of the steady increase of stateless refugees on their territories grew, the insight emerged that the refugee problem could not be solved with legal means. In the obvious knowledge of the inability of the nation-states, the totalitarian states consciously and systematically employed "denationalization" as "a powerful weapon of totalitarian politics" (*OT*, 269) to undermine the European nation-state order.

7.3 The Paradox of Rightlessness

The refugees of the interwar period were stateless and as such they stood outside any legal order. Notwithstanding, the factual situation forced states to deal with statelessness. Since the stateless refugee was not a "juridical person" (*OT*, 447) the situation could not be tackled on a legal level with the means of governance characteristic of a constitutional state. Arendt shows how stateless people endangered the "nation-state as a legal and constitutional state i.e. they

---

[47] The German version speaks of "legal undeterminierbar" (*ETH*, 581).

jeopardized it in its foundations."[48] Arendt justifies her assertions with the fact that the stateless person who was placed outside the pale of law and who represented the "anomaly for whom the general law did not provide" (*OT*, 286) forced every government "into admittedly illegal acts" (*OT*, 283). The paradox that became apparent was that the stateless person whose statelessness was due to the fact that he or she did not fit into the national order and even represented a danger for the order actually managed to maneuver the state into a position where it acted outside its own legal order and started "to undermine legality in the internal affairs of the affected states and its international relations" (ETH, 592).[49]

Arendt exemplifies the undermining of "international relations" on the model of deportation practices. The concept of a nation-state order and national sovereignty inhibited the nation-state from renouncing its "right" to deport the stateless refugees. The "right to expel" mirrors not only the core principle of territorial sovereignty but also expresses the state's fundamental right to national self-determination. However, it was not possible to expel stateless people on legal grounds, since no other state was there to receive them. If the respective state wanted to preserve its territorial sovereignty, it had to deport the stateless person without complying with, or even against, international agreements. The result was a steady increase of nonlegal deportation practices and the increase of "illegality in the inter-state border traffic" (*ETH*, 594).[50] In clandestine actions, the police smuggled stateless persons over the border to the territory of the neighboring country. Obviously, the refugees were in breach of the immigration laws of that country and thus offended its rights of sovereignty. The neighboring country, following the same logic in turn, took the stateless refugees to the next state one night later.[51] The spread of such deportation practices revealed in all clarity that it was impossible to acknowledge the legal and sovereign sphere on the basis of the principles of a nation-state order and that this led to the "deadly conflicts" one had wanted to avoid after the experiences of World War I. Arendt describes a spiral of disrespect for national sovereignty jurisdictions in favor of lawless assertions of sovereignty. From the perspective of the European nation-state order, sovereignty claims faced sovereignty claims and paved the way for the next war as *ultima ratio*.[52]

---

[48] Hannah Arendt, "Nationalstaat und Demokratie," available online at HannahArendt.net, Documents 2/06, 2006. In the paper, Arendt writes: "Der Einbruch der Staatenlosen und die ihnen zugefügte schlechthinnige Rechtlosigkeit gefährdeten den Nationalstaat als Rechts- und Verfassungsstaat, d.h. sie gefährdeten ihn in seinen Grundlagen."

[49] Cf. *OT*, 284. The German version says "...Legalität überhaupt im Innern der betroffenen Staaten wie in ihren zwischenstaatlichen Beziehungen zu unterminieren" (*ETH*, 592).

[50] The German version speaks of "Illegalität im zwischenstaatlichen Grenzverkehr" (*ETH*, 594).

[51] Cf. *OT*, 283f.

[52] Here Arendt is in line with Kelsen, who criticizes in "Reine Rechtslehre" that within the notion of state sovereignty, "the single state is in the center of the world of law." Kelsen, *Pure Theory of Law*, p. 345.

In addition to the illegality of the border traffic, which Arendt marks as "petty wars between the police at the frontiers" (*OT*, 284), undermining the legality of internal affairs is of defining importance in her critique. The implementation of principles of *Rechtsstaatlichkeit* (constitutionality) – which means the separation of powers, the authority of the legal order, an independent jurisdiction, and the actual effectiveness of laws – is at the same time the implementation of a nation-state order. These principles guarantee a durable and stable state order as well as legal reliability between state authorities and residents. In contrast, to dissolve the legality in the internal affairs implies an attack on the central characteristics of the nation-state. Arendt describes how this attack took place on different levels. At the first level, *the spread of illegality in society* resulted directly from the increasing number of refugees and was linked to the fact that people without residence and work permits were simply forced to act outside of the pale of law in order to secure their existence. Arendt explicates how an increase of illegal refugees changed everyday life in society, especially by certain forms of illegality, such as any kind of illicit work.[53] Moreover, she outlines that the "defiance of the authority of laws" should be regarded as an "explicit sign of the inner instability and vulnerability of existing governments and legal systems."[54]

Closely linked to the societal spread of illegality, Arendt additionally elaborates on the "transformation of the juridical system" (*ETH*, 594).[55] She writes:

For then a criminal offense becomes the best opportunity to regain some kind of human equality, even if it be as a recognized exception to the norm. The one important fact is that this exception is provided for by law. As a criminal even a stateless person will be treated worse than another criminal, that is, he will be treated as like everybody else. Only as an offender against the law can he gain protection from it. (*OT*, 286)

Her point seems to be that the rightlessness of the stateless refugee bursts the *structure of the legal rule* on both sides; on the side of the *legal condition*, as well as on that of the *legal consequence*. Since according to Kelsen the legal rule embodies the "basic form of law,"[56] the *Rechtstaatlichkeit* (constitutionality) of the nation-state implodes. What does this mean in detail? Legal condition and legal consequence determine what a law contains by establishing a certain punishment for a certain crime and, in this manner, determine and guarantee the formal character of law. This ordered union of condition and consequence "bursts" in the case of the stateless refugee. The first "burst" occurs on the side of the crime, the legal condition. To understand this, one has to remember that the "right of asylum" had been a sacred right since ancient times. It was always applied when a person was being persecuted for a crime that was against the

---

53 Cf. *OT*, 279.
54 Hannah Arendt, "Civil Disobedience," in Arendt, *Crisis of the Republic*, pp. 49–102, at 69.
55 The German version speaks of "eine genaue Umkehrung des juridischen Systems" (*ETH*, 594).
56 Hans Kelsen, "Reine Rechtslehre," in *Einleitung in die rechtswissenschaftliche Problematik* (Aalen: Scientia Verlag, 1994), p. 22.

law in his country of origin but not in the country in which he sought asylum. Therefore, the asylum seeker had to prove that he had committed such an offense. Although the "right of asylum" had become increasingly insignificant due to interstate treaties in the nineteenth century, Arendt points out the right of asylum immediately regained its political relevance with emergence of the refugees in the twentieth century. Now the tragedy was that the modern refugees could not provide evidence that they had committed any of the required offenses. They were what a refugee should never be: absolutely innocent. This kind of absolute innocence was "the greatest misfortune" (*OT*, 295) for the stateless refugees, because the punishment that awaited them despite or owing to this was the "deprivation of all rights."[57]

Jurists are so used to thinking of law in terms of punishment, which indeed always deprives us of certain rights, that they may find it even more difficult than a layman to recognize that the deprivation of legality, i.e., of all rights, no longer has a connection with specific crimes. *In our times absolute rightlessness is the punishment for absolute innocence* (*OT*, 295).[58]

Although the stateless refugee committed no offense and therefore no legal condition was violated, the nation-state "reacted" with the deprivation of all rights. By formulating a "law" that penalized absolute innocence with absolute rightlessness, the coherence of the entire legal system was called into question and the concept of law was led to an ad absurdum. If "absolute innocence" was punished with the maximum penalty, what should happen to a thief?

Here the extent of the legal paradox becomes apparent, because through a theft, the stateless refugee could obtain all those legal rights that a citizen qua citizen was guaranteed, if a crime was committed. In other words, by committing an offense, the stateless refugee again became a member of a legal-political community and received some of his civic rights back. This paradoxical reversal results from the fact that a legal process commenced that *normalized* the stateless refugee and granted him rights he previously did not have. If he did not have money, he was accorded a lawyer. Before, he was subjected to the inhumane treatment by the police. After committing an offense, he could complain about humiliating prison conditions and inspect the records on him, obtain information, and so on. In short, "he has become a respectable person" (*OT*, 287). The irritating fact is that the offense against the legal order of a society put the stateless person in the position to enjoy rights he hitherto did not have

---

[57] Arendt refers to the asylum policy of the United States during World War II. After the French defeat, the United States offered asylum to those who were endangered to be deported to Germany. To be entitled to this right, one only had to prove that he or she had undertaken something against Nazi Germany. Arendt points to the fact that there were neither a noteworthy number of refugees who could meet this condition nor were those who could the most endangered ones. Cf. *OT*, 294.

[58] In contrast to the English version, where this last sentence is missing, in the German version the paragraph ends with: "Absolute Rechtlosigkeit hat sich in unserer Zeit als die Strafe erwiesen, die auf absolute Unschuld steht" (*ETH*, 611).

despite his innocence. While in the first case the rightlessness of the stateless refugees destroys the structure of the legal rule by realizing an absurd legal condition, in this case the rightlessness leads to paradox legal consequences, which in the end ruin the structure of the legal rule. The punishment for theft, burglary, and bank robbery was being rewarded "civic rights." According to Arendt, the result is that the idea of legality collapses as soon as it comes into contact with people who "ceased to be a juridical person" (*ETH*, 609).[59]

The corruption of constitutionality caused by an insufficient handling of the problem of stateless persons was not at an end with the "reversal of the juridical principles." Since the authorities were afraid that humane treatment would lure potential refugees and also tempt other states to expel them, the police were bestowed with exceptional powers hitherto unknown. Thereby, according to Arendt, the foundation of the separation of power was steadily undermined and this, as a consequence, promoted the "transformation of legal relations and standards" (*ETH*, 597).[60] Completely detached from the political course of democratic governments, this led to a "police-directed foreign policy" (*OT*, 288) that did not make the police recoil from cooperating with the Gestapo and Soviet GPU in the 1930s. The police were allowed to choose their own methods to combat the refugee problem. With this direct power over people, they had the right to expel refugees without trial, without a judicial order, and without a legal examination of the facts. This generated a fundamental shift of power within the constitutional-political structure of a nation-state. The important decisions were no longer taken within the constitutional framework and under the control of the judicature and legislative bodies but executed by the police on location, without justifications and without further publication.[61] Through this "spectral mixture"[62] of law positing and law preserving, constitutional bodies lost their reputation and authority. As an example, Arendt describes how in France an expulsion order by the police received disproportionately higher priority and had more serious consequences than that of the Home Secretary, despite the fact that the police were constitutionally subordinated to the Home Secretary.[63]

Meanwhile, the relationship between the "normal citizen" and governmental bodies remained in the realm of the constitutional order. However, with

---

[59] If one argues with Freud that law always applies to a cultural-psychological dimension (Sigmund Freud, "Der Mann Moses und die monotheistische Religion," in *Gesammelte Werke, Band 16* [Frankfurt a. M.: Fischer Verlag, 1999], pp. 101–246, at 187ff; Sigmund Freud, "Das Unbehagen in der Kultur," in *Gesammelte Werke, Band 14* [Frankfurt a. M.: Fischer Verlag, 1999], pp. 454–60), then the stateless refugee undermines this dimension as well. Arendt sarcastically states that a person who is confronted with deportation every day just has to search his conscience whether he wants to rob a bank or not. Cf. *ETH*, 594.

[60] The German version speaks of "die Umkehrung aller gesetzlich vorgesehenen Verhältnisse und Maßstäbe" (*ETH*, 597).

[61] Cf. *OT*, 287ff.

[62] Walter Benjamin, *Reflections: Essays, Aphorisms, Autobiographical Writings*, edited by Peter Demetz (New York: Schocken, 1986), p. 286.

[63] Cf. *OT*, 287.

every new refugee, the police's "emancipation from law and government" continued with a process of "gradual transformation into a police state" (*OT*, 287). Besides an almost unlimited and arbitrary domination and new "form of lawlessness, organized by the police" (*ETH*, 599),[64] this situation contributed to the massive undermining of the legal order of the nation-state and also explains why there was "disgracefully little resistance from the police in those countries the Nazis occupied."[65]

Of course, one could argue with Carl Schmitt that to suspend constitutionality on nearly all levels of the political system demonstrates the state's claim for sovereignty. For Arendt, Schmitt's attempt, however, agrees with the traditional metaphysical approach to politics and its need for an Archimedean point while at the same time he completely ignores the historic, social, societal, political, moral, and legal dimensions of the idea of nation and nation-state. Certainly, Arendt would agree that police conduct as well as systemic shifts within the state resulted from the jeopardized order brought about by the refugee problem. However, unlike Schmitt, Arendt takes the liberal and constitutional characteristics of a nation-state structure very seriously and criticizes those systemic shifts. If we follow this discussion further, we have to ask what Schmitt considers a political order to consist of? Who is the sovereign? Who can declare a state of emergency and abrogate constitutionality for the sake of public safety and order? These questions lead further into the work of Schmitt and away from my attempt to explain Arendt's argument of the collapse of the nation-state. Nevertheless, in questioning Schmitt about these issues, one is confronted with plenty of inconsistencies and contradictions in his work. His definition of the concept of order varies from a Catholic-theological design in his early work,[66] to a cultural-national concept in *Crisis of Parliamentary Democracy*,[67] to a racist, national socialist one in *Über die drei Art des rechtswissenschaftlichen Denkens* ("On the Three Types of Juristic Thought").[68] Without doubt, Schmitt had always deemed man to be *subjectum*,[69] but subjected to whom and by whom remains completely unclear. Hermann Heller already criticized in his sovereignty paper in 1927 the concept of sovereignty in Schmitt's work. Heller states that Schmitt is "inherently contradictory and not

---

[64] The German version speaks of "eine Form polizeilich organisierter Gesetzlosigkeit" (*ETH*, 599).

[65] Arendt's account of the shift within the function of the police has a striking though unacknowledged affinity to Walter Benjamin's considerations in his *Kritik der Gewalt*. Like Arendt, Benjamin also points to this "gespenstische Vermischung" (spectral mixture) between law positing and law preserving within the police. Walter Benjamin, "Zur Kritik der Gewalt," in Walter Benjamin, *Zur Kritik der Gewalt und andere Aufsätze* (Frankfurt a.M.: Suhrkamp, 1965), pp. 29–65, at 43.

[66] Cf. Carl Schmitt, *Der Wert des Staates und die Bedeutung des Einzelnen* (Tübingen: Mohr, 1914), p. 7.

[67] Cf. Carl Schmitt, *Die geistesgeschichtliche Lage des heutigen Parlamentarismus* (Berlin: Duncker & Humblot, 1991), p. 88ff.

[68] Schmitt, *Über die drei Arten des rechtswissenschaftlichen Denkens*, p. 23.

[69] Cf. Günter Meuter, *Der Katechon. Zu Carl Schmitts fundamentalistischer Kritik der Zeit* (Berlin: Duncker & Humblot, 1994), p. 491.

tenable." Apart from his "inadequacies in reference to international law,"[70] for Heller too it remains unclear who should act as the sovereign in Schmitt's theory. Heller supposes that for Schmitt the Reichspräsident takes up this position but, as Heller continues, Schmitt actually avoided a clear answer.[71] In *Der Hüter der Verfassung*, written some years later, Schmitt explicitly repudiated that the Reichspräsident could be the sovereign.[72] From Arendt's perspective, the polemical remark springs to mind that the problem that many state theorists were faced with – namely, to define the sovereign, a problem that Heller did not satisfactorily solve at all[73] – possibly was due to the political situation of the interwar period and the fact that nobody was in the position to execute alleged sovereignty rights unilaterally.

In the undermining of constitutionality and the charge of an imminent police state, Arendt sees systemic changes to the extent that a decline of the nation-state order appeared conceivable – an order that had also once begun with the wish to realize political freedom. She concludes that the refugees and stateless people since the peace treaties of 1919 through 1920 "have attached themselves like a curse to all the newly established states" and bear for all, the new as well as the old, nation-states "the germs of a deadly sickness." For Arendt, it becomes clear "that the nation-state cannot exist once its principle of equality before the law has broken down. Laws that are not equal for all revert to rights and privileges, something contradictory to the very nature of nation-states" (*OT*, 290).

7.4 The Paradox of Human Rights

The paradox of human rights, one could elaborate on the basis of Arendt's considerations, expresses the danger that threatens a nation-state order by the *nonrealization* of human rights. In the declaration of human rights, the liberal and free democratic content of the nation-state found its most distinct expression. Therefore, it is not surprising that the French Revolution started with the declaration of inalienable rights that became the pillar of its constitution. In her examination, Arendt maintains that the traditional understanding of human rights could not be realized within a nation-state logic. Apart from the humanitarian consequences, Arendt argues that with an obvious political disregard of the human rights, the nation-state loses a central legitimation principle of its order. "[M]ass-statelessness" (*OT*, 298), the rightlessness that complemented the refugees, their difficult humanitarian situation, and their

---

[70] Heller, "Die Souveränität," p. 89.

[71] Cf. ibid., p. 89.

[72] Cf. Carl Schmitt, *The Concept of the Political* (Chicago: University of Chicago Press, 1996), p. 132.

[73] Cf. the illuminating critique by Otwin Massing, "Souveränität – ein unverzichtbarer Anachronismus," in Rüdiger Voigt, ed., *Abschied vom Staat – Rückkehr zum Staat?* (Baden-Baden: Nomos, 1993), pp. 51–93, at 58ff.

illegality, revealed that the moral and liberal aspects of a nation-state constitution and the talk of the inalienable human rights "were mere prejudice, hypocrisy, and cowardice" (*OT*, 269). Hereby the nation-state disavowed not only the enlightened and liberal idea of human rights but also ridiculed "the political apprehensions of the fully developed nation-states" (*OT*, xvii) and the "conscience of the nation" (*OT*, 133), thus undermining the authority of an entire political order. The result was that supporters of a nation-state order, such as politicians, parliamentarians, journalists, intellectuals, and so on, lost their power to convince people in the political debate about the interpretation and evaluation of events and developments. They thus missed the opportunity to highlight the vital differences between an authoritarian form of government on the one hand and a constitutional government on the other hand and to warn of the consequences of a systemic shift that the radical left-wing or right-wing parties and movements would create. But why does Arendt believe that the liberal principles of human rights can never be guaranteed within a political order based upon the idea of nation-states?

First of all, her discourse on human rights confronts us with the irritating assertion that the situation of stateless refugees cannot be understood within the framework that the traditional understanding of human rights provides. Arendt argues that one cannot speak of the loss of human rights if one is deprived of this or that fundamental legal entitlement that is usually considered a human right. In this case, one is proclaiming only individual rights that are designed to guarantee a constitutional minimum within a political community.[74] However, the stateless refugees did not belong to any community and, therefore, no laws exist for them at all. Together with their nationality, they lost their "place in the world which makes opinions significant and actions effective." They had to rely either on the "charity of private people or the helplessness of public bodies" (*OT*, 296). Their freedom of movement Arendt sarcastically calls "*Hasenfreiheit*" (*ETH*, 613) (freedom of a hare) and the freedom of speech, "[A] fools freedom because what he thinks or says is of no interest to anything or anyone" (*OT*, 296). In short, Arendt considers this rightlessness to be the real "human rights" violation. She points out that the authors of the human rights declaration had not realized that these individual rights were based on the right to be a member of a political group. But why had nobody thought of such a right? To what should human rights react if not to rightlessness?

To answer these questions that lead directly to the center of the contradictions in the traditional concept of human rights, we need to look at the dimensions of the human rights declaration. Arendt distinguishes four dimensions. The first, the *moral-enlightenment dimension*, emphasizes the fact that man liberated himself from all historic, societal, or religious authorities. It was no longer God or tradition that justified the state and its laws, it was the human being and his dignity that set the standard for right and wrong.[75] In

---

[74] Cf. *OT*, 295f.
[75] Cf. ibid., 290f.

the second, the *historical-functional dimension*, Arendt speaks of the "historic implication" (*ETH*, 602)[76] of human rights. With the abolition of holy certainties through secularization and the collapse of traditional customs and habits, human rights were expected to replace old guarantees and certainties. From then on, human rights were to guarantee something "that could not be guaranteed politically or that had never been guaranteed politically" (*ETH*, 602). With this, the idea of human rights "acquired a new connotation" (*OT*, 293)[77] and its thoughts of freedom, especially the postulation of inalienable rights for all human beings, changed in the political area to a "kind of additional law for those who had nothing better to fall back upon" (*OT*, 293). The tragedy about this change was that only those who were already powerless in the public realm called for human rights. Arendt specifies that not one important political figure or group referred to the human rights idea in their argumentations. The consequence was that human rights remained politically ineffectual as well as insignificant. Although this train of thought is pivotal for Arendt's political justification of human rights – which would open another discussion[78] – the third dimension of human rights is crucial for our considerations here. This *political-legal dimension* indicates that human rights were interwoven with the people's sovereignty and therefore were meant to be realized in the civil rights. Arendt writes:

Man appeared as the only sovereign in matters of law as the people was proclaimed the only sovereign in matters of government. The people's sovereignty (different from that of the prince) was not proclaimed by the grace of God but in the name of Man, so that it seemed only natural that the inalienable rights of man would find their guarantee and become an inalienable part of the right of the people to sovereign self-government. (*OT*, 291)

If one looks at the fusion of people's sovereignty and human rights against the background of the moral-enlightenment dimension of the human rights idea, this fusion is irritating. Had the intention of the human rights declaration not been the emancipation from all traditional authorities and to recognize Man as the only standard? Yet, the talk of a connection of human rights and people's sovereignty suggests that one would not remain long with the isolating absolutism of Man. The human being was directly sorted into the order and context of a political community – namely, the nation – and the right to

[76] The English text speaks only of "another implication of which the framers of the declaration were only half aware" (*OT*, 291). The German version speaks of a "geschichtlich sehr wesentliche Sinn" (*ETH*, 602).

[77] Arendt differentiates between the "idea of human rights" and "human rights." By doing so, she reflects the difference between principle and content, which is characteristic for the philosophy of the eighteenth century. In contrast, however, Arendt tries to explain why human rights concur with a special tenor and not just depict them as historically contingent.

[78] Elsewhere I have argued that there is a political justification of human rights in Arendt's work. Cf. Christian Volk, "Die Garantie der Menschenrechte als politisches Argument. Eine Skizze des Arendtschen Rechtsverständnisses," in Biegi, Mandana, et al., eds., *Demokratie, Recht und Legitimität im 21* (Jahrhundert, Wiesbaden: VS Verlag, 2008), pp. 129–44.

inalienable rights became dependent on the people's sovereignty. On the one hand, this "curious conversion" (*ETH*, 604) was the result of the structural design of the concept of human rights. On the other, it was linked to the historic origins of the nation-state. To speak of the structural design of human rights, I want to point to the specific subject of examination, namely, the concept of Man. Due to this concept of Man as an "abstract human being" (*ETH*, 604), human rights were granted on the grounds of human dignity and nature. For Arendt, the problem with this approach lies in the fact that the "abstract human being" was at no time and at no place a reality. Even indigenous people lived together in some form of human community and humans were known at best as men and women. Arendt, therefore, arrives at the irritating conclusion that the idea of human rights in this individualistic and abstract version was not operational in legal-political terms. The idea had to be changed in such a way that the concept of human rights could encompass the "plurality of human beings" (*ETH*, 604)[79] and, by doing so, apply to the condition of a political community. With the means of the historic-political facts of the eighteenth century, plurality could be realized only if the individualistic-abstract concept were identified with the people. At first sight, it is not directly clear why an individualistic-abstract concept of Man was politically not practicable. Why is identifying an individual with the term of people superior to the abstract concept of Man? *Concreteness* and *objectivity*. Although the proclamation of inalienable and indispensable human rights emancipated human beings from traditional historic hierarchies and annihilated feudal privileges, to believe in the nature and dignity of a human being is not more concrete than to believe in history.[80] Yet, a citizen of a state was visible and perceptible. Above all, he or she had a concrete authority that could deal with civic rights, in whatever form. In sum, Man was set as an absolute on the basis of philosophical consideration. But because no authority could realize the abstract absoluteness, this "idea of human rights" fell so low in the political arena that it finally came to rest in the lap of national sovereignty. The sovereign nation-state was the most powerful and most important political agent and the only authority that could guarantee any sorts of rights. This fact changed those inalienable and indispensable rights to which everybody should be entitled into rights that the respective state granted its citizens. In the case of the nation-state, they were the civic rights of the nation.

---

[79] The German text says: "Die Paradoxie, die von Anfang an in dem Begriff der unveräußerbaren Menschenrechte lag, war, daß dieses Recht mit einem »Menschen überhaupt« rechnete, den es nirgends gab, da ja selbst die Wilden in irgendeiner Form menschlicher Gemeinschaft leben, ja, daß dieses Recht der Natur selbst förmlich zu widersprechen schien, da wir ja »Menschen« nur in der Form von Männern und Frauen kennen, also der Begriff des Menschen, wenn er politisch brauchbar gefaßt sein soll, die Pluralität der Menschen stets in sich einschließen muß. Diese Pluralität konnte nur wieder aufgeholt werden im Sinne der politischen Gegebenheiten des 18. Jahrhunderts, indem man den »Menschen überhaupt« mit dem Glied eines Volkes identifiziert" (*ETH*, 604).

[80] Cf. *OT*, 297ff.

Apart from this internal explanation for the merging of human rights and sovereignty, Arendt also states a directly linked historic-political explanation. Human rights were anything else but inalienable and indispensable. On the contrary, the French Revolution especially demonstrated that they have to be fought for in battles against an absolute monarchy. At this point, we can speak of the *historic-political dimension* of the human rights idea. From the start, human rights were the result of national freedom struggles and, consequently, were connected to a people's right to self-determination. On the basis of historic experience, one was convinced that only the sovereign will of one's own people was in the position to guarantee human rights. The rights had been procured in battles against despotic usurpations and were proclaimed inalienable and indispensable in every civilized state. No other authorities were required to establish them. Hence, one believed that those peoples who still had to suffer under despotic or tyrannical rulers "had not yet reached that stage of civilization" (*OT*, 291). The human rights concept stigmatized these regimes as illegitimate and committed every thinking person to protest. This way, human rights functioned as a criterion that distinguished the civilized world from the uncivilized and wild rest. Rightlessness was not only a sign of uncivilizedness, but the assertion also prevailed that rightless persons did not exist in the civilized world. In Arendt's view, this belief was misleading.

At the latest, when millions of refugees moved from one European country to the next, it became apparent how deceptive the assumption of inalienable and indispensable rights in the civilized world organized in nation-states actually was. Even more, it illustrated that a human rights guarantee was infinitely far away and that a nation-state order could not create the necessary requirements. The only guarantee that could be effected was a guarantee for civic rights for the citizens of the same nation. Arendt argues that the reason why one could include the "plurality of human beings" in the concept of human rights in the eighteenth to the twentieth century only by linking the individualistic-abstract concept of Man with that of a people results from the centuries-old belief in state sovereignty to which the nation-state also adhered. Probably it is going too far to generalize Carl Schmitt's provocative statement, "Whoever invokes humanity wants to cheat,"[81] as being the statement of a whole era, but it does express the core idea of a political order that recognizes the sovereign will of a nation as the "the sole legitimate criterion." Within the political logic of the nation-state, the term "humanity" cannot be a "political concept"[82] for Arendt either. Although the term does exist on a moral or a moral-philosophical level, as Kant's *Perpetual Peace* shows, it never played an important role in political thinking.[83] To realize anything that resembles human rights and to guarantee

---

[81] Schmitt, *The Concept of the Political*, p. 54.

[82] Ibid., p. 55.

[83] Accordingly, Seyla Benhabib argues that in Kant's political thinking, "exclusionary territorial control...[is]...an unchecked sovereign privilege...which cannot be limited or trumped by other norms and institutions." Benhabib, *The Rights of Others*, p. 67.

every human being a place in the world, the term "humanity" must become a political concept – a concern to which Arendt's work is committed.

However, the sovereignty principle of a nation-state order is diametrically opposed to this concern. Arendt's criticism of this is not morally, ethically, or anthropologically motivated, but purely *politically motivated*. Her assumption of a "collapse of the system of nation-state" manifests itself as a massive loss of legitimation and authority in the paradox of human rights. Whereas the paradoxes centered attention on the inner-state and the interstate undermining of a nation-state order in Europe, here Arendt's criticism was that due to the politics of the nation-state,

> the mere phrase 'human rights' [. . .] became for all concerned – victims, persecutors, and onlookers alike – the evidence of hopeless idealism or fumbling feeble-minded hypocrisy. (*OT*, 269)

If one assumes that in the "idea of human rights" the liberal concept of the nation-states manifests itself in the "faith of the enlightenment"[84] – and Arendt does – then a "whole way of life" loses its authority, credibility, and persuasive powers. Trying to convince the world of the liberal and free democratic potential of this form of government becomes a farce.

7.5 Conclusion

If one follows Arendt's argumentation in *The Origins of Totalitarianism,* it becomes clear that her claim about the collapse of the nation-state is a direct attack on the terminology and principles of the leading state and sovereignty theorists of the Weimar Republic, who believed that they could create a state order on the theory of the national will as the "sole legitimate criterion." This led to the ethnic hatred that was prevalent in the 1920s and 1930s, and that made communication between the political entities difficult, if not impossible. The postulation of the homogeneity of a nation started the deassimilation process that held not only political conflicts in store, but also diminished a nation's sovereignty on issues such as "emigration, naturalization, nationality, and expulsion." Unilateralism in questions of security and public safety as an expression of state sovereignty ended practically in the inability of the nation-state to act and, therefore, forced it also to dissolve its constitutional foundation without solving the problem. Due to the enormous loss of authority and power, many European states had relinquished the nation-state as a form of government long before World War II and had instead either established totalitarian, fascist, or authoritarian regimes or had replaced the parliamentary constitutional state with a party dictatorship.

---

[84] Julia Kristeva, *Strangers to Ourselves* (New York: Columbia University Press, 1991), p. 152.

8

The Eichmann Trial and the Legacy of Jurisdiction

Leora Bilsky

Although the phenomenon of political trials has a long history that goes back to the beginning of Western civilization, to the trials of Jesus and Socrates, it has gained renewed interest of late. This interest was triggered by developments in international law, in particular the possibility of bringing heads of state to trial for crimes of genocide, crimes against humanity, and war crimes in national courts exercising universal jurisdiction. Although the legal cases vary, defendants such as Yugoslav president Slobodan Milošević, former Chilean dictator General Augusto Pinochet, and Israeli prime minister Ariel Sharon all raised one common defense: They claimed that the proceedings against them amounted to a political trial.

In my book *Transformative Justice: Israeli Identity on Trial*,[1] I tackled the dilemma of the political trial with the help of political theory elaborated by Otto Kirschheimer, Judith Shklar, and Hannah Arendt. In this chapter, I would like to develop the theory of political justice further and apply it to what I call "the new (international) political trial." I offer a reading of the Adolf Eichmann trial as occupying the intersection between *national political trial* and *international political trial*. I focus on one aspect of the trial – the *legacy of jurisdiction* – and on a neglected aspect of Hannah Arendt's writing on the trial. I argue that it is in this seemingly legalistic aspect of the trial that we can identify the roots of a crisis for modern criminal law that emerged in the wake of World War II. It reveals the deep sense in which an important source of legitimacy for the criminal law, its connection to a single and coherent political community, has been undermined and is in need of a new articulation.

One of the first moves toward better enforcement of international norms was taken by the Israeli court in the trial of Eichmann in 1961. It was here that the precedent of the authority of a national court to adjudicate "crimes against

[1] Leora Bilsky, *Transformative Justice: Israeli Identity on Trial* (Ann Arbor: University of Michigan Press, 2004).

198

humanity" committed outside its territorial jurisdiction was established.[2] For this purpose, the Israeli court had to provide an entirely new basis for its jurisdiction, one that transcended the traditional constraints that national sovereignty imposes on territorial criminal law.[3] The defense argued that since the crimes had been committed outside Israel and prior to the establishment of the state, the Israeli court lacked jurisdiction. The court could have responded to this challenge by relying on the Israeli law for punishing Nazis and their collaborators (1950), which invested the court with special jurisdiction over crimes against humanity and crimes against the Jewish people that were committed during the Nazi regime from 1933 to 1945.[4] However, the court was unsatisfied with such a positivist legal answer and provided an additional justification by offering an alternative basis for its jurisdiction based on principles of international law.[5] The court ruled that in judging crimes against humanity, there is no need to establish a territorial link or a personal link of the perpetrator or his or her victims to the state. Rather, every national court assumes the power to adjudicate the case, acting as the delegate of the international community. The idea behind this doctrine was that these are acts so deeply offensive to the entire international community that the case may be brought in any other state if the country of the culpable person takes no action. According to this doctrine, international law recognizes the authority of each state to enforce international norms when the infringement concerns humanity as such.[6] This new basis for the court's authority was called the principle of "universal jurisdiction." The new doctrine of jurisdiction allowed the court to circumvent the boundaries of state sovereignty, thus offering a way to adjudicate crimes against humanity that enjoyed de facto impunity from the national courts of their perpetrators' state and in the absence of a permanent international criminal tribunal. It thus purported to eliminate an important source of impunity for those engaged in crimes against humanity under the auspices of

---

[2] For an interesting article connecting the Eichmann trial to current debates about universal jurisdiction, see Gary J. Bass, "The Adolf Eichmann Case: Universal and National Jurisdiction," in Stephen Macado, ed., *Universal Jurisdiction: National Courts and the Prosecution of Serious Crimes under International Law* (Philadelphia: University of Pennsylvania Press, 2004), pp. 77–90.

[3] For elaboration on the connection between territory, sovereignty, and national law, see Jeremy A. Rabkin, *Law without Nations? Why Constitutional Government Requires Sovereign States* (Princeton and Oxford: Princeton University Press, 2005), pp. 45–70.

[4] Nazi and Nazi Collaborators (Punishment) Law, 5710/1950, 4, Laws of the State of Israel (LSI) (1949–50), 154.

[5] Cr.C (Jm.) 40/61, *Attorney General v. Adolf Eichmann*, 45 P.M 3.1965, *International Law Reports*, vol. 36 (Cambridge: Cambridge University Press, 1968) (hereafter *Eichmann Trial*), pp. 18–276; Cr. A 336/61, *Eichmann v. Attorney General*, 16(3) P.D. 2033, ibid., pp. 277–342 (Dist. Ct. Jerusalem 1961); *affd*, ibid., pp. 277, 279–304 (Supr. Ct. Jerusalem, 1962). This volume of *International Law Reports* (ILR) includes the full record of both district and supreme court judgments in the Eichmann trial. The English texts are translations made by the Israeli Ministry of Justice of Israel from Hebrew of the original record.

[6] Ibid., p. 299.

a sovereign state. This precedent, however, remained dormant for many years until its reinvocation in recent years.[7]

At the time of the Eichmann trial, various critics warned against the danger of its becoming a "show trial" as a result of its being held in a national court related to the community of the victims, which might be tempted to prefer particularistic national interests over juridical ones.[8] Today, however, the very willingness of national courts to recognize universal jurisdiction and to apply international norms over officials of third-party states is viewed as an advancement of the rule of law in the field of international relations. The doctrine of universal jurisdiction is presented as an answer to the inability (or unwillingness) of the concerned national courts to try state officials who commit war crimes or crimes against humanity in the name of "state interests."[9] This shift in understanding of the role of "third-party" national courts in applying international norms requires explanation. Are national courts the source of danger of the politicization of international law, or are they the best guarantee against "political justice," piercing the shield of sovereign immunity?[10]

We will not be able to solve this puzzle unless we clarify our concept of the political trial and the danger it poses to the rule of law. Hannah Arendt first articulated these concerns in the context of the Eichmann trial and proceeded to offer a unique way of addressing them. The solution she advocated, though, was different from the one advanced by the Israeli court. Since Arendt's commentary on the trial was not read with juridical eyes,[11] this part of her

[7] Luc Reydams, *Universal Jurisdiction: International and Municipal Legal Perspectives* (Oxford and New York: Oxford University Press, 2003).

[8] It might be argued that international criticism of the Eichmann trial did not stem from the court's exercise of universal jurisdiction as such, but rather from the tribunal's connection to the community of the victims. Under this view, the Israeli court lacked "impartiality" in exercising universal jurisdiction. This "purist" view, however, presupposes a certain understanding of the "rule of law," as detachment which I undertake to challenge in this chapter. Indeed, third-party courts, in Germany, Spain, and elsewhere, concerned about their legitimacy in exercising universal jurisdiction, have added requirements of proving a stronger nexus between the court and the case at hand. For elaboration and evaluation of this trend, see Anne-Marie Slaughter, "Defining the Limits: Universal Jurisdiction and National Courts," in Macedo, ed., *Universal Jurisdiction*, pp. 168–90. Bass adds another argument against the exercise of "pure" universal jurisdiction connected to the issue of incentives. He argues that the more disconnected the court is from the case at hand, the less interest there will be in conducting the trial in the first place. See Bass, "The Adolph Eichmann Case."

[9] See for example, Sally Falk Moore, "Egregious Crimes against Humanity: Some Reflections in August 2003," in John Borneman, ed., *The Case of Ariel Sharon and the Fate of Universal Jurisdiction* (Princeton: Princeton Institute for International and Regional Studies, Princeton University, 2004), pp. 116–30.

[10] For elaboration, see Paul W. Kahn, "Universal Jurisdiction or the Rule of Law," in Borneman, ed., *The Case of Ariel Sharon and the Fate of Universal Jurisdiction*, pp. 131–45.

[11] The exception being Jacob Robinson, an international law jurist who devoted an entire book to refuting all of Arendt's juridical mistakes and misconceptions: *And the Crooked Shall Be Made Straight: The Eichmann Trial, the Jewish Catastrophe, and Hannah Arendt's Narrative* (Philadelphia: Jewish Publication Society of America, 1965). Needless to say, Robinson did not find any merit in Arendt's ideas for the development of the jurisdiction of atrocity.

argument was ignored. The international community regarded the Eichmann trial as largely a "Jewish issue," concerning Jewish politics and Jewish memory of the Holocaust.[12] As a result, the legal implications of the doctrine of "universal jurisdiction" as interpreted by the Israeli court were not explored. Today, with the growth of interest in the doctrine of universal jurisdiction, and with the changing understanding of the role of the victims in the trial, the Eichmann trial is often posited as a legal precedent for the doctrine of universal jurisdiction. However, this legalistic approach fails to articulate the normative basis for the court's jurisdiction and the question it raises about the proper link between the tribunal and the community of the victims. In the following, I suggest reading the court's judgment together with Arendt's assessment of the juridical text in order to reconcile the two perspectives and develop a theory about the sources of legitimacy for a national court adjudicating crimes against humanity. This inquiry can help us gain a more precise understanding of the problems facing the jurisprudence of atrocity today.

8.1 Judgment in Jerusalem

The Nuremberg trials conducted in the aftermath of World War II are seen as a milestone for the international community.[13] For the first time, the political leaders of a defeated regime were brought to trial before an international tribunal for war crimes, crimes against the peace, and crimes against humanity. The London Charter that established the ad hoc tribunal had to overcome difficult legal obstacles in order to apply criminal responsibility over the defendants. Many of these obstacles stemmed from the fact that modern criminal law is based on the idea of state sovereignty and, as a consequence, it fails to address collective crimes that are conducted in the name of sovereign states.[14] This difficulty is exemplified in traditional criminal law doctrines such as "acts of state," "state immunity," "superior order justification," "territorial jurisdiction," and so on with which the Nuremberg court had to wrestle. After the conclusion of the Nuremberg trials, the challenge for the international community was how to turn this important precedent for overcoming state sovereignty and trying international crimes into a working precedent in the absence of a permanent international criminal court.

The Eichmann trial was an important precursor to current notions of universal jurisdiction. The Israeli court, being a national court, had to provide justification for its jurisdiction. The court articulated several bases for its jurisdiction

---

[12] For example, Judith N. Shklar, *Legalism* (Cambridge: Harvard University Press, 1964), p. 155.

[13] Gary Jonathan Bass, *Stay the Hand of Vengeance: The Politics of War Crimes Tribunals* (Princeton: Princeton University Press, 2000). Bass characterizes war crimes trials as a regular part of international politics that emerged well before Nuremberg. However, he argues that the discipline of international criminal law as a distinct legal field originated in the aftermath of World War II, in the Nuremberg trials.

[14] George P. Fletcher, "The Storrs Lectures: Liberals and Romantics at War: The Problem of Collective Guilt," *Yale Law Journal* 111 (2002): 1499.

that could be recognized internationally. First, the court based its extraterritorial jurisdiction on the doctrine of "passive personality" (also known as passive nationality), according to which a national court acquires jurisdiction over crimes committed outside its territory when it can show a special connection to the victim of the crime. Usually, this means that the victim is a citizen of the state, but since Israel did not exist at the time when the crimes were committed, the court extended its notion of citizenship and based its link to the victims on the fact that they were Jews and that Israel was established as a Jewish state. Aware of the difficulties that such ethno-religious reasoning raises for liberal thinkers, the court offered two other bases for its jurisdiction: the protective principle[15] and the principle of "universal jurisdiction" over crimes against humanity.[16] I will concentrate on the latter since it provides a novel basis for jurisdiction.[17] The court ruled that in judging crimes against humanity, there is no need to establish a territorial link or a personal link of the perpetrator or his or her victims to the court. Rather, every national court assumes the power to adjudicate the case, acting as the delegate of the international community.[18]

The new theory of "universal jurisdiction" allowed the court to circumvent the barrier of territorial sovereignty. Respect for the sovereignty of states is manifested in delineating the boundaries of criminal law according to territorial boundaries of states.[19] It means, however, that the criminal law is rarely applied to crimes against humanity, since they are often committed by state

---

[15] The protective principle recognizes that states may prosecute certain conduct committed outside their territory on the basis that it threatens the security interests of the state. For elaboration on the various instances where courts may be permitted to exercise extraterritorial jurisdiction, see Ian Brownlie, *Principles of Public International Law*, 5th ed. (Oxford: Clarendon Press, 1990), pp. 303–9.

[16] *Eichmann Trial*, p. 277. The Israeli Supreme Court stated: "There is full justification for applying here the principle of universal jurisdiction since the international character of 'crimes against humanity' (in the wide meaning of the term) dealt with in this case is no longer in doubt, while the unprecedented extent of their injurious and murderous effects is not to be disputed at the present time. In other words, the basic reason for which international law recognizes the right of each State to exercise such jurisdiction in piracy offences – notwithstanding the fact that its own sovereignty does not extend to the scene of the commission of the offence (the high seas) and the offender is a national of another State or is stateless – applies with even greater force to the above mentioned crimes." See *Eichmann Trial*, pp. 277, 299.

[17] As explained by Bassiouni, all bases for extending territorial jurisdiction still rely on the nexus to a territorial sovereignty, apart from universal jurisdiction. "The reach of a state may, therefore, be universal with respect to the forms of extraterritorial jurisdiction . . . but in all of them there is a connection or legal nexus between sovereignty and the territoriality of the enforcing state, or the nationality of the perpetrator or victim, or the territorial impact of the extraterritorially proscribed conduct." In contrast, "the theory of universal jurisdiction transcends national sovereignty, which is the historical basis for national criminal jurisdiction." See, M. Cherif Bassiouni, "The History of Universal Jurisdiction," in Macedo, ed., *Universal Jurisdiction*, pp. 39–63, at 42.

[18] *Eichmann Trial*, pp. 279–304 (basing jurisdiction on protective, passive personality, and universality principles).

[19] As explained by Bassiouni, "Sovereignty, jurisdiction, and territory have traditionally been closely linked. This is due to the recognized importance of avoiding jurisdictional conflicts

officials and in promotion of what is deemed to be "state interest." Indeed, this understanding underlies the justification for the establishment of the ad hoc international tribunal at Nuremberg, since German courts were not to be trusted to prosecute major Nazi war criminals.[20] The national state often does not view these acts as "crimes" (and so the perpetrators are not indicted in its courts) or is too weak to seriously prosecute them, and other states are prevented from interfering in the name of respect for state sovereignty.

The paradox of human rights that Arendt explored in *The Origins of Total-itarianism* highlights the difficulty of developing tools to adjudicate crimes against humanity. The paradox reflects a tension between two contradictory obligations that seem to originate in the same idea of human rights. On the one hand, in the name of human rights the international community recognizes the right of "self-determination" and upholds the right of all societies to govern themselves. On the other hand, the danger that unlimited sovereignty may be applied against the state's own citizens creates an acute need to protect minority groups against the power of their own state.[21] The doctrine of "universal jurisdiction" that was developed by the Jerusalem court and applied for the first time to crimes against humanity offered an elegant solution to this dilemma. It connected the substance of the crime (against humanity) to the means of prosecution (by each national court acting in the name of humanity). However, at the time of the Eichmann trial, the court did not articulate what conditions or limitations (if any), other than the presence of the defendant on trial, are needed in order to establish the competence of the court. This oversight might be the result of the strong link of the court to the Eichmann case, which was felt so dramatically through the testimonies of Israeli Holocaust survivors during the trial.

The Eichmann trial was the first time in which the victims as a group faced a perpetrator of the Holocaust in a courtroom. It was also the first case in which "crimes against humanity" occupied the center of the trial. However, since the case was brought before a national court, the difficulty of reconciling traditional doctrines of criminal law with the extraordinary character of the new crime had to be addressed. The court opted for a dual solution: to sit both as spectator

---

between states and providing legal consistency and predictability." "The History of Universal Jurisdiction," p. 40.

[20] For a historical discussion of the difficulties faced by the German court in adjudicating the crimes of Auschwitz according to German criminal law during the Frankfurt trial (1965), see Devin Pendas, *The Frankfurt Auschwitz Trial, 1963–1965: Genocide, History, and the Limits of the Law* (Cambridge: Cambridge University Press, 2006).

[21] For elaboration of this tension as the source of a crisis for political theory of the state, see Giorgio Agamben, *Homo Sacer: Sovereign Power and Bare Life*, translated by Daniel Heller-Roazen (Stanford: Stanford University Press, 1998). For a theoretical attempt to resolve some of these problems in the context of current controversies over global justice, see Seyla Benhabib, *Another Cosmopolitanism*, with an introduction by Robert Post and with commentaries by Jeremy Waldron, Bonnie Honig, and Will Kymlicka (New York: Oxford University Press, 2006); Seyla Benhabib, *The Rights of Others: Aliens, Residents, and Citizens* (Cambridge: Cambridge University Press, 2004).

and as actor in the trial of Eichmann.[22] As spectators, the judges opened the
stage of the trial to the testimonies of about a hundred Holocaust survivors,
thus allowing the court to become a forum for weaving collective memory out
of the individual threads of survivor testimonies. Nonetheless, as an actor in
the legal field, the court did not allow these voices to overwhelm its judgment.
Here, the court applied its juridical lenses to the case and focused on the ways
in which Israeli criminal law could be adapted to the crimes of the Holocaust
without creating dangerous precedents that would jeopardize the liberties of
ordinary criminal defendants in the future. The dilemma of how to reconcile
traditional doctrines of criminal law (based on the idea of state sovereignty)
with the postsovereign condition exemplified by crimes against humanity was
particularly salient here. This normative crisis of core tenets of criminal law
did not surface during the Nuremberg trials, due to its extraordinary status
as an ad hoc international military tribunal. It was only during the Eichmann
trial that it was first felt with all its urgency. However, due to the tendency of
judges and jurists to think via legal precedents and analogies, the judgment of
the court tended to obfuscate the problem. Only in the critical reports of the
trial by the political philosopher Hannah Arendt was the problem identified
with all its ramifications for the future of criminal law.

8.2 Hannah Arendt and the Eichmann Trial

Hannah Arendt is known for her criticism of the Eichmann trial and, in particular, of the conduct of the Israeli prosecution. In her report on the trial,
Eichmann in Jerusalem, she criticized the prosecutor, Gideon Hausner (and
Prime Minister David Ben Gurion) for using the trial as a means for promoting
a political agenda, a national version of the history of the Holocaust, through
the testimonies of Holocaust survivors and under the legal category of "crimes
against the Jewish people." In contrast, Arendt presented herself as the guardian
of law, advocating the complete separation of criminal law from politics and
denying any legitimacy to "external" political goals that go beyond the traditional aim of ascertaining the guilt of the defendant.[23] For that purpose, she
suggested that the prosecution should refrain from relying on the category of
"crimes against the Jewish people" and use instead the more general category
of "crimes against humanity."

During the heated controversy that erupted after the publication of Arendt's
report, it was convenient to stress the universalistic strand in her criticism

---

[22] For elaboration on the idea of the judge as spectator and actor, see Bilsky, *Transformative
Justice*, pp. 117–44.

[23] Hannah Arendt, *Eichmann in Jerusalem: A Report on the Banality of Evil* (London: Faber and
Faber, 1963). (Hereafter abbreviated *EJ*.) Arendt's view of the role of trials is challenged in
contemporary writings on transitional justice by proponents of the symbolic role of trials. For a
good example, see Lawrence Douglas, *The Memory of Judgment* (New Haven: Yale University
Press, 2001); Mark Osiel, *Mass Atrocity, Collective Memory and the Law* (New Brunswick and
London: Transaction, 1997).

and hence to depict Arendt in stark opposition to the official position of the Israeli political and legal establishment. This opposition was further stressed by the public exchange of letters between Arendt and Gershom Scholem in which he accused her of lacking love of Israel.[24] In retrospect, we can see that this simplistic dichotomy between universalism and particularism cannot be maintained. It is not easily reconciled with the various doctrines developed by the Israeli court (especially the emphasis on international law by Justice Simon Agranat of the Israeli Supreme Court).[25] Likewise, it cannot be easily reconciled with Arendt's support of the competence of an Israeli court to adjudicate Eichmann.

Arendt's criticism of the Israeli prosecution, which opens *Eichmann in Jerusalem*, has gained much public attention. Less known is her position regarding the jurisdiction of the Israeli court. Arendt thought that the best tribunal to judge Eichmann's acts would be a permanent criminal international court. But in its absence, she favored the jurisdiction of an Israeli court (*EJ*, 258–60). On this issue, Arendt was a lone voice against many in the international community who rejected outright the legitimacy of the Jerusalem court because of the identification of the judges with the Jewish victims.[26] Arendt, in contrast, argued that just as other national courts were competent to judge crimes of the Holocaust committed on their territory and against their nationals, so was an Israeli court. The real difficulty, in her view, was not the assumed "partiality" of the judges but a misguided understanding of "territory." She called for a new interpretation of the legal concept of "territory" in a way that would better reflect the legitimate boundaries of national courts exercising jurisdiction over crimes against humanity.

On a first reading, it seems that Arendt advocated two contradictory positions. On the one hand, she objected to the use of the category "crimes against the Jewish people" as too particularistic; on the other hand, she favored the jurisdiction of a national court whose judges belonged to the Jewish nation and were identified with the community of the Jewish victims. Indeed, one commentator who recognized this inconsistency suggested that it cannot be resolved and that we should take Arendt's writing on jurisdiction as a deviation from her general position.[27] I would like to advance a different reading, one that embraces this seeming contradiction as the key to understanding Arendt's position on

---

[24] Scholem raised the issue of Arendt's blaming the victims in the context of her focus on the responsibility of the Jewish Councils for cooperating with the Nazis. See Bilsky, *Transformative Justice*, pp. 146–51.

[25] Pnina Lahav, *Judgment in Jerusalem: Chief Justice Simon Agranat and the Zionist Century* (Berkeley and Los Angeles: University of California Press, 1997), pp. 145–62.

[26] A good example is Telford Taylor, the American chief prosecutor for the second round of trials at Nuremberg, who expressed his strong reservations about the trial in Jerusalem. Telford Taylor, "Large Questions in the Eichmann Case," *New York Times Magazine*, January 22, 1961, p. 11.

[27] Thomas Mertens, "Memory Politics and Law: The Eichmann Trial: Hannah Arendt's View on the Jerusalem Court's Competence," *German Law Journal* 6/2 (February 1, 2005): 407. The author identifies an inconsistency between Arendt's interpretation of the Jerusalem court's

how to articulate the jurisprudence of atrocity by national courts. I will argue that if we read Arendt's interpretation of the nature of the crime together with her interpretation of the principle of "territorial jurisdiction," we discover that she began to develop the novel idea about the need for criminal law to adjust to a fundamental change in the conception of community, one that would transcend geographical borders. This conceptual change could endow legitimacy to the court's "extraterritorial" use of coercive force against the accused. According to my interpretation of Arendt, criminal law (or courts applying domestic criminal codes) has to adopt a double lens, one that is capable of recognizing its simultaneous embeddedness in two communities: a national community and the community of humanity.[28] However, Arendt does not fully elaborate this theory, and we can detect it only when we link her interpretation of the unique nature of "crimes against humanity" to her interpretation of the principle of territorial jurisdiction.

8.2.1 *The Nature of the Crime: Crimes against Humanity*

"Crimes against humanity" are usually understood as being directed at the core of "humaneness," so that this category constitutes a legal barrier against "inhuman" actions. In contrast, Arendt attributed the unprecedented nature of the crime not to the inhumanity of the actors, but to the novel purpose of the crime. In this argument, she adopted the lens of a political philosopher, viewing the crime from the broader perspective of humanity:

> It was when the Nazi Regime declared that the German people not only were unwilling to have any Jews in Germany but wished to make the entire Jewish people disappear from the face of the earth that the new crime, the crime against humanity – in the sense of a crime "against the human status," or against the very nature of mankind appeared . . . [it is] an attack upon diversity as such. (*EJ*, 268–9)

In Arendt's formulation, crimes against humanity are not just "inhuman acts," as the Israeli court had it; neither are they similar to more familiar crimes like expulsion or mass murder. Rather, they threaten the very possibility of humanity (what she calls the "human status") even when they are perpetrated against particular groups (Jews, Gypsies, and so on). An attempt to annihilate one group should be understood as an attack on the condition of human plurality. It was on this point that Arendt differed from the district court, which stressed the unique nature of the crime as "crimes against the Jewish people." In contrast, Arendt saw the particular crime against the Jewish people as an instance of a universal crime against humanity.

Arendt wrote that this understanding was obscured from the court because it viewed the crime solely from the perspective of Jewish history. However, I would add that a further obstacle arose from the fact that the court was a

competence on the basis of territoriality, on the one hand, and her view that "crimes against humanity" should be adjudicated only by an international court, on the other. The author dismisses the former position as unsupportable.

[28] Benhabib traces this vision of dual citizenship in both a national republic and a cosmopolitan community to Kant's ideas. See Benhabib, *Reclaiming Universalism*, p. 124.

domestic court applying positive criminal law. Domestic criminal law tends to conceive the community that is harmed by the crime in terms of national borders. Thus, for example, the crime of murder is understood not in terms of the harm to the individual whose life was taken, but in terms of undermining the values and interests of the political community at large. But this is usually where domestic criminal law stops. Arendt wanted the court to go a step further and acknowledge that the harm to an ethnic or a religious group envisioned by crimes against humanity should be understood as harm to humanity as such.[29] This different type of harm is obscured by the category of "crimes against the Jewish people," which defines the harm in terms of the specific group harmed and does not point to the condition of human plurality as its protected value. Furthermore, from the perspective of domestic criminal law, it is hard to distinguish between the crime of genocide and mass murder. Arendt urged recognition of a different community that was targeted by the Nazi crimes: the community of humankind. Recognizing a community that transcends national borders helps Arendt explain the difference between mass murder and crimes against humanity. She wrote:

The supreme crime it was confronted with, the physical extermination of the Jewish people, was a crime against humanity, perpetrated upon the body of the Jewish people ... only the choice of victims, not the nature of the crime, could be derived from the long history of Jew-hatred and anti-Semitism. (*EJ*, 269)

We can understand Arendt's position as extending the logic of domestic criminal law to international crimes. Just as national criminal law conceives of a crime as an offense against the state as a collective, not merely against the individuals immediately harmed by it, so a "crime against humanity" should be understood as being directed against the core values of the international community or the community of humanity, and not merely against the victimized group injured by it.[30]

8.2.2 Jurisdiction
Although Arendt recognized the jurisdiction of the Israeli court, she rejected as unsatisfactory the two bases offered by the court in support of its jurisdiction (she did not elaborate on the protective principle). The doctrine of "passive personality," she argued, was not compatible with the foundations of modern criminal law because it put too much emphasis on the injury to the individual victim as the main justification for the criminal process and not on the more

---

[29] A similar approach was taken by Justice Agranat in the Eichmann appeal; see Lahav, *Judgment in Jerusalem*. For developments in this direction, including the emergence of state laws enacting universal jurisdiction over certain crimes such as slavery, war crimes, genocide, torture, and crimes against humanity, and the definition of the harm in terms of the larger international community, see A. Hays Butler, "The Growing Support for Universal Jurisdiction in National Legislation," in Macedo, ed., *Universal Jurisdiction*, pp. 67–76.

[30] For elaboration of this claim in the context of contemporary international criminal law, see Robert Sloan, *The Expressive Capacity of International Punishment*, Columbia Public Law and Legal Theory Working Paper 06100 (2006), pp. 10–20.

general injury to the community.[31] This might, in her opinion, bring criminal law too close to private revenge. Much more surprising was her rejection of the doctrine of "universal jurisdiction" as the basis for recognizing the authority of the Israeli court over the case. As Arendt advocated the adoption of "crimes against humanity," it would seem only natural for her to accompany this choice with "universal jurisdiction."[32] If the injured community is humanity as such (or the condition of human plurality), why not recognize every national court as competent to adjudicate such a crime? Arendt does not give a satisfactory answer to this question. She only explains that the Israeli court based its universal jurisdiction on an unfounded analogy to the law of piracy. A pirate, Arendt wrote, is an "outlaw" who has no flag and who acts on the high seas outside the territorial jurisdiction of any state. Far from being an outlaw, Eichmann had been a loyal member of his state and had acted in its name. In other words, the problem with Nazism was not the actions of outlaw individuals but rather the actions of an "outlaw state" – a criminal state (EJ, 262). The new crimes reverse the traditional understanding of the state as the locus of legality, and the analogy to piracy obscures the nature of the problem. However, given the formidable obstacles in the way of prosecuting Nazi atrocities, Arendt's point about piracy seems to be rather legalistic when made by someone who urges the court to be innovative and creative. I believe that behind the legalistic explanation lies a well-founded fear concerning the risk of politicization involved in the prosecution of state actors by third-party courts.[33] Indeed, the history of the doctrine of "universal jurisdiction" over pirates can give us a first hint of the problem it could pose. International law deliberately restricted universal jurisdiction over pirates to pirates acting on their own and not on behalf of states. It was reasoned that expanding this jurisdiction over "state" pirates might politicize the law too much, making it into another tool of political conflict between states.[34]

[31] "Criminal proceedings, since they are mandatory and thus initiated even if the victim would prefer to forgive and forget, rest on laws whose 'essence' – to quote Telford Taylor . . . 'is that a crime is not committed only against the victim but primarily against the community whose law is violated'" (EJ, 261).

[32] Arendt's interpretation of crimes against humanity made it synonymous with genocide as defined in the 1948 Convention on the Prevention and Punishment of the Crime of Genocide. Interestingly the convention also rejects universal jurisdiction. Article 6 of the convention states: "Persons charged with genocide or any of the other acts enumerated in article III shall be tried by a competent tribunal of the State in the territory of which the act was committed, or by such international penal tribunal as may have jurisdiction with respect to those Contracting Parties which shall have accepted its jurisdiction." Universal jurisdiction is not recognized by the convention. Convention on the Prevention and Punishment of the Crime of Genocide, December 9, 1948, United Nations Treaty Series, vol. 78, p. 277.

[33] A good example is Belgium's repeal of the law granting its courts universal jurisdiction over certain international crimes in the face of American pressure. See Falk Moore, "Egregious Crimes against Humanity," pp. 119–23.

[34] Madeline H. Morris, "Universal Jurisdiction in a Divided World: Conference Remarks," New Eng. L. Rev. 35 (2001): 337, 339–40; Alfred Rubin, The Law of Piracy, 2nd ed. (Irvinton on Hudson: Transnational, 1998). Orentlicher explains why the analogy to piracy law might be

Arendt rejected the two bases given by the court for extending its "territorial jurisdiction." She argued that instead of looking for the "exception" to the rule, the court should have reinterpreted the doctrine of territorial jurisdiction in accordance with the nature of the new crime. Her insistence on returning to the "rule" of territorial jurisdiction implies that the international community should rethink its concept of state sovereignty in its relation to criminal law. Arendt began this process by offering a new interpretation of the concept of territory. Since Arendt's interpretation of "territory" is so novel, it is worth quoting in full:

Israel could easily have claimed territorial jurisdiction if she had only explained that "territory," as the law understands it, is a political and a legal concept, and not merely a geographical term. It relates not so much and not primarily to a piece of land as to the space between individuals in a group whose members are bound to, and at the same time separated and protected from, each other by all kinds of relationships, based on a common language, religion, a common history, customs, and laws. Such relationships become spatially manifest insofar as they themselves constitute the space wherein the different members of a group relate to and have intercourse with each other. (*EJ*, 262–3)

On the basis of this cultural interpretation of "territory," Arendt justified Israeli jurisdiction over crimes against humanity since she understood them as directed against the Jewish "territory." She explained that Jews throughout the ages had kept their "territory" as a community, and that after the Holocaust, Israel inherited this cultural space (*EJ*, 263). The Nazis' very attempt to destroy the special "territory" that bound the Jews together as a community throughout the ages made their crimes unique, that is, different in quality from prior attempts to murder Jews as individuals (even on a massive scale). The State of Israel was created after the Holocaust, in part out of the world's recognition of what had happened to the Jewish communities. Israel was also the state that three hundred thousand Holocaust survivors had made their home. These facts justified trying Eichmann in an Israeli court.[35]

---

misleading. "For one thing, justifications for universal jurisdiction over piracy assume (perhaps not always correctly) that no state would consider prosecution an affront to its sovereignty. But when bystander states prosecute traveling dictators, indifference is the least likely response of the defendant's home state. Further, piracy can be truly indiscriminate in its choice of victims; to say that the pirate is an enemy of all mankind may be an exaggeration, but it is more than a metaphor. In contrast the claim that, 'like the pirate . . . before him,' the torturer is now an enemy of all mankind is fundamentally a moral claim." Diane F. Orentlicher, "The Future of Universal Jurisdiction in the New Architecture of Transnational Justice," in Macedo, ed., *Universal Jurisdiction*, p. 231.

[35] Arendt's interpretation of "territory" is in line with the logic behind the Nuremberg trials. The jurisdiction of the ad hoc international military tribunal was restricted to crimes not confined to one territory. Interterritorial crimes were given to the jurisdiction of national courts while the International Military Tribunal dealt with supranational crimes. Likewise, Eichmann's role in the "final solution" of the Jewish people was not restricted to German state borders but was directed against the "territory" of the Jews as a nation across national borders. Thinking of "territory" in a nonreified way allows Arendt to see that the State of Israel and its courts

Arendt's interpretation of territorial jurisdiction presupposes the need to find a stronger link between a national court and crimes against humanity, beyond the state's membership in the community of nations, as the interpretation of universal jurisdiction by the Israeli court suggests. The Israeli court did not dwell on this question because in the Eichmann trial, the strong link of the court to the case was evident (indeed, a link that undermined the impartiality of the court in the eyes of many in the international community).

We can now see that both theories advanced by the court for extending territorial jurisdiction can undermine the validity of the criminal law as a distinct field, connected to an imagined political community. "Passive personality" reduces the criminal law to the individual victim (undermining the distinction between tort law and criminal law). "Universal jurisdiction," on the other hand, threatens to turn the criminal law into a theoretical enterprise, one not burdened by any ties to a specific community, history, or tradition. In the following, I argue that only by introducing the "community" basis of criminal law can we find a proper balance between law and politics in post-Holocaust adjudication. In other words, we need to reintroduce the political community in articulating the proper relation between international criminal law and the jurisdiction of domestic courts.[36] I suggest that Arendt pointed in this direction when she offered a new interpretation of the "territorial principle" of jurisdiction instead of adopting the all-encompassing principle of "universal jurisdiction."

8.3 The Riddle of Jurisdiction

Every system of law grows out of and maintains a human community, and it remains connected to it as long as it is a living law. This fundamental insight is manifested in the beginning of each trial. At this initial stage, even before the parties present their arguments, the court requires that its jurisdiction over the dispute be established. It requires that the parties show a meaningful connection between the case in controversy and the court. The most important connection is based on a *territorial link* – that the disputed acts occurred on the territory over which the court has jurisdiction (the territoriality principle). Another link is a *personal* one, in cases where one of the parties to the dispute is considered a member of the political community over which the court is authorized to judge (the nationality principle). Finally, a *temporal* restriction has to be respected – that the adjudication is not premature and that there is no statute of limitations applicable to the acts under consideration. These three links that establish the court's competence are also the three basic relations that constitute a political

---

have the strongest link to the community of Jews as a nation and thus can claim "territorial jurisdiction."

36 For two recent attempts to articulate the role of a political community in the evolving practice of universal jurisdiction, see Orentlicher, "The Future of Universal Jurisdiction"; Sloan, *The Expressive Capacity on International Punishment.*

community: space, time, and people.[37] In other words, in order to establish its
jurisdiction, the court has to examine how "close" it is to the dispute – whether
it has some meaningful links to it. Jurisdiction requires a relation to the court
while the liberal ideal of the "rule of law" requires distance – that the judge be
a stranger to the dispute and exercise impartiality. Is there a real contradiction
between these two requirements? And what does it tell us about the danger of
a political trial? Does it exist when there is too much proximity or too much
distance?

The law of jurisdiction can give us pause. It teaches us that the key to solving
the problem of a political trial does not necessarily lie in trying to maintain
a strict separation between politics and law. "Blind justice" does not always
result in a just trial. We are used to thinking about the rule of law in terms
of maintaining a distance between the court and the parties to the dispute,
but at the same time the rule of law requires that a meaningful link be established between the court and the community injured by the deed. It seems that
underlying this tension is a basic assumption that the criminal law belongs to
a political community and is an exercise of its self-governance. The distance
that the rule of law instructs us to protect between the tribunal and the case is
a distance within the known boundaries of a state territory. Today these boundaries are questioned in transnational adjudication. Some argue that the developing jurisprudence of international crimes such as genocide and crimes against
humanity explode law's spatio-temporal coordinates.[38] The challenge is to
articulate anew the proper distance between court and case.[39] This, I maintain,
can be done only if we take into consideration the relation of criminal law to
a political community.

8.4 The Specter of the Political Trial

The dangers stemming from the exercise of "universal jurisdiction" were not
apparent to many at the time of its announcement in the Eichmann trial. During the 1990s, when various states adopted this doctrine into their laws, and
after the Cold War, when several attempts were finally made to apply it by
third-party national courts, the question became a pertinent one.[40] From the
perspective of many in the international community, the attempts to bring
to trial heads of state such as Pinochet, Milošević, and Sharon were signs of
advancement in the rule of law. It seems that by taking the issue away from the

---

[37] In legal terms, international law recognizes five bases for jurisdiction (the territorial principle,
the nationality principle, the protective principle, the passive personality, and the universality
principle). See Steven R. Ratner and Jason S. Abrams, *Accountability for Human Rights Atrocities in International Law: Beyond the Nuremberg Legacy* (Oxford: Clarendon Press, 1997),
pp. 140–1.

[38] Lawrence Douglas, "Beyond Nuremberg and Eichmann: Toward a Jurisprudence of Atrocity"
(paper presented at Tel Aviv Legal History Workshop, April 2009, on file with author).

[39] Bassiouni, "The History of Universal Jurisdiction," pp. 39–63.

[40] Ibid.

courts of the perpetrators to third-party courts this last vestige of state immunity is removed.[41] In what sense can we honestly claim that this development might be a move toward further politicization of the law? By defining the nature of the new crimes, removing the obstacle of territorial jurisdiction, and overcoming temporal limitations, it seems that finally the international community can bring to trial perpetrators of serious international law crimes. However, by removing these legal obstacles, we also undermine the juridical character of the crime, thus making it vulnerable to political manipulation. For example, from a political point of view, there was no sense in bringing Sharon to trial during his long years in the Israeli opposition. From a legal point of view, it was impossible to bring him to trial after his election as Israeli prime minister in 2001, both because too much time had elapsed since the Lebanon war of 1982 and because of the territorial obstacle (leaving aside the question of immunity). Once these obstacles were removed, it became all too easy to select the best political time for indicting Sharon in a Belgian court.[42] This is one sense of politicization of the law. It impacts the relations between states when used in a politically motivated manner or simply to vex and harass leaders of other states. Another sense of politicization involved in such adjudication, which I believe undermines in a more profound way our concept of criminal law, is an internal one. It stems from the disjunction that universal jurisdiction creates between the judge and the relevant political community, thus raising problems of democratic deficit.[43] This concern goes in two directions. First, some critics worry that to allow foreign judges to make law for societies to whom they are largely unaccountable threatens the democratic foundations of criminal law.[44] Second, since the courts exercising universal jurisdiction operate at a remote distance from the communities that are deeply affected by their judgments, the solidarity between judge and community is undermined. This in turn undermines the legitimacy of the court's judgments in the eyes of the concerned community, since the judges do not take the risk of living under the results of their judgments.[45] Another way to understand the concern of politicization

---

[41] Diane F. Orentlicher, "Whose Justice? Reconciling Universal Jurisdiction with Democratic Principles," *Georgia Law Journal* 92 (2004): 1057.

[42] For discussion of the various aspects of the case, see Borneman, ed., *The Case of Ariel Sharon*.

[43] Benhabib, *Reclaiming Universalism*, p. 133: "[T]he community that binds itself by these laws defines itself by drawing boundaries as well, and these boundaries are territorial as well as civic. *The will of the democratic sovereign can extend only over the territory that is under its jurisdiction*; democracies require borders.... Democratic rule, unlike imperial dominion, is exercised in the name of some specific constituency and binds that constituency alone." Emphasis added.

[44] Orentlicher, "The Future of Universal Jurisdiction."

[45] Anne-Marie Slaughter defines these two problems with universal jurisdiction as "external" and "internal." "The exercise of jurisdiction without a link either to people or territory raises two major problems: one internal and one external. The internal problem concerns the legitimacy of a court in concentrating the full power of the state against an individual defendant who, by definition, cannot be said to have in any way authorized the exercise of that power through

is in terms of the symbolic role of the court's judgment in shaping the collective memory of the concerned communities (of perpetrators and victims).[46] Supporters of universal jurisdiction are not unaware of this democratic deficit. However, they maintain that the gain to democratic values overrides this worry by removing the last vestige of impunity and enhancing the ideal of the "rule of law." In the eyes of supporters of universal jurisdiction, the dangers of unaccountable sovereign power seem to outweigh the new dangers of politicization. This position, however, takes for granted that the two alternatives are at the two opposite ends of the spectrum – universal justice versus national justice. It is worth turning again to the unexplored middle ground suggested by Arendt via her interpretation of the concept of "territory" to see what it can contribute to understanding the future direction of international criminal law.[47]

8.5 Criminal Law and the Community of Humanity

We saw that the Eichmann court introduced the doctrine of universal jurisdiction for crimes against humanity without elaborating any conditions for its legitimate use. In some parts of its decision, the court stressed the link between the State of Israel and the victims, but it did not connect this link to its theory of universal jurisdiction. Arendt, in contrast, believed that the territoriality doctrine should be reinterpreted to allow for a more plural conception of "community" as the basis for post–World War II criminal adjudication. I argued that without introducing some requirement of a link to a living community, the pure concept of universal jurisdiction introduces many dangers of politicization.[48] In other words, it is doubtful whether it would have been justified, according to Arendt, to try Eichmann in Switzerland, for example,

nationality or conduct within the state's territory. The external problem concerns the heightened danger of interference in the affairs of fellow states." Anne-Marie Slaughter, "Defining the Limits," in Macedo, ed., *Universal Jurisdiciton*, p. 172.

[46] Douglas, "Beyond Nuremberg and Eichmann." Douglas's emphasis on the symbolic role of the court gives support to the need to rethink the relation between law and community in trials that transcend traditional national borders.

[47] Bass maintains that this middle ground between universal justice and national justice was achieved in the Eichmann trial. See Bass, "The Adolph Eichmann Case." In my view, the court simply added a different basis for its judgment, and Arendt's criticism offers a much-needed theoretical formulation of how to arrive at this middle ground.

[48] Indeed, several authors have been urging to the development of principles of imposing conditions on the court's claim for universal jurisdiction. See Orentlicher, "The Future of Universal Jurisdiction," where the author argues that jurisdictional clashes caused by the introduction of universal jurisdiction should be resolved by weighing the respective interests of relevant communities. The need to articulate conditions for the exercise of universal jurisdiction and to create priorities is also reflected in the Princeton Principles of Universal Jurisdiction (in Macedo, ed., *Universal Jurisdiction*, pp. 18–25); Hari M. Osofsky, "Domesticating International Criminal Law: Bringing Human Rights Violators to Justice," *Yale Law Journal* 107 (1997): 191. Osofsky suggests that limits can be placed on the exercise of universal jurisdiction in the United States through an adaptation of the civil law doctrine of *forum non conveniens*.

while it was justified to do so in Israel, the home of many of the victims of the Holocaust. However, Arendt made it clear that Eichmann could not be tried in Israel under the narrower category of "crimes against the Jewish people," as this would be politicization of another sort, requiring us to narrow our conception of the injured community while ignoring its harm to the human community (the condition of plurality).

In what sense is Arendt's interpretation of territorial jurisdiction different from the alternative basis of "passive personality" jurisdiction that was upheld by the court? During the Eichmann trial, the two interpretations converged, so that it was difficult to perceive the different implications each would have in the political world. However, with hindsight, after the proliferation of universal jurisdiction clauses in national legislations, we can clarify the difference. Arendt's interpretation of the territoriality doctrine is more restrictive toward the jurisdiction of a national court than the one entailed by the universal jurisdiction theory or the passive personality doctrine. According to Arendt, an Israeli court cannot adjudicate all crimes against humanity, only those conducted against the body of the Jewish people. Likewise, not every crime directed against a Jew as a Jew justifies the court's jurisdiction, but only those crimes that threaten the continued existence of the Jewish community. In this way, a meaningful link between a third-party national court and the concerned political community (or communities) is maintained. As we shall see, a similar direction is pursued today by adding restrictions to the pure theory of universal jurisdiction and requiring that some nexus exists between the tribunal and the concerned political community.

Arendt's book deals with the nature of the crime (crimes against humanity) and the venue of adjudication in close proximity. She allows us to see the close connection between these two questions. This connection is not often noticed in legal scholarship due to their separation into two distinct stages at the trial.[49] In contrast, Arendt's interpretation of "crimes against humanity" and of the territoriality principle of jurisdiction makes the two issues complementary. On both issues, she rejected a more individualist interpretation of the law in order to reintroduce the political community into her jurisprudence. Thus, Arendt's interpretation of both the substantive law and the procedural rule of jurisdiction retains the connection between the court and a specific political community, without falling into the trap of either empty universalism or ethnocentric particularism.

By adding the political community to her theory of jurisdiction, Arendt stressed the important connection between the tribunal and the concerned community – a connection that is obscured under the pure theory of universal

---

[49] However, see the discussion of the *Finta* case in the Canadian court, *R. v. Finta* [1994] 88C.C.C. (3d) 417 (S.C.C.), by Slaughter, "Defining the Limits," who maintains that both the majority and dissent based their judgment upon the assumed relationship between the nature of the crime and the jurisdiction of the court.

jurisdiction. But it is this central place given to the political community in her interpretation of the law that raises an acute difficulty for the readers of *Eichmann in Jerusalem*. The starting point of the book is a note on the unique danger that lurks for the Israeli court, the danger of turning Eichmann's trial into a show trial, in the service of the Israeli executive. The question is whether recognizing the need to preserve the bond between a political community and the tribunal undermines the legitimacy of the trial altogether, when it is the community of the victims that undertakes to judge the perpetrator of collective crimes carried out against them.

I believe that by reintroducing the community to international criminal law adjudication and by giving priority to the concerned national courts, we can in fact reduce the danger of illegitimate politics. However, such a move must be accompanied by a clarification of the notion of the injured community. In this, I suggest that we follow Arendt's imperative and adopt a double perspective. Arendt insisted that crimes against humanity injured two communities simultaneously: a particular community of the victims group (Jewish community, for example) and an ideal community of humanity (condition of plurality). To adjudicate such crimes, we should find ways to link these communities together. One such possibility is offered to us today by the permanent International Criminal Court (ICC) in the Hague. It is interesting to note that during the debates over the Rome Statute that established the ICC, the possibility of universal jurisdiction was considered and rejected. Instead, it adopted the requirement of "complementarity" that gives priority to national courts.[50] The "complementarity" requirement upholds the concept of state sovereignty in the sense that the concerned states enjoy priority in trying the case.[51] Only in cases where it is proven that the state is unable or unwilling to adjudicate the crime can the case be taken up by the ICC.[52] It thus provides strong incentive for

---

[50] See, John T. Holmes, "The Principle of Complementarity," in Roy S. Lee, ed., *The International Criminal Court – The Making of the Rome Statute: Issues, Negotiations, Results* (The Hague: Springer, 1999), pp. 41–78. (The Rome Statute of the International Criminal Court was done at Rome, July 17, 1998, and came into force on July 1, 2002.)

[51] Sloan argues that "[c]omplementarity recognizes . . . that national prosecutions, *if* genuine, feasible, and fair, more effectively serve the manifold goals ascribed to international criminal law than do international prosecutions." *The Expressive Capacity of International Punishment*, p. 15. I would add that such national prosecutions are also more justified from a political theory perspective.

[52] Article 17 of the Rome Statute. Cassesse identifies two patterns of development for international criminal law in post-Holocaust jurisprudence. One follows the Nuremberg precedent and culminates in the establishment of the ICCY and ICCR tribunals. The other begins with the Eichmann trial and culminates in the establishment of a permanent international criminal court. The Nuremberg pattern gives priority to international tribunals in trying the highest officials of a criminal regime, while the Eichmann precedent gives priority to national courts of the relevant political community. Cassesse believes that the Nuremberg pattern is the better way to address the problem of sovereign immunity. See Antonio Cassesse, *International Criminal Law* (Oxford: Oxford University Press, 2001).

states to prosecute crimes they would have preferred to ignore.[53] ICC litigation is structured to remain the exception to the rule of national adjudication.[54]

Furthermore, the ICC, being a permanent court, is bound by its precedents and is required to apply them over time in an equal manner, thus reducing the danger of selective political prosecutions. This solution does not eliminate the sources of unjustified political immunities, but it is mindful of the need to retain the legitimacy of the court in the eyes of the concerned political community. The principle of complementarity indicates that the best path for adjudicating crimes against humanity, genocide, and the like is finding a middle ground – not the rule of power (as the doctrine of absolute sovereignty implies) and not empty legalism (as the doctrine of universal jurisdiction might indicate).

Interestingly, we can detect a similar development in the judgments of national courts and in national legislation concerning universal jurisdiction. The requirement of a meaningful link to the court is being added.[55] A similar rethinking can be detected in legal scholarship. Thus, for example, one supporter of universal jurisdiction, when addressing the criticism concerning the democratic deficit in such adjudication, suggests that a legitimate use of

---

[53] The possibility of a prosecution in the ICC creates a rift between state law agents (prosecutors and courts) and the executive branch. It gives law enforcement bodies a credible threat that by becoming accomplices to an internationally recognized crime they might be indicted in the Hague. This is a negative incentive to the executive to refrain from certain policies that can amount to international crimes. The existence of the ICC also creates a positive incentive to law enforcement bodies since if they choose to prosecute, they enjoy priority over the ICC, so they can explain their intervention to the local community in terms of the good of the national community (since otherwise the case will be adjudicated by the distant ICC). This newly created rift between law enforcement bodies and the executive might resurrect the triangle – among the court, the executive, and the victims – upon which the rule of law is premised. It creates a better balance between politics and law instead of a complete divorce between them.

[54] Two major questions arise concerning jurisdiction priority. First, what shall be done when the national legal system extends immunity to the perpetrator of crimes defined under the Rome Statute of the International Criminal Court? Second, what shall be done in cases of competition between various national courts? These are very large questions that deserve a separate discussion. For initial investigation of these jurisdictional puzzles, see Orentlicher, "The Future of Universal Jurisdiction"; Leila Nadya Sadat, "Universal Jurisdiciton, National Amnesties, and Truth Commissions: Reconciling the Irreconcilable," in Macedo, ed., *Universal Jurisdiction*, pp. 19–21.

[55] Thus, for example, although universal jurisdiction was indispensable to the Spanish proceedings against Pinochet, the case did not rely solely on that principle. The original complaints comprised seven individuals possessing dual Spanish-Chilean citizenship. Moreover, when the jurisdiction of the Spanish court was challenged, the court clarified that it could try crimes of terrorism and genocide pursuant to the principle of universal jurisdiction, bolstered by jurisdiction predicated on the nationality of the Spanish victims. For elaboration, see Orentlicher, "The Future of Universal Jurisdiction," p. 1074. Later, Spain's Supreme Court ruled that universal jurisdiction should be exercised over genocide only when there is a "direct link to Spanish interests." See Sentencia del Tribunal Supremeo sobre el caso Guatemala por genocidio (Judgment of the Spanish Supreme Court concerning the Guatemala genocide case), Sentancia de Tribunal Supremeo Sala Segunda, de lo Penal n. 327/2003 February 25, 2003 (No. 327) (Spain). Similarly, following criticism over the indictment of Prime Minister Ariel Sharon in a Belgian court, the legislator added various conditions that demand a link between the case and the court.

universal jurisdiction is dependent on meeting several conditions that address the disjunction between the court and the relevant political community.[56] This direction is still in its initial stages and much thinking has to be done on how to democratize international criminal law (in the sense of bringing a political community to bear on the legal proceedings).[57]

Can these developments of international criminal law answer Arendt's concern? Should we view a limited version of universal jurisdiction (with a required nexus to a political community) as equal to Arendt's conception of cultural "territorial" jurisdiction? Here we should note the unique circumstances of the Eichmann trial, in which the community of victims was transformed into a sovereign state. Under these unique circumstances, Arent opted for a reinterpretation of the territorial doctrine of jurisdiction. More often, however, the victimized community remains part of the larger community of the perpetrators. In this context, the "cultural" conception of territory should become part of the court's interpretation of the substantive crime. In particular, it should bear on the definition of the harmed community.

Let me close this chapter by returning to the nature of the community we should imagine in adjudicating crimes against humanity. Should national courts and international courts envision the same community when adjudicating international criminal law, or should they diverge and serve distinct communities? There are those who advocate that the ICC serve as a "proxy justice" to the specific political community being injured by the crime.[58] Others maintain that notwithstanding the "complementarity principle," once a case comes before the ICC, the relevant community should be that of humanity as a whole.[59] Following Arendt, I would suggest that we should understand the crime as involving two communities simultaneously, and define the unique detriments and goals of such adjudication, whether it is carried out by national or international tribunals. Arendt's important observation in *Eichmann in Jerusalem* on the necessity for criminal law to be connected to a living community should continue to guide us in our quest for a better way of implementing our basic values of human rights. When criminal law loses this insight in its attempt to adhere as closely as possible to moral strictures, it risks losing its power and meaning. On the other hand, when judges confine themselves to the narrow

---

[56] Orentlicher, "Whose Justice?"

[57] A step in this direction was undertaken by the Princeton Project on Universal Jurisdiction, which produced the Princeton Principles on Universal Jurisdiction. For the principles and commentary essays on the subject, see Macedo, ed., *Universal Jurisdiction*, pp. 18–25.

[58] Sloan argues that this is indeed the prevailing view, *The Expressive Capacity of International Punishment*, p. 12. See also Steven Glickman, "Victims' Justice: Legitimizing the Sentencing Regime of the International Criminal Court," *Columbia Journal of Transnational Law* 43 (2004): 229, 257; Ruti Teitel, review of M. Cherif Bassiouni, ed., *Post-Conflict Justice* (2002), in *American Journal of International Law* 98 (2004): 872, 874.

[59] Sloan, *The Expressive Capacity of International Punishment*, p. 16. Sloan maintains that the ICC should not serve as a "proxy justice" to local political interests. He learns this from Rome Statute article 1, which states that the mission of international criminal tribunals is to prosecute the most serious crimes of concern to the international community as a whole.

viewpoint of the specific community involved (of perpetrators or victims), they lose sight of the embeddedness of criminal law in the larger community of humanity. Instead of ignoring the community basis of criminal law, we should recognize the political aspects of the litigation as part and parcel of the power of criminal law to serve as a bridge between divided communities and our common aspiration to realize our moral ideals.

9

International Law and Human Plurality in the Shadow of Totalitarianism

Hannah Arendt and Raphael Lemkin

Seyla Benhabib

Hannah Arendt and Raphael Lemkin were witnesses to the twentieth century. They both experienced the dislocating transformations on the European continent as a consequence of two world wars; lost their states as well as their homes in this process; narrowly escaped the clutches of the Nazi extermination machine; and made it to the New World through sheer luck and fortuitous circumstance. Their thought is marked by the cataclysms of the last century, and they have in turn emerged as indispensable interlocutors for all of us in understanding this past.

Arendt and Lemkin were contemporaries and there are astonishing parallels in their early biographies. She was born in Hannover in 1906 (d. 1975) and grew up in Koenigsberg in East Prussia. After World War I, the Polish Corridor was created and cut East Prussia and Koenigsberg off from the rest of Weimar; in 1945 Koenigsberg was occupied by the Soviets and renamed Kaliningrad. Lemkin was born in Bezwodene in 1900, then part of Tsarist Russia. Between the two world wars (1918–1939), Bezwodene became part of Poland and today is Bezvodna in Belarus.

When Arendt was arrested by the Gestapo in the spring of 1933 and was forced to flee to Paris via Prague with her mother, she had been carrying out research in the Prussian State Library at the request of Kurt Blumenfeld on anti-semitic measures undertaken by Nazi nongovernmental organizations, business associations, and professional clubs to exclude Jewish members. Her Zionist friend Kurt Blumenfeld, in turn, was preparing to present this material at the Eighteenth Zionist Congress. During those very same years, Ralph Lemkin was a young clerk in the office of the Polish state prosecutor, who had been

This chapter has previously appeared in *Constellations. An International Journal of Critical and Democratic Theory* 16, 2 (June 2009), pp. 331–50. It has been revised for inclusion in this book. Many thanks to A. Dirk Moses, James Sleeper, and Roy T. Tsao for reading earlier versions of this chapter. Dirk Moses provided invaluable historical and editorial suggestions.

collecting documents on Nazi war legislation, particularly those affecting cultural, linguistic, and religious activities and artifacts of cultural and religious groups. In 1933, he had sent a paper to a League of Nations conference in Madrid, in which he proposed that "the crimes of barbarity and vandalism be considered as new offences against the law of nations."[1] In 1939, he fled from Poland and reached Stockholm, where he continued to do extensive research on Nazi occupation laws throughout Europe. On April 18, 1941, he arrived in the United States via Japan. That very same year, Arendt and her second husband, Heinrich Bluecher, arrived in New York via Portugal.

Yet in contrast to Arendt, who acquired worldwide fame after her arrival in the United States with her many works and university appointments, Lemkin, after the general acclaim he received with the passage of the Genocide Convention by the United Nations in 1948, fell into obscurity and died a lonely death, destitute and neglected in New York in 1959.

It is certainly fascinating to speculate whether these Jewish refugees, who were caught up in the great dislocations of their time, ever met one another in some location or association in the United States. We just do not know. What is even more astonishing is the lack of any discussion in Hannah Arendt's work of Lemkin's great book on the concept of genocide,[2] or of any evidence that Lemkin knew Arendt's work on totalitarianism, which certainly was the most powerful historical documentation and philosophical analysis in the early 1950s of the unprecedentedly murderous character of the Nazi regime. Arendt and Lemkin appear to have existed in the same time and space coordinates without ever encountering one another. It is thus incumbent upon retrospective readers of their work to put together the pieces of the puzzle in this missed encounter.

This missed encounter can itself be viewed as a metaphor for the ways in which not only their lives but also their thought ran so close to each other and yet remained so distant.[3] In 1944, Ralph Lemkin published *Axis Rule in*

---

[1] This, and other biographical information on Ralph Lemkin, is drawn from Ann Curthoys and John Docker, "Defining Genocide," in Dan Stone, ed., *The Historiography of Genocide* (New York: Palgrave Macmillan, 2008), pp. 9ff.; Samantha Power, *"A Problem from Hell": America and the Age of Genocide* (New York: Basic Books, 2002), pp. 17–87. See also Dominik J. Schaller and Jurgen Zimmerer, "From the Guest Editors: Raphael Lemkin: The 'Founder of the United Nation's Genocide Convention' as a Historian of Mass Violence," *Journal of Genocide Research*, 7, 4 (December 2005): 447–52.

[2] Cf. Raphael Lemkin, *Axis Rule in Occupied Europe. Laws of Occupation, Analysis of Government, Proposals for Redress* (Washington: Carnegie Endowment for International Peace, 1944). (Hereafter abbreviated *AROE.*) Upon the publication of *Axis Rule in Occupied Europe*, the *New York Times Book Review* devoted its January 1945 cover to this work. It is hard to believe that Arendt, who resided in New York City at that time, and in view of her general interests in and knowledge of these questions, would not have been familiar with Lemkin's book. See Otto D. Tolischus, "Twentieth Century Moloch: The Nazi-Inspired Totalitarian State, Devourer of Progress – and of Itself," *New York Times Book Review*, January 21, 1945, pp. 1, 24, as cited by Power, *"A Problem from Hell,"* p. 525, note 35.

[3] A subtle analysis of the sensibility of Arendt, Lemkin, and others in terms of the category of "citizen of the world" is given by Ned Curthoys, who writes, "As émigré scholars and public

Occupied Europe, in which he demanded that a new category in the law of nations be formulated in order to reckon with and bring to justice war crimes committed by Nazis and their allies against the many peoples of Europe. He was concerned that international law ought to recognize the unprecedented nature of genocide of the Jews and other peoples. In 1951, Hannah Arendt published *The Origins of Totalitarianism*, which also exposed the unprecedented political nature of totalitarianism as a novel form of political rule in history – in fact, as a transformation of the sphere of the political as such. Yet, unlike Lemkin, Arendt was quite skeptical that declarations of human rights, international conventions, and the like could help restore the destroyed political fabric of the world after World War II. In a passage that almost seems to take aim at Lemkin's efforts to pass the Genocide Convention, Arendt wrote:

Even worse was that all societies formed for the protection of the Rights of man, all attempts to arrive at a new bill of human rights were sponsored by marginal figures – by a few international jurists without political experience or professional philanthropists supported by the uncertain sentiments of professional idealists. The groups they formed, the declarations they issued show an uncanny similarity in language and composition to that of societies for the prevention of cruelty to animals. No statesman, no political figure of any importance could possibly take them seriously and none of the liberal or radical parties in Europe thought it necessary to incorporate into their program a new declaration of human rights.[4]

Did Arendt possibly have Lemkin in mind when she referred in dismissive terms of those "international jurists without political experience"? And could she have been referring to Eleanor Roosevelt, the tireless force behind the passage of the Universal Declaration of Human Rights in 1948, when Arendt takes a swipe at "professional philanthropists supported by the uncertain sentiments of professional idealists"? There are no references in Arendt's work, as far as I can tell,[5] to Raphael Lemkin.

Ironically, though, by 1963, when she wrote *Eichmann in Jerusalem,* Arendt has not only accepted the categories of the Genocide Convention, she goes even beyond Lemkin to provide a philosophical condemnation of the crime of

---

intellectuals, Arendt, Jaspers, Spitzer, Auerbach and Lemkin were dedicated to illuminating generous and unorthodox methodological approaches imbued with the restless exigencies of personal experience and hermeneutic intuition." Ned Curthoys, "The Émigré Sensibility of 'World Literature': Historicizing Hannah Arendt and Karl Jaspers' Cosmopolitan Intent," *Theory and Event*, 8, 3 (2005), accessed online at http://muse.jhu.edu/journals/theory_and_event/v008/8.3curthoys. html.

4 Hannah Arendt, *The Origins of Totalitarianism* (1951) (New York: Harcourt, Brace, and Jovanovich, 1979), p. 292. (Hereafter abbreviated *OT,* and all references in parentheses are to this edition.) Originally published in Britain as *The Burden of Our Time* (London: Secker and Warburg, 1951).

5 I am being tentative here because there is still no serious cataloging of the contents of some eighty odd boxes deposited in the Library of Congress in Washington, D.C., although microfilm collections exist in several universities. The same is true of the extensive Hannah Arendt and Heinrich Bluecher Library, which is located at Bard College. Attempts are under way to catalogue its holdings. The electronic catalogue contains no references to Lemkin.

genocide in the light of her concept of human plurality. Genocide, in Arendt's view, destroys plurality and is a crime against the human condition as such. In the dramatic epilogue to *Eichmann in Jerusalem*, she states that the "justice of what was done in Jerusalem would have emerged to be seen by all if the judges had dared to address their defendant in something like the following terms."[6] In astonishingly pointed language, she then delivers her own verdict against Adolf Eichmann:

You admitted that the crime committed against the Jewish people during the war was the greatest crime in recorded history, and you admitted your role in it.... Let us assume, for the sake of argument, that it was nothing more than misfortune that made you a willing instrument in the organization of *mass murder*; there still remains the fact that you have carried out, and therefore actively supported, a policy of *mass murder*.... And just as you supported and carried out a policy of not wanting to share the earth with the Jewish people and the people of a number of other nations – *as though you and your superiors had any right to determine who should and who should not inhabit the world* – we find that no one, that is, no member of the human race, can be expected to share the earth with you. This is the reason, and the only reason, you must hang. (*EJ*, 277–9; emphasis added)

I want to suggest that these two quotations – from *The Origins of Totalitarianism* and from *Eichmann in Jerusalem* – are like bookends marking the evolution of Arendt's thought from skepticism toward international law and human rights[7] in the 1950s toward a cautious confirmation of their role in shaping politics among nations in the 1960s. And this change of heart on Arendt's part was, whether or not she personally was acquainted with or knew Ralph Lemkin's work, indebted to his achievement. He remained one of those "obscure international jurists," in her words, who single-handedly and tirelessly worked to craft and eventually saw the Convention on Genocide adopted by the United Nations on December 9, 1948. I shall argue in this chapter that with her claim that Eichmann must die because he "carried out a policy of not wanting to share the earth with the Jewish people and the people of a number of other nations," Arendt not only confirmed Raphael Lemkin's understanding of the crime of genocide as the "intent to destroy, in whole or

---

[6] Hannah Arendt, *Eichmann in Jerusalem: A Report on the Banality of Evil* (1963), revised and enlarged ed. (New York: Penguin, 1992), p. 277. (Hereafter abbreviated as *EJ*.)

[7] There continues to be contentious exchanges around Hannah Arendt's concept and justification of human rights. See S. Benhabib, "Another Universalism. On the Unity and Diversity of Human Rights," *Proceedings and Addresses of the American Philosophical Association*, Presidential Address, 81, 2 (November 2007): 7–32; Seyla Benhabib, *The Rights of Others. Aliens, Citizens and Residents* (Cambridge: Cambridge University Press, 2004), pp. 49–61; Peg Birmingham, *Hannah Arendt and Human Rights: The Predicament of Common Responsibility* (Bloomington: Indiana University Press, 2006); Jeffrey Isaac, "Hannah Arendt on Human Rights and the Limits of Exposure, or Why Noam Chomsky Is Wrong about the Meaning of Kosovo," *Social Research* 69, 2 (2002): 263–95; Christoph Menke, "The 'Aporias of Human Rights' and the 'One Human Right': Regarding the Coherence of Hannah Arendt's Argument," *Social Research*. Hannah Arendt's Centenary, 74, 3 (Fall 2007): 739–62.

in part, a national, ethnical, racial or religious group, as such,"[8] she gave it a firm ontological grounding in the human condition.

In tracing this transformation in Arendt's thought, the first step will be to delve into her analysis of the dilemmas of the modern European nation-state and the role of this institution in the rise of European antisemitism; the second step is to consider her discussion of the problem of minorities and of statelessness in the interwar period. For Arendt, antisemitism is not an eternal aspect of the human condition or of human history. It originates with the interlacing of historical, socioeconomic, political, and cultural circumstances around the rise of the modern nation-state and the emancipation of European Jewry. These two political developments in turn fuel her profound pessimism about the role of modern political and legal institutions on the European continent and encourage her skepticism about their ability to resolve the paradoxes that they themselves create.[9]

Raphael Lemkin, by contrast, is a jurist trained in the law of nations, and for him the rise of European antisemitism and the eventual destruction of European Jewry need not be explained in terms of the fate of the Jews alone. He considers genocidal antisemitism to be *one* episode *among others* in the long history of the cultural extermination of human groups; the Holocaust is to be singled out for its intensity and extent rather than its logic. Lemkin retains his faith in the relative autonomy of legal institutions vis-à-vis the political process, but instead of documenting the folly of the League of Nations and of Minority Treaties, as Arendt does, he strives to put into legal code the unfulfilled promises of this institution, in particular with respect to minority rights and vulnerable peoples. In the 1950s, both agree, however, that the "rule of law" in the American republic had reached the right balance between politics and the law.[10] Above all, they believe that political traditions in the United States have helped ameliorate the fatal confusions that recurred on the Continent as

---

[8] United Nations Convention on the Prevention and Punishment of the Crime of Genocide. Adopted by Resolution 260 (III) A of the UN General Assembly on December 9 1948 (Chapter II). See the rather dramatic description of the events surrounding and leading up to the adoption of this convention in Power, *"A Problem from Hell,"* pp. 54–60.

[9] I have discussed these paradoxes extensively in Benhabib, "The Right to Have Rights. Hannah Arendt on the Contradictions of the Nation-State," in *The Rights of Others*, pp. 49–71. See also Christian Volk, "The Decline of Order: Hannah Arendt and the Paradoxes of the Nation-State," chapter 7 in this book.

[10] Ann Curthoys and John Docker report that only eleven months after the Genocide Convention went into effect, in December 1951, "a petition entitled *We Charge Genocide* was presented by Paul Robeson and others to the UN Secretariat in New York," on behalf of African Americans, charging that slavery was a form of genocide. See "Defining Genocide," pp. 15ff. The General Assembly did not adopt the petition and, furthermore, "Without exception, law academics were adamantly opposed because any attempt to apply the Genocide Convention to the U.S. situation would affect the integrity of 'our nation'." Ibid., p. 19. Lemkin was among these academics and, within the context of the Cold War, he saw these accusations as Soviet attempts to "divert attention from the crimes of genocide committed against Estonians, Latvians, Lithuanians, Poles and other Soviet-subjugated peoples." Interview, *New York Times*, December 18, 1951, as quoted in ibid., p. 19. See also for further discussion Anson Rabinbach, "The Challenge of

between the supremacy of the will of the nation, understood as a homogeneous
ethnocultural entity, and the constitution of a state, which ought to guarantee
equality in the eyes of the law and equal rights to all its citizens regardless of
their ethnic origin.[11]

I begin with a brief consideration of Arendt's analysis of the origins of
European antisemitism and the failure of the Minority Treaties in the interwar
period. I turn then to Lemkin's crucial innovations in international law with the
introduction of the legal concept of genocide. I argue that underlying this legal
concept is an "ontology of the group." While little noted in the literature on
Lemkin, this concept has two origins: One is the legal category of "minorities"
as defined by President Wilson's Fourteen Points, and the other is a Herderian
belief in the group as the *conditio sine qua non* of all human artistic and
cultural achievement.[12] Arendt, by contrast, only harbors skepticism toward
such group concepts. Yet, like Lemkin, she believes in the ontological value and
irreducibility of *human plurality*. It is because we inhabit the world with others
who are *like* us and yet always different *from* us that the world is perspectival
and can only manifest itself to us from a particular vantage point. Nevertheless,
plurality need not be constituted through the "ascribed" groups of ethnicity,
nationhood, race, or religion alone – quite to the contrary. It is only when
ascription is transcended through association and human beings come together
for a joint purpose in the public sphere that plurality, which is the human
condition, is most strikingly revealed. I shall argue that Arendt's philosophical
grounding of the concept of plurality provides the concept of genocide with
one of its strongest moral and existential underpinnings.[13]

the Unprecedented: Raphael Lemkin and the Concept of Genocide," *Simon Dubnow Institute Yearbook*, 4 (2005): 397–420.

   In Lemkin's case, as well, we encounter a certain "color blindness," an insensitivity to
the problem of race as color, as opposed to race defined through ethnicity, language, and
religion. Hannah Arendt has often been criticized on this account and in particular for her
controversial essay on school desegregation in southern schools, published as "Reflections on
Little Rock," *Dissent*, 6, 1 (1959): 45–56. See my analysis of Arendt on black-white relations
in the United States and on race in Africa in Seyla Benhabib, *The Reluctant Modernism of
Hannah Arendt* (New York and Toronto: Rowman and Littlefield, 1996, expanded new edition
with Preface, 2003), pp. 146–55; Richard King's essay on the invisibility of race among émigré
intellectuals, "On Race and Culture: Hannah Arendt and Her Contemporaries," chapter 5 in this
book.

[11] For a more skeptical consideration of these claims with regards to sovereign power and executive
     privilege in the U.S. experience, see Andrew Arato and Jean Cohen, "Banishing the Sovereign?
     Internal and External Sovereignty in Arendt," chapter 6 in this book.

[12] Daniel Marc Segesser and Myriam Gessler, "Raphael Lemkin and the International Debate
     on the Punishment of War Crimes (1919–1948)," *Journal of Genocide Research*, 7, 4 (2005):
     453–68.

[13] For further considerations on the concept of groups, see A. Dirk Moses, "Moving the Genocide
     Debate beyond the History Wars," *Australian Journal of Politics and History*, 54, 2 (2008):
     248–70, at p. 267. On the place of *existential* as distinct from *moral* values in Arendt's work,
     see the illuminating chapter by George Kateb, "Existential Values in Arendt's Treatment of
     Evil and Morality," chapter 16 in this book; an earlier version of Kateb's essay has appeared

9.1 Antisemitism and the Nation-State in Arendt's Thought

In her reflections on antisemitism in the aftermath of the Holocaust and after the fate of German Jewry had become sealed, Arendt put forth a radical contention: Antisemitism, she argued, far from being an "eternal" dimension of the relationship between Jews and gentiles, represented, rather, a thoroughly modern phenomenon.[14] As such, it reflected the disintegration of traditional political structures in Europe and, in particular, the decline of the nation-state in the aftermath of European imperialism in the second half of the nineteenth century. According to Arendt, antisemitism had to be understood not in isolation, but in the context of a crisis of Western civilization that far exceeded the importance of the "Jewish Question."

In thus framing the "Jewish Question" against a much broader political background, Arendt challenged a number of traditional views on antisemitism. Foremost among them was the idea that modern antisemitism simply represented a new form of religiously motivated "Jew hatred." Against this view, Arendt argued that, in effect, "even the extent to which the former derives its arguments and emotional appeal from the latter is open to question." As she wrote in a crucial and characteristically controversial passage from the *Origins of Totalitarianism*:

The notion of an unbroken continuity of persecutions, expulsions and massacres from the end of the Roman Empire to the Middle Ages, the modern era, and down to our own time, frequently embellished by the idea that modern antisemitism is no more than a secularized version of popular medieval superstitions, is no less fallacious (though of course less mischievous) than the corresponding antisemitic notion of a Jewish secret society that has ruled, or aspired to rule, the world since antiquity. (*OT*, xi)

Arendt's strong language in this passage is meant to drive home her point unambiguously: to understand the new in light of the old was, she suggests, to fundamentally misunderstand it. No amount of historical detail about the persecution of Jews could explain what she considered an unprecedented phenomenon. An adequate understanding of modern antisemitism therefore

---

in *Hannah Arendt's Centennary: Political and Philosophic Perspectives*, Jerome Kohn, guest editor, Part I, 74, 3 (Fall 2007): 811–55.

[14] Parts of this section have previously appeared in Seyla Benhabib and Raluca Eddon, "From Anti-Semitism to the 'Right to Have Rights': The Jewish Roots of Hannah Arendt's Cosmopolitanism," *Babylon: Beitraege zur juedischen Gegenwart* 22 (2007): 44–62; and also in Phyllis Lassner and Lara Trubowitz, eds., *Antisemitism and Philosemitism in the Twentieth and Twenty-First Centuries Representing Jews, Jewishness, and Modern Culture* (Newark: University of Delaware Press, 2008).

For general discussions on the significance of Jewish politics for Arendt's conception of politics and philosophy, see Benhabib, *The Reluctant Modernism of Hannah Arendt*; Richard Bernstein, *Hannah Arendt and the Jewish Question* (Cambridge, MA: MIT Press, 1996). Cf. also Jerome Kohn, "Preface: A Jewish Life: 1906–1975," in Jerome Kohn and Ron H. Feldman, eds., *Hannah Arendt: The Jewish Writings* (New York: Schocken, 2007), pp. ix–xxxiii.

required new categories of thought.[15] Underpinning all these contentions, and thus Arendt's theory of antisemitism as a whole, was a fundamental paradox: Modern antisemitism rose as the modern nation-state declined; therefore, the suggestion that antisemitism was a byproduct of extreme nationalism was simply mistaken. As she explained, "... unfortunately, the fact is that modern antisemitism grew in proportion as traditional nationalism declined, and reached its climax at the exact moment when the European system of nation-states and its precarious balance of power crashed" (*OT*, 3). It was only in light of these events, unfolding on a European and indeed a global scale, that it was possible to understand what would have been an otherwise deeply perplexing development: the enormous significance that the "Jewish problem" acquired for the Nazis.

The class of Jews who had inherited their wealth from the court Jews of the absolutist state seemed ideally suited to serve the purposes of the modern nation-state, since they formed the only group in society that "did not form a class of [its] own and ... did not belong to any of the classes in their countries" (*OT*, 13). As a result, they could offer the emergent state both the financial backing and the political loyalty it so desperately needed. The distance from court Jew to European banker seemed but a short step away. And indeed, the European banker continued to be of use to the state even as it subsequently achieved a higher degree of consolidation. Even as their political role diminished as the result of subsequent political developments, Jewish bankers nevertheless remained useful as international mediators *among* nation-states.

The peculiar economic position occupied by the Jews as lenders and bankers, bailing out and supporting first the absolutist regimes of Europe and subsequently national governments, gave them a unique and problematic profile. They were "within the nation" but never really "of the nation." They enjoyed a "supranational" and almost "protocosmopolitan" existence, which at one and the same time called forth and belied the universal belief in "the rights of man." The Jews seemed to represent "human rights as such." Yet at the same time, their problematic position within the nation also evidenced their vulnerability in virtue of not clearly belonging to a collectivity that would stand

---

[15] Arendt's insistence on the centrality of Jews to the larger story of the moral and political collapse of Europe reveals a complex and ambivalent philosemitism that underpins her theory of antisemitism. While she famously declared that "I have never in my life 'loved' any people or collective," and, indeed, that the "'love of the Jews' would appear to me, since I am myself Jewish, as something rather suspect," she nevertheless attributed to Jews a privileged cultural as well as political role in European history. See Hannah Arendt, *The Jew as Pariah*, edited and with an introduction by Ron H. Feldman (New York: Grove Press, 1978), p. 247. Cf. the expanded and revised edition of the essays from *The Jew as Pariah*, supplemented by other materials, in Kohn and Feldman, eds., *Hannah Arendt: The Jewish Writings*. In one sense, for example, in the figure of the *schlemiel* as embodied by Heinrich Heine and in Bernard Lazare's *pariah*, Arendt discerned a unique model of humanity, which, "excluded from the world of political realities," could at one time "preserve the illusion of liberty." While Nazi totalitarianism erased this illusion, Arendt regarded the pariah's humanity and independence of mind as eminently political qualities in her own time – indeed, as the conditions sine qua non of human freedom.

up for them. This is why for Arendt, as well as for Theodor Herzl, the Drey-fus case was so significant. Even after the legacy of the French Revolution, and within the "civic nation" of France, the Jews remained outsiders. After the Franco–Prussian War (1870–1871), Dreyfus, an Alsatian Jew and an offi-cer in the French army, was accused of being a spy for the Germans. Jewish existence thus revealed the fragile balance between the universalistic aspira-tions of the modern nation-state and the principle of "national sovereignty." Such sovereignty would repeatedly be defined not in terms of a community of citizens and equals but in terms of an ethnos of blood and belonging.[16] Particularly after the collapse of the nation-state system in Western Europe in the wake of overseas imperialism, and the destruction of the Kaiserreich, the Russian, the Austro-Hungarian, and Ottoman empires in Central and East-ern European territories, a political and legal chaos exploded to which the nation-state system as a model of "interstate order" was unable to provide answers.[17]

It is also at this point that the threads connecting the experiences of the failed liberal emancipation of the German Jews to whom Arendt belonged with the collective experiences of the majority of Eastern European Jews, as articulated for us most poignantly through Lemkin's category of "genocide," become visible.

In *Axis Rule in Occupied Europe*, Lemkin as well considers the legal status of the Jews in Chapter VIII (*AROE*, 75–8). He observes matter-of-factly that the definition of a Jew was based by Axis powers (among which are included not only Germany, but Italy, Hungary, Bulgaria, and Rumania, too) upon the Nuremberg laws. "A Jew is any person who is, or has been, a member of the Jewish faith or who has more than two Jewish grandparents" (*AROE*, 75–8). The latter are considered Jewish if they are, or have been, members of the Jewish faith. Lemkin is particularly attentive to differences in the treatment of Jews from France, Norway, Belgium, and the Netherlands in the hands of the Nazis in contrast with those hailing from the Eastern European territories; but after the deportation en masse to Poland of Western European Jews, he claims, these differences among different Jewish nationalities had evaporated.

In contrast to Arendt's reflections, there is no social, economic, psycholog-ical, or cultural analysis of European antisemitism in this work, but rather a very detailed account of the race policies of the Nazis and their attempts at the Germanization of the European continent. Whereas Arendt attempts to understand the *causes* of antisemitism, Lemkin focuses on the *consequences* of racialist Nazi ideology. Prejudice and genocide, among human groups – which in his unpublished *Notes* is extended as far as the colonization of the Aztecs

---

[16] These philosophical theses on the contradictions between "human rights" and "national sovereignty" are more clearly analyzed in Hannah Arendt's *On Revolution* (New York: Pen-guin, 1963). For a more detailed discussion of these themes, see Benhabib, *The Rights of Others*, chapter 2. See also Andrew Arato and Jean Cohen, "Banishing the Sovereign?", chapter 6 in this book; Dick Howard, "Keeping the Republic: Reading Arendt's *On Revolution* after the Fall of the Berlin Wall," chapter 12 in this book.

[17] Cf. Volk, "The Decline of Order."

and the Incas, the destruction of early Christians by the Romans, and, less controversially, to the genocide of Ottoman Armenians – appear rooted for him in a deep-seated anthropological predilection of the human species.[18] It is the law and human institutions that can counter this. "Only man has law," he is reported to have said.[19]

Arendts' and Lemkin's analyses of antisemitism then show little affinity: For her, the emergence of the Jewish Question in the heart of nineteenth- and early-twentieth-century Europe requires a full-scale analysis of the paradoxes of the modern nation-state system, whereas he sees deep-seated tendencies throughout human history toward the persecution of vulnerable groups, and among them the Jews. It is the goal of law to protect the vulnerable against the predator and the exploiter, but the law cannot eradicate evil from the human heart.

It is in their reflections on the minorities questions in Europe between the two world wars that Arendt and Lemkin tread on some common ground.

9.2 Arendt on Statelessness, the Minority Treaties, and the "Right to Have Rights"

The dissolution of the multinational and multiethnic Russian, Ottoman, and Austro-Hungarian empires and the defeat of the Kaiserreich in 1918 led to the emergence of nation-states, particularly in Eastern-Central European countries that enjoyed little religious, linguistic, or cultural homogeneity. These successor states – Poland, Austria, Hungary, Czechoslovakia, Yugoslavia, Bulgaria, Lithuania, Latvia, Estonia, and the Greek and the Turkish republics – controlled territories in which large numbers of "national minorities" resided. On June 28, 1919, the Polish Minority Treaty was concluded between President Woodrow Wilson and the Allied and Associated Powers, to protect the rights of minorities who made up nearly 40 percent of the total population of Poland and consisted at that time of Jews, Russians, Germans, Lithuanians, and Ukrainians. Thirteen similar agreements were then drawn up with various successor governments "in which they pledged to their minorities civil and

---

[18] "In my early boyhood, I read *Quo Vadis* by Henry Sienkiewicz – this story full of fascination about the sufferings of the early Christians and the Roman's attempt to destroy them solely because they believed in Christ.... It was more than curiosity that led me to search in history for similar examples, such as the case of the Hugenots, the Moors of Spain, the Aztecs of Mexico, the Catholics in Japan, and so many races and nations under Genghis Khan.... I was appalled by the frequency of evil, by great losses in life and culture, by the despairing impossibility of reviving the dead or consoling the orphans, and above all, by the impunity coldly relied upon the guilty." Raphael Lemkin, "Totally unofficial," manuscript, undated, New York Public Library, Manuscripts and Archives Division, the Raphael Lemkin Papers, Box 2; Bio- and Autobiographical sketches of Lemkin, as cited in Schaller and Zimmerer, "From the Guest Editors: Raphael Lemkin," pp. 450–1.

[19] The full quote is: "Only man has law.... You must build the law!" Quoted in Power, *"A Problem from Hell,"* pp. 47, 55.

political equality, cultural and economic freedom, and religious toleration."[20] But not only were there fatal ambiguities in how a "national minority" was to be defined, but the fact that the protection of minority rights applied only to the successor states of the defeated powers, and not to the victors – Great Britain, France, and Italy, who refused to consider the extension of the minority treaties to their own territories – created cynicism about the motivations of the Allied Powers in supporting minority rights. This situation led to anomalies whereby, for example, the German minority in Czechoslovakia could petition the League of Nations for the protection of its rights but the large German minority in Italy could not. The position of Jews in all successor states was also unsettled: If they were a "national minority," was it in virtue of their race, their religion, or their language that they were to be considered as such, and exactly which rights would this minority status entail? For Arendt, the growing discord within and the political ineptitude of the League of Nations, the emerging conflicts among so-called national minorities themselves, as well as the hypocrisy in the application of the Minority Treaties, were all harbingers of developments in the 1930s. The modern nation-state was being transformed from an organ that would execute the rule of law for all its citizens and residents into an instrument of the nation as a narrowly "imagined" ethnonational community. "The nation has conquered the state, national interest had priority over law long before Hitler could pronounce 'right is what is good for the German people'" (*OT*, 275). This statement from Hans Frank, the former German minister of justice and governor general of occupied Poland, is also cited by Lemkin, who renders it as, "Law is that which is useful and necessary for the German nation."[21]

The perversion of the modern state from an instrument of law into one of lawless discretion in the service of the ethnic nation was evident when states began to practice massive denaturalizations against unwanted minorities, creating millions of refugees, deported aliens, and stateless peoples across borders – special categories of humans created through the actions of nation-states.[22] In a territorially bounded nation-state system or in a "state-centric" international order, one's legal status is dependent upon protection by the highest authority that controls the territory upon which one resides and issues the papers to

---

[20] Carole Fink, "Defender of Minorities: Germany in the League of Nations, 1926–1933," *Central European History* 5, 4 (1972): 330 ff., at p. 331. See also Carole Fink, *Defending the Rights of Others: The Great Powers, the Jews and International Minority Protection* (Cambridge: Cambridge University Press, 2004).

[21] Cited by Lemkin in *AROE*, 31, note 25. Frank's Speech to the Academy of German Law in Berlin on November 1939 was reprinted in *Juristische Wochenschrift*, December 1939.

[22] Cf. the careful analysis by Christian Volk, who argues that for Arendt, peoples' right to self-determination, the democratic sovereignty of the people, state sovereignty, and *Rechtstaatlichkeit* (constitutionality) all constitute elements of the nation-state. But there are tensions among these principles and they can easily be perverted in their meaning. Volk notes that for Arendt, United States and Great Britain are republics, not nation-states, just as Nazi Germany, Fascist Italy, and Hungary under the regime of Horthy are not nation-states either. Volk, "The Decline of Order," chapter 7 in this book.

which one is entitled. One becomes a *refugee* if one is persecuted, expelled, and driven away from one's homeland; one becomes a *minority* if the political majority in the polity declares that certain groups do not belong to the supposedly "homogeneous" people; one is a *stateless* person if the state whose protection one has hitherto enjoyed withdraws such protection, nullifying the papers it has granted; one is a *displaced* person if, having been rendered a refugee, a minority, or a stateless person, one cannot find another polity to recognize one as its member and remains in a state of limbo, caught between territories, none of which desires one to be its resident. It is here that Arendt concludes:

We become aware of the existence of a right to have rights (and that means to live in a framework where one is judged by one's actions and opinions) and a right to belong to some kind of organized community, only when millions of people emerge who had lost and could not regain these rights because of the new global political situation.... The right that corresponds to this loss and that was never even mentioned among the human rights cannot be expressed in the categories of the eighteenth century because they presume that rights spring immediately from the "nature" of man... the right to have rights, or the right of every individual to belong to humanity, should be guaranteed by humanity itself. *It is by no means certain whether this is possible.* (*OT*, 296–7; my emphasis)

Written in 1951, three years after the adoption of the Genocide Convention by the UN General Assembly, this quotation betrays Arendt's profound ambivalence toward the nation-state system. It remains one of the most puzzling aspects of her political thought that, although she criticized the weaknesses of this system, she was equally skeptical toward all ideals of a world state and, in fact, at this stage in the early 1950s, toward all instruments of international law to resolve these problems.

Arendt's philosophical and political ambivalence toward the nation-state has complex dimensions. The nation-state system, established in the wake of the American and French revolutions, and bringing to culmination processes of development at work since European absolutism in the sixteenth century, is based upon the tension, and at times outright contradiction, between human rights and the principle of national sovereignty. The modern state has always been a specific nation-state.[23] This is the case even when this nationalism is civic

---

[23] William E. Scheuerman makes an excellent case about the dominance of the French Revolution as a negative model and counterexample that is often juxtaposed to America in Arendt's work. He argues that Abbe Sieyes' influential conception of the nation "is remarkably free of the ethnicist qualities...." See "Revolutions and Constitutions: Hannah Arendt's Challenge to Carl Schmitt," in David Dyzenhaus, ed., *Law as Politics: Carl Schmitt's Critique of Liberalism*, foreword by Ronald Beiner (Durham, NC: Duke University Press, 1998), pp. 252–80, at 259. Scheuerman concludes that "For her as for [Carl] Schmitt, the intellectual legacy of the French Revolution merely reproduces the most heinous features of Absolutism, particularly its vision of an indivisible, omnipotent, and legally unlimited sovereign." Ibid., p. 261. Of course, the critique that concepts such as the sovereignty of the nation reproduce absolutist tendencies was first voiced by Alexis de Tocqueville in his *The Ancien Regime and the French Revolution*,

in form, as is usually associated with the American, French, British, and Latin American models, or ethnic, as is usually associated with the German and East-Central European models. The citizens of the modern state are always also members of a nation, of a particular human group who share a history, language, culture, religion, and tradition, however conflictually this identity may be constituted, and however "imagined" the identity of the nation may be.[24] Between the principles of national self-determination and universal human rights, there are always potential, and often, actual conflicts. The ethnocultural nation can trample upon the rights of vulnerable minorities.

Ironically, although she never accepted Zionism as the dominant cultural and political project of the Jewish people and chose to live her life in a multinational and multicultural liberal democratic state, the catastrophes of World War II made Arendt more appreciative of the moment of new beginning inherent in all state formations. "The restoration of human rights," she observed, "as the recent example of the State of Israel proves, has been achieved so far only through the restoration or establishment of national rights" (*OT*, 179). Arendt was too knowledgeable and shrewd an observer of politics not to have also noted that the cost of the establishment of the State of Israel was the disenfranchisement of the Arab residents of Palestine and hostility in the Middle East until the present. She hoped throughout the 1950s that a binational Jewish and Palestinian state would become a reality.[25]

What can we conclude from the historical and institutional contradictions of the idea of the nation-state? Is Arendt's begrudging acceptance of this political formation a concession to political realism and historical inevitabilities?[26] Could Arendt be saying that no matter how contradiction-fraught the nation-state may be as an institutional structure, it is still the only one that defends the rights of all who are its citizens – at least in principle, even if not in practice?

The answer to this question in part depends on Arendt's own evolving appreciation of international law and international institutions. Between the 1951 publication of *The Origins of Totalitarianism* and the 1963 appearance of *Eichmann in Jerusalem*, post–War World II politics were transformed with the creation of the United Nations in 1946, the Universal Declaration of Human Rights in 1948, and the adoption of the Genocide Convention

translated by Gerald Bevan (London and New York: Penguin, 2008), originally published in 1856.

[24] Benedict Anderson, *Imagined Communities: Reflections on the Origin and Spread of Nationalism* (London and New York: Verso, 1991).

[25] For an extensive discussion of this issue as it relates to Arendt's reflections on Palestine, see Benhabib, *The Rights of Others*, pp. 61–70.

[26] There is renewed interest in Arendt's views of world politics and international relations. For an original reading, see Douglas Klusmeyer, "Hannah Arendt's Critical Realism: Power, Justice, and Responsibility," in Anthony F. Lang, Jr., and John Williams, eds., *Hannah Arendt and International Relations: Readings across the Lines* (London: Palgrave, 2005), pp. 113–78; Patricia Owens, *Between War and Politics: International Relations in the Thought of Hannah Arendt* (Oxford: Oxford University Press, 2007).

by the General Assembly that same year. Although Arendt never abandoned her belief in the priority of self-determination of peoples for guaranteeing human as well as citizens' rights, her faith in international law and institutions grew. The complex relationship between republican self-government and new developments in the international sphere, including international law, are part of the subtext of Arendt's reflections on the trial of Adolf Eichmann in Jerusalem.[27] And this new world constellation comes about, in no small measure, through Lemkin's tireless efforts in drafting and advocating the acceptance of the Genocide Convention.

9.3 From *The Origins of Totalitarianism* to the Genocide Convention

Transforming the memory of the persecution not only of Jews but of other peoples, such as the Gypsies, the Poles, the Slovenes, and the Russians, into a universal legacy for mankind, actionable under the law of nations, was Lemkin's desideratum. In the Preface to *Axis Rule in Occupied Europe*, he writes: "The practice of extermination of nations and ethnic groups as carried out by the invaders is called by the author 'genocide,' a term deriving from the Greek word *genos* (tribe, race) and the Latin *cide* (by way of analogy, see homicide, fratricide)" (*AROE*, xi). These few famous lines offered a term for what Churchill, referring not only to the extermination of European Jewry but to German war conduct in Eastern Europe generally, called "a crime without a name."[28]

Lemkin himself, it has been pointed out, did not insist on the uniqueness of the Holocaust but attempted to formulate "a broad theory and definition of genocide, in which the Holocaust served as prime example, not as an exception."[29] This broad conception of genocide in the meantime has spawned a new field of "comparative genocide studies."[30]

Lemkin's picture of Nazi ambitions and of the Holocaust was based on an immensely detailed knowledge of the legal framework of the occupation regimes. From a historian's point of view, Dan Stone writes that

... perhaps Lemkin's most original contribution ... is his inclusion of the murder of the Jews in a wider policy for the demographic reshaping of Europe. Historians ... have

---

[27] See Leora Bilsky, "The Eichmann Trial and the Legacy of Jurisdiction," chapter 8 in this book. For an in-depth discussion of the jurisprudential issues behind the Eichmann trial, see also Seyla Benhabib, *Another Cosmopolitanism: The Berkeley Tanner Lectures* (Oxford: Oxford University Press, 2006; issued as paperback in 2008), chapter 1, pp. 13–44.

[28] Winston S. Churchill, *The Churchill War Papers: The Ever Widening War*, vol. 3: 1941, edited by Martin Gilbert (New York: W.W. Norton, 2000), pp. 1099–1106; as cited by Power, *"A Problem from Hell,"* p. 29, note 32.

[29] Dan Stone, "Raphael Lemkin on the Holocaust," *Journal of Genocide Research*, 7, 4 (December 2005): 539–50, at 546.

[30] See the special issue of the *Journal of Genocide Research*, 7, 4 (December, 2005), devoted to the work of Raphael Lemkin; Michael A. McDonnell and A. Dirk Moses, "Raphael Lemkin as Historian of Genocide in the Americas," in the same issue, pp. 501–29; A. Dirk Moses, "The Holocaust and Genocide," in Dan Stone, ed., *The Historiography of the Holocaust* (Houndsmills: Palgrave Macmillan, 2004), pp. 533–55.

shown the extent to which the genocide of the Jews was part of a broader plan for the "resettlement" of ethnic Germans and the expulsion of millions of Slavs, as encapsulated in the *Generalplan Ost* (General Plan East). Where Lemkin does not adumbrate contemporary concerns is in his failure to see that attack on the Jews as driven by a radical ideology.... Today historians accept that the murder of the Jews was not the full extent of the Nazis' ambitions, but... there are good reasons why the Jews were targeted first and most tenaciously, and equally that the Jews had a special place in the Nazi *Weltanschauung*.[31]

Not only in terms of historical research but in terms of more technical legal considerations as well, Lemkin's various definitions of genocide are elastic, and exhibit an "'instability' between the historical and the legal, between the cultural and the 'ethnical,' between intent and consequence...."[32] According to the Genocide Convention, adopted on December 9, 1948,

...genocide means any of the following acts with intent to destroy, in whole or in part, a national, ethnical, racial or religious group, as such: (a) Killing members of the group; (b) Causing serious bodily or mental harm to members of the group;

---

[31] Dan Stone, "Raphael Lemkin on the Holocaust," p. 545. Arendt was well aware of this "imperialist" aspect of Nazi ideology and therefore distinguished between "overseas" and "continental" imperialism in *The Origins of Totalitarianism*, pp. 222–67. On further discussions of imperialism and the Holocaust in the works of Arendt and Lemkin, cf. McDonnell and Moses, "Raphael Lemkin as Historian of Genocide in the Americas," pp. 501–29. But see the following distinction made by Lemkin between the Nazi persecution of Slavs on the one hand (pragmatic colonization reasons) versus the Jews and Gypsies (purely racial reasons): "[T]he Nazi plan of Genocide was related to many peoples, races, and religions, and it is only, because Hitler succeeded in wiping out 6 million Jews, that it became known predominantly as a Jewish case.... [As] a matter of fact, Hitler wanted to commit G. against the Slavic peoples, in order to colonize the East, and to extend the German Empire up to the Ural mts. Thereupon after the completion of the successful war he would have turned to the West and to subtract from the French people the 20 million Frenchmen he promised in his conversation with Rauschning. Thus the German Empire would have reached from the Ural Mts. to the Atlantic Ocean. Nazi Germany embarked upon a gigantic plan to colonize Europe, and since there are no free spaces local populations had to be removed in order to make room for Germans. Nazi Germany did not have a fleet to protect overseas possessions. Moreover Germany had never had good experiences in the past with overseas colonization. It was thus much simpler to colonize the European continent.... [H]itler's plan covered the Poles, the Serbs, the Russians, the Frenchmen.... The main purpose of the Nazis was a commission of a G. against nations in order to get hold of their territory for colonisation purposes. This was the case of the Poles, and the Russians and the Ukrainians.... [T]he case against the Jews and the Gypsies was not based upon colonisatery [sic] but upon racial considerations.... The case against the Jews and Gypsies was of a purely racial rather than emotional political nature. The race theory served the purpose of consolidating internally the German people. The Germans had to be shown that they are racially valuable Nordics. Their favorable racial classifications could be understood better by comparing them with those who were called and classified as vermin of the earth – the Jews and the Gypsies." As cited by A. Dirk Moses, "Intellectual History and Conceptual Questions," in A. Dirk Moses, ed., *Empire, Colony, Genocide: Conquest, Occupation and Subaltern Resistance in World History* (New York: Berghahn, 2008), pp. 20–1. Moses is quoting from Raphael Lemkin, "Hitler's Case-Outline," Jacob Radar Marcus Center of the American Jewish Archives, Collection 60, Box 7, Folders 12 and 13. The spelling has been corrected in part by Moses.

[32] Anson Rabinbach, "The Challenge of the Unprecedented: Raphael Lemkin and the Concept of Genocide," in *Simon Dubnow Institute Yearbook* 4 (2005): 397–420, at p. 401.

(c) Deliberately inflicting on the group conditions of life calculated to bring about its physical destruction in whole or in part; (d) Imposing measures to prevent births within the group; (e) Forcibly transferring children of the group to another group.[33]

The degree of "intent" that must accompany these acts; the definition of "the group"; whether social classes should or should not be considered as groups; what degree of destruction of the cultural legacy of the group constitutes genocidal intent as distinct from forced assimilation, ethnic cleansing, or displacement – such debates have accompanied these words from their inception and will continue to do so. But Lemkin not only brought legal imagination and perspective to the understanding of antisemitism and the extermination of the Jews, he also introduced the category of "the group" and insisted that a genocidal plan would be characterized by the following:

The objectives of such a plan would be the disintegration of the political and social institutions, of culture, language, national feelings, religion, the economic existence of *national groups*, and the destruction of the personal security, liberty, health, dignity, and even the lives of individuals belonging to *such groups*. Genocide is directed against *the national group as an entity*, and the actions involved are directed against individuals, not in their individual capacity, but as members of *the national group*. (*AROE*, 79; emphasis added)

The famous Chapter IX of *Axis Rule in Occupied Europe* is dedicated to showing why Nazi and Axis actions in occupied Europe constitute a crime that requires a *new* conception. Admittedly, given his insistence that genocide against groups has been a constant feature of human history, it is at times unclear whether Lemkin thinks that this is an *old* crime that requires a *new* name, or a *new* crime that differs from historical precedents so radically that it must be called by a *new* name. He thinks it is the latter (*AROE*, 79). Lemkin is concerned to prove that the Nazis are waging an unprecedented "total war" since they make no distinction between the nation and the state: " . . . the nation provides the biological elements for the state" (*AROE*, 80, 90).[34] Such total war is the antithesis of the Rousseau-Portalis Treaty[35] that ought to have governed war among sovereign states and which were, he believes, implicit in the Hague Regulations of 1907: "This doctrine holds that war is directed

---

33 United Nations Convention on the Prevention and Punishment of the Crime of Genocide. Adopted by Resolution 260 (III) A of the UN General Assembly on December 9, 1948 (Chapter II).

34 Cf. the illuminating article by Stone, "Raphael Lemkin on the Holocaust," pp. 539–50.

35 The Rousseau-Portalis doctrine provides a basis for the combatant/noncombatant distinction. In the 1801 opening of the French Prize Court, borrowing heavily from Jean-Jacques Rousseau (*The Social Contract*, Book 1, chapter 4), Portalis said: " . . . war is a relation of state to state and not of individual to individual. Between two or more belligerent nations, the private persons of whom these nations are composed are only enemies by accident; they are not so as men, they are not so even as citizens, they are so only as soldiers." Quoted by William Edward Hall and A. Pearce Higgins, *A Treatise on International Law*, 8th ed. (Oxford: Clarendon Press, 1924), p. 611; in turn cited in Myres Smith McDougal and Florentino P. Feliciano, *Law and Minimum World Public Order* (New Haven: Yale University Press, 1994), p. 543, Notes.

against sovereigns and armies, not against subjects and civilians" (*AROE*, 80). The Nazis violated this principle not only by waging total war, but even prior to war, through their policies of Aryanization of the German race (by forbidding mixed marriages with Jews and others; employing euthanasia on the feeble minded and the retarded, and so on); imposing the Germanization of peoples such as Dutchmen, Norwegians, and Luxembourgers, and the Germanization of the soil alone of people *not related* to Germans by blood, such as Poles, Slovenes, and Serbs; and finally, when it came to the Jews, committing their total extermination (*AROE*, 81–2).

Lemkin is first and foremost concerned to establish that there are no existing instruments of international law to deal with such crimes. The Hague Convention on Respecting the Laws and Customs of War on Land (signed on October 18, 1907) has rules addressing "some (but by no means all) of the essential rights of individuals; and these rules do not take into consideration the interrelationship of such rights with the whole problem of nations subjected to virtual imprisonment" (*AROE*, 90). The Hague rules deal with "the sovereignty of a state," but not with preserving "the integrity of a people" (*AROE*, 90). In a subsequent essay, Lemkin names genocide a "composite crime."[36] By his own account, as far back as 1933, he formulated two new international law crimes: the crime of *barbarity*, "conceived as oppressive and destructive actions directed against individuals as members of a national, religious, or racial group" (*AROE*, 91); and the crime of *vandalism*, "conceived as malicious destruction of works of art and culture because they *represent the specific creations of the genius of such groups*" (*AROE*, 91, emphasis added). In 1944, he is convinced that neither these terms nor the Hague Conventions are adequate to deal with the crime being perpetrated by the Axis powers.

Yet why is the destruction of the life, works, culture, and life-form of a national group more heinous than the destruction of the individuals belonging to this group? According to Lemkin, insofar as "the actions involved are directed against individuals, not in their individual capacity, but as members of *the national group*" (*AROE*, 79), they violate the *moral* principle that innocents shall not be harmed; the *legal* principle that the law punishes individuals for what they do, not for what or who they are, as well as *the laws of war and peace* that innocent civilians must be spared and must not be treated as collateral damage. There is an added dimension of legal criminality and moral culpability when destruction is aimed at the *national group as such*. To make this point, Lemkin returns here to the Minority Treaties of the interwar period, much as Arendt did, and observes that "National and religious groups were put under a special protection by the Treaty of Versailles and by specific minority treaties, when it became obvious that national minorities were compelled to live within the boundaries of states ruled by governments representing the majority

---

[36] Ralph Lemkin, "Genocide as a Crime under International Law," *American Journal of International Law*, 41, 1 (1947): 147.

of the population" (*AROE*, 90–1). Not only the life and well-being but also the "honor and reputation" of such groups were to be protected by the legal codes at that time (*AROE*, 91). Thus legal developments in the interwar years already anticipated the need for special protection of the life and well-being as well as the "honor and reputation" of such groups.

But why privilege the national/ethnic/religious group in this fashion? In a passage that remains frequently uncommented upon, Lemkin lays bare what I will call his "ontology of groups":

The world represents only so much culture and intellectual vigour as are created by its component national groups. Essentially the idea of a nation signifies constructive cooperation and original contributions, based upon genuine traditions, genuine culture, and a well-developed national psychology. The destruction of a nation, therefore, results in the loss of its future contributions to the world. Moreover, such destruction offends our feelings of morality and justice in much the same way as does the criminal killing of a human being: the crime in one case as in the other is murder, though on a vastly greater scale. (*AROE*, 91)

This passage is noteworthy for a number of reasons. Lemkin is quite unconcerned about the definition of a "national group," considering it almost self-evident and using it interchangeably with "ethnos" (*AROE,* 79); he often includes race and religion as well as social groupings in need of protection (*AROE*, 93).[37] The Genocide Convention speaks of a "national, ethnical, racial or religious group," without much specification as such.[38] Whether one considers Lemkin's own formulations or refers to the text of the Genocide Convention, it is the "ascriptive" group, the group into which one is *born* or into which one is *thrown* (to borrow a phrase from Martin Heidegger), that constitutes his reference point. Such groups are not created, they are found; they are not invented, but discovered.

Most significantly, Lemkin's understanding of the group is culturalist, defined in terms of the "genuine traditions, genuine culture, and well-developed national psychology" (*AROE*, 91). Culture, in turn, is viewed fairly conventionally as "high culture," as "original contributions" to the world. In a popular piece addressed to a large audience in *The American Scholar*, Lemkin writes:

We can best understand this when we realize how impoverished our culture would be if the peoples doomed by Germany, such as the Jews, had not been permitted to create the Bible, or to give birth to an Einstein, a Spinoza; if the Poles had not had the opportunity to give to the world a Copernicus, a Chopin, a Curie; the Czechs, a

---

37 It is all the more puzzling therefore that Lemkin would be so resistant to extend the Genocide Convention to cover conditions of slavery in the Americas. See footnote 10.

38 United Nations Convention on the Prevention and Punishment of the Crime of Genocide. Adopted by Resolution 260 (III) A of the UN General Assembly on December 9 1948 (Chapter II).

Huss, a Dvorak; the Greeks, a Plato and a Socrates; the Russians, a Tolstoy and a Shostakovich.[39]

Is there a distinction to be made then between cultures that contribute to world civilization and others that have not or cannot? Is there a lurking distinction between "genuine traditions" and "genuine culture" and "nongenuine," inauthentic traditions and cultures? And would such distinctions affect the claim of some cultures to be preserved and protected more than others? Is Lemkin's ontology of the group based upon an implicit hierarchy of cultures and their contributions?

My goal here is not to engage in postmodernist skepticism about holistic concepts of groups and culture against Lemkin. Even beyond postmodern skepticism, however, the definition of the "group" that is deemed worthy of legal recognition remains a contentious matter in all debates on group rights, and has consequences for *which* collective rights groups are deemed to be entitled to as opposed to the individuals who are members of such groups.[40] Lemkin's own understanding of the national group has two sources. From a legal point of view, he reverts to the instruments of the Minority Treaties of the interwar period, which, as we saw previously through Arendt's analysis as well, were themselves hardly unproblematic. Philosophically, Lemkin is heir to a romantic and nationalist Herderian tradition that sees national groups, broadly conceived, as sources of a unique perspective on the world, as originators of a mode of disclosing the world.[41]

---

[39] Lemkin, "Genocide," *American Scholar* 15, 2 (1946): 228; quoted in Power, *"A Problem from Hell,"* p. 53.

[40] See Will Kymlicka, *Citizenship in Diverse Societies* (Oxford: Oxford University Press, 2000); Will Kymlicka, *Multicultural Citizenship. A Liberal Theory of Minority Rights* (Oxford: Oxford University Press, 1995); for a general discussion of these issues in contemporary debates, cf. Seyla Benhabib, *The Claims of Culture. Equality and Diversity in the Global Era* (Princeton: Princeton University Press, 2002); within the American context of dilemmas raised by group-based classifications, see Robert Post and Michael Rogin, eds., *Race and Representation: Affirmative Action* (New York: Zone, 1998); James Sleeper, *Liberal Racism* (New York: Viking, 1997).

[41] There has been ongoing debate about Johann Von Gottfried Herder's legacy. Some classify him as a "German nationalist." Karl Popper, for example, in *The Open Society and Its Enemies* (London: Princeton University Press, 1945), "includes Herder in a sort of Hall of Shame recapitulating the rise of German nationalism," as noted by Michael N. Forster, "Introduction," in Johann Gottfried Von Herder, *Philosophical Writings. Cambridge Texts in the History of Philosophy,* edited and translated by Michael N. Forster (Cambridge: Cambridge University Press, 2002), p. xxxi, note 33. Others, such as Isaiah Berlin and Charles Taylor, view Herder as a precursor of a kind of cultural and value pluralism that is distinct from relativism. See, for example, Charles Taylor, "The Importance of Herder," in E. Avishai Margalit, ed., *Isaiah Berlin: A Celebration* (Chicago: University of Chicago Press, 1992).

By pointing to this Herderian connection, my point is not to charge Lemkin with a kind of "relativist nationalism of vulnerable peoples." Rather, I wish to draw attention to the concept of the group in his writings, a concept which is philosophically underexplored, in as much as language, race, ethnicity, and religion are often used, either together or individually, as markers of group identities. Lemkin does not explore either the conflicts or ambiguities to which the use of these markers can give rise in the law or society. We know, by contrast, that for Herder

This privileging of national groups leads Lemkin to conclude that

genocide is a problem not only of war but also of peace. It is an especially important problem for Europe, where differentiation into nationhood is so marked that despite the principle of political and territorial self-determination, certain national groups may be obliged to live as minorities within the boundaries of other states. If these groups should not be adequately protected, such lack of protection would result in international disturbances, especially in the form of the disorganized emigration of the persecuted, who would look for refuge elsewhere. (*AROE*, 93)

Lemkin's thought here slides from the crime of genocide to the peacetime protection of "minority rights," which, as he admits, is a matter of civil and constitutional and not criminal law (*AROE*, 93). Whereas for Hannah Arendt, the division of people within a nation-state into minorities amid a majority is the source of the problem itself, Lemkin sees strengthening protection for minority rights to be necessary in peacetime as well. He thereby tries to use legal means to address political questions that are properly matters of state organization

the nation is a linguistic and cultural and not a racial group. See, for example, J. G. Herder, "Treatise on the Origin of Language" [1772], in *Philosophical Writings. Cambridge Texts in the History of Philosophy*, pp. 65–167. See also Letter 114 in "Letters for the Advancement of Humanity: Tenth Collection," and the fragment on "Purified Patriotism" (both in ibid., pp. 380ff, p. 406), for Herder's condemnation of wars among nations and of imperialism. Lemkin undoubtedly would have fully shared Herder's sentiments as expressed by the following: "What, generally, is a foisted, foreign culture, a formation [*Bildung*] that does not develop out of [a people's] own dispositions and needs? It oppresses and deforms, or else it plunges straight into the abyss. You poor sacrificial victims who were brought from the south sea islands to England in order to receive culture. . . . It was therefore not otherwise than justly and wisely that the good *Ch'ien-lung* acted when he had the foreign vice-king rapidly and politely shown the way out of his realm with a thousand fires of celebration. If only every nation had been clever and strong enough to show the Europeans this way." Ibid., p. 382.

In his famous essay on "Zum Ewigen Frieden" (On Perpetual Peace), Kant will respond to Herder that one needs to distinguish between desired contact among nations, which is grounded in the "right of hospitality," and imperialist, exploitative, and belligerent intentions harbored by some nations against others in seeking contact. Cultural isolationism is not defensible. See Immanuel Kant, [1795] 1923 "Zum Ewigen Frieden. Ein philosophischer Entwurf," in *Immanuel Kants Werke*, edited by A. Buchenau, E. Cassirer, and B. Kellermann (Berlin: Verlag Bruno Cassirer, 1923), pp. 425–74. For an English translation, see Immanuel Kant [1795], "Perpetual Peace: A Philosophical Sketch," in *Kant: Political Writings*, Cambridge Texts in the History of Political Thought, 2nd and enlarged edition, edited by Hans Reiss and translated by H. B. Nisbet (Cambridge, UK: Cambridge University Press, 1994), pp. 93–131.

Cf. also Arendt's very interesting reflections on Herder's significance for the Jews after the Enlightenment. She credits Herder with rendering Jewish history visible in Germany "as history defined essentially by their possession of the Old Testament." Hannah Arendt, "The Enlightenment and the Jewish Question," in Kohn and Feldman, eds., *Hannah Arendt: The Jewish Writings*, p. 12. At the same time, insofar as this history is theological history and not history connected to that of the world at large, for Herder " . . . the Jews have become a people without history within history. Herder's understanding of history deprives them of their past." Ibid., p. 16. Philosophically, as well as historiographically, the question is one of balancing the universal and the particular, the general history of humanity and the specific memories, trajectories, and suffering of specific peoples.

and that concern the design of political constitutions and institutions – whether these be federalist or unitary.

Arendt presents a rather different understanding of the value of the group.[42] For her, the group is not ascribed but formed; it is not discovered but constituted and reconstituted through creative acts of human association. The value of the group does not lie first and foremost in its "original contributions" to world culture and "genuine traditions" but rather in its manifestation of human diversity; in its disclosing a new perspectival outlook on the world.[43] The world is disclosed for us through diversity and plurality.

9.4 Plurality as a Fundamental Category in Arendt's Work

No passage better expresses the concept of plurality in Arendt's work than the following:

> If it is true that a thing *is* real...only if it can show itself and be perceived from all sides, then there must always be a plurality of individuals or peoples...to make reality even possible and to guarantee its continuation. In other words, the world comes into being only if there are perspectives.... If a people or a nation, or even just some specific human group, which offers a unique view of the world arising from its particular vision of the world...[that] is annihilated, it is not merely that a people or a nation or a given number of individuals perishes, but rather that a portion of our common world is destroyed, an aspect of the world that has revealed itself to us until now but can never

---

[42] I will conjecture that Arendt, emerging as she did out of the more liberal and individualistic tradition of German-Jewish emancipation, would not be as accepting as was Lemkin – an Eastern European and Polish Jew – of the concept of the group or of the moral and political imperative to preserve groups. Arendt was quite sensitive to the differences among the experiences of German versus east European Jewish communities. Cf. critical remarks about the "collective" versus "individualistic" orientation of the *Ostjuden* as opposed to German Jews in the letter to her husband Heinrich Bluecher. For further discussion, see S. Benhabib, "Arendt's Eichmann in Jerusalem," in Dana Villa, ed., *The Cambridge Companion to Hannah Arendt* (Cambridge: Cambridge University Press, 2000), pp. 65–86. For a philosophical analysis of antisemitism in the works of Arendt and the Frankfurt School, as refracted through the German Jewish experience, see my "From 'The Dialectic of Enlightenment' to 'The Origins of Totalitarianism' and the Genocide Convention: Adorno and Horkheimer in the Company of Arendt and Lemkin," in Warren Breckman, Peter E. Gordon, A. Dirk Moses, Samuel Moyn, and Elliot Neaman, eds., *The Modernist Imagination: Essays in Intellectual History and Cultural Critique. For Martin Jay on his 65th Birthday* (New York: Berghan, 2009), pp. 299–330.

[43] Does not this voluntarist concept of the group contradict Hannah Arendt's own assertive defense of her own Jewish identity? I would argue that it does not in that Arendt insists on defining the conditions and the meaning of her own belonging to the Jewish people. For her, it is not the Halachachic definition of the Jew, as one born to a Jewish mother, that is paramount, but rather one's conscious and self-chosen identification with the fate of a collectivity and a people. This individualist, perhaps existentialist, dimension of Arendt's Judaism is at the root of her conflict with Gerschom Scholem. It is also what distinguished her from other thinkers, such as Leo Strauss, who argued that one could not separate out the cultural and theological meanings of Judaism as sharply as Arendt herself wished to. I have explored these questions further in Benhabib, "From 'The Dialectic of Enlightenment' to 'The Origins of Totalitarianism' and the Genocide Convention," pp. 299–307, 316–17.

reveal itself again. Annihilation is therefore not just tantamount to the end of the world; it also takes its annihilator with it.[44]

As Patricia Owens observes,

[W]ars of annihilation that aim to wipe out a particular group attack the basic fact of human plurality and violate the "limits inherent in violent action." With genocide we are not "just" talking about large numbers of dead but something that is potentially immortal. The public, political world, the political constitution of a people, the outcome of people's living together, and debating their common affairs is also destroyed with genocide.[45]

Genocide violates "an altogether different order," writes Arendt in *Eichmann in Jerusalem* (*EJ*, 272).

The category of plurality is no less ontological in Arendt's thought than that of the group is in Lemkin's. That is to say, for both authors, these categories represent some element and principle that is part of the order of being human in the universe. Arendt names this "the human condition," that is, "the basic conditions under which life on earth has been given to man."[46] Plurality is the fact that corresponds to our irreducible sameness as members of the same species and yet at the same time expresses our irreducible difference from one another. "Plurality is the condition of human action because we are all the same, that is, human, in such a way that nobody is ever the same as anyone else who ever lived, lives, or will live" (*HC*, 8). This plurality is the precondition of the possibility of all political life: Because we are members of the same species who have speech and reasoning, or who are capable, of *legein* – reasoned speech – we can communicate with one another, build a world together, as well as destroy one another. And since we are all subject to similar bodily needs and face likewise the struggle with nature, we face the "circumstances of justice," that is, how to establish just institutions under conditions of vulnerability and scarcity.

Plurality is also what enables diversity and perspectivality:

In acting and speaking, men show who they are, reveal actively their unique personal identities and thus make their appearance in the human world, while their physical identities appear without any activity of their own in the unique shape of the body and sound of the voice. The disclosure of "who" in contradistinction to "what" somebody is – his qualities, gifts, talents and shortcoming, which he may display or hide – is implicit in everything somebody says and does. (*HC*, 179)

We live in a world constituted by narratives about the "who" as well as the "what" of action; this web of narratives is the medium through which the

---

44 Hannah Arendt, "The Promise of Politics," in *The Promise of Politics*, edited and with an introduction by Jerome Kohn (New York: Schocken, 2005), p. 175.

45 Owens, *Between War and Politics*, p. 110.

46 Hannah Arendt, *The Human Condition* (1958), new edition with an introduction by Margaret Canovan (Chicago: University of Chicago Press, 1998), p. 7. (Hereafter abbreviated as *HC*.)

multiplicity and diversity of perspectives on human affairs converge and conflict, are woven together and torn apart.

These ontological theses of Hannah Arendt's are well known.[47] Her concept of plurality enables Arendt to escape both the ascriptivism and the culturalism of Lemkin's concept of the group. Groups for Arendt are enduring associations, rooted in the human capacity to create a world in common that is shareable, yet diverse; that is communicable, yet open to misunderstanding; and that appears as one, yet is refracted through many different narratives and perspectives. While from a philosophical point of view, there can be little question about the brilliant acuity to Arendt's analyses, from a legal point of view, from the standpoint of the jurist, the protean aspect of Arendt's concept of plurality may be too volatile. The juridification of the category of the group brings with it inevitable ontological as well as sociological problems.

Ironically, her skepticism toward group concepts and her dynamic concept of plurality enable Arendt to deliver a trenchant account of the crime of genocide as constituting a "crime against the human condition" as such. This, I believe, is the meaning of the preceding quoted passage from *Eichmann in Jerusalem*:

And just as you supported and carried out a policy of not wanting to share the earth with the Jewish people and the people of a number of other nations – *as though you and your superiors had any right to determine who should and who should not inhabit the world* – we find that no one, that is, no member of the human race, can be expected to share the earth with you. This is the reason, and the only reason, you must hang. (*EJ*, 277–9; emphasis added)[48]

Genocide is "an attack upon human diversity as such, that is, upon a characteristic of the 'human status' without which the words 'mankind' or 'humanity' would be devoid of meaning" (*EJ*, 268–9).

It is hard not to see in these passages of searing eloquence a belated vindication of those such as Lemkin whom Arendt seemed to dismiss only a little more than a decade earlier as "those few international jurists without political experience or professional philanthropists supported by the uncertain sentiments of professional idealists" (*OT*, 292), but who through their tireless efforts transformed the meaning of the "human status." Abandoning her bitter irony of *The Origins of Totalitarianism* in 1951, Arendt in *Eichmann in Jerusalem* in 1963

---

[47] For further discussion of these dimensions of Arendt's thought, see Patchen Markell, "The Rule of the People: Arendt, *Archê,* and Democracy," chapter 4 in this book (an early version of this essay appeared in *American Political Science Review*, 100, 1 [February 2006]: 1–14); Roy Tsao, "Arendt's Augustine," chapter 3 in this book. For the roots of these Arendtian themes in Martin Heidegger's philosophy, see Seyla Benhabib, "The Dialogue with Martin Heidegger," in *The Reluctant Modernism of Hannah Arendt*, chapter 4; Dana Villa, *Arendt and Heidegger: The Fate of the Political* (New Jersey: Princeton University Press, 1996).

[48] Arendt's almost militant defense of capital punishment will shock and disturb many readers. Was she perhaps indulging in some form of human vengeance herself rather than just defending justice? These are questions that go beyond the scope of the present discussion. I am grateful to Hans Joas of the Max-Weber Kollegium in Erfurt for having pointed out this problem to me in the course of a discussion.

embraces and honors Lemkin's legacy, although it remains a mystery why she does not credit Lemkin by name.

9.5 Brief Epilogue: Arendt and Lemkin on Universal Jurisdiction

For Lemkin, no less than for Arendt, embracing the concept of "genocide" raised the question of jurisdiction. In *Axis Rule in Occupied Europe*, Lemkin is ready to include the crime of genocide as amended under the Hague Regulations (*AROE*, 93). He later insists, however, that this crime must be independent of any prior treaty or set of regulations. Furthermore, he notes that "the adoption of the principle of *universal repression* as adapted to genocide by countries which belong now to the group of non-belligerents or neutrals, respectively, would likewise bind these latter countries to punish the war criminals engaged in genocide or to extradite them to countries in which these crimes were committed" (*AROE*, 92; emphasis added). Universal repression makes the culprit liable not only in the country in which he committed the crime but also "in any other country in which he might have taken refuge" (*AROE*, 94). Astonishingly, Lemkin shows himself to be little concerned with difficulties that may arise with the application of the principle of universal repression, such as the capacity of prosecutors in other countries to be able to collect evidence, provide for adequate defense of the defendants, escape the semblance of "victor's justice," and myriad other procedural and substantive details that may go wrong in a criminal trial. By contrast, these and other details haunted Hannah Arendt with regard to the trial of Adolf Eichmann and cast doubts for her on its full legality.

For Lemkin, "genocide offenders should be subject to the principle of universal repression as should other offenders guilty of the so-called *delicta juris gentium* (such as, for example, white slavery and trade in children, piracy, trade in narcotics and in obscene publications, and counterfeiting of money)" (*AROE*, 94). There is something deeply unsatisfactory about singling out the radicalness of the crime of genocide, on the one hand, and comparing it to piracy, trade in narcotics, obscene publications, and such, on the other. The only crime to which genocide can be compared, insofar as it too is a crime against the human status and the human condition, is slavery, and this is what Lemkin was not willing to do.

In *Eichmann in Jerusalem*, Arendt notes that the analogy between genocide and piracy is not new, and that the Genocide Convention expressly rejected the claim to universal jurisdiction and provided instead that "persons charged with genocide... shall be tried by a competent tribunal of the States in the territory of which the act was committed or by such international penal tribunal as may have jurisdiction" (*EJ*, 262).[49] With the recognition of the crime of genocide as a "crime against humanity," Arendt believes that the path has

---

[49] For an illuminating discussion of the legal details of some of the issues involved, see Bilsky, "The Eichmann Trial and the Legacy of Jurisdiction."

been cleared to entertain the likelihood that "international penal law" will develop. Quoting Chief Justice Robert Jackson in the Nueremberg trials, Arendt points out that international law is viewed as an "outgrowth of treaties and agreements between nations and of accepted customs," and as long as that is the case, she believes that "in consequence of this yet unfinished nature of international law," it is ordinary trial judges who have to render justice by facing the unprecedented with the "help of, or beyond the limitation set upon them through, positive, posited laws" (*EJ*, 274). She does not consider the negative consequences of "judges making law," though on the whole, she is very sensitive that law, whether domestic or international, be seen by a self-governing people to be "its" law, and not be imposed upon it by other instances.[50]

Lemkin, on the other hand, in 1948 was fearful that an international criminal court would mean "too great an affront to state sovereignty."[51] Ironically, Arendt was willing to go beyond him in the principle as well as the practice of the persecution of the crime of genocide. Undoubtedly, though, both would have greeted enthusiastically the establishment of an International Criminal Court with the jurisdiction to try those accused of crimes against humanity and of genocide through the Treaty of Rome. They would also have been dismayed that their adoptive country, for whose constitutional traditions they had such reverence – the United States – first signed and then withdrew from the Treaty of the International Criminal Court. The weakening of the status of international law and the contempt toward international institutions is part of the "crises of our republic" in the contemporary period, very much as the violation of the laws of war and peace, the collapse of the League of Nations and of the nation-state system, and the Holocaust were those of Arendt and Lemkin.

---

[50] For a more detailed exploration, see Benhabib, *Another Cosmopolitanism*, pp. 13–44.
[51] Power, *"A Problem from Hell,"* p. 56.

PART III

POLITICS IN DARK TIMES

10

In Search of a Miracle

Hannah Arendt and the Atomic Bomb

Jonathan Schell

In the work Hannah Arendt published in her lifetime, there is a conspicuous gap. She reflected deeply and powerfully on the nature of totalitarianism, imperialism, nationalism, antisemitism, and almost every other horror and vexation of the twentieth century that might be mentioned, yet she devoted no sustained attention to nuclear arms, which of course were born into the world in July of 1945, a full six years before she published her first thoroughly political book, *The Origins of Totalitarianism*. The omission had a particular fascination for me. Beginning in the mid-1970s, I began to devote my attention to the nuclear dilemma. Notwithstanding her avoidance of the subject, I found her work more fruitful than anyone else's for thinking about it, and especially for riddling out the meaning of the possible self-extinction of human beings that nuclear arsenals had made possible. For example, in her thinking about the great crimes of the twentieth century, she gave primacy to genocide. As she was one of the first to understand, that crime has a special significance not only because of the shocking numbers of people killed but also because each act of genocide is an attack on the "plurality" of the earth's peoples. That is, it not only destroys living persons but also shuts down the unique culture and public world of a whole people and its traditions. Genocide is, to speak in contemporary terms, a kind of ecological crime within the human sphere: a crime against the diversity of human cultures. It is also a crime against the human future, inasmuch as its essence is cancellation of the regenerating power of a people, which thereafter disappears from the continuation of the human story. (If some of the people's murderers could have their way, it would disappear from memory as well.) Clearly, a nuclear holocaust would be an event of this kind, though raised to a higher order. It would be the highest crime of that type, destroying all peoples and, thus, the human future per se.

Likewise, Arendt's distinction between the "private realm" and the "public realm," or "common world," seemed to offer a way out of the impasse of imagination so often experienced by those who attempted to "think about the unthinkable." Instead of trying to multiply scenes of individual suffering in imagination beyond any human power to do so, we should acknowledge that what a nuclear holocaust uniquely threatens is that common world, which "is what we enter into when we are born and what we leave behind when we die," for it "transcends our life-span into past and future alike," and "was there before we came and will outlast our brief sojourn in it."[1] Was not it exactly this that was threatened by the human species' new capacity to do itself in? Equally helpful was her distinction between "immortality" – fame sustained within history – and "eternal life," which was supernatural and transcended history. The points of origin of the two concepts were ancient Greek civilization and early Christianity, respectively, yet were not they what was needed to comprehend the stakes involved in the modern threat of the physical annihilation of the world? For it was precisely human immortality – all human duration in the common world – that was newly put at risk by nuclear arms. The distinction seemed especially important in a time when some religious-minded people were confounding a nuclear holocaust with biblical Armageddon, and even looking forward to the latter as a path to eternal life. They were ready to sacrifice immortality for eternity.[2]

Why, then, did Arendt never take up the nuclear question directly? Over the years, I speculated on explanations. Could it be because her first husband, Gunther Anders, had written on the issue in his book of 1956 *The Outdatedness of Humankind* and she had decided to leave the matter to him? Or, more likely, could it be because her friend and admired teacher Karl Jaspers also addressed the dilemma in his book of 1958, *The Future of Mankind*, whose American edition she helped publish? Lacking any basis for these musings, I once had occasion, at a conference in Washington in the early 1970s, to ask her directly why she had avoided the nuclear subject. She answered, in the emphatic, sharply articulated, heavily accented English that was all her own, "*You* do it! You have it in your bones." Her "you" was the plural one, directed to my generation, which does literally have nuclear contamination in its bones, in the form of the strontium 90 deposited by fallout from nuclear tests.

The idea that she shied away from addressing the new topic on generational grounds finds some support in the published record. In the preface to *The Human Condition*, published in 1958, she comments, "The modern age is not the same as the modern world. Scientifically, the modern age which began in the seventeenth century came to an end at the beginning of the twentieth century; politically, the modern world, in which we live today, was born with the first atomic explosions." Her book, she tells us, will discuss the former, not the latter, "against whose background" it is nevertheless written (*HC*, 6). This passage expressed precisely my experience with Hannah Arendt and the bomb: She would not address it directly, but her work would provide a kind of intellectual foundation for doing so.

---

[1] Hannah Arendt, *The Human Condition* (Chicago: University of Chicago Press, 1958), p. 55. (Hereafter abbreviated *HC*.)

[2] I made use these ideas of Arendt's in my book of 1982, *The Fate of the Earth*, especially in its second part, "A Second Death."

To be sure, there are other mentions of the topic scattered throughout her writing. For example, although the body of *On Revolution* has little to say about the bomb, the introduction mentions it, once again as a backdrop. Her concern is to set the stage for the discussion of revolution, which, she finds, has loomed up with new importance in part precisely because political change through warfare has been so sharply delimited by nuclear arsenals, which can produce no political results but only "total annihilation."[3] Implicit is the idea that the political vacuum thus created is being filled by revolutions – an insight that bore fruit when the Cold War ended not with a hot war, whether conventional or nuclear, but through internal revolt within the Soviet system. She also takes the occasion to render an important judgment: Sacrifice of oneself for freedom, a noble act, cannot be equated with sacrifice of humankind for freedom, an absurdity. As she puts it, "To sound off with a cheerful 'give me liberty or give me death' sort of argument in the face of the unprecedented and inconceivable potential of destruction in nuclear warfare is not even hollow; it is downright ridiculous" (*OR*, 13). But the first words of the book are, "We are not concerned here with the war question," and we hear little more about war, nuclear or otherwise.

Something similar happens in the first part of her short work *On Violence*. Once more she observes that nuclear arms have short-circuited war at its upper levels. The combination of the nuclear paralysis of great-power war and the vigor of revolutions, often in small countries, leads her to foresee prophetically "a complete reversal in the relationship between power and violence, foreshadowing another reversal in the future relationship between small and great powers."[4] As in the preface to *On Revolution*, she delivers herself apodictically of a firm but frustrated (and frustrating) judgment. Observing that in the nuclear age, the great powers have been reduced to heaping up the means of annihilation in the hope of staving off that same annihilation, she simply declares, "To the question how shall we ever be able to extricate ourselves from the obvious insanity of this position, there is no answer" – and drops the subject. She seems to have come to a wall that she cannot or will not jump over. (A few pages later, however, she hazards the guess that the global eruption of student activism of the 1960s is rooted in its awareness of the possible immanence of "doomsday."[5]

Even the one very short essay that does turn out to be chiefly devoted to the bomb – "Europe and the Bomb" (1954) – shoehorns the great question into a discussion of the rather more modest topic of European attitudes toward the United States. This oblique procedure gives her occasion, in a highly compressed page or two, to situate the bomb in the Western political tradition. Historically, she writes, there have been two justifications for the violent sacrifice of life in political affairs. One was the conviction of the ancient Greeks and Romans

---

[3] Hannah Arendt, *On Revolution* (New York: Penguin, 1963), p. 11. (Hereafter abbreviated *OR*.)
[4] Hannah Arendt, "On Violence," in *Crises of the Republic* (New York: Harcourt Brace, 1972), p. 10.
[5] Ibid., p. 10.

that only the life that one was ready to sacrifice for something larger than oneself was fully worth living – a code whose touchstone was a belief in human freedom and whose highest virtue was necessarily courage. The other was the Hebrew-Christian respect for the bare fact of life. Its highest (if not absolute) virtue was "the sacredness of life as such," imposing a duty to protect it, even if some life was lost in the very process. Arendt finds that atomic weapons rendered both traditions "meaningless," and with them "the whole political and moral vocabulary in which we are accustomed to discuss these matters."[6] For sacrifice is possible only when there is something surviving the war for which the sacrifice might be made, but anything of that kind would be canceled in the general fall of the species. She offers no alternative formula for weighing the dilemma.

10.1 Ignition

It is quite a surprise, then, to come upon, in 2005, the fullest and most spacious reflections Arendt ever devoted to the nuclear question. They are to be found in *The Promise of Politics,* a selection of Arendt's previously unpublished writings made by her literary executor, Jerome Kohn. Of the highest interest and value in themselves, they also permit a reevaluation of the place of the nuclear question in the long arc of Hannah Arendt's thought. In a word, the atomic bomb appears to have been a starting point for her political thinking and showed marked signs of one day becoming an endpoint, although that day never came. She never offered a solution to the nuclear dilemma any more than she prescribed any program for dissolving totalitarianism. Yet both evils, which she came to see as twin expressions of a common, deep-seated crisis of the modern age, propelled her on a new path of reflection. "Mad Ireland hurt him into poetry," W. H. Auden wrote of W. B. Yeats. You might say that the insanity of the bomb, together with that of totalitarianism, hurt Arendt into thinking.

The publication of writings that the writer herself chose not to publish always raises questions. Should we give words that Arendt rejected for publication the same weight as ones she chose to publish? The question is of special concern regarding her thoughts about the bomb, since these are all but consistently missing from the published work, as if by a lifelong choice. In light of the new material, the question becomes why she never weighed in publicly on a topic she addressed at some depth privately, as it were.

One surprise of *The Promise of Politics* is to learn of the amount of writing Arendt did that she never brought to completion. According to Kohn's informative and illuminating introduction, Arendt, upon finishing *The Origins of Totalitarianism* (1951), embarked on another related book that would have delved more deeply than *Origins* had into the relationship of the thought of

---

[6] Hannah Arendt, *Essays in Understanding* (New York: Harcourt, Brace, 1994). (Hereafter abbreviated as *EU.*)

Karl Marx to Soviet totalitarianism. After writing as much as a thousand pages, she gave up the project. But before that happened, she had developed a new book project, to be called "An Introduction *into* Politics." This book would have sought to do for politics what her friend Karl Jaspers' *Introduction to Philosophy* had done for philosophy. Again she wrote at great length and again was unable to finish the book. It is from the material meant for these aborted projects that Kohn has drawn *The Promise of Politics,* an apt title that one imagines Hannah Arendt herself might have chosen. Surveying this record, one has the impression of a broad and flowing sea of thought that from time to time yields up a book, as if the author were a fisherman trolling in the streams of her own mind. Now Kohn has come along as a kind of second fisherman and made some prize catches.

It is the fragments from the unwritten "An Introduction *into* Politics," gathered under that same heading in the second half of the posthumous *The Promise of Politics,* that bear on the atomic bomb. One question is why Arendt abandoned this book. As Kohn reveals, the project, originally conceived as a short volume, grew into a colossal undertaking – at one point envisioned as a two-volume work, and later as a massive, one-volume systematic treatise on the nature of politics. It seems to me that Kohn gets to the heart of the problem that Arendt had encountered when he observes that the projected book "traces the entire trajectory of Arendt's thought after *Origins*: from the inception of the tradition of political thought to its end; to what politics was and is apart from that tradition; and to the relation, rather than merely the split, between active and mental life" (*EU,* xviii). Filled and overfilled with a fantastic richness of often incomplete thoughts joined by often awkward transitions, the newly published texts are a kind of plum pudding of Hannah Arendt's thinking to come, as if, setting out to write a single book, she realized she had stumbled into her life's work. In short, what she faced was an intellectual Big Bang, a universe of new thinking. Clearly, it could not be encompassed in any single work, not even a two-volume one. Many books would be needed, and, over the years, many were written. *The Human Condition* (1958) drew on the new material, especially in the chapter devoted to action. The projected first volume of the projected treatise, Kohn tells us, evolved into *On Revolution* (1963), while other fragments turned into the "exercises in political thought" published as the essays that make up *Between Past and Future. Men in Dark Times,* and, especially, *Crises of the Republic* also drew on the material. The themes were still being developed in her last book, *Willing.*

10.3 What the Stones Said

In "An Introduction *into* Politics," she gives a more compressed account of what prompted her to embark on the new path than she perhaps does anywhere else. The question she first poses is one that would preoccupy her on and off for the rest of her life: "What is the meaning of politics?" No sooner does she ask the question than she abruptly answers it: "The meaning of politics is freedom"

(*EU*, 108). No explanation is given, but readers of Arendt will recognize that she here introduces the keystone of her singular conception of politics that will be elaborated in her later work: Freedom is the root in "action in concert"; action in concert, taking such forms as direct action by revolutionary councils, town meetings, and the like, is the defining activity of politics; such peaceful activity (not force) in turn is the true source of political power; and this, as long as it lasts, is the arch stone of the "common world." Readers of Arendt will also appreciate the choice of the word "meaning," rather than, say, "goal" or "role" or "use," in her question "What is the meaning of politics?" It signals her conviction, explored in later work, that politics is one of those activities in life that has a value – a dignity, a splendor, a realization of human potential – in itself, independently of its usefulness as a means to other ends. And yet what has goaded her onto this path of thought are two dilemmas that fairly scream out for practical solutions, for results. They are the rise of totalitarianism and the atomic bomb. She writes, "Both these experiences – totalitarianism and the atomic bomb – ignite the question about the meaning of politics in our time. They are fundamental experiences of our age, and if we ignore them it is as if we never lived in the world that is our world."[7] She argues that the twin dangers composed a single Gordian knot that stands at the center of a broader crisis of modern civilization. They compel the question "What is the meaning of politics?" in its sharpest possible form. For in their presence, the issue was not only, as before, what, in a positive sense, the meaning of politics might be, but whether in fact political activity had "any meaning at all" (*PP*, 110), or, indeed, had simply become indeed an intolerable menace to human life.

It is scarcely surprising to find the author of *The Origins of Totalitarianism* hurt into further thought by that political system. But the coequal presence of the atomic bomb in this role was previously unknown. For her, totalitarianism of course represents a more radical extinction of freedom than any previous political system. If totalitarianism is what politics has become, she tells us, then the despairing conclusion would follow that whereas in ancient times freedom and politics were "deemed identical," "under modern conditions, they must be definitively separated." If so, then, by her lights, politics would have lost all meaning. Defenders of modern politics might then try to repair to the position that even if freedom is gone, politics is still necessary to guarantee survival – the bare existence of the body politic and its members. But the threat of atomic annihilation cuts off this retreat: "For here politics threatens the very thing that, according to modern opinion, provides its ultimate justification – that is, the possibility of life for all humanity" (*PP*, 110).

If these two unparalleled evils are what "politics" has brought – if *they* manifest the meaning of politics – then wouldn't it be better "somehow to dispense with politics before politics destroys us all?" (*PP*, 109). And yet Arendt is very far from offering any program for dealing with either of the evils – such

---

[7] Hannah Arendt, *The Promise of Politics*, edited by Jerome Kohn (New York: Schocken, 2005), p. 109. (Hereafter abbreviated *PP*.)

as a plan to overthrow totalitarian regimes or a proposal to ban the bomb. On the contrary, as she would later do in *On Revolution* and *On Violence,* she peremptorily rules out any proximate relief from the awful dilemmas. She writes, "No matter how hard we try to understand the situation or take into account the individual factors that this twofold threat of totalitarian states and atomic weapons represents – a threat only made worse by their conjunction – we cannot so much as conceive of a satisfactory solution, not even with the best will on all sides...." Only "some sort of miracle," she adds, might break the impasse (*PP,* 111).

It might seem that at this point the discussion would come to a dreary close, but on the contrary, it is precisely these apparently despairing conclusions that "ignite" the new eruption of thought in the material for "An Introduction *into* Politics" and, later, in her published works. For the expression of despair is followed by a startling U-turn. Acknowledging that a "miracle" is needed, she immediately announces that a miracle is precisely the sort of thing that can be expected of politics in its Arendtian incarnation. In an early eruption of ideas that Arendt readers will again find more fully developed later in her published work, she begins by asserting that life on earth itself is an "infinite improbability" (*PP,* 111). So also, within that life, is the rise of the human species. Why assume, then, that human affairs, characterized by even greater unpredictability than the natural world, are devoid of miracles? That would be especially unwarranted in view of the fact that human beings have "a most amazing and mysterious talent for working miracles," namely "action." Action, in turn, is the seat of the very wellspring of the unpredictable miracles in human affairs: that very freedom that gives politics its "meaning." Freedom for Arendt means much more than an ability to choose among alternatives. "The miracle of freedom is inherent in... [an] ability to make a beginning, which itself is inherent in the fact that every human being, simply by being born into a world that was there before him and will be there after him, is himself a new beginning" (*PP,* 113). In summary, there seems to be something in the bare fact of being physically born that undergirds a miraculous human power of action thereafter to bring forth the new and unexpected into the world – even in the face of such seemingly hopeless difficulties as the conjunction of totalitarianism and the bomb. Her point is that notwithstanding the current intellectual and practical paralysis of action, the very nature of politics guarantees that "we do indeed have the right to expect miracles" (*PP,* 114).

These observations, which point ahead to seminal passages on the subject of the "natality" of humankind in her published works, are in this text pressed into the merely structural, rather strained role (let us remember that we are dealing with texts she chose not to publish) of bridging the distance between the immediate crises of totalitarianism and the bomb on the one hand and her inquiry into the fundamentals of politics on the other. Although the impasse, urgent but intractable, does not permit an answer, which she has flatly ruled out, it does send her racing back through the centuries, all the way to ancient Greece, in search of the new starting point for political thinking and practice that, we cannot help thinking, might one day open up a solution to the impasse, an appearance of the hoped for miracle. We seem to have been dispatched on a long backward journey, all the way from the 1950s to Pericles and Plato, not to speak of Parmenides and Anaxagoras, but with the unspoken hope, implicit in the bleak point of origin, that she or someone else will make the return journey.

What follows, under the subtitle *The Meaning of Politics*, is a thirty-page summation-in-advance, almost a prospectus, of the Arendtian definitions of politics that will be at the heart of her forthcoming books.[8] Characteristically, her procedure is not to define one sort of politics that is benighted and another that is beneficial and then recommend that we choose the second. Rather, the inquiry is into what politics really is, and the implication is left between the lines that we would prosper by recognizing this nature and, so to speak, let politics be its true self. However, such an inference is unusually close to the surface in the text at hand, beginning as it does by associating totalitarianism and nuclear annihilation as a culmination of conventional understandings of politics. In this framework, the question, "What is the meaning of politics?" means: If not *this*, then *what*?

The new question is related to its dual starting points of nuclear annihilation and totalitarianism in several ways. In the first place, of course, it was the whole intellectual enterprise that was set in motion by the impasse that forced the new theoretical questions upon Arendt. In the second place, the new conceptions offer analytical tools for understanding the new stakes that have put been put on the historical table. In weighing these stakes, she always mentions totalitarianism and the bomb in parallel. What totalitarianism does to Arendtian politics is fully spelled out in *The Origins* and her later books, and needs no great elaboration here. To put it simply, totalitarianism, the form of politics that relies on violence more than any other, kills politics at its root by using "systematic terror to destroy all inter-human relationships," thus eradicating the freedom and spontaneity that are the taproots of a genuine politics, from the popular participation that springs up in revolutions to the common world that last through the ages (*PP*, 162). The atomic bomb, she writes in "An Introduction *into* Politics," threatens the common world from another angle – not by destroying all freedom directly, but simply by destroying all life. In Arendt's mind, the meanings of the two dangers are of a kind. The terror in totalitarianism "finds its equivalent in total war, which is not satisfied with destroying strategic targets but sets out to destroy – because it now technologically can seek to destroy – the entire world that has arisen between human beings" (*PP*, 162). The common world that totalitarianism destroys from within, you might

---

[8] It is tempting to recommend this protracted subsection for use with students as an introduction to Arendt's work, but the text is probably too cryptic in its condensation for the purpose. But if students should not *start* their experience of Arendt with reading this text, then probably neither should they *finish* that acquaintance without it, for what it lacks in development and detail, it makes up for in velocity and summarizing power.

say, nuclear war (but not conventional war) destroys from without. In both cases, historical and moral limits previously curbing the use of violence have been decisively overstepped. For in both, "murder is no longer about a larger or smaller number of people who must die in any case, but rather about a whole people and its political constitution, both of which harbor the possibility – and in the constitution's case, the intention – of being immortal" (*PP*, 161).

The two evils are related historically as well. It was Hitler's totalitarianism, she observes, that provided the justification for the United States to create the new, nuclear form of total war. The extent to which she draws the equivalence becomes clear when she states that, "When a people loses its political freedom" – as under totalitarianism – "it loses its political reality, even if it should succeed in surviving physically" (*PP*, 161). Physical survival, at stake in nuclear war but not under totalitarianism, thus seems to be assigned a kind of derivative value, as the undergirding of freedom and the common world. Even more emphatically, in a discussion of a world reduced to a single totalitarian state, she writes, "human beings in the true sense of the term can exist only where there is a world, and there can be a world in the true sense of the term only where the plurality of that human race is more than a simple multiplication of a single species" (*PP*, 176). If this perhaps troubling equation of an unfree people or species with an extinct people or species seems perilously close to a "better dead than red" (or maybe "just as bad red as dead") or a "Give me freedom or give me death!" approach to nuclear annihilation, we can remind ourselves of her indignant repudiation, previously quoted, of that very slogan. Still unaddressed, though, are other differences between nuclear annihilation and totalitarian domination that come to mind. Loss of freedom, or even genocide, may destroy the regenerative power and thus the immortal future of *a* people, or conceivably a few peoples, but nuclear war, as she acknowledged, puts *all* peoples at risk. Also, by severing the roots of the species at the biological level, it bars all hope of regeneration forever. If genocide cancels the power of peoples to bring forth new generation, human extinction cancels the power of the species to bring forth new peoples. That deeper abyss – compared to which, humanly speaking, none can by definition ever be greater – seems to transcend the equation with totalitarian dangers.

However that may be, Arendt was unique in her appreciation of the commonality in the threats of totalitarianism and the bomb, which did indeed both menace, as she wrote in an especially impassioned and eloquent passage, the human "relationships established by action, in which the past lives on in the form of a history that goes on speaking and being spoken about," and which "can exist only within the world produced by man, nesting there in its stones until they too speak and in speaking bear witness, even if we must first dig them out of the earth" (*PP*, 161).

In the third place, Arendt's new line of thinking bears on the origins as well as the stakes of the nuclear danger. For all its radical novelty, the bomb, too, showed continuity with the previous conceptions of politics that Arendt was challenging. Arendt of course wrote no *The Origins of Nuclear Annihilation*,

but "An Introduction *into* Politics" does offer some thoughts on the matter.
The commonest account is to trace the rise of the destructive powers delivered into human hands by science in the modern era. Arendt acknowledges the
central importance of this development, but also finds origins of the problem
in the evolution of politics that is here her concern. Central is the mistake of
identifying brute force as politics' essential means. It was thus not only "technical invention" that paved the way to annihilation; it was that the "political,
public space had itself become an arena of force both in the modern world's
theoretical self-perception and in its brutal reality" (*PP*, 147). The pathways
to the bomb were of course technical, but they also ran through a conception
of politics that she defines thus:

> In our current crises, the prejudices that stand in the way of a theoretical understanding
> of what politics is really about involve nearly all the political categories in which we are
> accustomed to think, but above all they pertain to the means/ends category that regards
> politics in terms of an end purpose lying outside of politics, as well as to the notion that
> the substance of politics is brute force, and, finally, to the conviction that domination
> is the central concept of all political theory. (*PP*, 152)

Standing on the brink of the annihilation to which these ideas have conducted
the world, it is no wonder, she writes, that "the hope arises that men will
come to their senses and rid the world of politics instead of humankind" (*PP*,
153). Unarticulated is the idea that if somehow politics had developed along
a different path, the one she has begun to set forth in these texts, the impasse
might have been avoided.

10.4 Annihilation, Ancient and Modern

The section of "An Introduction *into* Politics" subtitled the "Meaning of Politics" ends with a self-contained, twenty-seven page tour de force that Kohn
rightly calls "one of the greatest in all of Arendt's writings" (*PP*, xxix). Neither
precisely an essay nor a conceptual work, nor a work of historical analysis, nor
a literary exegesis, this passage is an extended and coherent meditative flight
combining elements of all of these into a genre that is sui generis. Whereas in
other parts of *The Promise of Politics* a superabundance of ideas seems all but
uncontainable in a bulging, stressed structure, this passage forms a perfectly
integrated and self-contained whole. The starting point, like a text for a sermon,
is Homer's *Illiad*. Her aim is to learn something about the total war threatened
by nuclear arms from the destruction of Troy, which she calls the "ur-example
of a war of annihilation" (*PP*, 163). Thus the passage moves through the entire
trajectory of her quest into the meaning of politics, from the earliest Greek
experiences down to the nuclear impasse. In her reading, the poem becomes
the starting point for a comparative exploration of the political achievements
of the Greeks and Romans – of "what politics actually means and what place
it should have in history" (*PP*, 163) – all construed as a kind of response to
the phenomenon of total annihilation revealed in the city's destruction, which

was so thorough that "until recent times it was possible to believe that it had never existed" (*PP*, 163). In its search *in war* for a politics that can, at least in a limited sphere, *supplant* war, the passage seems to embark on the quest for what William James called "the moral equivalent of war."

The text creates the foundation for such an exegesis because Troy's destruction, a Greek operation that became the central ancestral story for Greece, was also, according to the Romans, the point of conception of their city and empire, thanks to the wanderings of Aeneas, the Trojan who, according to Virgil's *Aeneid*, escaped the city with his father on his back to found Rome. In doing so, Aeneas in effect reverses Troy's destruction. Thus the Greek and Roman conceptions of politics, at least in their self-understandings, have a common root in the Trojan War. Rome's very existence, by continuing the Trojan line in the person of Aeneas, provided a sort of "full justice for the cause of the defeated" Trojans (*PP*, 174). That's why "Perhaps it is only from this Roman perspective, in which the fire is rekindled in order to reverse a previous annihilation," that we can "understand what a war of annihilation is truly about and why, quite apart from all moral considerations, it cannot be allowed a place in politics." The reason is that this survival guarantees a sine qua non of any politics whatsoever – "a plurality of individuals or people and a plurality of standpoints to make reality possible and to guarantee its continuation" (*PP*, 175). Rome's founding also honored Troy's memory in another way. Aeneas, instead of destroying Latium when he arrived on its shores from Carthage, ended the war with the Latins in a treaty that allowed them to survive within what would become Rome's world-spanning Roman Empire. Even as Rome's foundation undid the annihilation of Troy, it spared Latium from annihilation. Here seems to be the antithesis of the much-mentioned "cycle of revenge." Instead of one act of destruction leading robotically to another, the process is turned on its head: An act of destruction leads to an act of foundation, performed in a way that also spares, rather than destroys, a new foe, thereby cutting short new rounds of the infamous cycle.

What is more, according to Arendt, the Greeks forged out of the same Homeric experience the specifically Greek kind of politics that Arendt so admired and was to place at the center of her own conceptions. Arendt has a great deal to say about the continuities and differences between Greek and Roman politics and law. What is most relevant to the modern crisis, however, is her notion that the birth of a certain kind of politics, which she invites us to resume and foster and expand in our time, originally grew in ancient times in response to an experience of annihilation. For, "if wars are once again to be wars of annihilation, then the specifically political nature of foreign policy as practiced since the Romans will disappear, and the relations between nations fall back into an expanse that knows neither laws nor politics, that destroys a world and leaves a desert" (*PP*, 190). Thus did Arendt turn to the founding legends of Western civilization to find the conceptions she needed to begin to make sense of the threat that, more than two thousand years later, threatened that civilization's unmaking, its end.

Arendt was apparently able to embark on her intellectual journey only by foreswearing any ambition of finding solutions to either totalitarianism or nuclear peril, not to mention the crisis they jointly presented, as if only by turning away in a kind of provisional despair from the practical task at hand could she give herself the freedom to embark on the course of fundamental thinking that might one day open the way to solutions. More than a half-century later, it remains to ask whether such expectations had a basis. In regard to totalitarianism, the verdict is in. The hoped-for "miracle" occurred. In less than two decades after Arendt died in 1976, the Soviet Union collapsed. "Action in concert" of the kind identified by Arendt was very much involved, especially in Eastern Europe, where revolutionary councils were indeed formed and the structures of totalitarian rule were undermined from within. This event was both preceded and followed by the remarkable series of nonviolent revolutions that, starting in the 1970s and continuing into the new century, have brought down dictatorial governments in several dozen countries, from Greece, Portugal, and Spain in the 1970s to the Philippines, Chile, and South Africa later. These were "Arendtian" revolutions par excellence. Arendt had had at least an inkling of what was to come. She wrote soon after the events of the Hungarian revolution against Soviet domination in 1956 that if they "promise anything at all it is much rather a sudden and dramatic collapse of the whole regime than a gradual normalization. Such a catastrophic development, as we learned from Hungarian revolution, need not necessarily entail chaos. . . . "[9]

And what of nuclear danger? The end of the Cold War, which brought about the kind of action that Arendt, delving into antiquity, discovered, appeared to create a predicate for nuclear disarmament. The problem in the 1950s had been the seeming impossibility of disarming in the face of the totalitarian antagonist. In 1991, if not earlier, the antagonist disappeared, but the arms sailed on into the new era. The arsenals of the Cold War, though reduced, still glower at the world. The number of nuclear-armed countries in the world has risen to nine. Can we look forward to a second miracle, itself precipitated by the miracle that brought down totalitarianism but this time bringing nuclear disarmament? President Obama, it is true, has called for a world free of nuclear weapons. But the journey to the goal remains uncertain. Neither Arendt nor history has written that story – not yet.

[9] Hannah Arendt, *The Origins of Totalitarianism* (New York: Meridian, 1958), p. 510.

11

Hannah Arendt between Europe and America

Optimism in Dark Times

Benjamin R. Barber

Affecting to make sense of Hannah Arendt, every scholar tends to disclose herself, every writer (as Richard Bernstein rightly says) finds he is telling a story. Here is mine: In 1968, when I was writing my first published work to be called "Conceptual Foundations of Totalitarianism,"[1] a critique of the term *totalitarianism* as it was being used by social scientists during the Cold War to mark the Soviet Union as a Nazi-like regime, I read *The Origins of Totalitarianism,* just seventeen years after it had been published. Over the summer of 2006, nearly forty years later, I read it again, this time against the backdrop of a new war on terrorism, a war against a "Islamofascist totalitarian" enemy. Like so many young political theorists, I was a fan of Arendt on democracy back then; but I was far less sympathetic to her book on totalitarianism. Over time, however, while I did not come to share all of Arendt's political opinions, living as I do in the building on Riverside Drive where she lived, in the same line and just two stories above the apartment where she died, I do quite literally nowadays share her "view." The result of these quirky facts is this chapter, more sympathetic to Arendt than I might have thought possible before I started to write it.

It is a chapter about how Hannah Arendt's deep European pessimism, so heartbreakingly grounded in her European experience, was palliated by a newly acquired American optimism, rooted – if not in the black and white realities of American history (which she tended to colorize) – in her own liberating American experience. It is meant to help us understand the place of her seminal work on totalitarianism in the scheme of her thinking, and hence help us understand the term itself. This focus allows the chapter, if only incidentally in terms of its primary analysis, to illuminate and rebut sundry claims made today by increasingly hysterical critics of Islamic fundamentalism. These critics toss around terms like "Islamofascism" and "totalitarianism" in a manner that obfuscates the nature of the threat we face even as it distorts the conversation

[1] In C. J. Friedrich, Michael Curtis, and Benjamin R. Barber, *Totalitarianism in Perspective* (New York: Praeger, 1971).

about totalitarianism that has been under way since the early 1930s, when *The International Encyclopedia of Social Sciences* first gave the novel term currency.

Fundamentalist critics of fundamentalist Islam – such as Samuel Huntington and Bernard Lewis and, more recently, Hirsi Ali – have long been flirting with allusions to fascism in characterizing the excesses of modern Islam. A right-wing zealot named Jonah Goldberg has even written a silly little book called *Liberal Fascism*, claiming it is "impossible to deny that the New Deal was objectively fascistic."[2] Yet more serious liberal Europeans from Vaclav Havel and Adam Michnik to Andrei Glucksman and Josckha Fischer (who has written about a "third totalitarianism") have flirted with the term "totalitarianism" as a modern label for terrorism.[3]

Perhaps no one has made the argument against "fascist" Islam with greater ardor, more grandiloquence, and less discretion than Paul Berman, nominally a "liberal" himself, in his book *Terror and Liberalism*. There, after referring to Saddam Hussein as a "totalitarian menace" and to the "entire situation" in the Middle East as having "the look of Europe in 1939," Berman calls for an "anti-totalitarian war."[4] He concludes his book by asserting that "right now we are beset with terrorists from the Muslim totalitarian movements," so that "today the totalitarian danger has not yet lost its sting, and there is no wisdom in claiming otherwise."

It is my contrarian thesis here that there is a great deal of wisdom in claiming otherwise – at least if one wants to understand the term "totalitarianism," or if one cares about the seminal analysis of totalitarianism actually proffered by Hannah Arendt, especially as it shapes and is impacted by her own relationship with America.[5]

As the Enlightenment had once come to America in all its splendid certainty to rationalize the founding (as Henry Steele Commager had argued in his celebrated book),[6] it came again at the end of World War II, cloaked this time in a new ambivalence about modernity and reason, an ambivalence occasioned by the bald and seemingly inexplicable horrors of the Holocaust.[7] On this wave came Hannah Arendt. Like so many of the refugees who in becoming Americans helped invent America, Arendt was caught between the world from which she sought refuge and the land that would give her sanctuary: between

---

[2] Jonah Goldberg, *Liberal Fascism*, (New York: Doubleday, 2007), p. 158.

[3] See the interesting essay by Anson Rabinbach, "Totalitarianism Revisited," *Dissent* (Summer 2006), p. 82.

[4] Paul Berman, *Terror and Liberalism* (New York: W.W. Norton, 2003), pp. 2–6.

[5] Henry Steele Commager, *The Empire of Reason: How Europe Imagined and America Realized the Enlightenment* (Garden City, NY: Anchor Press/Doubleday, 1977).

[6] Berman, *Terror and Liberalism*, p. 214.

[7] See, for example, Max Horkheimer and Theodore W. Adorno, *Dialectic of Enlightenment*, New Edition (New York: Continuum International Publishing, 1976).

Europe and the United States, Auschwitz and Riverside Drive. While some of the immigrants went west to Hollywood to fashion the tinsel myths by which pop-cultural America would come to define itself, others came to New York and Cambridge and helped establish the University in Exile (the New School for Social Research) and a new social science that cast its gaze forward to the American morning, all empiricism and positivism and shiny tabula rasa on which the new country wrote only new stories, rather than backward in the direction of the receding but still dark European night void (at that moment) of promise.

Arendt nevertheless could not help but bring to America her preoccupation with Europe's darkest years. In an intellectual schizophrenia typical of reflective refugees, she seemed to forgive nothing associated with Europe's recent past while exonerating America of just about everything others might regard as dark in its history.[8] Totalitarianism began with the fantastic and dangerous conviction that "everything is possible." Yet did not America begin with a cheerful version of this same premise? And was not the premise itself redolent of Enlightenment empiricism, and the belief that the human mind was a blank tablet open to novelty and innovation? The child of the Holocaust harbored a profound pessimism about modernity; yet the émigré to America understood that modernity in its American incarnation could have outcomes utterly antithetical to the Holocaust. One can intuit that for Arendt, America's possibility hinted that the Holocaust, history's most daunting and horrific event and a perverse byproduct of the Enlightenment, might not be altogether foreordained or ineluctable. Monstrous as it was, it was contingent rather than predetermined. It may have sacralized laws of history and of nature, but it was not "caused" by them. Might America be the proof?

Like J. L. Talmon and Karl Popper, Arendt divined in totalitarianism a unique modern phenomenon in which the modern masses played a critical role. Yet unlike these theorists – perhaps because she became an American – she exempted democracy from the indictment. Or perhaps it was just America, masquerading as a paradigm of the political, she let off the hook, not the Enlightenment per se. In any case, she insisted instead on America's relationship to the saving idea of the *public* and hence the republic (*res publica*) – an idea she would rescue from the ancient Athenians in *The Human Condition*. For *The Human Condition* was the book, with its penchant for the communitarian aspect of democracy, for which she became best known among American political theorists and their student enthusiasts.[9] For all the cultural critique

---

[8] My own teacher, Judith N. Shklar, was similarly haunted by the European totalitarian past – she always focused on cruelty as the worst of the political vices and was drawn to a politics of fear that distrusted even democratic power. Yet she also found that America drew from her an unnnatural optimism, and her last book exuded an American form of hope. Judith N. Shklar, *American Citizehship: The Quest for Inclusion* (Cambridge, MA: Harvard University Press, 1991).

[9] Hannah Arendt, *The Human Condition* (Chicago: University of Chicago Press, 1958). (Hereafter abbreviated *HC*.)

of mass society being leveled at the Americans by her fellow refugees, such as Adorno and Horkheimer, and despite Alexis de Tocqueville's anxiety about America's lurking "majoritarian tyranny," Arendt was certain that "America knows less of the modern psychology of masses than perhaps any other people in the world."[10]

This is then a chapter about Arendt's voyage from Europe to America. In the path described by her intellectual journey from *The Origins of Totalitarianism* (1951), written as an immigrant, to *Eichmann in Jerusalem*, which she covered for *The New Yorker* in 1961, in a style that felt truly American, and then on to her most American work, *On Revolution* (published in 1963), where she seemed to celebrate her newfound land at the expense of much of European social history, she reenacted her original passage to America.[11] That passage involved a journey from the horror and despair of a totalitarianism born from contingency to the relative if terrible hope made possible by Jewish complicity (endowing the victims with responsibility was a kind of empowerment), and finally on to the real optimism of democratic politics in its bright American incarnation, which was, she believed, more or less permanently immunized against the dark spells of Europe.

Although Europe had stumbled into totalitarianism, in her view, she seemed torn by a vision of historical necessity and a vision of contingency: the contingency engendered by a collision between antisemitism, imperialism, mass society, and bourgeois economics. But contingency or no, dark times felt routine on the true "Dark Continent" (Arendt used the phase with conventional obliviousness to describe Africa in *Origins*, but it rings more true as a portrait of her Europe), while in the United States, all was light. The only American figure to appear in her collection of essays in *Men in Dark Times* was Randall Jarrell, and there was little dark about him or his times. In any case, he appears as an afterthought, presumably because there was a brief portrait of him already written that she decided to include in the anthology – despite the "cheerfulness" that was his most salient characteristic.[12]

If Europe was shrouded in shadows, Germany was at the very heart of that darkness. The poem she cites from Bertholt Brecht as the epigraph to her *Eichmann in Jerusalem* reviles the home of Kant, Goethe, and Schiller:

---

[10] Hannah Arendt, *The Origins of Totalitarianism* (New York: Schocken, 2004), p. 420. (Hereafter abbreviated *OT*.) Unless other texts are cited, all my citations from OT are from this edition. *OT* was originally published in 1951 by Harcourt, Brace.

[11] Hannah Arendt, *Eichmann in Jerusalem: A Report on the Banality of Evil* (New York: Viking, 1963). (Hereafter abbreviated *EJ*.) Arendt covered the Eichmann trial for the *New Yorker Magazine* in 1961 and the book arose out of that coverage, published in 1963; Hannah Arendt, *On Revolution* (New York: Macmillan, 1963). (Hereafter abbreviated *OR*.)

[12] Hannah Arendt, *Men in Dark Times* (New York: Harcourt, Brace, 1968). Aside from Jarrell, her subjects included Lessing, Luxemburg, Roncalli, Jaspers, Dinesen, Broch, Benjamin, Brecht, and Gurian. It was the "exuberance of [Jarrell's] cheerfulness" that she writes about in the brief five-page miniportrait that concludes her book. She admired Jarrell's ability to "laugh away the rubbish," but this was neither the aspect of a man born to dark times nor a sufficient response to the dark times that are this book's subject. Ibid., p. 267.

"O Germany – Hearing the speeches that ring from your house one laughs, But whoever sees you, reaches for his knife" (*EJ*, 2). Whether or not this reflects Arendt's own perspective on the "dialectic of enlightenment," it certainly suggests a distinction between the impact of the Enlightenment on Europe and on America. At home in the United States, she might easily have added a Whitmanesque line about the émigré from Europe who hears America singing and is induced to lay the Aryan blade aside and set sail for its welcoming shores.

It was in *On Revolution* that Arendt offered the stark dualism that defined so much of her writing on the old and new worlds at which she had already hinted in *Origins*: First stood the old French revolutionary obsession with the *economic* question (security) that had generated the first great "terror" and in time led to the vanishing of the *political* question (liberty) and to the coming of the masses; and which, with antisemitism and imperialism in the mix, had opened the path to totalitarianism. In contrast there stood the American revolutionary preoccupation with the *political* question that had saved the United States from social revolution and immunized it against the pathologies that would destroy Germany and doom the European experiment in economic salvation. Socialism bred terrorism, and in time Jacobins, Bolsheviks, and Nazis. Democratic politics engendered America the pure – never mind slavery, never mind the seventy-year social revolution that led to the Civil War, never mind the fledgling empire, never mind Hiroshima. Seen through eyes that had witnessed the Holocaust, the American way of politics promised salvation, precisely because it positioned politics and civic community (civil society) above issues of deep economic organization and social revolution. Like a true American, much as she admired equality, Arendt put liberty first. Whatever issues the United States had with justice, neither radical evil nor absolute terror nor total domination was among them. The spontaneity and pluralism that totalitarianism had to destroy in order to realize itself, as Arendt defined it, were securely ensconced in the United States. Perjuring American political will stood in the way of the myriad contingencies that in Europe generated and accumulated until totalitarianism became, although not ineluctable, historically unavoidable. Too many contingencies rose together in too great a wave until the tide, though never inevitable, was unstoppable.

The Christian Fall had unfolded on both continents, but in Europe a convergence of dire historical contingencies had led to a descent into hell on earth, conceived in Nazism's ideological womb, born on the Wannsee, and made manifest at Buchenwald and Auschwitz. America stood as an almost perfect antinomy: the place where hell was not, and could not be. In the land of the city on the hill, its residents being human, the Fall was of course an option. But Puritan redemption stood as America's safety net; or at least as a trampoline at the bottom of every hole and pit, assuring a happy bounce to every fall and an upbeat outcome to every downturn; a happy way out of the most tragic of circumstantial misadventures, whether those bred by slavery, by imperialism, or by mere political corruption.

Once in America, Arendt seemed to comprehend both perspectives present in Melville's poignant account of American innocence in his *Benito Cereno*, the story of a slave revolt on a Spanish slaver beyond the ken of an innocent American captain who boards the ship to find out what is the matter.[13] Captain Delano never "gets it." As a German Jew who had survived both assimilation and persecution, Arendt had been an intimate witness to radical evil – which became the subject of *The Origins of Totalitarianism* – and so she certainly could "get it," could fathom both slavery and the consuming revolt against it. But she fell in with Captain Delano too, oblivious in the new world that was now her home to what had been inescapably apparent in the old. There was much in the new world she simply did not or would not look at. Having encountered the blinding radiance of absolute evil, she was insensitive to such lesser vices as American history might display. After Hell, neither Purgatory nor Hades appears particularly awesome or even awful. Although mass society was one of the contingencies that opened the way to total domination over atomized individuals, Arendt still felt assured that American mass society was innocent of mass psychology and its psychoses.

There simply can be "no parallels to the life in the concentration camps. . . . It can never be fully embraced by imagination . . . [because] it stands outside of life and death" (*OT*, 572). Europe's horrors offer Arendt a back way into America's exceptionalism, which by comparison is both peerless and virtuous. America's worst sin, slavery, cannot compare to what happened in Germany, for slavery, horrendous as it might be, is rational and purposive; that is to say, utilitarian, and hence all too imaginable. The evil of the camps was unique – distinctive even from other camps in other systems of "total domination." The Nazi camps occupied the inner circle of damnation, the true "hell" at the core of evil. The other versions were mere Purgatory (the Soviet labor camps defined by malevolent neglect but not extermination) or Hades (nontotalitarian camps such as those of the Boers or the colonial powers in India).

Every pathology of the modern world, every calamity in Arendt's own history, culminated in the camps, which thus became the starting point for all of her postwar intellectual work.[14] Totalitarianism was finally an invention intended to explain the inexplicable, a device by which those "most consequential institutions of totalitarian rule" could be made accessible to human imagination (*OT*, 569). That was Arendt's principal challenge: how to help the world, but in particular her new fellow citizens in the new world, comprehend the incomprehensible horror of the camps in which the old world had found its terminus. *Origins* is not a historical explanation of the Holocaust, but a genealogy of radical evil, comprising six hundred pages of analysis in search

---

[13] For a full discussion, see Benjamin R. Barber, "Melville and the Myth of American Innocence," in David Scribner, ed., *Aspects of Melville* (Pittsfield, MA: Berkshire County Historical Society, 2001).

[14] An essay called "The Concentration Camps" appeared in *Parisian Review* in 1948 and found its way into *Origins*.

of a noncausal understanding of what had transpired in the camps. Because she sets out to do the undoable, she cannot really succeed in the project. The distance between mundane reality and the camps is too great, a study in radical evil beyond culpability. This is perhaps why fans and critics alike agree that *Origins* is something other than a work of social science.

The hard challenge Arendt confronts is dealing with "the inability of the non-totalitarian world to grasp a mentality which functions independently of all calculable action in terms of men and material, and is completely indifferent to national interest and the well-being of its people" (*OT*, 541). For this inability "shows itself in a curious dilemma of judgment: those who rightly understand the terrible efficiency of totalitarian organization and police are likely to overestimate the material force of totalitarian countries, while those who understand the wasteful incompetence of totalitarian economics are likely to underestimate the power potential which can be created in disregard of all material forces" (*OT*, 541).

Arendt honed her capacity to take the measure of an evil so radical that, as philosopher Richard Bernstein helped us see, it was voided of normal moral essence – of virtue and vice alike – and became metaphysically banal. Bernstein has rejected a simple dichotomy in comparing *Origins* with *Eichmann in Jerusalem*. The latter work is conventionally understood to equate banality with evil in some novel and dramatic fashion that exculpates the Nazis from radical evil-doing at the same time that it attributes to the Jewish Councils some degree of complicity. But what Bernstein actually argues is that "Arendt's judgment of Eichmann was far more damning than that of 'monster,'" because the "terrifyingly normal" (Arendt's words) "new type of criminal" Eichmann incarnated represented a new class of "desk murderers" for whom "thoughtlessness" was more awful than ever an abstract radical evil could be.[15]

In my view, the passage from radical evil to banality in Arendt may also have reflected the degree to which Arendt had come to despair not only of finally explaining the Holocaust to her fellow Americans, but of explaining it to herself. The tone of *Origins* itself grows increasingly dark, frightening, and unempirical in its bleak essentialism as it approaches the climax of Chapter 3 ("Totalitarianism in Power") of the final Part III, devoted to the secret police and the camps. The camps were the dark pit at the beginning and end of her thought, and presented an obstacle to thinking between or beyond them. In *Origins*, all of the expansive and detailed explanations about the decline of party politics, the unlimited economic expansion that occasioned imperialism, the growth of racial politics and the resulting decline of the nation-state, the convergence of mobs and elite, and the dissolution of the class system – all of these explanations that were meant to help understand how total domination had come into being had the feel of accretions on the corpse-like corpus that was the extermination camp. The idea of radical evil is coterminous with

---

[15] Richard J. Bernstein, *Hannah Arendt and the Jewish Question* (Cambridge, MA: MIT Press, 1996), p. 160.

the reality of the camps, for which "there are no parallels.... Its horror can never be fully embraced by the imagination for the very reason that it stands outside of life and death." The seemingly "helpful comparisons" arising out of forced labor, banishment, and slavery "all lead nowhere," since what is at stake is "the appearance of some radical evil, previously unknown to us" (*OT*, 572).

This focus on the Nazi camps created a problem for Arendt's larger totalitarian project. The putatively descriptive social science term found much of its currency in its assimilation of right and left fundamentalisms into a single category: the totalitarian state. Yet given Arendt's preoccupation with the extermination camps, the ambitious attempt to bring Soviet Russia into the totalitarian fold had a certain contrived feel, as if it were a necessary but irksome add-on. Stalin's depredations seemed to reach a plane somewhere between purgatory and hell, not quite the inner circle; and Stalinism was not all of the Soviet experience. Though he came later, Khrushchev would to some degree rescue the state from total domination.

To be sure, Arendt herself tried to bridge the seeming distance between the Soviet labor camps and the Nazi extermination camps: "The often maintained view that the Bolshevist concentration camps are a modern form of [labor] slavery, and are therefore fundamentally different from the Nazi death camps, which were operated like factories, is therefore mistaken." Mistaken, Arendt reasons, because of the terrorism associated with Stalin's purges, which "are obviously one of the most striking and permanent institutions of the Bolshevist regime."[16] But purges, even when associated with random slaughter, already fall short of radical evil and the superfluousness of man Arendt associated with it. The labor camps treated men not as superfluous but as crucial if disposable instruments of Soviet production schedules. Moreover, Arendt's portrait here is drawn before Stalin's death, and well before the 1956 revisionism that came with Khrushchev. Besides, how can the total domination state implode and end and still be defined as the total domination state? Later critics of the Soviets such as Ambassador Jeane Kirkpatrick had insisted that the essence of the distinction between authoritarian and totalitarian states was precisely that totalitarian states could never wither from within; yet that is exactly what had happened to the Soviets in 1989, a collapse from the inside that came after Arendt's death but in time to announce the insufficiency of the term "totalitarianism" as applied to the Soviet regime.

So finally, it seems to me, it is not the Gulag but Auschwitz alone that is at stake in the totalitarian essence depicted in Chapter 3 of Part III of *Origins*. There Arendt confronts the fantasmic and incomprehensible hyper-reality of the camps that all of the preceding analysis is meant to elucidate and clarify. Arriving at her scrutiny's actual historical object, however, she is reduced to a kind of dumbness, to meta-language about "superfluousness," nothingness,

---

[16] This from a 1950 or 1951 essay called "Mankind and Terror," reprinted in Hannah Arendt, *Essays in Understanding: 1930–1954* [1994] (New York: Schocken, 2005), p. 303.

and the end of all normal language; the end of both logic of teleology and the logic of utility of a kind we might associate with labor camps. Totalitarianism was finally shorthand for total domination and absolute terror, yet even these locutions remained abstractions incapable of capturing radical evil. For radical evil, quite simply, was not to be captured. It turned out to be beyond good and evil in ways not even Nietzsche's meta-ethics could plum. How to say it? Beyond the human. Outside human experience. Destructive of all human essence. Eluding human language and human imagination. The dismal essence of ineffability. Which is all to say that it is literally unspeakable.

Still, the analyst's task remained to speak: to explain the inexplicable, above all for Arendt to explain it to those who had defeated the system militarily, but had little grasp of what they had defeated. Knowing that, as Mary McCarthy had remarked, "radical evil is hard for Americans to grasp," Arendt tried to bring to them the meaning of Auschwitz and of the system that had produced it – without resorting to the "laws of history" by which it was being elucidated by Marxists and other determinists and historicists. (Arendt had worked on a study of Marxism and how it became totalitarian where incarnated as Bolshevism, but never finished or published it.) She affected to penetrate the American cloak of innocence, though, ironically, she did so at the very moment she was trying on that cloak herself.

Not until 9/11, however, well after Arendt's death, did Americans really get it – after which time, like their president, they got little else. Whether she would have approved of the appeals to a new Islamofascist totalitarianism we cannot know. I suspect not, since she did not even fully approve of the counterideological uses of her term "totalitarianism" during the Cold War. Extending the idea to the Soviets, although she made the effort, always seems far more daunting than applying it to its natural subject matter in the Nazi camps. About the term's popularity in the McCarthy era at the start of the Cold War, she said such "popularity is suspect because it occurs in a country where no danger of totalitarian movements exists, and for which the totalitarian threat is almost exclusively an issue ... of foreign politics. Popularity is even more suspect at a moment when the public authorities ... have become fully aware of all its external and internal implications."[17]

Compelled to honor the fascist/communist linkage by the logic that defined the totalitarian construct, the construct itself constantly rebuked her: Essentialist totalitarianism was incomparable. Neither the Gulag, nor slavery, nor Mao's early massacres, nor the murderous savageries of Stalin could live up to the paradigm of radical evil. Perhaps that is why she moved away from the radical evil idea over time, and hence away from the seminal analysis of *Origins*. Given her diffidence at standing by her original obsession with evil pure and simple, could she then have ever imagined that al Qaeda's deadly tactics, rooted in powerlessness and marginality, met the mark of that original construct as put forward in *Origins*?

---

[17] From a 1951 essay called "The Egg Speaks Up," in Arendt, *Essays in Understanding*, p. 270.

There can be little doubt that the story she tells in *The Origins of Totalitarianism*, written at the end of World War II and published in 1951, is not only the point of departure for understanding everything else Arendt wrote, but the book that allows pundits today to draw her into the new millennium, the age after 9/11. It is its very account of radical evil and its insistence on terror as an essentialist phenomenon that propel it into the headlines once again. To be sure, the Nazis are long gone, relegated to stock roles in Broadway musical comedies, while the Iron Curtain has been down for almost a generation. Indeed, as we have noted, Hannah Arendt herself gave up talking about radical evil. Richard Bernstein, in Chapter 13 of this book, and others have certainly tried to persuade us that there are affinities between radical evil and the cold indifference of banality, noting that even in *Origins*, Arendt denotes this cold detachment as an indicator of radical evil, suggesting that it is the critical marker: that the early, passionate, bestial S.A. that murdered for pleasure exhibited a kind of engaged sadism, while the coldblooded, systematic S.S. pursued an agenda of depersonalized slaughter – a slaughter from which, Himmler had insisted to his men, they should take no pleasure.

Nonetheless, I remain persuaded that Arendt moved away from that meta-idea of radical evil much in the manner she says she did, both because radical evil was ineffable, but also because as a new American she sought seeds of hope in the darkest places. This is where a certain kind of comfort is perhaps to be found in the competing notion of banality that appeared in her reportage on the Eichmann trial, initially almost as an afterthought, though eventually as the subtitle of her book. Even the egregious charge (if that was what it was) of Jewish responsibility some have associated with that reportage may have arisen out of a bent American hopefulness.

I do not wish to reopen the angry debate over whether Arendt was really suggesting Jewish complicity in her remarks on the responsibility of Jewish leadership in facilitating the Holocaust. But she did write in her account of Eichmann's trial that the "role of the Jewish leaders in the destruction of their own people is undoubtedly the darkest chapter of the whole dark story" (*EJ*, 117). And she notoriously charged that while it was "true" that the Jews, existing without real political organization or a state of their own, could hardly be seen as cooperating in their destruction, it was nonetheless more true – indeed, it was "the whole truth" – "that if the Jewish people has really been unorganized and leaderless, there would have been chaos and plenty of misery but the total number of victims would hardly have been between four and a half and six million people" (*EJ*, 125). That is to say, the Jews *were* organized if not as a state, and organized leadership played a role in the Holocaust.

What I do mean to suggest with this flashback to the controversy over Eichmann is that there may have been some element of American optimism in this Arendtian turn, a comforting aspect of possibility – the role of will – in the idea of complicity. Had Arendt thought she had discovered in Jewish complicity, however ugly, a weird kind of dignity? As banality and administratively sanctioned mayhem somehow humanized (banalized) radical evil, so complicity might render evil comprehensible, even conquerable. For with complicity came the possibility of choice and hence resistance, making totalitarianism less of a preordained death sentence. How sweet the idea "it might have been other-wise." Charges of complicity of any kind were of course bound to enrage Jews and others. Surely this was to blame the victims rather than the perpetrators of the world's worst genocide. Yet it might also inspire a perverse kind of hope, the hope that the behavior of totalitarianism's victims might count among the contingencies, and that adjustments in behavior might therefore alter the course of history, might actually alter the logic leading to extermination.

Her study of Eichmann did then lead her away from the dark pit of totalitar-ian essentialism and offered a tortuous methodology that, in positing banality and noting a certain Jewish responsibility on behalf of a too cooperative leader-ship (the *Judenraete*), exculpated historical determinism. It allowed her to speak of the unspeakable and escape the trap of *Origins*, which led to conclusions that nullified the entire work's premise.

Yet for all of this, for all the counterevidence provided by the evolution of Arendt's thought about totalitarianism, we cannot get around the fact that the enduring impact of her study of the Holocaust is founded on the analysis in *Origins* and on her attempt there to hold the mercury that was the idea of radical evil in her bare hands. And it is precisely the renewed concern with evil that came out of 9/11 and that dominates politics today that has brought *Origins* back into the rhetorical environment.

That totalitarianism is indeed once again back in the media rhetoric of politicians and pundits in the post-9/11 world is all too understandable. Yet for this very reason, I want to argue here that allowing it to remain there can only try our understanding of terrorism and distort our ever-changing understanding of Hannah Arendt herself. On the positive side, confronting terrorism directly does bring Americans finally to a glimmering of what Arendt was trying to do – since we now too are at pains to try to explain the inexplicable, which for us are the unprecedented (on American soil) horrors of 9/11, the murder of innocents, the resistance of Flight 903's doomed heroes, the motives of the millions who now "hate us" (as we see it) beyond all reason without our being able to fathom why. As once the Holocaust defied explanation, today terrorism defies imagination and leaves America uncomprehending, vulnerable to fear-mongering and extremist polemics.

It is hardly surprising then, foraging around for a term to elucidate the incomprehensible, the media and intellectual elites entrusted with making sense of it all have not only resuscitated the construct of totalitarianism but resur-rected memories of the Nazi era in which it arose. "The more apt epithet for Osama bin Laden," writes *New Republic* editor Peter Beinart, musing on bin Laden's political messianism and the Taliban's moralizing Puritanism, "is total-itarian," or, as he calls it, "Salafi totalitarianism."[18] President George W. Bush

---

[18] Peter Beinart, *The New Republic*, September 25, 2006.

himself has frequently employed the analogy between the Nazis and Islamic terrorists, referring to "Islamofascism" and an axis of evil and implying that those who do not fully embrace his war on terrorism may be so many Chamberlains buying peace in our time by selling out tomorrow's national security. More than a few books have been written exploring the linkage, not all of them by Bush administration acolytes or hawkish neoconservatives. With her husband, the former Danish Social Democratic Party cabinet minister Karen Jesperson has written a study called "Islamists and the Naïve," comparing Islam with Nazism and communism. "The link between politics and religion," Jesperson explains, "makes Islam a totalitarian movement, and it is gaining ground in the Middle East and Europe."[19] Yet for all of the attention, these works all tend to prove how desperate and counterproductive the appeal to totalitarianism is.

This is most evident in what is perhaps the most serious and extended argument of this kind from the liberal side. It comes from Paul Berman in a 2003 book cited at the beginning of this chapter called *Terror and Liberalism*. As we have seen, Berman is ready to apply the term retroactively to Saddam Hussein – "in Saddam Hussein and his government, we were facing a totalitarian menace – something akin to fascism" – as well as to the "entire situation" in Europe in 1939.[20] After superficially recounting the stories of prewar fascism and communism as totalitarian, and examining at greater leisure the Muslim Brotherhood and its fundamentalist ideological origins in the work of Egypt's radical intellectual Sayyid Qutb, Berman offers a warning to today's liberals, to him modern cousins of those earlier European cosmopolitans who would not grasp the meaning of the camps or accept that they could actually exist. Do not allow your good faith American optimism to blind you to the harsh new realities, Berman preaches: There has been too much wishful thinking on the left, a foolish need for an ideology that, "in its anti-imperialist errors, has lost the ability to stand up to fascism." But the reality "right now" is that "we are beset with terrorists from the Muslim totalitarian movement, who have already killed an astounding number of people." Far from being some historical movement that has supposedly "been defeated," totalitarianism is actually "reaching a new zenith."[21]

Such implicit historical linkages are common in Europe as well. Pope Benedict has not referred explicitly to totalitarianism, but he has associated historical Islam with *inherent* violence and has been defended against the hue and cry evoked by his statement by many who have said that while his words may be offensive, they are true.[22] And who better to recognize it than a German bishop?

What all of these examples tend to demonstrate is how the America that was once seen by Hannah Arendt as terminally uncomprehending in the face of

---

[19] Cited in Dan Bilefsky, *International Herald Tribune*, September 8, 2006.

[20] Berman, *Terror and Liberalism*, pp. 4–5.

[21] Ibid., pp. 206–7.

[22] At a speech at Regensburg University in September 2006, Pope Benedict cited Emperor Manuel II of the Byzantine Empire, saying, "Show me just what Mohammed brought us that was new and there you will find things only evil and inhumane."

totalitarianism has caught up to her, ready finally to open itself to a confrontation with radical evil in both its actuality and its metaphysical entailments –
if only it can find it. The events of 9/11 have become a kind of American
Auschwitz, our own experience of the camps compressed into the horrors of
a single morning. But I remain unconvinced and can still see the wisdom of
"seeing otherwise."

The comparison between Islamic Jihadism and totalitarianism is on its face
absurd, and may seem to camp survivors or other victims of systemic genocide
to be obscene. Yet it is meant to evoke a new American openness to arguments
about absolute evil to which America's exceptionalist innocence and preternatural sunniness once rendered America immune. The terrorists have now
penetrated the shell of our exceptionalism and led us to recognize that there is
a version of hell that may also serve as America's destiny. Our new Captains
Delano, President Bush and Vice President Cheney, recognize evil when they
see it. They are ready for all that total terrorism entails, including the total war
against it and the loss of liberty that total war must mandate.

Yet can any serious historian, any genuine moralist, really believe that
our experience of terrorism, however brutal, warrants calling the perpetrators "totalitarian"? As once the term was not enough for the essentialist horror
of the camps, today it is far too much for the complex realities of modern,
decentralized, multifactor terrorism. It neither lives up to the ferocious indicators Arendt adduced for its origins, nor corresponds to the inner circles of
absolute evil embodied by the essentialist hell it manifested.

Try this experiment: Take the measure of terrorism's characteristics by
Arendt's indicators for a totalitarian entity; you will find today's terrorism
comes up wanting on almost every one. Compare the portrait of absolute
radical evil with what terrorists have actually achieved, and the equation is
laughable. Moral bookkeeping is never very useful, but it is risible when a
comparison is made between three thousand terrible murders perpetrated by
deluded and otherwise impotent zealots and the systematic dehumanization
and liquidation of 6 million in a process embodied by extermination camps
whose sole purpose is genocide.

Now at one level we have already shown Berman's "analysis" and the arguments it mimics are really just so much rhetoric. As the term "totalitarian"
was once employed by the Cold War's political soldiers to vilify a communist enemy by assimilating it to the earlier Nazi enemy, it now has become a
blunt club with which to batter a new elusive foe by associating it with old,
more familiar, villains.[23] The postwar communists, our allies against Hitler,
once had to be recast as neo-Nazis themselves to provide ideological cover for
political and strategic changes that had turned them into our foes. Today, new
and unfamiliar (if not altogether incomprehensible) enemies require familiarly
disparaging labels. So why not equate terrorists with Nazis (and communists)
by applying the trustworthy totalitarian brand?

---

[23] See Herbert J. Spiro and Benjamin R. Barber, "Counter-Ideological Uses of 'Totalitarianism,'"
Politics and Society, 1, 1 (November 1970): 5–7.

There is more to recent and current usage than just rhetoric, however. All political language is value-laden and contested, and like the terms "liberty," "justice," "democracy," "equality," "legitimacy," and "sovereignty," the term "totalitarianism" is subject to permanent controversy. But as conceived and constructed by Hannah Arendt, Frederick Hayek, J. L. Talmon, and Karl Popper and later employed by sundry social scientists including Karl Deutsch, Zbigniew Brzezinski, Carl J. Friedrich, John Kautsky, and Franz Neumann, inter alia, the idea had powerful ideological and philosophical meanings that cannot be dismissed as merely rhetorical. That they were in every case incommensurable with one another and vigorously contested from one to the next does not mean they were without social scientific significance.[24] However, it is Arendt's account of totalitarianism that rationalized the effort to place fascism and communism – the one expressly collectivist, the other having a more liberal and individualist past that its practice abandoned – in a single common category that is the source for many commentators who today apply the term to Islam. Of the many conceptions, hers, with radical evil and terror at its core, seems especially pertinent.

Yet anyone who takes her analysis seriously, who surveys totalitarianism in all of its multiple definitional emanations, must conclude that its application to Islamic terrorism today is misguided, simply indefensible. Indeed, a careful analytic retrospective already has suggested the term can be used to assimilate communism and fascism only with great difficulty and at the cost of mounting incoherence. This much was clear from Arendt's own inconclusive attempts to do so, surveyed in the preceding paragraphs. What Arendt's work demonstrates is that totalitarianism's most compelling explanatory success was limited to explicating the inexplicable in Nazi terror: that communism was an accretion, an afterthought, the consequence of ideological impulses to revillify a former ally.

Hannah Arendt's analysis itself, we have already shown, gave rise to some of the problems associated with the later theoretical and social science usage she helped instigate. Surveying the term as it emerged in the late 1950s and the 1960s as a primary social science construct of cross-polity comparative political analysis reveals just how little social science rigor it possessed back then, and how unhelpful it really was as social science – precisely because, as Arendt ultimately revealed, it was not really intended (and did not succeed) as a tool of *comparative* political analysis at all, but was a way of labeling regimes at war with Western liberal societies, or more quintessentially a way of getting at a unique and diabolical turn in human affairs that made *comparative* political analysis impossible.

Radical Islam today certainly practices terrorism, but it meets few of the criteria Hannah Arendt or later social scientists set forth to mark totalitarianism. Brzezinski suggests that totalitarianism is "a new form of government falling

---

[24] Frederick Hayek, *The Road to Serfdom: Karl Popper, The Open Society and Its Enemies* (Chicago: University of Chicago Press, 1944); J. L. Talmon, *The Origins of Totalitarian Democracy* (New York, Praeger, 1961).

into the general classification of dictatorship ... a system in which technologically advanced instruments of political power are wielded without restraint by centralized leadership of an elite movement, for the purpose of effecting a total social revolution."[25] There is hardly a single element of this definition that applies to the decentralized system of backward political power represented by the Taliban or al-Qaeda. Or take Hayek's emphasis on totalitarianism as a "danger raised by the policy of economic planning."[26] Are the Taliban guilty of an overly planned welfare system? Then there is Franz Neumann's focus on the "total politicization of society by the device of the monopolistic party," a description that is nearly irrelevant to the Islamic terrorist approach.[27] Or take John Kautsky's "soft" definition of totalitarianism as "merely ... a set of methods used, under certain circumstances, by a group or several groups in control of a government in order to retain control of it."[28] Islamic terrorists precisely do not have control of governments and reject the notion of government itself. They are not zealots of secularism but antisecularists. Karl Popper takes us even further afield, suggesting that "what we call nowadays totalitarianism belongs to a tradition which is just as old ... as our civilization itself. ... Utopian social engineering ... historicism ... and the closed society."[29] Popper was worried about Marx, Hegel, and above all Plato; religious fanaticism was the last thing he worried about. On the other hand, J. L. Talmon believes that much of the totalitarian attitude is rooted not in the certainties of ancient Platonism but in modern democratic ideas, particularly as "contained in the eighteenth century pattern of thought."[30] The democracy Arendt prizes, Talmon fears. Indeed, Talmon's line of thinking led Brzezinksi to conclude that all fully developed modern industrial regimes, communist and noncommunist alike, were actually "converging" in their significant political and economic essentialism. Secularism and not religion is their essence, and totalism is their tendency. We are all totalitarians now!

Aside from the myriad contradictions that set these many definitions against one another,[31] not one really captures the peculiar kind of decentralized and

---

[25] Z. K. Brzezinski, *Ideology and Power in Soviet Politics* (New York: Praeger, 1967), pp. 46–7. This and other arguments discussed here are the subject of my extended essay "Conceptual Foundations of Totalitarianism," from which the material here is taken. Carl J. Friedrich, Michael Curtis, and Benjamin R. Barber, *Totalitarianism in Perspectiive: Three Views* (New York, Washington, and London: Praeger, 1969): pp. 3–39.

[26] Hayek, *The Road to Serfdom*, chapter 7.

[27] Franz Neumann, *The Democratic and Authoritarian State* (Chicago: Free Press, 1957), p. 246.

[28] Benjamin R. Barber, *Totalitarianism in Perspective: Three Views* (New York: Praeger, 1969), p. 9.

[29] Karl Popper, *The Open Society and Its Enemies* (Princeton: Princeton University Press, 1963), pp. 1–2, passim.

[30] Talmon, *The Origins of Totalitarian Democracy*, pp. 2–3.

[31] Most definitions are what I call "phenomenological" rather than essentialist, associating the term "phenomenological" with a variety of characteristics that can be present or absent to a certain degree, so that it becomes possible to talk about this or that regime as "to some degree" totalitarian.

marginalized religious sects – the disestablished and extremist versions of an established and conservative religious sect (extreme Sunni Wahhabist Islam) – that characterize the terrorists Berman and others want to designate as totalitarian to get our attention. Above all, whereas totalitarianism is a centralized, statist phenomenon rooted in a perversion of politics, Islamic terrorists are decentralized and stateless, aspiring to religious, not political, dominion and engaged in a perversion of religion rather than of the state. As a consequence, today's terrorists are antistatist and see themselves as *resisting* rather than embodying politics and the states that practice politics. Perhaps most importantly, while Arendt understood violence as an end in itself and the totalitarian party as a form of institutionalized, administrative violence, Islamic terrorists treat violence only as a means to nonviolent ends. The celebration of martyrdom is not a celebration of violence per se but of religious epiphany and permanent peace (as with all the monotheistic religions, martyrdom entails reunion with the godhead in a peaceful eternity).

Most tellingly, the modern Jihadists have no camps except the ones they train in, and no mission of extermination except the killing used to effect their political and religious goals. They wish to convert and, in religious terms, to dominate, but they do not wish to engage in genocide or even slaughter as an end in itself. So they not only fail to meet the benchmarks laid down by the social science phenomenology of totalitarianism, but they remain far away from Arendt's essentialist obsession with violence, race, and the camps. Today's terrorists are voluntarists (human choice is possible), not historicists and determinists. They make war on neither race nor ethnicity, nor even other religions (unless they believe those other religions are confronting and encroaching on them), but seek quite specific political and religious ends (to remove the infidels from Islamic lands).

It may not then be particularly surprising to discover that the approach Hannah Arendt developed to render transparent a system of profound evil whose essence was its opacity has become a seductive perspective for those wanting to explain evil in our times. But terrorism is in fact an entirely distinctive historical phenomenon that is not so much inexplicable as it is intolerable. In fact, we moderns actually have a pretty good idea of what Jihadic terrorism is – and what it precisely is *not* is totalitarianism.[32]

The analogizing fails for all the conceptual reasons noted here, but it also fails for historical reasons. Arendt's careful historical analysis in *Origins* focuses on the developments leading to the totalizing, one-party state and the Nazi ideology rooted in violence and genocide. The camps are not an incidental or sometime feature of totalitarian developments, but the totalitarian essence. There is nothing in the Taliban training camps of the 1990s or the Taliban

---

[32] For one perspective, see Benjamin R. Barber, *Jihad vs. McWorld* [1995] (New York: Times Books, 1995, new edition, 2001). But there are numerous thoughtful historical and political studies of Jihadism and religious fundamentalism that proceed without any reference to totalitarianism, such as Amy Chua and Hans Juergenmaier.

domination of the Afghan regime in that period, nothing in Baathist Syria or Baathist Iraq under Hussein, nothing in the mullah's Iran, and nothing in al-Qaeda's struggle to oust infidels from Islamic territories bearing the slightest resemblance to Arendt's totalitarianism. Neither Hussein nor Ahmadinajad nor al Zaharwi nor Osama bin Laden resemble Hitler. Iran is not Germany. The point of Arendt's careful attention to the details of German historical development was to root abstract essentialism in concrete historical context.

What is left when the sober analytic comparisons showing the utter incommensurability of Nazi totalitarianism and Jihadic terrorism are done is the obsession with evil – the effort to comprehend the incomprehensible. Here we do find a certain affinity between those trying to comprehend the Holocaust and those wanting to make sense of 9/11. But not everything that is similarly incomprehensible is similarly commensurable. The awesome turns out to be plural. Fear has many sources, not one.

One can see how we reach in the new millennium for the comfort of Arendt's old millennium term. The certainty of the Holocaust's evil can feel like solace to those who do not understand what is happening to them today. Perhaps that is how Americans feel who are experiencing for the first time what it means to live in dark times when the two oceans can no longer ward off evil, when not even the magic technical bubble of Star Wars imagined by Ronald Reagan can be regarded as preserving America from the mayhem that came from within on 9/11. Now that the paradigmatic extermination camp is a presence among us, we too must fathom radical evil. So why not resuscitate the idea of totalitarianism? Whether as innocent victims of terror or as terrorizing avengers, Americans finally recognize what may have always been the truth, despite the myths of exceptionalism: that we too are caught up in the world of empire, of entangling alliances, and of violence and war; and of genocide, too, if only by omission, caught up in ways that have delivered us forever from preternatural innocence.

We may not produce extermination camps, but with Abu Ghraib, Guantanamo, and those unnamed venues to which we outsource and redact prisoners whom our codes of law do not quite yet permit us to torture, we seem ready to join the rest of the human race in Purgatory. Our Arendtian politics of liberty persist, but the economics of social revolution she feared now shadow North/South relations and threaten our own society with deepening inequalities. The contingencies of Europe that led it to dark times are no longer precluded by our imagined exceptionalism. No wonder we reach for the clarity of the idea of totalitarianism that Arendt brought with her on her voyage from darkness to light as we embark on our own journey in the other direction.

No system is finally immune to the seductions and the horrific consequences of radical evil. The "banality" of an American Eichmann is, thank God, still a long shot in America, though our fierce soldiers armed with firepower that cannot help but overwhelm the good will they bear must sometimes make them look to their victims less like liberators than totalitarian administrators of death. And in times when the president of the United States can assert, as George W. Bush has, that Common Article Three of the Geneva Convention is hopelessly "vague" and that he does not really know what the phrase "outrage upon humanity" means, anything is possible and nothing impossible. If law is the strongest bulwark against totalitarianism, its diminishing force in America must make liberals and democrats anxious.

12

Keeping the Republic

Reading Arendt's On Revolution *after the Fall of the Berlin Wall*

Dick Howard

Democracy won the Cold War by default. The Berlin Wall seemed simply to collapse, its authority broken, its power shriveled. There was no revolutionary act; the conflicts of the past just faded away, almost before anyone was aware that they had gone. The once-dominant ruling communist parties and their ideologies shriveled overnight. But a revolution without revolutionaries left a political space without participants. As a result, triumphant democracy has become a threat to itself. It acts before it thinks. Alone on the political stage, it runs the classical risk of *pleonaxia*, overreaching. The Bush administration's attempt to impose democracy worldwide threatened to destroy its foundations at home; but many of the liberal critics of what they saw as "imperialist" adventurism fail to take seriously the very real evils that the American crusade seeks to eradicate. The democratic warriors have a valid point when they oppose tyrants like Saddam Hussein, but they cannot claim that their liberal critics are therefore antidemocratic. If democracy "won" the Cold War, what does its victory mean? This question provides the background for a rereading of Hannah Arendt's *On Revolution*, a book that tried to understand the uniqueness of the American form of democracy, the revolution that was at its origin, and the spirit that it bequeathed to contemporary Americans.

The 1962 introduction to *On Revolution* calls attention to the unique relation of war and revolution in the years after World War II. Because war has become impossible in the nuclear age, "those who still put their faith in power politics in the traditional sense . . . and, therefore, in war," will have mastered what is now an "obsolete trade." The only remaining justification for war, she adds knowingly, is a revolution that claims to defend "the cause of freedom." But like war, such a revolution would make use of violence, which is the "anti-political" province of technicians, whose use threatens the freedom that it professes. This dilemma had been seen already in the seventeenth century – which, as Arendt notes, had seen its share of violence. Philosophers invented the fiction of a prepolitical state of nature in order to show that the political realm – which is the locus of freedom – does not emerge simply from the fact

of people living together. The political is *created*; it has a beginning that sep-
arates it from prepolitical life just as the modern notion of revolution claims
to inaugurate a rupture with what preceded it. But this act involves a paradox.
The need to break with the past in order to found the new means that the
new order has itself no proper legitimacy; its only foundation is the violent
revolutionary "crime" that destroyed the old order. This was the rock against
which the French revolutionary hopes crashed again and again.

Jonathan Schell's introduction to the 2006 revised edition of *On Revolution*
makes a provocative proposal that avoids the oft-repeated cliché opposing a
bad French revolution to a good American version. He begins from Arendt's
account of the role of the workers' councils in the 1956 revolution in Hungary, which was published as an "epilogue" to the 1958 revised edition of *The
Origins of Totalitarianism*. He suggests that she never republished this essay in
subsequent versions because it reflected a transition from the bleak pessimism of
her account of *The Origins of Totalitarianism* toward the optimism articulated
in *On Revolution*. Schell defends the contemporary relevance of that new vision
by pointing to "the wave of democratic revolutions" that he claims was inspired
by the echoes of 1956 (rather than the more constitutionalist Greek, Portuguese,
and Spanish transitions of the 1970s). The Hungarian experience thus represents first expression of a subterranean fissure that began to resurface with Polish Solidarnosc, passing to the overthrow of military dictatorship in Argentina
and Brazil and then on to the Philippines and South Korea, before returning to the former Soviet Union and South Africa to culminate (provisionally)
with the fall of Miloševič, the Georgian Rose Revolution, and the Ukrainian
Orange Revolution. Schell insists on the fact that "most" of these cases looked
to the American Revolution rather than to the French model; they "aimed
at establishing conditions of freedom rather than solving social questions."
Further, "[a]ll were largely nonviolent," and "most interesting and important,
they repeatedly vindicated Arendt's new conception of power and its relationship to violence."[1] As a result of this chain of "opposition to regimes as
disparate as the military rule of southern Europe, the right-wing dictatorships
of South America, and the apartheid regimes of South Africa," Schell argues
that "Arendt was right" to claim that the "signers of the Mayflower Compact
had discovered the very 'grammar' and 'syntax' of any action whatsoever."[2]

This sweeping generalization, whose author may be said to take his wishes
for reality, will be doubted by the historian, but its theoretical premise is typically Arendtian: wide-ranging and deeply philosophical. Schell cites a lapidary
remark in which she makes clear the reach of her theoretical claims. One cannot
say, she insists, that totalitarianism is the problem and that workers' councils

---

[1] Cf. Jonathan Schell, "Introduction," to Hannah Arendt, *On Revolution* (New York: Penguin
   Classics, 2006), p. xxii. From this perspective, the transitions of 1989 were indeed revolutions;
   their model was the American experience. As will be seen in this chapter, this claim can be
   maintained only by concentrating on the activity of the dissidents as a form of civil disobedience.
[2] Ibid., p. xxvi.

are the solution. Rather, she argues, both totalitarianism and the councils are a response to "the age's problems."[3] But Schell goes on to reduce her philosophical argument to what he calls a practical and contemporary "debate" that asks whether "the wave of Arendtian democratization [has] run its course."[4] What worries him, rightly as a citizen, is the current American policy of "democratizing other countries by armed force."[5] But while it is true that, in *The Origins of Totalitarianism*, Arendt claimed that imperialism is one of the problems to which totalitarianism is a "fantastical attempted solution," it would be a leap to think that the same logic explained her opposition to the American war in Vietnam, as if she thought that America was on its way to totalitarianism. Jonathan Schell's hope that the "wave of democratic revolutions" could foreshadow a more general reversal of relations between small and great powers[6] forgets that Arendt rejected the idea of the simple replacement of a bad condition (totalitarianism) by a good alternative (workers' councils). Her concern with "the age's problems" was both philosophical and political. Although Jonathan Schell argues that "the United States, in pursuit of its war on terror, is losing track of its founding ideals," he does not explain what these are, and how they could manifest themselves two centuries after the foundation.[7]

12.1 Human Rights and "America's Ideals"

Jonathan Schell's "wave of democratic revolutions" has coincided with what some have called a "revolution of human rights." The reason that actions of a growing but small number of dissidents within the former Soviet bloc acquired a political weight was not simply the formal juridical framework provided by the "Third Basket" of the Helsinki Accords of 1975 (which the Soviets thought of as a victory for the *Realpolitik* affirmed by the Brezhnev Doctrine that had been invoked to justify crushing the Prague Spring in 1968). Although Hannah Arendt was no longer alive, the arguments she had proposed in her essay on "Civil Disobedience," written at the height of the protests against the American war in Vietnam, offer a more political explanation of how and why the assertion of individual rights came to acquire political significance.[8] She first clears away the usual (mis)interpretation according to which the civil disobedient is not a criminal because he acts in the light of day and because he

---

[3] Ibid., p. xviii.
[4] Ibid., p. xxvi.
[5] Ibid., p. xxvii.
[6] Ibid., p. xxviii (for these last citations).
[7] Ibid., p. xxvii.
[8] My reading of Arendt's argument is influenced by the seminal essay by Claude Lefort, "Droits de l'homme et politique," in *L'invention démocratique* (Paris: Fayard, 1981); it has been translated to English in Claude Lefort, *The Political Forms of Modern Society* (Cambridge, MA: MIT Press, 1986). Cf. also Lefort's essays on Arendt in order to appreciate the coincidence (and difference) of their independently developed arguments. I have discussed these issues raised by Lefort in Dick Howard, *The Specter of Democracy* (New York: Columbia University Press, 2002).

accepts the consequences of his act, as in the paradigmatic cases of Thoreau or Gandhi. She points instead to the political implication of the fact that protesting publicly means that the disobedient is appealing to others, even if the motive for the action may lie deep in the privacy of individual conscience. Action that seeks to speak to others presupposes the existence of a basis for mutual understanding that, when awakened, can result in collective action. While this might explain in part Jonathan Schell's "wave of democratic revolutions" and, more broadly, the emergence of an autonomous civil society, it is important to recognize that the success of the dissidents depended also on the fact that the weakened authority of the rulers made them incapable of crushing violently the new politics before it spread (as they did in the Polish coup d'état of December 1981). It is necessary to take into account the interplay of thought and event, authority and action, which form an indissoluble, and political, pair.

It seems that in East Central Europe the civil disobedience that Arendt understood as the renewal of the particular "spirit of American law"[9] took the form of a demand for "human rights" that acquired a power that transcended national boundaries. Although it appealed to international law, it cannot be reduced solely to a legal matter. The action of the dissidents became unavoidably political at the same time that the Soviet bloc – and what remained of its ideology – lost its legitimacy. But – again! – the simple opposition of good and evil dissolves the political problems that would emerge. After the fall of the Berlin Wall, when neither geopolitics nor leftist hopes for a "third way" that would save the "good" aspects of communism could justify the denial of rights, the question that rightly worries Jonathan Schell emerged in full force: Can rights be imposed at the point of a bayonet? Arendt had rejected the imposition of democracy by force. But in spite of the dissidents' challenge to the residual ("Westphalian") notion of national sovereignty on which the old power politics depended, no new political theory emerged to explain why some pleas for international intervention in the name of human rights are audible (Bosnia, Kosovo) while others fall on deaf ears (Rwanda) or mobilize international protests but only weak commitments (Darfur, Mynmar). This inconsistency is at least in part the result of a misunderstanding that Arendt had criticized in "Civil Disobedience": Liberal individualism's appeal to rights ignores their political foundation. It is necessary but not sufficient to punish violations of rights; the intervention must also (re)establish a political framework within which the preservation of human rights no longer depends on outside support but becomes, rather, the spirit that animates civil society.

12.2 The Politics of Civil Disobedience

In this context, Arendt's essay "Civil Disobedience" has a political significance that goes beyond any similarities between the American war in Vietnam (which

---

[9] Hannah Arendt, "Civil Disobedience," in *Crises of the Republic* (New York: Harcourt, Brace, Jovanovich, 1972), p. 85.

was her referent) and the dilemma facing Americans opposed to the Iraq invasion. The spirit animating her text recalls Benjamin Franklin's famous reply to a bystander who called out a sharp question to the departing delegates to the Philadelphia Convention: What have you made? "A republic, if you can keep it," was Franklin's lapidary reply, anticipating two major themes in American history: the difficulty of maintaining a republic, and the fact that there are no passive observers in its political life.

Civil disobedience, insists Arendt, becomes necessary only when the challenge to the authority of government results in "a constitutional crisis of the first order."[10] What constitutes a crisis of authority is *both* the government's overreaching its constitutional powers *and* a popular refusal "to recognize the *consensus universalis*" that founds the tacit agreement holding together the plural threads of the political republic. Arendt had denounced the excess of government elsewhere[11]; here she stresses the weakening of those voluntary associations whose foundational role in a democracy had been underlined already by Tocqueville. Civil disobedience is only "the latest form of voluntary association"; it is a mode of action "in tune with the oldest traditions of the country."[12] Those traditions are at the basis of a shared moral consensus; and as such, they are not merely subjective but profoundly political. While the law obviously cannot provide a place for the violation of the law, Arendt argued that the fact that the actions of the disobedients were changing majority opinion "to an astounding degree" suggested that their actions expressed the "spirit" of American law. But how could the spirit become letter? The Supreme Court refused to intervene in the conduct of the Vietnam War on the grounds that such a "political question" belonged to the other branches of government. This left Arendt only one option: to propose a constitutional amendment transcending the merely liberal guarantees of the First Amendment in order to actualize the practical republican politics of civil disobedience whose spirit she had described.[13]

The reader of *On Revolution* will recognize in this proposed constitutional revision some themes that led Jefferson to his idea of a participatory "ward system" that could preserve the spirit of "public happiness" experienced in the American Revolution.[14] Although she insisted that civil disobedience is "for the most part" an American tradition, Arendt added that its necessity stems from a

---

[10] Ibid., p. 89.

[11] Cf., for example, her reflections on the Pentagon Papers, "Lying in Politics," which is reprinted as the first essay in Arendt, *Crises of the Republic*, which also contains "Civil Disobedience."

[12] Ibid., p. 96.

[13] "The establishment of civil disobedience among our political institutions might be the best possible remedy for this ultimate failure of judicial review." Ibid., p. 101. The argument developed here is foreshadowed at p. 83 ff.

[14] Arendt was far from being a constitutional engineer; she was far more concerned with the spiritual aspect of politics. For example, writing about the May '68 movement in "Thoughts on Politics and Revolution" (1970), she suggested that "[t]his generation discovered what the eighteenth century had called public happiness." As she then weighted the chances for success,

danger imposed by a government that, because it refuses to admit its own limits, "has changed voluntary association into civil disobedience and transformed dissent into resistance.... [This threat] prevails at present – and, indeed, has prevailed for some time – in large parts of the world.... "¹⁵ Although these "large parts of the world" may not share in the experience that produced the American "spirit" on which her analysis of civil disobedience was based, her argument is at once ontological, historical, and based on political theory. The philosopher of *The Human Condition* stresses the ontological human ability to make promises; the political thinker of *On Revolution* recalls the historical experience dating from the Mayflower Compact and practiced in the New England townships; the political theorist underlines the Lockean idea that society is bound together by compacts even before it then creates a government. These assumptions are the primary justification of civil disobedience because they imply that it is the government that violates the compact; and therefore it is the covenanted society (*not* an individual disobedient *but rather* the political power of individuals acting together) that must reassert itself in the face of this abuse. This elegant argument is, however, only normative; it sacrifices the dynamic element of democracy – which was not, after all the concern of Locke, who was a liberal rather than a political republican.

In this context, the similarities of the Vietnam and Iraq experiences do need to be considered. Arendt's list of misdeeds by the Vietnam-era U.S. government ring familiar: an illegal and immoral war accompanied by executive overreach, chronic deception of the public, restrictions on First Amendment freedoms, and a government that forgets that the translation of the slogan *e pluribus unam* that figures on every dollar bill is not *union sacrée*.¹⁶ But why did the kind of disobedient action that she supported not appear in the context of opposition to the Iraq invasion? At one point, she seems to suggest that the American commitment to liberal pluralism had become an ideological commitment that replaces political action by ideological certainty.¹⁷ But elsewhere, after admitting, a bit reluctantly, that not everyone needs to participate in or even be concerned with public affairs, she hopes that a self-selection process that draws out a "true political elite in a country" will produce "a new concept of the state. A council-state.... "¹⁸ And her ever-renewed hope for a renewal of the political spirit only seems to fade (although it doesn't really) in her last public presentation, "Home to Roost" (1975), when she describes a series of disasters in foreign and domestic politics culminating in a "swift decline in political power... [that] is almost unprecedented."¹⁹ The institutions of

---

her bittersweet opinion was: "[v]ery slight, if at all. And yet perhaps after all – in the wake of the next revolution." Arendt, *Crises of the Republic*, pp. 203, 233.

¹⁵ Ibid., p. 102.
¹⁶ Arendt, "Civil Disobedience," p. 94.
¹⁷ Ibid., p. 98.
¹⁸ Arendt, "Thoughts on Politics and Revolution," p. 233.
¹⁹ Hannah Arendt, "Home to Roost," in *Responsibility and Judgment* (New York: Schocken, 2003), p. 259.

liberty that have sustained the American spirit may be exhausted after surviving "longer than any comparable glories in history."[20] Refusing to appeal
to the truths of philosophy,[21] she refuses to abandon the spirit of freedom.
"[W]hile we now slowly emerge from under the rubble of the events of the past
few years," she concludes, "let us not forget these years of aberration lest we
become wholly unworthy of the glorious beginnings two hundred years ago.
When the facts come home to roost, let us try at least to make them welcome.
Let us try not to escape into some utopias – images, theories, or sheer follies. It
was the greatness of this Republic to give due account for the sake of freedom
to the best in men *and to the worst.*"[22] I have italicized this last phrase for
reasons that will become clear in my conclusion. Democracies can and will err;
criticism is essential to their preservation.

Although she tried to avoid the traps of ontology and its historicist correlate of an "escape from politics into history,"[23] stressing always the diversity
and plurality of "the human condition," there is something troubling about
Arendt's constant return to the "spirit" of the American founding. The "facts"
on which she laid such great importance in her political essays play a sub-
sidiary role in *On Revolution*. As a result, it is difficult to know why and
how the Americans have, or have not, met Franklin's challenge – "a republic
if you can keep it"? Have they, as she at times suggests, fallen victim to the
pragmatic antipolitics of the party politicians? Have they, as she often fears,
adopted the French revolutionaries' concern with the social question? Or is
there, as I want to suggest, something about the very nature of democracy that
constantly threatens it from within even as – for the same reason – it reinforces
the power of a democratic polity *and* of its individual citizens? A closer look at
the dynamic history from which Arendt distilled the revolutionary "spirit" can
help to explain also why Arendt's problems cast light on our own, and why

---

[20] Ibid., p. 260.
[21] "If it is in the nature of appearances to hide 'deeper' causes, it is in the nature of speculation
about such hidden causes to hide and to make us forget the stark, naked brutality of facts, of
things as they are." Ibid., p. 261.
[22] Ibid., p. 275. The italics are mine.
[23] Hannah Arendt, "The Concept of History," in *Between Past and Future* (New York: Viking
Press, 1954), p. 83. "The Concept of History" returns repeatedly to the conflict between a
theory of politics and a theory of history. Arendt begins the essay's section on "History and
Politics" as follows: "[A]t the beginning of the modern age everything pointed to an elevation
of political action and political life, and the sixteenth and seventeenth centuries, so rich in new
political philosophies, were still quite unaware of any special emphasis on history as such. Their
concern, on the contrary, was to get rid of the past rather than to rehabilitate the historical
process." Ibid., pp. 75–6. She goes on to argue that "History in its modern version ... though it
failed to save politics itself from the old disgrace, though the single deeds and acts constituting
the realm of politics, properly speaking, were left in limbo, it has at least bestowed upon the
record of past events that shape in earthly immortality to which the modern age necessarily
aspired, but which its acting men no longer dared to claim from posterity." See also her remarks
on Hegel's philosophy of history: "Hegel's transformation of metaphysics into a philosophy of
history was preceded by an attempt to get rid of metaphysics for the sake of a philosophy of
politics." Ibid., p. 76.

ours in turn bring out the power of her understanding of the autonomy of the political. The "age's problems" on which she laid such stress are not defined by a specific historical conjuncture; they belong to a long epoch whose decisive characteristic is that it has repeatedly faced the challenge of maintaining a republican democracy that is constantly threatened by its own antipolitical tendencies.

12.3 Rethinking the American Revolution

Despite her rejection of philosophy,[24] Arendt's stress on the uniquely human ability to covenant, to make promises, and to exchange opinions among a plurality of participants in public life is based on deep-rooted premises that are constantly present in what she called "the human condition." Granted, she is not describing the world from the perspective of a monadic subject; plurality, publicity, and the fundamental concept of action guarantee a dynamic that makes humans capable of coming together to create a type of power that is distinct from the brute force of dumb nature or the antipolitical violence of war. But how does this potential to produce the singular events that are the matter for political thought acquire its historical uniqueness? In the American case, an originary moment,[25] the Mayflower Compact, is said to define the "condition" from which emerged the "spirit" that, in its turn, reappeared in the New England townships, in the Revolution, in the nineteenth-century form of associative life described by Tocqueville, and then in the twentieth-century political action of the civil disobedients. *Plus ça change, plus c'est la même chose.* But: *tant mieux*! I like this vision. But I am not sure how it helps to understand either the political achievements of the American revolution or, more generally, the way that historical experience illuminates contemporary political problems.

The foundation of Arendt's analysis of the American revolutionary spirit is her claim that "the great and, in the long run, perhaps the greatest American innovation in politics as such was the consistent abolition of sovereignty within the body politic of the republic, the insight that in the realm of human affairs sovereignty and tyranny are the same."[26] This question of sovereignty, which was crucial to the movement that led to each new phase of the Revolution, suggests the need to *think* today about the implications of an *event* that marked the culmination of the revolutionary wave: "the revolution of 1800," which

---

[24] For a polemical interpretation, cf. Miguel Abensour, *Hannah Arendt contre la philosophie politique* (Paris: Sens & Tonka, 2006).

[25] I use the concept of "origin" in a specific sense that I illustrate in Dick Howard, *Aux origines de la pensée politique américaine* (Paris: Editions Hachette, 2009). Its systematic foundation is developed in Dick Howard, *From Marx to Kant,* 2nd edition (New York and London: Macmillan Press, 1993). See also Dick Howard, *The Primacy of the Political. A History of Political Thought from the Greeks to the French and American Revolutions* (New York: Columbia University Press, 2010).

[26] Arendt, *On Revolution*, p. 144.

brought the republicans of Thomas Jefferson to power.[27] Reflection on that event, in turn, will suggest an interpretation of what Arendt may have meant by "the age's problems." Although she did make this distinction, the nature of sovereignty in a republican democracy such as the one that was created in the United States differs from the kind of popular sovereignty sought by a democratic republic such as the one that ultimately failed during the French Revolution. The basis of the one is judgment, which accepts the existence of a plurality of perspectives, whereas the other is founded on will, which is unitary. The difference is important, although it is often difficult to maintain in practice.

The American Revolution passed through three phases before its initial impetus was realized, and the classical unitary theory of sovereignty was rejected in favor of a republican-democratic practice. The first period, from 1763 to 1776, posed the challenge of sovereignty. After the British victory in the Seven Years' War, the colonists no longer needed the protection of the mother country; but Britain now needed to reorganize relations among the parts of its enlarged empire and to pay the debts it had incurred in the process. This led to a series of measures that, from the point of view of the colonists, seemed an impingement on their rights and liberties. Often summed up in the lapidary phrase, "No taxation without representation," the stream of pamphlets produced during these years began with attempts at conciliation only to be drawn, inexorably it seems, to articulate what Tom Paine expressed in 1776 as simply "Common Sense."[28] In retrospect, one theoretical argument brought to a head the conflict, making the rupture seem inevitable. John Dickinson, in his *Letters from a Farmer in Pennsylvania*, showed that the local self-government demanded by the colonists implied an *imperium in imperio,* which was a contradiction in political terms. This logical argument carried practical weight because of the experiences of self-management, such as the refusal of the Stamp Act or the nonimportation boycotts on the part of the colonies proved that political legitimation from Britain was not needed for the Americans to run their own lives. Thus was born in practice and theory the revolutionary spirit of republican self-government. This was, however, but a first step; the new spirit had to find an institutional incarnation.

The self-understanding won in the first period had first to be defended once independence was proclaimed. The war began poorly; in the bitter winter of 1776, at Valley Forge, General Washington ordered that Tom Paine's new pamphlet, *The American Crisis*, be read to the troops. "These are the times that try men's souls," wrote Paine, as he denounced "[t]he summer soldier

---

[27] This was the name given it by its contemporaries and repeated by Jefferson himself in 1819. Curiously, historians have neglected its implication. To my knowledge, there exists a single book on the topic, Daniel Sisson, *The American Revolution of 1800* (New York: Knopf, 1974). A collection of essays, James P. P. Horn, Jan Ellen Lewis, and Peter S. Onuf, eds., *The Revolution of 1800: Democracy, Race, and the New Republic* (Charlottesville: University of Virginia Press, 2002), does not pay sufficient attention to its theoretical implications.

[28] Paine's best-selling pamphlet appeared in early 1776; for his part, Jefferson denied any originality in his declaration, which he saw as expressing a shared sense of the colonists.

and the sunshine patriot. . . . " Political events do not just happen; individuals participate when they exercise their judgment, which is neither theoretical nor abstract. Finally, the army held; French help began to arrive. It remained for the Americans to give themselves the institutions for self-government.

As in the first political phase of the revolution, theoretical reflection joined with practical experience. The theory was condensed in the efforts of John Adams, whom Arendt invokes frequently. But while she rightly stresses his debt to the constitutional schemes of Montesquieu, it is Adams' insistence that government must be a "representation in miniature" of the people whom they represent that became crucial to the development of American political self-understanding. The implication of Adams' proposition for the development of a representative republican democracy was made clear by the practical experience of direct democracy in the State of Pennsylvania. For circumstantial reasons,[29] its constitution provided for frequent elections, a weak executive, periodic review of all laws by a "council of censors," among other popular measures. This directly democratic constitution proved to be a recipe for instability that served as a warning that became clear when peace was finally made in 1783. The sovereignty that had been won could not be maintained in the face of postwar economic problems made worse by interstate rivalries that blocked the functioning of the loosely knitted confederal government. The conception of sovereign self-rule for which they fought needed to be modified if the thirteen newly independent states were to remain a "United States."[30]

A new stage in American political thought and practice was reached not only with the creation of the new national Constitution in 1787 but also with its popular ratification. As Arendt recognized, the letter of the institution has to be structured in such a way that the spirit that presided at its origin can be maintained (or renewed). The new understanding that emerged in this third phase is presented in the *Federalist Papers*, which were at once a political act (affecting the ratification process) and a theoretical self-reflection (that retains its actuality). In the present context, two crucial arguments, and their relation, must be properly understood. The first is *Federalist 10*, which defends the possibility of a large republic by recourse to the idea that its safety and vitality will be guaranteed by the presence of competing factions. The second is elaborated in *Federalist 51*, which insists that the safety and vitality of the republic will be guaranteed by the checks and balances among the branches of the new

---

[29] Pennsylvania was a proprietary colony ruled by the Penn family. Those leaders who, in the other colonies, had directed the struggle with Britain had been attempting to give it greater independence by making it a crown colony. As a result, when independence came, they were discredited. An artisan class replaced them in the crucial period of constitution making.

[30] The passage from the Articles of Confederation to the Constitution of 1787 – as well as the different institutional forms adopted in Massachusetts and Pennsylvania – should not be interpreted in terms of economic interests. Arendt offers a stinging rebuke to those who follow Charles Beard's *Economic Interpretation of the Constitution of the United States* (1913). Their insistence on tactics of "unmasking" and denunciations of "hypocrisy" belongs to French-style historiography. Cf. Arendt, *On Revolution*, p. 89.

government. It would seem that if one of these claims is valid, the other is not necessary – or if both are indeed valid, the resulting constitution may limit itself too greatly, making swift and decisive action impossible. However, when put in the context of the debate over sovereignty, the two claims can be seen as saying one and the same thing: *Federalist 10* explains that "the" sovereign people as such does not exist, while *Federalist 51* draws the conclusion that any branch of government that claims to incarnate the vox populi is exceeding the power accorded it by the Constitution.[31] However, because the Constitution provides *both* checks *and* balances, the power of a democratic people will always produce the dynamic that, already in the first phase of the revolution, seeks to realize a democratic self-government at the same time that the separation of powers prevents its complete achievement. The inherent paradox of the American republic is that it solicits popular sovereignty even while making its complete realization impossible, thereby reinforcing each of the competing political institutions.

This historical dynamic reached a temporary resolution with the "revolution of 1800," which marked the first peaceful passage of political power from one party to another. After a bitter campaign foreshadowed by the repressive Alien and Sedition Laws (1798) and heated by reciprocal accusations of "monarchism" and "Jacobinism," Jefferson assumed the presidency and Adams returned quietly home to Massachusetts. Jefferson's inaugural address alluded to the campaign, but insisted significantly that "every difference of opinion is not a difference of principle. We have called by different names brethren of the same principle. We are all Republicans, we are all Federalists."[32] This did not imply that party differences would – or could, or should – be abolished (although the temptation noted by Arendt to replace *e pluribus unam* by a *union sacrée* would appear from time to time).[33] The unity that binds together the republic is what Jefferson calls here a "unity of principle." The nature of that principle was demonstrated in the second moment of the revolution of 1800, the Supreme Court's decision in *Marbury v. Madison* (1803). The court's ruling can be interpreted as arguing that although Jefferson's Republicans were now the majority, their power remained limited; it is the *principles* of the Constitution that constitute the always present but never fully realized,

---

[31] A third argument, that of *Federalist 63*, could be added to reaffirm the point being made here while raising also the question of representative democracy. That argument concerns the legitimacy of a senate in a society that has no constituted aristocracy. The justification offered in *Federalist 63*, which freely admits that American democracy is not direct but representative, depends also on the symbolic nature of the sovereignty that is to be represented by that upper branch of the legislature. For details, cf. *Les origines de la pensée politique américaine*.

[32] Thomas Jefferson, "First Inaugural Address," in *Writings* (New York: Library of America, 1984), p. 493.

[33] In fact, with the presidency of the third of the great Republican presidents, James Monroe (1816–24), America entered what was called the Era of Good Feeling, during which party competition had disappeared at the national level. The result was the "corrupt bargain" by which John Quincy Adams became president. The reaction was not long in coming: the populism that brought Andrew Jackson to power in 1828.

or realizable, sovereignty of the people.[34] It is the Constitution that guarantees that the people are one at the same time that its institutional structure assures that the momentary expression of that unity is realized only through the constant production of difference, debate, and deliberation. The "revolution of 1800" was thus an *event that is more than an event*; it confirms the experience of and reflection on the American Revolution and can be taken as the expression of that "spirit" invoked by Arendt.

This interpretation of the foundation of American democracy in terms of the problem of sovereignty can be developed further. As a "principle," sovereignty is symbolic; but there is an always-present temptation to seek its realization. Because it depends on particular judgments rather than on a unitary sovereign will, the momentary expression of popular sovereignty is always open to negotiation; it can never be incarnated once and for all, yet it is the constant presence without which neither a polity nor the individuals who compose it can subsist. More concretely, the history of American democracy can be interpreted as the constant competition among institutions that claim to represent the will of the sovereign. The actors in the resulting dynamic process are not only the legislative, executive, and judicial branches (and the federal states); new players emerge, be they legitimate, principled political parties or the nonviolent power of political disobedients. Perhaps, too, social groups will claim political power on the basis of their expertise, their specialized interests, or their shared moral values. While one or another institution may come to dominate for a time (even the "social" interests that Arendt denounced as ruining the French Revolution may acquire a dominant power at some historical moments), it is important to recognize that as long as the *principle* remains – as long as sovereignty remains symbolic – there will surely emerge others that will contest the legitimacy and dispute the monopoly that is asserted. Rather than a direct democracy in which the unitary sovereign will of society is expressed in its political institutions – what I have called a "democratic republic" – the Americans created what can be called a "republican democracy" whose institutional structure encourages individuals actively to judge among choices available, and to participate together in the self-determination that is needed to "keep" the republic they have inherited.

12.4 Conclusion: The Age's Problems and Our Own

At the beginning of this rereading of Arendt, provoked by Jonathan Schell, I asked why we have seen no serious civil disobedience in the United States in the wake of the Iraq disaster. One answer is suggested by the way in which a kind of thoughtless liberalism, unthinkingly adopted by neoconservatives as well, became the scarcely contested common sense of the post–Berlin Wall era. This ideology was nicely dissected in a *New York Times* op-ed by Orlando

---

[34] I cannot pursue the theoretical foundations of this argument, which is indebted to the work of Claude Lefort here. Cf. Lefort, "Droits de l'homme et politique."

Patterson.[35] Under the title "God's Gift?" Patterson points out that Americans generally, and the ideologues of the Bush administration in particular, assume that everyone longs for a personal kind of freedom whose realization demands only that oppression be lifted. "Once President Bush was beguiled by this argument he began to sound like a late-blooming schoolboy who had just discovered John Locke, the 17th century founder of liberalism." In his second inaugural speech, Mr. Bush declared "complete confidence in the eventual triumph of freedom... because freedom is the permanent hope of mankind, the hunger in dark places, the longing of the soul." Thus, the president told an Arab American audience, "No matter what your faith, freedom is God's gift to every person in every nation." He drew the implications in another speech that laid out the neoconservative agenda: "We believe that freedom can advance and change lives in the greater Middle East." It would not be unfaithful to Arendt to suggest that this thoughtlessness – this inability to understand that politics is based on plurality and that it is the result of action by the participants – that is "the age's problem." The problem is not the goals of those who govern us; the problem is their and our political naiveté (which goes together with a vengeful moralism) that forgets the interconnectedness of thought and event, authority and action, politics and possibility. The result is an antipolitical politics that dares not admit that it lives as if it enjoyed an eternal present – which is one reason that the Americans were so unprepared once their victorious arms fell silent after the Berlin Wall had fallen.

But the thoughtless liberal – and his neoconservative first-cousin – has a co-conspirator: the "liberal hawk," who thinks too much.[36] Formerly, or perhaps still, on the left side of the spectrum, this antipolitical species came to realize finally that the nightmare of totalitarianism is not just a bump in the progress of history toward smiling tomorrows and, enthusiastic as always, jumped on the bandwagon of the campaign for human rights. Having defied both the orthodox left and the pragmatic peddlers of *Realpolitik*, these political moralists

---

[35] Harvard sociologist Patterson, the author of *Freedom in the Making of Western Culture*, published this article as a guest op-ed in the *New York Times,* December 19, 2006. It is ironic that the first wave of neoconservatives (those of the 1980s) denounced the same naiveté, as Peter Beinart noted in the *New Republic* (January 1–15, 2007). Beinart quotes Jeane Kirkpatrick's famous 1979 essay, "Dictatorships and Double Standards": "[N]o idea holds greater sway in the mind of educated Americans than the belief that it is possible to democratize governments, anytime, anywhere, under any circumstances. This notion is belied by an enormous body of evidence...." Beinart's point is that the critics of the Bush adventurism are returning to the older "reality-based" position.

[36] The liberal hawk is a modern version of the Marxist militant whom Arendt's friend, Harold Rosenberg, defined as "an intellectual who doesn't think." Cf. Harold Rosenberg, "The Heroes of Marxist Science," in *The Tradition of the New* (New York: McGraw-Hill, 1965), p. 184. Since he knows the necessary *telos* of history, he has only to fit the particular events into that pattern (neglecting the distinction between subsumptive and reflective judgment that would be important for Arendt's later work). An example of this style of thought is found in my essay, Dick Howard, "The Use and Abuse of Democracy: Paul Berman's Generational *Bildungsroman*," *Constellations*, 14, 3 (September 2007): 445–53.

were not deceived by the bromides of soft-hearted American liberalism; they were certain that they could maintain their independence (and thus their influence) while supporting critically the unilateral war of the neoconservatives.[37] They were wrong; and they cannot blame Bush or Rumsfeld or criticize faulty execution of their plans any more than fellow-traveling leftists blamed the "cult of personality" or "the bureaucracy" for the failures of the Soviet Union. However, it would be wrong to throw out the human rights baby with the liberal bath water. The "liberal hawks" do not have the answer to what Arendt called "the age's challenges," but they do at least challenge the thoughtless liberals. They too are seeking to renew the ideals that found democracy, despite their mistaken choice of allies.

In this context, the account of the political significance of the historical events of the American Revolution proposed a moment ago returns us to what Arendt called "the age's problems." Every political actor of course claims to advance policies that are the incarnation of the united will of the nation and that its platform will open the path to smiling tomorrows. But they open the door to antipolitics if they fail to recognize that the symbolic – and therefore contested and plural – nature of the sovereign people cannot be reduced to its temporary reality. That, finally, is the crucial lesson to be drawn still today from Arendt's *Origins of Totalitarianism*, which is an attempt to think the most extreme expression of antipolitics. The extreme casts light on the everyday; and it underlines the actuality of Benjamin Franklin's elliptic assertion: "A republic, if you can keep it." That is why the politics of human rights – as a *politics*, not as simply the protection of private freedoms (as Arendt stressed in the discussion of "Civil Disobedience") – is fundamental to a republican democracy. It is an error to think that the "democracy" that triumphed in 1989 was the *solution* to the "age's problems." The nearly two decades that have followed those events make clear – yet again – that democracy is a dangerous game that can easily lose its way when democrats forget how to *think*, which means to recognize the paradox that it is necessary to find the limits of a political process that is by its very nature unlimited. Just before she insisted, in the passage cited earlier, that the "greatest American innovation" was the abolition of sovereignty, Arendt reminded her reader of Montesquieu's "famous insight that even virtue stands in need of limitation and that even an excess of reason is undesirable.... "[38] If too little democracy is certainly a default, the attempt to realize it once and for all (by force, if needed) can prove to be a more grievous threat to democracy itself.

---

[37] Did they still remember Lenin's ironic dictum (in "Left-Wing Communism: An Infantile Disorder"): Critical support is analogous to the rope offered to the hanged man?

[38] Arendt, *On Revolution*, p. 143.

PART IV

JUDGING EVIL

13

Are Arendt's Reflections on Evil Still Relevant?

Richard J. Bernstein

> I have always believed that, no matter how abstract our theories may sound or how consistent our arguments may appear, there are incidents and stories behind them which, at least for ourselves, contain in a nutshell the full meaning of whatever we have to say. Thought itself . . . arises out of the actuality of incidents, and incidents of living experience must remain its guideposts by which it takes its bearings if it is not to lose itself in the heights to which thinking soars, or in the depths to which it must descend.
>
> Hannah Arendt, "Action and the Pursuit of Happiness," 1962

This statement is especially revealing for understanding Hannah Arendt as an independent thinker. We know that many of the incidents that provoked her thinking were directly related to her attempt to comprehend what seemed so outrageous and unprecedented – the novel event of twentieth-century totalitarianism, especially Nazi totalitarianism. In the preface to *The Origins of Totalitarianism*, she declares: "And if it is true that in the final stages of totalitarianism an absolute evil appears (absolute because it can no longer be deduced from humanly comprehensible motives), it is also true that without it we might never have known the truly radical nature of Evil."[1] In 1945, she had already said that "the problem of evil will be the fundamental question of postwar intellectual life in Europe."[2] Few postwar intellectuals directly confronted the problem of evil, but it did become fundamental for Hannah Arendt. She returned to it over and over again, and she was still struggling with it at the time of her death.

But if we take seriously the opening quotation from Arendt, we have to ask whether her reflections on evil are still relevant in our attempts to understand

---

[1] Hannah Arendt, *The Origins of Totalitarianism*, 3rd. ed., rev. (New York: Harcourt, Brace, Jovanovich, 1968), p. ix. (Hereafter abbreviated *OT*.)

[2] Hannah Arendt, *Essays in Understanding, 1930–1954*, edited by Jerome Kohn (New York: Harcourt, Brace, 1994), p. 134.

This article has previously appeared in *Review of Politics* 70, 1 (Winter 2008): 64–76.

a very different world. We may be living through dark times, but we are not living through the *type* of totalitarianism that Arendt experienced. I will argue, however, that Arendt's reflections about evil do have contemporary relevance, and they can serve as a corrective to some of the current careless ways of speaking about evil.

I will focus on three issues. First, I discuss Arendt's warning about introducing absolutes (good and evil) into politics. Second, I want to show how her understanding of radical evil – making human beings superfluous as human beings – is relevant to contemporary issues about statelessness, refugees, and immigration. Finally, I want to show how her reflections on the banality of evil help us to understand evil and responsibility in a globalized bureaucratic world.

Before turning to my main discussion, I want to say something about Arendt as an independent thinker (*Selbstdenker*), especially in her thinking about the question of evil. One of the greatest sources of misunderstanding of Arendt results from the misreading of her as proposing explanatory theories that presumably have a universal scope. The most notorious example is the way in which many of her critics and defenders speak of her *theory* of the banality of evil – as if it were a theory intended to epitomize Nazi evil. Arendt never spoke in this manner; she explicitly denied that the banality of evil is a *theory*. Rather, it was "a phenomenon which stared one in the face at the [Eichmann] trial."[3] To think of Arendt as a theorist *in this sense* – as proposing universal explanatory theories – is to miss what is most distinctive about her thinking. To use a metaphor that she favored, her thinking consists of "thought-trains." These "thought-trains," provoked by incidents of living experience, crisscross and interweave. Sometimes they reinforce each other. But sometimes they also clash with one another, and cannot be easily reconciled.[4]

I begin my discussion with Arendt's remarks about good and evil in *On Revolution*, a text that is frequently neglected in dealing with the more striking themes of radical evil and the banality of evil. In her controversial chapter on "The Social Question," she introduces a brief discussion of Melville's *Billy Budd* and Dostoevsky's "The Grand Inquisitor." She tells us that "if we want to know what absolute goodness would signify for the course of human affairs . . . we had better turn to the poets. . . . At least we learn from them that absolute goodness is hardly any less dangerous than absolute evil. . . . "[5] By absolute goodness and evil, she means goodness and evil "that are beyond ordinary virtue and vice":

Claggart was "struck by an angel of God! Yet the angel must hang!" The tragedy is that law is made for men, and neither for angels nor for devils. Laws and all "lasting

---

[3] Hannah Arendt, *Eichmann in Jerusalem: A Report on the Banality of Evil* (London: Faber and Faber, 1963), p. 287. (Hereafter abbreviated *EJ*.)

[4] See Margaret Canovan's discussion of Arendt's "thought-trains" in her "Introduction" to *Hannah Arendt: A Reinterpretation of her Political Thought* (Cambridge: Cambridge University Press, 1992).

[5] Hannah Arendt, *On Revolution* (New York: Viking Press, 1963), p. 77. (Hereafter abbreviated *OR*.)

institutions" break down not only the onslaught of elemental evil but under the impact of absolute innocence as well. The law, moving between crime and virtue, cannot recognize what is beyond it, and while it has no punishment to mete out to elemental evil, it cannot but punish elemental goodness even if the virtuous man, Captain Vere, recognizes that only the violence of this goodness is adequate to the depraved power of evil. The absolute . . . spells doom to everyone when it is introduced into the political realm. (*OR*, 79)

The absolute spells doom to everyone when it is introduced into the political realm – this might well be taken as the epigraph for the corruption of politics in the United States since 9/11. From that infamous day, we have witnessed an abuse of evil – a simplistic dichotomy that divides the world into absolute evil and good. In my book *The Abuse of Evil*, I have argued that this discourse of good and evil reflects a dangerous mentality – a mentality that is drawn to absolutes, simplistic clear dichotomies, and alleged moral certainties. In the "War on Terror," nuance, subtlety, and fallibility are (mis)taken to be signs of weakness and indecision. But if we think that politics requires judgment, the formulation of judicious opinions, careful discrimination, and deliberation – as Arendt does – then this talk of absolute evil is profoundly antipolitical; it corrupts politics. The fashionable discourse of good and evil is being used as a cynical political weapon to stifle critical thinking and obscure complex issues. To speak and think in this way, to speak about the "evil ones," "the servants of evil," and "the axis of evil," as our political leaders so frequently do, may be highly successful in playing on people's fears and anxieties, but it corrupts politics.

Arendt's reflections on politics remind us of a human potentiality that is rooted in our spontaneity, natality, and plurality, and they serve as a critical standard for judging "really existing politics." Everything that we learn from Arendt about politics teaches us that politics involves (or rather ought to involve) judgment, debate, and the type of tangible public freedom that comes into existence when human beings act and speak together as equals. Whatever criticism we may want to make about the limitations of her conception of politics, Arendt does capture something that is vital for any genuine conception of democratic politics. Consequently, the first lesson we might learn from Arendt is to be on our guard when absolutes – absolute evil and good – are introduced into politics. Samantha Power eloquently describes the contrast between Arendt's more thoughtful responses to evil and the new stark opposition of evil (black) and good (white):

Arendt used the phrase "radical evil" to describe totalitarianism, and this idea has been brought back in circulation. Yet while Arendt did not allow such branding to deter her from exploring the sources of that evil, the less subtle minds who invoke the concept of today do so to mute criticisms of their responses. (Who, after all, can be against combating evil?)

But sheltering behind black-and-white characterizations is not only questionable for moral and epistemological reasons, it poses a practical problem because it blinds us from understanding and thus undermines our long-term ability to prevent and surmount what we don't know and most fear. "Evil," whether radical or banal, is met most often with unimaginativeness. Terrorism is a threat that demands a complex and elaborate effort to distinguish the sympathizers from the militants and to keep its converts to a minimum. Terrorism also requires understanding how our past policies helped to give rise to such venomous grievances.[6]

Although absolutes are disastrous when they are introduced into the political realm, it does not follow that we should neglect the character of evil in our time. Arendt thought it was unavoidable, and I agree with her. But it requires that we carefully rethink what we mean by evil. And this is what she sought to do in her struggle to come to grips with an unprecedented radical evil of totalitarianism. I think there are actually several different thought-trains that she follows in her discussions of radical evil, but I want to concentrate on the phenomenon that she takes to be at heart of radical evil: "making human beings as human beings superfluous."

In 1951, before *The Origins* appeared in bookstores, Arendt sent a copy to Karl Jaspers so it would arrive for his birthday. Delighted to receive the book, he quickly read the preface and conclusion, and dashed off a note with a cryptic question: "Hasn't Jahwe faded too far out of sight?" In her next letter to Jaspers, Arendt wrote that this question "has been on my mind for weeks now without my being able to come up with an answer to it." Jaspers' question did provoke the following response about radical evil:

Evil has proved to be more radical than expected. In objective terms, modern crimes are not provided for in the Ten Commandments. Or: the Western Tradition is suffering from the preconception that the most evil things human beings can do arise from the vice of selfishness. Yet we know that the greatest evils or radical evil has nothing to do anymore with such humanly understandable, sinful motives. What radical evil really is I don't know, but it seems to me it somehow has to do with the following phenomenon: making human beings as human beings superfluous (not using them as means to an end, which leaves their essence as humans untouched and impinges only on their human dignity; rather, making them superfluous as human beings). This happens as soon as all unpredictability – which, in human beings, is the equivalent of spontaneity – is eliminated. And all this in turn arises from – or, better goes along with – the delusion of the omnipotence (not simply with the lust for power) of an individual man. If an individual man qua man were omnipotent, then there is in fact no reason why men in the plural should exist at all....[7]

Arendt presents a three stage analytic model of the "logic" of total domination – one that has rarely been surpassed for its trenchant insight. She claims that the concentration and extermination camps are the "most consequential institution of totalitarian rule" (*OT*, 441); they "serve as laboratories in which

[6] Samantha Power, "Hannah Arendt's Lesson," *New York Review of Books*, 5, 17 (April 29, 2004): 37.

[7] Hannah Arendt and Karl Jaspers, *Correspondence, 1926–1969*, edited by Lotte Kohler and Hans Saner, translated by Robert and Rita Kimber (New York: Harcourt, Brace, 1995), p. 166.

the fundamental belief of totalitarianism that everything is possible is being verified" (*OT*, 437).

"The first essential step on the road to total domination is to kill the juridical person in man" (*OT*, 447). This started long before the Nazis established the death camps. Arendt is referring to the legal restrictions that stripped Jews (and other groups such as homosexuals and gypsies) of their juridical rights. "The aim of an arbitrary system is to destroy the civil rights of the whole population, who ultimately become just as outlawed in their own country as the stateless and the homeless. The destruction of man's rights, the killing of the juridical person in him, is a prerequisite for dominating him entirely."

"The next decisive step in the preparation of living corpses is the murder of the moral person in man" (*OT*, 451). The SS, who supervised the camps, were perversely brilliant in their attempt to break down human solidarity:

When a man is faced with the alternative of betraying and thus murdering his friends or sending his wife and children, for when he is in every sense responsible, to their death; and when even suicide would mean the immediate murder of his own family, how is he to decide? The alternative is no longer between good and evil, but between murder and murder. Who could solve the moral dilemma of the Greek mother, who was allowed by the Nazis to choose which of her three children should be killed? (*OT*, 452)

But this is not yet the worst. There is a third step on the way to total domination – and it is here that we come face to face with radical evil:

After the murder of the moral person and the annihilation of the juridical person, the destruction of individuality is almost always successful. . . . For to destroy individuality is to destroy spontaneity, man's power to begin something new out of his own resources, something that cannot be explained on the basis of reactions to environment and events. (*OT*, 455)

The camps served the ghastly experiment of seeking to eliminate any vestige of human spontaneity and plurality. They sought to transform human beings into something that is not quite human – beings who were at once human and nonhuman. This is what Arendt took to be the most extreme form of unprecedented radical evil; this is what she meant by making human beings superfluous as human beings. Arendt is referring to those *Musselmänner*, the living corpses that were later to be so graphically described by Primo Levi:

Their life is short, but their number is endless; they are the Musselmänner, the drowned, they form the backbone of the camp, an anonymous mass, continually renewed and always identical, of non-men who march and labor in silence, the divine spark dead in them, already too empty to really suffer. One hesitates to call them living: one hesitates to call their death death, in the face of which they have no fear, as they are too tired to understand.

They crowd my memory with their faceless presence, and if I could enclose all the evil of our time in one image, I would choose this image which is familiar to me: an emaciated man, with head dropped and shoulders curved, on whose face and in whose eyes not a trace of thought is to be seen.[8]

By dwelling on the horrors Arendt came to the shocking realization that the not-so-hidden aim of totalitarianism is the deliberate attempt to make human beings qua human superfluous, to transform human beings in order to eliminate their humanity – to destroy their plurality, spontaneity, natality, and individuality. This is the closest she came to grasping radical evil – a new unprecedented phenomenon that confronts us with its overpowering reality and breaks down all standards we know. Mass murder, genocide, torture, and terror have happened before in history. But the aim of totalitarianism is not oppression, not even "total domination" if this still is understood as the total domination of *human beings*. Totalitarianism, as Arendt understands it, strives to obliterate people's humanity.

If this is what Arendt means by radical evil, then the question arises: Is it relevant for us today? Since the time of the Shoah, we have lived through genocides, mass murders, and sadistic tortures. But this is not the same as the systematic attempt to transform human nature into something that is nonhuman, the condition that Arendt analyzes and that Primo Levi so graphically describes. Yet radical evil is the final stage of the process of making human beings superfluous. And the theme of superfluousness is one that runs through *The Origins* like a red thread. She takes up the theme of superfluousness in "The Decline of the Nation-State and the End of the Rights of Man." She tells us that statelessness is "the newest mass phenomenon in contemporary history, and the existence of an ever-growing new people comprised of stateless persons, the most symptomatic group in contemporary politics" (*OT*, 277). Arendt makes the disturbing but extremely perceptive observation that "if we consider the different groups among the stateless it appears that every political event since the end of the First World War inevitably added a new category to those who lived outside the pale of law" (*OT*, 277). What Arendt wrote more than fifty years ago is even more relevant in our own time. Arendt, who was stateless for eighteen years, poignantly highlights the plight of the stateless human being – the superfluous nonperson – who has no legitimate legal or political status. To be a stateless person is to be "unprotected by any specific law or political convention." She argued that the emergence of masses of refugees was one of the most intractable problems of the twentieth century – and it is turning out to be just as intractable, perhaps even more so, in the twenty-first century. In the final pages of *The Origins*, she presciently tells us that "totalitarian solutions may well survive the fall of totalitarian regimes in the form of strong temptations which will come up whenever it seems impossible to alleviate political, social, and economic misery in a manner worthy of man" (*OT*, 458).

[8] Primo Levi, *Survival in Auschwitz and the Awakening: Two Memoirs*, translated by Stuart Woolf (New York: Summit Books, 1986), p. 90. See also Giorgio Agamben's discussion of the *Musselmann* in *Remnants of Auschwitz: The Witness and the Archive*, translated by Danile Heller-Roazen (New York: Zone, 1999).

This recurring creation of masses of refugees and stateless nonpersons is at the heart of Arendt's sharp critique of appeals to abstract Rights of Man – the inalienable rights that a human being is supposed to possess qua human being. "The Rights of Man, after all, had been defined as 'inalienable' because they were supposed to be independent of all governments, but it turned out that the moment human beings lacked their own government and had to fall back upon their minimum rights, no authority was left to protect them and no institution was willing to guarantee them" (*OT*, 291–2). This is the condition where one becomes superfluous – a situation that is precarious and extremely dangerous. This is why Arendt argued that the most fundamental right is "the right to have rights" – the right to belong to a political community that will protect and guarantee one's rights as a citizen:

The calamity of the rightless is not that they are deprived of life, liberty, and the pursuit of happiness, or of equality before the law and freedom of opinion – formulas which were designed to solve problems *within* given communities – but they no longer belong to any community whatsoever. Their plight is not that they are not equal before the law, but that no law exists for them; not that they are oppressed but that nobody wants even to oppress them. Only in the last stage of a rather lengthy process is their right to life threatened; only if they remain perfectly "superfluous" if nobody can be found to "claim" them, may their lives be in danger. (*OT*, 295–6)

The problems of the stateless, refugees, "illegal immigrants," and even of legal immigrants who are treated as second-class citizens (or even as noncitizens) have become more diversified, complex, and fraught with explosive tensions in our time. We should take to heart Arendt's warning about what can happen when masses of people are suddenly rendered superfluous. Unless we find ways to address this phenomenon in humane ways that recognize as fundamental "the right to have rights," then totalitarian solutions to the problem of superfluousness will remain a strong temptation.[9]

In her famous exchange with Gershom Scholem after the publication of *Eichmann in Jerusalem*, Arendt wrote:

Indeed my opinion now is that evil is never "radical," that it is only extreme, and that it possesses neither depth nor any demonic dimension. It can overgrow and lay waste the whole world precisely because it spreads like a fungus over the surface. It is "thought-defying," as I said, because thought tries to reach some depth, to go to the roots, and the moment it concerns itself with evil, it is frustrated because there is nothing.[10]

In *Hannah Arendt and the Jewish Question*, I have argued that Arendt's statement is misleading insofar as it suggests that she repudiated her claims about the way she described radical evil in *The Origins* – the making of human beings

---

[9] See Jacques Derrida's perceptive discussion of the relevance of Arendt's discussion of statelessness and asylum in *On Cosmopolitanism and Forgiveness* (New York: Routledge), 2001.

[10] Hannah Arendt, *The Jew as Pariah*, edited by Ron H. Feldman (New York: Grove Press, 1978), pp. 250–1.

superfluous. She *never* repudiated her original analysis – not even in this passage. Rather, she questions whether it is appropriate to call this phenomenon "radical evil." The literal meaning of "radical" is of or from the roots, which suggests that evil is something deep and buried. But she came to believe that the metaphor of roots is misleading; a more appropriate metaphor is fungus, because it spreads quickly on the surface. The banality of evil is not only compatible with the radical evil of making human beings superfluous, it enables us to understand how desk murderers such as Eichmann accomplished this with such efficiency.[11]

What precisely is the banality of evil? Is this notion still relevant for coming to grips with evil today? The phrase the "banality of evil" is a primary reason that *Eichmann in Jerusalem* provoked – and still provokes – so much controversy. It might have been better if Arendt had used a less provocative expression such as the one suggested by Seyla Benhabib: the "routinization of evil."[12] But "the banality of evil" has a shocking power to compel us to stop and think – to face up to the new forms that evil has taken in our time.

Before turning to what Arendt means by the banality of evil, and why it is so relevant for us today, let me remind you of a few facts. The phrase "the banality of evil" appears only once in her report on Eichmann: in the final sentence of her main text, just before her epilogue. She quotes what were reported to be Eichmann's last words before he went to the gallows. "After a short while, gentlemen, *we shall all meet again*. Such is the fate of all men. Long live Germany, long live Argentina, long live Austria. *I shall not forget them*." Arendt then comments:

In the face of death, he had found the cliché used in funeral oratory. Under the gallows, his memory played him the last trick; he was "elated" and he forgot that this was his own funeral.

It was as though in those last minutes he was summing up the lesson that this long course in human wickedness had taught us – the lesson of the fearsome, word-and-thought-defying *banality of evil*. (*EJ*, 252; emphasis in the original)

That's it! – That's the only mention of "the banality of evil" in the entire report. When her report was published as a book, she did use the subtitle "A Report on the Banality of Evil," but this subtitle did not even appear in the original *New Yorker* articles.

One of Arendt's clearest statements about "the banality of evil" occurs in her 1971 lecture "Thinking and Moral Considerations":

Some years ago, reporting the trial of *Eichmann in Jerusalem*, I spoke of the "banality of evil" and meant with this no theory or doctrine but something quite factual, the phenomenon of evil deeds, committed on a gigantic scale, which could not be traced to

---

[11] See my discussion of radical evil and the banality of evil in Richard J. Bernstein, *Hannah Arendt and the Jewish Question* (Cambridge: Polity Press, 2005).

[12] See Seyla Benhabib, "Hannah Arendt and the Redemptive Power of Narrative," *Social Research*, 57, 1 (Spring 1990): 185.

any particularity of wickedness, pathology, or ideological conviction in the doer, whose only personal distinction was perhaps extraordinary shallowness. However monstrous the deeds were, the doer was neither monstrous nor demonic, and the only specific characteristic one could detect in his past as well as in his behavior during the trial and the preceding police examination was something entirely negative: it was not stupidity but a curious, quite authentic inability to think.[13]

Arendt calls into question one of our oldest and most entrenched moral and legal convictions: namely, that people who do evil deeds must have evil motives and intentions. They are vicious, sadistic, wicked, demonic, pathological. But Eichmann was not a pathological, sadistic monster – the way in which the prosecutor sought to portray him. He was "terrifyingly normal." "He was a new type of criminal who commits his crimes in circumstances that make it well-nigh impossible to know or feel that he is doing wrong" (*EJ*, 276). His deeds were monstrous, and he deserved to hang, but his motives and intentions were banal. So "the banality of evil" is not an expression that refers to Eichmann's *deeds*; there was nothing banal about these. Rather, "the banality of evil" refers to his *motives* and *intentions*. Historians have raised many questions about the factual accuracy of Arendt's portrait of Eichmann, but I do not think that this diminishes her main point – that normal people with banal motives and intentions can commit horrendous crimes and evil deeds.[14] Susan Neiman sums up why *Eichmann in Jerusalem* makes such an important contribution to our understanding of evil in the contemporary world:

Auschwitz embodied evil that confuted two centuries of modern assumptions about intention.

Those assumptions identify evil and evil intention so thoroughly that denying the latter is normally viewed as a way of denying the former. Where evil intention is absent, we may hold agents liable for the wrongs they inflict, but we view them as matters of criminal negligence. Alternatively, anyone who denies criminal intention is present in a particular action is thought to exonerate the criminal. This is the source of the furor that still surrounds Arendt's *Eichmann in Jerusalem*.... The conviction that guilt requires malice and forethought led most readers to conclude that Arendt denied guilt

---

[13] Hannah Arendt, "Thinking and Mortal Considerations: A Lecture," *Social Research*, 38, 3 (Fall 1971): 417.

[14] Christopher R. Browning, the eminent historian of the Holocaust, sums up the judgment of many historians when he writes: "I consider Arendt's concept of the 'banality of evil' a very important insight for understanding many of the perpetuators of the Holocaust, but not Eichmann himself. Arendt was fooled by Eichmann's strategy of self-representation in part because there were so many perpetrators of the kind he was pretending to be." In his recent biography of Eichmann, David Cesarani sets out to show how mistaken Arendt was in her characterization of Eichmann. David Cesarani, *Eichmann: His Life and Crimes* (London: William Heinemann, 2004). But ironically, as Barry Gewen remarks in his recent review; "Cesarani believes his details add up to a portrait at odds with Arendt's banal bureaucrat, but what is striking is how far his research goes to reinforce her fundamental arguments." Barry Gewen, "A Portrait of Eichmann as an Ordinary Man," *International Herald Tribune*, May 12, 2006.

because she denied malice and forethought – though she often repeated that Eichmann was guilty, and was convinced that he ought to hang.[15]

Although Arendt did not think that Eichmann was a satanic monster, he was *responsible* for his deeds; he was not a mere bureaucratic cog in the Nazi death machine. Arendt categorically rejects what she called "the cog theory." In response to the claim that one was merely a cog in a machine, it is always appropriate to ask: "And why did you become a cog or continue to be a wheel in such circumstances?"[16]

Why is the concept of "the banality of evil" so controversial? I suggest that the reason is related to Arendt as an independent thinker. She was convinced that with the event of totalitarianism, there had been a radical break in tradition. We can no longer rely on traditional categories, concepts, and standards to comprehend what has happened. The task is to forge news concepts and categories that illuminate the darkness of our times. We have to learn to break away from simplistic dichotomies where it is falsely assumed that if we deny that someone has deliberate evil intentions, we are affirming his innocence. We have to learn to understand how someone may not have evil intentions and be "terrifyingly normal," and yet be accountable and responsible for his or her deeds. We have to learn "to think without banisters" (*Denken ohne Geländer*). But when someone really challenges our conventional and deeply entrenched ways of thinking, it is threatening – it seems to leave us without any support. Arendt shows us that if we really want to understand what is new and distinctive about evil in our time, we cannot rely on our traditional notion that evil deeds are committed by persons with evil intentions, that monstrous deeds are caused by monsters. Ironically, this is a reassuring and comforting idea because it removes evil from everyday, normal life – we presumably "know" that *we*, at least, are not monsters! I believe that this *regression*, where our enemies are demonized, is all too characteristic of the rhetoric of our political leaders. Remember that on 9/11, in his address to the nation, George W. Bush said, "Today our nation saw evil, the very worst of human nature." And it behooves us to remember that Bush's rhetoric is matched by Islamic militants. On April 7, 2004, Moktada al-Sadr declared, "America has shown its evil intentions and the proud Iraqi people cannot accept it."

Arendt emphatically did *not* think that there is an Eichmann in each of us, but she might well agree with David Cesarani when he writes in the conclusion of his biography:

The *génocidaire* has become a common feature of humanity and to that extent Eichmann is typical rather than aberrant. This is not the same as saying that "we are all potential Eichmanns"; rather, that the matrices which generate the perpetrators of atrocity and

[15] Susan Neiman, *Evil in Modern Thought: An Alternative History of Philosophy* (Princeton: Princeton University Press, 2004), pp. 271–2.

[16] Hannah Arendt, "Personal Responsibility under Dictatorship," *Listener*, August 6, 1964, p. 186.

genocide have multiplied. In these circumstances normal people can and do commit mass murder or engineer it. . . .

Now, in the twenty-first century, in a world awash with refugees and the victims of "ethnic cleansing", when racism and fanaticism continue to dominate politics, and when international tribunals are trying the foot soldiers of genocide and their commanders in the military and political echelons, Eichmann appears more and more like a man of our time.[17]

This is the primary lesson of the banality of evil. One does not have to be a monster, a sadist, or a vicious person to commit horrendous, evil deeds. Normal people in their everyday lives, "decent citizens," even respectable political leaders, who are convinced of the righteousness of their cause, can commit monstrous deeds. The bureaucratic and technological conditions of modernity make this a much more likely and dangerous phenomenon. But, as Arendt emphasizes, this does *not* mitigate the accountability and responsibility of those who commit such deeds. Arendt wants us to confront honestly the "paradox" that even though normal persons may commit horrendous deeds even without deliberate intention, they are nevertheless fully responsible for these deeds and must be held accountable.

I have stated that the current fashionable discourse of good and evil is actually a *regression* to a primitive and mythic conception of evil where we divide the world in a simple (and simplistic) dichotomy between forces of evil and the force of good. The evil ones are demonic and satanic, but the good guys are innocent and virtuous. This is a quasi-Manichean world where there is the great battle of Good versus Evil. It is quasi-Manichean because, unlike the Manicheans, who thought that Good and Evil were equiprimordial, and engaged in an eternal struggle, our mythology – so pervasive in our Hollywood movies, popular culture, and political rhetoric – is one where we "know" that Good will ultimately triumph over Evil. Understanding evil in this way mystifies and obscures the new face of evil in a post-totalitarian world. Today when we are discovering the extent to which policies made in Washington encourage the terrible abuses that have taken place in Abu Ghraib and many other prisons, when we learn how lawyers in the White House, sitting at their desks, devise "sophisticated" justifications to "legalize" torture, the banality of evil takes on new meaning.

Arendt compels us to face up to difficult and painful questions about the meaning of evil in the contemporary world, the ease with which human beings are made superfluous, the feebleness of the "voice of conscience," the subtle forms of complicity and cooperation that "go along" with murderous deeds. These, unfortunately, are not issues restricted to Nazi horrors. They are still very much with us, and demand that we struggle with them over and over again.

It is important to remember that even though Arendt was critical – even scornful – of the melodramatic chief prosecutor, Gideon Hauser; she expressed

---

[17] Cesarani, *Eichmann*, p. 368.

the highest regard for the judges who tried Eichmann. She endorsed their judgment about Eichmann's responsibility. She wrote, "What the judgment had to say on this point was more than correct, it was the truth." I want to conclude with the passage from their judgment that she cited. The judges were, of course, speaking about Eichmann. But what they have to say about *responsibility* is as relevant today as it was for Eichmann:

[In] such an enormous and complicated crime as the one we are now considering, wherein many people participated, on various levels and in various modes of activity – the planners, the organizers, and those executing the deeds, according to their various ranks – there is not much point is using ordinary concepts of counseling and soliciting to commit a crime. For these crimes were committed en masse, not only in regard to the number of victims, but also in regard to the numbers of those who perpetuated the crime, and the extent to which any one of the many criminals was close or remote from the actual killer of the victim means nothing, as far as the measure of responsibility is concerned. On the contrary, in general *the degree of responsibility increases as we draw further away from the man who uses the fatal instrument with his own hands* (EJ, 246–7, Arendt's emphasis).

14

Banality Reconsidered

Susan Neiman

I would like to consider a phenomenon I have never encountered with any other work of philosophy: the violent – no, hysterical – reaction to *Eichmann in Jerusalem*, which accompanies a misreading of the text so crude and grotesque you would think it could only occur in the most ill trained of superficial readers.[1] The misreading does occur among such readers, but since I have often encountered it among masterful scholars, whose patience and erudition illuminated difficult texts for the rest of us – and even among masterful scholars who knew and revered Arendt personally – it cannot be a reaction born of sloppiness. The outrage that the book continues to produce, rooted in the claim that Arendt excused the criminals and blamed the victims, is so widespread that they point to something deeper.

Arendt herself was sufficiently hurt and bewildered by the reactions to beat a cheap retreat: The book was not a theory, nor did it propose a new analysis or understanding of evil; it was simple description. She wrote *Eichmann in Jerusalem* as a journalist doing nothing but reporting what she saw. In saying this, she was assuming at best an air of naiveté that ill became her. *Eichmann in Jerusalem* is not a piece of journalism; it is one of the best pieces of moral philosophy that the twentieth century has to offer. (Let us not get distracted by the fact that it was originally written for the *New Yorker* – Kant wrote fifteen of his most important texts for the *Berlinische Monatschrift*, the eighteenth-century version of the *New York Review*). The problems with *Eichmann in Jerusalem* are not, as sometimes suggested, problems of expression. Arendt's command of language was something awesome – particularly daunting in view of the fact that English was her fifth language. Nobody is perfect, but anyone capable of the range of irony and passion her writings invariably display is unlikely to make such a gross error of tone that would make the offending parts of the book simply mistaken.

[1] Hannah Arendt, *Eichmann in Jerusalem* (Viking Press: New York, 1963).

Briefly, I will argue that the book is so easily misread because it makes two large moves, which are conceptually revolutionary. They may be easy to miss because something in both of them is deeply archaic – but not, for that reason, false. The first move is a revival of theodicy. Elsewhere I've argued that *Eichmann in Jerusalem* is the closest thing to a modernist theodicy the twentieth century has produced, so I will sketch those arguments in briefest detail.[2] One thing that makes the book so hard to read is the conviction that theodicy has not only gone out of style, but out of taste. If, as Adorno suggested, it might be barbaric to write poetry after Auschwitz, must not writing theodicy be positively savage? Arendt would have agreed, if theodicy is understood in the terms Hegel took over from Leibniz: showing Auschwitz and even lesser evils to be necessary parts of God's plan for the best or most reasonable world as a whole would have been a project Arendt fought with all the resources at her command. Here as in many points she remained a Kantian: "Finally we shall be left with the only alternative there is in these matters – we can either say with Hegel: *Die Weltgeschichte ist das Weltgericht*, leaving the ultimate judgment to success, or we can maintain with Kant the autonomy of the minds of men and their possible independence of things as they are or have come into being."[3] Still she spent much of her life looking for the right formulation of the relationship we ought to have toward the world. "At home in it" is a bit too cozy for one so aware of its abysses; in considering titles, she must have decided that "in love with it" was too redolent with pathos or kitsch. (Everything sounds better in Latin.) Her best expression of the task occurs in a dedication to Jaspers: "to find my way around in reality without selling my soul to it the way people in earlier times sold their souls to the devil."[4] To find her way about in reality, she had to understand how a creature like Eichmann could be part of it.

It is this effort that explains critics' sense that Arendt was not simply offering description or engaging in simple journalism. Despite her protestations, she was clearly defending something. The object of defense was not, however, Adolf Eichmann, but a world that contained him. Young-Bruehl's choice of the phrase *Amor Mundi* to express the attitude that Arendt succeeded to convey in her life and her work was exact. It was this that allowed Mary McCarthy to write the most insightful comment that *Eichmann in Jerusalem* ever received. She wrote to Arendt that reading the book produced in her an exhilaration akin to what she felt when hearing *Figaro* or *The Messiah*, "both of which are concerned with redemption." Arendt's reply was revealing: "You were the only reader to understand what otherwise I

---

[2] "Theodicy in Jerusalem," in Steven Ascheim, ed., *Hannah Arendt in Jerusalem* (Berkeley: University of California Press, 2001).

[3] Hannah Arendt, *Thinking* (New York: Harcourt Brace Jovanovich, 1971), p. 216.

[4] Hannah Arendt, "Dedication to Jaspers," in *Essays in Understanding*, edited by Jerome Kohn (New York: Harcourt, Brace, Jovanovich, 1994), p. 213.

have never admitted – namely that I wrote this book in a curious state of euphoria."[5]

Arendt says McCarthy is the only person to have understood her, which means that if we want to understand the book ourselves, we had better try to summon up our experiences of listening to Mozart and Handel. McCarthy says they are both about redemption: Let us call this the idea that the world has, for all its horrors, enough bits in it that are good, or glorious, to make us believe that Creation on the whole is a gift. Arendt herself, playing on the Jewish legend that thirty-six righteous people, unknown and unnoticed, are the constant presence that holds the world together, writes this way about Anton Schmidt, a German sergeant executed in Poland for helping Jewish partisans, in the most moving and memorable passage of the book. Anton Schmidt and Hannah Arendt: a little of the good and the glorious is enough to convince us that the world is not a mistake. Ten righteous people, after all, would have saved Sodom and Gomorrah.

Eichmann in Jerusalem can function as a modernist theodicy, hence be redemptive in the ways McCarthy described, because it offers an account of evil that leaves Creation unscathed. Evil exists, to be sure, but it is not a necessary part of the world, or even a particularly deep one. Nor is it, therefore, a necessary part of the human condition: There is no such thing as original sin. Arendt's thinking was thus much like that of Rousseau, whose Second Discourse offered a naturalist account of the decline from the state of nature (a state marked not by goodness, contrary to many caricatures, but simply by moral neutrality). By describing a series of apparently harmless and certainly thoughtless procedures that resulted in a war of all against all, Arendt describes the development of an individual who began as nothing worse than a common careerist and ended as an engineer of the Final Solution.

The very offering of such an account challenges one of our deepest assumptions about evil, namely, that it has to be inexplicable. If you understand it, it cannot be evil. Religion plays a shadowy role in supporting this assumption, though it is often expressed by people who are resolute atheists. Where does the assumption come from? We are all partly convinced by the idea that explaining something is equivalent to justifying it; an idea that's furthered by the fact that its denial is always expressed on the defensive (and always for some reason in French: *tout comprendre n'est pas tout pardonner*). Evil is, by the only definition which comes close to commanding consensus, that which can never be justified. But why should we be certain that understanding it is tantamount to justifying it?

One reason for doing so is an unholy aura of the sacred and the erotic that surrounds many discussions of evil. If evil is as evil as it should be, it is too big and too deep for human understanding. So Shakespeare's Iago and Melville's

5 Hannah Arendt, *Between Friends: The Correspondence of Hannah Arendt*, edited by Mary McCarty (New York: Harcourt, Brace, Jovanovich, 1995), p. 168.

Claggart are archetypes of evil precisely because they are portrayed as black holes – not empty (the density is only suggested, but it is mind-boggling), but impenetrable. There is an inside, but we cannot ever see it. But classical literature presents other models of evil, in which emptiness is a central feature, most strikingly in portraits of the devil himself. Both Faust's Mephisto and the devil in Dostoyevsky's *The Brothers Karamazov* display characters and faults that are so common, and commonplace, that the notion of the diabolical drops out. Goethe's spirit who always denies is not a rebel but a pedant; Dostoevsky's demon is a whining flunky, who specializes not in tempting young idealists but in ridiculing them.

Arendt picks up this strand of tradition in calling Eichmann a clown, and using all her considerable command of the art of irony to underline his self-pitying, self-contradictory, and absurdly pretentious descriptions of what he was and did. Goethe's devil is a much more useful model than Milton's, for the latter is appealing enough to attract followers. He is grand and he is bold and he has the sort of power that makes wicked into a synonym for really cool. Who, by contrast, longs to imitate Mephisto? Torn as he is, the only figure of size and stature in the drama is Faust himself – as Mephisto often enough remarks, with the clever whimpering tinge of envy that is his major trademark. Arendt quoted Brecht as saying that comedy is a better form for dealing with evil than tragedy, for tragedy reinforces the apocalyptic quality that lends evil an air of the sublime. Both Brecht and Arendt were prescient: The fascination with fascism, and not just fascism, that twists evil into an eerie industry is the result of the Gnosticism that Arendt brilliantly – in 1961 – described as the most dangerous, attractive, and widespread heresy of the postwar world. It was in the interest of fighting that heresy that she used the fungus metaphor in the famous letter to Gershom Scholem.

If the first thing that makes this book's message major, and difficult to read, is the way it denies the assumption that evil must be unintelligible, the second is the way it denies that evil must be intentional. This denial was so radical and counterintuitive that it led to the worst misunderstandings. We have become so convinced that doing evil means intending to do so that we take Arendt's claim that Eichmann became an architect of the Holocaust without intending it to mean she was letting him off the hook – and in so doing even implying that the Holocaust itself was not really evil.

By describing Eichmann as the thoughtless clown who could be an object of disgust or contempt, but not shock or awe, Arendt was thought to excuse him. For here was a man who did not really mean it: He had nothing against Jews, he would have preferred not to be involved in murdering them, and the one time he actually watched somebody else do so he swore that it made him sick. Did not this sort of description, so very far from the proud and ruthless Nazi we love to hate, serve as a form of apology? Now for all Arendt's desire to remove evil from the realm of the demonic, there are in fact some perfectly acceptable satanic models: Goethe's and Dostoevsky's devils, unlike Milton's or the Middle Ages', have most of the features she found in Eichmann. But if she managed to forget this in the heat of the controversy, it's no wonder her critics did too. To compound the offense, Arendt devoted several pages to the ways in which the Jewish Councils contributed to executing the Final Solution. The apparently gratuitous blaming of the victims next to an apparently incomprehensible excusing of the criminals touched a nerve that has been hurting ever since.

Nobody really asked, however, why in the world Arendt should bring up the question of whether and how the Jewish Councils bear some share of complicity in the Holocaust in a book devoted to the Eichmann trial. She herself attacked the prosecutor for asking victims why they failed to resist – a question she called cruel and stupid. Those Arendt commentators who cannot imagine her being either cruel or stupid have thrown up their hands at the introduction of the subject, for there seems to be no good reason for talking of the Jewish Councils in this context at all.

This is true only so long as we regard the book as a theory-laden form of journalism rather than a practice-laden form of philosophy. If we view it as philosophy, the question of Arendt's use of the Jewish Councils solves itself. They are there for exactly the same reason Eichmann himself is there: to show that not intention but judgment is the heart and soul of moral action. What you mean matters far less than you suppose. The world will hold you accountable for what you do since it is what you do, not what you mean, that affects it. If the structure of *Eichmann in Jerusalem* itself revives a philosophical project last tried by Hegel, the means by which it does so rejects the ethics we have come to take for granted since Kant. The project I have called modern theodicy – showing how the world can be affirmed, even loved, without denying the evil within it – depends on showing that much, if not all, of the world's evil can be understood. This means it must be explicable without reference to mysteriously evil intentions.

Now even those who reject other parts of Kant's ethics tend to agree that the only thing good in itself is a good will. Arendt argues that when we think about the Holocaust, good will becomes irrelevant, for an astonishing number of people had it and even many of those involved in the Final Solution had wills that were not worse than outstandingly mediocre. A small number of racist fanatics proposed the Final Solution, and a small number of sadists took advantage of the opportunities the camps afforded. But neither would have gotten anywhere were it not for the support of millions whose intentions spanned the gamut between moderately low to positively good. Let us take them in turn. However you look at Eichmann, and however you look at intention, what he willed was not that Jews should be murdered in millions – he testified over and over that he'd have preferred other solutions to the "Jewish Question" – but that he do his job and get ahead. Shutting one's eyes to fascism, and even profiting from it, is not the same thing as willing the chain of events that ended at Auschwitz. So much the worse for intention.

Take those in Germany who called themselves inner émigrés. For one reason or another, they stayed in the country when the fascists took it over, but they were, they claimed, always opposed to them. Suppose, for the sake of argument, that both the inner émigrés and the far more culpable Eichmann are sincere and authentic: They mean what they say, and their reports about their inner states are completely true. All this does is to show us how little our inner states count.

Once we see this, it is easy to see why Arendt introduced discussion of the Jewish Councils, whose members acted from intentions that were not even moderately benign, but positively admirable. They proceeded in what they believed to be the best interests of the Jewish people, intending to save as many lives and prevent as much pain as they possibly could. Yet by cooperating with the Nazis, those very well-intentioned leaders enabled the murder of millions to take place with far more thoroughness and efficiency than would have been possible without them.

Look what we have come to: The Holocaust was carried out by millions of people with trivially bad intentions like those of Eichmann, who did not actively will the production of corpses, but was willing to walk over them, literally, if it advanced his career; the lukewarm well-meaning bystanders who wrung their hands and retreated to inner emigration as the catastrophe around them grew; and people whose intentions were often exemplary, but whose mistakes of judgment led them to actions that produced the opposite of what they intended. There are any number of shades in between, but these kinds of examples should suffice to show that where it really matters, intention may drop out entirely.

The claim here is so radical that it conflicts with any number of our deepest intuitions. Most of the more important moral scenes in our experience turn on questions about the subject's inner state. Just glance at literature: Is not the tragedy of Billy Budd the story of the noble innocent whose one unintended, impulsive movement will condemn him to hang? Is not the tragedy of Oedipus the story of the resolute adventurer who goes to every length to avoid committing evils he cannot in the end avoid? (If he did not care about it, he would not be worth our interest, and I refuse to accept the reading that views hubris as Oedipus' tragic flaw. It is hubris, after all, the attempt to defy the gods, that constitutes his greatest strength: Without it, he would never have left his original home and kingdom in the attempt to avoid the fate the oracle foretold.) But the reference to Oedipus reminds us that the relation between intention and moral judgment is not part of the nature of the world, nor even a part of the human. It is a relation with a history, and histories change. The fact that Oedipus not only did not intend his crime, but did everything he could to avoid it, may have mitigated his guilt but it could not erase it: For Greek audiences, his actions had damaged the world order, and every sort of plague might ensue until it was expunged. Oedipus should remind us that the consequences of intending an action are no more self-evident than the concept of intention itself. Both can change significantly, and thus change the ways we experience the world.

What if evil actions are committed by people whose intentions do not reflect the magnitude of their crimes? This is the central question of *Eichmann in*

Jerusalem, and with it Arendt set in motion a moral earthquake with which we have yet to come to terms. She argued that the judges missed the greatest moral and legal challenge of the case. Their judgment depended on the common assumption that intention is the place to locate responsibility and blame. The difference between murder and manslaughter, after all, rests on the defendant's ability to show that he didn't really mean it – where "meaning it" signifies that he neither willed the consequences of his actions nor acted out of base motives. "On nothing, perhaps," writes Arendt, "has civilized jurisprudence prided itself more than this taking into account of the subjective factor."[6] That you could do nothing but sign a paper and nevertheless be guilty of murder is a fact that shows how our categories are in need of change.

This point was missed equally by Eichmann's defense attorney, the judges whose strategy was to question his sincerity, and critics such as Daniel Jonah Goldhagen who sought to prove that Germany was riven by antisemitic passions of the sort that Eichmann failed to display. For all of them, guilt must turn on a subjective state, and the less offensive the subjective state looks, the less guilty the criminals must be. Yet far from trying to excuse Eichmann, Arendt argues against this assumption, that his guilt was not a matter of subjective state but objective fact. If mass murderers' intentions can be unexceptionable, we are not to conclude that nobody is responsible for anything, but to locate responsibility elsewhere. Indeed, Arendt goes so far as to make his guilt a matter not just of murdered people but of "a violation of the order of mankind" for which "the very earth cries out for vengeance." These are no pleas for relativistic mitigation, but tones that take us back to Oedipus. Reading them makes the fury with which this work is approached more surprising than ever. Why should we care whether Eichmann meant to commit mass murder? He did it, and was judged for it, was duly sentenced to hang – a sentence that Arendt, unlike many of her contemporaries, found perfectly justified.

At least part of the reason that the resistance to Arendt is so violent is our fear of consequences that follow. If Eichmann could do evil without intending it, so could I. If his motives were no better or worse than my own on shabbier days – ignoring the consequences of my actions, or lack thereof, in a rush to get through whatever business at hand will further my own and my family's narrowest interests – where might my own actions – or lack thereof – lead? These are questions – *mutatis mutandis* – that Arendt wanted us to ask. At the same time, she violently rejected the idea that there is an Eichmann in all of us. Not only does this come far too close to a notion of original sin, but the idea that everyone is guilty comes perilously close to the idea that no one is. (Cynics think this is the main reason that Germans love Goldhagen.) Many, and perhaps most of us, have the potential to behave as Eichmann did. Some of us do it, and some of us do not, and this is all that makes up moral difference – and gives us the right to act. (I am surely not alone in noticing that when all attempts to prove connections between Saddam Hussein and al-Qaeda or evidence of

[6] Arendt, *Eichmann in Jerusalem*, p. 277.

weapons of mass destruction had been exposed as lies, Bush reached for the handily untestable claim that Saddam intended to produce both weapons and terror.) Indeed, the need to mark the difference between actual and potential guilt may have been the most important reason for rejecting the necessary link between intention and morality.

Much of twentieth-century moral and legal philosophy has attempted to clarify the notion of intention – with very unsatisfying results. Is intention fundamentally cognitive, a matter of my ability to understand the consequences of what I will? Or is it primarily volitional, a feature of my desire that those consequences come about? Both features are part of the ordinary use of the concept and are often sidestepped in philosophical analysis of it, for ordinary discussion relies less on the metaphysics of inner states than on the assumption of a stable distinction between what you do and why you do it. Cases such as Eichmann's cast this assumption in doubt. The distinction exists, of course, but it is anything but stable.

Arendt's substitute for intention is judgment. Though very fragmentary, what she wrote suggests we are better off when we locate guilt and innocence in judgment than when we locate it in intention. If judgment cannot be taught, it can at least be shown – unlike intentions, which are in principle inaccessible. And judgment can be practiced, which allows us to do more about being good than merely wanting it. But let me be clear: If Arendt is doing something more than journalism, it is something less than theory. There is nothing resembling a systematic account of intention either in *Eichmann in Jerusalem* or the books that followed it. Perhaps she would have worked out a notion of judgment had she written the work her death prevented. Neither judgment, nor dignity – which plays a connected and central role – is an inner quality, for here the inner and outer are so thoroughly connected one cannot imagine one without the other. Neither can be reduced to a single moment, like Kant's good will. They are rather made up of bundles of – often ordinary – actions without being reducible to anyone of them. Both dignity and good judgment need to be shown: If we never see them, you do not have them.

Arendt's insistence that goodness must be manifest accounts for her early rejection of apologies for communism, despite the fact that unlike most anti-communists, she eschewed every turn to the right. Most of us on the left – yes, mea culpa – are inclined to overlook the evils of communism as excesses undertaken with the best of intentions. For communist hearts, and often even minds, seemed to be in the right place; and if we went so far as to say that their judgment was not, we had no conceptual tools to suggest this was the thing that mattered. We were uneasy with the classification of both communism and fascism as totalitarian. When one was undertaken from the same motives and commitments to universalism and liberation that every heart that beats on the left shared, how could one throw them into the same conceptual pot?

Arendt died before the *Historikerstreit*, in which conservative German historians argued that Hitler learned his trade from Stalin. Living in a German context, I remain uneasy about the impulse to relate the two too closely. Tzvetan

Todorov said that Germans should talk about the singularity of the Holocaust, and Jews about its universality. In fact, this claim itself could be derived from Kant's claim that most of the world's problems could be fixed if we worried about our own virtue and other people's happiness – against the general tendency to do just the opposite. When Russians begin to work through the crimes of the Soviet Union as the Germans have done with the Third Reich, the comparison between the two systems would be an act of taking responsibility. When Germans make the comparison, it is nearly always an act of avoiding it.

The attempt to come to terms with the ethical wreckage left in the wake of communism is barely beginning, and to do it well, we will need to acknowledge how messy our intuitions about intention are. They clearly matter for some things – there is a very real distinction, with very real consequences, between murder and manslaughter. It is less clear how they matter for others. To take a case closer to home: At first glance, Cheney's involvement in the war may seem worse than, say, Wolfowitz's. The fact that the former seems to believe in little besides the greater glory of Halliburton seems to make him more nefarious, while the latter's evident commitment to goals that may be shared by those opposing the war makes his warmongering less reprehensible. Nor is this merely a matter of subjectivity. Actions may include the intentions that brought them about. The fact that Iraqi and other Middle Eastern observers experience the rapaciousness of much of the war interest will poison attitudes toward America for decades to come (if we are lucky, and do a lot of penance – otherwise it will last much longer). On the other hand, without the driving conviction of neocons such as Wolfowitz, would the cynics have as much room to maneuver? Clearly not, if only because citizens will not in fact die or pay for actions in which they cannot believe. And if conviction may do more harm in the world than the lack of it, we may find ourselves agreeing with Kurt Tucholsky: *Das Gegenteil von gut ist, gutgemeint'*. The instability of our intuitions about intention becomes clear in curious ways.

For all the ire Arendt's claim about the banality of evil arouses, most of the left has internalized it. Something about the lesson that thoughtless, self-serving bureaucrats may do more harm than willful satanic monsters has seeped into general consciousness. We had learned to be wary of invisible evils – the kind that can belong to structures in which decent people play a part. The evil that Bush rightly called visible seemed an anachronistic throwback that we did not know how to name. This paralyzed much of the left's reaction to 9/11. Most of Bush's critics have been so appalled by the instrumentalization of the terrorist attacks – Richard Rorty compared it to the Nazi's use of the Reichstag fire – that we are loath to do anything that seems to feed it. The right is less scrupulous, and much quicker with moral reaction – and moral obfuscation. The first step to getting clearer is to resist the idea that evil comes in one form. One can applaud Arendt's insight into how much evil is banal without concluding that all of it is – a conclusion, of course, that she explicitly rejected.

Calling evil banal is a way of talking about its depth, but not its scope. One fairly stable intuition is a matter of dirty hands. Attending meetings and signing orders are actions that are themselves banal, even when their consequences are deadly. Blowing yourself up to kill the greatest number of strangers in your radius or burning a man in a lynching are not – even where the evil is magnified by eerily banal accompaniments like videos and postcards. Yet here one thought of Gunther Anders is profoundly relevant. Comparing the concentration camps with Hiroshima, Anders wrote that the ability to serve in the former required a far more damaged soul. And nevertheless, why should we care about the condition of the soul of the pilots of the plane that dropped the bomb that opened the first era in which humankind has the power to destroy the earth as a whole?

I suspect that Arendt would have no final answers to these questions had she finished that final book; for judgment, she knew from Kant, is a matter of relating particular rules to individual cases, and there are no rules that can be given for this kind of activity. We can begin by making that clear and showing that specious claims to moral clarity are just that. "What happened at Abu Ghraib was wrong," said Donald Rumsfeld recently, while passing on the responsibility for it to a couple of foot soldiers. "But it isn't the same as cutting someone's head off in front of a video camera." It isn't the same. From that, it hardly follows what Rumsfeld wants to imply: that one set of actions is pure evil, and the other is simply – too bad. Only if you think that evil has one essence can you draw this conclusion. For in fact, one of these evils is visible and the other – alas – still is not. One of them is the product of a large and complex system that makes it easy for individuals to evade responsibility, and the other is directly the product of ruthless individual will. One of them takes death as as unfortunate byproduct, and another as its clear-eyed goal. One of them reduces individuals to faceless bodies, the other exploits our inclination to pity and fear and shows us the tear-stained eyes and the shivering lips of grown-ups reduced to pale heaps of terrified flesh. The most significant difference between them, however, may be this one: Both of them use methods so loathsome as to create their own enemies left and right. But since one of them has significantly more power than the other, its effects are likely to be far longer lasting. The ways in which Abu Ghraib confirmed the world's worst nightmares may create hatred and bitterness toward America, toward the West, and toward anyone in the future who's ever inclined to say a word, however sincere, about defending human rights against dictators. Will good intentions help us if the consequences – in implacable hatred and mistrust of all that we are and could be – turn out to be worse?

These are questions that should guide analysis of different forms of good and evil, which now should take place. Here the discussions of evil and intention, of language and structures of responsibility, which Arendt sketched in *Eichmann in Jerusalem,* are invaluable tools. Examining differences in forms of evil is a way to give moral concepts reflective depth and nuance while still maintaining them with fullest voice. It is none too soon. In 2003, Paul Krugman wrote,

"Someday, when the grown-ups are back in charge, they'll have quite a mess to clean up."[7] One task for grown-up intellectuals is cleaning up the mess they have made of our moral concepts and going to work to reclaim them by building a better superstructure.

7 Paul Krugman, *New York Times*, August 29, 2003.

15

The Elusiveness of Arendtian Judgment

Bryan Garsten

> Truly political activities... cannot be performed at all without the presence of others, without the public, without a space constituted by the many.
>
> Hannah Arendt, "The Crisis in Culture"[1]

> ... as a spectator you may understand the "truth" of what the spectacle is about; but the price you have to pay is withdrawal from participating in it.
>
> Hannah Arendt, *The Life of the Mind*[2]

> ... exclusion from politics should not be derogatory... self-exclusion, far from being arbitrary discrimination, would in fact give substance and reality to one of the most important negative liberties we have enjoyed since the end of the ancient world, namely freedom from politics, which was unknown to Rome or Athens and which is politically perhaps the most relevant part of our Christian heritage.
>
> Hannah Arendt, *On Revolution*[3]

One of the freedoms that representative democracy protects is the freedom *not* to participate actively in politics, the freedom to stand on the sidelines and watch. In modern liberal democracies, most citizens take advantage of this freedom most of the time. Not participating seems to be the most common activity of democratic citizenship today. Among political scientists and political theorists, the overwhelming tendency is to lament this state of affairs and to long for a more participatory politics. This chapter emerges from a different perspective on how best to defend democratic politics. I am interested in

---

[1] Hannah Arendt, "The Crisis in Culture: Its Social and Political Significance," in *Between Past and Future* (New York: Penguin, 1968), pp. 197–226, at 217.

[2] Hannah Arendt, *The Life of the Mind* (New York: Harcourt, Brace, 1971), p. 93. (Hereafter abbreviated *LM*.)

[3] Hannah Arendt, *On Revolution* (New York: Viking Press, 1963), p. 283.

An earlier version of this article has previously appeared as Bryan Garsten, "The Elusiveness of Arendtian Judgment," in *Social Research. Hannah Arendt's Centennary. Political and Philosophic Perspectives*, Part II, 74, 4 (Winter 2007): 1071–1108.

understanding and defending a kind of citizenship that is closer to what most citizens do in modern liberal democracies. To be clear, this is not a defense of passivity. Passivity is not the only kind of nonparticipation that we find in our politics, and it is clearly not the best kind. But many citizens who do not participate are also not entirely passive. Instead, they watch politics and they judge what is going on. A certain type of watching and judging is, it seems to me, a defensible way of being a democratic citizen. Of course, there are also unattractive versions of this activity – the combination of watching and judging that I want to explore must be distinguished from close cousins, such as judging without watching (prejudice) and watching without judging (being entertained). To make such distinctions adequately, we first have to establish the potential dignity of the citizen understood as a judging spectator, and to do that we have to explain precisely what the faculty of judgment is.

The suggestion of this chapter is that Hannah Arendt's reflections on judgment can fruitfully be read as part of such a defense of the citizen as spectator-judge. This might be a surprising thesis about Arendt. She is best known as a theorist of action, not spectatorship, and her conception of politics in the strong sense of the word was one that seemed to give priority to those citizens who joined the controversy and debate of political life and disclosed themselves to others by taking action in the public arena. The American revolutionaries whom she admired in *On Revolution* were those who created a realm of politics through action. And her influence among political theorists is most obvious among those who defend a participatory conception of politics in which active contestation is central.[4] So I must admit from the beginning that my effort to enlist Arendt in the defense of any kind of non-action pulls against a major strain of her thought, and against the most important legacy that her thought seems to have left behind.

Still, it seems to me that the emphasis on political action as participatory politics leaves out certain interesting facets of Arendt's thinking and may interfere with efforts to understand her writings on judgment. Arendt wrote that her interest in judgment emerged out of her experience with the Eichmann trial, and in this chapter I draw mostly from the essays and lectures in which she was grappling with that experience.[5] Her main concern about Eichmann was not that he had failed to participate actively in politics; no true politics

---

[4] When Habermas summarized Arendt's position in remarks to the New School, he identified as her key philosophical point a "concept of action as 'praxis' which articulates the historical experiences and the normative perspectives of what we today call participatory democracy." Jürgen Habermas, "On the German-Jewish Heritage," *Telos*, 44 (1980): 127–31, at p. 128. For a more complete summary of his view of Arendt, see Jürgen Habermas, "Hannah Arendt's Communications Concept of Power," *Social Research* (1977): 3–24. Similarly, George Kateb's classic book on Arendt asserts that participation is the core of her philosophy: "Direct citizen participation is the element common to her ancient and modern commitments." George Kateb, *Hannah Arendt: Politics, Conscience, Evil* (Oxford: Martin Robertson, 1983), p. 7.

[5] Arendt's philosophical musings about the issues central to judgment do predate the Eichmann trial, but Ronald Beiner gives persuasive evidence that her most significant thoughts on the theme were closely intertwined with her reflections on Eichmann. Ronald Beiner, "Hannah Arendt on

was available for him to participate in. Nor does she seem to have expected him to create a realm of true politics in the way that the American revolutionaries had; that would seem to be asking too much of the subjects of the Nazi regime. She did, however, blame Eichmann for having declined to judge the rightness of his actions for himself and for refusing to take responsibility for them. Moreover, she thought that many of those who criticized her initial report on his trial often displayed an unwillingness to render judgment that was analogous to Eichmann's own attitude. "Who am I to judge?" asked her critics, ready to understand, if not excuse, Eichmann's actions. Arendt said she found this response to her writing particularly troubling. She thought that the disinclination to judge was an attitude brought on by modern mass democracy and one that paved the way for totalitarianism. Her interest in judgment was rooted in an effort to undermine the philosophical tendency of thought behind the disinclination to judge.[6] Thus, her effort to defend the possibility and the dignity of judgment was as important a response to the perils of mass democracy as was her defense of participatory action.

Since the role of a spectator is more prominent in modern representative democracies than it was in ancient participatory republics, finding a defense of it in Arendt's thought might help to rescue her from the accusation that she was lost in nostalgia for the Greek polis.[7] The importance of citizens' judgment to the modern liberal-democratic tradition is rooted not primarily in Aristotelian *phronesis* but in John Locke, who, in answer to the question, "Who shall be judge?" at the end of the *Second Treatise*, offered an inspiring reply: "*The people shall be judge.*"[8] If Arendt's writings can help to explain what it means for the people to judge, or to judge well, then they would offer a resource not only for nostalgic republicans, but also for defenders of modern liberty.

Once we turn to Arendt's writings on judgment, however, we cannot avoid confronting the fact that while her theory of judgment is very suggestive it is also notoriously difficult to understand; the standards of judgment are, in her account, difficult to describe or capture; they are *elusive*. In this chapter, I suggest that the elusiveness in Arendt's account of judgment arises from her effort to deal with what she regarded as a deep and fundamental philosophical problem confronting any theory of judgment: How is it possible to judge

Judging," in *Lectures on Kant's Political Philosophy* (Chicago: University of Chicago Press, 1982), pp. 97–101.

[6] Andrew Norris points to the importance of Arendt's defense of judgment to her treatment of totalitarianism in Andrew Norris, "Arendt, Kant, and the Politics of Common Sense," *Polity*, 29, 2 (1996): 165–91, at pp. 174–5.

[7] Kateb also explores Arendt's relation to representative democracy, but his argument does not challenge the supremacy of participatory action in Arendt's scheme. He argues instead that she underemphasized the fact that representative government is home to a variety of types of political action, including economic activity and civil disobedience. Kateb, *Hannah Arendt*, pp. 40–1, chapter 4.

[8] John Locke, in "Second Treatise of Government," *Two Treatises of Government: A Critical Edition*, 2nd edition, edited by Peter Laslett (Cambridge: Cambridge University Press, 1967), section 240. Emphasis in the original.

without putting oneself into a relation of obedience to the grounds of one's judgments? If we say that the grounds of our judgments have some authority over us, then we seem to cede authority, and thus responsibility, to those grounds. To defend the dignity and responsibility of a citizen-judge – and thus to defend the possibility of the role that Eichmann should have taken on – Arendt felt that she had to show how it was possible to judge without ceding responsibility to the principles or rules by which one judges.

In the first section of the chapter, I argue that we can see this problem shaping Arendt's thoughts on judgment if we read carefully her stance toward Kant's standard moral and political theory, especially in the lectures on moral philosophy edited recently by Jerome Kohn.[9] There is room to debate the weight that one should place on these lectures in relation to the rest of Arendt's work, but in this chapter, I take Richard Bernstein's advice about how to read Arendt: I follow one of Arendt's "thought-trains."[10] The train that is most apparent in these lectures on moral philosophy suggests that the reason that Arendt turned to the *Critique of Judgment* as a source of moral and political theory was that she had concluded that the *Critique of Practical Reason* and the associated writings, with their emphasis on rule following, were too easily turned into excuses for nonjudgment. A prime example of this misuse of Kantian thought could be found in Eichmann's testimony, which confused the Kantian notion of following rules with the Führer's requirement to follow Nazi laws. In the second section, I suggest that this worry about Kantianism led Arendt toward a fundamentally Nietzchean insight about the advantage of a deeply subjective account of judgment. When Nietzsche asserted, "my judgments are *my* judgments," he created a tight link between an agent and his or her judgments, and thus insured the agent's *responsibility* for those judgments.[11]

But Arendt was not a Nietzschean. Unlike Nietzsche, she wanted to make agents' responsibility for their judgments *moral*. She thus faced the difficult task of trying to remoralize her post-Kantian, Nietzchean account of judgment. What possible grounds could a moral but post-Kantian kind of judgment rest upon? One proposed answer, offered to Arendt by Jürgen Habermas and others, is that intersubjectivity provides an alternative ground for such judgments. In the third section of the chapter, I suggest that the worry about responsibility previously mentioned helps to explain why Arendt did not adopt this strategy. She could not propose Habermasian intersubjectivity, or communicative rationality, as a ground for judgments without threatening the Nietzschean responsibility that she wanted to preserve. Arendt's own understanding of intersubjectivity, or "representative thinking," had to remain ultimately a

---

[9] Hannah Arendt, "Personal Responsibility under Dictatorship," in *Responsibility and Judgment*, edited by Jerome Kohn (New York: Schocken, 2003), pp. 17–48.

[10] Richard J. Bernstein, *Hannah Arendt and the Jewish Question* (Cambridge: Polity Press, 1996).

[11] Friedrich Nietzsche, *Beyond Good and Evil*, translated by R. J. Hollingdale (New York: Penguin, 1990), p. 71.

subjective form of thinking; it had to remain grounded within the individual judge. A form of intersubjectivity that located the ground of judgment partially outside oneself might too easily have come to be viewed as an alternative source of responsibility for our judgments; it might too easily have become an excuse for our own bad judgments, and too easily have been used to justify the same sort of unthinkingness that Arendt worried had been the unintended legacy of Kant's moral theory. Arendt's "representative thinking" therefore had to remain subjective, in the sense of ultimately grounding judgments within an individual in order to preserve the individual's full responsibility for those judgments.

Nevertheless, Arendt's writings on representative thinking describe a certain *sort* of subjectivity, and in the final section of this chapter, I explore more precisely the character of this thinking and how it was linked to the responsible judgment that Arendt wished Eichmann, and citizens in general, would exercise more often. The key point about the mode of imaginative thinking that Arendt wanted to emphasize was that it required us *not* to be fully present to ourselves. The perspective of judge is one that requires me to imagine myself partly outside myself and my commitments, and yet still essentially belonging to the self doing the judging. The problem that Arendt was struggling with was how we could step outside ourselves in this way without thereby ceding a measure of our individual responsibility for our judgments. Her view, I will suggest, was that the element of self-alienation involved in representative thinking helps to protect us from relying upon any one set of external standards and so helps to preserve our personal responsibility.

15.1 Eichmann's Confused Kantianism

One of the simplest and most powerful responses that readers have given to Arendt's effort to find a "nonwritten" political philosophy in Kant's *Critique of Judgment* is to point out that Kant had a political philosophy that *was* written down. The written political philosophy emerged from and was congruent with the moral philosophy of his second *Critique* and the *Groundwork of the Metaphysics of Morals*, and it was articulated in some detail not only in the occasional essays such as *Perpetual Peace* and *Theory and Practice*, but also in the more systematic and complete *Metaphysics of Morals*. At the heart of Kant's political philosophy was the view that in the final analysis, politics must pay homage to morality; and at the heart of Kant's moral theory was the objective standard of the categorical imperative. Thus Kant himself distinguished carefully between moral judgment and aesthetic judgment. In the realm of morals there existed a "definite concept" in light of which we could judge our actions. Thus there was no need to search for a moral or political standard in the intersubjective common sense of aesthetic judgment, as a number of commentators have pointed out.[12]

---

[12] Richard J. Bernstein, "Judging – the Actor and the Spectator," *Philosophical Profiles* (Philadelphia: University of Pennsylvania Press, 1986), pp. 232–3; William Galston, "Lectures on Kant's

This response to Arendt's enterprise seems right, in one sense, but also inadequate. It fails to investigate why Arendt took the approach she did. For of course she knew as well as we do about Kant's written moral and political philosophy. To understand her interest in finding an alternate grounding for moral and political judgments, we first have to understand why she regarded the standard Kantian theory as inadequate.

Though Arendt's dissatisfaction with Kant's own account of his moral theory may have a number of theoretical roots, the nub of the matter as it appears in the lectures on moral philosophy can be summarized with reference to her reflections on Eichmann. She illustrated the reason for dismissing Kant's proposed objective standard, the categorical imperative, by pointing out Eichmann's statement during the trial to the effect that when he had followed the Nazi orders and participated in the work of extermination, he had been behaving in accordance with a version of Kant's moral theory that was appropriate "for a small man's domestic use." Eichmann stated the popularized version of the categorical imperative as the following principle: "True to the law, obedient, a proper personal life, not to come into conflict with the law." While Eichmann's testimony shows that he recognized his actions did not accord with true Kantian morality, Arendt's interpretation of his testimony emphasized the way in which he seems to have misread Kantianism into a prescription for following rules or laws. She thought that Eichmann had made the terrible mistake of substituting the Führer's will for the generalized will of the categorical imperative.[13]

But, somewhat surprisingly, Arendt was not content to simply dismiss Eichmann's move as a crude mistake. Instead, she thought it revealed a fatal flaw in Kant's own moral theory, a flaw associated with Kant's emphasis on rule following. She observed that those Germans who had been most likely to follow laws, those who had been the most traditional and respectable sort, the churchgoers and the secular moralists, had been the ones most likely to obey the new laws and codes of the Nazis: "They simply exchanged one system of values for another," she wrote. The ones who resisted, on the other hand, were "those whose consciences did not function in this, as it were, automatic way – as though we dispose of a set of learned or innate rules which we then apply to

Political Philosophy," *Journal of Politics* 46 (1984): 304–6; Patrick Riley, "Hannah Arendt on Kant, Truth and Politics," *Political Studies* 35, 3 (1987): 379–92. See also the response of Hans Jonas from November 1972: "Now it is not the case that Kant simply made appeal to judgment. He also made appeal to the concept of the good." Quoted in Beiner, "Hannah Arendt on Judging," pp. 114–15.

13 "What he [Eichmann] has failed to point out in court was that in this 'period of crimes legalized by the state,' as he called it, he had not simply dismissed the Kantian formula as no longer applicable, he had distorted it to read: Act as if the principle of your actions were the same as that of the legislator of the law of the land – or in Hans Frank's formulation of 'the categorical imperative of the Third Reich,' which Eichmann might have known: 'Act in such a way that the Führer, if he knew of your action, would approve it.'" Hannah Arendt, *Eichmann in Jerusalem: A Report on the Banality of Evil*, revised and enlarged edition (New York: Penguin, 1994), p. 136. The testimony itself is complex and confused; relevant portions of it are included as an appendix to this chapter.

the particular case as it arises." Instead, the resisters "were the only ones who dared judge by themselves."[14] These skeptics and doubters, because they were not in the habit of treating morals as a matter of rule application, had not been as tied to or dependent upon the presence of rules or codes; they had not so easily accepted the substitution of "thou shalt kill" for its opposite in the way that Arendt suggested the thoughtless Eichmann had.[15]

Rejecting the automatic or unthinking view of morality as a set of codes was also linked to the matter of responsibility for Arendt. For insofar as we think of ourselves as following rules, we can pass off responsibility for our actions to those rules. Arendt was much haunted by the defense that war criminals such as Eichmann offered – that they were only following orders or laws and thus were fulfilling their duties. But she was not content simply to reply that the orders and laws in this case were wrong. She sought a deeper explanation of the mistake made by the war criminals. The disposition to follow orders and rules was itself misguided, for it implied that *obedience* could be a human virtue. Arendt argued that obedience was never a virtue, at least not for anyone who lived in the modern, secular world free from religious obligation. What organizations and governments require, and are entitled to seek, is not obedience but "consent" or "support" – the only form of following that adult humans can engage in without giving away their dignity and status as humans, without turning themselves into slaves. And if, as Arendt insisted, "there is no such thing as obedience in political and moral matters," then the people who merely follow orders or laws cannot shift the responsibility for their actions onto the laws or lawgivers.[16]

Now it seems to me that we must admit that many of Arendt's concerns mentioned so far seem to follow in the spirit of Kant himself, if we read Kant sympathetically. Arendt's description of the resisters as those who "dared to judge for themselves" echoed Kant's challenge in "What Is Enlightenment?," *sapere aude* (dare to know), and her insistence on taking responsibility for one's actions rather than obeying outside forces seems a way of asking for autonomy. Eichmann's claim that his deference to the Führer's will was parallel, somehow, to Kant's injunction to follow the moral law is not tenable. Why, then, did Arendt pause to consider Eichmann's position as illustrative of a deep flaw in Kantian moral theory?

What Eichmann's claim revealed, she thought, was that Kant's moral law could come to play the same role that religious law had in earlier times: that of commanding obedience to a norm and thus teaching, perhaps in spite of Kant's own deepest intentions, that morality was primarily a matter of obeying laws. In Arendt's view, Kant had failed to fully separate morality from legality.

[14] Hannah Arendt, "Personal Responsibility under Dictatorship," *Responsibility and Judgment*, pp. 17–48, at p. 44.
[15] Hannah Arendt, "Thinking and Moral Considerations," *Responsibility and Judgment*, pp. 159–89, at p. 178.
[16] Arendt, "Personal Responsibility under Dictatorship," p. 48.

In "Some Questions of Moral Philosophy," she traced this aspect of Kant's thought carefully. First she identified the ethic of obedience as a distinctively religious view: "the all-important principle that in religion, but not in morality, sin is primarily understood as disobedience." She defined moral philosophy as a field that existed only where "emancipation from religious commands" had occurred, and she specifically credited Kant with having tried to introduce this emancipation.[17] While Kant allowed for the necessity of obedience in religion and in politics, he did not mean for the moral law, the categorical imperative, to be understood as requiring "obedience" to anything except one's own will. Nevertheless, he found that he could not avoid using the language of law. The use of this language was not incidental, Arendt argued. The legal language emerged from Kant's obsession with the problem of how to make morality "obligatory." Arendt explained this as the problem of how to explicate why the will should follow the dictates of reason. In the end, she concluded, Kant defined the good will as one that followed the dictates of reason unquestioningly, for the faculty of will, as he understood it, did not itself contain the ability to question. This is why he gave morality "the form of the imperative" and "brought back the concept of obedience, through a back door as it were."[18] In bringing the element of obedience to light, Arendt aimed to question Kant's understanding of autonomy on Kantian grounds. From the perspective of our will, the dictates of reason appear as a force that is external and heteronymous.[19] And insofar as we identify, as agents, with our wills, we may regard Kantian dictates of reason, or moral laws, as external sources of authority.

It is at this point that Arendt thought the notion of judgment could be useful. She noticed that if freedom from obedience depends upon us having a faculty of the will that is one of "pure spontaneity," one that is not bound to an external authority, then that faculty must in fact perform not one but two functions. It must not only spur us to action but must also "arbitrate between reasons without being subject to them."[20] This second, arbitrating function "is in fact the same as judgment," which she suggested might be a capacity separate from reason and, ultimately, from will. She described this faculty of arbitrating will, or judgment, as "one of the most mysterious faculties of the human mind." Presumably the mystery lay in how it was possible to listen to and arbitrate between reasons without *obeying* reasons. On what grounds is one's decision to endorse a particular reason one's own? The answer cannot be formulated in the language of reasons, and so there is something inscrutable about judgment so understood. Arendt quoted Nietzsche here: "If someone told us he needed reasons to remain decent we could hardly trust him any longer."[21] And in

---

[17] Hannah Arendt, "Some Questions of Moral Philosophy," *Responsibility and Judgment*, pp. 49–146, at pp. 66–7.

[18] Ibid., p. 72.

[19] Ibid., pp. 71, 277–8 note 9.

[20] Ibid., p. 131.

[21] Ibid., p. 131.

fact there is something deeply Nietzschean in the suspicion of reasons that she entertained at this point in the argument. A truer Kantian would point out that the language of spontaneity is one that comes precisely from Kant's description of the faculty of reason, and that the freedom of moral autonomy stems from the unity of practical and theoretical reason – reason helps to constitute the will rather than reigning despotically over it. But Arendt, looking at reason from the perspective of a separate willing faculty, saw how reason might appear to be a source of command and so a threat to spontaneity and freedom.

Arendt's talk about the mysteriousness of the faculty of judgment is linked to her ruminations on the insufficiency of philosophical accounts of the will in the last section of the second volume of *The Life of the Mind,* the section that was to lead into her final volume on judgment. There she spoke of the fact that no theorist except Duns Scotus had been "ready to pay the price of contingency for the gift of freedom" (*LM,* 195, cf. 198). This was because "nothing indeed can be more frightening than the notion of solipsistic freedom – the 'feeling' that my standing apart, isolated from everyone else, is due to free will, that nothing and nobody can be held responsible for it but me myself" (*LM,* 196). Contingency, spontaneity, freedom, and responsibility all go hand in hand in her account here, and all are threatened by philosophical understandings of freedom that try to give justifications for our actions. Philosophers had almost all, in one way or another, failed to appreciate "the bewildering spontaneity of a free act" (*LM,* 196). An act can be free only if it is not caused by something prior. But if an act is justified, the justification itself "will have to show the act as the continuation of a preceding series, that is, renege on the very experience of freedom and novelty" (*LM,* 210). Arendt ended her final work by returning to the direct philosophical question about "the abyss of pure spontaneity": to what degree can we be at home with a freedom so closely linked with contingency? The question about whether we could be at home with a freedom that remained inscrutable to philosophical justification came down to asking whether that freedom pleased us, she asserted, and thus the question could be pursued only by opening an investigation into the basis of our likes and dislikes, an investigation into the faculty of taste or judgment (*LM,* 217). This was the investigation that she planned but never was able to write. The passages at the end of *The Life of the Mind* are enough, however, to help flesh out the discussion of the mysteriousness of the faculty of judgment in the earlier lectures on moral philosophy and at least help to cast light on what she regarded as the central philosophical dilemma. The mysterious "contingency" of truly free actions that troubled her at the end of her life was closely related to the mystery she had mentioned in the earlier lectures: the mystery of how the arbitrating part of our will, or our judgment, can respond to reasons without being subject to them. This is the question that she thought Kant's moral theory could not adequately answer.

While our main concern here is not the validity of Arendt's interpretation of Kant, it is worth pointing out two ways in which Kant's moral and political thought does seem to open itself to the sort of criticism that Arendt was advancing. First, on the issue of responsibility, there is the fact that Kant makes an actor fully responsible for his or her actions only when he or she *departs* from the moral law. To be sure, the autonomy gained by following the moral law is a prerequisite of moral responsibility in one sense. Only if we have a free will can we be praised or blamed for our actions. But responsibility for the *consequences* of our actions is a different matter. For Kant, following the moral law actually *insulates* us from responsibility for those consequences. We can be held responsible for the outcomes of our actions only if we have acted against the categorical imperative, as Kant makes perfectly clear in the *Lectures on Ethics*: "If we do either more or less than is required of us we can be held responsible for the consequences, but not otherwise – not if we do only what is required, neither more nor less...."[22] Thus Kantian morality does seem to encourage an individual to retreat within himself in a way that recalls Eichmann's self-defense: "I have done my duty, obeyed the laws, and can't be blamed for what the world does with that," seems to be, in abstract form at least, a Kantian mode of thinking. Responsibility falls on the principles, not on the individual following them.

The second place in which Kant's writings open themselves to Arendt's criticism is in his explicitly political thought. Notoriously, Kant allows for no right of resistance or rebellion and asks us to consider whatever government happens to exist as if it were legitimate enough to warrant our obedience. This recipe for quietism is found in the famous "argue but obey" principle of "What Is Enlightenment?" in the *Metaphysics of Morals,* and in the following unambiguous passage in "Theory and Practice":

...all resistance against the supreme legislative power, all incitement of the subjects to violent expressions of discontent, all defiance which breaks out into rebellion, is the greatest and most punishable crime in a commonwealth, for it destroys its very foundation. This prohibition is absolute. And even if the power of the state or its agent, the head of state, has violated the original contract by authorizing the government to act tyrannically, and has thereby, in the eyes of the subject, forfeited the right to legislate, the subject is still not entitled to offer counterresistance.[23]

There is actually a more compelling argument for this view than might at first be apparent: Kant thinks we have a duty to act morally, that we can do so only when living under some form of government, and that resisting government is essentially a destructive action that puts us outside of government without

---

[22] Immanuel Kant, *Lectures on Ethics*, translated by Louis Infield (Indianapolis: Hackett, 1963), p. 59; cf. Immanuel Kant, "The Metaphysics of Morals," in *Practical Philosophy*, edited by Mary Gregor (Cambridge: Cambridge University Press, 1996), pp. 353–604, at 6:228.

[23] Immanuel Kant, "On the Common Saying: 'This May Be True in Theory, But It Does Not Apply in Practice,'" translated by H. B. Nisbet, in *Political Writings*, edited by Hans Reiss (Cambridge: Cambridge University Press, 1991), pp. 61–92, at p. 81.

any assurance of putting a new or better one in its place. Thus what seems to be a request for unconditional obedience is in fact a way of preserving the preconditions of our moral action and, in Kantian terms, a way of protecting our freedom.[24] This is why Arendt's criticism must target his conception of freedom itself, through calling into question his understanding of the relation between reason and will. Still, seeing the defense of obedience in his explicitly political theory – and the directness with which it could be deployed as an excuse for Eichmann – can only make her concerns about standard Kantian morals and politics seem more plausible. Obedience is an integral part of Kant's political theory.

There is in Kant's thought one apparent exception, or partial exception, to the ban on disobedience. This is his enthusiasm for the revolutionaries in France, an enthusiasm so strong as to have earned him the nickname "the Old Jacobin." I call this a "partial exception" because, as has been much commented upon, Kant defended his enthusiasm as appropriate only for *spectators* of the revolution. He insisted that as actors, the revolutionaries themselves were acting wrongly.[25] Still, the partial exception was enough to attract and intrigue Arendt, and it was by beginning with the perspective of the spectator that she aimed to arrive at a whole new Kantian political philosophy, one that would escape the demand for obedience by giving priority to the capacity exercised most of all by spectators, the capacity of judgment.[26]

15.2 Beyond Nietzsche to Good and Evil

If Kantian rules and reasons could function as excuses, scapegoats onto which Eichmann placed responsibility for his actions, Arendt's hope was that the Kantian faculty of judgment could not be so misused. Because our judgments cannot be fully explained as the necessary consequence of any set of rules or principles, the responsibility for them cannot be placed on any such rules.[27] If we want to explain a particular judgment, we cannot do so simply by pointing to the principles on the basis of which it was made; judgments are always more particular than those principles, so the individual, not the principles or rules, must remain the final explanation of any particular judgment. Since nothing external to the person is responsible for the final judgment, the responsibility for a person's judgment lies inescapably with the individual himself. On this point, Arendt was quite close to Nietzsche. In *Beyond Good and Evil*, Nietzsche

---

[24] Here I follow Christine Korsgaard, "Taking the Law into Our Own Hands: Kant on the Right to Revolution," in Andrews Reath, Barbara Herman, and Christine M. Korsgaard, eds., *Reclaiming the History of Ethics: Essays for John Rawls* (Cambridge and New York: Cambridge University Press, 1997), pp. 297–328.

[25] Immanuel Kant, "The Contest of Faculties," in *Political Writing*, pp. 176–90, at p. 182.

[26] Arendt, "Some Questions of Moral Philosophy," pp. 94–6.

[27] Elizabeth Young-Bruehl notes that Arendt was looking for a form of judging "that does not surrender its reflexivity to imperatives." Elizabeth Young-Bruehl, *Why Arendt Matters* (New Haven: Yale University Press, 2006), p. 207.

had described the free spirit as someone who was liberated from the external constraint of reasoning and explaining himself to others, and who insisted, against the calls for such self-explanation, "My judgments are *my* judgments, and no one else is entitled to them."[28]

But the inscrutability of Nietzschean judgment evident in this statement reveals the sense in which such judgments are also *irresponsible*. While Nietzschean judgment makes an agent more "responsible" for his judgments in one sense, tightening the link between agent and judgment, it does not make him responsible *to anyone else*. To the contrary, the liberation that Nietzsche described seems designed to dissociate the free spirit from any such interpersonal obligations. Nietzsche wanted to unlock the inner vitality of individuals that he thought social ties and internalized norms of conscience had stifled. This explains why Arendt could not simply adopt Nietzschean judgment. Her intention, as we have seen, was quite different from Nietzsche's. According to the line of thought that we have traced through "Some Questions of Moral Philosophy," at any rate, her goal was to refute the excuse of "just following the laws" that Eichmann had adopted from Kant's moral theory. Freeing the agent from the imperative of Kantian reason was Arendt's way of taking away the excuse that reason could provide, tightening the knot tying actor and judgment and action together in order to fix responsibility unmistakably on the actor. She wanted to do this for the old-fashioned reason that she wanted to preserve the possibility of blaming Eichmann, of delivering a moral verdict on his behavior. She could not follow Nietzsche in simply asserting that all judgments are merely subjective expressions of an individual's power because she wanted to claim that Eichmann was, in fact, wrong. Observing the "banality" of evil was never meant to raise any doubt about evil's badness. Arendt did not seek to bring us to a supra-moral perspective "beyond good and evil," but, on the contrary, to vindicate the possibility of a moral perspective that distinguished good from evil. She sought a perspective that could remoralize the judgment she had freed from Kantian moral theory without introducing standards or grounds that could be used to excuse an agent from taking full responsibility for his or her actions in the way that she feared Kantian law and reason could be used.

The distance between Arendt and Nietzsche can be seen most clearly in the fact that they took precisely opposite stances on the value of Kant's third *Critique*.[29] Nietzsche, in *The Genealogy of Morals*, devoted a section to ridiculing the *Critique of Judgment* and lamenting its influence on Schopenhauer. The problem that Nietzsche saw in Kant's approach was that "instead of envisaging the aesthetic problem from the point of view of the artist (the creator),

---

[28] Nietzsche, *Beyond Good and Evil*, §43, p. 71.

[29] Bonnie Honig does not account for this fact in her reading of Arendt as a Nietzschean. Bonnie Honig, "The Politics of Agonism: A Critical Response to 'Beyond Good and Evil: Arendt, Nietzsche, and the Aestheticization of Political Action,' by Dana Villa," *Political Theory*, 21 (1993): 528–33.

[it] considered art and the beautiful purely from that of the 'spectator,' and unconsciously introduced the 'spectator' into the concept 'beautiful.'"[30] The spectator's point of view was a disinterested, impartial one. For Nietzsche, this meant that it did violence to the beautiful. Arendt, in contrast, was attracted to precisely this part of Kant's account. In Kant's description of how a disinterested judgment could emerge even if there were no definite concept that everyone had to accept as a grounding for such a judgment, Arendt found a way of thinking about disinterestedness that she hoped could replace the objectionable objective standard that Kant had relied upon in his moral theory.

The validity of moral judgments was, in Arendt's view, "neither objective and universal, nor subjective, depending on personal whim, but intersubjective or representative."[31] The intersubjective point of view grounds moral judgments that are not based on a definite set of reasons or rules and yet are also not inscrutable to others. It arises from imagining ourselves in the place of others and seeking judgments that these imagined others could accept. And it estimates that acceptability by referring not to concepts or rules or abstract forms, but to particular examples, drawn either from history or from literature.[32] But this means that one's moral judgments depend on the imagined community of people with whom one shares particular understandings of particular cases. Those who regard Achilles as an exemplar of courage, for example, make up a different community, with a different "common sense," than those who regard Achilles as an exemplar of adolescent obstinacy. Thus Arendt concluded "Some Questions of Moral Philosophy" with the thought that "our decisions about right and wrong will depend upon our choice of company."[33] And near the end of her essay on "The Crisis in Culture," she defined a cultivated person, someone with taste, as "one who knows how to choose his company.... "[34] Putting these two passages about choosing company together, we arrive at her thought that culture and taste are the preconditions to choosing the imagined community in engagement with which one justifies one's decisions about right and wrong. The question that lingers over this suggestive set of ideas is, in what sense is the imaginative act of choosing our company *moral*? In what sense does the exercise of imagining one's company offer guidance to, or set limits on, one's personal, subjective whim?

15.3 The Subjectivity of Arendt's Intersubjectivity

It is helpful to think through exactly how the faculty for representative thinking might go to work in a case like Eichmann's. How would the advice to choose

[30] Friedrich Nietzsche, *On the Genealogy of Morals*, translated by Walter Kaufmann and R. J. Hollingdale (New York: Vintage, 1967), §6, p. 104.
[31] Arendt, "Some Questions of Moral Philosophy," p. 141.
[32] Ibid., p. 145.
[33] Ibid., p. 146–7.
[34] Arendt, "The Crisis in Culture," p. 226.

one's imagined company and "woo the consent" of everyone in it actually proceed, and how might it have awakened his conscience? Certainly no remedy
for his collaboration would have been found in asking him to imagine himself
consulting the opinions of his actual community. Arendt presumed that the
communal norms of those around him had themselves been perverted. The
strength of representative thinking comes instead from the way in which it
suggests one can step outside such norms through the use of the imagination,
creating a different, broader community whose common sense can inform and
ground judgments that depart from those supported by one's actual community. In articulating how we can bring before our minds examples that are not
actually present, Arendt showed how one could – and thus could be expected
to – leave behind the narrowness of one's particular situation and context and
adopt an "enlarged mentality." Eichmann could and should have imagined
himself as part of a community whose common sense would have revolted at
the actions he was asked to perform. But what community was that? What
directs the imagination as it constructs this new grounding for its judgments?
The danger is that this work of imagination is purely negative, an escape from
context that offers no positive guidance on how to create new horizons of
meaning. Arendt wrote that the more perspectives one imagines and consults
or woos, the more valid one's judgments will be. This is not so much a question
of numbers as it is a movement toward the broadest possible imagined community, that of "humanity" as a whole. The judgment that Arendt ultimately
sought to vindicate was, after all, that Eichmann and others had committed
"crimes against humanity."[35] But it is important to see that humanity as such
is an imagined community. It must be a product of "representative" thinking
because it is not *present* anywhere. We know humanity only through examples;
we know only particular humans, and there is no definite rule or simple concept
to apply to determine whether a particular specimen is or is not *human* in the
moral sense – that is a matter for reflective judgment. But here things become
difficult: With regard to which community's common sense is *this* judgment
about what counts as "human" to be made? The only possible answer seems
to be, with regard to humanity's sense of what humanity is. But that can mean
nothing other than the following: In deciding to keep company with humanity
as a whole, I must imagine for myself what humanity's sense of itself could
be. The ultimate criterion upon which I base my choice of company must be
nothing other than my own imagined sense of humanity.

Now two observations can be made about this exercise in representative
thinking, both of which may seem disappointing and yet both of which seem
true. The first is a familiar complaint about the emptiness or formality of
judgment so conceived. Arendtian representative thinking offers no substantive
account of how to distinguish good from evil, no hierarchy of ends in light
of which to evaluate particulars. We have already seen why Arendt avoided

---

[35] Young-Bruehl points out that on Arendt's account, "judgment is the faculty that prepares a
person to be the Kantian ideal: a world citizen." Young-Bruehl, *Why Arendt Matters*, p. 166.

introducing such definite grounds, but nevertheless we may be disappointed by
the lack of guidance that her alternative provides. Arendt herself raised this
worry near the end of "Some Questions of Moral Philosophy" by asking the
question of "whether there is really nothing to hold onto when we are called
upon to decide that this is right and this is wrong as we decide that this is
beautiful and this is ugly."[36] Her answer – and her final and most conclusive
statement in the lecture – is that while there is no *standard* to hold on to or
be guided by, there are *examples*: "We judge and tell right from wrong by
having present in our mind some incident and some person, absent in time or
space, that have become examples."[37] But as we have seen, the imaginative
work required to determine which particulars count as examples of what,
the work of choosing one's imagined community, seems to require precisely
the sort of judgments that we are attempting to ground. The circularity of
judgment guided by example is linked to the formality of judgment, and it has
the effect of leaving certain foundational judgments still seeming groundless.
Again, Arendt gestured at this difficulty herself in the final moments of her
essay. After saying that "our decisions about right and wrong will depend on
our choice of company," she wrote, in a crucial and remarkable passage, "In
the unlikely case that someone should come and tell us that he would prefer
Bluebeard for company, and hence take him as his example, the only thing we
could do is to make sure he never comes near us."[38] And that is all she can find
to say about this final decision about whose company to keep in our imaginative
reconstruction of "humanity." The implication is that there is nothing more
that can be said to justify or ground this judgment. Here is the Nietzschean
moment of final and inescapable individual responsibility in Arendt's thought
on judgment. My judgment is, in the end, *my* judgment, and there is nothing
more that can be said – importantly, no more "wooing" or persuading that can
be expected of us on this point.[39]

The second true but perhaps disappointing observation about Arendt's
understanding of representative thinking is that the "intersubjective" character
of the grounds of validity that Arendt's account provides is not a genuine third
way between objectivity and subjectivity. Intersubjectivity is still subjective in
the following sense: The individual must in the end choose his community
of cointerpreters or cojudges on grounds that may remain, to a large extent,
inscrutable to others; he must choose whose consent to woo, whom to try to
persuade or to imagine himself persuading – or, what amounts to the same
thing, choose his interpretation of humanity. To ensure his responsibility for
this choice, there can be no source or grounding for it outside of himself. In
Arendt's own words:

---

[36] Arendt, "Some Questions of Moral Philosophy," p. 143.

[37] Ibid., p. 145.

[38] Ibid., p. 146.

[39] Compare Korsgaard: "The moral life can contain moments when responsibility is so deep that
even a justification is denied us." Korsgaard, "Taking the Law into Our Own Hands," p. 322.

Morality concerns the individual in his singularity. The criterion of right and wrong, the answer to the question what ought I to do? depends in the last analysis neither on habits and customs, which I share with those around me, nor on a command of either divine or human origin, but on what I decide with regard to myself. In other words, I cannot do certain things because having done them I can no longer be able to live with myself.[40]

It is true that Arendt seems to have aspired to find in intersubjectivity a shared world of appearances.[41] But the line of thought explored so far in this chapter suggests that she would have had to be very wary about granting final moral authority to that world. Certainly that world could not be viewed as a source of morality in the Kantian sense, a source of authority analogous to the obligation of the moral law. If the shared world was to be viewed in that way, then its dictates, however intersubjective their mode of derivation, would offer the same possibility of shifting responsibility and making excuses: "I was only following the common sense of the community" is not very different in form from the excuse that Eichmann gave, and seems equally well suited to rationalizing a refusal to judge. If the purpose of Arendt's theory of judgment were merely to replace "the moral law" with "the common world" or "common sense," then the "arbitrating" part of the will, or judgment, would have simply taken on the function of reason with respect to the "instigating" part of the will, and Arendt would have done nothing more than change the terminology of the Kantian categories that Eichmann's example had led her to reject.

Only if we can identify the outcome of intersubjective consultation as wholly our own can we avoid this predicament. The importance of insisting on a judgment and action as ours, even through and after the process of intersubjective reflection, is something Arendt herself suggested: "Furthermore, while I take into account others when judging, this does not mean that I conform in my judgment to theirs. I still speak with my own voice and I do not count noses in order to arrive at what I think is right." She continued, "But my judgment is no longer subjective either, in the sense that I arrive at my conclusions by taking only myself into account."[42] I am not sure what to make of this last sentence, since a "subjective" view certainly can take into account the responses of others. Only if those responses created some ground distinct from myself would they constitute a real alternative to the subjective perspective – but if they claimed authority, then they would necessarily also threaten the responsibility that comes along with subjectivity.

This line of thought helps to explain why Arendt did not take the view of judgment that Habermas has urged upon her. Habermas views the intersubjectively validated ground of judgment that Arendt drew from the third *Critique*

[40] Arendt, *Life of the Mind*, p. 97.
[41] Lawrence J. Biskowski, "Practical Foundations for Political Judgment: Arendt on Action and World," *Journal of Politics* 55 (November 1993): 867–87.
[42] Arendt, "Some Questions of Moral Philosophy," p. 141; cf. Hannah Arendt, "Truth and Politics," in *Between Past and Future* (New York: Penguin, 1968), pp. 227–64, at p. 241.

as "a first approach to a concept of communicative rationality which is built into speech and action itself."[43] He laments the fact that Arendt did not quite take this step herself and that she shied away from asserting that "representative thinking" could in fact provide "a cognitive foundation... for the power of common convictions."[44] But the very essay that Habermas quotes, Arendt's "Truth and Politics," suggests that she shied away from finding in representative thinking anything like communicative rationality. In that essay, she was deeply concerned with the coerciveness of truth claims in politics. Communicative rationality, insofar as it claims to ground a rather firm sort of validity, may not technically be an assertion of "truth," but it cannot help but exert a similar force in moral and political life. Insofar as communicative rationality claims to reveal the dictates of reason in morals and politics, it might well seem (from Arendt's perspective) to threaten the spontaneity, freedom, and responsibility of an individual's judgment in the same way that Kant's dictates of reason did. Communicative rationality would seem to dictate what is right from a perspective external to the individual will of the person doing the judging.

Again, to be clear, it may be that Arendt was wrong to view reason as something external to the individual in this way. Both Kantians and Habermasians would argue, in different ways, that the thought-train I am following in Arendt fails to understand the way in which the will can itself be shaped by reason, that it fails to fully understand or accept what Kant called the "practicality" of reason, and that it overestimates the problem of motivation. They would argue, I think, that she was wrong to view the will's relation to reason as one of obedience. But while I cannot settle this difficult issue here, it seems to me that Arendt's view of the matter is at least not implausible. There is a sense in which her perspective illuminates a deep dilemma in the nature of judgment itself: Can judgments be based on nonsubjective foundations without thereby threatening the freedom and responsibility of those individuals doing the judging? Judgments are inscrutable or incommunicable if they are based entirely on an individual's solipsistic perspective – they are not truly judgments. But if they are based on anything outside that perspective, then they threaten to become irresponsible (in Nietzsche's sense of being alienated from the agent) and coercive (in Arendt's sense of being something obeyed). The elusiveness of Arendt's account of judgment stems in part from the seriousness with which she treated this dilemma. At times she seems to lean toward an account of judgment that was closer to Habermas's view, but at other moments she seems to have caught herself, noticing the coercive potential of such an approach, and pulled back toward a view more responsive to Nietzsche's point. In the thought-train that I am following, at least, she seems to have cared more about responsibility than

---

[43] Habermas, "On the German-Jewish Heritage," p. 130; cf. Seyla Benhabib, *The Reluctant Modernism of Hannah Arendt*, new edition (Lanham, MD: Rowman & Littlefield, 2003), pp. 199–203.

[44] Habermas, "Hannah Arendt's Communications Concept of Power," p. 23.

about communicability. It is the subjective character of judgment that preserves our distance from any set, external source of authority on which we might be tempted to blame our judgments. Therefore, the intersubjective mode of thinking that she described – representative thinking – is ultimately a particular form of subjective thinking.[45]

Another way of seeing that Arendt's intersubjectivity is subjective in this sense is to notice the various places in which she emphasized the *loneliness* of the judging citizen. In *Eichmann in Jerusalem*, she noticed that people capable of distinguishing right from wrong had only their own judgments to guide them, and that their judgments often "happen[ed] to be completely at odds with what they must regard as the unanimous opinion of all those around them . . . "[46] Her account of representative thinking followed Kant in asking the judge to refer to the possible judgments of imagined others rather than the actual judgments of concrete others. In that work of imagination and abstraction, there is a kind of loneliness. At certain moments in Arendt's writings, the loneliness of the judge is almost incomprehensible if not understood against the background of the dilemma about judgment described in the preceding. In her essay "Thinking and Moral Considerations," which began once again with Eichmann, she investigated the link between thoughtfulness and moral judgment through an analysis of the notion of conscience, which she etymologically defined as knowing "with and by myself."[47] She linked conscience to the Socratic injunction, reported in Plato's *Gorgias,* never to become out of harmony with oneself. Several commentators have voiced dissatisfaction with Arendt's use of Plato here. Seyla Benhabib points out that putting the emphasis on our individual desire "to be at home with ourselves" seems to lead Arendt toward a subjective, "quasi-intuitionist conception of moral judgment," a position that seems to fly in the face of Arendt's interest in plurality and intersubjectivity.[48] George Kateb, from a different perspective, concurs, noting, "Subjectivity is intrinsic to [Arendt's understanding of] Socratic conscience: It contains no principle that can be 'generalized.'"[49] Why was Arendt trying so hard here to find a basis for moral judgments in the activities of thinking and judging themselves, activities that occur within the psyche of an individual alone? One way of understanding what motivated Arendt at these otherwise perplexing points in her argument is to emphasize her anxiety about relying on any external grounds for our judgments, anxieties about the lack of responsibility that can arise from leaving the subjective point of view behind.

---

[45] Thus I agree with Young-Bruehl's emphasis on Arendt's effort to develop a "standard of the self." Young-Bruehl, *Why Arendt Matters*, p. 200 ff.

[46] Arendt, *Eichmann in Jerusalem*, p. 294.

[47] Arendt, "Thinking and Moral Considerations," p. 160.

[48] Seyla Benhabib, "Judgment and the Moral Foundations of Politics in Arendt's Thought," *Political Theory* 16, 1 (1988): 29–51, at pp. 44–5; cf. Benhabib, *The Reluctant Modernism of Hannah Arendt,* pp. 190–8.

[49] Kateb, *Hannah Arendt*, p. 102.

15.4 Representative Thinking and Judging-Spectatorship

If it is true that Arendt's representative thinking is ultimately subjective in this sense, in spite of her own occasional protestations otherwise, it is nevertheless true that when we go on to explore the *content* of the singular perspective of the lonely judge, we do not find Arendt describing a narrow or unified point of view. She did not leave behind her interest in plurality and intersubjectivity when she turned from political to moral questions.[50] The most interesting part of her analysis of Socrates' view of conscience as harmony with oneself, for example, is her observation that a certain sort of plurality enters into even the Socratic understanding of the harmonious soul: "Nothing that is identical with itself, truly and absolutely *one* like A is A, can be either in or out of harmony with itself; you always need at least two tones to produce a harmonious sound."[51] The Socratic desire for harmony therefore should not be described as a desire for unity; unison is in some sense the opposite of harmony. Human consciousness itself assumes plurality within the psyche, for otherwise explicit recognition of oneself as a being would not be possible; one can see oneself as a self only from the outside. Difference and otherness, Arendt wrote, were not only characteristic of the public world but were also "conditions for the existence of man's ego."[52] We could not be conscious beings if we were not "two-in-one," she asserted. Thinking and thoughtfulness presume an explicit dialogue with oneself, and while she sometimes contrasted that dialogue with the public debates of the political world, she also insisted that it was a *dialogue* rather than a monologue.[53] She was not so far, then, from Walt Whitman's lovely democratic insight that a single individual could "contain multitudes"; she merely insisted that the multitudes had to be able to live with one another in some form of harmony or, to use her word, friendship.[54]

It was the ability to divide ourselves in this way, to see ourselves and our commitments from the outside – to become spectators to ourselves – that lay behind Arendt's interest in the notion of disinterestedness found in Kant's third *Critique*. She wanted to divide and dissolve the unity of the soul that Nietzsche admired, which is why she defended thoughtfulness and self-consciousness rather than attacking it as Nietzsche had. In "The Crisis in Culture," she justified her interest in disinterestedness by saying that the spectator's perspective could rescue us from the means-end mentality that accompanied the maker's perspective, and thus that the spectator's perspective helped to prevent the modern emphasis on *poesis* from eclipsing all other modes of experiencing the world.[55] In "Truth and Politics," she gave a different argument for

[50] Benhabib, "Judgment and the Moral Foundations of Politics in Arendt's Thought," p. 44.
[51] Arendt, "Thinking and Moral Considerations," p. 183. Emphasis in the original.
[52] Ibid., p. 184.
[53] Arendt, "Some Questions of Moral Philosophy," pp. 96, 105.
[54] Benhabib, "Judgment and the Moral Foundations of Politics in Arendt's Thought," p. 44.
[55] Arendt, "The Crisis in Culture," pp. 217, 219.

disinterestedness: It was the condition of the use of imagination required by representative thinking. Disinterestedness liberated us from our private interests and our local partialities and thereby freed us to imagine the perspective of others, freed us to approach the "enlarged mentality" that Kant described. Behind the interest in disinterestedness lay Arendt's conviction that judgment, both moral and political, requires us to regard ourselves from a distance. In a sense, disinterestedness serves, for Arendt, to inject into one's own lonely consciousness and conscience the space or capaciousness necessary to judge. Considering the viewpoints of potential others is a work of imagination, and "the only condition for this exertion of the imagination is disinterestedness, the liberation from one's own private interests. Hence, *even if I shun all company or am completely isolated while forming an opinion, I am not simply together only with myself in the solitude of philosophical thought. . . .*"[56]

It was vital for Arendt that the imaginative work of representative thinking was not designed to create a new identity for oneself. Instead, she argued that when I engage in representative thinking, I aim at "being and thinking in my own identity where actually I am not."[57] This crucial and fascinating phrase explains why she referred to the form of thinking as "representative." Representation is necessary to put oneself where one is not. The formality of Arendt's mode of judgment can be criticized for removing us from our concrete circumstances (in spite of the concern with particulars), but its purpose is to make room for the work of representation. The emptiness of such a formalistic mode of judgment is designed to create an inner absence. If one were simply *present* to oneself in the direct, unmediated way that Nietzsche's playful, strong, free spirit is, there would be no opportunity to engage in the imaginative work of representation. As Hannah Pitkin pointed out in her classic study years ago, the paradox within the very idea of representation is that it posits something being present in some sense even where it is actually absent.[58] Arendt's notion of representative thinking is one in which the perspectives of others are somehow made present someplace where in fact they do not exist – inside of us. If those other people actually existed inside of us, we would be – literally – someone else. So instead they must be re-presented. Arendt's account does not quite remove the mysteriousness of this re-presentation, but she at least suggests why such a phenomenon must be possible if an individual psyche is to be capable of observing itself from some distance. The imaginative work of making absent others present to oneself, and of emptying oneself enough to admit those represented others, is the work of representative thinking and is what makes judgment possible for an individual. What judgment presumed, she thought, was precisely the lack of an identity so singular or unified as to remain closed to such representations or imaginations.

---

[56] Arendt, "Truth and Politics," pp. 241–2; cf. Arendt, "The Crisis in Culture," p. 210.
[57] Arendt, "Truth and Politics," p. 241.
[58] Hannah Pitkin, *The Concept of Representation* (Berkeley: University of California Press, 1984), pp. 8–9.

This point about identity suggests one understanding of the link that Arendt often made between judgment and persuasion, the effort to woo the consent of others. The phenomenon of persuasion seems to require something like representative thinking, insofar as it requires a certain flexibility or capaciousness in our conception of what constitutes ourselves. To be open to persuasion, we must be able to imagine ourselves believing something different and yet still being ourselves. Presumably, if all our convictions and beliefs changed, we would no longer be ourselves; every effort to persuade might therefore be seen as an assault on our identity. But the political life that Arendt defended was one in which persuasion had to remain a real possibility. And a condition of that possibility seems to be the capacity to imagine oneself as something other than oneself, and yet still oneself – the capacity to re-present oneself. The distinction that Arendt made between persuasion and "coercion by truth" depends upon this fact about persuasion, for it is the ability to imagine alternate selves that remain nevertheless the same self that allows us to assimilate new opinions actively as our own rather than merely be coerced by them.[59] Our own judgments are less coercive than Kantian dictates of reason only because we play a more significant role in creating and assimilating them, and that activity of assimilation cannot be understood without referring to the imaginative work of re-presentation.[60]

What Eichmann lacked, on Arendt's account, was the interior space in which that imaginative work could occur, the internal space that judgment requires. Too satisfied with his own identity, too comfortable in his own private life, his banality consisted in a lack of imagination. His failure did not lie, she thought, simply in choosing the wrong standards to use when judging. Nor did his failure lie in not knowing which standards to use. Instead, he failed by not judging at all, by not being able to see himself from a spectator's vantage point, and by not creating within himself the plurality and capaciousness that judging-spectatorship needs. And those writers who had condemned Arendt's own writings as too judgmental, those critics who had asked, "who am I to judge?" were guilty of the same sort of error. Like Eichmann, they were plagued by a disinclination to judge born not ultimately of doubt about the standards on the basis of which one might judge, but of an overly comfortable, settled identity too at home with itself and too little provoked to see and judge itself from the outside.

15.5 Judging-Spectatorship and Representative Government

We are now in a position to return to the opening theme of this chapter: Representative government is often said to lock citizens tragically outside the

---

[59] Arendt, "The Crisis in Culture," p. 223.

[60] I offer an account of the link between persuasion and judgment in Bryan Garsten, *Saving Persuasion: A Defense of Rhetoric and Judgment* (Cambridge, MA: Harvard University Press, 2006).

realm of participatory politics by trapping them most of the time in the role of spectators. But with the preceding reflections in mind, one might read this feature of representative government more positively. Representative government institutionalizes the role of spectator and so encourages citizens in viewing any existing orders or codes from a certain distance and with a certain detachment. In doing so, representative government aims to institutionalize what Arendt described as the precondition of judgment.[61] It also seems to model the stance that citizens should take with regard to their own commitments, encouraging us to see them as partial and provisional, not fully constitutive of one's identity, open to persuasion. Furthermore, if there is any truth in Kant's sense that people watching the French Revolution could reveal their moral natures through their enthusiastic judgments about it in a way that they could not through their actions, representative government would seem to provide a place for the expression of their moral natures by institutionalizing their role as spectators. Similarly, Ronald Beiner has suggested that Arendt's emphasis on history in her later reflections on judgment might seem to distance the faculty of judgment from the work of politics, since historians render their judgments only after the fact and rescue the meaning of events only with hindsight. Judgment can therefore seem only marginally related to politics, "a kind of vicarious action, a way of recouping our citizenship in default of a genuine public realm."[62] But again, the perspective that I am suggesting here would understand representative government as an effort to protect a place for the historian's judgment in the practice of politics, providing an opportunity for citizen-historians to dignify political action through their judgments from the sidelines. The public space and recognition that Arendt described as an integral part of political life exist only if an audience exists, and those citizens in liberal democracies who seem to do nothing more than watch and judge are the ones who provide the audience. True, more active citizens can watch and judge one another, but they are often too busy watching themselves in the eyes of others. Judging-spectatorship is a distinct role for the great majority of citizens who are not actively participating.

In promoting a certain alienation from politics, representative government also promotes a certain kind of self-alienation. But if Arendt is right about the reasons that democracy can veer toward totalitarianism, then this feature of representative government may be a blessing in disguise. In her essay "The Crisis in Culture," Arendt suggested that entertainment differs from culture in not being shaped by the faculty of judgment. A politics in which citizens decline to judge is therefore a politics of entertainment. Arendt viewed such a politics as a grave threat in mass democracies; she feared the consequences of citizens watching politics without accepting their responsibility to judge it.

---

[61] For a recent effort to make judgment central to an understanding of representative government, see Nadia Urbinati, *Representative Democracy: Principles and Genealogy* (Chicago: University of Chicago Press, 2006).

[62] Beiner, "Hannah Arendt on Judging," p. 153.

Of course, the presence of representative institutions does not guarantee the exercise of judgment, and the disinterestedness that these institutions promote can easily slide into lack of interest or apathy, a propensity to find nothing more than entertainment in political life. In this chapter, I mean only to suggest an argument about how the purpose of representative government might best be understood, not to examine the extent to which that form of government achieves its purpose. The purpose of representative government will elude our understanding so long as we think the only opposite of apathy is participatory politics. There is another opposite of apathy: attentive and judging spectatorship. The challenge to which Arendt's thoughts on judgment alerts us is that of finding a way to conceive of citizenship in mass representative democracies, a way of thinking that concedes the dominance of spectatorship in citizens' experience without collapsing into a defense of passivity and subjection.[63]

This chapter has not resolved the philosophical issues that make Arendt's account of judgment seem so elusive. Especially, the grounds of particular judgments remain elusive. In fact, it may seem fair to ask whether Arendt's worries about responsibility led her, at least in the train of thought explored here, to underemphasize the importance of other factors in evaluating moral judgments. Eichmann was culpable not only because he refused to take responsibility for his actions, but also because his actions were wrong.[64] Nevertheless, the elusiveness of Arendt's account of this wrongness is central to her point. She thought any standard that no longer eluded us threatened to become a source of unthinkingness and an excuse not to judge for ourselves. Elusive standards of judgment have the effect of preventing us from blaming the principles or dictates of reason for our actions and opinions. To say that the standards of judgment are elusive is to say that any particular standard always seems somehow incomplete, that one can always see the matter from outside the perspective provided by that standard, as a spectator. Seen in its best light, the elusiveness of judgment provokes continued thoughtfulness and imagination and ensures the continued need for making judgment-calls *ourselves*. Arendt's perspective thus provides a surprisingly compelling way of understanding and appreciating the strength and assertiveness of judging-spectators. To judge, to depart from the safety of rules, codes, and principles, to insist on one's own

---

[63] One project for political scientists that might emerge from this perspective would be a reevaluation of theoretical understandings of the act of voting. Instead of seeing voting as a moment of participation in ruling, as many contemporary political science treatments do, it might be more fruitful to think of voting as a moment of judging-spectatorship by those who are not ruling. Morris Fiorina's "retrospective voting" comes closer to this than, for example, accounts of civic engagement or participation that include voting alongside activities such as campaigning or organizing. See Morris Fiorina, *Retrospective Voting in American National Elections* (New Haven: Yale University Press, 1981). Another project for political scientists would be an effort to classify types of nonparticipation in a manner analogous to the way in which political scientists have classified types of participation.

[64] In this sense Kateb is probably right that "judging is too frail a support" for morality. Kateb, *Hannah Arendt*, p. 38.

personal stake in one's evaluations, requires a bold spirit that is quite different from the apathetic submissiveness often ascribed to those citizens of representative democracies who do nothing more than watch politics and render judgments about what they see. If Arendt's account of judgment does not offer a complete or satisfactory account of judgment, it nevertheless, through its very elusiveness, helps to highlight part of what makes judging worthy of attention and respect.

15.6 Appendix

From Eichmann's testimony, on his view of Kant's categorical imperative:[65]

PRESIDING JUDGE: The Accused will now answer questions from the Judges.

JUDGE RAVEH: I shall ask you a few questions in German. Do you remember at one point in your police interrogation talking about the Kantian imperative, and saying that throughout your entire life you had tried to live according to the Kantian imperative?

ACCUSED: Yes.

Q: There is no need to show this to you; do you remember it clearly?

A: Yes, I remember it clearly.

Q: What did you mean by the Kantian imperative when you said that?

A: I meant by this that the principle of my volition and the principle of my life must be such that it could at any time be raised to be the principle of general legislation, as Kant more or less puts it in his categorical imperative.

Q: I see, therefore, that when you said this you were precisely aware of Kant's categorical imperative?

A: Yes, I was.

Q: And so, do you mean to say by this that your activities in the course of deporting Jews corresponded to the Kantian categorical imperative?

A: No, certainly not, because these activities . . . at that time I had to live and act under compulsion, and the compulsion of a third person, during exceptional times. I meant by this, by the . . . by this living according to the Kantian principle, to the extent that I am my own master and able to organize my life according to my volition and according to my wishes. This is also quite obvious, in fact it could not be meant any other way, because if I am subjected to a higher power and a higher force, then my free will as such is eliminated, and then, since I can no longer be master of my free will and volition, I cannot in fact adopt any principles whatsoever which I cannot influence, but, on the contrary, I must, and also may, build obedience to the authorities into this concept, and then the authorities bear the responsibility. In my judgment, that also belongs to it.

[65] Available online at http://www.nizkor.org/hweb/people/e/eichmann-adolf/transcripts/Sessions/Session-105–04.html, accessed April 29, 2007.

Q: Do you mean to say by this that following the authorities' orders blindly signifies realizing the Kantian categorical imperative?

A: Since the Kantian imperative was laid down, there had never been such a destructive and unprecedented order from a head of state. That is why it was new, and that is why there is no possibility of comparisons, and no . . . one cannot have any idea of how it was. There was the War. I had to do just one thing. I had to obey, because I could not change anything. And so I just placed my life, as far as I could, in the service – I would put it this way – of this Kantian demand. And I have already said that in fact others had to answer for the fundamental aspect. As a minor recipient of orders, I had to obey, I could not evade that.

Q: I understood from the first part of your answer that you meant that these years in which you were a blind recipient of orders would be excluded from life according to the Kantian imperative. And I intended to ask you about this, from when till when did it last? But then you added something, and that again changed the whole thing. Now I do not know what your final position is on this.

A: Killing people violently cannot be according to the spirit of the Kantian imperative, because in principle it is not something God-given.

Q: That means that there was a time when you did not live by the categorical imperative?

A: Could not live, because higher powers made it impossible for me to live by it.

Q: From when to when was this?

A: Strictly speaking, that was from the moment when I was transferred against my will, and against my wishes, to Berlin.

Q: Till when?

A: Until the end.

Q: And throughout this time it was clear to you that during that period you could not live by the categorical imperative, although you had in principle arranged actually to live your life by it?

A: During this time I read Kant's *Critique of Practical Reason*.

Q: For the first time?

A: Then was the first time.

Q: So that it was only then that you encountered the idea of the categorical concept?

A: I had come across this earlier, but I had not concerned myself particularly with it; instead, the Kantian categorical imperative was disposed of shortly as follows: "True to the law, obedient, a proper personal life, not to come into conflict with the law." This, I would say, was the categorical imperative for a small man's domestic use.

Q: From where had you taken this definition of the categorical imperative for the small man? When you read Kant later, did you find it corresponded to his definition?

A: No, I sensed this earlier on, because for someone like myself it is not possible to understand all of the subject of Kant completely; instead, I only took from these writings what I could understand, and what my imagination could somehow grasp.

Q: So I understand that you learned the true concept at the time you were dealing with the deportation of Jews?

A: As to whether it was the genuine complete concept of the categorical imperative, I am still not able to grasp even today, but I have grasped one thing – that giving such orders by a supreme head of state cannot accord with the spirit of a divine order. But now I was trying to come to terms with myself, and I saw that I was unable to change anything and unable to do anything.

Q: What interests me more now is whether then, in the years when you came to Berlin – against your will, as you put it – until 1945, whether during that period you were aware, or became aware, that you were not living according to Kant's categorical imperative?

A: I first became aware of this in Kulm. But it would not be right for me to say I became aware that I was not living according to this Kantian requirement, but I said to myself: I cannot for the present live entirely according to it, although I would like to do so.

Q: And this realization remained with you up until the end? Until the end of 1944?

A: I did not think of it every day, but when I travel, it is my habit not to speak a lot, but to reflect.

Q: All right, then: When you thought it over, then did it become clear to you?

A: In fact, in the end that was also the direct reason for my approaching Mueller from time to time.

16

Existential Values in Arendt's Treatment of Evil and Morality

George Kateb

Existential values dominate Hannah Arendt's political theory. The result is that morality often ends up either subordinate in importance to existential values or sidelined by them. Morality must struggle to be heard. Most famously, her espousal of political action grows not out of moral concern, but out of her existential values, which political action is intended to serve. But the story does not end there. The existential values present in Arendt's writings that I consider are the two that I believe (with some encouragement from Arendt) constitute human dignity: human status and human stature. Human dignity for Arendt rests on human uniqueness, the human difference from the rest of nature. The salient element of Arendt's concept of human *status* is not being animal-like. The salient element of Arendt's concept of *stature* is the creative and audacious use of freedom in thought, art, and action. I do not quite mean to say that Arendt is a philosopher of existentialism, properly speaking, though she has noteworthy affinities to it, especially to some of its French variants.

Although my explicit discussion of *The Human Condition*, which is her most extended treatment of existential values, is concentrated in the last pages of this chapter, that book is always in the background of my discussion.

Hannah Arendt's understanding of political evil is hard to match. The depth of her understanding, however, does not stop her from condemning such evil with a force that is also hard to match. The more she perceives, the more unforgiving she grows. She has no doubt as to what evil is and why certain political phenomena should be called by that name, the most condemnatory of all names. Is there anyone more trustworthy in illuminating this darkness and

A version of this article has previously appeared as George Kateb, "Existential Values in Arendt's Treatment of Evil and Morality," in *Social Research. Hannah Arendt's Centennary. Political and Philosophic Perspectives*, Part I, 74, 3 (Fall 2007): 811–55. It has been revised for inclusion in this book. I wish to acknowledge the help of Sharon Cameron, Jerome Kohn, Jeremy Waldron, and James P. Young.

guiding people's response to it? Yet I think that it is fair to say that thinking about morality is not congenial to her talent. One might expect that one who writes so powerfully about evil would publish a general view of all kinds and degrees of wrongdoing and, at least by implication, right conduct. Even if political evil is in some respects discontinuous with, say, either oppression or injustice, even if evil is qualitatively different and not only worse in intensity of inflicted suffering, isn't it a bit odd that a great theorist of evil showed such a reluctance to publish more extensively on the general subject of morality and immorality? She seems suspicious of morality, as if she had an allergy to it. Perhaps evil blots out all other phenomena of wrongdoing? Are they only to be taken as inevitable and as posing no great philosophical mystery or even perplexity? Another possibility, which I take more seriously, is that Arendt believes that too much attention to morality would dilute adherence to existential values, which I take to be her deepest commitment.

Thanks to the splendid editorial labors of Jerome Kohn, to whom any student of Arendt's work owes a tremendous debt, Arendt's relationship to morality, and the connection of morality to evil, has become much fuller. The volume he put together, *Responsibility and Judgment* (2003), with a fine introduction, helps us see Arendt's hardest thinking about morality and immorality in themselves and in relation to evil. The main text is "Some Questions of Moral Philosophy" (1965–6), but the full version of "Personal Responsibility under Dictatorship" (1964) and several other items, including the hitherto unpublished presentation at the American Philosophical Association, "Collective Responsibility" (1968), also enhance our knowledge of what Arendt thought about the general subject of morality and its relation to evil. I do not say that in these texts Arendt gives us a fully worked-out view of morality, much less that the view that appears is free of difficulties. But we can now make a better sense of Arendt's moral thinking; and just by that, we can, I believe, make something more of Arendt's thought as a whole.

In this chapter, I first sketch Arendt's conception of morality and its connection to evil. Then in the next section, I address Arendt's characterization of evil. I go on to examine Arendt's treatment of the proper moral response to evil, either when violent and carried out by groups or individuals or when nonviolent and carried out by particular individuals. In the last section, I turn to the familiar theme of the place of morality in politics when politics is free of evil, if not of smaller kinds of wrongdoing. I do not think there is a paradox in hating evil while remaining suspicious of morality. It all depends on what one means by morality. Arendt offers a case that is worth serious study. But her case has its unsettling aspects. And as always, her sensitivity to philosophical difficulty is so great that her ideas are full of qualifications, and more than that, she sometimes turns on herself and seems to countenance what she had elsewhere criticized. Reading Arendt is always an adventure. Trying to prepare a short commentary on any aspect of her work necessitates making a few matters more explicit than she does, while omitting more than a few details that are enriching to the student but that do not fit easily into anyone's scheme.

Before turning to our first theme, Arendt's conception of morality and its relationship to evil, I would like to mention some comments that Arendt made in one of the few personal accounts that appear in the works that she published or intended for publication. Perhaps Arendt's comparative reticence about morality becomes more comprehensible when we attend to these comments, which seem to reflect Arendt's lifelong disposition.

Early in the full version of "Personal Responsibility under Dictatorship," Arendt tries to explain "how uncomfortable most of us are when confronted with moral issues."[1] She then says that her early intellectual formation "occurred in an atmosphere where nobody paid much attention to moral questions."[2] We could add that her doctoral dissertation was a treatise not in moral philosophy, but in moral psychology and even more in those existential questions that are a large part of philosophical anthropology. Insistence on moral rectitude "would have appeared to me as Philistine."[3] Moral rectitude did not therefore figure decisively in the common evaluation of any person. The reigning attitude in her circles when she was a young woman was that "moral conduct is a matter of course."[4] That is to say, people knew what moral behavior was, and mostly practiced it unremarkably. But the events starting in 1933 and lasting until 1945 changed all that, because "monstrosities no one believed possible at the beginning" manifested themselves.[5] (Arendt does not speak of the protracted horrors of World War I, as if the horrors were not monstrosities; but weren't they?) Thus Arendt went from – what shall we call it? – a tacit and untested moral sense to an initially "speechless horror"[6] that was in some part moral in nature, but that usual ideas of morality could not begin to address. She says that it took many people twenty years (since the end of World War II) "to come to terms with what happened."[7] She complains that she had "so little mental or conceptual preparation for moral issues.... We had to learn everything from scratch," and learn without the assistance of moral categories and general rules that had no relevance to evil.[8] Worst of all, it will turn out, as Arendt's analysis proceeds, especially in "Some Questions of Moral Philosophy," that totalitarian evil could not have sustained itself as a system of atrocious crimes against humanity unless large numbers of people were in some sense moral. Morality, in its most customary meaning, facilitated totalitarian evil and always facilitates any evil.

[1] Hannah Arendt, "Personal Responsibility under Dictatorship" (1968), in *Responsibility and Judgment*, edited by Jerome Kohn (New York: Schocken, 2003), p. 22.
[2] Ibid.
[3] Ibid.
[4] Ibid.
[5] Ibid., p. 23.
[6] Hannah Arendt, "Some Questions in Moral Philosophy" (1965–6), in *Responsibility and Judgment*, p. 56.
[7] Arendt, "Personal Responsibility under Dictatorship," p. 23.
[8] Ibid. p. 25.

I go through these comments by Arendt because they may help elucidate the reasons for the lack of sustained theoretical interest in moral issues – apart from "Some Questions" – despite her steady attention to evil. Immorality is one thing, and evil absolutely another. Evil is so different that even words like villainy and wickedness are not adequate to it; they fit extreme immorality, not evil.[9] She nonetheless lectured extensively on moral philosophy in the mid-1960s and established a connection between evil and the proper immediate domestic response to it, which was moral conduct (nothing more) in one particular sense of moral. (Violent response to it is another distinct but related moral matter.) Yet she did not publish the lectures on moral philosophy.

We can also make a more general point: Were it not for the occurrence of political evil in the form of totalitarianism, Arendt might never have interrupted the flow of her primary and most profound concerns, which were not moral at all, but – loosely and broadly speaking – existential. It is roughly true that Arendt does not find moral conduct existentially interesting except when it requires a distinctive human capacity like thinking or judging, or a trait like courage, or an expression of selflessness, all of which testify to human stature. It is a major fact of life that what is properly called immorality causes suffering, but suffering is not in itself an existentially interesting fact. All creatures suffer. The virtues and vices were originally defined by classical antiquity as assertive political traits, not ameliorative private ones.[10] As for love and friendship, about both of which Arendt writes so powerfully, they are not in the moral sphere. Even her interest in totalitarian evil, as I will later suggest, is also finally existential more than it is moral. To anticipate, the horror of totalitarianism was human degradation, the victims' loss of human status – what she calls dehumanization – more than the physical and psychological suffering that effected the degradation. Morality is about suffering, but there are existential considerations that matter for Arendt more than suffering as such. On the one hand, evil is discontinuous with immorality; on the other, moral values can claim no superiority to existential values. Morality is confined.

Let us now turn to Arendt's conception of morality and morality's relationship to evil. I concentrate first on what she means by morality. One thing to notice is that Arendt works with the assumption that the moral agent is always the individual, whether the agent acts as an individual in private life or an office-holder in political life, or as one who thinks that he or she is a mere "cog,"[11] or is a follower, or an uncommitted but dutiful cooperator. Without elaborating, she says in "Some Questions" that "Legal and moral issues are by no means the same, but they have in common that they deal with persons, and not with

---

[9] Arendt, "Some Questions in Moral Philosophy," p. 74; cf. Hannah Arendt, "Thinking and Moral Considerations," in *Responsibility and Judgment*, p. 188.

[10] Hannah Arendt, "Collective Responsibility" (1968), in *Responsibility and Judgment*, p. 151.

[11] Arendt, "Personal Responsibility under Dictatorship," p. 31.

systems or organizations."[12] She wants to block such defensive maneuvers as an agent's appeal to superior orders or acts of state, both of which work to exonerate individuals from responsibility for the evil (or other wrong) they do as participants or dutiful, nonresistant cooperators.

Incidentally, I think that she nonetheless favors the "double standard of morality" that the state allows itself by the doctrine of reason of state.[13] She approvingly cites more than once Machiavelli's advice that the prince must learn how not to be good (*essere non buono*) while denying (not merely ignoring) that Machiavelli's additional advice is that the prince must know how to do the worst sorts of wrong (*male*), which is usually translated as evil because of the extremism of Machiavelli's examples.[14] To be sure, Machiavelli says that his second piece of advice merely repeats the first. In any event, I am not sure how her acceptance of reason of state goes with her rejection of the claimed innocence of impersonal role behavior.

Only persons, then, not reified abstractions, can be held responsible, even when their behavior is free of any self-conscious will to do or allow evil or other wrong. They are responsible when they go through the motions of their work or just go along. From the start, people are responsible for the organizations they join at any level, or allow to continue and flourish, and for the policies that ensue. There may of course be other conceptual reasons for Arendt's refusal to adopt "the moral viewpoint" when assessing "systems or organizations,"[15] but for her one conceptual reason could *not* be that the deeds of organized groups are impersonal and hence beyond the individual agent's or the philosopher's judgments of right and wrong.

What does Arendt mean by morality? She means more than one thing, but does not systematically sort the several meanings that figure in her work. I have found the following meanings. The two most important are, first, morality as mores, which are the conventions of right and wrong conduct that are acknowledged and practiced in a given society. Mores change with time, even though they are "solidified through tradition," and they are valid only "on the ground of agreements."[16] We should add, however, that there are conventions common to many societies. One of those common conventions is the basic definition of justice: Preserve each in what is rightfully his or hers. Justice is primordially an avoidance of injustice as improper dispossession. I am not sure that Arendt ever discusses this notion, though her arguments need it. I think that she just assumes it. That means that some part of the content of the morality of mores usually includes primordial and common justice, even if dedication to it is unreasoned and shallow. In any event, the natural home of mores, of

---

[12] Ibid., p. 57.

[13] Arendt, "Collective Responsibility," p. 154.

[14] Arendt, "Some Questions in Moral Philosophy," p. 80; Machiavelli's two pieces of advice are in *The Prince*, chapters 15, 18.

[15] Arendt, "Some Questions in Moral Philosophy," p. 57.

[16] Hannah Arendt, *The Human Condition* (Chicago: University of Chicago Press, 1958), p. 245. (Hereafter abbreviated *HC*.)

routine morality, is everyday life, but people carry their mores into their public engagements. On the matter of mores, therefore, Arendt establishes no sharp line between private and public. The "intrusion of [personal] criminality into the public realm" is always possible.[17]

The second major meaning of morality is contained in the Socratic precept that is found in the *Gorgias*: It is better for the person to suffer wrong than to do it to another person. Although Arendt does not fill out the precept, we can do so with the help of the *Crito* and Book I of the *Republic*: Not only is it better for the person to suffer wrong than to initiate it, but it is also better for the person to suffer wrong without retaliation than to suffer wrong and then retaliate against the wrongdoer. Arendt thinks that the Socratic precept is definitive of morality. It silently governs the everyday life of the truly moral person, and it may also have political applications in unusual circumstances. But as we shall see, her view of this precept does not rule out self-defense or defense of others.

Other meanings of morality found in Arendt's work include the following. There are the moral commandments of God as revealed to Moses in the Jewish scriptures. These commandments give no reasons for their content and imply no order of importance among them. But the commandments are absolute because they come from God; they are not to be doubted or quarreled with. Does Arendt believe in the existence of the divine source of the moral commandments? She seems to say both yes and no. Then, there is the selfless morality of Christian goodness as taught by Jesus in the gospels. Actually, Christian goodness, a kind of love, goes beyond morality and even supererogation. What comes from love, as Nietzsche says (with Jesus in mind), occurs beyond good and evil.[18] Last, there is the morality that authentic political action engenders from its own nature and needs, the morality internal to politics and practiced by individuals committed to the political life. As we all know, promise keeping and forgiveness define this morality for Arendt.

In sum, Arendt takes up in varying extent five versions of morality: mores, Socratic morality, God's commandments, the teachings of Jesus, and the morality of authentic politics. Let us notice again that evil as embodied in murderous totalitarianism necessarily offends every version of morality that Arendt discusses, except the morality of mores, which it offends only contingently; it also obviously offends the primordial notion that dispossession is to be avoided. But nonetheless, evil is not merely immorality.

How does Arendt regard violent resistance (massive or not) to evil, but also to tyranny, despotism, and dictatorship? If it is moral, under what version of morality does it go? That is, is the use of violence in resistance to evil or to something lesser, like oppression or injustice, a moral activity of some kind? When people act to avoid or resist being improperly or even cruelly

---

[17] Arendt, "Personal Responsibility under Dictatorship," p. 24.
[18] Friedrich Nietzsche, *Beyond Good and Evil* (1886), translated by Walter Kaufmann (New York: Vintage, 1966), section 153, p. 90.

dispossessed, are they acting morally? Is there any morally significant difference between acting violently to preserve ourselves and acting violently for the sake of preserving others when we are otherwise safe? I will take up some of these questions more fully later. Here I would just say that Arendt thinks that violence is not always simply immoral; it can be morally allowed or justified, but its use is – so far as I can tell – not in itself purely moral or just, even in cases of literal personal self-preservation. However, she seems to consider retribution a moral act. Retribution is right, but self-preservation is not right or wrong, just allowable. This is a rather awkward position, isn't it?

I know of no way of aligning Arendt's views of self-preservation, resistance for others, and retribution, and then incorporating them into any of the versions of morality she takes up. These views must derive from or bear some relation to the indispensable maxim that each person is by right to be preserved in his or her own, in what belongs to the person. Leaving aside resistance for the sake of others, I think that Arendt often relies on a tacit and certainly untheorized notion of a right of self-preservation, violent where need be, possessed by people against all those who are trying to dispossess them of their basic human rights, to destroy or oppress them. Even Socrates did not lay down his weapons on the battlefield.

The five kinds of morality that Arendt discusses do not exhaust the field of morality; nor are they quite sufficient for her, I believe, when she attempts to deal with all the questions in moral philosophy that concern her.

In passing, I wish to mention Arendt's occasionally voiced moral skepticism. Here and there in her work, Arendt appears to express some sympathy for the view that without belief in God, morality has no foundation. In periods of widespread unbelief, morality is therefore subjective. In addition, the very activity of thinking, which may develop conscience and hence help to inoculate a person against wrongdoing and complicity with evil, may also move in the opposite direction by tending to erode moral certainty. She says that "conventions, the rules and standards by which we usually live, don't stand up too well under examination."[19] Furthermore, Arendt sometimes conflates moral skepticism and the abdication of morality (in the form of the hitherto prevailing morality of mores) by millions of people. In *Origins*, she says, for example, that when a society gives "silent consent" as "hundreds of thousands" of people are rendered homeless and stateless, and "millions" are made "economically superfluous" by unemployment, amid political disintegration, the only conclusion is that "[t]his . . . could only happen because the Rights of Man, which had never been philosophically established but merely formulated, which had never been politically secured but merely proclaimed, have, in their traditional form, lost all validity."[20] Rights are thus both philosophically uncertain and in many

---

[19] Arendt, "Some Questions in Moral Philosophy," p. 104.
[20] Hannah Arendt, *The Origins of Totalitarianism* (1951), 2nd enlarged edition (New York: World, 1958), p. 447. (Hereafter abbreviated *OT*.)

circumstances politically ineffective; but I do not think that Arendt means that they often prove ineffective mainly because they are philosophically uncertain.

I will not explore Arendt's skeptical moments; I will only emphasize the fact that she has no doubt as to what evil is. It seems to me, however, that if you are sure what evil is, you will be sure what immorality (in various kinds and degrees) is, even if you think that evil is discontinuous with immorality. I also surmise that she was not too deeply troubled philosophically by the wish to validate morality. She says that for truly moral people, the content of morality, understood as Socratic morality, is self-evident, even though its practice is never routine.[21] Then again, most people are not truly moral and no philosophical argument will persuade them to be moral. It is not that every man is a self-aggrandizing Callicles, but that every man is only everyman, given over to conformity and self-love.

A part of her conception of morality is her view of the space that morality fills. It is, in brief, the field of the "not at all horrible."[22] From the perspective of reflection on evil, moral issues look like "harmless side issues" in comparison.[23] (We should notice, however, that she is bemused by the thought that many people feel that any wrongdoing short of the worst policies of totalitarianism does not have much weight.[24]) She says there is "a distinction between transgressions, such as those we are confronted with daily and with which we know how to come to terms or how to get rid of either through punishment or forgiveness, and those offenses where all we can say is 'This should never have happened.'"[25] Evil is what should never have happened, whereas immorality is woven into life and hence irremovably woven into that for which we should feel gratitude.

Even more severely, Arendt says that "the invocation of allegedly moral principles for matters of everyday conduct is usually a fraud."[26] Arendt is averse to seeing a moral issue implicated in every choice or act as people lead their lives. She is almost as far removed from modern consequentialism as it is possible to be. Temperamentally, experientially, and theoretically, Arendt keeps her distance from morality (in all the senses she specifies), for the most part. Yet when evil becomes the subject, morality in the two meanings of mores and Socratic morality makes a vivid appearance in Arendt's thinking. We turn now to the nature of evil as Arendt conceptualizes it. What is especially noteworthy is that morality in the sense of mores can allow evil to flourish, while both Socratic morality and the quasimorality of allowable violence define resistance to evil. Thus, one kind of morality facilitates doing evil whereas other kinds battle against it. That is the main part of Arendt's complex story.

[21] Arendt, "Some Questions in Moral Philosophy," pp. 77–8.
[22] Arendt, "Personal Responsibility under Dictatorship," p. 23.
[23] Arendt, "Some Questions in Moral Philosophy," p. 56.
[24] Hannah Arendt, "Home to Roost" (1975), in *Responsibility and Judgment*, p. 266.
[25] Arendt, "Some Questions in Moral Philosophy," p. 109.
[26] Ibid., p. 104.

Arendt's most concentrated discussion of the nature of evil is in what originally was the last section of the last chapter of *The Origins of Totalitarianism*
and retained in the second edition (chapter 12, section 3). *Responsibility and
Judgment* fills out some aspects of this discussion. What is evil? The evil that
especially concerns Arendt is totalitarian evil as manifested in death and slave-
labor camps. Arendt defines totalitarian evil as "the crimes which men can
neither punish nor forgive" (*OT*, 459; see also *HC*, 241). Thus when Arendt
refers to some atrocious individual act such as murder as evil, the fullness of her
definition – unpunishable and unforgivable crimes – is not present. Wickedness
or villainy, in private or public life, is evil, but not absolute evil, because it can
be either punished or forgiven, at least in principle. Still, we should notice that
when she deals at length with Socrates, as the hero of moral awareness and
hence of refusal to become an instrument of serious wrongdoing, she is working with someone who opposed tyranny, both oligarchic and democratic, not
totalitarianism. Nonetheless, Socrates is the model for one kind of resistance
to totalitarian evil. Let it be added: He is the model for individual nonviolent
resistance. Totalitarianism is not in its essential motivation and practices a
system equivalent to the historically familiar forms of arbitrary or repressive
systems such as tyranny, despotism, or dictatorship, but, in Arendt's account,
the moral person's resistance is of the same nature under all these systems. The
historically familiar forms of wrongful government could be said to have done
particular acts that were evil, but not evil in the same full sense of absolute evil
represented by the system of totalitarian extermination.

Arendt refers to the unforgivable sin, the irremovable stumbling block, the
skandalon, that Jesus talks about, and about which he says it were better for
the perpetrator "that a millstone were hanged about his neck and he cast into
the sea."[27] By these words, Jesus condemns without mercy the sin of causing
young ones to sin or stumble. It would be better for the perpetrator had he
never been born. Arendt seems to run together this sin with the unforgivable
blasphemy against the Holy Ghost.[28] Be that as it may, she is intent on making
unforgivable the evil whereby "the fact of existence itself" is destroyed (*OT*,
442). Some transgressions come about to be forgiven; others must be legally
punished when they violate the order of society. Murder itself, the worst form
of immorality, is, however, only a "limited evil" (*OT*, 442). She says that, after
all, the murderer "still moves within the realm of life and death familiar to
us"; she adds rather shockingly and quite by the way that the man whom the
murderer slays "has to die anyway" (*OT*, 442). The inference one can make
from this reckless phrase is that the fact of premature, violent death is less
important than the victim's existential condition at the time of death: degraded
or undegraded.

[27] Matthew 18:6, other gospels; Arendt, "Personal Responsibility under Dictatorship," p. 109.
[28] Matthew 12:31–2; other gospels.

Although totalitarian extermination is murder, it is more than murder. But what makes it unpunishable and unforgivable murder – absolute evil? Perhaps it is the scale of murder – murder in the millions that transforms the crime of murder into evil? However, she does not seem to think that the numbers of the dead reach to the heart of the matter, as someone enclosed within a theory of morality might. No, the most important point is not reached "by counting the many millions of victims." The fact is that "extermination of whole peoples had happened before in antiquity, as well as in modern colonization."[29] (Again, she does not mention the mass casualties of either world war.)

In differentiating the evil of totalitarian extermination, she says that what is crucial is that mass murder not only took place within a legal framework but that it was animated by the command "'Thou shalt kill,' not thy enemy but innocent people who were not even potentially dangerous, and not for any reason of necessity but, on the contrary, even against all military and other utilitarian considerations."[30] Indeed, "Hitler believed he needed a war as a smokescreen for his nonmilitary killing operations."[31] The immemorial highest necessity was simply a pretext. These features help to make the evil of Nazi and perhaps Stalinist mass murders unpunishable and unforgivable.

The initiation and command of such atrocities cannot be attributed to the vices of greed, envy, resentment, and vengeance that drive villainy and wickedness. The motivation seems not human, as if real evil, absolute evil could not come from human beings but only from some force more than human that inhabited and goaded human beings. As we know, however, Arendt produces a great theory of the mentality of initiative and command that relies on the notion of compelling the world to conform to a fiction, to a construction of the possessed imagination. It is the uncontrolled passion, as it were aesthetic, for an all-embracing fiction, also known as an ideology, that supplies the motivation of leaders and initiators, which is only human, for absolute evil.

But there is more to Arendt's account of the nature of evil. Death is the endpoint, but on the way to physical death, there is degradation – the degradation that results from the daily slow torture in the camps. The degrading or dehumanizing effects of this torture account in large part for Arendt's speechless horror at evil. Degradation is the destruction of existential values; this destruction matters more to her than her moral wish that people not suffer so terribly or die violently before their time. More terrible than pain or death is what extreme pain and fear of immediate death can and usually do make of people. They die before they die.

The application of the word "existential" is mine, but the thought is Arendt's. Let us remember that she says that totalitarian evil destroys "the fact of existence itself" by destroying what is distinctively human about its victims' existence. A crime against humanity is a crime, above all, against the

---

[29] Arendt, "Personal Responsibility under Dictatorship," p. 42; cf. ibid., p. 288.
[30] Ibid., p. 42.
[31] Ibid.

humanity, the humanness, the human *status*, of the victims. The crime is absolute: It makes human beings into the semblance of human beings; it is of a more terrible nature than the worst immorality. There is nothing more condemnable than systematically effacing human status as a matter of policy; this is the ultimate reason for calling totalitarianism absolute evil.

When human status is effaced as a result of continuous suffering, the cost is not only moral – that is, in the suffering endured. In any person's life, bad treatment can inflict irreparable losses, but the existential loss, the deliberately inflicted loss of one's principal human qualities, while one is still alive, is beyond reckoning. I believe that Arendt lends substance to the view that the status component of human dignity is not exclusively a moral idea, but also an existential one. On the other hand, her conceptualization of the stature component is closer to standard. It is not in itself a moral idea, even if in some versions, such as that of John Stuart Mill, it must be morally circumscribed.

In some recent theories, the state's respect for fundamental human rights is seen as an acknowledgment of the existential significance of the status component. Arendt is thus not alone in attributing existential worth to a morally valuable practice. Certainly, acknowledgment of rights serves to protect persons from injustice and oppression, both of which deny human dignity by inflicting needless and often atrocious suffering. The theoretical defense of rights is thus in large part a moral defense because human status is in large part a moral idea. Yet even in these theories, fundamental human rights have been defended not only as barriers to injustice and oppression but also for two other reasons of human status that are existential in nature. First, just by helping to avoid or reduce state-inflicted injustice and oppression, respect for rights, at the same time, testifies to the official recognition that human beings are not mere animals or things to be used as the state wishes, or, even worse, as useless objects to be thrown away, or as sacrificial stray dogs, or as a poisonous ingredient to be extruded forcibly from the system. Instead, all human beings are ends in themselves. Second, rights create opportunities for persons to lead their lives on their own terms without having to anticipate punishment for doing so. Recognized rights, again, reduce the load of suffering in society. At the same time, however, the idea of rights as the creation of opportunities for action honors agency, which is not a mere animal capacity for instinctive purposive action, but an invaluable and distinctively human attribute. In this regard, too, the idea of rights is not solely a moral idea, but also an existential one. To be sure, moral agency is one main manifestation of human agency, but even moral agency has an existential significance that simply comes from being one of the forms that a unique human capacity takes.

What distinguishes Arendt from other theorists of rights, then, is that she seems to give greater importance than others do to the existential importance of rights. Recognition of rights is a tribute to the human essence. When rights are recognized, the state renounces the will to turn people into instruments or invidiously categorize them, and also the will to cripple human agency. For her, both of these existential implications of rights matter more than the moral achievement of reducing suffering for the sake of reducing suffering.

In general, existential values matter for Arendt more than moral ones – if we are allowed to think that these two sets of values are commensurable and hence able to be ranked. When the subject changes from the injustice and oppression inherent in the state's failure to recognize rights to the evil of totalitarianism, the same pattern holds. That is why I contend that in Arendt's analysis, the deepest evil of the totalitarian systematic destruction of rights is existential, not moral. Obliterated existential values matter more than savagely violated moral values. What is more, Arendt holds that the existential values that define human *stature* and are intrinsic to authentic politics – and authentic politics is the sector of the *vita activa* where existential values are realized to the highest degree – matter greatly more than the moral values that such politics may achieve or the moral costs it may exact. She gives little attention to the moral circumscription of authentic politics by the harm principle.

What, then, is the extreme point of the evil of degradation that is inflicted by totalitarianism? It is to be in the condition of "living corpses" (*OT*, 447, 451). Arendt says that in the slave and death camps, the "juridical person" of each victim is killed while the victim is still alive (*OT*, 447), and that "the next decisive step ... is the murder of the moral person in man" (*OT*, 451). The human status is bound up with recognition of the juridical and moral capacities in every individual. The system of societywide terror also subjects the whole population to something like a condition of living corpses; that is, the system achieves a significant degree of destruction of the juridical person and the moral person in each member. But the camps are an intensification of the condition of the whole totalitarian society and therefore serve as a kind of laboratory for its intentionally murderous total domination. Outside the camps, the camp system can be reproduced "only imperfectly" (*OT*, 456). When both the juridical person and the moral person are destroyed through the horror of camp conditions, there is no person, no personhood, no human status left – "being a person as distinguished from being merely human."[32] Arendt also speaks of the "killing of man's individuality" (*OT*, 454), defined as anything that distinguishes one man from another (*OT*, 457) or as the individual's "uniqueness" or "unique identity" (*OT*, 453). Thus, both the common human status and the unique selfhood of each are effaced. No human spontaneity remains – the power that allows human beings to "begin something new out of his own resources" (*OT*, 453). (Notice the similarity in wording to Arendt's idea of authentic political action as exemplifying natality, the ability to begin something new.) "Nothing then remains but ghastly marionettes with human faces, which [notice: which, not who] all behave like the dog in Pavlov's experiments" (*OT*, 455).

As bad a horror as any, Arendt thinks, is the destruction of the will to harm the guards, even by a futile gesture; there were no spontaneous massacres of the

---

[32] Arendt, "Some Questions in Moral Philosophy," p. 95.

guards in the moment of liberation. To endure degradation without resistance is not anything like preferring to suffer wrong than to do it. In David Rousset's formulation, "Nothing is more terrible than these processions of human beings going like dummies to their death" (*OT*, 455).[33] The inmates became only natural; in a formulation Arendt uses earlier in *Origins* about African natives, "they behaved like a part of nature" (*OT*, 192) and hence became interchangeable, like "beasts" (*OT*, 455). Such a condition of naturalness in human beings is "highly unnatural" (*OT*, 455). To become merely natural, a docile creature of instincts and reflexes, is the total loss of human status; it is the ultimate degradation, the last step in dehumanization.

It is right to insist that Arendt is not blaming the victims. She says in a climactic passage: "When a man is faced with the alternative of betraying and thus murdering his friends or of sending his wife and children . . . to their death; when even suicide would mean the immediate murder of his own family – how is he to decide?" (*OT*, 452). Subjected to such treatment, (almost) everyone would become what most of the inmates of the camps became. But she wants us to know that though suffering matters in itself, the effects of suffering on human status matter apart from the suffering and must be perceived unblinkingly.

Arendt's powers of articulation are brilliant. She knows that silence would be more truthful than brilliance, which may feed prurience; but she overcame her speechless shock in order to enhance our understanding. Aware of the limits of any inquiry into the subject of totalitarian evil, she says that "the truth, the whole truth" about Auschwitz cannot yet appear, if ever. "No generality – and what is truth if it is not general? – can as yet dam up the chaotic flood of senseless atrocities. . . . "[34] In Bernd Naumann's book on the 1965 trial of some of the SS men posted at Auschwitz, the reader will find, she says, "moments of truth," which are anecdotes. These anecdotes "tell in utter brevity what it was all about."[35] But Arendt does more than tell anecdotes. She produces a general analysis of totalitarian evil that has not been equaled.

How does evil enter the world? Arendt's proposal is that the initiative is taken by a small group that is possessed by a fiction, by an ideology, which recognizes no boundaries on the ambition to realize it. But how does evil take hold? By means of the very morality of the mass of citizens. The reason is that, much of the time, morality is for most people nothing different from conformity to mores and hence they can comply with any command or practice, and do so with an easy or good – that is, unactivated – conscience. They casually think they are doing the right thing, no matter how wrong it is or would have been once thought – by them – to be. (Just think of the overnight conversion of decent neighbors into ethnic cleansers.) By mores, Arendt does not mean what Nietzsche means by the phrase "Sittlichkeit der Sitte": the habits of custom

33 See also Arendt's quote of Rousset in Hannah Arendt, *Eichmann in Jerusalem,* revised and enlarged edition (New York: Viking, 1964), p. 12.
34 Hannah Arendt, "Auschwitz on Trial" (1966), in *Responsibility and Judgment,* p. 255.
35 Ibid., p. 255.

so deeply and painfully ingrained as to become second nature,[36] but rather a set of prescriptions that are not more seriously regarded than table manners.[37] Socially accepted modes of conduct "could be exchanged for another set with no more trouble than it would take to change the table manners of a whole people."[38] Mores are mimesis and have no inwardness.

The terrible irony is that unthinking conformity joined to unexamined self-preferment (self-love) suffices to produce in normal people an everyday version of the loss of human status endured in the death camps. The practice of pseudo-morality not only sustains the systematic dehumanization of victims, it turns its practitioners by painless degradation into pseudo-human creatures. Chosen normality is a hideous parody of atrocious victimization and in certain circumstances facilitates the atrocious victimization of others. In Kant's sense of radical evil as being at the human root – which is not Arendt's sense, as she makes clear (*OT*, 459) – the radical evil of the masses makes possible the absolute evil of the death camps. If the relation of persons to what counts for them as moral conduct is merely social, there is little of personhood left, little genuine agency, except the daily reenactment of the choice not to choose. Not needing the pressure of totalitarian terror to conform, human beings appear close to indifferent as to what the content of morality is. The morality of mores is not real morality and can therefore transform itself from the conformity that ordinarily keeps normal society in motion into the conformity that allows and even encourages the ideological passions of a comparative few to create a whole system of evil. Eichmann's banality is an active and highly placed example of the morality of mores.

There is one more awful irony that Arendt barely touches on. It is the coexistence in many persons of the ability to treat their family, friends, and associates, who are seen as like them, with affection and thoughtful decency, while officially or unofficially cooperating with the atrocious victimization of a group of others who are designated as enemies or even as subhuman. In Thoreau's *Journal* (c. June–July 1846), there is an excellent passage on this human tendency to compartmentalization as illustrated in the U.S. slave society at the time of the Mexican War.[39]

In any event, Arendt says that "the true moral issue" of the Nazi crimes did not arise with the behavior of the Nazis, "but of those who only 'coordinated' themselves and did not act out of conviction."[40] If numerous people had cared only about the most elementary justice, these policies, which explode all categories of immorality, could not have been carried out. The general point

---

[36] Friedrich Nietzsche, *Genealogy of Morals* (1887), translated by Walter Kaufmann (New York: Vintage, 1966), essay 2, section 2; also *Daybreak* (1881), translated by R. J. Hollingdale (Cambridge: Cambridge University Press, 1982), book 1, section 9.

[37] Arendt, "Personal Responsibility under Dictatorship," p. 43.

[38] Ibid.

[39] Henry D. Thoreau, *Journal*, vol. 2, *1842–1848*, edited by Robert Sattelmeyer (Princeton: Princeton University Press, 1984), pp. 262–3.

[40] Arendt, "Some Questions in Moral Philosophy," p. 54.

is that, at all times and everywhere, unless morality is a commitment, it can degenerate into mores, merely social behavior, and thus turn into the path of least resistance, which is one of the greatest sources of the strength of recurrent evil. Arendt's suspicion of morality is actually a conviction that people who say they are moral are only conformists who love themselves. It is no wonder that a steady motif in Arendt's writings is a detestation of the politics (and economics) of self-interest.

I now turn to Arendt's views on the proper resistance to evil and to the place of morality in it. We must discuss Arendt's idea of genuine morality, which is Socratic, as a proper form of resistance to totalitarian evil (section 16.1) and then notice again some remarks, not systematized, on the morality of violence in resistance to such evil (section 16.2).

16.1 Socratic Resistance to Evil

Evil as a system issues from the readiness of the many to abandon one set of mores (acted on as if it were the sole content of morality) for another set, but resistance to evil includes the practice of genuine morality, and even more, the exertions of vigilant citizens to prevent its emergence. It is clear that Arendt believes in resisting evil. Although she admires Jesus of Nazareth enormously, she nowhere accepts his admonition "resist not evil,"[41] either in private or public life. She cannot move beyond good and evil. To be sure, the evil that Jesus had in mind is not crimes against humanity; but his precept has been usually read to demand nonresistance even to serious oppression or injustice, as by Paul and Augustine. In contrast, Arendt believes in resistance; it is a large part of the politics she praises, and it includes not only resistance to totalitarian evil, but civil disobedience and also, though in a qualified way, violent revolution when systems or particular policies are oppressive or unjust.

It is important to notice first that Arendt gives a sympathetic statement of what she calls the "political answer" to Socratic morality. "'What is important in the world is that there be no wrong; suffering wrong and doing wrong are equally bad.' Never mind who suffers it; your duty is to prevent it."[42] Arendt wants a world where sincere everyday morality is, in the good sense of the expression, a matter of course. (Perhaps her whole theory of ideal or authentic politics rests on the assumption of a society in which most people do not commit serious crimes and also in which a fortiori the problem of evil in the full sense, evil as a protracted policy of torture-filled extermination, never arises. I will return to this matter in the last section of this chapter.)

Arendt does not specify in this context what deeds the prevention of the spread of suffering would take, but we know from *Origins* that widespread economic misery and political deracination after World War I demanded a

---

[41] Matthew 5:39.
[42] Arendt, "Collective Responsibility," p. 153.

moral response that they failed to receive. The elementary notion of morality as preserving each person in his or her own, unmentioned by Arendt, is the version of morality at issue here. More primordially, a moral response can be triggered by what she calls in her book on Eichmann the "animal pity by which all normal men are affected in the presence of suffering."[43] (Is this the one good word about pity she ever says?) This is perhaps more reliable than any deliberation, which is too rare. It may also be the case, however, that the same mental process by means of which some people come to act as individuals who resist evil is also at work when some aroused persons act as real citizens to prevent or ameliorate conditions of terrible misfortune in the name of elementary morality. Be that as it may, in Arendt's reflections, evil gives Socratic morality its undesired chance to appear and then makes its appearance urgent. Yet there are existential purposes served by genuine morality, not only moral ones. I mean that certain admirable human capacities and traits of character, which give testimony to the human *stature*, are displayed by those who resist evil as individuals. This is not to say that those who resist do so deliberately for the sake of the human stature. Indeed, they often do so for the sake of the human *status* of others. But the observer will take in the significance of resistance for the human stature.

Now, the subject of resistance to evil involves not the camp inmates, but, first, nonviolent individuals on the outside but still within societies under totalitarian control, and second, nations (or movements) prepared to resist evil with armed might. Arendt's treatment of individuals who resist occupies many pages of "Some Questions" and other writings, while she makes only some suggestive remarks about massive violent resistance. I do not chide her for the latter brevity: No thinker can attend to everything.

Let us begin with her consideration of individuals who resist nonviolently. We might think that this phenomenon is dwarfed in importance by the organized efforts of armed forces. Why devote so much attention to a heroic but minor moral phenomenon? Perhaps the answer is that a minor moral phenomenon is a significant existential one. On the moral response of individuals, "Some Questions" contains a perceptive analysis of Kant's contribution to thought about genuine morality and the role of the first statement of the categorical imperative in it.[44] Arendt does not drive the point home, but we are free to make it. Kantian morality, despite Kant's own theoretical position on the morality of resistance to any authority, may lead a small number of people to resist on the grounds that it is morally imperative for everyone around them to do so. The fact that most people do not resist, but actually cooperate or go along, makes no personal difference to the true moral agent, for whom we could say, though Arendt does not, that the problem of the moral free rider is hopelessly beside the point. Yet there is one problem here, and that is that

[43] Arendt, *Eichmann in Jerusalem*, p. 103.
[44] See, for example, Arendt, "Some Questions in Moral Philosophy," pp. 60–72.

resistance is a highly dangerous act; it could lead to the agent's imprisonment or torture and death.

Does Kantian morality require self-sacrifice? Yes and no. It seems that Kant incorporates extreme self-sacrifice into the first statement of the categorical imperative; he may also allow conscripted self-sacrifice on the part of soldiers as a matter of civic duty. Yet he also says that when one drowning person violently shoves another off a plank, he has done something against the moral law that is nonetheless not to be punished by the penal law; in such circumstances, no one can be expected to defer to another, and it is uncertain whether any jury would ever convict the offending party.[45] (Cicero's nearly hilarious discussion is the source of the example of one plank and two drowning men, *On Duties*, book 3, section 23.) The question of the extent of self-sacrifice in genuine morality will stay with us. Arendt's remark that "it is obviously not everybody's business to be a saint or hero" is not quite her definitive judgment.[46] But the truth is that only a few are able to be either one.

I think that Arendt's discussion in "Some Questions" comes into its own when, forsaking Kant for a while, she takes up Socrates (not for the first or last time in her body of work). Her account of Socrates is continuously instructive and instructively restless. To repeat: Although Socrates did not know about totalitarianism, he experienced tyranny. Arendt employs his resistance to tyranny as a model for individual resistance to a system that is immeasurably worse than tyranny.

In the background of Socratic morality is the commitment to begin thinking about morality by asking, what do I owe? This is the question that dominates not only the Platonized Socrates in the *Crito*, the *Gorgias*, and the *Republic*, but also, I believe, the "real" Socrates as he is presented in the *Apology of Socrates*. Other interlocutors in the dialogues appear to begin with the question, what is owed to me? I will think of what I owe others only if I am forced to do so. The social contract tradition, perhaps even the ambiguous John Rawls, also begins with or eventually adopts an egocentric perspective, but requires everyone, as an equal to all others, not only to ask what he or she is owed, but to acknowledge that he or she owes the same to others. What do we owe each other? To preserve each person in his or her own rights is the common answer. The egocentric perspective is implored to become at least narrowly moral, not merely prudential: to treat others rightly for their sake, but to treat them ill if they do not treat me right. But the truly moral person thinks first of what he owes others, whether or not others treat him as he is owed. Arendt does not explore this background, though her judgment is that genuine morality is Socratic morality. She goes directly to the guiding precept, taken from the *Gorgias* (469c), that it is better (for the agent) to suffer wrong than to do it,

45 Immanuel Kant, *The Metaphysics of Morals* (1797), translated by Mary Gregor (Cambridge: Cambridge University Press, 1991), p. 60.
46 Arendt, "Personal Responsibility under Dictatorship," p. 34.

though as Socrates says, he would prefer neither to suffer wrong (or injustice) nor to do it.

In the *Gorgias*, the precept emerges in a political context, and is intended to answer the question whether it is desirable or undesirable for a person to be a tyrant. Socrates does not want to possess the tyrant's power to do wrong with an apparent if perhaps temporary impunity; if he had to choose, he would prefer to suffer at a tyrant's hands than to be a tyrant himself. But the precept suits everyday life as well or better. The full force of the precept comes into play when a third party is involved. The paradigmatic act of Socratic political morality occurs in 404 B.C., when Socrates refuses an order by the Thirty (tyrants) issued to him and four others to apprehend and deliver Leon of Salamis to them. Leon was innocent of any crime; the Thirty wanted to spread complicity in their guilt as bloody usurpers. Socrates refused to obey and went home (*Apology*, 32c–d). He refused, that is to say, to help make a third party suffer wrong and accepted for himself the risk of suffering wrong instead; he refused to cooperate with the evil of destroying an innocent life. He put others ahead of himself when forced by circumstances to do so. He sided with the weak against the strong when he could have joined the strong or stayed on their good side. That is what genuine morality is: You treat people rightly, no matter how you imagine they would treat you if the roles were reversed. Arendt assumes these details, but I think they must be spelled out in order to highlight the great demands that genuine morality makes on people.

When it comes to individual acts of resistance to Nazi evil, the Socratic precept would change a bit. It would read: I would rather suffer wrong (because it is better for me) than allow evil to go uncontested. Unlike Socrates, I am not asked to be a direct agent of evil and also unlike him I can remain in comparative safety by doing nothing. But I would still feel as if I were an agent of evil even if I only went along and did nothing active to support the policies of evil. I suppose that a model act would be to harbor a persecuted person. A close but not exact model is Thoreau's civil refusal to pay the head tax in his state in 1846; even closer is his involvement in helping escaped slaves flee to freedom in Canada, after 1850, when new fugitive-slave laws made potentially all citizens active agents of evil. (It was then that Thoreau's thoughts turned to violence against the institution of slavery, not just helping escaped slaves.) In a crisis, if you want to count yourself as moral, you put victims or potential victims of atrocious policy ahead of yourself. You may risk torture or death, but your aim is to suffer only if there is no alternative. There is a steady hope that one can get away with the dangerous act for the sake of oneself, but also of course to perform future acts of resistance.

The question remains, however, as to whether Socratic morality teaches that one must die (or risk some terrible fate like torture, squalid imprisonment, or impoverished exile) rather than assist or otherwise countenance evil policies. Social contract theory, at its most consistent and hence most morally (not politically) radical, insists that one can never be morally obliged to sacrifice one's life for others or for any purpose. But does that hold for Socratic morality?

How much self-sacrifice is required by the Socratic precept that it is better to suffer wrong than to do it? Is it really better *for me* to die than do one gravely wrong deed – call it evil – when compelled by the fear of a dire penalty? (Leave aside whether it is better for others.) If I do such a wrong deed, am I so impaired by it that I am thereafter forever doomed to repeat it or forever unable to do the right thing in difficult circumstances? Is not such a view fanatical?

Suppose you could save another person's life by calmly giving your own in exchange. (Again, leave aside the possibility of saving more than one life by giving your own.) I think that this would be a case of martyrdom. Arendt does not discuss this situation; in any case, she is not theorizing martyrdom. The example has the oddity of allowing a fellow sufferer, an equal to oneself, to accept one's martyrdom while not imagining the possibility of rejecting it, much less thinking of becoming a martyr in turn for someone else. Socrates is a hypothetical martyr when he says that he would never give up philosophizing on state command, even if he had to die many times (*Apology* 29c–30c). In his actual and purely political acts of dissent and noncompliance, he did believe that he was courting the danger of being imprisoned or put to death in opposing the mass trial of the admirals after the battle of Arginusae (406 B.C.), or the danger of death in refusing to join the group that the Thirty ordered to seize Leon. He insists that "there is no man who could make me consent to commit an unjust act from the fear of death, but that I would perish at once rather than give way" (*Apology*, 32a). This seems to indicate that Socratic morality entails the readiness to endure the ultimate self-sacrifice. If martyrdom is like saintliness, moral heroism, in contrast, consists of incurring the risk of death for the sake of avoiding becoming the agent of evil or grave wrongdoing. (Socrates compares himself to Achilles. Isn't that a bit odd, unless displaying courage matters more to the agent or observer than any cause?) Jesus said, "Greater love hath no man than this, that a man lay down his life for his friends."[47] But the context indicates martyrdom rather than heroism: the friends are joined in a godly cause that rises above any moral relation, including samaritanism, between ordinary friends or toward strangers.

Genuine morality shows greatness when it confronts evil, but can *morality*, to be genuine, require the ultimate self-sacrifice? Whatever Socrates thought, what does Arendt think? I have already quoted Arendt to the effect that not everyone can be a saint or hero. Other philosophers (for example, J. O. Urmson in his influential paper of 1958, "Saints and Heroes"[48]) define acting like a saint or hero as supererogation – as doing more than moral duty requires. Does the extraordinary quality of evil demand a commensurately extraordinary response, if that response is to count as moral at all? I do not think that Arendt intends a version of Socratic morality that is as radical as Socrates' own. Her model is the person who, when confronting evil, takes chances but

[47] John 15:13.
[48] J. O. Urmson, "Saints and Heroes," in A.I. Melden, ed., *Essays in Moral Philosophy* (Seattle: University of Washington Press, 1958).

who also takes every precaution to get away with it; the person acts in secret and picks his or her occasions for bravery with some caution; presumably most of those who performed acts of nonviolent resistance or noncompliance in the name of morality survived. Often the moral act was simply not to join in – a parsimonious negative morality that did not always exact a terrible cost. Arendt more than once says that some of the worst deeds were done by volunteers, who had a choice not to do them. The strange fact is that people expect all conscripted soldiers to risk death and many of them to die, yet do not expect individuals, acting on their own, to be self-sacrificing. There are role duties, however, that do or once did incorporate self-sacrifice in civilian as well as military life: Think of mothers sacrificing their lives for near-term fetuses; parents for their young children; and firefighters and police officers for us all. But our interest here is in the place of Socratic self-sacrifice in political resistance. On this theme, it is obvious that my remarks are not satisfactory. I cannot improve them.

Let us turn to another aspect of Socratic morality. Most of the time, as I have said, Arendt indicates that Socratic morality has only "negative" qualities: It is abstention from participation in acts of evil or qualitatively smaller wrongdoing "even though they are done by everybody around you."[49] It turns out that Arendt does not consistently describe Socratic morality as entirely negative, as avoiding harming others when one is under pressure to harm them. After all, resistance to totalitarian evil by individuals was marked by positive acts of charity (for example, harboring the persecuted) – to leave aside acts of violence, which can never be acts of Socratic morality.

Furthermore, she says, the qualities of Socratic morality are "marginal," suited only to "borderline situations ... times of crisis and emergency," when "Socratic morality ... has revealed itself as the only working morality."[50] But in a remarkable statement that is casually introduced, Arendt seems prepared to convert the exceptional temporary condition into a normal condition that stretches over long periods of time. She says, "When standards are no longer valid anyhow – as in Athens in the last third of the fifth century and in the fourth century, or in Europe in the last third of the nineteenth century and in the twentieth century – nothing is left but the example of Socrates."[51] What does this statement mean? We could read it as saying that there are whole historical periods in which evil, atrocious policies – but not evil in the full Nazi or Stalinist sense – are regularly and systematically enacted, and that therefore the political expression of Socratic morality was much more than marginal in theoretical importance, though scarcely present in actuality. Socratic morality would have been necessary throughout the most glorious period of ancient Athens, and it is therefore a permanent necessity in our time and perhaps indefinitely into the future. This is not to say that individual acts of abstention from wrongdoing or

[49] Arendt, "Some Questions of Moral Philosophy," p. 106.
[50] Ibid.
[51] Ibid.

risky charitable undertakings are by themselves adequate to combat evil – they never were. But their example can inspire some scattered noncompliance or a large-scale refusal to cooperate with evil or wrongdoing. These acts dramatize moral urgency.

Arendt breaks effortlessly with many of her published reproaches of those who seek to inject serious moral considerations into concerted political action – including those reproaches found in her great essay "Civil Disobedience" (1970) – when she celebrates the moral passion of students, who acted as individuals but in concert, in *On Violence* (1970) and "Thoughts on Politics and Revolution" (1970).

The next question is what motivates those who are moral in the manner of Socrates? For one thing, it is certainty about what evil or lesser wrongdoing (say, injustice) is. Socrates is explicit. He says that though he has no wisdom, certainly no knowledge about the afterlife, he does "know very well that it is evil and disgraceful to do an unjust act.... I will never do what I know to be evil" (*Apology*, 29b). Knowledge might supply its own motivational impetus. But Arendt inclines to the view that Socrates had doubts about everything, including the most elementary notions of right and wrong. He believed, she suggests, that thinking was an endless process of revision.[52] But I do not see how her argument about the relation between thinking and moral considerations could hold together unless the one who was given over to the activity of thinking was sustained in moral conduct by an invincible conviction that some things can never be rightly done and that, positively, some right things had to be done. To anticipate: If I am always "thinking matters through by myself,"[53] and I therefore choose to have to live with myself, I must, to begin with, have a more or less settled idea of what is evil and what is not, what is wrong and what is right. (Naturally, the emphasis is on evil and wrong, but not to the total exclusion of positive charity.) I must know in advance what actions would force me to shun myself and hence what other actions would prepare me to feel, even if I could not do so with a whole heart like Socrates, that I would rather die than do some things or abstain from doing other things.[54] Why would it be so awful to live with oneself as an imagined accomplice of evil if I believed that thinking about evil always landed me in an aporia, if I believed that I did not know what evil is, or had only a hesitant hunch? Such a picture lacks psychological plausibility. Just like Arendt, Socrates knew what was so wrong that noncompliance with it was called for.

I do not wish to take issue with the overall conception that Arendt elaborates. The quintessential moral disposition is to prefer suffering wrong to allowing or doing wrong – especially when one stands a better chance of avoiding suffering by doing nothing to resist evil. One cannot choose oneself without qualification and still be moral. But if, instead, one thinks – that is, if "I speak with myself

[52] Ibid., p. 86.
[53] Ibid., p. 279, editor's note 12.
[54] Arendt, "Collective Responsibility," p. 156.

about whatever happens to concern me" – one is less likely to do evil or allow it to go on unresisted.[55] By making thinking – the continuous activity of going over what one has done, is doing, or contemplates doing, which is also necessarily the continuous activity of interpreting oneself and others and interpreting the situation in which we have found or find ourselves – the source of a kind of secular conscience, Arendt has illuminated the meaning of genuine morality.

This is not the place to go into all the difficulties inherent in the notion of the silent dialogue between me and myself. Whatever it is, it is not the relationship between the self and the Socratic inner "voice," which does not converse but only issues infrequent prohibitions. One trouble stands out and deserves a quick mention. I refer to the origin of the dialogue. Isn't it the case that much of the content of thinking emerges unbidden into the mind and often not fully shaped? After it emerges, the active power of the mind cannot help but notice the content and may choose to respond to it and shape it. Arendt's metaphor of internal dialogue may hide the continuous interplay of active and passive by making the participants two identical and active speakers in the present, as if every thought triggered another one in response. But I may misunderstand. Or, we can follow Mary McCarthy's lead, when she put it this way at Arendt's funeral: "in the agon of consciousness," there are "always two, the one who says and the one who replies or questions."[56]

Arendt appears disposed to explain the Socratic preference for suffering wrong over doing it *exclusively* by what she considers a concern for the self of the agent rather than a concern for the political world (such as that of good citizens) or even a concern for those others who are suffering evil (such as that of good secularists or Christians). In an interesting formulation, she says that "it is not a question of loving myself as I love others" when I act morally. Concern for the self is thus not self-love. Who could accuse Socrates of loving himself, or perhaps even of liking himself, in the usual sense of these phrases? Nonetheless, Arendt makes the imperatives of living with oneself in the mode of "unending" thinking – is there any regular mode of living with oneself except thinking? – the *sole* reason that people are prepared to practice Socratic morality when the emergency arises. To be sure, she makes it clear that the self that is the object of concern is "not so much this entity of I-am-I (Richard III)."[57] It is not, we might say, either the active ego or the distinctive personality. It is the self divided into two speakers who take turns in speaking and listening in dialogue, not one part that only speaks and one part that only listens. It is invisible and inaudible verbal self-division. Yet something is missing. Arendt is not explicit on the nature of the desiring or emotional self

[55] Arendt, "Some Questions of Moral Philosophy," pp. 95–6.
[56] Hannah Arendt and Mary McCarthy, *Between Friends: The Correspondence of Hannah Arendt and Mary McCarthy, 1949–1975*, edited by Carol Brightman (New York: Harcourt, Brace, 1995), p. 392.
[57] Arendt, "Some Questions of Moral Philosophy," p. 279, editor's note 12.

behind the process of thinking who wants passionately not to have to bear the lacerating burden of harboring the recollection that one has done evil or allowed it unresistingly.

Arendt says, "A good conscience does not exist except as the absence of a bad one."[58] If nothing simply hedonist lies behind the desire to avoid self-laceration, Arendt still maintains that self-regardingness of a refined sort does – a fierce avoidance of self-contempt and even of self-loathing. She goes to the extreme of saying that for the moral agent, "the argument would not be that the world would be better off without the murder being done, but the unwillingness to live with an assassin."[59] I do not doubt that these feelings may have a place. What I find untenable is the attempt to locate the exclusive motivation for genuine morality in concern for the self, no matter how much proper self-concern rises above self-interest and selfishness. Just as strong doubts about one's ability to define and identify evil are incompatible with Socratic morality, so is exclusive concern with how one lives harmoniously with oneself. When Socrates acted, he adopted without question the determination to be guided by the question, what do I owe? Benefits to his soul from right conduct follow from that determination much more than they inspire it. In fact, concern with the benefits to oneself of acting rightly seems like a rationalization meant to persuade interlocutors who are either moral skeptics or, more likely, egocentrics who start with the wrong question, which is what is owed to them. Socrates cared about others (and not only about the condition of their souls). How could the Socratic primacy of the question of what I owe others go with the primacy of concern for one's soul?

I want to work, however, against what I just said. I may have been misled in the past by my own moralizing preoccupations in saying that Arendt writes as if concern for the self is a sign of an imperfect character. I mean, first, that Arendt herself, whatever her readers may feel, does not find in a proper concern for the self any degree of *moral* fault. Second, if she prizes existential values more than moral ones, proper concern for oneself is more praiseworthy than moral concern for the suffering of others. Last, her commitment to the existential values lodged in authentic politics may be just as deep as or deeper than her commitment to concern for the freedom and worldliness of the city. Her theory of political action in the polis, after all, is permeated by more concern for the self of the political actor than for the well-being of the city. At least, that is how I read *The Human Condition*. For all these reasons, I now doubt my previous and long-standing supposition that Arendt intends even gently to impeach Socratic morality by tracing it to a moral person's concern for the self – as long as such concern is not just another, although subtle, manifestation of self-interest.

To reinforce this view, I propose that it is symptomatic of Arendt's uncomfortable orientation to even the best morality that she sees Socrates as purely nonmoral in his passion for thinking and claims that for him the "moral

[58] Arendt, "Thinking and Moral Considerations," p. 161.
[59] Arendt, "Collective Responsibility," p. 156.

by-product of thought is in itself of secondary importance."[60] Does not this remark make his aversion to wrongdoing merely incidental to his passion to think? I believe this judgment may actually reverse Socrates' commitments. He was a seeker of wisdom about how to live. To say that this gadfly "does not examine things to improve either himself or others" is, I am afraid, wide of the mark. Sometimes, even when Arendt writes most admiringly about morality, she still shows reluctance to admit that there is or could be a moral germ to philosophical thinking. Nietzsche was only too happy to make the point in order to shake up the mystique of philosophy[61]; apparently Arendt thinks too well of the philosopher who was the founder of genuine morality to encourage us to believe that his driving passion could be moral.

We may have to think, then, that Socratic concern for the self accounts in part for Arendt's admiration of morality, so that the prevention or relief of suffering is "secondary" for her, just as she claims (I think mistakenly) that it was for Socrates. She goes too far in seeing concern for the self as the only cause of moral action against evil, but her view reinforces her larger effort of eliciting existential value from genuine moral conduct.

Notice the existential values, all of them aspects that display human stature, that crop up in her discourse on genuine morality. Just as her deepest concern with regard to evil is existential (human beings lose their human status as victims of evil or as its conformist facilitators), so her deepest reason to admire those who are genuinely moral is existential (they demonstrate human stature). Thinking itself, which makes genuine morality possible, is the highest human activity, or at least as high as any. It matters apart from morality because it testifies to what human beings alone are capable of. Morality is therefore intimately linked with an inestimably valuable nonmoral activity. She gives an eloquent defense of the view that Kant "puts the duties man has to himself ahead of the duties to others."[62] This concern with the self evinces "self-respect," not self-love and not even "the love of some neighbor." She claims that what is involved is "human dignity and even human pride."[63] Such pride – what I call an awareness of the need to demonstrate human stature – "goes against the grain of Christian ethics."[64] Kant makes duties to oneself part of *morality*. I infer that Arendt thinks that one way we have of praising genuine morality is to see that it is allied with a sense of human dignity, which in its two components is not primarily for her a moral idea but an existential one.

The activity of thinking and certain praiseworthy qualities, including concern for one's integrity, are only secondarily moral, but of the highest existential significance. There is another quality of existential significance, and that is courage. I think that it stands above all other traits of character in Arendt's

---

[60] Arendt, "Some Questions of Moral Philosophy," p. 107; also p. 123.
[61] Nietzsche, *Beyond Good and Evil* (1886), translated by Walter Kaufmann (New York: Vintage, 1966), part 1, section 6.
[62] Arendt, "Some Questions in Moral Philosophy," p. 67.
[63] Ibid.
[64] Ibid., p. 68.

estimation. She recurrently calls courage the highest virtue. There are kinds of courage: It can be physical, moral, or intellectual. They may (but need not) sustain or intensify one another. Heroic courage is most of the time physical. Arendt shows special respect for "the willingness to suffer," which she thinks can demonstrate the "authenticity" of one's moral position.[65] It is not that a willingness to suffer may be demanded as a necessary means to a moral end; rather, a willingness to suffer gives evidence of one's serious commitment to one's moral position and spreads respect for it and for oneself in the eyes of others. In sum, genuine moral activity is in the eyes of the observer, whatever it may be in the eyes of the agent, an existential accomplishment, not only a contribution to the prevention, reduction, or elimination of evil (whose greatest harm is itself existential). Morality can help to show what human beings distinctively are, what they are made of, what they are capable of, what they can be proud of. In the form of individual resistance to evil, but also resistance to smaller wrong, moral agents can create memorable, perhaps immortal, examples of political action.

16.2 Violent Resistance to Evil

Here we must briefly discuss Arendt's view of the morality of violent resistance to evil, especially when the resistance is massive. Socratic or genuine morality is only one element of resistance. In general, nonviolence cannot possibly defeat absolute evil, though it might occasionally defeat oppression or, more often, injustice. Those who organize and lead a system of exterminationist evil are never open to the sort of persuasion that scattered or concerted individuals, who act nonviolently and are prepared to suffer rather than obey or cooperate, can sometimes exercise on opponents who inflict oppression or injustice and who (like, say, the British in India eventually) are open to persuasion.[66] Only armed and organized forces can sustain the major effort of resistance. When it comes to resisting evil, Socratic morality is more important existentially than it is practically. For all that, I think that Arendt inclines to the view that, as I have indicated, when it comes to violent resistance – by individuals, movements, or societies – the issue is not perhaps what morality requires but rather what it merely permits. Although "violence always needs justification," it can be "justifiable."[67] But if violence can be justifiable, she says that "it never will be legitimate"[68] – a radically moral assertion, indeed. Two things that make violence justifiable are rightful self-defense (which is not properly understood as merely self-interested action) and the defense of human beings against ferocious assaults.

---

[65] Arendt, "Collective Responsibility," p. 156.

[66] Ibid., p. 152.

[67] Hannah Arendt, "On Violence" (1970), in *Crises of the Republic* (New York: Harcourt, Brace, Jovanovich, 1972), pp. 151, 174.

[68] Ibid., p. 151.

Evil, totalitarian or other kinds, will be and should be resisted. But Arendt mentions in a slightly opaque passage, with apparent approval, "the Greek [tragedians'] version of the Christian insight that every resisting of the evil done in the world necessarily entails some implication in evil...."[69] Orestes killed his mother to avenge her murder of his father. Arendt's view may be that the use of violence in a good cause is not simply evil or unequivocally immoral, on the one hand, or purely moral, on the other. This is not to say that she would ever have called it the lesser (and necessary) evil – an idea she finds repugnant because she is haunted by the thought that Jewish leaders under Nazism were allowed to try to save the lives of some of their own people by choosing others to die. The choosers themselves were killed at last. She is happy to learn that the Talmud says never surrender one man for the safety of the whole community or allow one woman to be ravished for the sake of all women.[70] She adds that, politically, "the weakness of the argument [in defense of doing the lesser evil] has always been that those who choose the lesser evil forget very quickly that they chose evil."[71]

I am afraid, however, that Arendt does not give a fair hearing to the argument for doing the lesser and necessary evil. It may be that the Jewish leaders were wrong to do the work of the Nazis. But that case is not paradigmatic of the lesser and necessary evil, and neither is Orestes' vengeance. On the other hand, political actors, especially when they use violence (but not only then), regularly claim that they do a lesser evil to prevent a greater evil and hence that they do the necessary evil. There is no political life without this calculation, despite the frequency of its disingenuous invocation. And if you say, as Arendt does, that resisting evil implicates the agent in evil, you are then committing yourself, I think, to accept the calculation of greater and lesser evil – namely, to do or allow the lesser evil when it is the only way of preventing, reducing, or ending the greater evil.

The lesser but necessary evil is, by definition, still evil, but it is not pure evil, and ideally it is stamped with reluctance and regret. At the same time, the doctrine of the lesser evil rarely lends itself to a clear and straightforward application and its use is not likely to be free of consequences that make the act or policy more morally lamentable than it was originally foreseen to be. Furthermore, to compare the relative importance of means and ends is not easy; it assumes a hierarchy of values. For example, how do we show that an amount of death and suffering is allowable when it is required to achieve an end like constitutional freedom or national sovereignty or honor? Historically, peoples are almost unanimous in the mistake of never giving morality supremacy over all other ends. Arendt is scarcely alone in subordinating morality. Or the perplexities inherent in the notion of the incommensurability of values disparage the very idea of according comparative weight to various values. The idea of

[69] Arendt, "Collective Responsibility," p. 152.
[70] Arendt, "Personal Responsibility under Dictatorship," p. 36.
[71] Ibid.

the lesser evil is more acceptable when the evils compared are of the same kind: numbers of avoidable deaths and extent of suffering that occur in a given condition as against deaths and suffering that would occur, in speculation, if there were resistance rather than acceptance. But no matter how hard we try, we can never be entirely persuaded or persuasive to others that the evil we do is strictly necessary and actually lesser, not even when we defeat aggressors or punish criminals, perhaps.

The conceptual trouble is compounded when the strict limits that Arendt sets on violence make it suitable only to the domestic politics of non-evil and even good political systems or to an individual faced with an immediate threat to his life.[72] (She sides with Billy Budd unequivocally as the murderer of Claggart,[73] in contrast to her earlier ambivalence in *On Revolution*.) She says that violence as a method of concerted action can remain rational only if it pursues the short-term goals of an aggrieved group.[74] But the use of violence against the Axis powers was not at the behest of short-term goals or for the sake of preserving lives, in the first instance. That the Allies committed evil in defeating evil Arendt does not deny. She believed that the American use of atomic weapons was a crime of war. But if the Allies did evil to destroy greater evil – even leaving aside the use of atomic weapons and other mass destruction of civilian life – then we must say that they thought they were practicing the doctrine of the lesser and necessary evil; and we surely do not have to say that they fought a just war, only that their good cause – the destruction of absolute evil – allowed them to use justifiable violence. How can the use of so much violence ever be called just, even if all of it was necessary? Necessity does not transmute evil into good. Then, too, some of it was surplus violence, unnecessary evil of an incalculable weight and used in part for ends other than destroying absolute evil. Officials tend to have more than one purpose, and to do more harm or inflict more pain on adversaries than they have to. The good results of a total effort do not excuse or even extenuate incalculable evil incidental or more central to that effort. Of course, I do not speak for pacifists when I say that the Allies fought, on balance, a morally allowable war; but pacifism is not needed to hold that the conduct of the war was so gravely impure morally that it should leave a residue of indelible shame.

The subject of war tends to muffle Arendt's critical powers, even though here and there she produces an invaluable insight. The horror of war – it is estimated that many more civilians died in World War II than combatants – occupies little of her theoretical attention. She does not like to moralize about war because, as she says in her laudatory introduction to J. Glenn Gray's splendid and quite existential book, *The Warriors*, his work gives voice to the "inevitable conclusions of the soldier's basic credo – that life is not the highest good."[75]

[72] Arendt, "On Violence," p. 151.
[73] Ibid., p. 161.
[74] Ibid., p. 176.
[75] J. Glenn Gray, *The Warriors*, 2nd ed. (1959) (New York: Harper Torchbooks, 1970), p. xiv.

This echoes her own existential, nonmoral (or antimoral) sentiment about the subordinate importance of the sheer and unadmirable value of staying alive that is expressed elsewhere in her writing.

We now turn to the last main aspect of Arendt's thought about morality. When evil is not systematically present, what role does Arendt give morality in political life? This question covers a wide range: Arendt's view of past and present constitutional politics; her understanding of the harm intrinsic to tyranny, despotism, and dictatorship; and her idea of authentic politics. There is too much to discuss at any length. What I say is sketchy.

Where evil is absent, Arendt's writings only touch on moral issues. It should come as no surprise when I express my belief that the most salient kinds of judgment, whether in praise or condemnation, that Arendt makes of the various non-evil forms of government that she considers, are existential (and sometimes aesthetic) rather than moral. The following points stand out.

On constitutional politics, her judgment is unreservedly favorable. She never speaks of the rule of law without reverence. Furthermore, whatever net impression of reserve about the United States Constitution that *On Revolution* may leave, her praise for it in the early 1970s is unstinting. In 1973, she exonerates the Constitution of responsibility for the "loss of revolutionary spirit."[76] She would blame the loss of the revolutionary tradition on the failure of Americans to continue to regard the Constitution as "sacred."[77] In 1975, the year of her death, she says that "the American institutions of liberty...have survived longer than any comparable glories in history...they survive splendidly in thought to illuminate the thinking and doing of men in darker times."[78] Indeed, two hundred years of liberty "have earned Herodotus' 'due meed of glory.'"[79]

This praise is of course moral in part. The Constitution has provided a framework for a decent and unoppressed life for many people. Although the political system under the Constitution has inflicted pain on millions, it has promoted happiness for other, perhaps more, millions. (Forgive the absurdity of this utilitarian calculation.) But Arendt is so averse to the encouragement of self-interest that she never says a good word for the daily stuff of politics engendered by the system of representative government under the Constitution. Nor could the political project of social democracy – greater socioeconomic equality – win her favor. It is for the most part yet another specimen of the politics of self-interest and hence of the instrumentalization of politics. I also do not think that she ever abandoned the idea that representation establishes political passivity, which does not cripple human agency but does deprive it

---

[76] Hannah Arendt, "Remarks," American Society of Christian Ethics, unpublished manuscript, January 21, 1973, p. 2.

[77] Ibid., p. 3.

[78] Arendt, "Home to Roost," p. 260.

[79] Ibid.

of its political relevance. For her, political passivity is, when freely accepted, a kind of human diminishment.

If the U.S. Constitution is morally praiseworthy, it must remain existentially deficient. To be sure, the enumerated rights protect human dignity; but we have seen that from Arendt's perspective, dignity (in its two components) is more an existential concept than it is a moral one: Guaranteed rights help to spare people injustice and oppression, but what matters the most is that they spare people, at the extreme, degradation. Rights also give people the standing (status) to enter political life and show by their agency what they are made of (their stature). (In general, good laws are rules that direct the "great game of the world" for those who are willing to play by the rules.[80]) But the only American political episode after the Constitution that Arendt ever celebrates is the student movement of the 1960s, which demonstrated the underlying capacity of Americans for at least an episode of authentic politics. This showed what it means to accept your rights and use them to act politically. When she praises the moral motivation of the students in the 1960s, it is only to ward off the possible imputation of group self-interest. But the movement mattered existentially at least as much as it mattered morally – not only to her, but also, it must be said, to the participants. In sum, although the common inclination, which I share, is to praise the Constitution for mainly moral reasons, Arendt goes beyond them.

In regard to un-free politics – the systems of tyranny, despotism, and dictatorship – Arendt does not spend much time on the moral cost: the cost of increased suffering of the people who endure them. I do not mean that she is indifferent to the moral critique. Rather, the powerful impression that her condemnation of un-free politics leaves is that what counts more than the moral fact of suffering is the existential fact that people are denied a regular chance to be political. If representative government diminishes people with their consent (what could be worse?), systems of un-free politics impose an involuntary and even more thorough diminishment (not the same as totalitarian degradation) on the people. On the one hand, repression and arbitrariness block the emergence of the safety and self-confidence needed for assertive citizenship; on the other hand, the public "space" that provides the setting and the opportunities for citizenship is closed off. People are domesticated: They are made tame and fit only for domestic and other private relations. All these effects assault human dignity and thereby affront the highest existential values. The worst effect is popular acceptance or unbitter resignation to their condition, whether in poverty or comparative sufficiency. The existential miracle occurs when people rise up against un-freedom, and in their insurgency, practice, if only for a time, authentic politics, with as little violence as possible. In the twinkling of an eye, rebels lose their impotence and discover the power of acting in concert. In Arendt's theory, rebellion against un-freedom sometimes appears as the supreme existential expression of the vita activa.

---

[80] Arendt, "On Violence," p. 193, note 11.

What of the place of morality in authentic politics? Arendt just presupposes, I think, a generally law-abiding people, even though in the tangle of human relations, "trespassing is an everyday occurrence" (*HC*, 240). Beyond that, she is so undisposed to think about moral issues when evil is absent that she is driven to the effort of devising a morality that is internal to politics, that grows out of the nature and the needs of authentic politics. She will not suffer the dependence of politics on something external to itself or the dependence of action on a logic that is not political. Is it possible that morality would be for her the most alien or obnoxious external consideration? Nothing is more insidiously harmful to genuine politics than genuine morality, whether Socratic or Christian. If politics is authentic, it does not occasion the need for real morality, except in untypical circumstances. (Arendt of course does not defend – but she barely mentions – the long career of Athenian imperialism.) Most important, the spirit of genuine morality, whether Socratic or Christian, is fundamentally hostile to the world-centered, world-loving spirit of authentic politics.

How successful is the effort that Arendt makes in *The Human Condition* to devise a morality internal to politics? She gives two necessary elements: forgiving, which is the "readiness to forgive and be forgiven" (*HC*, 245), and promise keeping, which rests simply on the principle of the Roman legal system, *pacta sunt servanda*, and applies as a matter of course (*HC*, 243). Both moral elements belong to Arendt's idea of authentic politics because they facilitate and stabilize the life of speech and action. But they hardly constitute a full political morality, even for a small and insular city. When deemed necessary and sufficient, they make up at best only a code for a small band of roving confederates who search the world for adventures, or for a group of insurgents in the early period of their movement; or, more conventionally, a code for many kinds of close and voluntary associations. These two elements, however, are not adequate to govern all the ties among a body of citizens, much less to guide the dealings of a city or country toward enemies or friends. A morality internal to political action must be attentive to a fuller range of the internal relations of the participants; it must also be mindful not only of internal relations but of the effects of political action on outsiders.

Despite its shortcomings, Arendt's writing is unusually interesting on forgiveness and its limits and is all the more interesting when we recall her view that absolute evil is unforgivable. Let us notice that the readiness to be forgiven is part of the concept of forgiving, as if to say that it is no less difficult to accept forgiveness than it is to grant it. Her phenomenology of forgiving is sublime for face-to-face relations, where "constant mutual release" liberates everyone from the cycle of receiving wrong and seeking retaliation for it (*HC*, 240). It may be that forgiving wrong and accepting forgiveness is Arendt's own version of the highest element of morality in all contexts, not only the political. It is closer to Christianity than to the Socratic precept that it is better to suffer wrong than to do it. Thus, at least one aspect of the Christian ethos is, at least at first sight, integral to Arendt's theory of authentic politics, while Socratic morality almost never is.

Yet, she acknowledges that forgiving "has always been deemed unrealistic and inadmissible in the public realm" (*HC*, 243). That leaves promise keeping to do the whole work of a morality tailored to politics. To keep political promises means to respect agreements, covenants, treaties, and (I think) social contracts such as the American Constitution. Perhaps a large part of a citizen's allegiance is to this principle of consent; perhaps a significant part of a theory of the content of political action is lodged in the enterprise of defending a free constitution. But of course there are other kinds of political action besides preserving a constitution, and they require more morality than promise keeping.

It really would be better not to moralize too much the internal morality of authentic politics. Forgiving and promise keeping are virtues, and like the virtues in many conceptions, especially the classical ones, they matter as much for what they show that human beings are capable of – thanks to either cultivation or self-overcoming – as for their practical benefits. Both forgiving and promise keeping are kinds of self-extension; neither is routine; both are difficult and unnatural; both reveal individual identity; neither is only a means but also an end in itself; neither is egocentric or narrowly self-interested. They manifest human dignity. It is as if authentic politics existed for the sake of forgiving and promise keeping as much as they exist for its sake. The two virtues (and other political virtues) matter existentially, not only morally, just like the authentic politics they make possible now and then, in those moments when a better world appears – only to vanish.

The Human Condition is the culmination of Arendt's existential outlook. But the outlook precedes it and continues after it. Arendt's work is always existential, whatever else it may be. Her fundamental commitment is to human status and stature: the absence of anything that degrades or diminishes, and the positive presence of individuality and initiative in resistance or creativity. Her deepest hatred of totalitarian evil is not moral but existential. Her deepest admiration for political action is not political but existential. To put it slightly differently: *The Origins of Totalitarianism* is existential in its horror; *The Human Condition* is existential in its affirmation.

16.3 Note on Secondary Sources

I would like to mention just a few of the works that bear on the themes of this chapter. In my book, *Hannah Arendt: Politics, Conscience, Evil* (Totowa, NJ: Rowman and Allanheld, 1984), I dealt with the challenge to morality made by Arendt's affirmation of the existential values intrinsic to political action, especially in her Greek conceptualization of action. The emphasis in this chapter is on existential values that suggest themselves when we contemplate the presence of the human species among other species in nature. The claim, though surely contestable, is that human dignity depends on human distinctiveness, on the human difference from all other species. In addition, I have broadened the consideration of existential values in Arendt's work in order to encompass their total destruction by totalitarianism and, secondarily, to identify their occurrence in moral action that resists totalitarianism and lesser forms of bad rule. When I refer to the French variants of existentialism, I have in mind especially André Malraux's novels; they give a brilliant anticipation of some of Arendt's ideas about the existential worth of action. And, despite her skepticism concerning the merits of Sartre as a philosopher, his elaboration of the philosophy of human freedom, including the notions of project and sudden upsurge, has an important affinity to what Arendt is saying about human distinctiveness. In his work-in-progress, *On the Margins of Hannah Arendt*, Peter Baehr provides an instructive discussion of the importance for Arendt of Karl Jaspers' attempt to preserve the idea of human freedom by discrediting any naturalist or materialist reduction of humanity's being. Dana Villa's *Arendt and Heidegger: The Fate of the Political* (Princeton: Princeton University Press, 1996) is a comprehensive analysis of the influence of Heidegger's ontology on Arendt's vision of the existential value of action and, at the same time, of Arendt's substantial departure from Heidegger. Mary Dietz's *Turning Operations: Feminism, Arendt and Politics* (New York: Routledge, 2002) discusses many aspects of Arendt's thought from a broad perspective of what counts as existentialist. On Arendt's concept of evil, Richard J. Bernstein's work is most valuable: see his *Hannah Arendt and the Jewish Question* (Cambridge, MA: MIT Press, 1996), especially chapters 7 and 8; and *Radical Evil: A Philosophical Interrogation* (Malden, MA: Polity, 2002), chapter 8. An excellent work on the moral psychology of those individuals who rescued persecuted people, in the face of serious risk to themselves, is Kristen Renwick Monroe's *The Heart of Altruism: Perceptions of a Common Humanity* (Princeton: Princeton University Press, 1996).

Index